Tambora and the Year without a Summer

Tambora and the Year without a Summer

How a Volcano Plunged the World into Crisis

Wolfgang Behringer

Translated by Pamela Selwyn

polity

First published in German as *Tambora und das Jahr ohne Sommer* © Verlag C.H. Beck oHG, Munich, 2016

This English edition © Polity Press, 2019

The translation of this work was funded by Geisteswissenschaften International – Translation Funding for Humanities and Social Sciences from Germany, a joint initiative of the Fritz Thyssen Foundation, the German Federal Foreign Office, the collecting society VG WORT and the Börsenverein des Deutschen Buchhandels (German Publishers & Booksellers Association).

Polity Press
65 Bridge Street
Cambridge CB2 1UR, UK

Polity Press
101 Station Landing
Suite 300
Medford, MA 02155, USA

ISBN-13: 978-1-5095-2549-2

A catalogue record for this book is available from the British Library.

Library of Congress Cataloging-in-Publication Data

Names: Behringer, Wolfgang, author.
Title: Tambora and the year without a summer : how a volcano plunged the
    world into crisis / Wolfgang Behringer.
Other titles: Tambora und das Jahr ohne Sommer. English
Description: English edition. I Medford, MA : Polity Press, [2019] I
    Originally published in German as: Tambora und das Jahr ohne Sommer : wie
    ein Vulkan die Welt in die Krise sturzte. Based on 3rd German edition
    (Munchen : C.H. Beck, 2016). I Includes bibliographical references and
    index.
Identifiers: LCCN 2018038779 (print) I LCCN 2018040297 (ebook) I ISBN
    9781509525522 (Epub) I ISBN 9781509525492 (hardback)
Subjects: LCSH: Tambora, Mount (Indonesia)--Eruption, 1815. I Volcanic
    eruptions--Social aspects--History--19th century. I Weather--Effect of
    vocanic eruptions on--Case studies. I Climatic changes--History. I World
    politics--Environmental aspects.
Classification: LCC QE523.T285 (ebook) I LCC QE523.T285 B4413 2019 (print) I
    DDC 363.34/95--dc23
LC record available at https://lccn.loc.gov/2018038779

Typeset in 10.5 on 12 pt Sabon by
Servis Filmsetting Ltd, Stockport, Cheshire
Printed and bound in Great Britain by TJ International Limited

For further information on Polity, visit our website: politybooks.com

For my mother, Margit Behringer (1925–2015), who taught me the joy of exploring new things.

I would like to thank Dr Justus Nipperdey, Johanna Blume, Judit Ruff, Sebastian Weiß, Pascal Steinmetz, Johanna Ungemach and Areti Karanikouli for their assistance during corrections to the German edition.

CONTENTS

— 1 —

INTRODUCTION:
THE TAMBORA CRISIS

Would anyone be interested in reading a book about a volcanic eruption? In the case of Tambora, there is good reason to believe they
would. This book is less about geology than about the societal reactions to an event that affected the climate worldwide – the largest volcanic eruption in human history. The explosions of April 1815 were
so powerful that they could be heard thousands of kilometres away.
The lava and pyroclastic flow devastated the immediate surroundings,
and cyclones, tsunamis, ash fall and acid rain the adjacent region. The
explosion cloud reached a height of 45 km. Large parts of Asia suffered for months under a 'dry fog' that obscured the sun. Upper winds
distributed the gas and suspended particles around the world. The aerosols reduced solar radiation and led to a global cooling. The winter of
1815/16 was one of the coldest of the millennium. Glaciers expanded.
Torrential rains caused flooding in China and India. In Europe and
North America, 1816 became the 'year without a summer'.[1] In many
parts of the world, 1817 became the 'year of famine'.[2]

The years that followed were devoted to coping with the results of
the crisis. Epidemics paralysed entire regions; mass migration shifted
social problems to other corners of the globe; and mass demonstrations, uprisings and suicide attacks generated a pre-revolutionary
mood. The eruption of Tambora served as a great experiment in
fields where we normally cannot conduct experiments: the economy,
culture and politics. The question is, how do different countries,
legal systems and religions respond to a sudden worsening of living
conditions imposed by external forces? To changes in nature, failed
harvests, inflation, famine, epidemics and social unrest? As the Indian
historian Dipesh Chakrabarty has noted, climatic events are uniquely
suited to being viewed from a global perspective.[3]

1

Throughout the world, the volcanic eruption forced the affected societies to confront a current problem using their own specific mechanisms for coping with an unexpected change in the climate that – whether through cold, drought or constant rain – challenged their usual means of supplying the population with basic necessities. Nearly all societies in the world had to demonstrate virtually simultaneously how capable they were of managing such a subsistence crisis, which almost always coincided with a spiritual crisis. Some of them seemed to do so effortlessly.[4] The Tambora Crisis caused others to slide into a protracted decline.[5] The sudden and simultaneous appearance of acute problems worldwide has the character of an experiment whose design we cannot determine, but can reconstruct. From the distance of two centuries, this allows us to analyse the vulnerability and resilience of the societies of the time when faced with sudden climatic turmoil.[6]

That is the topic of the present volume, which is interested not in the volcanic eruption as such, but in its cultural consequences as well as the capacities of societies at the time to respond to sudden climate change. The time period of this study is 1815 to 1820, dates that are familiar from political history as well. In 1815, participants in the Congress of Vienna resolved to reorganise the world, and in 1820, the Final Act of the Viennese Ministerial Conference integrated the intervening experiences of crisis into a set of regulations. The future US Secretary of State Henry Kissinger (b. 1923) wrote his doctoral thesis about this period, in which an excess of wars and crises led, through diplomatic negotiations, to a political order that assured peace and stability for a generation.[7] The European post-war politician Robert Marjolin (1911–1986) also wrote a study of this period, one devoted specifically to the unrest and revolts unleashed by famine in France.[8] The struggle for political stability took place in domestic politics as well, without some knowledge of which one cannot truly understand the foreign policy of the time. The domestic policy of these years was coloured by the climate crisis.

The period from 1815 to 1820 will be treated here as a coherent period of crisis – I call it the Tambora Crisis, to define it by its triggering factor. When the literature refers repeatedly to a crisis in the wake of the 'European wars',[9] it reveals more than the authors' refusal to meet the challenge of a worldwide crisis that was precisely not rooted in the political or military processes so familiar to them. It is almost touching to watch the same historian trying over and over again to attribute the same crisis to a different cause in every European country.[10] After all, this crisis had no logical cause. The volcanic

2

eruption could just as easily have occurred a few years earlier or later, and it could happen again today or tomorrow. It was an event 'external' to human society. This presents historians and sociologists with a methodological problem. The universal 'rule of sociological method' that it is 'in the nature of society itself that we must seek the explanation of social life'[11] does not apply here. Emile Durkheim's 'social facts' are abrogated when the conditions are set not by Napoleon or the bourgeoisie but by a volcano.

From the standpoint of global history, it is easy to see that the traditional explanations do not work everywhere anyway. Why should there be famines in China and South Africa or a cholera outbreak in India because Napoleon lost a war, the British Army demobilised its troops or more machines were used in European industry? Even in Europe, one would be hard-pressed to find documents showing that anyone connected the constant rain, floods and failed harvests or the unrest that followed with the wars and their end, or with nascent industrialisation. Historians who nonetheless make this claim have used the simple facts of chronology to draw a causal connection, along the lines of the post hoc fallacy, which psychologists call a logical fallacy.[12]

The dimensions of the Tambora Crisis were so extraordinary because its roots lay in nature, in processes of geology, atmospheric physics and meteorology. These forces of nature respect no borders. Their effects are not merely global, but also on a very particular scale. Without knowing anything about Tambora, contemporaries recognised the unusual character of this crisis by comparing it to earlier ones. According to the Swiss professor of theology and writer on poor relief Peter Scheitlin (1779–1848), 'In 1760 people in the country earned handsomely and all foodstuffs were extremely cheap – in 1771 they earned handsomely and all foodstuffs were very dear – in 1817 they earned nearly nothing but the inflation was terrible – in 1819 they earned nearly nothing but everything was very cheap. What a strange diversity! What an interesting distribution of all the possible cases in a period of 50–60 years, that is within a human lifetime!'[13] As we shall see, 'famine year' does not mean that there was no food available, but merely that it was unaffordable for the many people who, as described by the Indian economist Amartya Sen, had no access to it.[14]

The theme of climate and history has gained in influence ever since the world's scientists agreed that we are living in an age of global warming.[15] When climate change was put on the international agenda there were still fears of an immediately impending ice age, but by the time the international summits on climate change became established the broad consensus was that the problem for coming generations would be warming, not cooling. Since 1990, reports from the Intergovernmental Panel on Climate Change (IPCC) have regularly informed the public about the state of research in the field.[16]

In the 1960s, when the idea of studying the climate systematically emerged in the United Nations, a series of long, severe winters left an impression on western societies. In connection with the eruption of the Gunung Agung volcano on Bali, data was gathered for the first time from an airplane that proved that its emissions changed the composition of the air as high up as the stratosphere.[17] These were important additions to the first global study of a volcanic eruption in the wake of the eruption of Krakatoa in 1883.[18] One hundred years previously, following the eruption of the Icelandic volcano Laki, Benjamin Franklin (1706–1790) had already observed that the same weather phenomena occurred in Europe and North America.[19] However, the obvious hypothesis that Gunung Tambora had been the catalyst for worldwide climatic phenomena was not proven until 1913, in a study by the American atmospheric physicist William Jackson Humphrey (1862–1949).[20]

The research on volcanoes and their eruptions has progressed in the meantime. One of the principles of climate science is that violent volcanic eruptions can change the composition of the atmosphere through their emissions of ash, gases and fine particles, which can affect the climate worldwide.[21] The number of volcanoes was determined, and, based on ice cores,[22] tree rings[23] and sediment analyses, a chronology of volcanic eruptions over a period of several hundred million years was established.[24] Using the Volcanic Explosivity Index (VEI), the strength of volcanic eruptions was classified in seven stages, measured by the amount of matter emitted and the height of emissions.[25] The scale was calibrated according to the oldest precisely described larger volcanic eruption, that of Vesuvius in 79 CE (= VEI 5).[26] Even larger volcanic eruptions are described as 'ultra-Plinian' events. Their influence can be enormous. The eruption of the volcano of Thera/Santorini (= VEI 6) more than 2,650 years ago probably led to the extinction of the Minoan culture.[27] The eruption of Toba (= VEI 8) in present-day Indonesia some 70,000 years ago nearly led to the extinction of humankind.[28] The eruptions of supervolcanoes, for instance those under Yellowstone National Park or the Phlegraean Fields near Naples, surpass any scale. They could lead to a 'volcanic winter', a global cooling, which due to feedback effects could last for decades or even centuries.[29]

The eruption of Tambora (= VEI 7) in 1815 was the largest eruption in human history – with history traditionally defined here as the period from which we have written sources, that is, approximately the last 5,000 years. This eruption brought summer snowfalls in many areas, but there was no danger of a 'volcanic winter'.[30] The characterisation of the year as 'eighteen hundred and froze to death' is found just once in an undated poem from the USA.[31] It reads

> Months that should be summer's prime
> Sleet and snow and frost and rime
> Air so cold you see your breath
> Eighteen hundred and froze to death.[32]

The designation 'year without a summer' is an exaggeration, although it has gained a certain currency.[33] Today, with the help of land weather reports and ships' log books, we can reconstruct historical weather maps globally.[34] They show a varied range of weather anomalies for 1816. In some areas it was much too wet (e.g. western Europe and China), in others too dry (USA, India, South Africa), in most too cold, but in some also warm (e.g. Russia). These years appeared to be 'unnatural' in the eyes of contemporaries and anomalous in the analyses of modern climate scientists.[35]

The eruption of Tambora and its effects were only studied in greater detail in the 1980s. The research was strongly influenced by Anglo-American scientists: Henry Stommel (1929–1992) was an oceanographer at the Massachusetts Institute of Technology,[36] Charles Richard Harrington (b. 1933) was a zoologist at the Canadian Museum of Nature,[37] Clive Oppenheimer (b. 1964) is a volcanologist at the University of Cambridge,[38] and the American Nicholas P. Klingaman is a meteorologist at the University of Reading.[39] The recent study by Gillen D'Arcy Wood, a professor of English literature at the University of Illinois, is the first to include selected international cultural aspects, for example the emergence of vampire literature.[40] Alongside this there exist a number of very good studies that explore the crisis of 1816/17 on a local or regional level.[41] There is no lack of work on individual aspects such as the origins of the global cholera outbreak.[42] Many events such as the fall of governments, the discussions surrounding constitutions for newly founded states, political murders, pogroms and planned coups have not thus far been viewed in connection with the Tambora Crisis. And yet, as I shall argue here, they are virtually impossible to understand without this context.

The Tambora Crisis – and the present volume profits from this – occurred in a more modern media environment than any previous climate or subsistence crisis. In the early nineteenth century, when European expansion had reached its height, newspapers and periodicals already existed all over the world. Everywhere we find well-trained, curious and sometimes very opinionated government officials who wrote highly competent reports on all manner of subjects or events. To name but one example, the British governor of Java, Sir Thomas Stamford Raffles (1781–1826), undertook a survey with a standardised questionnaire among all the British residents of the Indonesian archipelago to explore the causes and consequences of the explosion of Mount Tambora. Many economists, 'political scientists' and also theologians wrote expert testimonies or detailed accounts and analyses of the famine. Scientists from the emerging disciplines of geology, physics and chemistry sought explanations for the extraordinary natural phenomena. Agronomists and technicians, but also nutritionists, architects and town planners, looked for ways of mitigating the effects of the crisis and preventing future suffering. They presented their ideas for discussion in specialist journals. The correspondence, diaries, travel accounts and memoirs of politicians, artists and scholars afford profound insights into their thinking. Frequently, these commentaries came from well-known personalities such as the Russian Tsar Alexander I, the English poet Lord Byron, the Prussian diplomat Karl August Varnhagen von Ense and his wife Rahel, née Levin, or the Weimar minister of state Johann Wolfgang von Goethe.

The task of the present volume is to construct a new synthesis, based on the rich contemporary sources, out of the many individual aspects. The aim is to redefine the Tambora Crisis as a part of world history, an event with a rightful place not just in natural history, but also in cultural and social history. Until now, regional or national histories have cultivated their own modes of dealing with this crisis because scholars have not been thinking outside the box. Often, it has also been swept aside because it apparently does not fit into our historical narrative of human progress from servitude to liberty. Readers need to leave such ideas behind if they are to dive into the complexities of the years 1815–1820.

The eruption of Mount Tambora was the beginning of an experiment in which all of humanity became involuntary participants. The reactions to the crisis offer an example of how societies and individuals respond to climate change, what risks emerge and what opportunities may be associated with it. This book shows how the climate crisis of the early nineteenth century was overcome. Anyone who is interested in the problems of current and future climate change should know about the historical example of the Tambora Crisis.

— 2 —

THE YEAR OF THE EXPLOSION: 1815

The end to all wars and the reorganisation of the world in 1815

The year 1815 witnessed the end of more than twenty years of warfare in Europe and beyond. Between 1792 and 1815, the Revolutionary Wars and the subsequent Napoleonic Wars fundamentally changed Europe.[1] The French occupation of broad swathes of the continent under Napoleon Bonaparte (1769–1821) had repercussions for the entire world. Thus, with the annexation of the Netherlands, Dutch colonial possessions passed to France. In order to prevent the French from regaining a foothold in 'Farther India', the United Kingdom took over the colonial possessions of the Netherlands in Southeast Asia, as well as Dutch Guiana in South America, the Cape Colony in South Africa and the island of Ceylon off the coast of India.

The Russo-Turkish War was fought on the edges of Europe from 1806 to 1812, concurrently with the Napoleonic Wars, with the Ottoman Empire aiming to recapture the Black Sea coast. After their defeat, however, the Ottomans were forced by the Treaty of Bucharest to cede Bessarabia to Russia as well.[2] The War of 1812 began around the same time.[3] This war between the USA and their former colonial masters escalated to such a degree after the American invasion of British Canada that in August 1814 English troops captured the US capital Washington and burnt down the White House and the Capitol. President James Madison (1751–1836) was forced to flee to Virginia.[4] When the Treaty of Ghent was signed in February 1815, the indigenous peoples also involved in the war were the actual losers.[5]

The Wars of Liberation against Napoleonic occupation ended in April 1814 with Napoleon's defeat and deposition, followed by the First Treaty of Paris (30 May 1814). After his wraithlike return from banishment in March 1815, Napoleon was defeated a second time by the Grand Alliance (England, Russia, Prussia and Austria) at the Battle of Waterloo on 18 June 1815. Even before these last hostilities had ceased, the Congress of Vienna (1 November 1814–11 June 1815) set the stage for the unfolding of the European drama in the years that followed. The term 'Restoration' has become established in the historical literature to refer to the results of these peace negotiations, as specified in the Final Act of the Congress of Vienna (9 June 1815), because they allegedly re-established the conditions of the period preceding the French Revolution. Restoration was, however, more of a battle cry of 1830s liberalism, for the Congress of Vienna restored literally nothing to its condition at any previous point in time. Instead, the negotiators sought new forms for the plethora of changes that had occurred in the preceding twenty-five years, with the aim of creating a lasting peacetime order.[6] The objective was to prevent future wars and revolutions by establishing a new peacekeeping power and options for political participation. The Congress of Vienna thus served as a model for the negotiations following the First and Second World Wars.[7]

The political order created in Vienna was revolutionary, sweeping aside the ancien régime world of states, including the Napoleonic state system. Major new states were created which were supposed to guarantee a European peacetime order. Virtually none of these states – and this is important for our story – had ever existed in this form before.[8] This had its price: in the period that followed, they suffered from serious legitimation problems and had first to gain the loyalty of their new populations. Within Germany, the tendencies to a realignment of state boundaries continued. The recasting of property relations in the preceding decades, the secularisation of ecclesiastical holdings and the ecclesiastical states, the mediatisation of the imperial cities, knights and counts and even of some principalities by the larger states remained in force. And these expropriations were joined by further annexations. Of the more than 300 territories that had existed under old German particularism, only thirty-four principalities and four city-states survived. They were combined to form a confederation of states, the 'German Confederation', whose parliament – the Federal Assembly – was to meet in Frankfurt. On 8 June 1815, the great powers signed the Deutsche Bundesakte (German Federal Act).[9] Article 13 stipulated that all states were to provide themselves with constitutions. The Tambora Crisis contributed considerably to the speedy passage of these constitutions in many states, since the new parliaments were needed not just in order to pay off the state debts, but also to remove injustices by harmonising the national law of the various states and to pacify unrest in the individual regions.

Tsar Alexander I,[10] patron saint of the German Wars of Liberation and the true victor over Napoleon, became the guiding spirit of the Holy Alliance, a coalition of the Christian monarchies of Russia, Prussia and Austria formed at a conference of the victorious powers in Paris on 26 September 1815. The monarch's manifesto issued an appeal for Christian fraternity. England roundly rejected this religious claptrap, however, and refused all support. Apart from the pope, nearly all of the other European monarchies joined, including France, which had once again been accepted into the circle of the great powers in the Second Treaty of Paris on 20 November 1815. Thus all major hostilities had ended by late 1815. A golden age was supposed to ensue.

Explosions in the Far East: a new war?

The sound of heavy explosions could be heard in eastern Java on the evening of 5 April 1815 and continued at intervals throughout the night and into the next morning. They led to hectic activity among locals and in the garrisons of the British colonial power. People imagined cannon fire from a siege or a French invasion, since there had been news of Napoleon's return and the resumption of hostilities in Europe. Troops marched out from Yogyakarta in anticipation of a possible enemy attack, as the governor of Indonesia reported in his memoirs. Then boats began to search along the coast for ships in distress.[11]

Sir Thomas Stamford Raffles, who had been appointed governor of Java at the age of thirty after a career in the service of the British East India Company,[12] soon realised that the noise must have come from an extraordinarily large volcanic eruption. But where was this volcano located? At first, contradictory reports arrived, according to which the eruption had allegedly been noticed on the 1st of April in Banyuwangie, but not until the 6th in Batavia (present-day Jakarta). The ash fall began throughout the area between the 10th and the 14th of April. Raffles therefore ordered a systematic investigation. To this end he designed a questionnaire that was sent along with a circular letter to all British residents of Indonesia in May 1815. Question 1 related to the chronological and physical circumstances. It enquired after the day and the hour when people had noticed the ash fall, how long it had lasted, and what had been its chemical composition. Question 2 explored the medical and economic effects of the eruption, the impact on the health of people and animals and on the harvest, as well as the presumptive causes. Question 3 asked about the source. Where did they believe the eruption had occurred?

With his survey, Raffles elicited eyewitness accounts of immediate reactions to the volcanic eruption. Such accounts had existed for 2,000 years, beginning with the observation of Vesuvius by Pliny the Younger. Spanish colonial officials had reported on the explosion of Huaynaputina in Peru in 1600,[13] while their Danish counterparts had written of the eruption of Laki in Iceland in 1783.[14] But Raffles was not satisfied with the incidental or regular reports he received, and instead sought a systematic and structured overview. The quality of the responses to his survey can be surmised from the response of a resident of Surakarta (Central Java). People there had heard the first explosions on Thursday, 5 April, between four and six in the afternoon. With its clear and distinct thunderclaps, and the irregular intervals between them, the noise had resembled a military operation, sounding more like mortar fire than a cannonade. On 6, 7, 8 and 9 April there had been occasional sounds like distant thunder. During those days, however, an increasing opacity in the atmosphere had suggested the true reason, since it was familiar from previous volcanic eruptions. On 10 April the explosions had continued, and dust had begun to rain down lightly. On Tuesday, 11 April the explosions became more frequent and powerful, lasting all day, with an especially loud bang around two o'clock in the afternoon. For approximately one hour, the explosions were accompanied by a tremulous motion of the earth, making large windows vibrate. Late that afternoon people heard a second loud thundering noise, and the air was filled with such dense vapour that the sun was scarcely visible. From 5 to 18 April the sun appeared to have vanished, and when it was briefly visible, it was only through a dense fog. In early May the air was still hazy and visibility reduced. The mountain above Surakarta remained invisible throughout the month, and even nearby objects could only be seen as if through a veil of smoke.

The situation worsened on 12 April when dust began to fall more thickly. It stayed dark all day, and no work was possible indoors. At the same time the temperature dropped rapidly. At ten in the morning the thermometer showed only 75.5 degrees Fahrenheit (24 degrees Celsius). The earthquake and precipitation seemed to come from the west. Some of these phenomena were familiar from previous volcanic eruptions, but the sudden rise of the sea level was extremely unusual, occurring quite close in time to the most violent earth tremors. The day and hour had not been recorded precisely enough. The dust was ash grey with a brownish tinge, and almost imperceptibly fine, and when dissolved in water it smelled like clay. It was not magnetic, and its chemical composition differed from that of the ash produced by the eruptions of Guntur in 1803 and Kelut in 1811.

When it came to the after-effects, the observer from Surakarta was remarkably optimistic. Buffaloes and cows were dying, but this could be the result of the continuing effects of a cattle epidemic. His enquiries had revealed that animal health more generally had not been damaged. Horses, sheep and goats were scarcely affected, but the rice crop might be. However, there had rarely been a year of such abundance. The mature rice was scarcely damaged, but an adverse effect on the growth of fresh plantings was to be expected. Depending on how heavy the precipitation had been, the clayey ash could cause the young plants to wither by absorbing needed water. The report's author commended himself to the governor with a promise of economic profit, suggesting that the ash fall with its high clay content might be used to make pottery.

The explosions of Mount Tambora: 5–15 April 1815

Now that we have heard about the situation from the viewpoint of a contemporary, what had actually happened? Mount Gunung Tambora, or as many contemporaries called it, Tomboro, was no longer considered an active volcano, since it had not erupted in human memory. In 1812, however, a cloud had formed over the summit, though nobody had paid much attention to it because of the mountain's great height, an estimated 4,200 metres. The cloud had remained ever since, growing darker as the months passed. It was thought to be a tropical storm cloud, but in later years the scholar John Crawfurd claimed to have seen a rain of ash even before the eruption, whilst travelling by ship to Macassar on the island of Celebes (now Sulawesi). In the weeks before the explosion people noted an increasing rumbling and trembling of the earth, and the fearful inhabitants of Sumbawa had asked the British Resident in Bima to investigate. He in fact sent a certain Mr Israel, who unfortunately travelled on the very day that Mount Tambora erupted. He was never heard from again.[15]

11

Map of Indonesia

The powerful explosions that could be heard for thousands of kilometres throughout the Indonesian archipelago began on 5 April 1815. On 14 April a Major Johnson reported from Solo on the main island of Java for the capital newspaper: 'The explosions were extremely violent and very frequent, and resembled the discharge of mortars. It commenced on Wednesday the 5th in the evening with repeated explosions, and ceased about 8 o'clock. It again commenced on Monday night or Tuesday morning, and continued extremely violent until a late hour the next night. Yesterday the ashes fell so thick that it was quite uncomfortable walking out as it filled our eyes and covered our clothes.'[16] And Crawfurd reported from Surabaya: 'The day after the sounds and shocks of earthquake which accompanied them were heard at Surabaya, the ashes began to fall, and on the third day, up to noon, it was pitch dark; and for several days after I transacted all business by candlelight. For several months, indeed, the sun's disk was not distinct, nor the atmosphere clear and bright, as it usually is during the southeast monsoon.'[17]

The climax of the eruption began on 10 April. One of the few survivors, the sultan of Sanggar – one of the six sultanates on Sumbawa – described it to Governor Raffles' envoy Lieutenant Owen Phillips as follows: at five o'clock on the evening of 10 April three distinct pillars of flame could be seen erupting near the summit of the volcano, presumably from the volcano's crater. They rose into the sky, coming together in turbulences at a great height. Viewed from Sanggar, the mountain afterwards appeared from all directions as a body of liquid fire. The flames could be seen raging until about eight o'clock, after which the mountain was obscured by the masses of falling ash and other ejected material. The stones that rained down on the relatively distant Sanggar consisted of debris ranging in size from a walnut to two fists. Between nine and ten o'clock ash rain began in Sanggar, and soon thereafter came a whirlwind that blew down nearly every house in the village, carrying off roofs and anything light. Even large trees were uprooted and flung through the air along with people, houses and animals. Then came the tsunami, which at 12 feet was higher than any seen before. The tsunami devastated the low-lying rice fields of Sanggar and everything else in its path.[18]

After its violent eruptive phase (5–15 April) the volcano remained active for several more weeks, albeit less powerfully so. From its original height of 4,200 metres, calculated from the reports of various captains who had passed it regularly before and after the explosion, only 2,850 metres remained after its peak blew off. This led to the formation of the six-kilometre wide caldera with a crater lake in the middle that Heinrich Zollinger found in 1847 during what is considered the first ascent of Mount Tambora.[19] Estimates still accepted today suggest that the eruption ejected some 150 cubic kilometres of volcanic material.[20] The release of aerosols into the atmosphere was far higher than that of any of the more recent volcanic eruptions that have been studied using better measurement techniques.[21]

The disaster of the principalities on Sumbawa

The island of Sumbawa measures some 280 km from east to west, ranges between 15 and 90 km wide and comprises approximately 15,550 square km in all. In the early seventeenth century the island was conquered by the sultan of Macassar in the south of the island of Celebes, the king of Gowa. The minor princes on Sumbawa ended up in a relationship of tributary dependency to him, and were forced to convert to Islam. Macassar was an international commercial centre with Portuguese, Chinese, Dutch, English, Spanish and Danish trading outposts. In 1669 the Dutch vanquished the kingdom of Gowa militarily, expelled the other Europeans and made Macassar a protectorate of the Dutch East India Company (VOC). The British took over this protectorate in 1811 and the kingdom of the Netherlands in 1816. The eruption of Mount Tambora occurred during the reign of King Mappatunru I Manginyarang Karaeng Lembanhparang, known as Sultan Abdul Rauf (r. 1814–1825).[22]

Sumbawa itself was divided into six principalities. On a peninsula in the north lay the three small sultanates of Tambora (near the volcano), Pekat and Sanggar with the port city of the same name. On its own peninsula in the west of the island was the sultanate of Sumbawa (now the Sumbawa district of the Nusa Tenggarat Barat province, Indonesia). In the centre of the island lay the sultanate of Dompo with its capital city of the same name, and in the east the sultanate of Bima. According to the accounts of Dutch correspondents, before the eruption the population lived from the cultivation of rice, maize and beans. In a bay on the south coast of Dompo people dived for pearls. The salt flats of Bima provided the local people with that commodity. Exports included rice, horses, honey, beeswax, birds' nests, pepper, salt, cotton, coffee, teak and sandalwood, the last of which was also needed for the production of red dye.[23]

As an agent of the Dutch East India Company emphasised in 1786, the principality of Tambora was located in the infertile, rocky part of the island, where not much grew in the mountains but rice. This principality east of the volcano even had to import rice from other

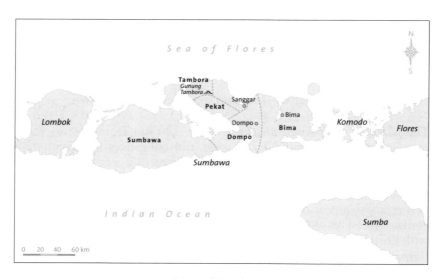

Map of Sumbawa

parts of the island, in exchange for forest produce – honey, wood and birds' nests – as well as horses. These products were so abundant that the sultan, nobles and subjects were in a position to compensate well for the barrenness of the land.[24] Excavations have confirmed contemporary information about a certain level of wealth in the sultanate of Tambora and have expanded our knowledge of trade relations. Apart from objects of old Indonesian culture, the excavations also unearthed imported goods such as Chinese porcelain, glazed ceramics, precious stones, copper implements and iron tools. According to these findings, Tambora probably had trade relations with Indochina.[25]

The effects of the eruption proved catastrophic for the island of Sumbawa. Lava and pyroclastic flows devastated the area around the volcano. Pumice stone and ash rained down on the entire island. Near the volcano, the ash attained a height of 120 cm. The principalities of Tambora and Pekat were wiped off the map. In neighbouring Sanggar, too, most of the population – an estimated 10,000 people – were killed by the eruption, the subsequent cyclone or the tsunami.[26] The sultan, however, miraculously survived and served as an eyewitness. Most survivors fled to the neighbouring principality of Bima. According to contemporary accounts, some 95 per cent of the rice harvest on Sumbawa was destroyed and the drinking water polluted. The result was famine and a wave of diarrhoea and fever, to which most of the remaining inhabitants of the principalities of Bima and Dompo succumbed.[27] People were so desperate that they sold their children into slavery and opened graves to look for any items they could sell. An additional 38,000 people are estimated to have died on Sumbawa.[28]

The disaster on the island led to mass emigration. Some 36,000 people fled to the neighbouring islands of Bali and Java, with others leaving for the sultanate of Macassar on South Sulawesi or for smaller islands. They paid dearly. One Dutchman who visited the island of Ceram Laut (Moluccas) in 1824 found a number of Sumbawans there who had sold themselves to slave merchants in order to pay for the voyage and secure their survival.[29] Zollinger – whose figures are still used by scholars today – estimated that after the mass death and emigration, fewer than 50 per cent of the original population of some 170,000 remained on the island.[30] Nowadays, around 1.5 million people live on Sumbawa.

The anthropologist Peter R. Goethals has pointed out that life changed utterly for the remaining inhabitants. First of all, the economy collapsed. Horses disappeared along with bees and birds. The flooding of the lowlands rendered traditional villages uninhabitable. It became impossible to grow rice in the paddy fields. The forests were also devastated. For several years, survivors had to depend on rice imports from Java. The governor of the sultan of Macassar exempted the principalities of Sanggar, Bima and Dompo from paying tribute and taxes, and all treaties had to be renegotiated after 1817. The survivors – and later the returnees – had to search for new land and establish new villages. Goethals concluded that all present-day settlements on the island can be traced back to those newly founded after 1815. The 'Tambora holocaust' depopulated the island and completely altered the forms of settlement and economic activity. Today's settlements are no longer located on the water, but on the mountainsides. Instead of paddy fields, the lower-yield method of dry rice cultivation was used. The first harvest in Bima was only possible five years after the disaster, and in the west of the island it took even longer. Nine years after the catastrophe, in 1824, the government officials Schelle and Tobias reported that the principalities of Sumbawa and Dompo were gradually recovering, but that Pekat and Tambora still resembled abandoned scenes of devastation.[31] In 1847 Heinrich Zollinger noted that the port city of Bima had recovered, unlike the rest of the island. In the principality of Bima, tobacco, indigo and sugarcane were now cultivated, in addition to the earlier export products. One interesting detail: the locals believed that the climate had changed. There was less rain, it was hotter, and many springs had dried up. Zollinger attributed this to the loss of vegetation.[32] To this day, Sumbawa remains drier and less fertile than neighbouring islands.

The eruption as divine punishment

After his first ascent of Mount Tambora in 1847, Zollinger learned that 'the natives believed the eruption to be divine judgement of a wicked deed committed by the king of Tambora'. He had heard the following story from the inhabitants of Dompo. One day, the Arab trader Seid Idrus had found a dog outside the Tambora mosque. He became very angry and wanted to drive the dog away, but was prevented from doing so because he was told that this was the king's dog. A dispute then erupted between the Muslim and the king and nobility of the principality. In the end the angered king ordered the foreigner to be killed at Mount Tambora. His subjects obeyed, carried the Arab off and set about killing him with spears, knives and clubs, and by stoning. They threw his body into a hole. But when the murderers tried to return to the city to report to the king, fire spouted

16

from the mountain and followed them. In Zollinger's rendering of the tale:

> By the power of God the most high, who is to be praised in all eternity, the fire pursued the people wherever they fled, and even pursued them to the sea, so that the sea of Tambora was in flames. The fire on the mountain burned for several days, and also in the villages, on land and sea. And there was darkness and ash rain. Nothing saved the inhabitants of Tambora, many thousands were burnt to death. The city of Tambora sank and became part of the sea. To this day the ships can drop anchor on the spot where the city of Tambora lies.[33]

Many elements of this account in which Allah defends his mosque are familiar to narratologists from *Wandersagen*, fragments of folklore spread by casual diffusion, for instance the image of the sunken city. Since the stories were transmitted orally, there are numerous versions, for example one in which Seid Idrus was immortal and now lived in the mountain, or in which the king hid a treasure before his demise. Zollinger himself was at first suspected of being a treasure hunter. Stories also circulated about evil spirits or dragons dwelling in the mountain who must not be disturbed because they tried to devour anyone who dared to scale it. The last destination of Zollinger's expedition was the small principality of Sanggar, which was completely buried in 1815 and had only re-emerged quite recently at the time of his visit. The raja of Sanggar, who had survived the disaster as a twelve-year-old boy, gave Zollinger some forty men to accompany him. Zollinger noted that they received a rousing welcome upon their return:

> Many people touched our bodies and could not believe their eyes when they found us alive and unharmed. They had never imagined that we would return so hale and hearty and so soon. In the village we were received by the priest, who solemnly blessed me. It was a great celebration, all day and into the night ... I had a buffalo slaughtered for the populace and rice distributed among them. Now they believed the land had been released from its curse, and the evil spirits banished. The misfortune of 1815 would never occur again, we hoped. The shooting, crowing and singing continued until the break of day.[34]

Consequences in the Indonesian archipelago

Apart from Sumbawa, the volcanic disaster also affected the other Lesser Sunda Islands. Because of the northwest wind, it had less impact on the islands of Flores, Timor and Komodo to the east (which saved the lives of the famous Komodo dragons) than on the western islands of Lombok and Bali. Only in the western part of Flores, Manggarai, which belonged to the principality of Bima, did mortality rise significantly. The population took the opportunity to rebel against the overlordship of Bima and stopped all payments of tribute to the sultan. It took thirty-five years for Bima to regain sufficient strength to launch a successful military expedition, which restored the previous power relations.[35]

The blanket of ash that covered Lombok and Bali was 20–30 cm thick. This does not sound so dramatic, but it sufficed to poison the fields and water. Many people died when their houses collapsed under the weight of the ash.[36] The rice harvest of 1815 was completely destroyed, and cultivation remained all but impossible in the years that followed. As a consequence, Lombok, Bali and the smaller islands suffered severe famine. Here, too, the population depended on rice imports from Java, which most people could not afford. Malnutrition and contaminated drinking water led to the outbreak of fevers and diarrhoea, accompanied by a plague of rats. In the autumn of 1816, the *Batavische Courant* newspaper reported that there were few survivors on Bali, and they were too weak to ensure the proper burial of the people who succumbed daily.[37] The higher social classes were also affected, and victims included the king of Badung (today Denspar), Gusti Ngurah Made Kaleran (c. 1780–1817). When the Dutch Governor H.A. van den Broek visited Bali in 1816 he saw thirty-four bodies lying in the road. Three years later, a passing sailor sighted numerous corpses on the beach. When Johannes Olivier asked in the early 1820s why there were so many dead children lying on the beach, he was told that they had been killed by their parents, who could no longer support them.[38]

Estimates of the number of dead on Bali and Lombok vary widely. The contemporary van den Broek believed that little more than 10 per cent of the original 200,000 inhabitants of Lombok had survived, that is, he assumed that some 175,000 had died. The estimates became smaller and smaller as time went on, perhaps because people found it increasingly hard to imagine the extent of the disaster. The German botanist and geologist Franz Wilhelm Junghuhn (1809–1864) was still able to imagine 44,000 dead, and Zollinger 10,000. Add to this the deaths on Bali, which the Dutch administration estimated at 25,000, a figure that present-day anthropologists consider too low. Bernice de Jong Boers combines the conservative figures from Bali, Lombok and Sumbawa and arrives at an estimate of 117,000 dead,[39] which does not include casualties on the smaller islands. All of this shows that the Lesser Sunda Islands experienced a catastrophe. It took more than ten years for the flora and fauna to begin to recover, but afterwards the volcanic ash acted as a fertiliser and the rice fields became more fertile than ever. Bali's success story as a tropical paradise was beginning. Twenty years after the eruption, the island had become the region's largest rice exporter.[40]

The southern part of the island of Celebes (present-day Sulawesi) was also hard-hit. It was reported from Macassar that the sun darkened on 11 April and was only faintly visible again at noon the next day. The air was full of ash, which continued to rain down for two days. The beach of Moressa was covered with several centimetres. The young rice plants were crushed, fish floated belly-up in the ponds and many small birds lay dead on the ground.[41] The Greater Sunda Islands were also affected. As Raffles' surveys indicated, both the east of Java and the south of Borneo (now Kalimantan) experienced the ash fall. These were also approximately the regions where people had heard the explosions.

Volcanism as normality

Earthquakes, tsunamis and volcanic eruptions are nothing unusual for the Indonesian archipelago. Here, in a long subduction zone, the Indian tectonic plate slides under the Asian. Most of Indonesia's seventy-eight known volcanoes are strung like pearls on a string along the islands of Sumatra and Java, and over the Lesser Sunda Islands to the Banda Sea. Even without knowing about plate tectonics, contemporaries realised that they were living in a particularly active seismic zone. Modern volcanology, using a combination of all methods – from eyewitness accounts to precipitation in ice cores in the Arctic and Antarctic – has counted no fewer than forty volcanic eruptions in Indonesia between 1800 and 1820. Most of them measure low on the explosivity index (VEI 1–3). In 1812, when Tambora first attracted attention, the large volcanoes of Merapi and Raung on Java erupted (both VEI 2), and Awu on the island of Sangihe experienced an internationally significant eruption (VEI 4). In 1815, when Tambora erupted on a massive scale, the volcanoes of Guntur, Tengger/Bromo and Raung (all VEI 2) on Java rumbled. And in 1817, when three volcanoes on Java and Sumatra were smoking (all VEI 2), Raung increased its violence to VEI 4.[42] At VEI 7, however, the eruption of Mount Tambora was by far the most powerful volcanic activity in

19

Ultra-Plinian Eruptions Worldwide, 1800–1820

Year	Volcano	Location	VEI
1800	St Helen's	(present-day) USA	5
1812	Soufrière	Caribbean	4
	Awu	Indonesia	4
1813	Suwanose-Jima	Ryukyu	4
1814	Mayon	Philippines	4
1815	Tambora	Indonesia	7
1817	Raung	Java	4
1818	Colima	Mexico	4

the region. On an international scale it has also remained the largest recorded eruption. The second decade of the nineteenth century, however, also saw a series of other ultra-Plinian eruptions that may well have influenced the climate worldwide.[43]

The cool 1810s

The concentration of volcanic eruptions between 1812 and 1818 was in keeping with meteorological observations in Europe, where a growth in glaciers had been noted since 1812. In the Tyrol, all of the summers from 1812 to 1816 had been much too cool and wet, although the last of these was the worst. In many Alpine valleys, the fruit failed to ripen in the summer of 1812. The winter of 1812/13 was snowy and bitterly cold all over Europe. In his history of weather patterns, the contemporary Bremen meteorologist Wilhelm Christian Müller (1752–1831) pointed to the effects of the cold climate on the history of events. The weather was frigid from late October 1812. By mid-November there was a hard frost, and in December too the temperatures remained below freezing. According to a footnote, 'From 15 to 24 November bitter cold throughout Europe. This paved the way for the downfall of Napoleon and the French in Russia.'[44] The winter of 1813/14 lasted into May and even prevented the fruit harvest. Because of a lack of hay in 1814, the summer grain was mown to use for livestock feed during the winter months. During the dog days (24 July to 23 August) it snowed in the Inn Valley. On 8 September it snowed in Bozen/Bolzano (South Tyrol), on 10 September in Innsbruck as well. This year had already seen a serious rise in prices for all grains. In the South Tyrolean wine-growing region the grapes never ripened. The winter of 1813/14 was icy cold.[45] As had often occurred during the more extreme winters of the Little Ice Age, the Thames froze near London and fairs with mass entertainments were held on the ice. One inventive publisher even printed a book on the phenomenon – using a printing press set up on the ice.[46]

During the Tambora Crisis, the unusually mild and fertile year 1811, which preceded the cold sequence of the second half of the decade, was often cited as a reference year.[47] In the Franconian wine-growing areas the wine harvest had already begun in July, yielding a vintage of the century. In the Nördlinger Ries in southwest Germany, the grain was ready for harvest in the first half of July. This backward look was a bit too rosy, however: because of the great heat, the harvest had been merely average. It was only the retrospective view from 1816/17 that made 1811 seem like a golden year.[48]

The peace year 1815 began in Europe with mild temperatures. Even in the mountains – for example the Brenner Pass – the trees were already blooming in March. The first reversal came in May, one month after the eruption of Mount Tambora, when late frosts destroyed the fruit harvest. The summer months were rainy and ranged from cool to cold. In Innsbruck, June had twenty-one days of rain and July twenty-four, and it snowed in the mountains. Only in mid-August did it become warm, even hot on some days, but it was too late to save the grain harvest.[49] Bremen reported ice at the end of November, and in December the Weser froze over, a rare occurrence.[50] A citizen of Montreux, in the Swiss canton of Vaud, wrote that it had rained incessantly from November 1815 into the first week of March 1816.[51] The same picture emerges from the notes of the pastor of Knetzgau in Lower Franconia, Heinrich Kessler, who wrote, 'The entire winter of 1815–16 was wet; scarcely a day passed without rain; snow fell seldom, and when it did fall, it did not remain for more than a few days. This drenched the winter seeds and they were eaten by snails, so that everywhere many fields had to be ploughed over.'[52]

Celestial events

It is hardly surprising that the volcanic eruption on the Lesser Sunda Islands caused a darkening of the sky in the region, and in some cases totally obscured the sun. Large parts of Indonesia, but also of India, Indochina and South China directly and indirectly felt the effects of the volcanic eruption: first with the appearance of the famous dry fog and the attendant cooling of the atmosphere, and then with the

21

torrential rains and flooding that signalled massive interventions in agricultural rhythms and yields.

Scant research has been done thus far on whether the dry fog known from the Laki eruption of 1784 was also observed in other parts of the world, or whether other celestial events were noted. In a study of the effects of the Krakatoa eruption – which began on 20 May 1883, continued through several phases, and ended on 27 August with a massive explosion – the Royal Society was able to record optical phenomena by analysing the log books and reports from weather stations in some 800 locations worldwide, beginning with the strange sunsets on three days in May 1883 in Natal, South Africa. Observers in Munich reported peculiar sunsets on three days in May, four days in June and two days in July. There were reports from Belfast for the same months, for example 'hazy overhead' on 15 July, which referred to the famous dry fog. Similar phenomena were noted on 28 August on the island of Diego Garcia and in Japan. At the beginning of September people in wide swathes of Latin America reported seeing a 'blue sun', which appeared shortly thereafter in the Philippines, Ceylon and India. In New Zealand the unusual sunsets continued until January, and in Wisconsin even until March 1884. The radiant sunsets over Europe and the Americas reached their greatest intensity in late December 1883, and lasted to a lesser degree until March, and in South Africa even until June, the following year.[53]

We can only dream of such a density of observations for the Tambora period. The log books, which survive in large numbers, have not yet been analysed, and meteorological journals were only founded in response to the climate phenomena of the era. We do at least have some written accounts. In his note in the *Annalen der Physik* on the observation of sun dogs on 16 June 1815, the physics professor Joseph Weber (1753–1831) wrote that the 'sky was covered with semi-transparent clouds'.[54] On 1 May 1816, the *Daily National Intelligencer* from Washington described the whole atmosphere as 'filled with a thick haze'. On 9 May, the *American Beacon* from Norfolk, Virginia mentioned the 'fine dust' in the atmosphere, which was 'injurious to respiration'. On 15 July, Boston's *Columbian Centinal* wrote 'the Sun's rays, it has been frequently remarked, have not their usual power'. The author attributed this to sunspots, going on to note 'there appears to be less intensity of light as well as heat'.[55] A German medical doctor remarked that this haze had nothing in common with damp fog and closely resembled the smoke visible above Europe thirty years before – that is, at the time of the eruption of Laki.[56] This observation is important because at the time Benjamin

Franklin had been the first to discover that the Laki eruption affected two continents, Europe and North America. In India, the military doctor Reginald Orton connected the 1817 cholera outbreak with the 'thick, "heavy" state of the air, giving it a *whitish* appearance'.[57] As far as we know, dry fog was first observed again in Germany by the Göttingen professor Johann Christoph Daniel Wildt (1770–1844).[58] This, however, was followed by a debate over whether it was truly dry fog, or whether the optical effects had been caused by other natural phenomena.[59]

Other observations related to the intense red glow of the sky at sunset and dusk. In England, unusually colourful sunsets were observed in the summer and autumn of 1815. Letters and newspaper articles from London reported on the glowing sky, which differed from the usual celestial events occasioned by air pollution.[60] In this context the question arose of whether people were seeing such a play of colours because the artist J.M.W. Turner (1775–1851) was painting them, or whether conversely Turner was painting such sunsets because he saw them.[61] Some precipitation also revealed unusual colour effects. Teramo (Abruzzo) on the Adriatic experienced 'a greater quantity of snow than has been known in the memory of man'. The snow was red and yellow, leaving locals with the impression that 'something extraordinary has taken place in the air'. Penitential processions were organised. It remained unusually cold and snowy all that winter in Abruzzo. In Hungary a blizzard raged for two days, causing stalls to collapse, claiming the lives of several thousand sheep and hundreds of oxen. News reports emphasised the fact that the snow was not white but brown or flesh-coloured. In April 1817 there were similar snowfalls at the Tonale Pass (Lombardy), which appeared brick red and left behind an earthy powder.[62]

Corn Laws

The end of the wars – and with them of the wartime economy – brought all manner of problems. During the continental blockade, landowners in the United Kingdom had been encouraged to plant the increasing amounts of grain needed to provision the troops. They had not only invested their profits in increasing production, but had also taken on additional loans. When the continental system ended, this calculation threatened to end in disaster. There was also an especially good harvest in the British Isles, which led grain prices to drop from 118 shillings in January 1813 to 60 in January 1815. A number of farmers had trouble meeting their interest payments, which encouraged the banks to call in the loans. Many farmers and even some banks faced ruin.[63]

It is against this backdrop that the more recent history of the Corn Laws begins, with the Importation Act of 1815, which, together with its successor laws, was abolished only in 1846. The purpose of the Corn Laws was to protect British grain producers from cheap imports from the continent, Russia or the USA, that is, to keep prices artificially high by means of import tariffs. This legislation put ordinary consumers at a disadvantage, for in Britain, too, the diet of the lower classes was still based on bread, so that grain prices had a direct impact on the cost of living. Because of the peculiarities of the British electoral system, which was based on a property qualification, those without property had no representatives of their own in Parliament. The House of Commons was dominated by the wealthy middle classes and the gentry, who profited from high grain prices as landowners, leaseholders or merchants. In the House of Lords the great landowners were virtually among themselves anyway.

The Tory government under Robert Jenkinson, Lord Liverpool (1770–1828), who had led the country through the vicissitudes of war as the youngest prime minister of all time, pushed the Corn Laws through Parliament on 23 March 1815, after the landowning lobby had pressed ever more vociferously for the protection of their interests. Over the course of 1815 the price of wheat in London had fallen to about 50 shillings, and that of other grains was even lower. Members of Parliament knew what they were doing when they passed the Corn Laws. Just in case, the army was ready to protect Parliament in the event of major protests. Many people vehemently opposed the Corn Laws. Petitions sought to prevent them, there were riots in London and other cities, the private houses of ministers were attacked and windows smashed.[64]

The cartoonist George Cruikshank provided a prophetic image of the critique even before the Bill's second reading in Parliament on 3 March 1815: a French sailing ship arrives at England's shores where an attractive blonde offers temptingly cheap grain with the words, 'here is the best for 50 s'. But the four rich landowners speaking for England reject the cheap grain. An older man leaning on a walking stick replies, 'We don't want it at any price. We are determined to keep up our own to 80 s, & if the Poor can't buy at that price, why they must starve, we love money too well to lower our rents again, tho the Income Tax is taken off.' A stout man with gouty legs adds, 'Aye aye let 'em starve and & be D__d to 'em.' And a third agrees,

George Cruikshank, The Blessings of Peace or the Curse of the Corn Bill,
London 1815

'No no, we won't have it at all.' One of the Frenchmen thereupon tips
a sack of grain into the sea, saying 'By gar if they will not have it at all
we must thro it overboard.' John Bull, the personification of England,
stands in the foreground, holding two children by the hand and
looking angrily at the landowners. He comments, 'No no masters,
I'll not starve but quit my native country where the poor are crushed
by those they labor to support & retire to one more Hospitable, &
where the Arts of the Rich do not interfere to defeat the providence
of God.' Behind him stands his wife with another child in her arms.
In the background we see a warehouse filled with sacks of grain with
'80 s' stamped on them.[65]

— 3 —

THE YEAR WITHOUT A SUMMER: 1816

'A new year smiles kindly upon us today'

Cheered by the hope of merry times to come
A new year smiles kindly upon us today
It shall prepare for us, freed at length from woe,
The sweet tranquillity of lasting happiness.[1]

Despite the cold, rainy winter of 1815/16, the climatic turmoil in Southeast Asia seemed far away to people in Europe. At first, only specialists took note of it: colonial officials, ship's captains, officers of the East India Company and a handful of scholars of Asia. Not even volcanologists and geologists were particularly interested in the distant events. The year 1816 was supposed to be a good one. This is evident from all the New Year's poetry with which newspapers and magazines opened their first editions of the year. Historians and political scientists summed up the devastation of war, the human losses, the gaps that billeting and contributions had left in stores of provisions, the interrupted trade relations and the lost markets, and naturally also the burden of debt that all countries and most municipalities had to bear as a legacy of the war years. And then there were the disappointed hopes and the mourning for friends and relations. But the war era appeared to be over. Restless France had been pacified, the revolutionary forces seemed to be under control, and international treaties had reorganised the world.

The USA also looked to the future with confidence. The last attempted invasion by the former colonial power had been pushed back, and it had brought Americans together. Everything seemed calm and peaceful, excellent preconditions for a peace dividend.

Business would revive, the economy would blossom and prosperity would grow. People had only positive things to say about the beginning of 1816.

In a New Year's poem, the Swabian poet Friedrich Rückert (1788–1866) alluded to both the vicissitudes of the war and the hopeful future, using the metaphor of the expected good grain harvest as the symbol of good times:

O most blessed of time's children
When destiny offers you the task,
Of binding the sheaves
The harvest has scattered before you!
From heaven today I wish for you
The finest sunshine, which ensures
That the wheat will ripen unsoaked
In the great barn of peoples.[2]

Sightings of sunspots with the naked eye

These expectations were mixed with the first worries, however. In January and February, scientific journals such as the *Edinburgh National Register* noted increased sightings of sunspots,[3] signalling the rise of a topic that would claim attention throughout the Tambora Crisis. All journals reported on these sightings, and the discussions were heated and intense. Anyone could look directly at the sun with the naked eye and the aid of a tinted or sooty shard of glass and count an increasing number of spots, which is impossible under normal circumstances. The 'contamination' of the sun became a subject of public debate and religious interpretation. The sun's appearance was inevitably associated with the vagaries of the climate and weather in 1816. As in earlier phases of the Little Ice Age, there were fears that the central star would weaken or even that the world would end.[4]

Sunspots had been discovered by Galileo Galilei (1564–1642) shortly after the improvement of the telescope, and were first described in print in 1611.[5] Over the course of the next hundred years scientists found that the number and size of the spots varied. After people became used to their existence, the next surprise was their complete absence for several years. At the peak of the reign of Louis XIV in France this absence coincided with a period of unusually cold temperatures.[6] When the English royal astronomer William Herschel (1738–1822) compared the development of grain prices in Windsor with the statistical frequency of sightings of sunspots over a period of nearly a century, he concluded that the decline in or absence of sunspots tended to correspond to inflation and famine.[7] From the seventeenth century there was a presumed association between sunspots and climate. Since the temperature on our planet largely depends on the sun, and periods of cold coincided with sunspot minima, scientists concluded that sunspots indicated a higher degree of solar activity. This view is still shared today: the sunspot's central umbra arises because of strong magnetic fields, leading to the eruption of solar matter which is catapulted out into the corona. The sunspots are surrounded by especially hot regions, which emit energy-rich radiation. The surface cooling caused by the eruptions becomes visible as a 'spot'. During a sunspot cycle the spots become more frequent and larger. The causes of this variability are no better understood now than they were at the time.

Interestingly, the Tambora Crisis by no means coincided with a phase of increased sunspot activity, although an especially large number of spots were sighted at the time. On the contrary, in the period between 1790 and 1830 astronomers found a low sunspot count, which was recently named the 'Dalton Minimum', after the astronomer John Dalton (1766–1844). The sighting of sunspots in 1816 had nothing to do with solar activity, but only with the darkened atmosphere that made it easier to observe them.[8]

Many amateurs in Europe and North America began to record sunspots. The town clerk of Nördlingen, Johannes Müller (1752–1824), even painted examples of the sunspots he observed in his chronicle, much as Galileo had done two centuries earlier. He was not particularly worried.[9] In Pietist circles and among Christian sectaries, in contrast, people saw the wrath of God at work and not mere 'aberrations of nature'.[10] As an enlightened Württemberg sectary put it, 'We were able to understand that among Christians in name only, love has been transformed into rage and bloodlust, pride and ambition, stubbornness and arrogance, dissimulation and imperiousness, lying and cheating, drinking and gorging and all manner of other abominations.'[11] The Bavarian councillor of state Joseph von Hazzi (1768–1845) wrote:

> Many there dreamt of spots noticed on the sun, which impede its beneficial powers forever, thus heralding the chilling and sinking of the earth. Others even saw a stripe resembling a scythe as proof that this scythe would soon cut down and destroy the human race like blades of grass. Prophets rose up on all sides to proclaim that the end of the world was nigh. There was even a scientific proof that the comet of 1811, which brought a torrid summer, had drawn the phlogiston from the sun, hence

the spots, and hence the fact that there had only been cool, wet and lightning-filled summers since 1811.[12]

In the autumn of 1815 the enlightened public ridiculed the mania for sunspots. An author calling himself Syntax Sidrophel published a poem in the London *Times* revealing that the sunspots were actually Napoleon, who after his second defeat had been left with no refuge but the moon. If one looked through the soot-tinted glass, one could see quite plainly that the spots were his head and limbs. Thus Napoleon Bonaparte was making trouble once again, this time as a sunspot causing cold weather and perpetual rain.[13]

The cold spring of 1816

While the sunspots were more a topic for leisured nature lovers, the majority of the population were more worried about the sluggish start to the agricultural year. To be sure, January and February had been rather mild, with alternating snow and rain. On 10 February 1816, however, the River Weser near Bremen froze, and the frost continued until early April.[14] In Scotland, severe winter storms hindered agricultural work, and winter seeds and root vegetables rotted in the damp fields. The wintry temperatures lasted far into the spring, and the sown grain failed to develop. There was not even enough grass for the sheep, and most of them died from lack of food after the lambing in April. The herds diminished in size and grain prices began to climb.[15]

In southern Germany, according to notes from Gunzenhausen in Middle Franconia,

the year 1816 began with rain and snow, very occasionally interrupted by frost. January and February were changeable, pouring rains that flooded everything, often suddenly followed by bitter cold, which soon gave way to snow, thaws and rain. March resembled its predecessor in wetness, inclemency and cold – that was the sort of weather we had when we were supposed to prepare the field for planting. April was as cold as December, rain constantly alternated with cold, and everyone was worried about the harvest. On 19 April a warm rain finally brought the desired change and we enjoyed dry and sunny days until the end of the month ... But most of May lacked sun ... Lightning brought rain and storms, sometimes also snow, and the young seeds grew only slowly. Many gloomy days resembled those in November.[16]

A chronicle from Bolzano/Bozen in the Tyrol summarises the concerns in northern Italy: at the beginning of the year an unusual amount of snow lay on the ground, joined in March by a bitter cold. In the first half of April there was another massive snowfall, and snow and frosts kept the vegetation from developing into May. It was only at the beginning of June that the first blossoms appeared on the trees. But on the 7th of June snow fell again and the temperatures dropped sharply.[17] A Belgian chronicle stresses that it began to rain at three o'clock in the morning on the 5th of May and continued without a moment's interruption until the morning of the 10th.[18] Placidus Heinrich (1758–1825), a naturalist and Benedictine father, reported the following weather in Regensburg in June 1816: 'Bright days 0, windy 14, days with fog 5, days with rain 12, days with hail 1, days with lightning 3 . . . The sun never shone without spots. A strange month because of the many cloudbursts and floods: because of the destructive hail and the cold when the sun was at its highest: all of this throughout southern Europe, from the 20th to the 30th parallel; and if I am not much mistaken, also reaching Asia and America at the same latitude.'[19] The rains led to the flooding of rivers and lakes and to increasing soil instability. Roads became impassable, there were landslides and entire vineyards slid away. Some cities witnessed even more serious incidents. In the middle of June, after torrential rains, several houses in Bamberg collapsed, burying fifteen people beneath them.[20]

Unrest and the emergence of class society in England

In England, grain and bread prices had reached a low point in January 1816. Since the weather already gave early indications that the next harvest might not be a good one, prices began to rise. By May they had increased from 50 to 76 shillings, before rising to 103 by December. Grain producers, who had been desperate at the start of the year, were feeling more sanguine as the year went on. For consumers the opposite was the case. Contemporary observers found the effect interesting. Agricultural labourers, who were also affected by the rising bread prices, joined forces with urban factory workers against their employers. Their dissatisfaction was especially high because they suffered not just from the high bread prices, but also from unemployment. Since many soldiers had returned from the wars in America, India and the European continent, there was an oversupply on the labour market. As prices rose, wages began to fall.[21]

The unrest began to assume wider dimensions in May 1816, when people called for fixed prices for grain and meat. Acts of vandalism occurred from Suffolk to Essex: barns were set alight and rebels armed with pikes and rifles took power in some towns. The authorities enlisted the help of the military. The ringleaders were captured and put on trial, but the wave of protest spread to the Midlands and the industrialised North. On 28 May strikes began against the low wages and high bread prices in Newcastle-upon-Tyne. In Shropshire and Staffordshire unemployed agricultural labourers migrated to the towns and demanded public assistance. The unemployed demonstrated in industrial cities such as Birmingham, Liverpool, Leicester, Coventry and also London.

The social protests did not just unite rural and urban workers; they were also directed against the wealthy more generally, whether they were grain producers or factory owners. For the disadvantaged, market developments were simply a conspiracy of the propertied, whose headquarters was Parliament. Whigs or Tories, the two great parliamentary parties represented the rich. For the nascent working class, they were all the same. The two parties were equally responsible for passing the Corn Laws and maintaining the political abuse of the census suffrage. Conversely, the union of the poor heightened fears among the rich of a conspiracy of revolutionaries bent upon shaking the existing order. Older lines of conflict became meaningless in comparison. The landed aristocracy no longer lamented the high cost of maintaining the army, which now protected their interests in their own country. Factory owners no longer complained about the rule of justices of the peace drawn from the high nobility, which quite clearly also protected their own property. English class society emerged in the wake of the Tambora Crisis.[22]

The cold, rainy summer in Europe

The young Mary Wollstonecraft (1797–1851), who had left England in May 1816 to escape the eternal winter of that year's spring, wrote from Geneva on 17 June about the final stage of her journey from Paris to Switzerland:

> The spring, as the inhabitants informed us, was unusually late, and indeed the cold was excessive; as we ascended the mountains, the same clouds which so rained on us in the vallies poured forth large flakes of snow thick and fast . . . As the evening advanced, and we ascended higher, the snow, which we had beheld whitening the overhanging rocks, now encroached upon our road, and it snowed fast as we entered the village of Les Rousses, where we were threatened by the apparent

31

necessity of passing the night in a bad inn and dirty beds . . . We hired four horses, and ten men to support the carriage, and departed from Les Rousses at six in the evening, when the sun had already far descended, and the snow pelting against the windows of our carriage.[23]

Once arrived at Lake Geneva, the summer weather did not meet the expectations of the English travellers, who complained:

Unfortunately we do not now enjoy those brilliant skies that hailed us on our first arrival to this country. An almost perpetual rain confines us perpetually to the house . . . The thunder storms that visit us are grander and more terrific than I have ever seen before. We watch them as they approach from the opposite side of the lake, observing the lightning play among the clouds in various parts of the heavens, and dart in jagged figures upon the piny heights of Jura, dark with the shadow of the overhanging cloud. One night we *enjoyed* a finer storm than I had ever before beheld. The lake was lit up, the pines on Jura made visible, and all the scene illuminated for an instant, when a pitchy blackness succeeded, and the thunder came in frightful bursts over our heads amid the darkness.[24]

'The earth is so extraordinarily sodden', the Swiss hospitaller Dufour wrote in his diary on 8 July 1816, 'that fountains spout from every hole. Streams form where none existed before.'[25] Since it rained all that summer, the rivers and lakes everywhere swelled and spilled over their banks. The lakes of Neuchâtel, Bienne and Morat joined to form a single large body of water. On Thursday 9 August the head-waters of the Rhône presented a terrifying sight: the river had been replaced by a mighty flow that swept away everything in its path and flooded large swathes of the valley near Montreux.[26] Lake Geneva swelled, and in some districts of the city boats became the only means of transport. A fifteen-pound trout was caught inside the Hotel de la Couronne. The rivers carried tree trunks and all manner of flotsam, including dead cows.[27]

Northern Italy and Austria also experienced cold, rain, snow and storms. The *Boten aus Tyrol* for 6 July noted, 'Here, too, we have had no lasting fine summer weather; it rains almost daily, and in the high mountains it snows. The small grain, such as wheat, rye and barley, is growing quite well in our region, but needs protracted fine days to ripen; matters are all the worse with the Turkish wheat or maize, which is poorer than in previous years, and risks not ripening at all, for in the uplands this crop has already being harvested in several places to use as animal feed, and buckwheat planted in its stead.' It soon became evident that even this assessment was overly optimistic, for the periods of fine summer weather continued to make themselves scarce. All of July was very wet, and the fruit harvest was meagre. The inflation of grain prices had begun in June, and in September the wheat had to be mown for use as animal feed, since it was unsuitable for making flour. In the climatically favourable wine-growing region around Bolzano/Bozen, the grapevines only flowered in August, several weeks later than usual. Innsbruck experienced only seven days of good weather all summer.[28]

Unusual storms, often paired with lightning and hail, were typical of this summer in Germany. 'Wherever in the countryside one travelled in the summer, one encountered trees felled by the wind. In Karlsruhe and the surrounding regions, the storm was so violent that it tore the roofs off houses, toppled heavily laden wagons on the roads and uprooted 36,000 trees in the woods around Karlsruhe alone.'[29] In Lower Franconia the farmer Johann Georg Kell noted that it had rained uninterruptedly for the five weeks from 23 May until 29 June, 'so that one scarcely got to the fields'. After a three-day pause, the rain set in again on 3 July. It was not merely unusually sustained, but also of a previously unknown intensity. Sebastian Pfister, the forester of Sailershausen (now part of Haßfurt), noted that on 21 June he was prevented from entering the woods all day 'by the extraordinarily inclement weather and heavy rainstorm', as he was on 28 June, 'because it didn't stop raining torrentially all day for a minute. In short, it was a day such as I and several of my fellows had never seen before.' The constant rain was followed by flooding. According to the parish chronicle of Lendershausen (now part of Hofheim), there were ten floods in the short period from 21 June to 19 July alone, which destroyed the entire hay harvest. July was also rainy and stormy.[30] There are even separate contemporary publications about specific days of inclement weather, such as the 15th of June in Tiefenhöchstadt (today part of Markt Buttenheim in Lower Franconia).[31]

Thuringia was also greatly affected, as the diaries of the Gotha geologist Ernst Adolf von Hoff (1771–1837) show.[32] In Middle Franconia people still had to light their heating stoves in June:

Lightning, terrible downpours, indeed cloudbursts, followed by devastating flooding. Throughout the summer, the beautiful meadow-rich Altmühl valley resembled a large lake . . . July began as June had ended. More lightning and rain showers. Almost no day remained bright and warm, and the hope of a hay harvest was drowned. The first half of August was warmer and sunnier, but rarely without lightning, but the second half was mostly raw and gloomy. Everybody was starving or hungry, everybody waited longingly for the sun, in vain, and nothing ripened. My children cried out for bread, their hunger was painful to see. What the rain spared the hail destroyed, and many stood lamenting before the ruined seeds that rotted in the fields alongside the animal feed. All the barns and granaries were empty and we looked towards the coming winter with heavy hearts. The fog and rain lasted almost without interruption into the middle of September.[33]

The weather in Swabia was hardly less terrible. In the Ries region there was exactly one day of sunshine in July, otherwise it rained nearly every day. August was also 'abnormally rainy and cool'. Eyewitness accounts agree that the sun was virtually invisible the entire summer, and when it did show itself, it was behind a veil of mist or fog. On 8 August the Ries was visited by a hailstorm, which destroyed the harvest across the region. The first frost came on 14 September, and between the 16th and the 23rd nighttime temperatures were below freezing. October remained wet and cold. On 12 November 'the farmers' last hopes were buried under the white shroud of falling snow'.[34]

Things were no better on the North Sea coast. The Bremen meteorologist Müller recorded 'rainstorms and lightning nearly every day from May to August, with persistent winds from the west and southwest. This was the wettest year since 1770, with the least warmth. Many ailments in the countryside . . . Constant rain until November, damp, cool days. Grain and hay rotted in the fields. The Weser was 15 feet high. Several dykes broke. Some harvest only on high sandlands. Inflation, famine in Thuringia, Bavaria, on the Rhine, etc. There was no wine at all.'[35]

In Scotland, agriculture suffered from the persistent cold. In this country, which already had a short growing season, all of the crops were four weeks behind. Only in mid-July did the wheat, barley and hay plants gradually develop ears. The grass was too sparse to feed the flocks of sheep. Here, however, there was too little rain. The months of August and September were overcast and stormy and further slowed the ripening of the grain, while the prices rose.[36] In England, Ireland and Wales, in contrast, as on the continent, the cold was paired with precipitation. The harvest of basic foodstuffs – wheat, oats and potatoes – was in danger. The inflation led to famine in Wales and Ireland, and large numbers of otherwise settled families took to the roads to beg. On 20 July 1816 *The Times* observed drily, 'Should the present wet weather continue, the corn will inevitably be laid, and the effects of such a calamity cannot be otherwise but ruinous to the farmers, and even to the people at large.'[37]

People in England observed events on the continent very closely, and worried about the future, as one can read in the *Norfolk Chronicle*: 'Melancholy accounts have been received from all parts of the continent of the unusual wetness of the season; property in consequence swept away by inundation and irretrievable injuries done to the vine yards and corn crops.' The calamities in neighbouring western Europe were particularly noted. For example, the river systems in the Netherlands and France were suffering from the surfeit of water: 'In several provinces of Holland, the rich grass lands are all under water, and scarcity and high prices are naturally apprehended and dreaded. In France the interior of the country has suffered greatly from the floods and heavy rains.'[38]

The Yankee Chill

Unlike in western Europe, in North America the summer of 1816 was marked by drought. What the two major regions in the western hemisphere had in common was extraordinarily cold temperatures. In North America people thus spoke of the Yankee Chill.[39] On average it was 1–2.5 degrees cooler than in other years, but the average was less decisive than certain cold spells: the sudden encroachment of cold polar air. The four cold snaps all came at just the right time to do permanent damage to the grain crops: in mid-May, then from 6–11 June, 8–10 July and finally from 20–30 August.

In his diary, the Vermont farmer Hiram Harwood (1792–1874) first described the delay in growth due to the sustained cold weather in May. It rained and stormed throughout the night of 5 June, and when he awoke the next morning he experienced the 'most gloomy and extraordinary weather' he had ever seen. The mountains were covered in snow, the fields and pastures frozen. The frost had blackened the leaves on all the trees overnight. The water was covered in a thick layer of ice. It was impossible to work without gloves. On 8 June the icy north wind brought snow. The next day, a Sunday, was still frosty, but clear. It was still cold on 10 June, and the wheat plants had died.[40] It snowed from Canada to Massachusetts. But even south of the snow line the cold wave was palpable. In New York, frozen birds fell from the trees. In Connecticut, the cold summer left the pastor and diarist Thomas Robbins (1777–1856) 'very much oppressed with anxiety'. On Sunday 9 June, in light of the frost damage to his parishioners' fruit trees, he preached a sermon on the parable of the barren fig

Thomas Jefferson's handwritten weather records, Washington, Library of
Congress, Manuscript Division, William C. Rives Papers

tree (Luke 13).[41] The cold wave could be felt even in the southern
states.

The period of frost in late August proved the most devastating,
since it dashed all hopes of an abundant harvest. Governor William
Plumer (1759–1850) of New Hampshire travelled from Salisbury to
Hanover on 20 August and noted that the maize crop was ruined
all along the route.[42] Optimists that the Americans were, farmers
had planted new seeds twice, but after the last cold snap it became
apparent that this year would no longer see a sufficient harvest. To
be more precise, it was the worst harvest ever recorded in North
America. On 1 September 1816, the Moravian Brethren[43] in North
Carolina summed the situation up as follows: 'The very cool and dry
weather in spring and summer hurt our grain fields badly, and it was
with sorrowful and troubled hearts that we gathered our second crop
of hay and our corn crop, which were so scanty that we reaped only
a third of what we usually get, and wondered how we would subsist
until next year's harvest.'[44]

Goethe in the rain

'I have become aware of the English poet Lord Byron, who begins to interest us', wrote the minister of state of Saxe-Weimar Johann Wolfgang von Goethe (1749–1832) in that very June of 1816 when Byron and his entourage were rained in on Lake Geneva.[45] Naturally he had travelled in Switzerland long before the English party, viewing the mountains and glaciers and making contacts in and around Geneva. As he did every year, he was planning his stay at a spa, intended to provide relief for his various physical complaints. That he was plagued 'by a curious, not dangerous but strongly rheumatic ailment', which sometimes forced him to keep to his bed, only reinforced this intention. The abnormal weather was already playing a role in the summer, though, as we can see from his correspondence. 'I cannot survive wholly without an excursion to the baths, since our Cimmerian summer is more liable to oppress than to enliven us'.[46] In his diary for that same date he notes that 'very cold air' prevailed in Weimar.[47]

Goethe felt oppressed not just by the weather, however, but also by the acute illness and later death of his young wife Christiane. He dedicated a poem to the anniversary of her death. With the help of weather conditions, it expresses his mood, which corresponded to that summer's climate:

'The 6th of June 1816'
Thou seekest, O sun, in vain
To shine through the dark clouds!
My life's entire gain
Is to lament her loss.[48]

The death of his wife did not, however, keep Goethe from his travel plans, which usually took him to one of the Bohemian spas. That year, though, his friends wanted to lure him to southwest Germany, and after his wife's death he was all the more ready to take up this invitation, especially because he could meet his mother, relatives, friends and his publisher Johann Friedrich Cotta (1764–1832) there. The first idea was to go to Wiesbaden, then Baden-Baden, where Cotta was supposed to book lodgings for Goethe and his companions from late July.[49] Unwittingly, the poet prince was making plans to travel to the heart of the European famine. 'The evil weather' caught up with Goethe before he even left home. In his diary he complained on 23 June of the 'horribly sodden state of the garden'.[50] This further inspired his plans to travel to the southwest, 'in the hopes of moving towards a better climate and favourable weather'. He formally announced his impending departure from Weimar to Grand Duchess Louise, citing the 'highly unpleasant, irksome and harmful weather in these parts'.[51]

Goethe left Weimar at seven o'clock on the morning of 20 July 1816, but the journey soon took an unexpected turn, as he wrote in a letter: 'At 9 o'clock, shortly before reaching Münchenholzen, the most inept of all carter's men toppled the carriage; the axle broke and the good fellow Meyer hurt his forehead.' Now it proved a disadvantage that Goethe was travelling in his own carriage and could not simply exchange it for another. He had to send to Weimar for help, which took several hours to arrive, and the injured Aulic Councillor Meyer needed treatment. It would take at least fourteen days for him to recover. In order not to lose the best month at the spa, Goethe changed his plans. Instead of Baden he travelled on 24 July to the sulphur baths at Tennstedt in Thuringia, between the posting houses of Langensalza and Weißensee.[52] But first the journey went back to Weimar, and that same evening Goethe dined with the physicist Ernst Florens Friedrich Chladni (1756–1827). According to Goethe's diary the conversation revolved around meteors, which Chladni had been one of the first to identify as fallen celestial bodies.[53] Meteorology, i.e., the science of weather, had taken its name from meteors. And it seems likely that the men also discussed the current climate crisis, which preoccupied many scientists.[54] Chladni was after all among those authors who had developed their own theories of the 'causes of the wet, cold summer of 1816' in the pages of the *Annalen der Physik*.[55]

Goethe was anything but satisfied with his stay at the new Electoral Saxon sulphur baths at Tennstedt, which had only been in operation for three years. Neither the guests nor the bathhouse could compete with those in Carlsbad or Baden-Baden. Above all, however, it was 'this weather . . . [that turned] the stay into such a miserable affair . . . The weather is awful . . . and so we are once again obliged to persevere in Islam' [i.e., in complete submission to God]. It rained day and night, with only lightning and downpours bringing a bit of variety. This hampered even the business of taking the cure: 'The bad weather prevents us from drinking the waters regularly. The bath does me good, but the weather hinders everything good.' The 'kind sunshine' showed itself for the first time on 31 July, but 'the terrible roads prevent us from making excursions'. The 'mucky' paths impeded even the simplest of promenades.[56]

Back in Weimar, Goethe was completely overtaken by the winter blues, since 'the uncertain days of fog and rain are by no means cheering'.[57] And the end of the year was no better. Throughout December Goethe battled a 'terrible catarrh', from which he had not yet recovered by the year's end. He noted in a faintly ironic tone, 'I have been tormented by a catarrh for four weeks, so that in the interval, because some things do need to get done, I can undertake only feverish activities.'[58] It was not until the new year that Goethe was back on his feet. On 20 February 1817 he read an account of the eruption of Mount Tambora in Cotta's *Morgenblatt für die gebildeten Stände*, about which his diary reports, 'Newspapers. Read the Morgenblatt. Story about a new volcano on Sumbawa.' Neither he nor the commentators on his writings saw any connection between this and the cooling, constant rains, and failed harvests of 1816.[59]

Literary historians usually study Goethe the lyric poet, dramatist, epicist, correspondent and autobiographer. As a minister of state, however, Goethe was also responsible for mining and the natural sciences more generally, and he retained an interest in these matters throughout his life. Climate scientists have recently become interested in Goethe as a mineralogist or early theorist of past ice ages. Things become more interesting if we examine his life and research interests together. During preparations for his spa stay, he spent 28 June 1816 considering both the 'persistent rainy weather' and the oxygen content of the atmosphere, and engaged in a 'discussion of sunspots' together with the other Weimar mining councillors Döbereiner, von Münchow and Voigt. On 29 June he explored 'grain rust' – that is, the failed harvest – and the local flooding in the wake of constant rain. On 1 and 2 July, between conversations with several experts, he studied a publication by Georg Friedrich von Jäger (1785–1866) on the 'deformation of plants'.[60] On 21 July, Goethe observed 'storm clouds dissolving into summer lightning', which fitted well with the theory of clouds he had been grappling with repeatedly since December 1815, inspired by an essay in the *Annalen der Physik* by the meteorologist Luke Howard (1772–1864), the pioneer of cloud classification.[61] This penchant may be viewed in connection with the abnormal weather and extraordinary cloud formations of those years.[62]

The end of the world on 18 July 1816

A growing host of farmers, economists and politicians observed nature with concern. People of a religious disposition awaited God's vengeance for the corruption of the world. And so in the summer of 1816 a prophecy from Italy, launched perhaps by an astronomer in the papal university city of Bologna, enjoyed a certain popularity. The English press referred to him as 'the mad Italian prophet'. He had purportedly predicted that the growing number of sunspots would lead to the sun burning out and losing its power on 18 July 1816. This would signal the end of the world, for without warmth all life must perish. The cold spring had been but a prelude. On 20 June 1816, the London *Morning Chronicle* reported on this apocalyptic prophecy, which was circulating in Paris and London, as well as 'in every other part of Europe'. The next day, the newspaper noted the astronomer's arrest: the government had deemed this announcement of an impending solar disaster to be too dangerous.

Was this report intended merely in jest? The name of the alleged prophet is never mentioned, but even serious newspapers continued to report on the affair. The London *Times* reported on 29 July that 'Italian mountebanks' had originally announced the disaster for 25 May, and only after it did not transpire changed the date to 18 July.[63] But the 'mad Italian prophet' from Bologna was not alone: in early June, a priest in Naples by the name of Carillo also announced that the end of the world was nigh. In the church of San Giacomo degli Spagnoli (now the Palazzo Giacomo, seat of the municipal government of Naples) he preached that the city would be completely destroyed on 27 June by a four-hour rain of fire. In other Italian cities that spring, 'prophets' also announced the dates of the impending end of the world.[64]

The 18th of July remained the most important of these dates. On 9 July, under the title 'General Conflagration', the *London Chronicle* reported on the advertised end of the world, but referred to such announcements as 'outrageous fooleries'. These fooleries spread to Austria via northern Italy, however. On 14 July, the *Wiener Zeitung* stated that the announcement had now spread everywhere, and rioting, which had to be broken up by the army, had already erupted in Udine (Friuli), Klagenfurt (Styria) and other Austrian towns.[65] On 17 July a resourceful publisher in Paris brought out a pamphlet entitled *Détails sur la fin du Monde*.[66] The London *Morning Chronicle* reported that this work sold like hotcakes, and that many Frenchmen and women fully expected the world to end the next day. The same issue of the newspaper noted that all over Paris, public prayers for better weather had been mandated, which underlines the connection to the Tambora Crisis. The 'silly report' on the end of the world was creating more excitement overall in Paris than in London. On

17 July, *The New British Lady's Magazine* also reported from Paris on the effects of the prophecy: 'Alarm and consternation pervade all ranks; even those who affect to laugh at the prediction evidently feel its influence ... and all wait the event with patient horror, though ashamed of openly avowing it; for as a Frenchman's sensible part is ridicule, they are afraid of being laughed at if the event does not come to pass.'[67]

Punctually on 18 July 1816, the *Morning Chronicle* published a satire on the end of the world under the title 'The Dreaded Eighteenth of July'. The author was allegedly the ominous 'Cassandra', named after the tragic daughter of the Trojan King Priam.[68] Cassandra confirmed that the end of the world prophesied by the Italian astronomer had indubitably come. That is why she had personally composed a 'code of instruction' for everybody to follow. This set of instructions contained useful advice on how to survive the end of the world. For instance, one should not arrange any duels for the morning of 18 July, soldiers should give up cursing and drinking, poets should return stolen verses and women should exchange the latest French novels for volumes of homilies. Thus the *Morning Chronicle*, central organ of the Whig party, mocked and ridiculed superstition. A laconic note in the diary of the writer John Cam Hobhouse (1786–1869) – 'The day the world was to be at an end' – shows that the educated were also well aware of the date.[69]

After the date had come and gone the newspapers continued to write about it. The landscape painter Joseph Farington (1747–1821) wrote in his diary on 19 July: 'Another wet morning: the season very remarkable. A foolish prediction has prevailed on the Continent & with some in England that spots in the sun indicated that the world would be at an end yesterday. A poor woman mentally affected by this impression hung herself last week.'[70] The *Gazette de Lausanne* noted on 23 July that the day had brought the sun, not the end of the world, although 'enlightened persons' had already predicted the extinction of that star.[71] That same day, under the headline 'Predicted End of the World', the *London Chronicle* reported that the mad Italian's prophecy had aroused such fear among some people in Flanders, France, Germany and other parts of Europe that they had stopped doing business and sunk into despondency. In Bath, a woman lapsed into a coma out of sheer terror, and in Ghent the population fell to their knees for a final prayer when cavalry troops rode through the city during a storm. They had taken the soldiers' trumpet call for the sounding of the seven trumpets from the Book of Revelation.

Farmers watch their fields in horror

In a journal entry dated 16 July 1816, the Alsatian farmer Johann Peter Hoffmann (1753–1842) reported:

> On the 6th of July I was in Pfalzburg. Yesterday wheat was 23 f per Frl, a loaf of bread costs 27 S. The rainy weather continues. The hay has not been made anywhere. The grass is rotting on the meadows, all the mountains are full of water. There is nothing but misery everywhere. The beggars are so frequent that there is nothing to be done, the poor suffer greatly. Potatoes are almost impossible to find. The sester [c. 12 bushels] costs 30 to 40 S and is hard to get. Nothing can grow, it is always too cold, I do not know what will happen until the harvest, which will be very late. Fortunately, as concerns ourselves, we suffer no want.[72]

As early as 20 July, the London *Times*, well informed as ever, predicted the ruin of British farmers if the wet weather continued.[73]

The Swiss clergyman Peter Scheitlin, who travelled from St Gall to Glarus on 7 October, made the following observation:

> The day was quite fine, but cold. A fine day was a very rare thing in 1816. Nearly the entire year was cold and rainy. That is why the grain was far behind, and none of it well formed. The later seeds in our region were not yet ripe, and the oats were still green. The grapes threatened to freeze on the vines, green and unripe. Garden vegetables had been largely devoured by innumerable snails. The hay and aftermath had grown crooked in the constant damp, and could only be laboriously dried in the rare moments when the sun appeared. Where in dry years one could harvest 30–40 *Viertel* of potatoes, this year one harvested only five or ten. In some places they were left in the ground for the mice because it was not worth the effort for the farmers to dig them up. The potatoes were mostly miserably bad, pale, glassy and scabby. Little fruit grew, and what there was lacked vigour.[74]

The farmer Johann Georg Kell from Nassach in Lower Franconia wrote in his diary:

> It began snowing on the 10th of November and a good deal fell. The field was was still full of oats. It was so cold on the 20th and the 23rd that the windows were covered from top to bottom with ice, which scarcely thawed by midday. And the people went out and scratched the oats out from under the snow, bound them together and took them home. This snow lay on the ground until the 12th of December, and then it began to rain and in the evening the wind grew so strong that it

42

uprooted trees and chased the tiles from the roofs, and the water came down hard. On the 18th it started snowing again and stayed on the ground until the 25th of December. Then it melted in places.[75]

Adopting the farmer's perspective, Bavarian Councillor of State Joseph von Hazzi reported:

In the meantime, the agriculturalist was tearing his hair out. The continuous rain and the advanced season scarcely permitted him to till his winter fields. He could not even think of going to the grain market. The long period had also completely exhausted his stores. It was time for the threshing, but how much stranger did it seem to him that upon threshing most of the grain turned into empty straw, that is, two-thirds less harvest and far less fodder than expected. For the hay and oats were paltry, the cold had even left the clover very low and weak. Finally, his grain fields were also not much to his liking. Countless snails, mice, vermin and weeds appeared as they had in 1570, 1770 and 1771. Very hard days indeed awaited man and beast, and matters were more terrible still in the regions hit by hail.[76]

Warnings of crop failure foment government fears

The prophecies of doom from some parts of the country caught the government of the kingdom of Bavaria unawares. In the spring, they had still anticipated an especially good harvest. But in early June, Minister of State Count Maximilian von Montgelas (1759–1832) informed the king of warnings of a potentially poor harvest because of the wet weather, as well as of the expected unrest in the countryside. The commissioner-general of the Isar district, Baron Ferdinand von Schleich (1766–1833), had told the minister that the farmers were 'in a state of near desperation', while the citizens of Munich were responding rather calmly to price rises. This was to change, however. On 6 July the minister of state told the king: 'When the topic turns to the present dearness, the populace curses policing and the government, and cites Baron Stengel, who supposedly once told the people here that if they could not fill their bellies with a 1-kreuzer bread, they should buy one for 2 kreuzers.'[77] Nothing was more feared than hunger riots, especially in the capital Munich, where another perennially important factor was the price of beer, which was closely tied to the price of grain, whether barley or wheat. In fact, popular anger was initially directed at bakers and brewers. Soon, though, because of alleged price speculation, it also turned to businessmen and especially to a Jewish banker who was involved in grain and potato speculation together with the electoral widow. Members of the ruling dynasty found themselves doubly in the line of fire: aside from their failure to ensure the survival of the people, they were also accused of lining their own pockets.[78]

The dramatic rise in prices meant that life became unaffordable for many people with low incomes. It is surely no coincidence that the first complaints came from large cities such as London, Paris or Vienna, where servants and day labourers could not fall back on gardens or small domestic animals of their own, making life costly even in normal times. In early July a certain 'F.G. v. K.', whom librarians have identified as Count Fedor von Karacsay (1878–1859), published his 'Frank Thoughts on the Dearness in Vienna'. The author, who began his treatise with a quotation from the Enlightenment cameralist Josef von Sonnenfels, calculated the composition of the incomes of small earners and simple civil servants, and what difficulties they encountered during times of inflation in supplying their families with food, clothing and firewood when they also had to pay rent. As soon as any unexpected expenses arose because of accident or illness, these families faced extreme hardship. And the author was not speaking here of the poorest stratum of the workforce, servants and day labourers, or factory workers. Karacsay supported the widespread view that the greed and profiteering of middlemen were responsible for the inflation. His publication called on the government of the Habsburg monarchy to restrain profiteering and set upper limits for the prices of basic foodstuffs.[79]

On 20 July, the government in the kingdom of Naples began receiving reports that the harvest that year was expected to be poor. On 7 August these fears became certainty, and it was clear that the wheat harvest would be wretched, barely one-third of the usual yield. The previous year's wheat harvest had already been disappointing, but in 1816 the gap could not be filled by maize, since the yield of this crop was similarly miserable.[80] In the Palatinate, official inspections in the individual districts beginning in August revealed substantial hardship in many towns and villages, and a growing displeasure among the population. By September, District President Zwackh had reached the conclusion that a wave of emigration was a real danger.[81] It was widely believed that 'profiteering in grain' must be involved in the inflation.[82] In Munich the scenario appeared so disquieting that in August Montgelas established a system of daily reports on developments in the popular mood. The ensuing flood of information was so overwhelming that a new order was issued stipulating that beyond the daily horror reports, they should only be sent accounts of truly important incidents. These included, for instance, the report in early October that most of the population in the district of Erding had fallen ill after eating mouldy bread. Later that month, the commissioner-general of the Isar district noted that the fact that 'unrest has not long since broken out among the citizenry in these hard times' was likely a result of educational efforts since the beginning of the reform era. He added, however, that the military should be kept in readiness just in case.[83]

The spectre of profiteering

While the Conseil d'Etat of the newly independent Swiss canton of Vaud (Waadtland) reacted quickly, already imposing a ban on grain exports in July 1816 as well as promoting imports and deliberately building up stocks,[84] the governments of other countries needed longer to do likewise. In Bavaria, tariff policy had been liberalised after the end of the continental blockade, and most members of the government were staunch supporters of Adam Smith's doctrine of free trade. Motions to raise export tariffs or lower import tariffs on grain, as recommended by the commissioner-general of the Upper Main district in Upper Franconia, were deemed inappropriate, as was the old European method of the 'grain embargo', a ban on exports. At the end of July the government was still hoping for a better than usual harvest, and accordingly instructed the regional governments to refrain from taking action and to distribute stores to the public on written application in case of emergency. Such corn stocks – a means of provisioning the population since the Middle Ages, as evidenced by the large granaries and corn warehouses in the cities – no longer existed, though, after years of war. They had been exhausted during the march-throughs by troops. This illustrates the degree to which the central government initially misunderstood the situation.[85]

Economic experts were sceptical of an export blockade, but also bewildered by the looming crisis. Clearly, the scarcity of grain and the inflation of food prices that so inflamed public sentiment were not connected with Bavarian economic policy or the failings of individual officials or speculators, but rather with widespread crop failures. Since Europeans had not heard of the eruption of faraway Mount Tambora even a year after it took place, or at least saw no connection between it and their own crisis, they sought the causes beyond the bad weather, partly in politics and partly in economic mechanisms. In December 1816 the director of finance for the Regen district, Albrecht

Ludwig Seutter (1773–1850), author of an 'Account of higher agrarian science',[86] believed there was a connection with the incessant European wars, which had brought with them a constant diminution of operating capital in agriculture and thus a decline in the cultivation of the soil as well as an emptying of warehouses. He also suspected errors in economic policy, and saw problems in consumer buying power.[87]

More generally, the famine of 1770 served as a parameter, for example for the statistician Joseph von Hazzi.[88] In December 1816 people tried to comfort themselves that, compared to the earlier famine, there were bottlenecks at the moment but not yet any substantial lack of grain. The Würzburg professor and later Bavarian prime minister Ignaz von Rudhart (1790–1838) even concluded that while there might be local shortages, there were by no means national ones, and that the inflated prices were a result of speculation.[89] Statistical material published later contradicted this interpretation,[90] but reports from the administrative districts were themselves contradictory from the beginning. While in the Isar district (Munich) people complained of rising unemployment, in the Upper Danube district (Augsburg) there was a labour shortage. Some farmers became impoverished, while others profited.[91]

This caused Montgelas to conclude that the inflation had been brought about 'purely artificially' by the machinations of a few speculators and fostered by 'wrong and excessive measures',[92] not least under pressure from the 'noisy pronouncements of the upper and lower Munich rabble', who thereby 'played into the hands of the monopolists'.[93] The minister of state's interpretation appeared to suggest that taking action against the grain profiteers would alleviate the inflation of prices, but the proponents of free trade were not convinced. 'All prohibitions, even the death penalty, have proven ineffective thus far against usury [*Wucher*] and smuggling. There is not even any proper definition of usury. The word is only used with regard to grain when grain becomes scarcer, and thus dearer, as we saw; it appears to be more spectre than reality, and only free trade banishes or releases this spectre.'[94]

Corn Jews

Despite its unanimous rejection by economic policymakers, the stereotype of the 'corn Jew' was revived during the Tambora Crisis. The negative image of a grain speculator of the Jewish faith, the term for

Potato speculator, painted shooting target 'To commemorate the famine of 1817', 1817, Erlangen, Hauptschützen-Gesellschaft

which has thus far been traced back to the seventeenth century (but no further),[95] may be rooted in the antisemitism of Martin Luther.[96] We know of several prints and medals by the Gotha engraver Christian Wermuth (1661–1739) from the famine year 1693, depicting the motifs that reappeared during the famine of 1816/17. One variant was the greedy corn Jew carrying a sack of grain on his back, with the Devil riding along and driving him onward. Another version was the corn speculator who has hanged himself from a branch after his speculation was foiled by a good harvest. Both iconographic variants appeared in 1817, in some cases – likely for fear of punishment by the authorities – without the label 'you corn Jew', but certainly as a clearly identifiable motif for many beholders.

This stereotype reached its height in the decades around 1800,[97] because the fundamental debate over equal rights for Jews peaked at the time of the political reorganisation of Europe. The 1789 Bill of Rights in the USA and the revolutionary constitution of 1791 in France had ended legal discrimination against Jews in those countries and their colonies. The Revolutionary Wars benefited German Jews, since French law applied in all those territories annexed by France. And in the French-influenced Grand Duchies of Berg, Frankfurt and the kingdom of Westphalia, the Napoleonic Code was introduced accordingly. The future belonged to equal rights. Both Prussia and Austria called for its introduction in the German states. It was even included as Article 16 in the German Federal Act of 1815, but only in mitigated form at the request of the smaller member states: the introduction of legal equality was left up to the individual states.[98]

The Free City of Frankfurt – seat since 1815 of the German Federal Assembly – became the focus of attention because the city government sought to rescind the grand ducal edict introducing equality and to return the Jews to their previous status.[99] These discussions happened to coincide with the period of the Tambora Crisis, but the latter rendered them more topical and more explosive, since interested circles carefully cultivated the stereotype of the profiteer and the corn Jew against this background. Political writers such as the Berlin historian Friedrich Christian Rühs (1781–1820), who wrote a nasty antisemitic pamphlet opposing the policy of equality promoted in Prussia by Wilhelm von Humboldt,[100] and the professor of theology Jakob Friedrich Fries (1773–1843), who taught first in Heidelberg and then in Jena, inflamed the public mood at the height of the inflation crisis, opining that 'Jewry is a remnant of an uncultivated prehistoric era, which should be not [merely] restricted but eliminated altogether'.[101]

The Bavarian councillor of state von Hazzi pointed out that Pope Pius VII (1742–1823) had provided a direction for the critique in his anti-usury edict of 7 August 1816. 'Soon the cries became louder when the granary was less well filled and grain prices rose. A general war cry against profiteers and corn Jews quickly ensued. People no longer recognised farmers, seeing in them only the spectres of the grain clippers.'[102] And in another passage Hazzi continues, not without irony, 'The grain prices rose in all regions and countries, and in the manner of our forefathers one heard everywhere the same war cry about corn profiteers as the cause of the dearness. It sounded throughout Europe, for the same weather dominated nearly this entire region of the earth. The horizon looked as if it was covered with a shroud, and the sun was thus always veiled. This and the incessant rain left the ground wet and cold and the products of the soil – grain, fruit and wine – were meagre and poor.'[103] From Rome the first thunderbolts rumbled against the corn merchants as profiteers and clippers. The preamble to the papal edict of 7 August already stated: 'His Holiness has learnt to his great dismay that the class of avaricious speculators, corn profiteers and wholesale grain buyers are constantly seeking to enrich themselves through the misfortune of others etc., that these despicable monopolists are traversing the provinces to buy up the grain, scarcely has it been harvested.'[104]

Both under Napoleon and in the years of the Bourbon restoration, Jewish merchants were regularly convicted of profiteering in the French départements of Haut-Rhin and Bas-Rhin (in the Alsace region) – few Jews lived elsewhere in France in those days. In the neighbouring Palatinate, in contrast, accusations of profiteering were levied exclusively at Christian farmers and landowners who hoarded their own grain and smuggled it over the border illegally.[105]

A research project studying credit networks in the Saar-Moselle region has shown that during the Tambora Crisis Jewish bankers were naturally involved in providing the small loans necessary to weather the period of crisis. The number of such private loans increased exponentially in the years 1816–1818 because the public banking system was not well developed at the time. However, Jewish moneylenders tended to provide larger loans with clear schedules of payment and were barely involved in small consumer loans. To the extent that one can tell from the records, they offered the same interest rates as their Christian competitors, generally 5 per cent.[106] In cases of small loans to farmers or day labourers, the usual agreement was that the loan would be repaid after the harvest. The volume of credit was highest in 1818, and still relatively high in the two years that followed, which may mean that farmers were investing in the expansion and modernisation of agriculture. The extensive documents contain no evidence of conflicts with Jewish lenders.[107]

Presumably, Jewish merchants traded in grain during the inflation crisis as much as Christian merchants or millers did.[108] However, since a revision of Napoleonic legislation in 1808, which was retained under Prussian rule, they were required to obtain official confirmation every year that they were not engaging in profiteering. This was discriminatory, but the official attestation protected them from accusations of profiteering.[109] In 1816, the government of the kingdom of Bohemia placed a general ban on Jews trading in grain.[110] In Munich, the mood was so inflamed that some feared a pogrom might break out in the autumn.[111] In September the astonished government, which was planning nothing of the kind, heard rumours of an impending expulsion of all Jews from Bavaria. In August 1817 it was claimed – again with no factual basis whatsoever – that 6,000 Jewish families had been expelled from Switzerland and resettled in Bavaria.[112] Anonymous forces were deliberately stirring up fears, and the effect was soon felt: in the autumn of 1817 travellers reported from Ingolstadt and Augsburg that the Jews there no longer felt safe and feared for their lives.[113]

A concrete case of violence can be found in the chronicle by Pastor Philipp Scherer, who reported, albeit only second-hand, on a riot in the Prussian city of Koblenz on 14 August 1817:

> The profiteers endeavoured to keep the price of grain high, and thus paid close attention to the prices on the grain market in order to take measures accordingly and adjust their purchases. One farmer who had 7 *Malter* [an old measurement that varied locally] of corn with him asked for 9 fl. per *Malter*. A Jew, a negotiator, hearing this, ran over and said, I'll give you 15 fl., closed the sacks and put them aside. A citizen of Mainz who was standing nearby and heard this assailed the Jew straight away and beat him. This noise attracted many others, eager to see what was happening, and they were told the story, whereupon all of them fell upon the Jew and beat him so severely that, as I was assured, he died of his injuries.[114]

This story cannot be confirmed by other sources, but suggests that the inhibition threshold for violence had been lowered.[115]

The crisis mechanism sets in

Cold snaps and bad weather are nothing unusual in northern and central Europe, and farmers are prepared for them as they are for periods of rain or drought. There are some exceptions to this rule, however. Frost too late in the year damages nearly all crops, even fruit trees. Grapevines need enough sun in the summer to ripen, and cereal grains can cope with substantial water in the growth phase, but not in high summer before the harvest. In June 1816, with the onset of constant rain in most regions of Europe, it became obvious that there might be a problem. And this affected cereals most of all. Moreover, the typical alternative crops such as protein-rich legumes also failed, as Scheitlin noted in his travel account:

> There were almost no peas, they completely failed, likewise the beans. The cabbages were like water, so paltry and immeasurably dear. Oats were not to be had. Not one foodstuff that grew here or in the environs was cheap, not one was good or healthy. The warm sun gives strength, the sun gives nourishment, the sun is and gives life. Even the milk yielded little butter, and even meat provided little nourishment. Thus a small portion of food no longer satisfied – hence the universal complaint that foods had lost their power to nourish and strengthen, and hence the enfeeblement of many people.[116]

Paradoxically, meat prices did not rise. Since livestock had to be slaughtered in large numbers because too little fodder could be stored given the constant rainfall and flooding, there was even an oversupply of meat. This was of little help to the poor, however, because they could not afford meat even in normal times, and still less when their sources of income were destroyed by unemployment.

Once the harvest was endangered the prices for cereals began to rise relentlessly, peaking after more than a year in late June 1817. As we know from the research of Wilhelm Abel (1904–1985), the demand for cereal grains was relatively inflexible in ancien régime Europe because they were the basis for the most important foodstuffs – bread, porridge, noodles, dumplings etc. – as well as roux for soups and sauces and, in fermented form, for beer. In northern Europe, people could substitute cheaper rye for the more popular wheat, while in Italy people could switch to maize or rice. In some areas potatoes were already established as an alternative staple, but the 1816 potato harvest also fell victim to the rain. The extent of the price rises differed from region to region. In southern Italy a doubling of grain prices already led to serious difficulties. In many parts of Germany, Switzerland and France, however, corn prices increased fivefold, and in some places tenfold. At the Würzburg corn market, trading was suspended at the height of the inflation on 28 June 1817 because no grain was offered for sale and it was impossible to set prices.[117]

On the part of simple consumers, the immediate effect of the inflation of grain prices was an attempt to reduce costs in other areas in order to ensure basic subsistence. Initially this meant a reduction in consumption. This in turn fed back into the crisis. Falling demand led to a decline in commerce, which led to can-celled orders from industrial producers. This in turn meant there was no longer enough work for all. Factories dismissed workers, merchants and tradesmen their employees and servants. Even in the countryside farm labourers were fired as extra mouths to feed who burdened the household when there was no work for them to do. Dismissed servants lost their lodgings along with their jobs. As a consequence of the crisis, the army of jobless and often homeless people, who were desperately searching for work because they lacked the means to absorb even the smallest loss of wages, swelled in the course of the summer. You did not have to be a prophet to imagine the consequences, which were all too familiar from previ-ous crises: a growing number of beggars would become a burden on local communities or go out on the road, social tensions would rise and with them the number of crimes recorded against property and persons.[118] The older historical school of economics has already described this crisis process.[119]

The structural crisis of the textile industry

The Swiss textile industry expected the lifting of the continental blockade to usher in a new golden age. The war-related disruptions to trade relations were over, and high-quality Swiss products had access to all markets once again. This was especially significant for the industrial regions of eastern Switzerland, since industrialisation was so far advanced there that not only had the population grown substantially, but agriculture had been reduced so far in some areas that food had to be imported from southern Germany. As soon as sales stagnated – as in wartime – there was not enough money to import food, or among industrial workers to purchase it.

The end of the continental system did not have the expected effect, however. On the contrary, the European markets were flooded with English goods. Since Swiss manufacturers could not compete with the prices of English cotton textiles, the textile industry suffered a crisis. Traditional hand spinners became unemployed virtually overnight. Since other countries underwent similar experiences, the mercantilist idea of protective tariffs gained ground from 1816. All countries tried to protect their own industries. France was the first to close its markets to foreign cotton cloth, which targeted the English but also affected the Swiss. Shortly thereafter Austria prohibited the import of Swiss textiles into its Italian possessions, and the kingdom of Naples raised its import tariffs. Swiss industry faced ruin.[120]

In his micro-study of the small Swabian town of Laichingen, Hans Medick has shown that, even in normal years, not all inhabitants of the villages and agricultural towns could live from their own agricultural produce. Because of the inheritance laws in this region, where land was divided equally among the children, farms were split into such small parcels that most people needed another occupation to feed their families.[121] On the Swabian Jura, linen weaving had developed over several decades into the most important branch of the economy. The weavers were small-scale entrepreneurs who bought the raw materials and processed them into linen cloth in their own workshops. Because of the wars between 1793 and 1815 and the blockade, these linen weavers had lost their markets. They also faced competition from cheap industrially produced cloth from England.

The tradespeople of the Swabian Jura – and other traditional areas of the domestic textile industry in central Europe – found themselves in a structural crisis.

Because of their diminishing purchasing power, tradespeople were especially dependent on being able to supplement their incomes by growing food for sale and/or their own consumption. An account by the pastor of Laichingen places this problem in a historical context:

> Our town, which numbers 300 citizens, has relatively few farmers and 250 artisans, all of them from the weaver's trade. Twenty years ago they gave life to the place, and at the same time provided for and fed the poor by giving them work and good wages. They were of great benefit even to the farmers. The latter could make a bit of money cultivating their fields and compensate for what they spent on taxes and the services of tradesmen such as wheelwrights and blacksmiths. But now things look quite different. Many years of war and the lasting stagnation of trade as well as four lean years owing to adverse weather and failed harvests on the one hand, and the excessive taxes as a result of wartime events and other obligatory payments and the scarcely affordable grain prices on the other, have reduced most of the local weavers to dire poverty and many to beggary.[122]

The crisis in the weaver's trade led to the collapse of the mainstay of the economy. Workers were dismissed with no prospect of future employment; farmers lost their sources of additional income and could no longer hire village artisans. The commercial crisis had been going on for twenty years, and famine and inflation for four, but things had never been as bad as they were in 1816, when all of the crisis factors were compounded.

Much as in Swabia or Switzerland, reports by the Electoral Hessian regional governments describe stagnation in the textile industry, leading both to the unemployment of large segments of workers, artisans and journeymen and the helplessness of merchants in these sectors. Also affected were all of the subsidiary trades, which – for example in the linen city of Hersfeld, where two-thirds of the inhabitants lived from that business – were involved in the dyeing, cutting, pressing and finishing of cloth. Because of the crisis of sales, all masters had to let their journeymen and workers go. The *Oberschultheiss* of Hersfeld reported that the unemployed begged for work with tears in their eyes, and when told there was none demanded passports so they could emigrate. Here, too, the background of the current crisis, which was a product of the bad weather, was a structural crisis, since Hessian fabrics also could not compete with cheaper English products.[123]

The army of beggars grows

With the inflation came the expected droves of beggars. Hazzi described them memorably: 'The advance guard of the approaching enemy already announced themselves. Beggars appeared on all sides, as if they had just crawled out of a crypt. These gruesome figures surprised and shook us, the plague on display at every turn. For in Munich we were not accustomed to this fatal sight, at least not since the hardy times of Rumford.'[124] In France, streams of beggars appeared from Normandy to Alsace, and what most disquieted the authorities was the fact that they walked abroad in loosely organised gangs, as they had at the time before the Revolution of 1789.[125] It is only against this backdrop that we can understand the spectre of Jacobinism, which raised its terrible head as the famine continued. Older people were reminded of the pre-revolutionary crisis, the time of the 'grande peur'. In May 1817 the prefect of the département of Aisne (Picardy) concluded that the number of beggars was so vast that it was utterly pointless to attempt to impose sanctions to combat this degree of disorder.[126] From Switzerland came reports that

> the people flowed through the towns and villages in droves, loudly crying out for the first necessity of life. The roads were filled with these unfortunates like armies on the march; market squares were their gathering places, entire streets were as if besieged. Throngs of them assembled outside buildings, on the door-steps, thrusting their way inside the houses, into the rooms and meeting-places of their more fortunate brethren; and their fearful cries and their tears and their ruined forms rent the hearts of the more sensitive ... Children called out for bread; one could not refuse their small, entreating hands a bite of nourishment; old folk stumbled along half-decayed, like shadows of death ... Fragile women, naked babes in arms, defied the harshest storms of winter; nearly rigid with the cold, the even more fragile children trudged alongside their mothers, often sinking into the Alpine snow masses. As their strength left them, older siblings urged them on, carrying them with arms strengthened by love into the greater mass of humanity in order to awaken hearts to new benevolence through this grim scene.[127]

The masses of beggars annoyed townspeople and tourists alike since they hindered all movement. As Zollikofer described it, 'Men going about their business were often followed by whole throngs of unfortunates, and when the stranger approached his lodgings in search of refreshment, he frequently found himself surrounded by one hundred unfortunates, as if blown in by a tempest; if he gave one of them even the smallest offering, he was often occupied for hours merely to satisfy for a few moments the laments of all who had assembled in a single place.'[128]

A flurry of legislation began in the autumn of 1816 that – as observers noted – was directed less against begging than against the beggars. In Bavaria a decree of 17 November ordered all towns to set up poor relief to place social life on a new basis, but this was followed on 28 November by a major regulation threatening beggars and vagabonds with severe sanctions. Bavarian beggars were distinguished from foreign ones, and first-time from 'repeat' offenders. Age, sex and conduct were taken into account when deciding on the length of gaol sentences and the threatened (and surely also implemented) number of lashes. 'Foreign beggars and vagabonds captured in the kingdom are to receive 15 to 30 lashes and be incarcerated in a workhouse.'[129]

The reaction of civil society was less heartless. One Nuremberg pastor explained in his New Year's sermon at the end of 1816, 'Moreover, may those of you not plagued by anxious fears for your survival, those who have not felt the sorrows of poverty; oh let him turn his complete modest senses to the thousands of his poor fellow men, and gratefully acknowledge: Who gave you preference?' Many people 'sigh in silence with suppressed, shamefaced tears, for the burden of livelihood lay heavy upon their hearts . . . feeding upon the sorrow that ate away at them.'[130] To be sure, this pity remained ambivalent. The town clerk of Nördlingen mocked the burghers who had to sell their worldly goods to weather the crisis 'honourably' with their families, while the 'more carefree' simply trained their children to beg: 'The more the dearness increased . . . the larger the number of beggars, the more studiously people learnt the tricks and artifices necessary to find one's sustenance . . . Unscrupulous parents did their best to school their children from the age of five in all the arts of beggary, sending them around the town and admonishing them with threats and beatings to amass a certain amount of alms every day. Children from the neighbouring villages arrive in droves daily, especially on Saturdays, and beg the city dry.'[131]

Enlightened economists and political scientists harshly criticised the return to state absolutism. Von Hazzi believed that

Every beggar is and always remains a living reproach to the government. A reproach because society and the state have a duty to ensure that everyone works and that those who do not work and can support themselves find sufficient sustenance. Whip lashes ad posterioria and the scourging of young people may be wholly unsuited here, merely heightening the state of barbarism. The great barracks for beggars are

55

equally unlikely to be effective. I saw such dépots de mendicité in France and noted, looking back with a shudder, that the people are herded together to get rid of them en masse through quick death from infectious diseases. Rome made use of the same method last year and in two days caused the horrendous number of beggars to disappear from the streets. They were penned up in their thousands like cattle . . . One thus finds no beggars in well-ordered states such as Tuscany, in Switzerland, in the manufacturing region on the Rhine, etc. Everyone works and earns.[132]

Everything seemed better to the author from a distance, but we have already heard of the hordes of beggars in Switzerland. And in northern Italy the poor wandered as trains of beggars from village to village, just as they did in the Rhineland.

Polarisation between rich and poor

After visiting some of the poorest Alpine villages to distribute alms, Peter Scheitlin travelled onward – after the snowstorms set in – into the Swiss Plateau. The contrast between rich and poor inspired him to offer the following comparisons:

> The areas around Lake Zurich seemed like an Elysium to me, the houses like palaces, the gardens like fairy lands, the people in their garb like the rich man in the Gospels, when I think of the poor Lazaruses in their holes in Dornhaus and Ennertlinth. Hopefully the inhabitants of the Lake Zurich region would not resemble that rich man if those poor people were lying before the doors of their cottages. But what a difference there is in a few hours' distance and between two neighbouring brother cantons! Hunger, hardship of every kind, rags and grim, dirty poverty there – wealth, gardens and silks here. How differently God distributes His bounty! Such thoughts rendered me cheerful one moment and dejected the next.[133]

Throughout 1816, the English caricaturist Cruikshank, who the year before had already pointed out the injustice of the Corn Laws, followed the growing polarisation between rich and poor. One highpoint of his oeuvre is his commentary on the purchase of the Elgin Marbles, great works of art from the Acropolis in Athens, which the Ottoman Empire had sold to Thomas Bruce, 7th Earl of Elgin (1766–1841).[134] In Cruikshank's cartoon, Foreign Minister Lord Castlereagh commends the antique statues to John Bull like a salesman while the latter's hungry children tug at his coat-tails crying 'Daddy, don't buy it! We don't want Stones. Give us Bread! Give us Bread!

Give us Bread!' Castlereagh argues that the stones are a bargain, costing just 35,000 pounds. 'Never think of Bread when you can have Stones so wonderous cheap!' John Bull, however, responds, 'I don't think somehow that these here Stones are perfect! & had rather not buy them at present – Trade is very Bad & provision very Dear & my family can't eat Stones! Besides they say it will cost £40,000 to build a place to put them in.' At John Bull's feet is the legend, 'Good news for J Bull – In consequence of the Glorious Peace – Increase of Taxes & Decrease of Trade, the Quartern Loaf will be sold in future for one Shilling & Sixpence.'[135]

Hans Medick has pursued the question of inequality in villages and small towns with the help of a wealth of primary sources – poor lists, tax registers, inventory and partition documents, etc. – and has discovered that the majority of the population quickly became impoverished because of debts, since they had been forced to exhaust all their resources for sheer survival. In the small Württemberg town of Laichingen in the Swabian Jura, 61 per cent of inhabitants had no cash reserves left at all by January 1817, and thus qualified for state poor relief. Aside from day labourers, this also included most of the linen weavers. By May 1817 the proportion of paupers had swelled to an incredible 80 per cent of the population. Some groups also benefited from the crisis, though. They included the local *Ehrbarkeit*, the traditional upper class, which consisted of bakers, innkeepers, butchers, merchants and some rich farmers as well as the pastor. They were still in a position to lend money at interest or profited from those who had to sell in a hurry. All those plots of land and houses that people had to sell in hard times found buyers among this stratum. The lean years thus led to a large-scale restructuring of property ownership.

The figure of the much-detested corn smuggler and profiteer, recognisable in various texts and even pictures, can still be precisely reconstructed for Nördlingen. In this case, he was the prosperous farmer Egidius Huggenberger, tenant of Strauß Farm in Hohenaltheim, who at the height of the inflation tried to sell a bushel of hulled spelt for the fabulous sum of 100 florins, ten times the normal price. In 1817 he sought to buy up the new harvest while it was still on the stalk in order to engender an artificial scarcity and speculate on the price. The people of Nördlingen resisted by painting a picture of the profiteer on a large panel and displaying it at the local corn market. The archprofiteer 'Gide' (dialect for Egidius) also found his way onto some souvenirs of the famine sold beyond the region.[136] But Gide merely served as a symbol for entire professions whose members exploited the misery of their fellow citizens and used their newly acquired riches

The grain speculator Egidius Huggenberger, Oettingen, Heimatmuseum

to dominate small-town civil society for the rest of the nineteenth century. Apart from profiteers in the stricter sense, brewers, innkeepers, bakers, butchers, millers and grocers did a good business, sometimes managing to siphon off additional, more or less legal profits for themselves. They invested their profits in real estate. In the small town of Nördlingen, property deals were made to the tune of 175,000 florins, an astronomical sum in those days. As one chronicler noted, 'The large purchases and exchanges became so substantial that such sums have not been seen for many years.'[137]

Contemporaries also addressed the topic of social polarisation during the crisis. 'While the farming class became richer, which also has other sources of income in cattle and sheep breeding, (mountain) dairies, poultry farming and the cultivation of other grains, the burghers become poorer, and civil servants are cast into debt. Is it a political principle that while one class of society rises, two others must be ruined?'[138] The question of grain exports and the state's role therein is addressed here, even though the author assiduously avoids naming those he sees as the beneficiaries of this 'system of buying up and exporting'. It was certainly not the local population. This polarisation during the famine raised issues of the justice and legitimation, or rather legitimacy, of state power.[139]

The rise in criminality: the prisons fill up

In keeping with the proverb 'Needs must when the devil drives', moral standards crumbled during the crisis. Developments ranged from the desperate trickeries of small borrowers to attempts by owners of grain stocks to hold back their products until prices rose further in order to make additional profits at the expense of the poor. This applied both to the direct producers, such as wealthy farmers, and to aristocrats or clerics who held back grain levies or tithes. All of those involved in selling grain, flour or bread – that is, millers, flour merchants, bakers and innkeepers – were subject to the temptation of profiteering. Some were wholesale buyers who purchased grain in the fields and hoarded it with the prospect of speculative profits. Contemporaries referred to this practice as *Fürkauf* (advance purchase). Finally, profiteers could also be the church or the state, which held back the grain tithe or the produce of their lands. Since this violated the commonweal, many contemporaries regarded *Fürkauf* and profiteering as a form of property crime.

Above all, however, we find a rise in crimes against property. Hans Medick gathered typical cases from the local government records of Laichingen, in which apprentices stole small amounts of money, grain or bread from their masters, neighbours from neighbours, or craftsmen from their colleagues. In today's parlance this was a kind of *Mundraub* or petty larceny of food. But there were more serious cases in which members of town councils or church boards tried to privatise the communal stores for their own benefit.[140] Rangers patrolled the forests, since the ever-common theft of wood assumed new forms in the cold months of the Tambora Crisis. Farmers and communes resorted to hiring paid guards to watch their fields around the clock. Theft from fields, woods and pastures was no harmless affair, but an illegal form of struggle over scarce resources. Naturally, storehouses, tithe barns and granaries had to be supervised at all times. In 1817, the annual report of Monheim district court noted, 'Morals have declined greatly during this sad famine year and theft has become an everyday occurrence.'[141]

Because of the general rise in criminality and the simultaneous growing vigilance of the authorities, 'we observed an unprecedented number of convicted smaller and larger civil offences in communes and districts in the year 1817, and we shudder when we hear that our state prisons were packed with unfortunates, that in the principal town [St Gall] in that one year alone 181 persons were processed criminally and 328 by the police; ... we shudder to consider the reason for their misfortune in moral decline, and when we find it in the situations, circumstances and the gravity of the times!'[142] J.F.K. Falkenberg, director of the Prussian Police Security Office, published a first handbook of criminology, which was intended to help police officers 'discover the various classes of robbers, thieves and thieves' accomplices' and prevent their crimes.[143]

In some regions the rise in criminality can be expressed statistically. In the Grand Duchy of Baden, the number of cases of theft that came to trial tripled between 1815 and 1817. The London *Times* complained that the courts were overworked, and wrote that never in recent history had the prisons been so full of inmates of all kinds. The numbers of the accused as well as the convicted were three to four times higher than in normal times. According to the statistics, the property crimes of larceny and robbery were not the only ones on the rise; crimes against persons or the public order, as in the case of riots, had also increased. Other, less common crimes increased as well, such as child murder, which in famine times generally referred to the killing of newborns by mothers who had no idea how to support them. In France the prisons were also full to bursting. In the département of Meurthe in Lorraine the number of cases of theft dealt with by the courts rose from just thirty-one in 1816 to 184 in 1817.[144] According to figures from the French interior ministry, the number of cases heard in court almost tripled, from 5,785 in 1814 and 9,890 in 1816 to 14,084 in 1817.[145] In some départements (but not in Alsace and Lorraine) the authorities exhibited a certain laxity towards the petty larceny of food. Louis XVIII even elevated this to official policy in a general amnesty of 1 September 1816, arguing that one must not confuse the unfortunates who fell into temptation because of scarcity and inflation with wicked criminals. In Switzerland, in contrast, punishments were meted out quite strictly, and the death penalty was imposed with according frequency.

In parts of France criminality assumed such dimensions that we must speak of an almost total loss of control on the part of the authorities such as had previously existed only on the eve of the French Revolution. In the départements of Eure and Seine-Inférieure armed gangs ruled the highways. On the one hand, they confiscated grain transports – according to the pattern of the 'moral economy', as during the hunger riots – but they did not hesitate to waylay other commercial transports or travellers. In the spring of 1817 broad swathes of the countryside were out of control. The unemployed marched from farm to farm in search of food, and often enough they did not come in peace.[146]

Property crime also rose sharply in Italy during the Tambora Crisis. Here, too, it was no longer a matter of 'simple' theft, but increasingly also of highway and street robbery. In 1815, the Criminal Tribunal in Trento passed only thirty-four sentences for grand larceny; in the following year the number was fifty-three, and in 1817, eighty-nine. The municipal court of Riva on Lake Garda heard no fewer than sixty-four cases of theft in the last three months of 1816 alone. The lack of safety on the streets and roads became so severe that applications to set up armed citizen militias were made and approved in many northern Italian towns.[147]

A special form of property crime was directly associated with the famine: birds, hares and badgers were not the only animals who had to fear for their lives. Even moles and rats ended up in cooking pots. Poaching reached new heights at this time of general hardship. Domestic animals were not spared either. Cats vanished from the streets, and goats and sheep were stolen from their stables. Even chained dogs, who were supposed to guard property, were killed and eaten. In Munich, 'handsome and well nourished dogs were snatched from the streets, which, because they have not been seen again, were most likely consumed', stated an administrative note of December 1816.[148] In Switzerland the authorities warned people not to eat cat brains, while the other body parts of dogs and cats were deemed safe for human consumption.[149] In many regions, cattle and horses were made available for eating if there was insufficient fodder to keep them over the winter. The starving even ate the cadavers of animals found dead.

The Spa Fields riots: the invention of the mass demonstration

In the autumn of 1816, social hardship in large parts of the country and dissatisfaction with government policy led to a series of mass rallies that went down in English history as the Spa Fields riots. Some 300,000 demobilised soldiers and sailors swelled the army of the half-starved unemployed, which in some suburbs of London numbered in the tens of thousands. One of the main aims of these unprecedented mass demonstrations was to democratise Parliament by introducing universal suffrage and thereby abolish the Corn Laws. Faced with

61

social polarisation, the philanthropic circles of the high aristocracy, which often supported such reforms for religious reasons, proved unable to control the movement. Within a few weeks, radical orators, some of them Members of Parliament, others religious preachers, spread the idea of lowering taxes and reforming Parliament and the suffrage throughout Britain. They were met with enthusiastic audiences. Mass rallies attracting several hundred thousand participants were held in industrial cities such as Glasgow, Liverpool and Manchester, and made a great impression on the public.[150]

The core demonstrators at Spa Fields were supporters of the social philosopher Thomas Spence (1750–1814), who had aimed to abolish social inequality by establishing the common ownership of land. 'Spence's Plan' foresaw the elimination of the aristocracy and large-scale landownership, the 'democratic' cultivation of the land by local self-administration, universal suffrage for men and women in elections to local government and Parliament, a 'social guarantee' for all those unable to work and rights for children, which were intended to prevent abuse and childhood poverty.[151] In the Spa Fields riots and later in the Cato Street conspiracy, the Society of Spencean Philanthropists sought to put their radical ideas into practice.[152] From a programmatic perspective, the Spenceans were early socialists, but because of their radicalism they were viewed as Jacobins. A toast attributed to one of their leaders, John Castle, was 'May the last of kings be strangled with the guts of the last priest.' It later came out that he was a government spy.[153]

Prime Minister Lord Liverpool's fears that the coming winter would be a stormy one were to be proved right, in both climatic and political terms.[154] The Spa Fields meetings continued with a mass demonstration in Islington on 15 November 1816, which was attended by 10,000 people and remained largely peaceful. The intention was to collect signatures for a petition to the prince regent, the future George IV, who had already taken over the official duties of the mentally ill George III.[155] The petition called for electoral reform, since the existing law privileged the propertied, as well as relief from the social hardships facing the population. The charismatic politician Henry 'Orator' Hunt (1773–1835), known for his gifts as a speaker, fired up the mass protest and was supposed to present the petition.[156] After the prince regent refused to accept it, the next mass rally was held on 2 December, this time with some 20,000 participants eager to hear Hunt speak. A minority of Spenceans hijacked the event, however, before Hunt could even reach the podium. They wanted to use the rally to gather as many people as possible to carry out a coup d'état. Their plans included capturing the Tower of London, which they believed to contain weapons, and the Bank of England, the commercial heart of the British Empire. While 'Orator' Hunt was still speaking several hundred radicals left the rally for the Tower, looting an arms shop along the way. The putschists were quickly intercepted by the troops of the Royal Exchange and either dispersed or arrested.

Revolutionary actions like those of December 1816 were terribly new for England. For that reason, the outcome of the sensational trial of the insurgents is rather surprising: the main defendant, James Watson, who had unmasked the government agent, was released in June 1817, and the charges against the other rebels were dropped. Orator Hunt distanced himself from the whole affair and gave the credible impression that he had known nothing about the plans. Arthur Thistlewood (1774–1820) tried to flee to the USA but was caught in May 1817 and charged with high treason, along with three other ringleaders. Like James Watson, all of them were released that same year. Dissatisfaction continued to rumble on, however, along with the radicals' underground activities. Thistlewood is believed to have been part of the 1820 Cato Street conspiracy, which had the fine plan to murder the prime minister along with the entire cabinet and the king.[157]

The main effect of the Spa Fields riots was to frighten the propertied classes with the extent of the protests and the 'spirit of Jacobinism' in England. The violent actions thus brought about a lasting shift in public opinion. The government succeeded in dividing the radicals, and the street terror legitimised a quiet but all the more effective terror from above, which was supposed to prevent future rebellions. In fact the tumults were used to restrict the Habeas Corpus Act and make it easier to arrest suspects. A commission of enquiry discovered the existence of a network of radical clubs with revolutionary intentions and activities. Since the government and both Houses of Parliament were persuaded of their dangerousness, the great majority voted to curtail the civil liberties of those suspected of treasonous activities. Henceforth, any act against the king or the prince regent could be construed as high treason and brought to trial accordingly.[158] In principle, anyone who expressed displeasure with the government in any way could now be put behind bars. In March 1817 this law was used against the leaders of a demonstration in Manchester who had protested against the suspension of the Habeas Corpus Act. In a circular letter to all magistrates, Home Secretary Henry Addington, Viscount Sidmouth (1757–1844), encouraged them to use the new laws as a basis for banning all suspicious writings as well.[159]

Export bans on basic foodstuffs

Continuing strong pressure from the population led most govern-ments to further restrict the trade in grain, to the point that some states imposed total export embargoes. Against their own better judgement, they gave in to public opinion, as von Hazzi noted:

> The public papers were all preoccupied with the dearness of food prices and raged against grain profiteering. They delighted in announcing where and when strict measures had been taken. One was constantly hearing of blockades, bans on distilling brandy, emergency granaries, maximum prices, compulsory stocks. For example in Baden, Hesse, Württemberg etc. The bakers also became targets, and many a poisoned arrow was shot in their direction. As in 1771, there were those who lauded the policies of the Turkish emperor, who undertook his own visitations and had the first baker nailed outside his shop by the ears.[160]

Christian governments found themselves admonished by their citizens to emulate the sultan of the Ottoman Empire as a model of justice – how humiliating!

It was the Swiss canton of Berne, of all places, that first initiated trade restrictions on 8 July 1816. Its 'Ban on Exports and *Fürkauf* [Advance Purchase]' violated the previous year's Swiss Confederation state treaty, whose Article 11 guaranteed all cantons duty-free trade in all goods within Switzerland. As soon as the neighbouring canton of Valais began to suffer from the restrictions imposed by Berne, it in turn closed its borders.[161] Other Swiss cantons followed that same month.[162] Even Austria-Hungary, which had access to relatively good harvests in the east, imposed an embargo on exports to the German states and Switzerland. The wartime alliance with Prussia no longer counted when a more perilous foe loomed: in this case, starvation. For its part, Prussia, whose possessions since 1815 had included the Rhineland up to Saarbrücken, imposed a ban on exports to all states that had done the same. At first this only applied to Austria, but gradually to more and more countries. In 1816, England could no longer import grain from North America as usual, since the USA and Canada were themselves struggling with scarcity. British Canada thus imposed an embargo on exports to the USA fairly early on.

The government of Bavaria, which did not officially recognise any grain shortfall and had only just introduced free trade in grain in 1813, restricted it ever further in the summer and autumn of 1816. It was already ordered on 17 July that the clearance of grain would no longer be conducted locally, but only by the main customs offices. On 28 September they conceived the idea of levying duties to the state not in money but in kind, a practice that had been out of use for some time. This was supposed to ensure on the one hand that the state gathered stores and on the other that extra grain would not be hoarded privately or sold abroad. According to a decree of 17 October, only grain that had been sold on the public marketplaces of the towns with privileges to hold a corn market could be exported. This prevented 'secret' dealings, above all the opportunity for speculators to buy grain still on the stalk – if they had not already done so long before. In order to close further loopholes, this was followed only three days later by an additional decree allowing grain to be exported only in sacks, which made it readily identifiable as such. On 17 November the export duties for wheat, rye, peas, spelt, barley, oats and potatoes were increased sharply.[163] On 11 December, the transit of grain loads through the kingdom was also subjected to strict controls.[164]

In the spring of 1817 Bavaria experimented with making imports even cheaper and exports dearer and tried to discourage grain exports without enacting formal prohibitions. On 13 September, after prices had not normalised after all, the free trade in grain was de facto lifted after four years. Foreigners were forbidden altogether from dealing in grain and Bavarians were subject to strict conditions: they had to own a house, have no debts, possess assets of at least 3,000 fl. and be of good reputation. Moreover, members of all interested trades (bakers, flour sellers, millers, brewers, etc.) were excluded. All registered dealers were permitted to sell at the approved corn markets under the limited conditions. In all towns, grain had to be stockpiled in emergency storehouses. This was the end of the free market.[165]

In the electorate of Hesse, whose heart was the former landgravate of Hesse-Kassel, the central government waited a relatively long time before giving in to the increasingly urgent warnings of the district governments. On 21 November 1816, Elector Wilhelm I (1743–1821) imposed a whole packet of measures including the establishment of emergency storehouses that grain owners were to stock compulsorily to feed the poor. They were allowed to keep only the grain they needed for their personal use. The grain in the emergency storehouses was to be distributed at the usual pre-inflation market price. The grain trade was severely restricted. Even brandy distillers who purchased grain abroad had to supply half of it to the emergency storehouses. They were forbidden to sell it in Hesse. The aim of the decree was to curb profiteering and secure a 'just price' for small consumers. Despite these regulations, prices continued to rise in Hesse as well.[166]

The economy comes to a standstill

By the end of 1816 it was clear that the famine was not a regional but an intercontinental crisis. Dr Charles Maclean, a specialist in tropical diseases with the British East Indies Company who believed that ailments were caused by malnutrition, wrote: 'We hear alarming accounts of scarcity from almost every quarter: Sweden, Switzerland, Germany, France, and the Netherlands. We *feel* it at home. Nor does the message of the American President, Mr. Maddison [*sic*], to both Houses of Congress, which has just been received, give any promise of a superabundance beyond the Atlantic. It is not by shutting our eyes against danger that we can hope to avert it.'[167]

There was no escaping the scarcity, and it affected all branches of the economy. Scheitlin described this powerfully for eastern Switzerland: the harvest failed everywhere, from fodder for animals to basic foodstuffs – cereals and potatoes, fruit and vegetables – and export products such as wine. Not even the vintners were solvent. The trade collapsed because demand disappeared not just in the region, but also in the customer countries such as France and Italy. Manufacturers dismissed a large proportion of their workforce.[168] Wilhelm Joseph Behr (1775–1851), professor of constitutional law in Würzburg, explained in a memorandum why the economy had come to a standstill: inflation on this scale affected not only marginal people or the pauper class, but also ate into the savings of the middle classes and thus into the capital for future investments. Even the well-to-do had to spend most of their liquid assets on food, so that the demand for manufactured goods fell and markets collapsed.[169] John Dexter Post has developed an impressive scenario of the economic standstill based on newspaper accounts from England and Germany.[170]

The blockades hindered more than just cross-border trade. Transports of grain, flour or bread could be held up even within larger states such as the kingdoms of Bavaria and Prussia, the Austro-Hungarian Empire and the Swiss Confederation, or between French départements, sometimes even between neighbouring towns.[171] The partial collapse of the infrastructure also played a role: the roads were soggy because of the constant rain, and the heavy snow made many mountain passes impassable. Numerous bridges had been destroyed by flooding. Quarantines were also imposed in response to epidemics of fever, diarrhoea and typhus. In some regions of England and France, however, roadblocks set up by insurgent peasants became a menace, as they had been in the summer before the French Revolution.[172]

These obstacles conflicted with an increased need for mobility by the large numbers of unemployed, beggars, vagabonds and the bands of highwaymen and footpads who soon put in an appearance, making the roads outside the town unsafe, especially in Italy and France. They were joined by the incipient streams of emigrants, who in Germany either followed the Danube to Russia or set off on their journey to America via the Rhine. In Ireland, England, Scotland, France and the Netherlands, but also on the Black Sea, emigrants crowded the large port towns awaiting their ships. In Britain they competed with the convicts who were to be transported to other corners of the earth.

Another reason why the economy came to a standstill was connected with the cold weather: as soon as winter temperatures fell below freezing, water power, the most important source of energy in the early modern period, literally dried up. Economic and more recently climate historians have been too fixated on 1784 – the year when James Watt was granted a patent for an improved steam engine – as a symbolic date for industrialisation. But scarcely anyone needed it, since hydropower was available nearly everywhere in Europe and was far cheaper than coal-fired boilers. These were only truly worthwhile for the owners of coalmines, who got the fuel for free. The rest of industry, like urban manufacturing in the mediaeval period, was based on water power.[173] As in the winter of 1788/89, the winter before the French Revolution, industry also came to a standstill in parts of Europe in 1816 because the watermills froze.

'Demoralisation and silent horror': the public mood reaches a nadir

In October 1816, a landowner in Moravia poured out his heart, committing his misfortunes to paper: all of the winter wheat was still green, and all of the seeds intended for next year had been used up already. Nobody could afford to buy anything, thousands were ending the year in poverty. The farmers were dismissing their servants, their farmhands and maids were unemployed, and they were selling off their cattle because of scarcity and a lack of fodder.[174] The Swiss hospitaler Dufour of Montreux was travelling from place to place – a difficult undertaking because of all the flooding – but could not find fodder to buy anywhere. The potatoes were rotten, the little wheat to be had was of poor quality, and when the wine harvest was cancelled due to the constant rain and early frosts, people were 'tristes et consternés'.[175]

Peter Scheitlin offers distressing images in his *Armenreisen* ('Travels to the poor') through Switzerland. In one passage, about his visit to the high valleys of Glarus, he subtly interprets the uncanny calm in the households of the starving, asking 'Is this tranquillity truly tranquillity? Is it dullness and indifference? . . . Oh, for those who lead such a sad, terrible and loathsome domestic life, even the most sublime nature must ultimately become mere bare stone, wild cliffs and oppressive sadness. And how do such people treat each other? All of them are famishing. Once one has nearly starved to death, one no longer has anything to say to one's fellows. All stare dumbly at the ground or are startled to recognise themselves in the person sitting opposite.' Scheitlin saw very precisely that these paupers lacked nourishment for the mind as well as the body, when children could no longer go to school, men to work and women to church – out of shame over their ragged appearance and ultimately out of weakness and malnutrition.[176]

In the highly industrialised Prussian canton of Neuchâtel, where many lived 'almost exclusively from handicrafts', people were doubly affected by falling incomes due to the sales slump and by the dearness of foodstuffs. 'For that reason, the unrest was great throughout the entire canton. Dissatisfaction, anxiety, demoralisation and silent horror dominated in nearly all communities, for this canton too (like St Gall, Appenzell and Glarus) suffered under the double scourge of stagnating trade and universal crop failure.'[177] The Nuremberg newspaper *Friedens und Kriegs Kurier* printed an account from the canton of Glarus where families were vegetating in absolute destitution:

> Three to four households with numerous children live crowded together in a single room, dressed in colourless rags, half naked, completely naked. Tables, chairs, bed-clothes have long since disappeared. Their nourishment consists of roots, herbs and some scrapings of yeast. People are dying for want of a drop of blue milk. Summer and winter they all lie in their rags on the hard floor, near the stove if old age or sickness affords them that privilege. Not a few resemble skeletons dragged from the grave, and the infant who should be a joy to the world emerges like a corpse from the mother's womb.[178]

Some lost any will to live. 'In the most terrible moment of desperation some ended their days by suicide, casting themselves into deep waters or using still crueller methods. Mothers abandoned their children or withdrew from them, or sent them away from the paternal home to distant misery and probable death; and the fathers were often hardened enough to refuse their children the last bite.'[179] A sermon from Wertheim in Lower Franconia given after the end of the famine mentioned that 'desperate fathers murdered themselves and their children to spare them slow death from starvation'.[180] The situation was desolate in Bavaria, too.

> If one saw so many suffering and starving in the capital, one could only imagine conditions in the countryside, the misery that reigned in many a cottage. Horses, guard dogs, the poorest oaten bread and all manner of roots served as nourishment. Scarcely had spring appeared than people threw themselves ravenously upon the mushrooms. Cattle and people were so exhausted from the winter that in the spring the horses could hardly pull, and labourers could scarcely do half the work their hands normally managed. It is not hard to imagine that quite a few turned prematurely to their graves.[181]

A new government in Württemberg

At first, most governments displayed a lack of sensitivity towards the suffering of their populations. Württemberg's King Friedrich I (1754–1816) was considered particularly insensitive. After taking power in 1797 and piloting his country through the vagaries of the Revolutionary Wars and the French occupation, he became king by the grace of Napoleon in 1805 and expanded the old duchy by incorporating a number of small states. He also took the opportunity, however, to abolish the old system of participation in decision-making by the estates and to set himself up as an absolutist monarch. Even as a despot, the obese monarch introduced a series of significant reforms, but still aroused the ire of many reformers and ultimately was held responsible for the famine in his country.[182]

His unexpected death on 30 October 1816 offered an opportunity for a change of government, which had every sign of ushering in a new era. The new royal couple, the handsome heir Wilhelm I (1781–1864) and his like-minded (second) wife Katharina Pavlovna, daughter of the Russian Tsar, were well versed in the necessary politics of symbols. The king confidently ignored his father's testament, which stipulated that everything should continue as before. His first act was to establish a foundation for the poor in Stuttgart, which was to be funded from the treasury of the princely domains; then he issued a general pardon for all deserters and convicts from past wars and reversed compulsory transfers in the civil service. He granted an amnesty for a series of smaller offences such as the theft of wood, abolished the secret police and reinstated postal secrecy. Negotiations also began over the reintroduction of a constitution and a parliament. The king was most admired for three regulations that seem rather trivial nowadays. First, by a decree of 19 November, he permitted all subjects, of whatever estate, to petition the king directly. Second, he loosened the ban on the possession of weapons and allowed the traditional marksmanship societies to resume their associational life. Third, he eliminated the royal menagerie, the zoo in Stuttgart, which had become a public nuisance. While segments of the population were starving, they could watch every day as a caravan of mules brought feed for the animals. Feeding the animals white bread, meat and vegetables at a time when many people were going hungry, along with the old king's insatiable appetite, had symbolised his mismanagement of the country.[183]

The crisis in Württemberg virtually demanded that the new generation present itself as sympathetic and actively engaged. The queen grasped the opportunity and promoted the founding of charitable associations in the more important towns, which called upon the wealthy to donate and establish soup kitchens for the poor. The associations' central headquarters was in Stuttgart, but district headquarters were set up in all administrative seats to supervise the local charitable associations. On 29 December 1816, the queen invited the members of the central board she had installed to the first meeting in the Old Palace in Stuttgart. There, the aim of the associations was defined as aiding the needy (*Dürftigen*) by helping them to help themselves rather than merely distributing alms.[184] The politics of symbols succeeded so well in entrenching memories of the queen that a new monument to the benefactress was unveiled not long ago in the palace gardens of Hohenheim.

'Silent night': the winter of 1816/17

The winter of 1816/17 began early. In northern Italy there was frost in October even in the low-lying, favourable valley locations. The harvests of cereal, hay and potato could not be brought in. In late November and early December the crops were dug out from under the snow. In Bolzano/Bozen recorded temperatures fell as low as –19 Celsius in November, and in Innsbruck –20 Celsius was measured for several days in late December. After these cold spells it remained relatively mild, until Candlemas (2 February) ushered in three full months of frigid weather and heavy snow. Northern Italy received an unusual amount of snow. On 7 April 1817, the *Bote für Tyrol* newspaper reported from Landeck in the Inn Valley, 'No one recalls such immense and destructive snow masses and avalanches as fell in this season, ... neither from experience nor tradition, nor from chronicles.'[185]

An observer in Franconia reported:

> Fog, rain, fearful wind- and snow storms and hoar-frost, very hard frosts from 18 November on, alternated with one another in November and indeed until the end of this joyless year. In many cases the oats and barley could not be harvested and potatoes and cabbage were buried under the snow. Much went to ruin. In December, people were still out in the fields digging fodder for the animals from under the snow. The failure of the harvest was universal and soon the dearness extended to all foodstuffs ... The poor folk boiled grass and hay and chopped up potatoes and clover as vegetables ... The suffering was agonising, and only exacerbated by the diseases resulting from frequent privation and the consumption of spoilt food. Begging and thievery increased greatly.[186]

In December 1816 a 'Kommission zur Unterstützung der Armen' (Commission to Aid the Poor) in Salzburg noted, 'The dearness has risen to a degree unprecedented in the history of our fatherland.'[187] It was in this situation that the twenty-four-year-old Joseph Franziskus Mohr (1792–1848), assistant curate in his native town of Mariapfarr in the Lungau, composed the song 'Silent Night, Holy Night'.[188] As Joseph Benedikt Huber described it, the entire Lungau district was a sort of poorhouse at the mercy of the inclement weather: 'In winter Nature is so severe and stubborn that she does not permit the post sleighs [to cross the Alpine passes] at all. They live in uncertainty about what is happening in the rest of God's world. Such an enormous amount of snow collects in this district that one can scarcely believe that the milder rays of the sun will be capable of melting it by the end of July.'[189] The parish of Mariapfarr extended 'out into the deep side valleys, which are difficult and perilous to reach, particularly during the long winter and the snowstorms so common in the Lungau'.[190] Although the lyrics of Mohr's song, with its naïve language, revolve around the Christmas story, the arrival of the saviour is sometimes interpreted as a reference to liberation from Napoleon. But that had occurred two years before. The connection with the brutal winter of 1816/17, in the midst of which those dwelling in mountain solitude (the first stanza of the German text contains the words *einsam wacht*, 'keeps solitary watch') could appeal to faith alone, is a far more plausible context.[191]

71

At the end of 1816 the mood had reached a nadir in many places, and the usual winter festivities did little to raise spirits. Scheitlin writes, 'In St Gall we call the last day of the year *Singabend* (song evening). But it was no evening of song. We remained silent. Anxiety weighed upon town and countryside. It was an evening of mourning.'[192] In Montreux, Dufour closed his 1816 diary with the remark that this had been one of the saddest years ever experienced by humankind. It was cold and barren and the harvest could not be brought in. The huge masses of snow that had gathered in the mountains due to the immense precipitation stayed on the ground and the usual thaw failed to occur. One would therefore have to rely on providence for the coming year. Given the unrest in France and England, and worries over how to survive the winter at all, there could be no more mournful day than 31 December 1816. All were mired in sadness and melancholy. But shortly before midnight the sky cleared. The moon suddenly appeared in all its beauty and the church bells welcomed the new day. The citizens stood at their windows and wished each other 'all the best for the New Year'.[193]

— 4 —

THE YEAR OF FAMINE: 1817

The *Neujahrsblatt der Zürcherischer Hülfgesellschaft* (Magazine of the Zurich Aid Society) opened its New Year's issue with the appeal: 'Sons and daughters of our natal city! The times in which we live are sober ones: misery is all around us. It reminds us daily, and at close quarters, and it ill befits an aid society to conceal it.'[1] Zollikofer also noted:

> The New Year 1817 had just begun, young and old usually celebrated on this day; many places were [normally] the scene of lively activities, but now there was an unusually hushed and solemn atmosphere everywhere; one heard only laments, and cries of woe evoked by the seriousness of the fearful times ... Natal city! ... You saw among your walls the most terrible, distorted face of your neighbours' misery; in your streets you heard the cries of your old folk and your infants; before your very eyes once hearty youth sank exhausted to the ground; deathly pallor touched the cheeks of maidens; men, in the full bloom of life, have vacant eyes; neighbour wives and mothers walked like shades in your midst.[2]

The usually effusive New Year's poetry now revealed a reflective side. Ludwig Uhland (1787–1862), whose work as a lawyer in paupers' trials scarcely kept his head above water, put it this way:

New Year's greeting 1817
He who means his nation well
Wishes it a blessed year
May the angelic host preserve us
From crop failure, frost and hail.

New Year's greetings cards became a category in their own right in the early nineteenth century. In 1817, one of the masters of the genre, the Salzburger and director of the Prague art academy Joseph Bergler junior (1753–1829), produced a card showing a young man who, while still rather well dressed, has no shoes to wear. He sits at a table in a sparsely furnished room, balancing two small loaves of bread in his hands. On the table stand a candlestick, a water jug and a pot with a spoon. The caption reads: 'One for today, one for tomorrow! How this fills poor men with sorrow.' On the wall hangs a note reading '1817'; another reading '1816' is lying under the table next to a crumpled hat, which resembles a beggar's cap set down to collect coins.[3]

The New Year's prayers in the churches also referred to the current problems: 'Lord of Nature, almighty eternal God, let thy sun shine kindly, when winter's rest has slept its last, upon our fields, awaken to life the precious seeds of our nourishment, let them thrive and ripen at the appointed time, so that the earth may have bread and the rejoicing of the harvest may praise thy name.'[4] Warmth and food had become scarce commodities. What could be done to bring them back?

Experimenting with ersatz foods

The inflated prices for cereals meant that people went out into the woods and fields to gather and try anything that might prove edible. The prominent role of bread in the food hierarchy is evident from the fact that at first even other foods such as potatoes, root vegetables and legumes were ground into flour to bake bread. In January 1817, the Stuttgart government newspaper reported that the master baker Dürr of Unterturckheim was trying to make dough from ground roots and sugar beet syrup.[5] In Würzburg, the doctor of agriculture and forestry Josef Carl Bayrhammer (1786–1821) published his *Erinnerungen an nahrhafte Pflanzen welchen, in das Brod aufgenommen, einen Theil des Brodkorns ergänzen* (Reminders of nourishing plants that, when incorporated into bread, supplement a portion of the cereal grain). Although his suggestions were hardly original, the first edition of 1,000 copies quickly sold out.[6] The baking experiments using flour made from fodder beets that Bayrhammer commissioned in January 1817 were extremely popular and were reported in a regional Bavarian newspaper, the *Intelligenzblatt für den Regenkreis*. Bayrhammer lectured throughout the kingdom of Bavaria. At these events, organised by local notables, participants discussed additional recipes. In Wunsiedel, for example, an apothecary presented his 'moss bread'. The government of the Upper Main region applied for Bayrhammer to be put on leave 'for the purposes of creating more bread using lichen and potato flour'.[7] Newspaper accounts and the support of Interior Minister Count Friedrich Thürheim (1763–1832) made Bayrhammer famous outside Bavaria. The Saxon government requested his services, the king of Sweden awarded him the Order of Vasa,[8] and the Prussian provincial government in Koblenz published his recommendations in their official gazetteer.[9]

An article in the *Nördlinger Intelligenzblatt* suggested: 'We should encourage the eating of old bread only, so that far less will be eaten because of the laboriousness of chewing, reducing consumption by one quarter, thereby compensating for the shortage until the (new) harvest.' Moreover, it advised that recipes should be 'stretched' with ingredients such as peas, beechnuts, blueberries, horse chestnuts, fodder beets, kohlrabi, sawdust, bark, wheatgrass, straw and oxhides.[10] Also in March, the *Wöchentliche Anzeiger des Polytechnischen Vereins* in Munich published reflections on making bread from inferior materials under the title 'Bemerkungen, veranlaßt durch den gegenwärtigen Mangel an Getreide' (Remarks occasioned by the present grain shortage). The author referred to suggestions by the Irish professor of chemistry Edmund Davy (1785–1857), who recommended the use of chemical means, which, however, were viewed sceptically because of the possible health risks. Stretching dough with 'Iceland moss' (cetraria islandica), which grew in Bavaria and could be processed to yield a nourishing food once its bitter compounds were neutralised, was discussed quite seriously, however.[11] Not long afterwards, the same weekly periodical discussed the use of brewing by-products in bread baking.[12] One reviewer, while praising the work of the Rosenheim cleric Schmid, who sought to produce 'hardship bread' from wild plants, pointed to the dangers of such experiments: 'Considering the continuing very high prices for bread and the inflated cost of living more generally . . . some poor folk have resorted to measures that unfortunately sated their hunger forever at the cost of their lives.' Because Schmid only enumerated edible plants, one could recommend his publication 'not just to the poor, but also to all friends of the poor'.[13]

In his *Brunecker Chronik*, Johann Nepomuk Tinkhauser (1787–1844) wrote that roots and herbs were increasingly being included in foodstuffs. Barley had become so scarce since late 1816 that beer was no longer being brewed in many places because the grain was needed for food instead. 'Loaves became ever smaller, dearer and poorer, and finally consisted only of bran stretched with chopped thistles and hay flowers, peas, chestnuts, ground vetch and crushed tree bark.' Interestingly, in the Tyrol, potatoes had mainly been used as fodder up to that point. It was only with the famine that people became increasingly willing to consider them as food for themselves. According to the farmer Johann Gasser of Lana in the South Tyrol, in the spring of 1817 many people even had to eat boiled grass, which was neither filling nor nourishing. There are many similar reports from the Trentino as well.[14]

In a letter of 29 April 1817 from Karlsruhe, the writer Rahel Varnhagen (1771–1833) told a friend in Berlin: 'Famine at the door: dearness that inconveniences everyone; such hardship that one hears nothing else *whatsoever*, and *everyone* hears it, and one hears it *from* everyone; in the uplands, a few miles from here, people are eating bread made of bark, and digging up dead horses; the farmers are losing their cattle for lack of grass and fodder. We are facing every horror. Do you know how fearful I am?! – At the same time, my heart is ready to leap from sorrowful pity.'[15]

Private versus state poor relief

The end of the ancien régime also brought with it the disappearance of the old European institutions of social relief that had worked quite well for centuries. The property of churches and monasteries and the capital of municipal foundations were nationalised, and in many places local self-administration was abolished. In many states, the municipal or communal administrations most familiar with the local situation were no longer responsible for social welfare. The new states that emerged after the French Revolution, most of them ruled by economically liberal elites, were wholly unprepared for a social crisis on this scale. Thus in many places, organising initial emergency aid was left to private initiative. Ruprecht Zollikofer, co-initiator of the private Hülfgesellschaft in St. Gallen (St Gall Aid Society) founded in September 1816, memorialised these private organisers of social assistance in eastern Switzerland in volume 2 of his near-contemporary account *Denkmal jener Schreckens-Epoche* (Monument to that epoch of terror), *Denkmäler des Wohltuns* (Monuments to benevolence).[16]

At first, the central state or the municipal governments – whose political leadership often overlapped with philanthropic circles – merely supported these efforts. In the kingdom of Bavaria, the government issued 'Regulations for the Establishment of Poor Relief' on 17 November 1816, which were intended to help coordinate aid efforts. Most towns in Bavaria already had charitable associations founded by their wealthy citizens. In Nuremberg, the authorities in the guise of Police Commissioner Christian Wurm (1771–1835)[17] instigated the establishment of such an association in early November. Since the 'usual revenues of the poor chest cannot cover the additional expenses incurred by the inflation, we must appeal to the charity of the friends of the poor, so that they may alleviate the hardships of their fellow citizens by generous subsidies'.[18]

Apart from private philanthropy, the municipalities and later the administrative regions were the first to intervene. Finally, the central government recalled its responsibilities and in early May set up a 'permanent central committee' expressly 'on the model of the welfare committees that already exist in the regions of our realm'.[19] Before doing so, the government began to reverse its economically liberal abstinence from poor relief policy and, in an edict of 17 November 1816, once again permitted local institutions to support the poor. Poor relief was placed in the hands of local *Pflegschaftsräte* (councils of wardens), which were to be run by mayors, pastors and deputies from all the estates. As during the ancien régime, these bodies were supposed to check whether the needy were deserving of assistance, that is, to determine whether and why the applicants could not support themselves and where they came from or were registered. Children, invalids and the elderly were generally eligible to apply for assistance. Poor relief was to be financed with voluntary endowments and targeted collection campaigns. Only when these funds had been exhausted could money be drawn from the local coffers or borrowed. Moreover, the able-bodied poor were to receive help to find employment.[20] For the towns, caring for the poor was a source of both worry and pride, since it gave them back some of the autonomy they had lost in 1808 even before municipal self-administration once again became part of the constitution.[21]

It is worth noting that the old princely houses, which had been mediatised in 1806, regained some of their relevance by providing poor relief. In the Ries district both the Catholic princes of Oettingen-Wallerstein and the Protestant house of Oettingen-Oettingen maintained aid associations and soup kitchens in their capitals. The upper classes of the former imperial city of Nördlingen also became involved in poor relief with a 'welfare association'. From January to August 1817 this association had nearly 100,000 pounds of bread baked and distributed to the needy at a low, subsidised priced. The completely penniless received the bread free of charge. In a sermon in Wertheim, the pastor called upon his congregation to give thanks to God for the efforts not only of King Maximilian I Joseph of Bavaria but also those of a series of individually named representatives of the various lines of the (previously ruling) princes of Löwenstein-Wertheim on behalf of their suffering (former) subjects, efforts which included donations of food and clothing and the creation of jobs in road building: 'Oh, it was a source of refreshment for many, falling like a drop of water upon an arid land.'[22]

The Tambora Crisis forced the states that had emerged from the reorganisation of Europe to confront the social plight of their populations. Poor relief had to be fundamentally recast, as occurred for example on 19 October 1816 in the duchy of Nassau. According to the rules of subsidiarity, the state was to intervene only as a last resort, but then thoroughly. Poor relief required trained personnel, beginning with government agencies. The relationships among these agencies, and their dealings with their staffs, the government and the various responsible bodies, had to be regulated administratively and legally. Job descriptions, qualification criteria and salary lists had to be devised for all staff positions. Documentation, correspondence and accounts had to be organised and checked. Finally, printed forms were needed for all conceivable aspects of poor relief administration. In the precision with which they scrutinised the living conditions of applicants, the forms devised during the Tambora Crisis are not very different from those used in today's social welfare offices.[23]

Women's associations

Emmermann's 'Handbook of Poor Relief' addresses the interesting point that separate women's associations had formed in the area of social welfare, which provided assistance as autonomous institutions. He gives them pride of place among the 'private welfare associations', and sees this as a consequence of the 'penchant, specific to the female sex, for helping the needy and alleviating human misery'. According to Emmermann, the authorities supported the establishment of these women's associations, whose main task was 'to support the shamefaced poor, the sick and indigent and helpless new mothers, to supervise orphaned children and to instruct female children of the poorer classes in various useful handicrafts'. Some women's associations took on all of these tasks, while others focused on individual ones, he noted. He also remarked that these 'institutions have ... begun to spread to the rural communities, now that the preconception that they could only thrive in the towns has almost completely disappeared'.

The women's associations were accorded complete autonomy. Even where they had been founded at the instigation of the *Amtsarmenkommissionen* (official poor relief commissions) this was not allowed to influence their 'internal arrangements': 'It is not at all the intention to control the efficacy of these women's associations or to force regulations upon them, nor to impose rules upon them regarding their expansion over wider regions and to several neighbouring administrative districts.' They did not have to account to the authorities regarding either their activities or the use of donations, but were completely free in their actions, 'as is in the nature of these associations, which can thrive only when the innate inclination for benefaction, purified by the progress of culture, is subject to no restraints'. To be sure, the poor relief commissions expressed the wish that private charity should concentrate on those who received too little aid from the local poor funds to support them, and the women's associations even had the right to consult the official poor lists. However, women's social competence was very highly regarded, particularly when it came to helping the 'shamefaced poor', because their sensibilities made it easier for them than for any government agency to discover what the genteel poor required.[24]

Although the women's associations were meant to be free to organise as they saw fit, the 'Handbook of Poor Relief' offered the sage advice that they should 'elect leaders from among their midst who were free of all influence, who pursue the chosen aims as organs of their benefaction and formally inform members from time to time about their charitable activities'.[25] The civil law of association did not yet stipulate that charitable associations had a duty to render accounts to their members, and to that extent the women's associations played a pioneering role in democratic associational life within civil society.

The triumphal march of Rumford's soup

In the winter of 1816/17, the so-called Rumford soup was used to combat hunger in public soup kitchens throughout Europe and the USA. In October 1816, the council of state of the Swiss canton of Vaud even printed a 'Notice sur la composition des soupes économiques d'après le système Rumford'.[26] In northern Italy 'la zuppa detta alla Rumford' was distributed to the needy in the spring of 1817.[27] The recipe was devised by the American Benjamin Thompson (1753–1814), a graduate of Harvard University and member of the British Royal Society. During his time in the service of Elector Charles Theodore in Munich, Thompson had worked on social reforms (school buildings, poorhouses, workhouses, manufactures) and planned the English Garden. The American had been granted the (imperial) noble title of Count Rumford in 1790 for his services. Among his many inventions were the energy-saving 'Rumford stove' and the 'Rumford soup' of 1795, which would henceforth feed the poor everywhere in Europe.[28]

Rumford wrote, 'After more than five years' experience feeding the poor of Munich, during which time every imaginable attempt was made not merely with respect to the choice of victuals but also to their various mixtures and proportions, and the manifold manners of their preparation in the kitchen, it transpired that the cheapest, tastiest and most nourishing food was a soup consisting of pearl barley, dried peas, potatoes, slices of fine white bread, wine vinegar, salt and water (in the appropriate proportions).'[29] After the cooking instructions – all components had to be boiled for hours in a certain order and were then to be poured hot onto the plate over bread – and numerous potato recipes, Rumford closed with a recommendation to all rulers and state officials: regardless of their varying attitudes to the proper state constitution and form of government, in order to prevent 'popular unrest' it was essential 'at all times . . . to diminish the general misery of the poorer classes'.[30]

The recipe for Rumford soup was adapted in various ways, with the proportion of potatoes frequently being increased. Later cookbook authors improved the soup with onions and vegetables such as carrots, celery root, swedes, leeks, kohlrabi or cabbage, replaced the water with bone broth and left out the vinegar. When there was more scope, the product could also be made richer by adding meat, bacon or offal. Aside from pepper, thyme and marjoram were suggested as seasonings.[31] In 1817 there were soup kitchens not only in the main cities of Innsbruck, Bolzano, Lienz and Bregenz, but in nearly every larger town in the Tyrol – the recipe for feeding the local poor consisted of 'water, sour beer, grated potatoes, pearl barley, dried peas and bread'. Even in the rich wine-growing towns of Kaltern and St. Pauls (Eppan) in the South Tyrol, the starving had to be fed. In the Franciscan and Capuchin monastery of Bolzano, 800 poor and needy people were fed every day.[32] After the experiences of 1816/17, feeding the poor would remain a necessity for decades to come. Whether in Hamburg, Berlin, Munich or Innsbruck, soup kitchens served a version of the Rumford soup.[33]

From the beginning of the famine, the Augsburg foundation of the banker Johann Lorenz von Schaezler (1762–1826) distributed 30,000 portions ('a substantial Bavarian half litre each') of Rumford soup a month to the poor, from the former Dominican monastery.[34] The distribution of alms, the feeding of the poor by the rich, and of beggars by princes, was naturally a business that benefited both sides, as Prince Ludwig of Oettingen-Wallerstein (1791–1870) noted in retrospect: 'The universal acknowledgement showed us that our efforts were not in vain, and we are happily conscious of having wrested hundreds of families from ruin and indeed starvation in the famine years of 1816 and 1817 alone.'[35]

Work-creation schemes

By the time of the begging act of autumn 1816, it had become clear that combating idleness was not a matter for the Protestant lands alone. In Catholic-dominated countries like Bavaria people also worried about the many involuntarily unemployed who could no longer earn their own living. Creative thinking was needed in this situation, and solutions were required not just of the central state, but once again also of the cities and communes, which had lost their right to self-administration since 1808. The bureaucracy had high expectations, as von Hazzi noted:

> Should each such commune not be able to find the means to create work for all of its members, in a land still completely lacking in good roads, where villages and hamlets are mired in muck, where much still remains to be done to improve fruit trees and where nearly every branch of industry is still very backward? In extraordinary cases, to be sure, the state must also provide funds. It can do so easily, since it needs so many important institutions such as canals, large buildings, highways, etc. These measures would provide an income for thousands, which would bear rich interest and indeed spread abundant prosperity.[36]

As today, the question thus arose of whether the public sector should or could jump in as a replacement for private sector employers. The search went on everywhere for suitable projects where investments could be brought forward or labour-intensive measures tackled in the first place. Examples were river straightening or canal building, which could employ thousands of unskilled workers for many years. Contemporary daily and weekly papers reported on these efforts. The newspaper of the Polytechnic Association, for example, quoted from 'the diary of a traveller' about the beneficial effects of a

Beschäftigungs-Institut für Weibliche Jugend aus der Armen-Klasse (Institute for the Employment of Female Youth from the Pauper Class), founded in 1816 in the former imperial city of Kempten in the Allgäu: 'Much moved, I saw in two bright, newly built halls there some seventy poor children aged from seven and eight years to between twelve and fifteen occupied in remarkable silence and with cheerful industry in embroidering muslin under the supervision of a teacher.'[37] In Munich in the winter of 1816/17 hundreds of families were employed in public works such as demolishing old walls, levelling land for future suburbs and 'beautifying the city'. The rapidly growing population meant that entire districts had to be opened to new construction, beginning with the Maxvorstadt between Schwabing Gate and the village of Schwabing, which was still some distance outside the city.

A secondary aim of these work-creation schemes, then as now, was to prevent the emergence of an age cohort accustomed to doing nothing. 'Institutions for providing work and occupation are beneficial everywhere; however, those people who grew up in idleness or lived an irregular life until a mature age rarely improve if they work solely out of hardship and compulsion.'[38] The Augsburg soup kitchen had a 'voluntary employment institution' attached to it, in which some 200 persons found work at the new spinning machines in February 1817, as well as a charity school and a care institution with room for seventy-five invalids. The school took in orphans and street beggars, and soon after its founding was looking after thirty-one boys and fifty-seven girls, instructing them in all subjects as well as their own religion.

In the United Kingdom, the Poor Employment Act of 16 June 1817 placed such work-creation schemes on a national basis. This law was a departure from previous liberal economic policy to the extent that it recognised the state's duty to provide relief for the unemployed. Public works projects were intended to help them to earn their own living again. The form of relief payments sounds modern: the state offered loans to public bodies interested in realising large-scale, labour-intensive projects such as roads, bridges or canals. A Public Works Loan Board considered the applications and decided upon the loans, giving preference to ongoing projects whose completion seemed likely.[39] In fact, the public works projects proved so successful that the population theorist Thomas Robert Malthus (1766–1834), who had still been opposed to them at the beginning of 1817,[40] changed his mind after only three years.[41]

In promoting the Poor Employment Act, Chancellor of the Exchequer Nicholas Vansittart (1766–1851) followed less the contradictory opinions of economic theorists than the practical exigencies of the Tambora Crisis and the unrest it sparked. Lobbying by the canal building companies, which had lacked capital since the beginning of the crisis, proved important, however. Since paying direct subsidies to a canal-building firm was out of the question, the financing occurred indirectly via a general work-creation scheme. The main argument put to Prime Minister Lord Liverpool emphasised the public interest in a speedy completion of this major infrastructure project – 'being public works of great utility for the kingdom at large' – through which one could, incidentally as it were, also help the poor. This argument appeared so logical that the Act was approved by both Houses of Parliament and the king in the record time of just seven weeks.[42]

The many roads, bridges, docks and canals built or repaired within short periods of time with the aid of the Poor Employment Act likely contributed to Britain's economic recovery and development in the medium term. Some of them, like the Regent's Canal, already exerted an immediate effect on the economic upturn. Above all, however, this law, in concert with the laws establishing savings banks and facilitating emigration, showed that even the conservative Liverpool government was not unmoved by the widespread suffering of the population.[43] The straightening of the Rhine begun in 1817 and the building of the Erie Canal in the USA (see Chapter 6) are evidence that the promotion of large-scale projects in the wake of the Tambora Crisis, especially in labour-intensive hydraulic engineering, was not limited to England.

The New York Society for the Prevention of Pauperism (SPP)

In the context of rapid urbanisation and nascent industrialisation, the hardships of the Yankee Chill combined with the effects of mass immigration provided the impetus for the founding of an institution that would prove highly influential for poor relief policy in large American cities: the Society for the Prevention of Pauperism (SPP). This New York society served as a model for numerous similar institutions in the USA in the years that followed.[44] In 1815 the number of relief recipients in New York was some 19,000, or approximately 20 per cent of the population.[45] In February 1817 a private soup kitchen employed ten cooks around the clock and distributed 103,312 portions of soup in just three weeks. Throngs of immigrants populated the city's hotels, sheds and cellars.[46]

In a spirit of active charity, the poor relief system in New York under Mayor Jacob Radcliff (1764–1844) sought to supply the mostly poor immigrants with food, shelter, heating and cooking fuel, as well as with work.[47] Meanwhile, a trio of members of the city's upper class used the Tambora Crisis to place poor relief policy on a new footing. In their view, existing poor relief actually created pauperism in the first place rather than helping to alleviate it. This opinion was shared by the New York entrepreneurs Thomas Eddy (1758–1827) and John Pintard (1759–1844), who had much in common. Born around 1760 in Philadelphia and New York, respectively, they had lived through the American Revolution in their youth. As a Quaker and a Huguenot they belonged to morally inspired minorities that corresponded to Max Weber's ideal image of the Protestant ethic. Their self-made wealth enabled them not only to intervene successfully in various branches of business (banking, insurance, communications), but also to engage in local politics and public affairs. Eddy served not just as a prison superintendent but also as a commissioner for the poorhouse, the hospital, the New York Free School Society, a society for the promotion of industry, and the New York Bible Society.[48] After a stint in debtors' prison, Pintard worked among other things as an employee of a fire insurance company, a steamship company and the Chamber of Commerce. He was a member of the city council and a leading member of the Society of Fine Arts, the Literary and Philosophical Society, the State Library, the New York Historical Society and of course also the Bible Society.[49] The third in the trio was the Quaker John Griscom (1774–1852), since 1813 the first professor of chemistry and natural philosophy in the USA. The three reformers met for the first time in 1816, during the attempt to found a self-help savings bank for working people, an early project to tackle the effects of the Tambora Crisis.[50]

In a letter of February 1817, Eddy told New York Governor DeWitt Clinton (1769–1828), the former mayor of New York City, that it was pointless simply to give money to the poor. What was needed instead was a plan to prevent poverty by rooting out its causes and giving the poor employment. That same month a committee was founded to study the causes of poverty, and in April a city council commission was established to explore the means to prevent a poor relief crisis such as that of the previous two winters. In August 1817 a New York publisher printed the programme of the recently founded Philadelphia Society for the Promotion of Public Economy, which recommended radical alternatives to existing poor relief. At the instigation of Griscom, Eddy and Pintard, the SPP was then founded in New York in December 1817 under the direction of the banker Matthew Clarkson (1758–1828), and tasked by Griscom with preparing a 'Report on Pauperism'.

The SPP saw itself not as simply another aid organisation, but as a research institute dedicated to studying the causes of poverty. Its first report, in February 1818, concluded that 90 per cent of relief recipients were not genuine but rather artificial paupers. If they needed support, it was mainly because of their ignorance, indolence or lack of thrift.[51] Thus simple charity could never diminish poverty. What the poor needed was improvement:

> Let the moral sense be awakened and the moral influence established in the minds of the improvident, the unfortunate, and the depraved. Let them be approached with kindness and an ingenuous concern for their welfare; inspire them with self-respect and encourage their industry and economy; in short, enlighten their minds and teach them to take care of themselves. Those are the methods of doing them real and permanent good and relieving the community from the pecuniary exactions, the multiplied exactions and threatening dangers of which they are the authors.[52]

The religiously motivated attitude that 90 per cent of poverty could be attributed to laziness and vice remained typical of the SPP, and determined the direction of its programme. The city was to be divided into small districts in which special visitors would go to the homes of the poor to admonish and advise them. Savings banks were to be set up so that workers could provide for themselves privately.[53] Workhouses should be established for self-support, and schools, churches and Sunday schools for education, especially in the poor districts of the city. The Poor Law needed to be amended so that only the truly helpless (children, the elderly, the sick and disabled) would be supported, after careful scrutiny of each case. Street begging should be banned and the selling of alcohol greatly reduced. Private poor relief should be prohibited since it undermined the new policy. All private endowments were to be combined into a central public fund.

In nine permanent committees, the SPP set about putting its programme into practice. Thus, for instance, the Committee on Idleness recommended the employment of the poor in public works, especially road and canal building and the construction of public buildings. Although the SPP's programme seemed to be directed against the recipients of relief, it created a number of institutions that improved their situation in the longer term. Notable among them, apart from the founding of a savings bank, were the Fuel Fund, which was intended to help the poor keep their dwellings heated in the severe winters, and institutes for the (re)education of youth, established to counteract the neglect of poor children, which had been identified as a problem.[54] Thus in the first ten years of its existence the New York House of Refuge took in more than 1,000 boys, and soon found emulators in Boston and Philadelphia.[55]

An International of social reformers

One of the most interesting aspects of the social reforms instituted following the Tambora Crisis was the international reception of the most important publications. It is thus not surprising that the prescriptions for solving the crisis were similar throughout the western world. Many of the protagonists of social reform even knew each other personally. These acquaintanceships were sometimes based on existing networks, such as those of the Quakers or the Bible societies that, not coincidentally, had sprung up everywhere in the USA and Europe in 1816/17. In some cases, social reformers tailored their itineraries expressly in order to meet like-minded individuals. During his European travels, Griscom met John Colquhoun (1748–1827), Thomas Chalmers (1780–1847) and Walter Scott (1771–1832) in the United Kingdom,[56] Alexander von Humboldt (1869–1859) in Germany and Johann Heinrich Pestalozzi in Switzerland, before returning to New York where he helped found and eventually run the SPP.[57]

Griscom presented the SPP's first scientific report during another European tour, which he undertook in 1818–1819 and during which he studied and assessed the various social institutions (hospitals, shelters, institutions for deaf mutes, insane asylums, foundling homes, prisons, penitentiaries and workhouses, schools, libraries and universities). His travel account can be read as a veritable overview of the most important reform projects in England, Scotland, France, the Netherlands, Germany, Switzerland and northern Italy.[58] Everywhere he went his presentation of the SPP's first report was met with great approval. The Glasgow reformer Thomas Chalmers had just begun a similar project of combating poverty through home visits.[59] The Economic Society of Geneva, which had organised a competition for the best suggestions on how 'to prevent the evil of pauperism', was so enthusiastic about Griscom's report that Professor Pictet, a member of the prize committee, immediately commissioned a translation.[60]

The New York SPP also became a model for similar organisations in the USA. The Pennsylvania Society for the Promotion of

Public Economy in Philadelphia, the second-largest city in the USA at the time, soon followed the same path, and in the third-largest city, Baltimore, an association of the same name was founded in 1820. In Boston, the Society for the Moral and Religious Instruction of the Poor was even renamed by the Unitarian Joseph Tuckerman (1778–1840) as the Society for the Prevention of Pauperism. What all of these religiously inspired societies had in common was that they located the causes of poverty among the poor themselves, and sought to render the latter fit to help themselves through moral instruction. The economic effects of the Tambora Crisis provided the impetus for their work, but they had no inkling that the misery in the USA as well as the wave of immigration from Europe were the consequences of a climate crisis.[61]

International solidarity with the disaster area in Switzerland

At the height of the famine we find remarkable signs of solidarity, as is evident from the Swiss example. This is how Zollikofer put it:

> And the great expenditure of effort inside the canton was also met magnanimously by charity from foreign lands. Germany's noble sons, especially in the north, honoured the terrible hardship in our country with the tenderest of sentiment: Frankfurt, Hamburg, Lübeck, Prussia's lands sent substantial support. The most distant and powerful monarch of the north, the great Alexander, revived many thousands in our land and neighbouring Glarus with his imperial gift of 100,000 rubles. And many noble private individuals from abroad as well as sons of the fatherland residing in distant lands remembered our misery with particular generosity.[62]

The major donation from Tsar Alexander I confronted the Swiss canton with problems of distribution. While Russian Minister of State Capodistra had noted the Tsar's wish that half of the sum be placed at the disposal of a colony for the reclamation of the Linth swamp, the rest of the donation had to be fairly divided. The details would take us too far here however.

The other gestures of solidarity were quite small compared to the Tsar's donation. As we can see from the accounts of the St Gall Aid Association, the city of Frankfurt am Main sent something over 1,000 florins, Hamburg slightly more than 700, Leipzig just over 200 and Livorno slightly over 1,000 florins. Swiss officers in French service donated 550, and Swiss living in Livorno, Florence and Pisa

330 florins. There were also some interesting individual donations: the Augsburg banker Schaezler donated 240 and the *Alt-Landvogt* Blanc d'Alby in Geneva 140 florins. The firm of Duchapeau, Rouge et Comp. in Hamburg donated nearly 300 florins. Some Swiss living abroad apparently collected money for their hometown. Thus, for instance, J.J. Mayer collected 422 florins in Paris and another local patriot 567 florins in London. In Geneva a total of some 1,000 florins was collected. By May 1818, the donations from abroad amounted to some 12,000 florins, and another 8,000 came from the canton of St Gall itself.[63]

Municipal governments – and in Switzerland cantonal governments as well – generally tried to encourage their wealthier citizens to donate voluntarily by appealing to their pity and their social conscience or reminding them of their religious duties. In some cases this worked surprisingly well, in others less so. For that reason, people had already begun to experiment with alternative forms of fundraising. For example, the Lausanne Société de Musique organised a benefit concert for refined society on behalf of the poor at which an oratorio was performed, most likely *The Creation* (1798) by Joseph Haydn (1732–1809).[64]

Flood disasters

Even today, floods often wreak greater destruction than other forms of disaster because they devastate such large areas. When entire river systems are affected, dwellings as well as industry and agriculture or the infrastructure of commerce and communications suffer. Mountains and slopes slide, rivers and lakes burst their banks, streets are buried under rubble or flooded, bridges and milestones are washed away. Wastewater and debris spread across the fields poisoning the pastures and killing cattle. Floods wash away seeds and cause the hay in the pastures and the grain in the fields to rot.

After the floods of 1816 the disaster continued the following year. While in 1816 the constant rain had led to flooding, in 1817 the rains were accompanied by the snowmelt. This involved not just the snow from the preceding winter, but the accumulated sum of all the cold winters of the 1810s. As Scheitlin recorded:

> The summers had been cold and rainy since 1812, and also very snowy at the higher altitudes. The masses of snow had increased fearfully with every winter; the glaciers had grown continually. The föhn wind (known

in the mountains as the snow eater) had melted away the old snow masses. The waves on the Rhine became higher and more powerful and brought monstrous floating blocks of ice on their crests. Moreover, the whole summer was punctuated by lightning storms. Downpours and cloudbursts fell from day to day, now in one place, then in another.[65]

Zollikofer painted the situation in dramatic terms:

The sun's otherwise so blessed glow, accompanied by stormy south winds, melted entire mountains of snow and fearful masses of ice, which had lain one atop the other for five years, to the terror of the country. Rivers and forest brooks swelled repeatedly to new, terrible heights: their waters broke through the protective banks in raging earnest, carrying the fruits of the land away in prideful fierceness, depositing in the depths of the earth the valley's more solid products and covering them with dense, sandy, infertile mud to prevent any possibility of new germination. Day and night, the awful echo of the alarm-bells' sombre tones often sounded from village to village, to awaken and admonish the unfortunate inhabitants of the valleys and their brothers in the neighbouring elevations and the more distant, secure plane to offer earnest and vigorous aid. Lake Bodmer's [Constance] wide, smiling shores were filled with wild and devastating waves, the highways were under deep water, consumed and destroyed; entire broad swathes of country, valleys and fertile lands resembled nothing more than a wild ocean. Villages and human habitations were empty and deserted, in danger of imminent devastation. Where friendly seeds had not long before borne the finest promise, people travelled around on light and fragile skiffs, amongst the houses and villages. Bridges and dams were destroyed, and human industry and precious works lay sunken in the depths of the cruel waters.[66]

Lake Constance was the great reservoir for the Rhine and other mountain rivers of northern Switzerland, and its waters reached quite unusual levels in the summer of 1817. In Scheitlin's words:

It already raised its back in June. Its waters are always highest in July, because it is only then that the snow in the high mountains begins to melt. But it retained its dangerous level even through all of August, rising some ten feet above its usual level. What quantities of water! What a weight, since a single cubic foot of water weighs 64 pounds. All of the shores around the lake with their villages were under water. Rorschach, the splendid market town, looked as if it had been built into the lake. High over the landing-place the waters heaved, turbid with mud from the roads.[67]

The flood attracted disaster tourists who rented boats to travel about the city. From shipboard one could pick fruit directly from the trees

Nikolaus Hug, Flood waters from Lake Constance on the market square in
Konstanz, 1817, Konstanz, Rosgartenmuseum

in the suburbs and villages. In Konstanz, the highest water level of all
time – 6.36 metres – was recorded on 7 July 1817. Six years later, at
low water, the level measured was only some 2 metres.

While in Europe it was the great river systems of the Rhine,
Danube and Rhône that overflowed from the mass of precipitation
and snowmelt, in India the great river systems of the Ganges and
the Brahmaputra were affected and in China the Yellow River and
the Yangtze. In the drainage area of the Yangtze there were heavy
snowfalls in January 1816, and several calamitous floods devastated
the Chinese heartland from early spring until early summer. The
drainage area of the Yellow River was likewise affected. The territory
(Heze) reported constant rain from January into the summer, and
many regions along the river experienced heavy flooding especially in
June. The floodwaters reached a highpoint in China in that month.[68]
India reveals a different pattern: there, 1815 had already been marked
by extreme precipitation and severe flooding. In contrast, 1816 was
a year of drought, since there was no monsoon. The next year, 1817,
tended towards the opposite extreme with torrential rains and protracted floods, with worldwide consequences, as we shall see. In the
Bengal lowlands the new scourge of humanity, cholera, broke out

during these disaster years, and began its triumphal march across the globe.

Climate anomalies and famines in China

In China, the Tambora Crisis coincided with the reign of Emperor Jiaoqing (1760–1820, reigned 1796–1820), whom recent research has identified as the monarch under whose rule the economic decline of the empire began.[69] Only in the 1990s did it seem certain, after a systematic analysis of chronicles, official histories and reports to the emperor, that the eruption of Mount Tambora had also left obvious traces in China. Abnormally cool and stormy weather was noted for the period from the winter of 1815/16 to the summer of 1817 for a total of fourteen provinces and the large cities of Shanghai and Tianjin, which resulted in crop failures and exceptionally high food prices. The first cold weather events were already reported in the southern provinces in the final months of 1815: in Sichuan it snowed in November, which was highly unusual, and in the months that followed it rained very frequently. On the islands of Hainan and Taiwan the cold periods occurred in December. It remained freezing cold on Hainan throughout the winter of 1815/16. Half of all trees, the rice plants and most other cultivated plants fell victim to the frost. The southern provinces – Fujian and Jiangxi – experienced metre-high snowfalls in February 1816. Water buffalo succumbed to the cold. In Jiangxi there were severe floods in April. An official administrative report from Tibet speaks of such heavy snowfalls in June 1816 – lasting three days and nights – that houses collapsed or threatened to collapse under the weight. That year's harvest was a complete loss. In Jiangxi province it rained incessantly all summer long. Autumn 1816 saw crop failures throughout China. The worst-affected provinces were Gansu (north), Hubei (central) and Guangdong (south).[70]

The floods in the major river systems also suggest a cold and wet summer. In the drainage area of the Yangste there were heavy snowfalls in January 1816, and from early spring to early summer several severe floods that affected the Chinese hinterland. In the summer of 1816 serious flooding was reported along the Yellow River, which indicates unusual rainfall in its drainage area. While only one region (Heze) reported constant rain from January into the summer, many accounts from other areas along the river agree that June was marked by heavy rainfall. The waters reached their highpoint in that month. Huang Jiayou concludes that the entire decade from 1811 to 1820 suffered from overly cool temperatures, but notes that in China's major river systems, 1816 can be identified as the most problematic year. At all twenty measuring stations, without exception, this year was referred to on a five-point scale as either 'very wet' (8) or 'wet' (12). In contrast, 1811 was referred to as wet at only two stations. The classification 'very wet' appears not a single time between 1811 and 1815. Nine stations were called 'wet' in 1815, but only seven in 1817, with none reporting a 'very wet' climate. In contrast, four stations spoke of a very dry and one of a dry climate. Therefore one can say that the regions of the major river systems in China – the Yellow River and the Yangtse – experienced an especially cold and wet year in 1816, a climatic anomaly that must have resembled what was happening in western Europe.[71]

In 1817 the province of Zhejiang reported virtually no sunny days between January and November. This was China's year without a summer. The rice harvest failed completely and prices rose sharply as a consequence. Jiangxi province experienced severe storms in May with hail and constant rain as well as cold temperatures until the end of June. The coldest day was 29 June; the next day, the mountains were covered with snow. In parts of the province the cold weather and heavy rain continued until early July. Some people wore furs, while others stayed by their hearths. In the more northerly province of Heibei the summer and autumn cold was accompanied by a drought, which also damaged the crops. Early frosts were also reported from here as well as from the province of Heilongjiang in Manchuria, where drought and frosts in July and the early autumn caused a meagre harvest. In the autumn of 1817, too, crop failure was widespread in China. As in 1816, the provinces of Gansu (north), Hubei (central) and Guangdong (south) were the most severely affected.[72]

Since these studies, a good deal of new research has appeared dealing with the manifestations of the Tambora Crisis in China, which apparently affected not merely the climatically more susceptible north, but also the Chinese heartland, the Yangtse river system and even regions in the south of the empire. The economic and cultural heart of the Qing Empire, the province of Jiangnang with the delta of the Yangtse, was also among the worst affected areas.[73] One study examines the terrible famine in Yunnan province in southern China. This region bordering on 'Indochina' is closest to the Sunda Islands and is known for its mild climate. The cold temperatures had already reached Yunnan in 1815 and persisted throughout 1816, accompanied by heavy rains. Occasionally there was even frost and snow in the summer months. In the capital Kunmin the temperatures in

August 1816 were at least 3 degrees lower than usual. The rice harvest failed along with the buckwheat crop. Although weather conditions improved slightly in 1817, from 1815–1817, in the so-called Jiaqing Famine, Yunnan province experienced the worst hunger catastrophe ever recorded there. The results were high mortality, begging and famine refugees as well as great social unrest including uprisings. Normality did not return until 1818.[74]

Another study looks at the effects of periods of cold and wet weather in the early nineteenth century on food crops on the Jiaodong peninsula in the eastern province of Shandong. Here, a cold- and damp-resistant type of millet (ragi or finger millet) replaced the one traditionally grown there, which thrives in a warm, dry climate and is resistant to drought. While the yields per hectare were lower, finger millet was better adapted to the new climate regime and promised greater crop security. The worsening of the climate led to a diminished cultivation of sweet potatoes, which had already been well established in the late eighteenth century. The cultivation of maize and peanuts also experienced a setback and, along with the sweet potato, only recovered after 1870.[75]

The Chinese Empire was too large for uniform climatic conditions. Despite the existing gaps in the literature, it is safe to say that the Tambora Crisis probably did not affect the entire empire, just as there were regions in eastern Europe that were not merely unaffected by the crisis, but in fact profited from the scarcity in western Europe. In the capital Peking, for instance, supplies were probably adequate. All through 1816 it was rather warmer than usual there. Its climate may have resembled that in Korea and Japan, where the winter after the eruption of Tambora was marked by colder and snowier weather than normal, but the summer that followed was a bit too hot and the harvest did not deviate from the norm. In Japan, 1783 had been the 'year without a summer' followed by a famine, when the islands themselves experienced one of the strongest volcanic eruptions in Japanese history. The twenty measuring stations in Japan and Korea registered no anomalous climate data for the years 1816/17. Like Russia, Japan seems to have escaped the cooling trend.[76]

Demographic anomalies

In the traditional cycle of agrarian crisis, crop failure and inflation were consistently followed by malnutrition and rising morbidity. As Charles Maclean suggested, 'The body being prepared by famine for falling into disease, a slight deterioration of the atmosphere would be sufficient to produce an epidemic malady.'[77] This worked differently than expected in the famine of 1816/17, however. The *Laichinger Hungerchronik*, which as we now know was written nearly a century later[78] and is considered a forgery,[79] speaks of elevated mortality among infants, toddlers and the elderly between June 1816 and February 1817. The forger met readers' expectations, but the reality was different. In Laichingen, the group most affected by increased mortality were fifteen to thirty year olds, perhaps because other age groups had already been reduced in the years before. The reason for this pattern was sought in the spread of typhus – which the sources call 'ardent fever'. But there were also cases of kwashiorkor. Mortality reached an apex in the months of March to May 1817, when food prices were highest and the nutritional situation of the poor reached its nadir.[80] Parts of Württemberg also experienced a smallpox epidemic.[81]

More striking than the clustering of incidences of illness and the increased death rate is the absence of major epidemics in many places. In Bavaria, for example, people were surprised that the feared outbreaks of typhus and dysentery did not materialise, and sought explanations. According to von Hazzi, 'It was likely mainly the medical arrangements that Bavaria has possessed for many years in the form of the district court medical doctors and apothecaries that prevented the spread of epidemic diseases.'[82] Clearly, hygiene had improved in the preceding decades. The system of poor relief that the local upper classes, municipalities and the state had improvised into existence was effective enough to avoid acute famine and malnutrition. The immune systems of the European and North American population were thus at first sight not so weakened at the end of 1816 that new diseases could gain a foothold and cause high mortality rates.[83]

In France both the famine and the demography of the crisis years have been studied in depth. In the département of Meurthe, part of the former duchy of Lorraine around Lunéville, climatic conditions were just as bad as elsewhere in France or in southern Germany. The harvests were so poor in all the arrondissements that people spoke of a 'catastrophe agricole', especially since the region was still suffering under occupation by German and Russian troops at the beginning of the year. Foreign and French soldiers had exhausted the grain stores from 1815, and the greatly diminished yields in 1816 were insufficient to refill the granaries.[84] In Lorraine, too, no epidemics broke out, but mortality rose nonetheless. Colette Girard has shown that this occurred with surprising selectivity. Throughout 1815 there was a sharp rise in infant mortality during the first three months of life,

Mortality in July in the département of Meurthe (Lorraine)

Year	Deaths
1816	641
1817	1084
1818	697
1819	693

and one might ask whether the parents did not help this along. Small children up to the age of five had a relatively high mortality rate as well. This suggests the spread of a childhood illness, especially since the mortality rate began to fall from April 1816, having been highest among all age groups in the winter months. It is striking that during the crisis year 1817 the mortality rate did not fall in March, but continued to rise, reaching a high point in July and August, that is, in the months before the new harvest brought relief. In the starvation summer more people died than usually did during the winter months, with the fifty to eighty age group being most affected. In the years that followed mortality remained elevated, but not as high as it had been in spring and summer 1817.[85]

The classic pattern of the demographic crisis was evident not only in the elevated mortality rates but also in the sharp fall in marriages per month. While there were 670 new marriages in February 1816, the number for the entire département at the absolute low point in March 1817 was just seventy-one. In January 1818 marriages then reached a new high point at 432.[86] As a consequence of this refusal to marry the number of births also fell to a low point. Before the beginning of the crisis nearly 13,000 children were born annually in the département, or more than 1,000 per month. Immediately before the crisis, in April 1816, the figure was even 1,228 children. Those born nine months later in January 1817, however, were no longer welcome. Their parents could scarcely feed them, and as a consequence far fewer children were conceived. Whether this was owing to abstinence by couples or infertility as a result of malnutrition remains unclear. In any case, up to April 1818 births fell to 693. The frequency of conception had thus reached a nadir in July of the preceding year at the height of the crisis. After the harvest was brought in, people became more willing to conceive: 1,199 babies were born in October 1818, but births fell again when it became clear that the harvests were not good enough to ensure a life free of want. The birth rate in Lorraine only returned to pre-crisis levels in 1819.[87]

If we look at the interplay of mortality and natality, there was a break in generative behaviour even without epidemic diseases. In his study of the Swiss canton of Berne, for example, Christian Pfister discovered that the watershed of the Tambora years remained recognisable in the age structure of the population well into the nineteenth century. In the 1860 census, the effects of the crisis were still clearly evident as indentations in both the female and the male population profiles even after forty-five years. This was the case even though western Switzerland was characterised by lower vulnerability and an absence of epidemics. Pfister thus speaks of a 'hidden crisis', which could be rendered visible only in the interplay of demographic factors – and optically through notches in the age pyramid.[88]

Typhus

Perhaps Bavaria, Berne and Lorraine simply got lucky, for in many regions of Europe typhus was typical of the crisis. Nowadays, the bacterial infection, which is transmitted by contaminated water or food, occurs almost exclusively in developing countries. In international classification the disease known in Germany as typhus is now called typhoid fever, while typhus (typhus exanthematicus) refers to the disease known in German as *Fleckfieber*, which is transmitted by ticks, fleas, mites and lice. Since this disease often appeared on an epidemic scale in times of hunger, it was also referred to in German as *Hungertyphus*.[89]

Because of the similar symptoms, the two diseases could long not be told apart. In the first week after an outbreak of typhoid fever, the temperature rises in stages, combined with lassitude, headache and constipation, sometimes stomach ache, coughing and nosebleeds. The next two weeks are characterised by a fever around 40° C, a slow heartbeat, swelling of the spleen, skin rash and disorientation ('nervous fever'). In the third week complications may arise from bowel perforation, internal bleeding, diarrhoea, hair loss, osteomyelitis, meningitis and delusions. If the patient survives the third week the fever gradually diminishes over a long period of recovery. When treated with antibiotics only 1 per cent of cases are fatal, but if left untreated up to 20 per cent of patients die. Children and young people are most at risk. The 1817 epidemic in Italy described by Bell displayed precisely the symptoms listed here. Mortality ranged from 3 per cent in Livorno to 1.5 per cent in Florence, where the recommended protocol – separation, good hygiene, nutrition and treatment in hospitals – was apparently followed more effectively.[90]

In eastern Switzerland, the epidemic diseases broke out in the winter, as Zollikofer noted:

> At the beginning of 1817 a malignant putrid and nervous fever raged in some places to great concern. It seemed to have disappeared altogether, but with the coming of October new, far more perilous traces of it appeared. Typhus arose in fearful form first in our mountain regions; to be sure, it struck down only few people, but the misery was terribly increased once again. Entire families were laid low by this ailment . . . The disease now spread more and more, soon reaching many villages and towns and individual dwellings in our land, and became ever more devastating – and even now [December 1818] expresses itself terribly. For months the many unfortunates languished on their hard sick-beds; their recovery was slow; many a family remained long incapable of working to support themselves . . . It did not seek out its patient sufferers or sacrificial victims in the pauper's hut alone; nay, it also turned, often threatening and fearful, to the homes of the wealthy; and mortally seized them, as well as many a pious, honest, frugal family; it gripped entire villages . . . Once again, melancholy and lamenting filled the land![91]

Apart from typhus there were also some cases of smallpox and naturally dysentery as well. Zollikofer gave precise figures for the victims: 'Circa 12,600 inhabitants of the cantons of St Gall and Appenzell had died within the year. At least 5,000 fell victim to the great scourges of the time, hunger and want and nameless misery. Only circa 5,300 children were born; c. 950 marriages were consecrated. Circa 7,400 people were a pure loss.'[92]

In the British Isles every imaginable fever epidemic raged, and the ailments are often hard to diagnose accurately in retrospect. In Ireland a fever epidemic whose causes could not be precisely determined spread, beginning in 1817 and continuing until 1819.[93] In Scotland, too, the diagnosis was at first unclear, and people debated the causes, therapies and modes of prevention.[94] The well-trained doctors in London, in contrast, were certain that the 'epidemic fever' raging in parts of the country and also in London in 1817 and 1818 was typhus.[95] Today we know that the fevers in Scotland and Ireland were also typhus. In Ireland alone 100,000 people were said to have died during the epidemic. The figures vary, however. According to a different estimate, 1.5 million Irish men, women and children were infected with typhus, but in the end 'only' 65,000 died of it.[96]

The American John Bell described the typhus that spread through large swathes of Italy from the autumn of 1816 according to his own experience. His Italian colleagues in Rome, Florence, Lucca, Livorno, Bologna, Pavia and Milan had observed that it spread mainly among the poor who had been unable to feed themselves adequately during the crisis. In Tuscany the poor also migrated to the cities, where they had no proper housing and crowded together to protect themselves from the raw winter weather. The first victims of the disease were beggars in prisons and hospitals. So-called camp typhus was considered one variant of the illness.[97] Most Italian doctors also identified the disease as 'typhus fever' or 'contagious typhus'. The years 1630 and 1766, which in Italy had also been marked by crises of scarcity and malnutrition, were cited as precedents for typhus epidemics.[98]

Pellagra

In the course of the Tambora Crisis a new ailment appeared, pellagra, a disease of malnutrition named for its symptoms, rough skin (*pelle*) that flakes and peels off (*pelare* means to peel). Pellagra is a deficiency disease that occurs when people eat nothing but maize or millet.[99] It was particularly interesting for medical doctors because there was no known evidence of its existence in antiquity or the Middle Ages. It is also absent from the encyclopaedic works of the Baroque. Pellagra was first described during the famine of 1771 in the Milan region, with the information that it was called 'pellagra' in common parlance, that is, by the population without medical education.[100] But pellagra had never before been as widespread as it was during the famine of 1816/17. Since nearly all of northern Italy was affected by it, this region was considered the 'homeland of pellagra'.[101] Medical doctors discussed whether the disease might be a type of scurvy, a later form of leprosy or a variant of an illness that appeared in Asturias.

The reason for the spread of pellagra was the introduction, since the late mediaeval period, of new food crops alongside cereals in the densely populated region between the urban centres of Venice and Milan, in the Po Valley, which were intended to make nutrition less susceptible to crisis: rice from Asia, millet from Africa and – after the discovery of America – maize. The duchy of Milan, which for two centuries had belonged to the Spanish Crown, was predestined for this import from New Spain. All early descriptions of the illness come from physicians in Milan or its environs, as well as Lyons. While pellagra is a disease of malnutrition like scurvy, it has different causes: it arises from a one-sided diet of maize or millet, not, as a contemporary doctor believed, 'through specific atmospheric and alimentary conditions'.[102] The reason it appears in times of famine is that when cereal crops such as wheat fail in maize-growing areas, people eat maize instead. As a consequence, polenta became the sole basic foodstuff. This one-sided nutrition led to deficiencies and the outbreak of pellagra.

From a present-day perspective, pellagra does not have the same status as the major epidemic diseases – plague, typhus and cholera – which claimed millions of victims. For contemporaries, though, it was not merely new and terrifying for that very reason, it was also a dangerous disease. At the height of the Tambora Crisis, there was scarcely a poor family in northern Italy that was spared pellagra. According to estimates by Milanese physicians, some 20 per cent of the population in Lombardy suffered from it.[103] Mortality was not as high as for other diseases and, more importantly, pellagra was not contagious. But the illness was terrible enough: in the first stage, aside from languor and exhaustion, patients suffer from numbness in the limbs, dizziness and colicky abdominal pain along with depression and sadness. In the second stage, they experience intense itching and burning in the skin of their hands and feet as well as their neck and chest. Reddening of the skin, swellings, 'extremely strong, piercing, sharp, throbbing headaches' and an uncanny tingling in the spine follow. The feet become weak and the gait unsteady, accompanied by limb pain and a salty taste in the mouth. The third stage brings a distortion of the facial muscles and facial deformity, flickering and double vision, a ringing and buzzing in the ears, along with muscle contractions that resemble epileptic fits. Sometimes the patients lie there stupified, sweating, and emitting a smell like silkworms. Insomnia, diarrhoea, strong melancholy and delirium set in, sometimes quiet, sometimes raging. Blisters filled with fluid appear on the skin. The eyes become vacant, red and threatening, known to the inhabitants of Belluno as 'occhi imburidi'. In the final stage, the patients are so weak that they can only lie down. The blisters burst and the fluid escapes with the 'scent of mouldy bread'. Cracks appear in the joints and the skin begins to peel, 'detaching itself in tender scales or bran-like flakes'. The fingernails become bent and chunky, and deep melancholy leads the patient to fall silent.[104]

It was typical of the stage of mental confusion that the *pellagrosi*, as sufferers were known, felt as if they were burning up from the inside. Some jumped into bodies of water. Those who could not swim or were not rescued drowned. If the apparent suicide failed, the confused patients were often confined in insane asylums or hospitals.[105] When Henry Holland visited the asylum in Milan he found some 500 *pellagrosi* of both sexes there. Doctors were surprised at the number of mental symptoms exhibited by sufferers: anxiety, hypervigilance and increasingly severe depression.[106]

Physicians were bewildered by pellagra, since unlike most ailments it was determined neither by age nor sex nor heredity nor physical constitution. Dissections also yielded no usable findings. For that reason, they looked instead at the 'occasional moments', or what we would now call environmental influences. In a logical process of elimination they considered the air, the seasons and solar radiation, and, after not being able to prove any influence by these factors, diet. Doctors agreed that the poorest elements of the rural population were hardest hit. Since they represented 88 per cent of patients, attention focused on their diet. 'One wished to discover which food bore within it the *causa efficiens*, and in this way fell upon the Turkish grain (Zea mays L).'[107] This one-sided diet affected even infants, since when their own milk dried up many mothers fed their babies a solution of maize and water.[108] Milan doctors soon discovered an effective treatment for the disease: the patients simply had to be fed a nutritious diet.[109]

Limoctonia, or death from starvation

Since occasional doubts have been expressed that people actually died of starvation in central Europe, I will quote from a report of 24

A family facing death by starvation, 1817, illustration from the Montafon valley in Voralberg (Austria)

September 1817 compiled by the St Gall health commission, a section of the Aid Association:

> The sad circumstances of an unheard-of dearness and a complete lack of earnings in our and the adjacent cantons gave rise to a different ill, to be sure not contagious but no less destructive in its effects to the population, one not observed for nearly half a century and thus scarcely anticipated, namely limoctonia,[110] or death from starvation, which was visited upon the dwellings of the poorest class in the form of the following manifestations, and also snatched away its sacrificial victims. First there was a complete disappearance of the muscular parts, weakness of the limbs, especially the knees, dizziness, hoarseness, an aging, decrepit and sunken appearance ... Next comes, as the habitual companion of starvation, a ravenous hunger (bulimia), which torments the patient until the end ... With the advancement of the disease there are alternately sharp pains in the stomach and across the abdomen; in adults, the latter becomes thin and constricted, but in children tympanitically and atrophically distended ... The urine is meagre and colourless; no sweat or transpiration. If the patient is not provided with food, the life force diminishes, the pulse becomes weak and slow ... the limbs grow cold and stiff ... activity in the outward parts ends, the senses vanish, only the sense of taste persists, the patients retain consciousness or sigh in a shallow delirium, and death moves from the periphery of the body to its centre. The agony lasts unusually long; even when the pulse can no longer be felt and the breath appears to stop, the dying person rallies for a brief time, deceiving those who surround him awaiting the end.[111]

This report by a Swiss doctor, and other eyewitness accounts, show that we need to take the reports of starvation deaths seriously. Regionally, the European epicentre of the climate anomaly and the crisis – southwest Germany and eastern Switzerland – appears to have been most affected, but even there the famine mainly touched more remote areas such as high mountain valleys, and there only the poorest of the poor. Scheitlin sought them out deliberately on his 'travels to the poor' in order to present them with clothing donations. The misery he already observed in the high valleys of Glarus in the autumn of 1816 surpassed his worst imaginings, and for that reason he recorded it in a book 'for young people'. He described one such visit to a poor family in Linth:

> In a tiny room some eight persons were gathered in black rags, shreds so tattered they could scarcely stay upon them. The dirt and vapours were terrifying. The females were half naked. In a cradle lay a newborn child, conceived by a corpse and born a corpse by a corpse. Like death it lay in the fragments of the cradle, pale, with no life force of its own,

with no noticeable care from its parents. Its nourishment was potatoes which, as the fruits of this year, must have been miserable enough. The most natural source from which it might have drawn nourishment had dried up. All those present looked as if they had been exhumed from the grave; the most miserable was the child's emaciated father, whose hollow eyes and sunken cheeks and consumptive cough announced the imminence of death, or rendered visible death itself. There were no tables, benches or chairs, not a single household device or piece of bed linen, nor any item of clothing. The walls, floor, ceiling and windows were black. They all sleep on the floor and eat on the floor, and otherwise lie on the floor. They were just boiling potatoes outside the door. I engaged them in conversation. They calmly answered my question of what they thought of their nameless misery, what they were planning to do about it. 'Sir, we are going to die! We can no longer help ourselves. We are simply going to starve to death. Our potatoes have been consumed and winter is coming. We cannot go begging anymore. We cannot go out the door or onto the street in these rags', replied the man I asked. Do you never go to church, don't your children go to school? 'Oh Sir! Judge for yourself whether we can go to church and school dressed like this! We have not been to church in three or four years, and our children have not been to school. Oh, if we could only go out begging like others and could walk down to Glarus!' The women said nothing. They watched me in silence.[112]

The mountain dwellers already had the misfortune to live on marginal soils, with no right to poor relief from the wealthy towns in the valley and no lobby. When they did appear in the valley like ghosts they caused a stir, but hardship in the towns and an aversion to beggars from outside meant that they often received no help and were driven away. When they were offered work they were often too weakened to do it. According to the accounts, in their hopeless situation these poorest of the poor retreated to their huts to die. Even the generosity of the people of St Gall had its limits: 'Unfortunately it was not in the power of the health commission to remove or even alleviate an affliction produced by the scarcity of a famine year, which was heightened to the utmost through various cooperating circumstances; they had to limit themselves to providing here and there, for the refreshment of such patients, a portion of thickened curds donated by humanitarians.'[113] In other regions of central Europe the poorer mountain regions also seem to have been affected: in Germany the Central Uplands and in the Habsburg lands the remote Alpine valleys. Thus in the Veneto such reports came from every district, so that the individual accounts combine to form a terrible overall picture.[114]

The beginning of the cholera pandemic in India

1817 was the key year for one of the most terrible epidemic diseases in history. All later cholera pandemics, which claimed millions of lives worldwide, can be traced back to the pathogen that appeared for the first time that year.[115] According to a contemporary description, the attack of this disease was 'usually sudden and violent'. It generally began at night with diarrhoea that continued for several days. Then the patients developed symptoms such as uneasiness, giddiness and headache. Sometimes they felt pains in the limbs like those that accompany a high fever or influenza. Soon the symptoms grew worse, including fits of vomiting and muscle spasms with excruciating pain. Their faces became so gaunt that masters sometimes scarcely recognised their servants. Restlessness and mortal fear gripped the patients, and their vital powers drained away until they finally died.[116]

Diarrhoeal diseases followed the Tambora Crisis from the beginning, as the result of contaminated water or as an accompanying symptom of many other illnesses such as typhus. This disease was different, however. Cholera, caused by the bacterium Vibrio cholerae and spread by contaminated drinking water and food, leads to a rapid loss of electrolytes and dehydration. People with a weakened immune system are especially susceptible: toddlers, the elderly and the malnourished. Untreated, its lethality is 20–70 per cent, much higher than that of typhus or pellagra. The disease can appear in epidemic form and even today is widespread in developing countries in the tropics as well as in Sub-Saharan Africa, India, China, Japan and Russia. When treated medically with salt and sugar solutions and antibiotics, the mortality rate drops to under 1 per cent. At the time of the Tambora Crisis neither the pathogen nor the proper treatment was known.

Since 1757 Bengal – now Bangladesh and the Indian states of West Bengal, Bihar, Jharkand, Tripura and Orissa – had been under the control of the East India Company, which made Calcutta (present-day Kolkata) its capital. Diarrhoeal diseases were nothing unusual there, since this densely populated and water-rich tropical region with wet rice agriculture was the home of the cholera pathogen. Forms of the disease had long been endemic in the tropical lowlands, defined by the course of the Ganges with its tributaries and the Ganges-Brahmaputra delta. European and Chinese travellers, scientists and traders had described the illness from the sixteenth century, and older Muslim and Indian accounts make it likely that it had existed there

103

since antiquity or even earlier.[117] An especially serious outbreak began in June 1817, though – perhaps caused by a mutation of the cholera pathogen. The mortality rate was disproportionately high even by Indian standards, as a British military doctor determined: 'Cholera is well known as a disease of tropical climates and warm seasons, but, as far as our information extends, it has rarely prevailed to any great degree in this country, until the autumn of 1817; when it appeared in Bengal, in the form of a very peculiar and malignant epidemic.'[118]

Contemporary physicians suggested that they might be dealing with a new pathogen, but the changed environment also played a role. Bengal was now part of the British Empire, with many contacts to other imperial territories, and merchants and troops were constantly travelling between these different outposts. This facilitated the rapid spread of cholera and made it a worldwide problem.[119] Contemporaries already recognised a connection between the outbreak and extraordinary climatic events. In India – as a result of Tambora – 1815 had been a year of extremely heavy rainfall with serious flooding and crop failures. The next year, in contrast, was extraordinarily dry and hot because of the delayed monsoon. Now the drought led to failed harvests and starvation. The year 1817 again tended towards the opposite extreme with heavy precipitation and flooding. Since these conditions were especially conducive to the spread of the cholera pathogen, the epidemic broke out with particular violence. In Bengal itself no town or village was spared. Within three months tens of thousands had died in the epidemic. Doctors were forced to recognise that cholera had become one of the most dangerous diseases in human history.[120]

Calcutta, which is dedicated to Kali, the Hindu goddess of death and destruction,[121] lived up to the name of its patroness. After breaking out at the Khumbh Mela, the largest Hindu festival on the Ganges, from where it was spread by pilgrims through water bottles, the epidemic reached the capital of British India in early August 1817. From here the pathogen spread first to other parts of Asia and East Africa and then to the rest of the world. Neither natural nor other barriers or quarantine measures could stop the disease. It spread not only up the river valleys as usual, but also along the coastline and across the Indian subcontinent. The disease followed British troops to Burma (now Myanmar), an independent kingdom under King Bodawpaya (1745–1819, reigned 1782–1819), and spread from there to China by land.[122] The epidemic had probably already reached the Chinese metropolis of Canton in 1817. British troops also spread the disease to Nepal and Afghanistan in 1818. Hindu pilgrims took it with them to the Punjab and Bombay on India's western coast. The pandemic raged throughout the subcontinent until 1820, after which it retreated to individual towns and villages.[123] A French doctor estimated the number of deaths in India as 1.25 million per year for each year between 1817 and 1831, which would be nearly 20 million people.[124] Modern estimates of deaths for some years are even higher.[125]

The large Indian cities had British medical facilities and even their own medical journals, in which academically trained doctors reported on the development of the epidemic and discussed possible treatments. While they were powerless to stop the spread, scarcely another major epidemic disease was so well documented at the time.[126] In 1817, the military doctor Reginald Orton at first speculated about a causal connection between the disease and the colonial wars, but soon rejected this hypothesis because the number of victims was equally high outside the areas of the military campaigns. Next he considered that the tropical climate might be responsible, and finally he developed the theory of a 'cholera cloud',[127] an idea that some medical historians have found especially curious.[128] If, however, one connects the 1817 cholera epidemic with the eruption of Mount Tambora, then the contemporary observation that the epidemic was accompanied by a 'cloudy, overcast state of the sky, ... giving it a *whitish* appearance', is quite fitting.[129]

Foreign rule and misery in Italy

Italy was as much affected by the cold wave of the Tambora Crisis as the countries north of the Alps. The temperature figures for Milan, Rome and even Palermo resembled those for Zurich, Munich or Paris. In 1816, it was 1–3 degrees colder on average than in a normal year of this period. In Italy, however, the usual hardships were exacerbated by foreign occupation: by Habsburg Austria in the north and Bourbon Spain in the south. By around 1800 conquest by Napoleon and his brothers had abolished the last independent Italian states – Venice and Rome – and even the end of Napoleon and the Napoleonids installed in Italy brought no improvement. Austria acquired Venice along with northern Italy, and the two were combined to form a new province, the Lombardo-Venetian kingdom. After the capture and execution of the Napoleonid Joachim Murat (1767–1815), southern Italy – the kingdom of Naples-Sicily – once again fell to the Bourbon Ferdinand I (1751–1825), who was married to Maria Carolina of Austria.

105

An American who travelled through Italy in 1816 and 1817 and who, as a passionate supporter of Napoleon, was hardly impartial, blamed Austria for all of the hardships. In his eyes, the climate was by no means responsible for the prevailing misery, but rather the refusal of the Austrian Emperor Francis I and his administration to institute reforms. James Sloan, who began his travelogue in Trieste, described the situation as follows:

> Since the war, Trieste has been inundated by beggars; an evil which is considered by its inhabitants as a consequence of its annexation to Austria . . . But this scene of misery in the inferiour [*sic*] walks of society, is not confined to Trieste. It comprehends the neighbouring towns and villages, and extends over the adjacent districts and provinces. Many well attested cases of persons dying of absolute hunger, were cited to confirm the representations, made on all hands, of the sufferings of the poor. I have repeatedly seen groups of these unhappy wretches, eagerly searching the polluted offal of the kitchen, for something to satisfy the imperious cravings of nature. In some parts of the Venetian and Milanese territories, many of this unfortunate class of sufferers, have supported life by feeding on grass and raw vegetables.[130]

In Udine, travellers were stopped at every corner by groups of begging old men, women and children 'whose dress and aspect bespeak a condition of wretchedness, of which we have no example in America'.[131]

Recent studies have shown that the Austrian administration commissioned very precise reports from all provinces of the Veneto in order to take appropriate steps to alleviate the suffering. Apart from charitable measures such as distributing Rumford soup, these mainly included employment programmes in road building, but tax relief was even considered.[132] After he reached Rome it became clear to the American that the Italian princes were no better than the Austrian rulers, but actually even worse, since they were also out to enrich themselves personally. He closed his travel account with the words: 'No country, perhaps, has suffered more than Italy, from the oppression of overgrown land-holders, and the imbecility inherent in her present governments, helps to nourish and perpetuate this abuse. Her tenures of landed property are upon the worst footing. This is the reason why vast tracts of her soil lie waste and uncultivated; this is the cause of the indigence, in general, of her peasantry; and the source of that frightful poverty, which exists in a country enjoying the kindest influences of heaven.' The large landowners and rulers of the petty states presented a particular problem, according to Sloan: 'When I was in Tuscany,[133] a lively indignation was excited throughout the lower orders of the people, against prince *Corsini*,[134] who monopolised the sale of grain in that country; and at a time, the people were literally starving throughout Italy, the Duke of *Modena* was purchasing grain in his dominions, and retailing it out at an enormous profit to his own subjects.'[135]

For Sloan, the fundamental evil of this European society lay first in the monarchy, then in the structure of domination over land and people, as it was still practised by the Italian aristocracy, and finally in the persistence of some barbarous features of outmoded feudalism.[136] Since he only travelled in 1816 and 1817 he does not seem to have realised that all of Italy and the rest of western Europe were experiencing a state of emergency because of the climate crisis. Particularly in southern Italy, that is, in the kingdom of Naples,[137] the famine of 1816–1817 is remembered as the worst in history.[138]

Recent studies have revealed that the entire Mezzogiorno (southern Italy) was affected by the famine and that here, too, rising grain prices led to great hardship. As in many regions of Europe the increased cultivation of potatoes was considered here.[139] In northern Italy the administration of the Lombardo-Venetian kingdom began hectic activities to prevent the starvation of villagers and their protest marches and plans to emigrate. They adopted the same measures as all surrounding countries, whether republics or monarchies: They organised donation campaigns, soup kitchens and employment programmes, took steps to combat begging and crime, and wherever possible bought up grain.[140] Sloan noticed none of this, and the conclusion he drew from witnessing the suffering mirrored the convictions of all middle-class liberals: 'If so much misery is to be found, we may fairly conclude that government is in fault.'[141] Sloan apparently had no idea that the USA was being affected by the same crisis and that soup kitchens and other modes of assistance were springing up everywhere there as well.

Rise in religiosity

For centuries, the Christian world had reacted similarly to climate anomalies, crop failures, hunger and epidemic diseases, interpreting them as signs from God. In this world-view, nature resembled a semiotic system in which one had to be on the lookout for hidden messages. Natural disasters and famines were understood as signs that God used to point to the excessive sinfulness of humankind, if not of concrete individuals in specific regions.[142] In such times of crisis people sought scapegoats and persecuted and murdered outsiders. In the late Middle Ages Jews sometimes served as a projection screen.[143] In the early modern period, during the Little Ice Age, climate anomalies were blamed on witches.[144] The mainstream of the major religions or confessions, however, had always been sceptical of such murderous actions.

As Gregory Monahan (1927–2011) has shown, in the age of Enlightenment the religious pattern of crisis interpretation gave way to a more modern response.[145] During the famine of 1709 in France, apparently for the first time, people blamed not minorities or the wrath of God, but the political authorities – the town magistrates, provincial governors and ultimately the monarch. Starvation was no longer considered a natural phenomenon or divine punishment. Instead, it was now deemed to be a sign of deficient concern, a lack of grain stores and the foresightedness to buy up stocks, a miserable infrastructure and pointless customs barriers which made it impossible to bring in supplies from other regions quickly.[146]

This secular pattern of interpretation also dominated in the Tambora Crisis, but one can observe a simultaneous marked rise in religiosity as well. Whether, as John Dexter Post (1926–2012) has suggested, it is possible to draw a direct connection between the intensity of the religious reaction and the intensity of the crisis, measured by the example of the level of price rises,[147] remains an open question. More generally, it seems that people flocked to churches of all denominations, Catholic as well as Protestant or free churches in continental Europe, Puritan, Baptist or Methodist churches in the Anglo-American world. In 1816, higher church attendance was noted in all the New England states. Contemporaries in the United States spoke of a religious revival.[148] In October 1816, after the results of the harvest had become clear, churchgoers seemed to be praying with unusual earnestness.[149]

In Spain, where the summer of 1816 was unusually cool and dry and the harvest was therefore under threat,[150] the number of processions and pilgrimages against the drought increased.[151] In Catholic Bavaria, where pilgrimages had been prohibited under the regime of Minister of State Montgelas, the practice gained a new lease on life. At this time of great suffering, people recalled their old helpers in hardship, the saints and their veneration.[152] Some even believed that the enlightened ban on pilgrimages was responsible for the famine. From all parts of the country came petitions asking that supplicatory processions be permitted again, and unofficial, illicit pilgrimages were conducted like protest demonstrations despite the prohibition.[153] Given this growing popular displeasure, the government hastened to give in to the pressure. Rogation services, processions and pilgrimages were allowed once more and placed in the hands of the regular parish clergy to channel the newly awakened religious sentiment.[154] The bishops emerged stronger from this crisis and, like the Pietists (but unlike the orthodox Lutherans), they returned to a traditional rhetoric of sin, albeit less out of their own convictions than for tactical reasons: they yielded to the expectations of rural popular piety in order to strengthen the Roman Catholic Church's position vis-à-vis the state.[155]

The example of the kingdom of Westphalia shows that, unlike in previous centuries, when cold, constant rain, famine and epidemics were explained in terms of the traditional economy of sin, Lutheran orthodoxy now dispensed altogether with such assignments of blame.[156] Perhaps pastors avoided penitential sermons because they wanted to avoid any appearance of criticising the church authorities, which in the old duchy had long maintained a strict orthodox Lutheran regime. The printed feast-day sermons for the Reformation jubilee of 1817 contain no hint of cares and woes.[157] Similarly, they avoided all political criticism. Not even the opening of the state parliament in 1817, which began with a sermon, was used to such ends.[158] The new role model on offer was the mercy of Jesus. Since special days of penance were no longer imposed as they had been in the past,[159] events organised by the newly established charitable associations served as occasions to propagate the new attitude.[160]

Orthodox Lutherans had no monopoly on sermons, however, for the new kingdom of Württemberg also had Pietist regions, which did not feel bound by the rules of the Stuttgart church leadership, as well as Catholic enclaves under the influence of the Allgäu awakening movement, whose piety formed a counterpart to Protestant Pietism.[161] The old moral interpretation of suffering lived on in these religious movements, underpinned by a prophecy by the theologian Johann Albrecht Bengel (1687–1752) that the world would end and Christ would return in 1836.[162] Because of its inwardness, Pietism also held an attraction for aimlessly wandering intellectuals like the Karlsruhe Aulic Councillor Heinrich Jung-Stilling (1740–1817), who predicted the end of the world in 1817.[163] Many believed that the end of days could come anytime, and waited for the corresponding signs.

Authors like Johann Michael Hahn (1758–1819) and his followers, the 'Michelians', interpreted the weather events and famine months as signs of the imminent last days.[164] The popular Pietist rhymed:

Here on earth, all of nature
Is at the mercy of temperature

Now cold, now heat comes to the fore
And all are baffled to the core
So that no living thing does thrive
And all are hindered in their lives.[165]

Hahn had quite a simple explanation for the temperature swings. Satan had been unleashed and dwelled in the lower atmosphere: 'Hence the suffering that is also evident in the disorders of the elements, and hence the misery of recent times.'[166] Similarly, members of the Catholic awakening saw the cooling trend as a portent of the impending last days, during which the world would grow cold and the end of humanity would be at hand.[167] For those known as 'the quiet in the land', hardship was a sign from God to prepare for the coming end of the world. This included looking inward and praying 'to implore God, the father of our Lord Jesus Christ, with the aid of the Holy Spirit, because of the great hardship and affliction that has affected our dear homeland and many other countries'.[168]

Pöschlianism: the end of the world on 30 March 1817

What the Michelians were for the Protestants, the 'Pöschlianer' were for a group of awakened Catholics. The originator of this sect was the priest Thomas Pöschl (1769–1837), who became known for having accompanied the bookseller and publisher Johann Philipp Palm (1766–1806) on his way to execution by Napoleon's governor in Braunau am Inn. Ever since that time, Pöschl had identified Napoleon with the Devil. Because of his growing obsession with Satan, penitential sermons and exorcism, in 1813 he was transferred to the remote village of Ampflwang (Hausruckviertel, part of the Salzachkreis in Bavaria until 1814, and thereafter in Austria), where he found a willing community of prayer who became his core followers. Pöschl made the visionary Magdalena Sickinger (née Schlichting), who regarded him as the founder of a new church, his medium, through whom he received his 'revelations' of the dawning of the millennium. Practical love and penitence as well as the conversion of the Jews were to prepare the way for its coming. After three years Pöschl himself would walk to Jerusalem and be crucified as the new Christ. Because his itinerant preaching stopped work wherever he went, since his growing group of followers considered it unnecessary given the impending end of the world, Pöschl was at first admonished by the ordinariate. He was taken out of circulation altogether and interned

110

in Salzburg in late March 1814 and declared insane in November 1815. A farmer from Ottnang, Johann Haas, then announced that he was God's chosen successor to Pöschl.

The famine caused the sect to run wild. Members increased their penances and exorcisms because they believed that all human beings were 'possessed by demons of gluttony, envy and lust'. They expected the world to end on Palm Sunday, 30 March 1817. In anticipation of Judgement Day, sect members gave away all their worldly possessions. On the eve of 30 March they erected a huge pyre upon which they burnt their finest clothes, jewellery and other valuables. In the end, God was to be propitiated by a human sacrifice. The local priest of Ampflwang managed to flee in time, however, and the sect member Joseph Haas was chosen as a substitute; since he did not want to die he convinced his thirty-one-year-old goddaughter Anna Maria Enzinger (1786–1817) to perish in his place. As part of the cleansing of the world before this human sacrifice, the sect set upon a family of neighbouring farmers, the only ones in the village who did not believe the world was about to end. The wife was beaten to death and her husband and daughter so grievously injured that they succumbed a few days later. Finally, Anna Maria Enzinger was killed as a 'sacrifice' in the presence of many sect followers. When sect leader Haas wanted to kill another young woman her father stepped in and prevented it. Haas thereupon began to beat his own wife and smash up the room.[169] These events attracted international attention. *The Times* of London reported on a further human victim, a thirteen-year-old girl killed on Good Friday 1817, who was allegedly possessed by the Devil, but this was presumably a garbled version of the same story.[170]

The son of the murdered neighbour family reported the incident and the police arrested the ringleaders. Under the impact of the orgy of violence, many Pöschlians begged for forgiveness, but later the mood changed. When the faithful tried to free the prisoners, riots ensued. The police shot into the crowd, leaving one person dead and several wounded. Austrian troops finally crushed the sect, whose followers were estimated (with much exaggeration) at 12,000. Of more than 100 arrestees, eighty-six sect members went to trial. The leaders had to be declared *doli incapax* because of mental confusion. Most of them were released, and only the murderer Haas was kept in permanent custody. The sect founder Pöschl, who distanced himself from the killings but stuck to his revelations, was taken to Vienna in April 1817 and interned for the rest of his life in the Deficientenhaus, a hospital for sick and mentally ill priests.[171]

The spectre of Pöschlianism had not yet been banished, however.

The Pöschlians regrouped and decided to move to Prague to convert the Jews. Lightly dressed, they set forth in the middle of a snowstorm, accompanied by their children and livestock. The police stopped this procession and committed the half-frozen sect members to the hospital in Vöcklabrück. The government in Munich took measures to prevent their incursion into Bavaria. On instructions from the minister of the interior, the vicariate general in Freising warned all clerics that 'nearby, a wild fanaticism' was committing 'the most terrible atrocities'.[172] It was evident that like-minded individuals in the Allgäu awakening movement were at work in Bavaria: the so-called *Herzbüchlein* (Little book of the heart) by Johannes Goßner (1773–1858) in Munich, which was banned by the state censors as well as the Church, was the Pöschlians' favourite book.[173]

In April 1817, when a journeyman artisan arrested in Rosenheim declared that he intended to seek work in Munich or become a Pöschlianer ('for they have a good life'), the ministry of the interior saw their fears confirmed that the fanatical sect could become a gathering place for the era's many malcontents. Followers could be found even among civil servants. Moreover, additional sect leaders were also coming forward. In Lower Franconia in 1817 a group gathered around a certain Bernhard Müller, who already had followers in Baden and Hesse.[174] The apocalyptic priest Ignaz Lindl (1774–1846) was preaching in the Allgäu, and Baroness Juliane von Krüdener in southwest Germany and Switzerland. Interior Minister von Thürheim began to believe in a great conspiracy among the sects. One year later, however, it became evident that such fears were groundless. Most of the Catholic and Protestant sectarians mentioned called for emigration to Russia; only Müller emigrated to the USA.[175] Lindl, who was deprived of his Bavarian parish in 1818 on orders from the king because of dangers to the peace, moved to Russia at the recommendation of Juliane von Krüdener. After an audience with the Tsar he was assigned a piece of land, and in 1822, along with twenty-two immigrant families, founded the village of Sarata in Bessarabia.[176]

The 'woman clothed with the sun' in Revelation and the war between rich and poor

The above-mentioned Juliane von Krüdener (1764–1824) was the heavyweight among the sectarians, and her appearance on the scene reveals the state of agitation in which southern Germany and Switzerland found themselves during the Tambora Crisis. Her father

Otto Hermann von Vietinghoff (1724–1792) had made a military career in Russian service, was minister of health under Catherine II and owned estates and factories in Livonia. Money was no object. Krüdener's birthplace, Riga, had been part of the Russian Empire since 1710. Her husband, the Baltic German nobleman Alexis von Krüdener (1764–1802), from whom she had separated in 1791, was Russian ambassador to Venice, Munich, Copenhagen, Madrid and finally Berlin. Krüdener had a religious conversion experience in 1804 that would take her far from her family's Lutheran faith. She first joined the Moravian Brethren, but soon evolved into a prophetess sui generis, seeking contact with all manner of evangelical gurus. Johann Heinrich Jung-Stilling helped her make contact with great figures in Germany, Sweden and Russia. Her religiosity – marked by outward Catholic-connoted signs such as crossing herself, kneeling, invoking the Virgin Mary, miracles, etc. – and her preaching to large crowds proved quite confusing to Protestants.[177] Because of her visions, her followers referred to her as 'the woman clothed in the sun' from the book of Revelation.[178]

Baden became her base of operations, which would become significant not least thanks to the Russian Tsarina Elizabeth Alexeievna, née Louise of Baden (1779–1826).[179] She mediated the contact with Tsar Alexander I, who was pleased by Krüdener's prophecies about his 'great mission' in Europe. This made her a political force. In the weeks before the battle of Waterloo she lived at the new Russian headquarters in Heidelberg, where she spent the evenings in conversation and prayer with the Tsar. She followed him to Paris, where she became a much sought-after member of society. Her gatherings were major events. When Talleyrand attended one of the Baroness's soirées he found the seven rooms of her apartment filled with some 500 people, and after fighting his way through to the last room he found the prophetess between the Tsar and the king of Prussia. Talleyrand surmised that so many people had come because they knew they could meet the Tsar there.[180] It is impossible to know what role Krüdener played in the realisation of the Holy Alliance of 26 September 1815, which was intended to place European power politics on Christian foundations.

She continued to advise the Tsar until she was compromised by a sex scandal involving members of her entourage and was not allowed to travel to Russia.[181] In November 1815 Krüdener arrived in Basle, where she mesmerised the people with her sermons on the end times. She also met with immediate resistance, however, because her public appearances challenged the ecclesiastical hierarchy of the Reformed city-state. The municipal authorities expelled her from the city because of the 'arising unrest'. She was able to remain in Switzerland, though, because her son Paul Alexander von Krüdener (1784–1858) was appointed Russian ambassador in Berne. During the famine years her radius of action encompassed Switzerland, Baden and Alsace, where she travelled around with an entourage of up to eighty persons.[182] Clerics such as the Genevan Henri-Louis Empaytaz (1790–1853) fell under her influence, which extended to evangelical sects in the British Isles.[183]

At the high point of the famine, the Baroness specialised in agitating among the lower classes, for whom she prophesied a 'day of vengeance'.[184] When she appeared once again before the gates of Basle, the city pastor felt compelled to argue against her in a sermon. Johann Jakob Faesch (1752–1832) reminded his audience of all that the Basle authorities, relief associations, grain purchases and soup kitchens had achieved, emphasising the numbers of paupers who had received support and the size of donations by wealthy citizens who cared about the needy. 'What does she want, this fanatic praised by so many gullible persons, what is the point of all the bitter accusations she directs ceaselessy at the well-to-do of our native city?', asked the pastor, who then answered his own question: her aim was 'to turn the beggars into lords'. And she purportedly sought personal revenge because the 'millionaires have not offered up millions to her'. The poor would only harm themselves if they left Basle, for nowhere else would they receive so much assistance.[185]

Juliane von Krüdener sparked a mass movement with her sermons. Wherever the prophetess appeared with her entourage, soup was cooked and blankets were distributed, much like in the disaster relief operations of today in developing countries. Not just the poor and the needy, but also the wealthy and learned – celebrities like the educator Pestalozzi – were moved to tears during her sermons. The Baroness gained followers from all walks of life, since along with physical hunger she also addressed the hunger for justice. She predicted that in the Final Judgement, government ministers would have to justify their actions. In an open letter of 14 February 1817 to the minister of the interior in Baden, she wrote, 'No, Sir, far from cultivating idleness, I have accused the millionaire city, this Basle that hates me . . . of not caring better for its many poor, and of diminishing the working class instead of providing work. But the poor in the congregations are again allowed to care for the poor, and the rich care for the rich in Basle. One depends on a few charitable institutions that completely stifle any love. Streams of the destitute come and demand bread from me, from the same Basle where people claim to attend to all their needs.'[186]

The masses who came to hear Krüdener's sermons now appeared dangerous not just to the Swiss authorities. Chancellor of State Metternich told the Russian ambassador in Vienna that he believed her aim was to 'incite the propertyless against the propertied. What did this foreign noblewoman want?'[187] Her sermons were viewed as attempts to foment war between poor and rich, and thus insurrection.[188] This suspicion found direct confirmation in a pamphlet entitled 'To the Poor', probably written by her supporter Johann Georg Kellner. In it, the poor are described as 'God's chosen people', and contrasted with the unprincipled rich.[189] Scheitlin described an appearance in Arbon in the Thurgau:

> The preaching soon resumed. A woman preached on the steps, a young lad preached in the entry next to the kitchen, a man preached on the upper storey; a fourth preacher lay face-down, as if poured out on the floor, like a dead man without a sign of life for more than a quarter of an hour. Then he stood up and preached the imminent demise of his small native town of Arbon. The Baroness thereupon gave a long sermon devoid of new ideas. The main preacher told of the Plague in Roja (Italy), of the flooding of the Seine (France), of the suddenly dried-up lake (also Italy), of a sickle-shaped drawing on the sun, of the centre pin of a compass that no longer points west, but now deviates to the east, and drew the conclusion that a new time of misfortune was on its way. He prophesied conflagrations that had already come; floods on the lake that had just retreated; dearth and famine that God was just in the process of alleviating.[190]

Finally the Swiss authorities put an end to the spectre and, despite the protection of the Russian ambassador, expelled the prophetess from every Swiss canton. In August 1817 she was brought to the Swiss border with a police escort, from whence she continued on to Prussia via Bavaria and Saxony with further escorts.[191] On 22 January 1818 she managed to give another speech at Beeskow on the Spree in which she emphasised the significance of the Holy Alliance and her closeness to the Tsar and the king of Prussia.[192] In March she was deported to Russia, where she was prohibited from settling in St Petersburg and Moscow. In the years that followed Krüdener mainly lived on her estates in Kosse (Livonia)[193] and continued to lobby on behalf of Germans immigrating to Russia, support for whom was organised by her daughter Juliette von Krüdener (1787–1865) and her son-in-law Franz Karl von Berckheim (1785–1836), now a Russian councillor of state and 'commissioner of immigration'.[194] Juliane von Krüdener wanted to visit the 'communities of the awakened' and her Zürichtal Colony in the Crimea one more time,[195] and died there on Christmas Day 1824. Tsar Alexander I visited her grave in the Greek chapel of Princess Anna Golitsyna at Koreiz.[196] Her followers memorialised her in books and continued to build a legend around her.[197]

Food riots in the spirit of the 'moral economy'

E.P. Thompson (1924–1993) has shown that food riots were among the classic forms of protest in ancien régime Europe. The common people confronted both feudal power and capitalist market mechanisms with a 'moral economy' that determined how much the necessities of life should cost according to experience and tradition. If the price of 'daily bread' rose to improbable levels, protests ensued in which transports were set upon and the goods sold at a 'fair price'. The perpetrators of such robberies regarded them not as crimes but as legitimate actions. The language of the critique was religiously inspired and, especially among Protestants, liberally laced with Biblical quotations. For example, one preacher noted that 'Exaction of any kind is base; but this in the Matter of Corn is of the basest Kind. It falls heaviest upon the Poor, It is robbing them because they are so . . . It is murdering *them* outright whom they find half dead, and plundering the wreck'd Vessel.'[198] During the Tambora Crisis, food riots in England already assumed forms of labour protest to the extent that factory workers in East Anglia not only set food prices, but also sought to establish a minimum wage to replace poor relief.[199]

In Lombardy and throughout northern Italy from September 1816 there were fears that the hungry would stage protests and uprisings. In Trento the rioting was so severe that a high-level commission was charged with finding solutions.[200] In the Prussian city of Koblenz, where protesters stopped a Cologne-bound barge carrying potatoes on 20 May 1817 and attempted to force the traders to unload the cargo, the military had to intervene to restore the rights of ownership. In his report to the Prussian government, the director of police still sought to create some understanding for the attacks by appealing to empathy: 'As unjust as the action itself was, it can nevertheless, in my unpresuming opinion, be excused by the great hardship that oppresses the poorer class at present, and with the desperate mood created by this situation, which increases their irritability. In such a mood it is, to be sure, a painful sight for the rougher element to watch potatoes, which they otherwise enjoy as their daily bread, and which now can scarcely be had for money, passing by in great boatloads.'[201]

Women were often in the forefront of food riots, not just because they were directly confronted with price rises at the markets, but also because they could see the effects of want on their children, and perhaps also because they could expect lesser penalties if convicted than their men. Thus on 16 August 1817 in Mainz (grand duchy of Hesse) the women complained of the prices demanded at the market. 'On the 16th the women also caused a nuisance at the market. They sought to bring down the prices by force. They asked the price, made a far lower offer, and when the seller refused they made short work of the matter, emptying the potato sacks, overturning the baskets of beans and other vegetables, mixing eggs and butter with them and stamping the whole underfoot. The noise was so great that the military was despatched to restore peace', as Father Philipp Scherer (1742–1827) recounted in his chronicle.[202] Thompson commented as follows on a similar incident in England: 'These women appear . . . to have been unaware that they should have waited for some two hundred years for their Liberation.'[203]

France as the centre of social protest

There were more riots and protest actions in France in 1816/17 than in any other country in Europe. The protests reached nearly every region, from Picardy to the Pyrenees and from the Côte d'Azur through Burgundy to the Ardennes. If climate historians are correct, France experienced the greatest deviations in summer temperatures; on average, they were 3 degrees lower than normal in 1816. That still tells us little about crop yields and grain prices, since crop failures were less severe along the coast, and it was easy to import food by sea. The price differences for grain were accordingly large. As French minister of police and the interior, Élie Decazes (1780–1860), noted in his memoirs, at the height of the crisis a hectolitre of wheat cost 30 francs in the arrondissement of Niort (Poitou-Charentes) near the Atlantic coast, while the same quantity cost 100 francs in Strasbourg, Colmar (Alsace) or the Vosges (Lorraine).[204] Now people were of the opinion that the crops – regardless of property relations – 'belonged' to the region where they were harvested. If grain was transported to other regions, the price would fall there and rise in one's own market. That is why local people sought to stop the transports. This view stood in flagrant contradiction to free trade ideology, which stated that free trade would compensate for price differences and ensure rational provisioning.

Marjolin distinguished between two phases of rebellion: in the first phase, which encompassed the summer and autumn of 1816 and lasted until January 1817, resistance remained rather passive. Locals tried to prevent the transport of 'their' harvest to other regions. After a relatively peaceful February, a second phase began in March in which resistance not infrequently culminated in open rebellion and assumed the characteristics of an uprising. During this phase, the anarchy in some regions resembled the situation in 1788. An uprising lasting several days already broke out in November 1816, when grain dealers tried to ship the harvest to Marseilles. Cereal prices had risen sharply in the days before, and wagons carrying grain were stopped at the city gates and forced to turn back. Then the grain was 'appraised' at a far lower price. When the affected traders called the police and the authorities called the military, the insurgents did not give up but barricaded themselves in the suburb of St-Cyprien. Only the diplomatic talents of a general kept the protest from ending in a bloodbath.[205] The same thing happened with potatoes in Lille in December. In this case, the uprising proceeded from the garrison and the local population joined in.[206] Bloodshed ensued in January 1817 in Doudeville (Normandy), when soldiers were deployed against looters at a granary. In Yvetot two protestors were shot dead, after which the furious crowd stormed the town hall and looted the wheat stocks. Such looting also occurred elsewhere in Normandy, including Dieppe, Rouen and Pont-Audemer. The anger was especially great when wheat was destined for transport to the capital, Paris.[207]

Just as at the time of the Great Fear in the early days of the French Revolution,[208] crowds stopped food transports on the roads, forced traders to sell their goods on the spot and paid the prices set by the protestors, a practice referred to as 'taxation populaire'.[209] While food riots were still sporadic in the autumn of 1816, they spread during the following spring and became veritable insurrections. 'Starving townspeople joined forces with desperate peasants to form large mobs who roamed the countryside, plundering manors of their stores and occupying towns. Entire provinces were in turmoil. The crowds resisted the soldiers and in some cases even forced them to retreat.'[210] In Reims, a popular movement tried to block all grain transports beginning in February 1817. Vierzon (Centre-Val de Loire) was in open revolt. In the eastern départements, which were most strongly affected by price rises and famine, transports were halted and grain sold at a 'just price'. In the spring, the crisis reached the political

118

centre, the Île-de-France. Champagne, Bourgogne, the Nivernais and the Orléanais were all heavily affected. Marjolin speaks of a 'véritable jacquerie', a general uprising in which farms were plundered, towns besieged and even regular troops attacked.[211]

Peasants planned to besiege the town of Chateau-Thierry in Picardy in July 1817. The alarm bells were rung en route so that people streamed out of all the villages and hamlets they passed to join the protest march until it had swelled to some 5,000. The demonstrators occupied the small town and forced the sub-prefect to sell all available grain stores at moderate prices. When the granaries had been emptied the crowd boarded the ships on which the grain bought up by the government had been loaded for transport. Only after all the grain had been distributed among those present did the uprising die down.[212] The centres of the insurrection were the départements of Aisne, Seine-et-Marne, Marne, Aube and Haut-Marne, where the textile workers also revolted beginning in April 1817. Gatherings of more than 1,000 demonstrators seized the grain in many places and sold it for a 'just price' of 34 francs per hectolitre.[213] On 31 May 6,000 peasants occupied the provincial capital of Bar-sur-Aube, and the police found themselves unable to restore order or make arrests. Farms throughout the region were set upon and looted. Large swathes of the country were in turmoil, and the authorities were powerless. Finally, weapons were distributed in the towns for self-defence against looters.

According to a report of 31 May from the département of Haute-Vienne (Limousin):

> There was an insurrection in Saint-Junien on the 29th. Three wagons transporting grain were stopped and unloaded by a substantial crowd, who wished the grain to be appraised. When the mayor saw that his efforts were fruitless, he had the prefect and the sub-prefect informed. The last-mentioned immediately set off for Saint-Junien at the head of all the forces he could muster. He tried without success to persuade the mutineers, and saw himself compelled to order an attack. Only one woman was wounded. The grain was loaded back onto the wagons, which departed under escort. The prefect himself arrived a few moments later with an impressive show of force. Thirteen individuals were arrested. The high court has been charged with investigating the matter.[214]

In the département of Maine-et-Loire (Pays-de-la-Loire) too, where the procureur général of Angers had long observed the rising agitation, the authorities managed to arrest eleven looters in Chalonnes in June. In other towns and in the neighbouring département of Sarthe, however, the National Guard refused to cooperate with the gendarmerie.[215]

Whether in Prussia or France, the local authorities were anxious to play down the dangerousness of events when reporting to the central government, since too much dissatisfaction among the population let alone ungovernability would have reflected badly on them. For that reason their reports tended to make the situation appear more harmless than it was. Thus, for example, the procureur général of Aix-en-Provence wrote that no notable crimes had been committed in the south in connection with the subsistence crisis, although we know of insurrectionist movements in the départements of Gironde, Landes, Basses-Pyrénées, Bouches-du-Rhône and Var.[216] One can also lend little credence to newspaper reports, since the publishers had to be cautious because of pre- and post-publication censorship. Thus the unrest in Koblenz was less likely to be reported in the Prussian papers than in the London *Times* – that is, if the news travelled that far.

What is striking about these rebellions and tumults during the Tambora Crisis is the absence of a political dimension in the stricter sense. The insurgents did not arrive wearing liberty caps and they did not propagate social revolution. The authorities reacted with astounding pragmatism, even if the odd shot was fired and a few people were killed or injured. France did not, however, experience a calamity like the Peterloo massacre of 1819 in England (see pp. 197ff). The authorities noted that they were in no position to combat the unrest effectively, among other things because the National Guard often refused to participate. The Decazes government concentrated its military means on securing the access roads and canals in the capital in order to ensure provisions for the population of Paris.[217]

Tumults in the kingdom of Bavaria

Wilhelm Abel supported the consensus that massive protests occurred only in France, but not in Germany. The more recent scholarship contradicts him, and not only with respect to the incidents in Mainz and Koblenz. The annual report of the Bavarian interior ministry for the administrative year 1816/17 states that tumults requiring military intervention to put them down had broken out in five locations in the kingdom. There had also been a whole series of further tumults that had been quelled 'often without military assistance'. 'Tumult' was not an everyday term, but a legal one rooted in the 1813 penal code. The 'crime of tumult or uprising' referred to excesses involving at least ten persons. There were two degrees of tumult: the first applied to demonstrations whose participants responded to orders to disperse

120

with non-violent resistance. The penalty was nonetheless one to eight years in the workhouse. If the 'tumulters' deployed violence against persons or property and if military force was needed to disperse them, their leaders faced the death penalty.[218]

It was mainly the self-confident citizens of former free imperial cities such as Schweinfurt, Memmingen, Lindau, Regensburg, Weissenburg and Dinkelsbühl who initiated serious incidents. The first tumult protesting rising prices broke out in the autumn of 1816 in Schweinfurt, where the local authorities had taken it upon themselves to accord the population a right of purchase at lower prices in the granary ordinance (*Schrannenordnung*). The grain merchants tried to get around this arrangement by simply offering nothing for sale until better-off customers – mainly from Saxony – were allowed to buy. Since the Schweinfurters felt cheated a tumult arose that the local police failed or refused to control. The first military deployment ensued. The judicial treatment of the case revealed behaviour that would remain typical over the course of the crisis: not wishing to fan the flames, the authorities played down the events. The annual report for the government states laconically: 'The judicial authorities did not deem the maltreatment of a few individuals to be grave enough to warrant a criminal investigation', which meant that they feared that wielding the sword of the criminal law might lead to an uncontrolled escalation of the conflict.[219]

The situation in Memmingen was even more serious. Here the problem was the systematic purchase of grain by Johann Heinrich von Sulzer-Wart (1768–1840) of Winterthur, who hoped that this would alleviate the hardship in the Swiss cantons. The merchant, who also served the king of Bavaria as commissioner of the salt trade and had been ennobled for his services in 1814, had obtained an export permit through his connections with the king. His purchase campaign had already led to price rises and unrest in Augsburg, and now the town of Memmingen was affected, which was located on the route to Switzerland. Although later reports by state officials tried to portray the events as the work of a few hot-headed students, the unrest appears to have been coordinated. On 3 December 1816 all of the town gates were occupied and closed. The grain transports were violently blocked. The local police could not get the uprising under control, or preferred not to. The insurgents requisitioned the grain and forced all the bakers to bake free bread for the poor. Minister of War Count Johann Nepomuk von Triva (1755–1827) then sent two companies, which marched into Memmingen on 10 December – that is, only after a week had passed – and occupied the main guardhouse

121

and the town gates. The occupation lasted about one month. The remaining grain was brought to the Swiss border at Lindau under military escort.[220]

There the conflict entered the second round, for in this port town on Lake Constance, through which cereals were to be transported by ship to Switzerland, people feared those who were buying up the grain for resale. In Lindau the uprising acquired a face, since the city commandant Johann Nepomuk von Harscher (1769–1834), a much-decorated military officer, placed himself at its head.[221] In the autumn of 1816 he had already taken it upon himself to have merchant store-houses searched and grain transports to Switzerland stopped. The confiscated grain was sold at the central market of Lindau, with great approbation from the townspeople and the local police. In December, Minister of State Montgelas demanded that this 'unappointed representative of the public' be deposed. Minister of War von Triva gave the troops from Kempten unlimited authority to use armed force 'as the circumstances warranted' and put troops in Augsburg on alert. Harscher was removed from office but did not face prosecution, and was merely transferred to Middle Franconia. He defended himself, arguing that he had merely followed up on suspected grain smuggling and demanded a public investigation of the incidents. It goes without saying that the government refused to conduct such an investigation.

Press censorship prevented the publication of any accounts of the uprisings in Memmingen and Lindau.[222] The Nuremberg *Korrespondent* explicitly refuted a report in the Swiss *Aarauer Zeitung* claiming that there had been 'incidents of unrest' in Augsburg. Such reports were attributed to people 'who at least find satisfaction in invented domestic upheavals and outrages'. In January 1817, the London *Times*, in contrast, reported from Memmingen that there had been 'some disturbance' there approximately three weeks before, 'occasioned by the people opposing the departure of some corn for Switzerland'.[223]

In February 1817 serious incidents occurred in the Bavarian Rhenish Palatinate, after news spread that 900 tonnes of flour and 400 of grain were to be delivered to Saargemünd in Lorraine to provision a Bavarian army corps under General Peter de la Motte (1765–1837), which was stationed there as part of the occupying army. Although the Rhenish Palatinate reached directly to the Saar opposite Saargemünd, and Palatine Bavarian troops were supposed to be provisioned beyond the river, an insurgency erupted in Zweibrücken. The wagons were stopped and, faced with threats from the population, the freight had to be unloaded. Although the contracts had already been drawn up before the export ban, the district administration in Speyer refused to let the transport continue. District President von Zwackh justified this refusal by arguing that flour and potatoes had been unaffordable for ordinary people since December 1816 and that it was necessary to avoid a famine.[224]

Amidst this commotion a lawyer from the former imperial city of Donauwörth intervened with a wholly unwelcome contribution to the discussion on the 'fountainheads' of the 'present dearness' and the ensuing tumults. The notary Felix Joseph Müller supported restrictions on the free trade in grain, since he located the sole cause of the inflation 'in the excesses of grain clipping (*Kipperey*) – grain profiteering and unrestricted export, which was now out of control'.[225] He dedicated his 'frank thoughts' to the 'Most August Ministry of State' in Munich. The ministry immediately censored the book, since Müller wrote that the increasing tumults in Bavaria, 'as in France', were the necessary consequence of free trade policy. 'In the earlier history of the world, too, one finds examples of popular uprisings produced by the dearness of foodstuffs.'[226]

In Regensburg 'grievous violence' erupted on 8 July 1817 when a grain seller from the estate of Köferung, which belonged to the family of Interior Minister von Lerchenfeld, was urged to charge the highest possible prices. During that day many country people had tried to buy bread in the city, and in the evening there were 'excesses as several mobs, consisting mainly of young men and women, became impatient when they were not served immediately, breaking the windows of five bakery shops over the course of five hours and smashing the ovens in five bake-houses, and also purloining some of the effects'. It is striking that the Nuremberg *Korrespondent* newspaper stressed that no citizens of Regensburg had participated in the tumults and that the citizenry and military had soon managed to restore order.[227] In fact, the rioting was suppressed with difficulty. The tumults only ended after the deployment of the cavalry, 'whose wise and cool-headed conduct' was much praised by the government of the Regen district.[228]

The 'Lower Main District' was on the verge of revolt. In early June 1817 the Würzburg government ordered the appropriation of all grain stores and prohibited any export not just to neighbouring states, but even to other administrative districts in Bavaria. The government of the Lower Main District had virtually placed itself at the head of a potential uprising and acted as if it were a sovereign government. As a consequence of this policy, grain from the Netherlands or Prussia could not be transported through the kingdom to southern Bavaria, but had to take detours. This was vexing because it endangered the supply to the capital.[229] People in Munich were shocked by 'Such a spirit of tyranny, which violated all lines of competence; such a propensity for opposition, which defied the most explicit instructions for conduct, and such an expression of egotistical imbalance that, guided solely by provincial self-interest, sought to elevate itself above the interest and the unity of the whole, could not be tolerated for a moment, but, to create an example, had to be forcefully reprimanded and suppressed, as then occurred.' In fact, the Würzburg government called upon the administrations of the neighbouring districts to emulate this practice, and the government of the 'Rezat district' in Ansbach actually followed their lead, decreeing a compulsory survey of the grain stores. Since the central government could not tolerate this, the compulsory measures were lifted by royal decree on 3 July. Interestingly, once again, these arbitrary acts went unpunished. Instead, the king assured his general commissioner in Würzburg, Franz Wilhelm von Asbeck (1760–1826), of the recognition of his 'particular services to the state'.[230]

Existential crisis and a new era in Bavaria

In the capital Munich, too, something was brewing in January 1817. Soldiers left their barracks in droves, the army of beggars increased, prophets of doom appeared and grain prices were the talk of the town. Contrary to the government's free trade policy, people demanded fixed prices and export restrictions as well as drastic measures against profiteers. Anger grew at the inaction of the government, which not merely misjudged the crisis but in its intransigence also ignored or even blocked possible solutions. This resulted from Montgelas' political and economic principles – the insistence on a centralised system paired with free trade. The government was not merely blind to the hardships of the population, however, but also repressive towards its critics: rogations, processions and pilgrimages continued to be prohibited as unauthorised demonstrations, and any open reporting on the dissatisfaction and unrest was suppressed with the argument that it endangered the unity of the state. The Montgelas government was interested in the well being of the state, not of the people, and had lost all awareness that the one was impossible without the other.

The hard line was softened somewhat nonetheless. Beginning in November, civil servants received inflation supplements to their salaries, graduated by income. The government wanted to prevent a return to the venality of the pre-revolutionary period: a functioning administration was the great achievement of the reform era. In November the government also agreed to a sharp rise in grain export tariffs. The Montgelas cabinet was, however, so dogmatically opposed to importing grain that in late December the king saw himself compelled to intervene directly in the business of governing – which he never did otherwise – and, despite the misgivings of the finance ministry, to order the purchase of additional grain in a decree of 28 December 1816. Citing formal details, Montgelas postponed the implementation of this decree until the purchase eventually fell through. State policy measures towards the poor consisted largely of a campaign against beggars. Eberhard Weis (1925–2013) thus concluded: 'There is no doubt that the inadequate response to the suffering up to 1817 severely damaged Montgelas' reputation among the population and supplied his enemies with further arguments against him . . . Since he dominated the government, public opinion also held him responsible for everything.'[231]

The misjudgement of the crisis was not the sole reason for the toppling of the minister in early February 1817. It is not, strictly speaking, among the causes cited in the traditional historical literature: a change of system through rapprochement with the Church; a change of generation; a change of system by subordination to the German Confederation; as well as a crisis in the Confederation of the Rhine because of the overextension of bureaucratic absolutism.[232] However, proceeding from Aretin's observation that many contemporary reflections never made their way explicitly into the written record, and picking up Hofmann's overextension thesis,[233] it seems likely that the social crisis played a significant role in Montgelas' downfall. Eberhard Weis has recently published what the older literature leaves out. In his conversation with the king on 2 February 1817, in which he demanded the immediate dismissal of the minister of state, Karl Philipp Josef, Prince von Wrede (1767–1838) pointed to Montgelas' failures at crisis management, culminating in the dramatic statement that 'At this moment, half a million are on their knees imploring God that their pleas may reach your ears.'[234]

One reason for the misjudgement was the centralism of the administration, which had been established on the French model and lacked any counterweight in the form of parliamentary control or communal self-administration. It is doubtless true that the old minister of state – who had pursued the process of reform for two decades – had his best days behind him. It was time for a new generation, and Crown Prince Ludwig, the future Ludwig I, supported this change.[235] It is telling that the new regime placed the person and property of the deposed minister of state under police protection, which was intended to 'safeguard him from the effects of the universal hatred that he had allegedly incurred'.[236] In his memoirs, Montgelas revealed his failure to recognise the seriousness of the famine – he still believed that it had been an artificially induced speculation crisis.[237]

The reforms introduced after he was deposed read like a response to the problems of the Tambora Crisis. First of all, in 1817 the office of minister of state was split in three, so the country now had a minister of the interior, a foreign minister and a minister of finance. Second, a concordat was signed with the Catholic Church. The state bureaucracy once again made room for religiosity, permitting the psychologically significant processions and pilgrimages, fearing that preventing them 'could lead to unrest and probably also violence',[238] as well as the reopening of convents and monasteries with their charitable institutions, which had been missed during the famine. Third, the municipal edict of 1818 reintroduced communal self-administration with elected representatives, since it had become clear during the crisis that the communes were best equipped to deal with their own problems. And fourth, that same year a new constitution was passed, which turned the kingdom into a constitutional monarchy and established a parliament that could introduce legislation and control government spending.[239]

An arson attack on the king?

Montgelas' removal from office did little to lessen tensions in the capital. On the evening of 16 April 1817 a fire broke out in the courtyard of the armoury, directly behind the royal court theatre, as the Augsburg *Allgemeine Zeitung* informed its readers. Favourable winds and the efforts of the fire brigade helped to contain the source of the fire and prevent 'the looming danger for the surrounding buildings'.[240] There was only one building in the immediate vicinity, however – the royal palace. August von Platen (1796–1835), then serving as an officer of the First Infantry Regiment, reported on the fire-fighting operations and the suspected cause of the blaze: 'I arrived at the site of the fire quite early on and along with Schnizlein joined the line of bucket carriers. It burnt all through the night. The place was dangerous, because the building in the armoury courtyard stood near the palace and the theatre. The fire was obviously set deliberately, since there are many malcontents among the common people, especially because of the dearness.'[241] The future director of the court library (now the Bavarian state library) Johann Andreas Schmeller (1785–1852) provided even more detailed information in his journals: 'Bivouac on a snowy, cold windy night at a fire that some starving cannibal had kindled with the timber (worth some 30,000 fl) from the roof truss for the new theatre that lay piled up in the armoury courtyard.'[242] The Prussian ambassador reported from Munich on 18 April: 'The day before yesterday the palace was endangered by fire ... The fire must have been set deliberately. The damage amounted to 40,000 fl.'[243]

No one in Munich believed that the fire was unconnected with the king. This conflagration was no accident, but an assassination attempt. Rumours circulated about 'insurrectionist posters' found in the city.[244] The fire-fighters, the Austrian ambassador reported, had found slips of paper at the court theatre reading 'Fire or bread'.[245] According to him, the king's first reaction had been that he could move his residence to another city in his realm.[246] The Munich city council then gave the king public assurances that the local citizenry remained loyal to him. King Maximilian I Joseph in turn assured his citizens, 'Notices of attempts and intrigues that have disquieted the inhabitants of our capital have not for a moment diminished the trust that our dear citizenry as a whole deserves.'[247]

Arson remained present in the subsequent crisis discussion as well. In early October 1817, posters announcing new arson attacks appeared in connection with the Oktoberfest. All of Munich was alarmed by these 'threatening handbills', a report to the government noted. People were also concerned by the rumours circulating that revenge would be taken against the assembled grain profiteers during the Oktoberfest. For this reason, regular troops were deployed to Munich in place of the usual militia to guard the national festival. Rumours of an impending 'veritable bloodbath' kept tensions high even after the Oktoberfest was over. The protection for the king was intensified: the sentries now stood with loaded weapons at the ready, since there were apparently plans 'to harm the Bavarian nation by such criminal assassination attempts'. On 14 November the French ambassador reported to Paris that there was rioting in Munich because of the inflation and even sentries had been killed at their posts. He was apparently simply repeating a rumour that reveals a city under strain, since the sources provide no evidence of such incidents.[248]

Rebellions from Norway to Tunisia

Based on his survey of protests in western Europe in the years 1816–1817, John Dexter Post concluded that the grain riots showed a degree of violence not seen since the Great Fear at the time of the French Revolution.[249] The first rebellion of the Tambora Crisis began in England in the early months of 1816 at the first sign of rising prices, and soon spread from West Suffolk, Norfolk and Cambridgeshire. The Ely and Littleport riots in May were among these early responses to the crisis, and were violently suppressed after three days by the Royal Dragoons.[250] In the spirit of the Luddite movement, which had already existed for a few years, in the spring of 1816 a few machines – which deprived workers of their livelihood – were destroyed and a barn set on fire. But in mid-May the protest movement took on a different quality. Some 1,500 men armed with long, iron-spiked cudgels marched through the streets, destroying the houses of those they considered harmful. They carried a banner emblazoned with the words 'Bread or Blood'[251] and demanded a reduction in the price of bread to a permissible maximum that they would set themselves. Similar violent protests occurred in Norwich, where buildings were looted and a grain mill destroyed. As elsewhere, the protests targeted those who profited from the rising prices: millers, bakers, grain merchants, etc. In Guildford a crowd of 400 gathered and broke the bakers' windows. But bakers and butchers were attacked in London too.[252] The summer of 1817 was marked by radical uprisings that greatly unsettled the Tory government, especially in Huddersfield and Nottingham. Under the circumstances it was easy to get Parliament to renew the Habeas Corpus Suspension Act.[253]

Scotland, Ireland and Wales also experienced protests. Bread riots were most common in the north. The military had to be deployed in Glasgow to put down a bread riot. In Dundee a crowd of 1,000 stormed shops and looted the house of a grain merchant before setting it on fire. In Ireland, hunger and fear had reached such levels in 1816 that the island slid into a state of social anarchy. In early 1817 Louth, Tipperary and Limerick were placed under the Insurrection Act, which had just been lifted the year before. Since the people were occupied with sheer survival, the unrest was ultimately milder than expected. In central Ireland, however, the houses and businesses of grain merchants were attacked and grain transports to Dublin halted. In many parts of Ireland – Kerry, Kildare, Londonderry, etc. – violence erupted and was suppressed with bloodshed. It was no different in Wales, which became a centre of the protests. In Merthyr Tydfil in South Wales, a centre of iron working, 8,000 miners went on strike. Their demonstrations were put down by force. Riots also took place in Aberystwyth and Tredegar. In 1817, the copper working town of Amlwch spent four weeks under a state of emergency,[254] and the uprisings became endemic. In Carmarthen crowds impeded food transports and could not be subdued by the military until 1818.[255]

In April 1817, the British ambassador reported from Switzerland to Foreign Minister Castlereagh in London that inhabitants of the mountain valleys of the Vaud were planning a hunger march to Lausanne, which the cantonal government was trying to prevent by negotiations.[256] In Geneva a series of bread riots followed the 1817 harvest. Shops were looted and farmers forced to sell their grain below the market price. The police simply looked on. When the rebel mob grew larger and larger, the city council called in grenadiers and the military dispersed the stone-throwing crowd. In Italy there were attacks on suspected grain speculators and bakers, and granaries and bakeries were looted. Although there was still a recognisable connection here with the inflation of grain prices, some of the forms of protest seem simply irrational from a present-day perspective. Near Bologna, for instance, thousands of peasants destroyed the rice fields because they believed they were emitting poisonous fumes. They wanted to remove this possible source of sickness despite or perhaps even because of the looming famine. In Catalonia, a part of the Spanish kingdom, the food shortage led to a wider rebellion in the spring of 1817. The unrest even affected North Africa. In Norway, which had long belonged to the kingdom of Denmark but was ceded to Sweden in 1814, the peasants of Christiania looted grain stores and set 'just prices'.[257]

A witness to these developments tried in retrospect to develop his own popular psychology of the riots:

> The barrenness of the previous year spread across the greater part of Europe: in most states of this corner of the world this sad event revealed an irregular national character. In England, looming symptoms of seditious and revolutionary sentiments manifested themselves. The displeasure rife in France is well known from the newspapers. The gangs of robbers growing in numbers in Spain and Italy shook the two foundations of civil society: the security of persons and of property. A large segment of penniless Swiss pulled up stakes and migrated to America. The German nation alone, trusting in almighty divine providence and the paternal concern of their rulers, bears this period of tribulation with mental tranquillity and German steadfastness. This faithfulness, this lawful perseverance will not go unrewarded.[258]

Was this intended to be satirical? At any rate, it hardly corresponded to German reality at the time of the famine.

For the time being, we lack the research to know whether bread riots of the moral economy type also occurred outside Europe during the Tambora Crisis. Bin Wong has demonstrated that this was generally the case in China into the nineteenth century, and that there were structural parallels to the bread riots in Europe, but his scattered examples do not show whether this was also the case in 1816/17.[259] Earlier studies on Burma and Vietnam suggest a pattern of protest that was more typical of peasant societies generally than tied to a specific civilisation.[260] Alongside bread riots and rebellions, however, protest in the countries of the future developing world took another form: the anti-colonial uprising or war of liberation.

Anti-colonial uprisings in Asia

Some Indian historians view 1817 as a milestone because an anti-colonial uprising occurred that year. The so-called Paik rebellion of Khurda was even referred to as the 'first war of independence'. The kingdom's conquest by the British East India Company was of quite recent date, since the last raja of Khurda, the heart of Orissa (present-day Odisha), had only been deposed in 1803. This made the warrior caste, the Paiks, superfluous and engendered great dissatisfaction. Moreover, their traditional landed property was to be taken away from them as well, which proved to be the last straw. When an anti-British demonstration of 400 Khandas (an ethnic group) erupted in the neighbouring state of Ghumsur in March 1817 – that is, after the external impulse of an independent rebellion – the Paiks joined in and placed themselves at the head of the movement. They stormed a police station and government building in Banpur and killed more than 100 staff members of the British Foreign Office. The new British tax demands on a society already on the verge of starvation played a role in increasing support for the uprising, as did switching the taxation system from cowries (shells) to silver coin to which local people had no access, along with chicanery by lower officials.[261]

The insurgents marched on Khurda, their numbers growing with every kilometre they walked. The uprising spread throughout the province and British officials in Khurda took to their heels. All government buildings were burnt to the ground and any money found was confiscated. When news of the insurrection reached Cuttack, regular troops were deployed, but they were routed by the insurgents, now 3,000 strong. On 12 April the rebels stormed Puri and set the governor's courthouse ablaze. Then they began to attack the colonial officials, who had entrenched themselves in their settlement by the sea.

In the meantime, the former raja's household had joined the rebels, and the priests proclaimed the end of English rule and the restoration of the sacred kingdom.[262] When regular British troops finally arrived the Paiks were overwhelmed by superior force and retreated to the jungle. Although the fighting in the forests continued until 1826, the English began to try the insurgents in May 1817. The rebels faced execution, deportation or long prison sentences. The last monarch of Khurda, Raja Mukunda Deva, died in custody in November 1817.[263]

In November 1817 rebellions broke out in another part of the empire, on the island of Ceylon (Sri Lanka). The island had long lived under its own kings, was partially colonised by the Portuguese in 1518 and annexed by the Netherlands in 1658. The British captured the island in 1796 and made it a crown colony in 1803. The last king, Sri Vikrama Rajasinha (1780–1832), was deported to India.[264] Only the kingdom of Kandy in the central highlands remained. The British Resident in Badulla, Sylvester Douglas Wilson, wanted to confirm the report that a member of the royal family of Kandy had arrived to revive the kingdom. Wilson sent a Muslim deputy to arrest him, but he was in turn captured and murdered by a group of insurgent Sinhalese armed with bows and arrows. When Wilson himself set off for Kandy he was also killed and his interpreter taken prisoner. The British made several attempts to end the uprising peacefully. Thus they reduced the grain tax from 1/10 to 1/14 for all those who had not participated in the insurrection; this failed, however, to persuade the freedom-loving Sinhalese.

The flooding that winter made it impossible to deploy regular troops from the capital Colombo, and even the lines of communication were interrupted. This made it easy for the rebels to attack the British using guerrilla tactics without revealing themselves. The population hid in the jungle. The colonial troops, who did not dare to advance along the narrow jungle paths, set native houses and villages on fire, killed livestock and destroyed the fruit plantations as well as the irrigation systems for the rice fields. Although the British sent more troops and established thirteen new military bases they were unable to capture the rebel leaders and the insurgency spread throughout the kingdom. After nearly all of the local chiefs joined in, the governor imposed martial law. All men in Uva over the age of eighteen were killed, which further fomented the resistance. The conduct of the war was so brutal that observers like the British military doctor Henry Marshall were horrified.[265]

Three factors helped the British to regain the upper hand in 1818: the unity among the rebels crumbled until the movement finally split;

additional troops from Madras and Bengal arrived; and one rebel leader after another fell into British hands. The colonial power set a warning example in Ceylon in 1817/18. The insurgency had, however, kept them busy for an entire year under the difficult circumstances of the Tambora Crisis. The British lost an estimated 1,000 men, and the natives nearly 10,000 to combat, starvation, sickness and execution. The war and the destroyed harvests brought hunger and disease. Ceylon remained British from 1818 and became a favoured tea-producing area for the British Crown. In 1948, after independence, the rebel leader Keppetipola was declared a national hero, and his skull was returned to Sri Lanka in 1954.[266]

Food prices reach a high point in June 1817

In southern Germany the usual price of grain was around 10 florins per bushel (*Scheffel*), even during the Revolutionary Wars. This period of 'normal' prices ended in Germany with the 'normal year' 1811. Prices rose from the beginning of the great volcanic eruptions and the deterioration of harvests. During the Tambora Crisis, the prices for wheat at the south German grain markets developed as shown in the accompanying table (rounded up per bushel, in Würzburg per *Malter*), reaching a highpoint of 85 florins in June 1817 in Ansbach.[267]

The expected good harvest of 1817 at first produced the opposite dynamic, since anybody with reserves brought them to market quickly to gain extra profits from the high prices. The sudden rise in supply meant that grain prices fell to 25 fl. by the end of June, but they rose again with the beginning of the harvest in July and by the middle of

Development of Wheat Prices in Bavaria and Franconia, 1816–1818

Grain market Administrative District	Passau Lower Danube	Regensburg Regen	Ansbach Rezat	Würzburg Upper Main
1816 January	18	16	17	12
July 15	30	28	27	25
Dec.	41	33	40	25
1817 May 15	56	49	57	42
June 15	72	74	85	56
July	28	59	59	46
Sept.	43	38	32	28
1818 Jan. 3	35	36	33	23

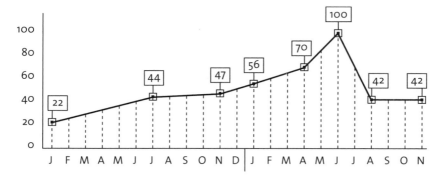

Inflation in Heilbronn in 1816/1817

Note: Price in *kreuzer* for an eight-pound loaf

the month were once again at 30 fl. or even a good deal more. After the end of the harvest, when the actual return could be estimated, the prices mostly fell until September, although in some places they continued to rise. In general, the prices were still on a level similar to that at the end of 1816, far removed from their previous normal level. The euphoria over the good harvest soon gave way to disillusionment.[268] At the end of 1817, the cost of wheat in Bavaria stood at a scandalous 52 fl. on average, so that the government tried to lower the price by the deliberate market placement of grain reserves. Since Austria had loosened its block on exports, 100,000 bushels of grain were bought up in Bohemia and Austria with the permission of the imperial court. This succeeded in lowering the price of wheat at the Munich corn market to 42 fl., which was still four times the normal price.[269]

In his well-received treatise 'On the Dearness of Grain in the Years 1816 and 1817', which he presented to the king in early 1818, the judge Franz Haecker in Rothenburg ob der Tauber emphatically noted that 'The period of this study is not yet finished, the dearness in all its horror is still with us, and a large portion of all peoples still await rescue from universal impoverishment, rescue from the hardship that grows daily as the sources of private assistance dry up'.[270] Councillor of State von Hazzi was pessimistic about the outcome of state interventionism. According to him, 'The results are such that all of these very well meaning provisions did not serve their purpose, that the grain prices have increased more than fourfold since January 1816 and are now more than half again as much, and with this inflation of grain all other necessities of life also cost more than half as much again, and consequently every family's household feels the greatest perplexity, and this perplexity in all circumstances proves daily more worrying and unfortunate.'[271] Hazzi believed that the supply crisis would have been easier to resolve without trade restrictions.

In practice, the apparently natural development of prices after the harvest year differed markedly from region to region. In the kingdom of Naples (Terra del Lavoro province), the price for durum wheat (*grano duro*) in May 1815 was 3.04 (ducats per *tomolo*), but it continued to rise after the harvest and peaked at 5.07 in June 1816, temporarily fell a bit after the harvest and reached an absolute highpoint of 5.35 in January 1817. The price then dropped slightly and after that year's harvest ended in November at 3.21, that is, close to the starting price. The price evolution was similar for other types of wheat (*grano tenero, grano mischio*), maize, which was somewhat cheaper, and barley (*orzo*), which was cheaper still. The price rises were less severe than in Switzerland, France or Germany, but the prevalence of subsistence agriculture meant they also had a serious effect.[272] When Raffles travelled through the Franche Comté in June 1817 the people in Champagnole (Jura département) where he stopped were still living in great hardship. The high prices for food had forced them to sell their horses, and the number of travellers had also dropped significantly. Raffles was dismayed by the large number of beggars and the widespread poverty in the Jura. Children ran alongside his coach and kept calling out 'Monsieur, s'il vous plaît, donnez moi charité.'[273]

Corn associations

Among the inventions of the crisis era were the *Kornvereine* (corn associations), which, in the absence of state assistance, represented self-help organisations on the local level. The background to their establishment was the circumstance that individuals possessed neither the contacts nor the capital to buy up bread cereals (that is, 'corn') over greater distances. Moreover, small-scale sales over long distances were not profitable for either buyers or sellers and were very difficult to organise. By bundling demand, the associations could amass capital, gather organisational experience and purchase in large enough quantities to obtain good prices – or at least this was their hope. Responsibilities could also be shared and social conflicts veiled: by investing capital, a merchant who had become the target of envy or protest could appear as a benefactor, and by using his organisational knowledge he could become a manager of social welfare or a guarantor of social peace. Beyond such functional issues, we should not underestimate the religious or philanthropic motivations behind the practical willingness to help.

The best-known such association was the 'Elberfelder Verein gegen Kornteuerung' (Association to Combat the Dearness of Corn), a joint-stock company for the purchase of grain – in this case rye – that was run on a charitable basis. The 'civic-mindedness' of the Elberfelders was already described as exemplary in 1817,[274] and a century later during the famine winter of the First World War in neighbouring Barmen (the two cities were later combined to form the new munici-pality of Wuppertal) this model appeared worthy of further study.[275] One leading representative of the Barmen bourgeoisie was the Pietist manufacturer Johann Caspar Engels (1753–1821), the grandfather of Friedrich Engels, who managed a factory with some 300 workers and also engaged in wholesale trade with Italy and western Europe. During the famine he was active in financing poor relief and the soup kitchen as well as in organising the Kornverein.[276] 'Aid associations' (*Hilfsvereine*) intended to serve the same purpose were founded during the crisis years in the Catholic Rhineland as well.[277] Historians have estimated that the private aid associations in the Prussian Rhineland had a purchase volume at least equal to the size of credits from the state.[278]

The formation of the corn associations is interesting for another reason as well. They claimed terrain that in old regime European society had been occupied by the church or the state. The latter were now supplanted by civil society, which used the tools offered by the new law on associations for self-organisation. Their instrument was the free association of citizens who looked for new ways of doing things with the means available to them – clubs and associations, cor-porations – and without the previously common religious trappings. Unlike state administrations, their organisational form was flexible. The Elberfeld Corn Association could even make a profit through clever contract negotiations, and paid 5 per cent interest on invested capital.[279]

Grain purchases in Russia and the rise of Odessa

Crop failures and inflation drove most governments in western and central Europe to purchase additional grain in autumn 1816 and spring 1817. Buying grain in the neighbouring areas became increasingly difficult, however, because all states had to attend first and foremost to the well being of their own subjects. In the end, only one country in the world was in a position to export grain in large quantities: Russia.[280] Since the sixteenth century, grain had been exported to western Europe from the Baltic region, which after the Napoleonic Wars largely belonged to Russia. The ports of export were Archangelsk on the White Sea and Riga or Reval (present-day Tallinn) on the Baltic. The second export region was Novorossiya on the Black Sea. Just as Peter the Great had pushed open the gateway to the west with the founding of St Petersburg, Catherine the Great opened the gateway to the south by subjugating the Crimean Tatars and driving back the Ottomans. In the Treaty of Küçük Kaynarca (1774), the northern Caucasus (Georgia) and the mouths of the Bug, Don and Dnieper rivers came under Russian rule. The Ottoman Empire had to allow the Russians free shipping in the Black Sea and guarantee them passage through the Bosporus. The Crimean Khanate was annexed by Russia in 1783.[281] In the Treaty of Jassy (29 December 1791) the entire northern coast of the Black Sea was ceded to Russia. The Russian port city of Odessa was founded in 1794 on the site of the fortified Ottoman town of Hacibey. After the seventh Russo-Turkish War of 1808–1812, the Treaty of Bucharest gave part of the principality of Moldavia to the Russian Empire as well as Bessarabia (now in Moldova), one of the most productive grain-growing regions in Europe.[282]

Although the transport costs were lower from the Baltic ports to central Europe, massive demand and the great supply of grain meant that Odessa became the most important Russian port of export from 1816/17. Europeans first had to get used to this shift. As Scheitlin wrote: 'South Russia has become a breadbasket. Odessa on the Black Sea is now a rich corn market. During this inflation, France, Italy and Switzerland had grain brought from there. The corn travelled by water to Trieste on the Adriatic Sea, and thence by wagon through the Tyrol over the high Adlerberg [Arlberg?] and via the Splügen and Septimer passes to the Grisons and from thence to north-eastern Switzerland. We even brought other grain here via Genoa.'[283] From Odessa, exports travelled to Italy and France, but during the famine of 1816/17 for the first time also to Hungary, Austria, Switzerland, southern Germany and Spain. According to the contemporary author Johann J. Eichhoff (1762–1827):

In the meantime, cultivation had expanded significantly in the southern provinces of Russia; the ports on the Black Sea, notably Odessa, offered the greatest ease of export . . . the famine year 1817 came to pass and thus the grain trade, like some other branches, soon took a new direction. News from all quarters at that distressing time could not say enough about the quantities of grain with which Odessa helped everywhere; for instance, the Austrian government signed very significant supply contracts with that newly flourishing commercial centre to provide for their southern provinces, namely Dalmatia, and meanwhile the most substantial dispatches arrived there via Trieste.[284]

The Bavarian government, with its theory of profiteering, had proved itself particularly resistant to imports, but as scarcity grew it was forced to capitulate. On 2 February 1817 the commission for the liquidation of the national debt, which was responsible for paying off the war debts from the Napoleonic Wars, was authorised to use a loan of 3 million florins to purchase grain from Russia. A government agent was supposed to buy 100,000 bushels of 'Russian corn' in Holland via the Baltic. On 16 February the Prussian envoy von Küster reported from Munich, 'The king has purchased substantial amounts of grain abroad to lower the price. In order to cover these expenditures, a loan of three million [fl.] has been taken out through bonds at 5 per cent interest. Prices have fallen markedly since the arrival of the first grain deliveries from Russia. It has become apparent repeatedly that true scarcity arose almost nowhere.'[285] Independently, the administrative districts also bought grain on their own accounts; the welfare committee of the Isar district, for instance, spent 150,000 florins.[286]

In Bolzano, where 800 paupers had to be fed every day, wealthy citizens learned that the merchants of Augsburg had bought up wheat in Russia. Following this example, they purchased 'Odessa wheat' for the princely sum of 30,000 florins to alleviate suffering in South Tyrol.[287] Similarly, Switzerland also looked to Odessa, as Zollikofer explained: 'We had to look for help from distant Asia, from Russia's abundant surplus of corn.'[288] During the famine France substantially lowered import tariffs. While they were raised again in 1819 after protests by farmers, in return Odessa was declared a free port for a term of thirty years starting that same year, allowing for the duty free export of grain.

The stimulus of the Tambora Crisis allowed southern Russia (now the Ukraine) to become Europe's most important supplier of bread cereals. The export tonnage rose from some 30,000 tonnes in the decade 1806–1815 to 125,000 between 1815 and 1826, with wheat making up some 90 per cent of the total.[289] After the victory over Napoleon, Russia with its surplus crops rescued Europe for the second time within a decade. And the trade relationships made during the famine continued afterwards, as Eichhoff noted in 1820: 'The western countries of Europe are supplied more easily and cheaply hereby than was possible by the North or Baltic Sea, which largely wrested the market in these countries away from the Dutch and the Hanseatic cities, and consequently their demand for Baltic and Rhenish grain necessarily diminished.'[290]

Russia, land of liberty

Paradoxical as it may sound in the light of tsarist autocracy and serfdom, for immigrants, early nineteenth century Russia was a land of freedom. Since the ascension to the throne of Catherine the Great, Russia had been ruled by a German dynasty that felt bound by Enlightenment ideas and guaranteed religious tolerance. French and German aristocrats and intellectuals had fled there in droves during the years of the Terror in France and the Napoleonic occupation. From the universities and the military to the civil service, these immigrants occupied important positions in Russian society. The first two governors general of Novorossiya were Armand Emmanuel du Plessis, duke of Richelieu (1766–1822), the future prime minister of France,[291] and Alexandre Andrault de Langeron (1763–1831), both of them aristocrats who had sought refuge in Russia before the Revolution and made names for themselves in the Russo-Turkish wars. They developed the hinterlands of Odessa and created the infrastructure for several waves of German migration to Novorossiya beginning in 1803. The 'New Russian Welfare Office' in Odessa was responsible for the integration of newcomers, including medical care, the allocation of land and initial financial assistance. The 'Black Sea Germans' were allowed to set up their own municipalities with self-administration. Many of them pursued their trades in newly founded villages or contributed as farmers to the boom in grain cultivation.

In Germany, the Tambora Crisis instigated the largest wave of emigration since the mediaeval settlement of the east. Faced with acute hardship, many Germans saw no future in their homeland. The first forty families from Württemberg set off for Russia in the summer of 1816 from the region of Schweikheim. From Ulm they travelled down the Danube to Vienna and from there through Hungary, past Budapest to the Russian border, which they reached at the end of the year. They spent the winter months near Odessa in the village of Groß-Liebenthal, which had been founded ten years previously.

Ten families decided to stay there, and the Russian government gave the others wagons and money for provisions so that they could continue on their way. In the late autumn of 1817 they reached the Caucasus, where they founded the first German colony, the village of Marienfeld.[292] A chronicle from Ulm notes laconically, '1817. The dearness continued. At the beginning of this year and the end of the last, Ulm boatmen transported many hundreds of families down the Danube to Vienna. They came from the districts of Reutlingen, Urach, Waiblingen etc. and emigrated to South Russia.'[293]

The Danube was navigable from Ulm. Since the sixteenth century, religious dissidents had travelled down the river from here to Moravia or Hungary on boats known as 'Ulmer Schachtel' (Ulm Boxes). During the Tambora Crisis, too, the Danube offered the cheapest and quickest way to emigrate. The targeted recruitment of German emigrants began under Empress Catherine II, and they came in a steady stream, interrupted only by the prohibition of emigration imposed in the Confederation of the Rhine in 1807 under pressure from Napoleon. The German Federal Act (Article 18), however, stipulated that all Germans had a fundamental right to freedom of movement. A Württemberg edict of 1817 also granted the basic right to emigrate. The constitutions of most German states adopted a similar stance, even if their governments were rarely happy to see subjects leave and sought to prevent it.[294]

Emigration to Russia appears to have been largely a phenomenon of the German-speaking region, including German Switzerland, Alsace and parts of Lorraine. Many factors were responsible for the decision to move to Russia, first and foremost the 'cultural knowledge' of the scope it offered. Russia offered immigrants free land, travel expenses and initial capital, the duty-free import of their belongings, free health care, interest-free loans to build houses and freedom from taxation for thirty years. Germans and their descendants were guaranteed exemption from military conscription and feudal services, freedom of movement, complete self-administration and jurisdiction and their own market rights in autonomous settlements. Freedom of conscience and religious practice were also guaranteed, which was important for the followers of dissenting churches, some of whom still faced oppression.[295] A ukase of 1804 issued by Alexander I imposed restrictions intended to dissuade penniless migrants. Craftsmen and farmers had to submit certificates proving their qualifications. Prospective emigrants had to document an initial capital of 300 fl. and were only permitted to come as families (that is, no individuals or childless couples). From that time on, the Russian government paid only transport costs in advance.[296]

Because of the absence of statistical data, the extent of emigration to Russia can only be roughly estimated. Thus on 17 June 1817
some 5,000 Württembergers alone spent the night in Neuburg an der
Donau, the first rest stop after Ulm.[297] They were probably part of the
largest group travelling to the Caucasus that summer. On the road, the
emigrants fell victim to an epidemic, which killed some 1,000 persons
in a quarantine camp near Ismail, the first Russian town they reached.
During the winter encampment at Groß-Liebenthal, 300 families
(some 1,500 persons) decided to remain there. The settlement authority assigned them a piece of land north of Odessa, where they founded
the village of Hoffnungstal. The rest of these Pietists had to fight to
continue their winter journey against the opposition of the Russian
administration. Elected deputies travelled to Moscow in December
1817, where they were granted an audience with the Tsar. In the end
they were able to travel with Russian financial support to Russian
Georgia, where they founded six villages, which – with the exception
of Neu-Tiflis – were named after members of the Tsar's family.[298]

Alongside emigration to Novorossiya, several heart-rending auto-
biographical accounts of which survive,[299] there was also significant
emigration to the Russian-dominated Baltic region and Russian
Poland. This is evident from the notes of the Prussian ambassador in
Karlsruhe, who could grant visas for such journeys: 'It was not only
Prussian journeymen artisans who frequently turned to me when
compelled to travel; the many emigrants whose passports I had to sign
camped outside my door in their hundreds, often with wife and children in such a state that it became impossible not to grant them travel
provisions as well along with my signature. It is estimated that in
those years some twenty thousand souls emigrated from Baden alone,
more than one-tenth of whom were bound for Russian Poland.'[300]
The only other European country with any notable emigration to
Russian Poland was Scotland.[301]

The press reported in detail on emigration from southwest
Germany. In the *Schwäbischer Merkur*, emigrants from Württemberg
had to announce their emigration with their names, so that anyone
to whom they owed money could make their demands in time.[302]
The venerable, 143-year-old Nuremberg newspaper *Friedens und
Kriegs Kurier* issued a stern warning: 'According to several accounts,
swindlers and the evil-minded, clad in all manner of disguises, creep
around, painting charming pictures of distant Russia to the gullible, firing their imaginations with fine simulations of a decent and
comfortable life, tempting the foolish into emigrating. These seducers
care nothing for the well being of their fellow man, however, but are

interested only in fattening and enriching themselves at the expense of others.'[303] Former inhabitants of the imperial cities accustomed to liberty had their doubts about the Russian promises of freedom. People spoke more plainly still in Switzerland, where freedom meant not just religious tolerance but also political self-determination. 'To Russia? That's all well and good. But the Swiss, if he is Swiss, fears Russia more than hunger. He would like to have free soil under his feet, but he is accustomed to understand it as soil where one may hold cantonal assemblies (*Landsgemeinden*).'[304]

Go West! Emigration to North America

Emigration to North America around the same time followed a different pattern to that to Russia. The majority of emigrants came from Britain and Ireland, whose old ties to 'New England' continued after American independence. A large proportion of migrants from England, Ireland, Scotland and Wales were bound for North America rather than the British colonies in South Africa, India, Australia or New Zealand. And in North America their destination was usually the USA rather than British Canada. The first great wave of emigration from Ireland began at the time of the Tambora Crisis.[305] But emigration from England and Scotland also rose sharply in 1816.[306] The number of British emigrants has been estimated at 100,000 in the years 1816–1818, and of German emigrants, especially from the Bavarian Rhenish Palatinate, Baden, Württemberg, Hesse and the Prussian Rhineland, at c. 20,000.[307]

The letters of family and community members who had emigrated earlier also played an important role in emigration to the USA. There were also published accounts of migrant experiences. More or less serious travel agents used newspaper advertisements and other means of drawing attention to their services, mentioning concrete conditions, dates and prices. An advertisement in a Heilbronn newspaper featured two sailing ships and the text: 'Emigration to America. On 1 and 15 November I am expediting two ships to New York, New Orleans and Texas, and these will likely be the last this year. Register right away. C. Stählen, notary in Heilbronn.'[308] Finally, a kind of advice literature emerged indicating the best ways to get to America, which even at that time was already equated with the USA, although there was also emigration from Britain and France to Canada ('Nouvelle France') and from Spain to Mexico and Latin America ('Nueva España') as well as from Portugal to Brazil. Moritz von Fürstenwärther (1781–1826),

141

who had studied emigration on the ground for the German Federal Assembly, recommended *The Western Gazeteer, or Emigrant's Directory, containing a geographical Description of the western States and Territories, viz: Kentucky, Indiana, Louisiana, Ohio, Tennessee and Mississippi, with the Territories of Illinois, Missouri, Alabama, Michigan and North-Western [Territory]*.[309]

German and Swiss emigration to America occurred via the Rhine and the Dutch ports, usually Amsterdam, and sometimes also Rotterdam. As in the case of emigration to Russia, the concrete data is spotty. Thus we know from the Prussian customs office in Mainz that no fewer than 5,517 persons travelled down the Rhine in the first half of June 1817.[310] According to one report:

> Daily we see German emigrants travelling through our city. This spring the number passing through by water surpassed 10,000, not counting the substantial number slowly driving along a cart full of children pulled by exhausted horses. All of them assure us that unemployment and unaffordable taxes are the reason for their emigration . . . Many of these unfortunates expect in vain to escape death by starvation, [but] it follows and catches up with them at the frontier of Europe, or in the middle of the ocean.[311]

Some 6,000 emigrants from Germany landed on nineteen ships from July to December 1817 in Philadelphia alone, with more arriving in New York, Baltimore, Boston and a few smaller ports.[312] Based on official statistics from Württemberg, von Hippel demonstrated that especially large groups of emigrants came from the mountains of the Black Forest and the Swabian Jura. Whether the emigrants were truly 'desperate' is not clear. In any case, they doubted their own opportunities for personal development in crisis-ridden Europe. Many emigrants were by no means poor; they could not have afforded to emigrate otherwise. Aside from the price of the passage, they also needed provisions along the way and capital to begin again in the new country. If religious motivations were not dominant, one could even venture the hypothesis that the emigrants were especially adventurous and prepared to take risks, that is, that they came from precisely that segment of the population who were most needed to shape the future at home as well.

Morris Birkbeck as a prototypical emigrant

The story of the Quaker Morris Birkbeck (1764–1825) is one such case; he not only emigrated to the USA and brought several colonies of emigrants with him, but also advised generations of British, French, German and Swedish would-be emigrants in his publications. Birkbeck emigrated not because of poverty, but because he hated oppression. As a Quaker in England he was not only denied the right to vote, although he paid taxes, but also had to pay a tithe to a church that was not his own. In London he had the opportunity to speak to Edward Coles (1785–1868), private secretary to President Madison, who was undertaking a diplomatic mission to Russia,[313] and decided to emigrate. Birkbeck and his family embarked in March 1817. After acquiring land in Illinois he returned to England to recruit settlers. His travel account *Notes on a Journey in America from the Coast of Virginia to the Territory of Illinois* already appeared in 1817 in Philadelphia, London, Dublin and Cork, and went through eleven editions in just two years. The book was translated into German and Swedish in 1818. The follow-up volume *Letters from Illinois* was published in Boston, Philadelphia and London,[314] soon went through seven editions in English, and was translated into German and French in 1819. Birkbeck wrote that the USA was 'a land of plenty, and we are proceeding to a land of abundance'.[315]

At the height of the Tambora Crisis, he had his finger on the pulse of the age: a land of plenty! Birkbeck affirmed that this could be found in the USA, especially 'on the western territory: a delightful region; – healthy, fertile, romantic'.[316] And for the religious, this is how he described what he found: 'Having crossed the Ohio, we have now fairly set our foot on the land of promise': There were no harsh winters like those in Pennsylvania (he claimed), no slavery and no difficulties acquiring land as in Kentucky. The Promised Land could be found in Illinois![317] This was followed by tips for immigrants who, however humble their beginnings, could become rich Americans, complete with practical examples with which the reader could identify. What attracted many to this author, alongside his irrepressible optimism, was his anti-feudal tone. Everyone in Europe who believed themselves too highly taxed, deprived of their political rights, limited in their freedom of conscience or in some way treated as inferior felt that this author was speaking to them personally. He portrayed America as the land of equals in which people were not embittered and disenfranchised – as they were in Europe – but friendly and civilised.[318] Anyone could purchase land, young people could marry and make their own way as best they could. The government was effective because it was elected. The state was better, because simpler, than any ever dreamt of by a utopian.[319] Freedom captivated the heart: 'It is enchantment, and Liberty is the fair enchantress.'[320]

In 1819, the English Prairie Settlement – now the small towns of Albion and Wanborough – on the Wabash River already numbered 400 English and 700 American settlers. Birkbeck became president of the newly founded Agricultural Society of Illinois and propagated scientific agricultural techniques.[321] Together with Coles, now the governor of Illinois, Birkbeck, who became secretary of state, actively prevented the introduction of slavery.[322] However proud Birkbeck was of his Englishness, he clearly stated that the Germans and French should also feel welcome to emigrate to the Promised Land: 'The most perfect cordiality prevails between the Americans of German and those of English extraction, in every part of the United States, if the assertions of all with whom I have conversed on this interesting topic, are to be relied on. National antipathies are the result of bad political institutions; and not of human nature. Here – whatever their origin, whether English, Scotch, Irish, German, or French – all are Americans.'[323]

Emigration to Brazil

After the Napoleonic occupation of Portugal in 1807, the émigré prince regent Joao/John (1767–1826) proclaimed the Portuguese colony an independent empire. Following the restoration of the Braganza dynasty in Portugal, Brazil became a kingdom in 1815. In November 1817, Crown Prince Peter I (1798–1834) married the Archduchess Maria Leopoldine of Austria, a daughter of Emperor Francis I, in Rio de Janeiro. It is no coincidence that Brazil became a favoured destination for German explorers. While German expeditions set off for the jungle, clever publishers were printing travel accounts from previous eras.[324] It was during the Tambora Crisis that Prince Maximilian zu Wied-Neuwied (1782–1867) explored the Amazon, a sensational account of which appeared in 1820.[325]

Brazil was the natural destination for Portuguese emigrants, but the emperor's 'German' marriage made it interesting for Germans as well. German artists, craftsmen and scholars followed the Archduchess, and soon the first farmers and farm labourers arrived and founded the first agricultural colonies, Leopoldina and San Jorge dos Ilhéus in Bahia. Georg Anton Schäffer (1779–1836) from Münnerstadt organised the first German emigrants' society in 1818. The immigrants were granted land near Salvador de Bahia, where they established the colony of Frankental. Tips for German emigrants bound for Brazil were soon published.[326] Peter I appointed Schäffer an agent of the Brazilian Empire for the recruitment of immigrants. To this end he set

144

Swiss emigrants to Brazil during the famine of 1816/17 crossing Lake
Neufchâtel, 1819, votive panel, Fribourg, Musée d'art et d'histoire

up a recruiting agency in Hamburg in 1823, lectured in the Hanseatic
cities, in Frankfurt am Main and at some German courts. His agents
promoted emigration to Brazil in the German provinces. The result
was a wave of emigration from Mecklenburg, but also from the
Hunsrück and parts of present-day Saarland. Between 1824 and 1828
some 5,000 Germans left for Brazil.

The search for the causes of 'emigration mania'

During the Tambora Crisis Europe was suffering from 'emigration
fever'.[327] Never before had so many people wanted to leave the old
continent at the same time. Unfortunately, we have no precise figures,
since many countries kept no statistics on emigration. England and
Württemberg were exceptions here. Matters were not much different in the host countries. Russia, Brazil and South Africa kept no
immigration statistics, and in the USA they only begin after 1820,
following the passage of the Steering Act of 1819.[328] This helps to

explain why a number of historians have missed the wave of migration in 1816–1818. There was, after all, a good reason for the Steering Act: the wave of immigration from Europe in 1817/18. Within just one year 20,000 people arrived from southwest Germany alone. The numbers for the years of the Tambora Crisis were likely a good deal higher than those in the 1820s.[329] In 1820, 8,385 persons immigrated to the USA, the largest group being the Irish (43 per cent), followed by the English (29 per cent). The next largest groups came from the German states, France and Canada. The year in the 1820s with the highest number of immigrants was 1829, with 22,500 people.

That mass emigration began with the 'famine year' can be demonstrated very clearly with the example of Württemberg, since this new kingdom saw itself threatened by out-migration and kept statistics. In an official warning of 14 February 1817 'Concerning the prevailing emigration mania', published in the government gazetteer the *Staats- und Regierungsblatt*, the ministry of the interior wrote: 'The mania for emigration, which has become evident for some time now in several regions, seems to be increasing at such a rate of late that it is not merely deleterious to the state, but also threatens to submerge a large number of citizens and their families in predictable misery.'[330] In reality, it was the other way round: families in Württemberg were willing to take upon themselves the difficult lot of emigration precisely because they were threatened with sinking into misery. Von Hippel was able to show that the emigration curve followed the curve of grain prices quite closely for many decades. The spring of 1817 with its maximum prices also witnessed the largest number of emigrants.[331]

Since this emigration disturbed the government, one of its most capable civil servants, the young Friedrich List (1789–1846), was entrusted with the task of studying the extent of and reasons for emigration. In early May 1817 he reported with surprising frankness to the interior ministry in Stuttgart: 'It appears from the statements of emigrants recorded yesterday that excessive levies and oppression of all kinds in civil life are the fundamental reasons why these emigrants have not felt comfortable in their situation thus far, that the great dearness prevailing at present and the resulting lack of work has increased this displeasure leading to a conviction that matters cannot continue thus, and that on the other hand they harbour sure hopes of a better life in America.'[332] In the Grand Duchy of Baden, too, as in many countries of the post-war period with their enormous public debts, heavy taxation and the arbitrary invention of ever-new duties provided the occasion for complaints. Arbitrary not least because no elected parliament had a say in how taxes were levied and spent.[333]

Official Emigration from the Kingdom of Württemberg

Year	Number of Persons	Index Number*
1812/13	409	010
1813/14	324	008
1814/15	444	011
1815/16	3,000	072
1816/17	17,500	417
1817/18	2,130	051
1818/19	2,592	062
1819/20	1,352	032
1820/21	1,066	025
1821/22	938	022
1822/23	809	019
1823/24	777	019

* Von Hippel, *Auswanderung*, 138. The index number refers to the average annual number of emigrants in the period 1812–1870: 4,195 persons = index number 100.

A few days later List sent an even harsher report from the administrative district of Weinsberg, criticising the deficient institutions of the Württemberg state, the unaffordable taxes and duties, the patronising treatment and harassment of the people by local and state officials, the abuses within the class of scribes (*Schreibereiwesen*), the slowness of justice, and oppression by aristocratic hunting and the manorial system:

> The pressure that all of these ills exert upon the citizen has been heightened by the crop failures of recent years and the attendant great dearness of foodstuffs and the scarcity of work to such a degree that the worse off are driven to desperation. For it is doubtless desperation speaking when the emigrants from Weinsberg state that they see no hope of improvement, and would rather be slaves in America than citizens in Weinsberg, or when emigrants from the surrounding villages state that even if they see death before them they cannot change their resolve, as they have no desire to live any longer under these conditions.[334]

The destinations of the 17,383 registered Württembergers are shown in the accompanying table.

The population rise in the years before the famine was also part of the background to the wave of emigration. Scholars have shown for the Rhenish Palatinate that the population never rose as rapidly as during the years 1802–1815. Despite the protracted wars and troop

147

Destinations of Emigrants from Württemberg, 1816–1818

Destination	Number	%
Russia	9,233	53.1
USA	6,009	34.6
Austria-Hungary	1,559	9.0
Prussia	43	0.2
Other German states	539	3.1

movements, the population rose by an incredible 34 per cent,[335] and this was probably also the case in the other southern German states. The causes were the abolition of previous marriage restrictions, early marriage to escape military conscription, the fall in mortality as a result of better hygiene, and the relatively good food supply before the Tambora Crisis.

Interestingly, emigration behaviour from the United Kingdom differed markedly from that in Germany. To be sure, a wave of emigration also began there in 1816, with some 150,000 officially registered emigrants within seven years, but this wave did not diminish immediately after the end of the Tambora Crisis. Because of the continuing economic crisis, the annual emigration figures rose up to 1819 and ebbed only slowly thereafter.[336]

Most of these emigrants went to North America, to the USA but also to British Canada. Other large groups of emigrants travelled to South Africa and India. Thousands of Britons emigrated to South America, where they joined the movements for liberation from Spain. The troops of the liberator Simón Bolívar alone had at least 6,000 British members in 1818. Cruikshank commented acerbically upon emigration from the British Isles, calling it 'a strong proof of the flourishing state of the country'. He depicted the migrants as a group of ragged beggars who could not support themselves at home, and called South Africa the 'Cape of Forlorn Hope'. Instead of ensuring

Emigration from the United Kingdom, 1815–1821[338]

1815	2,000
1816	13,000
1817	21,000
1818	28,000
1819	35,000
1820	26,000
1821	18,000

George Cruikshank, 'All among the Hottentots Capering ashore'!! or the
Blessings of Emigration to the Cape of Forlorn Good Hope (ie) To be half
roasted by the Sun & Devoured by the Natives!! Recommended to the
serious consideration of all those who are about to Emigrate, London 1819

prosperity in their own country, politicians were busy dreaming up
new British lands across the globe.

Amsterdam as focal point

Not all attempts at emigration were successful. In May 1817 some
30,000 would-be emigrants from southern Germany, Alsace and
Switzerland were stranded in Amsterdam and had to change their
plans because of poverty or broken contracts. The 'band of soul
sellers', as Friedrich List called them, who deceived would-be emigrants with visions of dream destinations, organised the first leg of the
journey down the Rhine to Amsterdam. The migrants were welcome
cargo for the Rhine boatmen. The same was true of the sailing ships
to America, which could transport the emigrants in steerage. Ship
owners and captains were the actual profiteers of emigration, but
local recruiters were essential for contact with customers. Swindlers

who took the cost of the passage and then made off with the money mingled with the honest agents. Their victims found themselves in Amsterdam without a ticket and often without a penny as well. As a consequence, the problems of mass begging and petty crime, which had arisen in their countries of origin as a result of the famine, were transferred to Holland. The streets 'were teeming' with emigrants, 'most of them begging'.[338]

An unexpected problem for many emigrants was that they had to wait so many months for a ship to America that life in the expensive city exhausted all of their funds. The differences in the responses of the various diplomatic missions are interesting. Part of the reason that Germans had so many problems was that their homelands did little to help. Württembergers even had to relinquish their citizenship before emigrating. The Swiss, in contrast, not only retained the right to return, but the Swiss consul issued them with a 'home certificate' and provided disappointed emigrants with the sum of two Louis d'or to help them return to Switzerland. The Swiss received support in case of illness, too. People from Alsace and Lorraine could expect similar assistance from French representatives.[339]

According to a Württemberg official in the Hague, 'In the environs of Amsterdam, in towns and villages, there are several thousand people from Alsace, Switzerland and Württemberg, most of whom can pay nothing and find themselves in the greatest poverty and hardship. Many parents die before their children, the poor, abandoned and helpless orphans wander around and must alas seek their bread at the doors of strangers. This misery is beyond words.'[340] On 9 May 1817 a benefit for the some 3,000 stranded German and Swiss emigrants was held at the French Theatre in Amsterdam, but this was just a drop in the ocean. On 3 July 1817 Fürstenwärther wrote from Amsterdam:

> I have found the misery of most of the emigrants greater, and the situation of all more perplexed and helpless, than I could have imagined ... During my journey here, on all the roads I already met droves of returning families who, deprived of everything, could survive only by begging. In Cologne, the government ensured that a large segment of them were stopped, fed and transported on to their homelands. The number of these unfortunates in Holland is however still indescribably large; all of the towns are flooded with them.[341]

The stranded emigrants became a social burden for Amsterdam and some other Dutch seaports, for a lack of money meant they could travel neither onward nor backward, but they also could not earn their own livelihood. Only a few succeeded in finding work in Holland. The authorities were faced with the task of organising social assistance for thousands of migrants. The willingness to help was there, but the scope of the problem soon led to attempts to slow migration by restrictive measures. We are familiar with this today, from EU or US border controls turning back people without identity papers and capital, and expelling or deporting those who manage to enter illegally. All this did was displace the problem, however. Migrants now became stranded at the border instead of in Holland. In 1817, this meant that they became the problem of the Prussian Rhine province, which in turn raised the hurdles for entry. In this way, southern German emigrants already ran up against obstacles in Koblenz or Mainz and became the problem of the Nassau or Hessian authorities. This shift across borders led to countries with out-migration such as Württemberg introducing travel restrictions. Thus, in a series of decrees beginning on 5 May 1817, the interior ministry of the kingdom of Württemberg issued instructions to stop giving out passports to America unless applicants could demonstrate sufficient assets to cover at least the travel expenses to their final destination.

Internal migration in Europe

Less spectacular than emigration to Russia or other distant corners of the earth was migration within Europe. Francophone Swiss tried their luck in France, apparently unaware that the famine was just as severe there as at home. German Swiss, in contrast, tried to migrate to Germany, to Prussia's eastern territories (the canton of Neufchâtel/ Neuenburg still belonged to Prussia at the time) or to the vast regions of the Habsburg Empire, for example Hungary. For people from Swabia, Hesse and the Palatinate, Prussian and Russian Poland and Hungary also became destinations. For those from the Rhineland and Westphalia, which now belonged to Prussia, migrating to Prussia's eastern territories meant moving within the same state entity. Berlin was nevertheless less than pleased with this option and tried to encourage people to stay home by offering them aid. In the Rhenish Palatinate, in contrast, the new district president Joseph von Stichaner suggested to the government in Munich that overpopulation could be reduced by deliberately resettling people in the Bavarian Upper Palatinate or in uninhabited areas of Altbayern.[342]

In general, it is safe to say that the European governments were less than enthusiastic about the individual migratory initiatives of their

151

citizens, whom they still regarded as subjects. According to the old mercantilist maxim, a growing population primarily meant wealth and power, while a drop in population meant a diminution of these desirable national objectives. Despite all the Malthusian warnings, these ideas were so deeply rooted that the authorities were unhappy about emigration even when the population was rising rapidly. In Italy, the government tried to prevent it by all available means. In the autumn of 1817 the extreme suffering in Lombardy-Venetia had set people in motion well into the Italian-speaking areas of the Trentino. For them, Spain seemed a desirable destination. The old duchy of Milan had belonged to Spain for hundreds of years since the time of Emperor Charles V, but apparently Spanish agents were now also trying to recruit immigrants. In November 1816, an instruction from the Podestà to the commissariat of police in Trento stated that a certain Giuseppe Angeli was organising the transfer of emigrants to the port of Genoa, where the 'commissari spagnoli' were supposed to meet and take over the group.[343]

More and more communities in northern Italy were dreaming of Spain, and the Austrian authorities tried with all their might to convince would-be emigrants that their hopes were illusory and they would return even poorer than before. The authorities were no more enthusiastic about the alternative of internal migration from Habsburg northern Italy to the Austro-Hungarian region of Banat. In order to dampen the impulse to emigrate by alleviating the suffering, they purchased grain at the market of Livorno and began to set up soup kitchens where they offered the official panacea: 'la zuppa detta "alla Rumford"'.[344] They were also willing to risk further increasing the war-related indebtedness of the communes.

Internal migration in North America

According to Frederick Jackson Turner's (1861–1932) famous theory, American culture was shaped by the experience of the frontier, the shifting border to a wide open land that inspired adventurousness and entrepreneurship.[345] The causes of westward expansion are usually sought in incipient overpopulation and the erosion of the soil in the East Coast states. John D. Post has pointed out, however, that this does not go far towards explaining the booms in westward migration, which swelled in precisely those years when Europeans were emigrating to the USA in larger numbers and for the same reasons. North America was as much affected by the Tambora Crisis as western

Europe. It also suffered from the consequences of war. The capital in Washington, which had been destroyed by the British, had to be rebuilt, as did the port cities on the East Coast. Administering this task fell to President James Monroe (1758–1831, in office 1817–1825), who was elected in 1816, in addition to managing the increased internal migration as a result of the Tambora Crisis.[346]

The harvest of 1816 in North America was so poor that many people sold their houses and packed their belongings onto wagons. Writing in the 1950s, Joseph B. Hoyt already pointed to the cold snaps, drought, crop failures and diseases of the summer of 1816 as catalysts for the wave of internal migration, and demonstrated statistically that the New England states were worst affected.[347] Between 15,000 and 20,000 left for the west from Maine alone, where people feared a famine. We have similar accounts for New Hampshire and Vermont. In most towns in Vermont, the population fell or stagnated during the crisis years, despite immigration from Europe. The same was true of mountainous areas more generally, where crop yields suffered particularly from the colder temperatures. According to a contemporary report, farmers feared the cooling trend would continue – the years 1812–1815 had also been significantly cooler than usual in North America even before the Tambora cold wave of 1816 – and regarded Ohio 'with its rich soil, its mild climate, its inviting prairies' as something akin to the Promised Land. But as in emigration from Europe, these expectations were not always met. 'I remember very well the tide of emigration through Connecticut, on its way in the West, during the summer of 1817 . . . Many of these persons were in a state of poverty and begged their way as they went. Some died before they reached the expected Canaan; many perished after their arrival, from fatigue and privation.' Even in the south, in North and South Carolina, farmers explained their westward migration by the failed harvest of 1816.[348] Among the most famous migrants were the family of Abraham Lincoln (1809–1865), who moved across the Ohio River from Kentucky to Indiana in 1816.[349]

When Morris Birkbeck and his family moved west from Washington, DC in the spring of 1817, they joined a broad stream of migrants. 'Old America seems to be breaking up and moving westward', he noted.[350] The Great Migration, as it is also known, continued for five years, from 1815 to 1819. The push to the west also accelerated the formation of political structures, the foundations for which had been laid by settlement and the constitution of new territories. A new territory gained statehood in each of the years from 1816 to 1821, a pace not matched before or since.

The Expansion of the USA, 1800–1840

Year	State	Total Number of States
1792	Kentucky	15
1796	Tennessee	16
1803	Ohio	17
1812	Louisiana	18
1816	Indiana	19
1817	Mississippi	20
1818	Illinois	21
1819	Alabama	22
1820	Maine	23
1821	Missouri	24
1836	Arkansas	25
1837	Michigan	26

The 'formative period' of some territories that were later incorporated into the USA as states is connected with migration during the Tambora Crisis.[351] As one can show using census data, in percentage terms all of the new states experienced the greatest growth in their history in the decade between 1810 and 1820.

Emancipation and antisemitism in the wake of famine

The 1815 Congress of Vienna not only resolved to abolish slavery, but also called for legal equality for the Jews. The ground had been prepared by Enlightenment notions of human rights, as expressed in the English Naturalisation Bill of 1753, the Tolerance Edict of Emperor Joseph II of 1781, and above all in the American Bill of Rights of 1789 and the first constitution of Revolutionary France of 1791, which granted Jews full civil rights. The more important states in central Europe (the Netherlands in 1806, Westphalia in 1808, Baden in 1809, Frankfurt in 1811, Prussia in 1812, Bavaria in 1813,

Population Growth in the New US States, 1800–1820

Year	Indiana	Mississippi	Illinois	Alabama
1800	2,632	7,600	2,548	1,250
1810	24,520	31,306	12,282	9,046
1820	147,178	75,448	55,211	127,901

Denmark in 1814 and Hesse in 1816) issued emancipation laws that granted civil rights, but usually attached to conditions such as the adoption of a family name, the German language, etc.[352] After the end of the wars, Prussia and Austria were the main proponents of equality apart from England and France. Prince Hardenberg (for Prussia) and Prince Metternich (for Austria) tried to inscribe Jewish emancipation into the major agreements of 1815 – the German Federal Act (Article 14) and the Final Act of the Congress of Vienna – against opposition from the small and middle-size German states.[353]

The stereotype of the Jewish usurer and profiteer lining his pockets by speculating on grain at the expense of the poor resurfaced during the crisis. This was the case in the affair surrounding Marie Leopoldine of Austria-Este (1776–1848), the widow of Elector Karl Theodor (1724–1799), who became notorious not just for her gambling addiction, series of young lovers and illegitimate children, but also for speculative trading in potatoes and grain. She maintained her own storehouse near Nördlingen, and entrusted the Jewish banker Simon Spiro with the management of her business affairs. A crisis arose at the turn of the year 1816/17 when two Munich banks went bankrupt after speculation in lottery tickets in which Marie Leopoldine was involved. The bankers implicated were the aforementioned Spiro and Franz Nockher, who committed suicide. In the autumn of 1817 the king asked Interior Minister von Thürheim to investigate and dispel rumours of the former electress's 'usurious speculation and intrigues in the grain trade'.[354]

As in other German lands, the banking sector in Bavaria was built up largely by Jewish bankers (Seligmann/Eichthal, Hirsch-Gereuth, Westheimer, Feuchtwanger, Rau and Aufhäuser) before the first state bank, the Bayerischer Hypotheken- und Wechselbank, was founded by the court banker Simon von Eichthal at the king's behest.[355] However, once the wars had ended, a functioning state administration had been established, and the solvency of the states had been restored, the role of Jewish bankers in state finance waned rapidly. At the same time, emancipation meant that Jews were no longer restricted to the financial sector. They became involved in wholesale trading and industry, and the settlement of Jewish craftsmen was also promoted, leading to a rapid change in the occupational composition of Jewish communities.[356]

Stereotypical resentments persisted nonetheless. In violation of the law of 1813 granting Jews legal equality, the city of Weißenburg in Franconia refused to allow them to settle there, and during the famine stated that 'the present is not at all the right time'. Crown

155

Prince Ludwig (1786–1868) intervened in the city of Schweinfurt's conflict with the interior minister in a letter in his own hand stating that he 'devoutly wished that Schweinfurt might remain free of Jews'. In Landshut in Lower Bavaria, a rumour arose in September 1816 that 'the Jews' had bought up all the potatoes: 'if they collect 100,000 fl, the starvation or satiation of 1,000 persons is in their hands'.[357] The stereotype of the 'Corn Jew' also persisted, once again with no concrete examples, as can be gleaned from an April 1817 tract by a jurist from Donauwörth, who wrote that the suffering could only be alleviated 'by abolishing Jewish interference and transactions in sales at the grain market'.[358] The political class did not take the antisemitism that emerged during the famine seriously. This would soon come back to haunt them.

From the Munich Oktoberfest to the Cannstatter Wasen festival

After the collapse of the ancien régime and the political reorganisation of Europe in the years between the Peace of Lunéville (1801) and the Final Act of the Congress of Vienna (1815), central Europe found itself in the midst of a nation-building process. Political decisions taken at conference tables to merge many small territories meant that people who had never had anything to do with each other previously, who came from different legal circumstances and religious traditions, suddenly found themselves living in the same country. The ruling dynasty was unfamiliar to many inhabitants of these newly constituted countries. Bavaria and Württemberg may serve as examples of this process. The ruler who came to power in Munich in 1800 came from Zweibrücken in the Palatinate. Some larger territories, like the old duchies of Bavaria and Württemberg, annexed a great number of smaller ones: Catholic Bavaria annexed the former archbishoprics of Passau, Freising, Regensburg, Augsburg, Eichstätt, Bamberg and Würzburg, the great Catholic imperial monasteries of Kempten, Ottobeuren, Ochsenhausen, etc., but also the Protestant margravates of Ansbach and Bayreuth, the former imperial cities of Augsburg, Nuremberg, Kempten, Memmingen, Lindau, Nördlingen, Regensburg, etc., plus dozens of independent territories formerly ruled by imperial knights or imperial counts and other small principalities. How were all these heterogeneous areas to be integrated?

In order to consolidate these territories and their inhabitants, the new states preferred to regard themselves as 'nations'. National symbols – national colours, costumes, languages, theatres, museums, etc. – had first to be created, however. An important measure was the establishment of national festivals. In Bavaria, the marriage of Crown Prince Ludwig to Princess Therese of Saxe-Hildburghausen (1792–1854) on 12 October 1810 offered an appropriate occasion. The event was celebrated with a popular festival (*Volksfest*), a horse race held on a meadow outside the old city walls that had been christened Theresienwiese (Therese's meadow) in the bride's honour. Because it was so successful, the fête was repeated the next year and called Oktoberfest, with new attractions added: a tombola, a try-your-luck stall, shooting at the popinjay, riflery contests,[359] races and other sporting competitions. The fête was organised by the Landwirtschaftlicher Verein (Agricultural Association), which combined it with an agricultural exhibition. Both parts of the event featured competitions and prizes, for example for the fastest runner or the most beautiful animal. Henceforth, this Oktoberfest, which married anniversaries of the ruling dynasty (the king's name day, the crown prince's wedding anniversary and the bride's name day) with popular entertainments and an agricultural exhibition, was held annually. Both the organisational form and the term *Volksfest* were completely new and tailored to the current state of socio-political upheaval,[360] in which the creation of a new 'fatherland' was the order of the day.[361]

The Munich Oktoberfest would become a model for similar events throughout southern Germany,[362] in part because territories like the new kingdom of Württemberg faced very similar problems, but also in part because the combination of an agricultural fair and popular entertainments was an ideal response to the Tambora Crisis. One of the main goals of the festival was to improve agriculture. According to its statutes, the aim of the Agricultural Association was 'to enliven and elevate agriculture wherever possible'.[363] To this end, prizes were given for the best stallions, mares, steers, cows, sheep, pigs and goats. Beginning in the famine year 1816, the Oktoberfest was extended to a several-day event at which new farm implements were displayed, and not long thereafter prizes were also awarded for inventions such as the 'potato shovel plough' or 'potato double-turn plough'. Aside from stockbreeders and inventors, particularly successful farmers, village mayors and male and female farm labourers were also recognised. In the famine year 1817, an industrial exhibition was also added, organised by the newly founded Polytechnischer Verein (Polytechnic Association).[364] Even the horse race was no mere sporting event, but was intended at the same time to inspire improvements in horse breeding.[365]

In September 1816, one of the initiators of the festival formulated a programme for the establishment of an Oktoberfest Verein, which shows the extent to which the festival placed itself at the service of improving agriculture.[366] Agriculture and industry were not the only focus, however; the event was also intended to exert a psychological influence on young people. Learning 'patriotic folk songs' was supposed to awaken 'sentiments conducive to the public good', while another objective was to 'develop and heighten their physical strength through appropriate gymnastic exercises and games'. Building projects, such as the construction of stands for spectators, were also intended to reduce unemployment. The author of this programme, Andreas Michael Dall'Armi (1765–1842), spent more than a decade designing the Oktoberfest. The innovations suggested in 1816 included try-your-luck stalls with products of local industry as prizes, shooting contests, and sporting competitions for the young.[367] The aims of the Munich Oktoberfest – to unite the Bavarian 'nation', display Bavarian achievements and bring the population closer to their dynasty – proved an ideal combination in 1816–1817. The festival not only distracted visitors from the crisis, but was also eminently suited to propagating reforms in agriculture and industry.[368]

The connection with the Tambora Crisis can be shown even more directly for the example of the Cannstatter Wasen, which was founded in 1818 as an agricultural festival.[369] The Stuttgart festival closely followed the Munich model.[370] The kingdom of Württemberg also faced the problem of integrating territories with widely divergent traditions. Here, too, the population had to develop ties to a new king, Friedrich I, which he attempted to foster with a penchant for autocracy following a career in Prussia and Russia.[371] After his unexpected death in October 1816 he was succeeded by his son Wilhelm I, who had just married a Russian princess. In keeping with the impact of the Tambora Crisis in Württemberg, the king adopted agricultural reform as his project. When the Württemberg National Festival was established, the agricultural exhibition was given pride of place. It was founded as the 'Agricultural Main Festival'.[372]

Relief institutions and agrarian reforms in Württemberg

Many towns in the kingdom of Württemberg set up spinning and weaving rooms to keep the unemployed occupied and enable them to support themselves. The authorities also wanted to reach the 'shame-faced poor' – those who hid their poverty – so that they could earn an income by selling their wares. Collection points were established for handicrafts and goods manufactured at home, which were delivered both by the poor themselves and by women of the wealthier classes. The sale of these products was also intended to generate income. Indigent artisans who, due to the inflation of food prices, could no longer afford the raw materials needed for their trade were provided with those materials free of charge so they could continue to work. Many of these initiatives required money. In order to set a good example, the king pledged to provide an annual subsidy of 10,000 florins. Other members of the dynasty followed his lead, including the Tsar's mother Maria Feodorovna, a native of Württemberg who was visiting Stuttgart at the time. Child employment institutes, which already existed in some towns, were introduced more generally under the name 'Katharinen- und Marienpflege' and placed under the aegis of the local associations. In addition, a school was established for 400 poor boys and girls, which was supposed to save them from neglect.

Many of these institutions were born of acute hardship. One such was a 'poor colony' in which those who had unsuccessfully tried to emigrate to Russia and returned penniless, with no hope of support from relatives, were prepared for reintegration into society. A colony expressly for returnees from Remstal was established on the royal demesne of Ottenhof in the Adelmannsfelden/Ostalb district. In 1818, King William appointed a poor commission assigned to the interior ministry, by means of which the various poor relief institutions were placed under state supervision and thus integrated into the administration. The founding of the Württemberg Landessparkasse (state savings bank) in May 1818 may also be counted among the immediate responses to the crisis, as it was intended to make it easier for citizens to provide for themselves come the next crisis. 'Small capital sums could be put aside with ease and security' in the Landessparkasse. The queen had drawn inspiration for this measure from Switzerland and England. Aside from the economic benefits, it was hoped that people would 'become accustomed early on to thrift with all of the moral consequences that spring from it'. A further initiative was the establishment of a modern hospital, which had hitherto not existed in Württemberg. It was only realised in 1828, however, with the founding of the Katharinenhospital.[373] Many of these projects were advanced by Goethe's publisher Johann Friedrich Cotta (1764–1832), who had a feel for the necessity of establishing a new infrastructure in economic and social policy and served as an advisor and provider of ideas to the young king.[374]

The initiatives to improve agriculture, which were all the more significant because they sought to tackle the root of the problem, were part of efforts to increase 'national prosperity' (*Volkswohlstand*) and 'national health' (*Volksgesundheit*), as they were referred to. The king and queen made a point of being the first to join the newly established Agricultural Association based in Stuttgart, whose aim was to make the cultivation of land and animal husbandry more effective through targeted advice for farmers and the dissemination of innovations and new implements. The association organised agricultural competitions, granted awards and patents, and tried to promote inventions by involving technicians and machine builders. In 1819 the king founded a separate association for matters of trade and tariff policy, which also affected the agricultural field.[375] At the same time as the Agricultural Main Festival at the Cannstater Wasen was introduced, a Landwirtschaftliche Unterrichts-, Versuchs- und Musteranstalt (Institute for Agricultural Instruction, Experimentation and Models) was established at Hohenheim, the predecessor to the University of Stuttgart-Hohenheim.[376]

Celebrating the first harvest wagon in the summer of 1817

The terrible weather of the previous year appeared set to continue in early 1817. The first months of the year were cold, snowy and stormy. The prices for food, especially bread grain, reached a highpoint in May and June 1817, but as June wore on it became clear that this year's harvest would be better than that of 1816, and perhaps better than the previous five years. After a long, cold and snowy winter in the Tyrol, 1 May brought good weather that was rarely interrupted by bad days up to harvest time. The *Eisheiligen* (Ice Saints, whose days on 11–13 May are often very cold and frosty) failed to appear, and brief showers provided sufficient water. People began to feel more confident of a good harvest to come.[377]

The vegetation recovered quickly over the summer and the harvest was bountiful.[378] Wheat and rye stood healthy on their stalks and people only had to pray that inclement weather did not return to destroy all their hopes. When it did not come in July either – although hail did damage crops in some regions – they just had to wait for the ears to ripen. Prices began to fall in anticipation of the harvest. Farmers started bringing in the crop as soon as possible. And given the famine year just passed, the harvest was celebrated as never before. In many places, the event was immortalised for posterity in word and image. Thanksgiving speeches and sermons were published.[379]

J.S. Dirr, Procession of thanksgiving in Überlingen on 4 August 1817,
Karlsruhe, Generallandesarchiv

Printed accounts of the thanksgiving celebrations appeared in some
places as well.[380]

What is especially interesting is that the 'celebration of the first
harvest wagon' was something completely new. To be sure, villages
had traditionally marked the bringing in of the harvest. Independent
of the harvest festivals often celebrated in parish churches in central
Europe on Michaelmas (29 September) or the first Sunday thereafter,
there are a number of customs surrounding the arrival of the *last*
harvest wagon, which signalled the completion of harvest labour.
Folklorists speak here of a closing ritual, in which the participants
bring the harvest to a close, for example by decorating the harvest
wagon.[381] What is more, in the age of Enlightenment, states had tried
to fix the day of the harvest festival in order to combat any religious
excesses. This was no different in the new kingdoms. In Bavaria, the
regional governments even dictated the Bible passages the priests
were to base their sermons on, and set the date of the harvest festival
as the last Sunday after Trinity.[382]

Everything was different, however, at the end of the famine of
1816/17. The relief was so great that people celebrated not the

last but the *first* harvest wagon. We do not know how this reversal of custom came about, but it crossed territorial and confessional lines. No authority could have mandated this. As soon as the new custom arose it spread like a fashion. There was scarcely a town or village that did not practise this jubilant new ritual. The date was whenever local farmers brought in the harvest, and this could differ from village to village. There were substantial differences even within small regions because of microclimates. Fürth in Middle Franconia made a start with its celebration on 18 July 1817, followed by Nuremberg on 21 July.[383] Wörth near Nuremberg was not ready until 25 July,[384] Ansbach on 30 July,[385] Uffenheim on 1 August,[386] the village of Kolmberg near Ansbach on 7 August,[387] Gunzenhausen on 11 August, and the village of Lendershausen near Hassfurt (Lower Franconia) only on 17 August.[388] Celebrities of the era, such as the Catholic theology professor and future bishop Johann Michael Sailer (1751–1832), also showed up to give speeches and sermons.[389]

The entry of the first harvest wagon was accompanied by large public festivities. In Thuringia even Minister Goethe had to pay tribute to this event, albeit between his many other appointments. On the afternoon of 1 August 1817 he wrote rather desultorily in his journal, 'To the market square, because arrival of first harvest wagon.'[390] Almost everywhere, the wagons were adorned with flowers, wreaths and inscriptions. In Stuttgart, the citizenry organised a joyous festival. The ride through the streets of the city was arranged as a triumphal procession, with bands playing, schoolchildren singing, bells ringing from the steeples, an official reception by the secular and church authorities, speeches on the central squares and services of thanksgiving in all the churches.[391]

The surviving illustrations of the entries of harvest wagons give an impression of state control. Nearly all such prints come from the kingdom of Württemberg or the Grand Duchy of Baden, two of the states worst affected by the crisis. The works were nearly always printed in the respective district seats (*Oberamtsstadt* in Württemberg, *Amtsstadt* in Baden). Absent are the old episcopal cities (e.g. Konstanz, Rottenburg, Speyer, etc.) and the main centres of the mediatised high nobility, who still lived in their residences. It seems highly likely that these events were actually promotional actions for the newly established states. Several of the places of printing (Aalen, Nördlingen, Ravensburg, Überlingen, Ulm, Wangen, Weil der Stadt) had only recently been free imperial cities, while others had been part of other territories not long before. It is striking, however, that the capitals (Munich, Stuttgart and Karlsruhe) as well as other large cities (Augsburg, Nuremberg and Mannheim) in all three states of the former Confederation of the Rhine are missing. There was one printed sermon from Nuremberg, in which the pastor of St Johann's apologised for the style, explaining that he had only learnt the day before the celebration that he was to give a sermon on Monday, 21 July.[392] This might indicate that the celebrations were improvised at the last minute. This sermon also stated that the owner of the fields had 'decided quite willingly, indeed without any outward request ... to make this year's first harvest blessing ... memorable for himself and the entire local community by means of a religious ceremony'.[393]

In fact, the state governments issued official orders to hold harvest festivals throughout the country. The government of Grand Duke Karl Ludwig Friedrich of Baden (1786–1818, reigned 1811–1818) ordered a general festival of thanksgiving on 17 August, in addition to the local festivities. The harvest festivals in the district capitals of Mosbach and Überlingen, however, show that some towns did not wait until this date. In Walldürn, in contrast, 'a feast of thanksgiving for the blessed harvest that God has bestowed upon us was held on the 17th of August'.[394] Many sources also contradict the idea that the management of the famine was regarded as a success for the state authorities. In Catholic areas, the thanksgiving celebrations regularly ended with a mass, and Protestants at the very least joined the pastor in singing the hymn 'Holy God We Praise Thy Name'. Not just sectaries but nearly all believers understood the famine year as a reminder of divine wrath at human sinfulness, and the rich harvest of 1817 as a sign of divine benevolence. A poem of thanks penned by the nightwatchman of Adelsheim in the Odenwald sounds somewhat disheartened but nonetheless grounded in religion:

> Although it may seem at times
> As though God has forsaken his people
> Still this I believe and know:
> In the end God's help is sure.[395]

It seems that in the end, despite all efforts made by the authorities, the crisis was grist to the mill not of the state but of the church. On the other hand – and this was probably decisive for politicians – the crisis had not delegitimised the new state formations. It was over for the time being, and politics, though somewhat late, had responded decisively and successfully. Even if the celebrations for the harvest of 1817 were organised by the authorities, they nevertheless

163

corresponded to a universal need and took account of people's relief that the crisis was past.

The inflation continues

The bringing in of the first harvest wagon was celebrated as much in the press as it was in speeches and sermons. This raises the question of the role of newspapers and magazines in the Tambora Crisis more generally. The economic historian John D. Post, for example, has described this in very plain terms for the protest movements. These journalistic accounts 'not only tended to minimize the gravity of social upheaval, but they also adopted a tone of unrealistic optimism concerning the possibility of an immediate end to the crisis'.[396] He cites as an example the Parisian press, which scarcely reported on price rises in order not to foment the speculation in foodstuffs, and which, when speaking of tumults and protests, generally reprinted verbatim the articles from the official organ of the police ministry, the *Journal des Maires*. We can assume that under the conditions of press censorship, the latter, like all other periodicals of the era, reflected reality only in highly filtered form. Thus if we find little in the Bavarian newspapers about the riots in southern Germany this does not mean that none occurred.

Similarly, the optimistic accounts of the end of the crisis following the 'good harvest' of 1817 do not mean that it was actually good. Although far better than the previous year's, it was not good enough. It was not even average when compared to the first decade of the century. While the prices for basic foodstuffs fell accordingly, they did not return to pre-1812 levels, but remained comparatively high and for many people too high. In some regions they quickly rose again after the first jubilation. In Normandy they did not fall at all, but continued to rise in mid-November 1817.[397] In Hesse, too, the euphoria over the good harvest soon dissipated. In October, the grain trade had been largely relieved of the previously imposed restrictions, with the exception of the distilleries. But by November the restrictions had been reintroduced, since the rye harvest had proved unexpectedly poor. The district government of Fulda suggested that larger stocks should be collected in state storehouses to prevent a renewed dearth of grain, and to that end recommended importing rye from the Baltic. The farmers were to be informed of the continuation of the emergency grain storage project. In the winter of 1817/18, too, hardship was omnipresent. The cloth makers' guild in Fulda lamented the 'incomparable impoverishment of our members, caused not least by non-guild production methods and the "Jewish cloth trade"'. The theft of firewood also continued unabated, a sign that the poorer population still could not afford fuel. It was reported from Hersfeld that begging in the streets and door-to-door persisted, despite the distribution of meals to the poor. The reason was continuing unemployment in the textile trade. Only with the next year's harvest and the subsequent fall of prices for basic foodstuffs could all trade restrictions be lifted in Hesse in August 1818.[398] Despite the harvest celebrations, the atmosphere in the autumn of 1817 remained tense.

The emergence of pauperism

Poverty and hardship continued in many parts of Europe despite lower food prices. Many households had fallen into debt during the famine, when people had sold their property, both movable and immovable, to secure the survival of their families. When businesses collapsed or people lost their jobs they fell into poverty and became dependent on relief payments. In July 1818 it was reported from Kassel that many inhabitants of the city were so deep in debt that their property had to be sold at compulsory auction, but the general lack of money meant that frequently no solvent buyers could be found even for land. In February 1819, taxation was reportedly also contributing to indebtedness in Schmalkalden, although even tax abatement often offered no escape from the debt trap. The labouring classes frequently had neither cooking pots nor beds in their miserable hovels, and their clothing consisted mainly of rags. There was usually nothing left to seize to pay off their outstanding taxes. 'Taken together, all of these accounts give the impression of widespread indigence and desperate sadness in the [Hessian] electoral state in 1819/20.'[399]

In the wake of the Tambora Crisis, we find a new stratum of people who could no longer find a way out of the poverty trap and remained permanently dependent on state assistance. What we see here is the emergence of the pauperism that would preoccupy politics in Europe and America in the decades that followed, until the boom of rising industrialisation once again offered employment opportunities for all who were able to work. Unlike before 1800, it was no longer only children, the ill and the elderly who needed support, but also able-bodied men and women who were looking for work but found none. The phenomenon of mass poverty and pauperism existed mainly in the period between 1816 and 1850, while contemporary literature of the period afterwards tended to focus largely on the 'social question' and the problems society experienced with the new 'proletariat'. By then, people expected to contend with the spectre of 'communism', but in the period of pauperism – apart from the riots during the famine of 1816/17 – the poor tended to be silent.[400]

The observations presented here on the emergence of pauperism – as the result of a climate crisis which arose from 'external' causes – correct two of the usual explanations simultaneously: Friedrich Engels (1820–1895) propagated the idea that the new poverty was a result of industrialisation; the economic historian Wilhelm Abel, in contrast, introduced the notion that pauperism was an offshoot of the old, pre-industrial poverty, exacerbated by population growth combined with the same low level of economic productivity. The industrial system was not the cause of poverty, but the remedy for it.[401] Neither of these theses appears to stand up to the data on the Tambora Crisis. Instead, the sources presented here give the impression that the middle classes became impoverished within a relatively short time. This new form of poverty was unknown during the ancien régime and could not be resolved with traditional methods. Contrary to the claims made in the literature, the term 'pauperism' was not an innovation of the 1830s, but rather, as the founding of the Society for the Prevention of Pauperism (SPP) demonstrates, of the year 1817 – as a direct response to the Tambora Crisis.[402]

'From the Grand Society': the Würzburg crisis at the end of 1817

During the first three weeks of December fires were set in eight villages around Würzburg, immediately calling to mind the blaze at the royal residence in Munich and the subsequent arson threats there. Two unknown individuals also tried to break into the Würzburg palace inhabited by Crown Prince Ludwig of Bavaria, later King Ludwig I (1786–1868). In their reports, the general command attributed these incidents to 'the continuing enormous dearness, which has left at least half of the common folk poor and wretched'. After two incidents on the city walls, which are not described in detail, the district president of the Lower Main district, the liberal commissioner-general Franz Wilhelm von Asbeck (1760–1826), saw the safety of Bavaria's second-largest garrison town endangered and requested troop reinforcements. Even soldiers on leave were to be enlisted 'until this crisis is over'.[403]

166

Three printed posters appeared on Christmas Day, threatening to set fires in Würzburg itself if grain prices did not fall drastically on 1 January 1818:

From the Grand Society!

We are sick of our life
And thus fear neither gallows nor wheel.
Our hand is forced, as our suffering proves
So give us cheap bread or give us death
We are determined now,
As we demonstrated once before
With fire, murder and strangulation
In town and country too
Profiteers and bigwigs, your time is up
We'll burn your houses down
And clear them out.
Now iron breaks
We shall prove it.

This anonymous Christmas message was dated 20 December and closed with the ominous words 'To be continued'.[404] This proved to be no exaggeration. Five more arson attacks occurred between Christmas and New Year. At the sites of the fires notes were found signed 'Hauptmann der großen Gesellschaft' (Captain of the Grand Society). The 'grand society' thus referred not to the profiteers and their enablers in the government, as a sort of counterpart to the 'common man', but rather to a previously unknown secret society with a military structure that intended to stand by the 'common man'. The written claim of responsibility had an immediate effect. The authorities were in a state of high alert, and grain prices fell because the vendors feared attacks, as the Würzburg general command noted in their report.[405]

There is a direct line from the crisis in Würzburg in late December 1817 and early January 1818 to the anti-Jewish pogroms of the following year, in which arson attacks and threatening letters also played a role, and a secret terrorist society claimed to be combating profiteers (*Wucherer*) and bigwigs (*die Großen*). The only difference was that this time they were more specific. The profiteers were the Jews, and the attacks targeted the representatives of the Bavarian 'occupying power' – with King Maximilian I Joseph at the top – which had only taken over the government in the former grand duchy of Würzburg in 1816, following a decision at the Congress of Vienna.[406] One of the threatening letters stated that, 'As the closest kin to the

167

Bavarian Chamber of Finance [finance ministry],[407] the Jew is allowed to engage in his criminal usury with the poor oppressed citizens . . . and if one asks why all this is so, the answer is that blackguards and Jews have joined forces to guide the reins of power.'[408] Against this backdrop, the arson attacks and the break-in at the palace of the crown prince must be viewed in connection with the arson attacks against Jews and their friends one year later. The threatening letters of September 1819 would also speak of 'our society', which would proceed against the profiteers 'with dagger and fire', but the rhetoric had become more radical, announcing nothing less than the 'total destruction of the Jewish people'.[409]

This was associated with the threat of political revolution, for the mysterious Würzburg 'society' also warned that 'the moment . . . has now come in which the oppressed Franconian will untie his fetters, recognising neither military nor civilian authority. Our assembly, united for a good and just cause, is strong enough to resist anyone. With fire, dagger and sword we are firmly determined to cleanse ourselves of the Jewish vermin.'[410] Just who was behind the Würzburg secret society was never discovered. The state-appointed city commissioner of Würzburg, Franz Anton Gessert (1770–1834), suspected ties to 'German populist nationalists [*Volkstümler*], . . . actually wild republicans', who sought to incite the mob against the Bavarian state authority with the aim of overthrowing the existing order.[411] The term 'wild republicans' could refer to students or members of the gymnastics movement. But since the author of the threatening letters clearly had a difficult time with spelling he probably did not come from academic circles. Unless, and this is not impossible, he was deliberately trying to cover his tracks.

Farewell to 1817

Many newspapers ended the old year with a backward look. This is how a commemorative broadsheet to mark the first harvest wagon in Ulm, which apparently appeared at the end of the year, put it:

> 'Twas a gloomy year, of woes across the earth,
> The lands hard pressed by wretched dearth
> The poor spake tearfully each morn'
> How shall I find my children's daily corn!
> Joy went veiled and hid her head
> Where otherwise she dwelt was still and dead.

Oh Mother Earth, thy bounty open please,
We begged for aid on bended knees.[412]

The editor of the Weimar magazine *Zeitschwingen*, Johann Baptist Pfeilschifter (1792–1874), inserted a 'Funeral Oration at the Grave of the Year 1817' into the New Year's 1818 issue, in which he addressed the most noteworthy phenomena of the year just ended, including the Bavarian concordat, the union of the Lutheran and Reformed congregations in parts of Germany, the jubilee of the Reformation and the cometic career of Baroness von Krüdener.[413]

The weekly paper *Regensburger Wochenblatt* looked back in horror at the old year:

Down to your brothers' halls,
Oh fatal year,
More awful still in weighty fate
Than any that e'er went before.

Where is the man whose tears fell not
Upon a deeply furrowed cheek
Whose noble heart did not bleed and grieve
At the sight of his brothers' distress?

Who shall paint the full picture of woe,
The sign of this time,
The joyless cares, hunger, sorrow and nakedness
Visited upon so many innocents?[414]

Maximilian Joseph Schleiß von Löwenfeld, the vicar of Rannungen near Schweinfurt, found the following hopeful words at the end of 1817: 'The year has closed its circle of sorrow and fear, and serene, more cheerful hours now step back onto the course of time. – Europe's hunger- and terror-filled worries are at an end.'[415]

— 5 —

THE TURBULENT YEARS THAT FOLLOWED: 1818–1820

The beginning of 1818

At the beginning of 1818 people celebrated the end of another terrible year and believed that things could only get better. The man who delivered the *Düsseldorfer Zeitung* began his New Year's poem as follows:

> As awful a year as ever seen
> Is over now, thank the Lord;
> What a year it was! 30 stivers the loaf
> We paid for bread
> And the muck in the streets,
> Nearly did me in
> From one house to the next.

> Bad or not I had to go,
> So often with an empty belly,
> To bring our dear readers
> Reports of the latest news;
> And the worst thing of all,
> I always had catarrh
> In that accursed weather . . .[1]

In its *Neujahrsblatt* for 1818, the Zürcherische Hülfsgesellschaft (Zurich Aid Society) stressed that after the 'indescribable hardships of the past year' the worst was over: 'But this struggle is not yet at an end', since the suffering continued despite the better harvest of the previous summer.[2] The New Year's poems addressed not just the negative consequences of the famine years 1816/17, for in some areas

170

the food prices remained elevated until the harvest of 1818. In the Palatinate, for example, grain prices were twice as high as normal. Only later did they fall more generally, and not until 1819 can one speak of a year with normal prices.[3]

The *Regensburger Wochenblatt* greeted readers with a hopeful poem dedicated 'To the New Year 1818':

> Hail to us! – A presentiment vibrates through the soul,
> At the new cycle of the year,
> The future dawns to us mild and bright
> A better lot to bring.
>
> The storm of fate scatters like dust; the sun breaks through
> After the long night,
> And nurtures with new happiness and delight
> The weary pilgrim choir.
>
> The seed thrives: – Business and industry blossom
> In newly rejuvenated splendour,
> And the spirit of usury must flee the earth
> When bounty smiles upon us.
>
> Fulfil Almighty Father what the soul surmised
> And the spirit warmly asked,
> Be gracious to King and Fatherland,
> And merciful to our city.[4]

Utopia realised: Korntal

The years of hardship saw the revival of nearly forgotten words and phrases and the coining of new ones that revolved around the object of desire – corn. Corn (German *Korn*) was a generic term in the Germanic languages that referred to the regionally dominant type of cereal and its starchy grains: wheat in England, barley in Sweden, oats in Westphalia and spelt in Franconia.[5] Only in North America did the word corn usually refer to maize, a plant that originated in Mexico.[6] Corn/*Korn* is related etymologically to *Kern* (hence the English kernel) and grain.[7] A land with rich yields was known as a *Kornland* or *Kornkammer* (granary). Planting corn in a cornfield yielded the staple food of the era, cereals (*Kornfrucht*, *Brodkorn*), but also the raw material for beer and *Kornbrand*, or *Korn* for short, a colourless distilled liquor.[8] Before the harvests, the cornfields were protected by 'guardians of the corn' (*Kornschützen*). The harvest was known as the cutting (*Kornschnitt*) or blessing (*Kornsegen*) of the corn. In

171

Catholic regions, the corn was consecrated in a 'christening of the corn' (*Korntaufe*). The corn transporter (*Kornführer*) took the grain to the corn market. The corn was subject to inspection (*Kornschau, Korngeschau*) and the corn laws, corn fees and corn levy (*Korngeld* or *Kornungeld*), an indirect tax. From the late Middle Ages, in times of scarcity, corn blockades (*Kornsperre*) and prohibitions on the use of corn for distilling had been imposed, or the price fixed by a so-called *Korntaxe*. The corn harvest was the most important date in the agricultural calendar. Parts of the harvest were traditionally stored in granaries (*Kornspeicher, Kornhäuser* or *Kornkästen*), large storehouses in central locations, and in Hungary also in corn pits. In the eighteenth century people also began to speak of 'corn magazines'. The corn stocks were supervised by 'corn lords' (*Kornherren*). Officials such as the corn clerk (*Kornschreiber*) and the corn measurer (*Kornmesser*) guaranteed the orderly management of the grain stores. The price of corn was decided at the corn market. The much-hated corn speculators who were held responsible for inflated grain prices were referred to as corn pedlars (*Kornkäufler*), corn clippers (*Kornkipperer*) or corn churners (*Kornschinder*). Antisemites were convinced that 'corn Jews' were at work.[9] A corn shortage affected prices and led to corn inflation. Corn thieves and corn beggars appeared in larger numbers during the famine. The corn pests (such as the *Kornbock*) were too numerous to list here.[10]

This family of words was joined in 1815 by the Corn Law in England, in 1816/17 by the corn association (*Kornverein*), and in 1818 by the toponym 'Korntal' in Württemberg. In the course of the Tambora Crisis, the possibility of (re)settlement within the country was developed as an alternative to emigration. The king of Württemberg opened a sort of special zone in his own country where evangelical Protestants could live in religious freedom according to their own lights. He gave the place an enticing name: Korntal (corn valley).[11] In 1818, the Brethren assembly under the leadership of the eschatological preacher Gottlieb Wilhelm Hoffmann (1771–1846) was permitted to purchase the Korntal estate and establish a Pietist model settlement there. The following year, on the occasion of the consecration of the large vestry, King Wilhelm I granted the community privileges for religious practice and permission to settle families from throughout the kingdom.[12]

That Korntal was a utopian settlement along the lines of its founders' image of early Christianity is evident from the fact that property was held in common and placed under the authority of a purchase association (*Güterkaufsgesellschaft*). Like their role model, the

Moravian Brethren in Herrnhut, the Korntal Pietists aspired to a sort of communist community. Hoffmann aimed to 'pulverise' the various parties of evangelical Christians 'with the mortar of love and make new men and women of them'.[13] Korntal became the centre of Pietism in Württemberg. Hoffmann wanted to establish it as a mother congregation that would serve as a model for additional settlements in the kingdom. Wilhelm I refused his consent, however, fearing the emergence of a Pietist parallel society. Korntal only lost its privileged status a century later with the German Constitution of 1919. From that time on, the town had to be opened to non-members of the Brethren. Korntal attained city status in 1958, but in the course of communal reform in 1975 was joined to the municipality of Münchingen to form the new city of Korntal-Münchingen (Ludwigsburg district). Korntal has, however, reportedly retained its peculiarities.[14]

From emigration to remigration

While at the height of the crisis all migration streams from central Europe led outward, after news of the good harvest in 1817 spread they began to reverse direction. Returning was not always easy, however. Angered by the emigration of its subjects, the kingdom of Württemberg had from the outset decreed a ban on returning.[15] But just like emigration, remigration was extremely difficult to control by legal means.

The first impoverished emigrants who, because of the catastrophic conditions in the Dutch ports, had waited in vain for their ships to the USA began to return to Württemberg and Baden in early 1817.[16] In July 1817 – even before the fall in prices – the administrative district of Heilbronn alone reported the return of some 1,000 Württembergers. The district of Brackenheim asked the government how to proceed and was instructed to allow the resettlement of individuals with proper travel documents, despite the ban. They were to be separated as quickly as possible from vagabonds and other 'itinerant riffraff' and sent to their communities of origin. But even this regulation proved untenable and it was modified in July 1817 to mandate the issuing of passports to Württembergers without papers so they could return home. This loosening of the ban in turn encouraged others wishing to remigrate.[17]

The returnees were by no means welcome in all of their places of origin, since at first they placed an additional burden on local relief institutions. They were resented in particular for having taken their assets and spent them elsewhere only to return penniless. The state of Württemberg was thus compelled in the years that followed to address the problems of returnees. The kingdom had to adjust its legislation several times, both to force home communities to accept returnees and to repel undesirable arrivals. In the process it had to take into account the interests not just of remigrants, their home communities and the state, but also those of neighbouring territories unwilling to let Württemberg dispose of its social burdens elsewhere. Without agreements between states there was a danger that former emigrants would turn into a new class of displaced persons.

The overwhelming majority of remigrants, however, succeeded in returning home after living for months or even years in their destination countries. Sometimes homesickness or the desire to spend their final years in the old country played a role. This was the case for the wine grower Joseph Asmus, who in 1841 applied through his brother in Großingersheim to reclaim his Württemberg citizenship, although he had made his fortune in Russia and owned two houses in Odessa and two estates in the surrounding countryside. In the case of this wealthy returnee, who also had relatives and an inheritance awaiting him at home, the authorities found it easy to give their consent.[18] Other emigrants had found it hard to adjust to living conditions in the new country, or returned when they learnt that close relations had fallen ill or died. In contrast to emigration, where religious, political or economic motives dominated, the motives for returning were often more familial in nature. Arguments in applications for permission to return that stressed a preference for the old homeland, in contrast, may well have served a rhetorical function.[19]

Return to the principle of self-administration

While in Württemberg the capable young civil servant Friedrich List had studied intentions to emigrate, in neighbouring Baden a head of department at the interior ministry evaluated the administrative reforms of the turbulent years since the small margravate on the Rhine had become first an electorate (1803) and finally a grand duchy (1807) extending from the Swiss border to Hesse. In the spring of 1817, Ludwig Georg von Winter (1778–1838) was charged with undertaking 'a journey to study the parts of the country oppressed by crop failure and inflated prices'.[20] The results of this enquiry have been lost, but the surviving fragments on his visit to Emmendingen reveal that Winter – like List in Württemberg – took notes registering the complaints and wishes of the local population. Henceforth, Winter would dedicate himself to scaling back the absolutist governmental structures taken over from France to a degree that allowed local administrations more responsibility, and he did so with the delightful argument that 'the German' desired 'a monarch, but not a satrap'.[21]

The reversal was especially drastic in the kingdom of Bavaria, with its centralism on the French model. The reason for the gradual placement of the towns under state trusteeship from 1802 until the municipality laws of 1808, and for the abolition of their self-administration, lay in the strong individual traditions of the communes. In Swabia and Franconia they had previously belonged to other territories or, as in the case of Augsburg, Nuremberg or Regensburg, had enjoyed the status of free imperial cities. Placing the local administration under state direction was intended to end the autonomy of these foreign entities. The local authorities lost control of jurisdiction, policing, schools and the management of the assets of communes and foundations. State commissioners replaced elected mayors. Important matters were decided by the district government or even the central government in Munich. Lacking a knowledge of local conditions, however, the central authorities were completely overwhelmed by this task. For that reason, many problems remained unresolved and the work of governing came to a standstill. The attempt to centralise local administration had proved a failure.[22]

As early as May 1816, the privy council had elaborated draft legislation for the return of competences to the communes. It failed because of the opposition of Montgelas, who remained firmly dedicated to French centralism. Nevertheless, there was no alternative to initiating the decentralisation of poor relief. The return of the assets of communes and foundations rendered the towns operational again, and the old urban elites resumed their political responsibilities. The resignation of Montgelas cleared the way for the re-establishment of communal self-administration. In the preamble to the municipal edict of 17 May 1818, the responsible director at the interior ministry, Georg Friedrich von Zentner (1752–1835), a native of the Palatinate, established the principles that would apply in future:

> Each member of the commune must be accorded the appropriate degree of participation in communal affairs; when the individual feels himself thereby to be an immediate member of a whole, or of a public community, he ceases to see himself as the sole end. A sense of the public, of the community, arises, even if it is only local at first, as soon as members of the commune are permitted to contribute to the common interest with

their own might, and not constantly hindered in their actions by outside interventions.[23]

Self-administration was re-established by electing municipal representative bodies along a uniform pattern throughout the kingdom. They then elected the Magistrat, the local executive body. The communes were given a broader scope, encompassing the management of local assets as well the right to levy their own duties or municipal taxes. They were again permitted to manage their own finances and to take on sovereign tasks. These included admitting new citizens, issuing licences, local policing, running the primary school system or local church administration. The central state did not withdraw altogether, however. State trusteeship remained in the guise of the city commissioner, who supervised self-administration as the eyes of a mistrustful state.[24]

The inclusive constitutional state

There were many reasons for the introduction of relatively modern constitutions. One was the fact that the most progressive country of the day, the United Kingdom, with the introduction in 1688 of a parliamentary monarchy in which power lay not with the king or queen but with an elected parliament, had advanced from being an island on the edge of Europe to a dominant world power. England had foiled Napoleon's claims to power. With its booming agrarian sector and free trade within the empire, England had little trouble surviving the Tambora Crisis. It was now the model for all reforming states.[25] But there was also a far more pressing reason for the implementation of constitutions: popular anger over government mismanagement of the crisis. Governments were not merely experienced as aloof and out of touch, they were also often foreign to their own people. The fact that the states were new virtually everywhere and behaved as occupying powers in their newly acquired territories also played a role here. National symbols were insufficient to integrate the regional forces; elections were also needed to a common parliament, in which the legitimate interests of all regions and population groups could be expressed.[26]

One of the great advantages of the English political system was that the state had credit thanks to the control of state finances, while monarchies on the continent were all so deep in debt that they had trouble avoiding state bankruptcy. This was a result of the long period of war as well as the uncontrolled state and court expenses that had remained hidden by a system of non-transparent and corrupt administration. In England, the control of finances was the responsibility of representatives of the state, whose rights were guaranteed in Parliament. France, having been defeated in war, also faced the problem of restoring credit, and for that reason enacted a constitution on 4 June 1814 that bound the king to the law. This guaranteed citizens basic rights, while elected deputies in the parliament controlled taxation and the government. The ministers were answerable to the parliament.[27]

Although the German Federal Act envisioned the introduction of constitutions in the federal states, all monarchies were reluctant to share power voluntarily. To be sure, Bavaria had enacted a constitution in 1808 that established the unification of law, equality before the law and religious tolerance. Lenders, however, were unimpressed by this revolution from above, since communal self-administration, which had existed even under the ancien régime, had not been reinstated. It is typical that the unfettered state of this period attempted to acquire money by decreeing compulsory levies. The social and political unrest of the Tambora Crisis helped to overcome resistance to democratisation.[28]

The enactment of the constitution in the kingdom of Bavaria in May 1818 put pressure on the other German middling states. In August, Bavaria's example was followed by the grand duchy of Baden, which was competing with Bavaria over the old Palatine territories around Heidelberg and Mannheim. The kingdom of Württemberg, which was located between these two countries, followed in 1819, and the grand duchy of Hesse immediately to the north in 1820. All of the constitutions followed the English model, setting up a bicameral system where the actual power lay with upper and lower houses chosen by general elections. The constitutions restricted the privileges of monarchs, granted basic rights to all people and civil rights to all citizens. These included freedom of conscience, opinion and assembly but also freedom of movement and the right to emigrate. They guaranteed the independence of the judiciary and the irremovability of judges, and thus the separation of powers and the rule of law. Although the parliaments did not yet elect the government, the ministers were answerable to the parliament and could be impeached if they abused their power. The strongest weapon wielded by members of parliament was the power of the purse, which placed governments in a certain dependence. It was precisely this that restored the creditworthiness of governments and helped to secure the national budget. The state could borrow money only with the consent of parliament, which limited the risk for lenders.[29]

Despite the deficiencies of these constitutions – census suffrage, privileges for the nobility, etc. – their introduction nonetheless represented a great step forward. This was evident in the sessions of the first *Landtage* (state parliaments), where the committees did serious work on substantive issues. From now on, lively discussions were conducted on policy in the various countries, and thanks to the parliaments future crises could be handled better than the Tambora Crisis had been. Not least for this reason, the latter remained 'the last great subsistence crisis in the western world'.[30] It was no accident that the only subsequent European famine took place in a country that, like a colony, was subject to external domination, namely Ireland.[31]

The suicide attack on August von Kotzebue

The Wartburg festival of 18/19 October 1817 had brought student organisations and universities to the attention of governments as potential sources of revolutionary unrest. The participants may have seen themselves as the avant-garde of national liberation, but the Wartburg festival also served as the jumping-off point for the political assassinations and riots of the years that followed.[32]

A few months later, the student Carl Ludwig Sand (1795–1820), co-organiser of the Wartburg festival, made the leap from words to deeds and murdered the author August von Kotzebue (1761–1819). At the festival, books by numerous liberal intellectuals accused of being Francophiles or promoting Jewish equality had been consigned to the flames. This action had been a long time in the planning: the nationalist founder of the German gymnastic movement Friedrich Ludwig Jahn (1778–1852)[33] had compiled the list of books, and his student Hans Ferdinand Maßmann (1797–1852) had organised, carried out and later reported on the book burning,[34] which he had discussed beforehand with the Jena philosophy professor Jakob Friedrich Fries, one of the event's masterminds.[35] The Prussian minister of justice Karl Albert von Kamptz (1769–1847), whose books had also been burnt, intervened with the government of the grand duchy of Saxe-Weimar concerning the 'riotous assembly of unruly professors and seduced students'.[36] With the Wartburg festival, a small minority of German professors and students had succeeded in making the universities, and the students' societies known as *Burschenschaften* in particular, appear as dangerous breeding grounds for revolution.[37] Naturally, at first, many people considered the disciplinary measures taken against individual professors and students to be excessive. But that was about to change.

178

On 5 May 1818, Sand confided in his diary that he intended to murder August von Kotzebue, whom he referred to as a 'traitor to the nation' and a 'deceiver of the people'. The following autumn he travelled from Jena to Berlin, where he spent some time with the ardent German nationalist and proponent of physical education Friedrich Ludwig Jahn (1778–1852), popularly known as *Turnvater* (father of gymnastics). In February 1819 Sand journeyed from Jena to Mannheim to commit the murder. He stopped at the Wartburg on his way, where he wrote in the guest book, thus reinforcing the connection with the Wartburg festival.[38] On 23 March 1819, using a false name, Sand went to see Kotzebue in his Mannheim home. After a brief exchange of words he pulled out a dagger and stabbed his victim several times in the chest. Kotzebue died just a few minutes later as a result of his grave injuries. Sand was carrying a second knife with which he intended to kill himself. His suicide attempt failed, however, allowing him to hand a written justification of his actions entitled 'Death Blow to August von Kotzebue' to a servant who had rushed to the scene. Sand considered his act to be tantamount to tyrannicide; he felt no regret and stood by his murder. There was no doubt that he would be convicted of the crime. The court at Mannheim sentenced him to death and he was beheaded on 5 May 1820. Sand had the story of another suicide assassin read aloud to him before his execution.[39] Henceforth, he was accounted a martyr by those who shared his views, including members of the educated middle classes.[40] The Nazi historian Karl Alexander von Müller (1882–1964) still glorified Sand as a 'murderer out of patriotism'.[41]

Sand was the kind of fanatical suicide assassin familiar to us today mainly from the political terrorism of Islamic fundamentalists. Through a politically motivated murder, he sought to light a beacon in the name of a purportedly sacred cause, and was prepared to sacrifice his own life in the process. For that reason, contemporaries already compared him to the Muslim sect of Assassins.[42] Like modern terrorists, he had formulated a written message claiming responsibility. Born the youngest of eight children to a Prussian jurist in Wünsiedel, he was considered 'slow-witted' at school and 'narrow-minded' and 'obstinate' at university. After reading Jahn's *Deutsches Volkstum*, which contained a section on 'unGerman books',[43] and whose author was one of the leading propagandists of antisemitism,[44] Sand felt called to higher things. In 1816 in Erlangen he founded a 'German-minded' student society, which was known by its opponents as Teutonia. In June 1817, as a student of Protestant theology, he gave his trial sermon. After the Wartburg festival he continued his studies in Jena under the antisemitic Professors Fries, Heinrich Luden and Lorenz Oken.[45] Sand was a member of the inner circle of the student fraternity known as the *Urburschenschaft*, which sought to replace the existing regionally based student organisations with a universal German one. Under the influence of another antisemitic professor, Karl Follen (1796–1840),[46] he joined the group of the *Unbedingten* (the Uncompromising), who promoted the 'uncompromising deed', including politically motivated murder. Any act performed in the interest of the fatherland was legitimate. The *Unbedingten* saw them-selves as the cadres of a coming 'German revolution'.[47]

Kotzebue was neither a member of the government nor a capitalist. What made him a target? A look at Ludwig Börne's theatre reviews reveals that Kotzebue was by far the most successful playwright in Germany at the time. His plays were performed far more frequently than all of Schiller's and Goethe's dramas together. As director of the Weimar court theatre Goethe even put on more of Kotzebue's plays than his own. Beethoven and Schubert set Kotzebue's libretti to music.[48] The ultranationalists had several reasons to hate Kotzebue. Like many other Germans, the son of a Weimar merchant had made a career in the Russian service. He married the daughter of a Russian lieutenant general, was elevated to the aristocracy and appointed assessor at the Oberster Gerichtshof (high court of appeals) in Reval (present-day Tallinn). In 1785 he became president of the Magistrat of the governorate of Estonia. His career made him a wealthy man. He wrote his novels and plays on the side.[49] His son Otto von Kotzebue (1787–1846) was also in the Russian service and spent the years 1815–1818 on his much-noted second circumnavigation of the globe.[50] Russia was a guarantor of peace in Europe and sought to exert influence as a great power. For that they needed personnel.

In 1816, Kotzebue was given a position at the Russian foreign ministry and in 1817 he was sent to Germany as a consul general. The accusations of espionage appear ridiculous against this back-ground. The real bone of contention was his attack on the student societies and gymnastic associations as breeding grounds for revolu-tion in his *Literarisches Wochenblatt*, and his mockery of *Turnvater* Jahn and the nationalist movement.[51] He was also one of the few writers in Germany to openly champion full legal equality for Jews.[52] In comparison to his German nationalist critics, Kotzebue was 'an enlightened, independent and liberal spirit'.[53] These were the reasons why a copy of his *Geschichte des deutschen Reichs* was burned at the Wartburg festival.[54]

The significance of the gymnastic associations must be stressed in this connection. Since 1811, *Turnvater* Jahn had placed his sporting exercises in the framework of military education to create a foundation for the wars of liberty against the French occupiers. From that time on, outdoor gymnastic practice areas appeared all over Germany, often complete with instructors from Berlin. Together with their knowledge of gymnastic equipment and exercises, these apostles of Jahn also spread his ideology: a blend of patriotism, nostalgia for the Middle Ages (Jahn incorrectly derived the term 'Turnen' from the chivalric tournaments), republicanism and a hatred of Jews and the French. Wherever they went, Jahn's emissaries met local fanatics – Maßmann, for example, met Sand in Erlangen in 1816 – and used these contacts to create a broad network of zealous nationalists. With the success of the Wars of Liberation, proponents of the gymnastic movement (*Turner*) gained great popularity with the public and even with some governments. Gymnastic meets became mass events in which youth as well as younger adults from all social strata participated, at least as spectators. Jahn urged his disciples to use the events for propaganda purposes, supplementing the physical exercises with lectures.

The *Turner* began organising several years before the student societies, which is why they became the political leaders. At Jahn's instigation they organised the annual ceremonies throughout Germany to commemorate the 18th of October, the day of the victory over Napoleon near Leipzig in 1813. Nearly all of the protagonists of the Wartburg festival can be found among the organisers of the local gymnastic groups. For that reason, some governments began to proceed against the *Turner* immediately after the festival. It now became evident that they were playing a role in political assaults. The gymnastic groups represented a greater danger than the student societies, for in 1818, when political parties did not yet exist, there were already some 12,000 organised *Turner* in Germany, and their organisation extended far beyond the academic milieu. Although the majority of these gymnasts were only interested in sport, they nevertheless formed a pool of possible recruits for political terrorism.[55]

Terror threats and the fear of revolution

Friedrich von Gentz had already raised the spectre of revolution on the occasion of the general mobilisation in Prussia to expel the French armies from central Europe. In a diary entry of 7 October 1813 he wrote: 'The spirit awakened by the universal resistance to French domination in Germany, powerfully heightened by Stein's proclamations, which, proceeding from Prussia in particular, had grown to such a degree that the War of Liberation rather resembled a War of Liberty, gave occasion for earnest reflections and worries for the future, and in those discussions I especially proposed the idea that toppling a despotism based on revolution might lead backward to further revolution rather than to true restoration.'[56] The entirety of politics after the victory over Napoleon may be understood as an attempt to contain the threat of revolution. In keeping with the Tambora Crisis, revolutions during this period were often compared to the danger of a volcanic eruption.[57] If people believed that the 'end to all wars' and the provisions of the Congress of Vienna would rein in these primal forces, they would be proven wrong in several respects. First of all, the Wars of Liberation had awakened hopes of political reform. Second, a generation of university students had been excited and brutalised by participation in the wars. And finally, everywhere in Europe tensions rose during the course of the Tambora Crisis. Every minor rebellion and every assassination attempt fomented government fears of revolution.

The spring of 1819 had begun with death threats made by radical students against the Russian diplomat Alexander von Stourdza (1791–1854), a Greek from the entourage of Tsar Alexander I, who propagated the ideology of the Holy Alliance.[58] In a pamphlet, Stourdza had referred to the German universities as hotbeds of revolution and called for them to be more tightly controlled.[59] In 1819, having just married the daughter of the well-known German physician and author Christoph Wilhelm Hufeland (1762–1836),[60] he escaped the threat of murder by fleeing to Russia, as the Prussian envoy Varnhagen von Ense noted.[61]

The murder of Kotzebue was met with especial interest in Vienna against the background of the threats against Stourdza. When the news arrived on 31 March, Friedrich von Gentz, secretary to the Congress of Vienna and advisor to Metternich, wrote two diary entries on the 'atrocity in Mannheim'. And in the days that followed he returned to it repeatedly, particularly since he received a death threat of his own on 2 April, in an anonymous letter 'in which I was reminded of Kotzebue's fate!'[62] Gentz, too, had an inkling of why he was being targeted: he had close contacts with Vienna's leading Jewish families (Eskeles, Arnstein, Herz, Rothschild, Ephraim and Levi), and had promoted their interests in legal equality at the Congress of Vienna.[63]

The terrorist act in Mannheim aroused horror among governments, the aristocracy and bourgeoisie and probably also many ordinary people. A diplomat in Munich wrote that 'The murder of Kotzebue has caused an extraordinary stir here, since Sand is Bavarian. The ministry has begun investigations about whether he was in league with other zealots (*Schwärmer*) who encouraged him to commit the deed.'[64] Sand was a Bavarian because his home town of Wunsiedel had become Bavarian shortly before. He had been born a Prussian and lived in Berlin for a time. He had studied in Tübingen (Württemberg) and Jena (Saxe-Weimar-Eisenach). And much to the dismay of the grand duke of Baden he had committed his murder in Mannheim, the former capital of electoral Palatine, but now part of Baden. The murderer had roots in many German territories, but it was Grand Duke Karl of Baden who had to sign his death sentence. He was not keen in the first place, but in this case he also feared the vengeance of radical students, as he rather naively explained to the Prussian ambassador, 'I cannot pardon him, and if I have him executed – is it not the case, my dear Varnhagen – that I must brace myself for some little student to shed my blood next?'[65]

In July 1819 the Idstein apothecary Carl Löning (1791–1819), a member of the German Society in Idstein and in contact with the radical student group the Gießen Blacks, to which his brother belonged,[66] made an attempt on the life of Carl Friedrich Emil von Ibell (1780–1834), president of the government of the duchy of Nassau. Löning intended to stab him to death and then kill himself, following Sand's model.[67] In the literature this attack is often portrayed as rather minor, but it can also be viewed quite differently. Unlike Stourdza, Kotzebue and Gentz, Ibell was no 'reactionary' author, but the leading statesman of a German territory, a liberal reformer who swept aside aristocratic privileges, abolished serfdom, introduced freedom of movement and played a decisive role in introducing a constitution to the duchy of Nassau. What did the Hessian liberal have in common with the so-called reactionaries? He, too, was a proponent of Jewish emancipation.[68]

Metternich expected that he and his family would become the targets of assassination attempts, but he did not let fear guide his actions. Instead, he was determined to capitalise on the fear of revolution in the smaller German states.[69] In the summer of 1819 representatives of the governments of many German territories were considering stricter controls on developments that had unnerved them for years: secret societies, student associations, prophets of doom and religious fanatics, but also the constitutional movement and the freedom of the press that went along with it, about which Gentz prepared a written report for the meeting of ministers in Carlsbad.

It was worrying that Sand's supporters were busy constructing the image of a 'murderer out of patriotism'. People well into the ranks of the Protestant middle classes expressed sympathy for his terrorist act, although it was hard to paint the murder of a playwright as tyrannicide. Even a few professors with no involvement in the assassination, such as the Berlin theologian Wilhelm Martin Leberecht de Wette (1780–1849), showed themselves to be on the side of the murderer. And there was a minority among students and young academics who, if we are to believe their diary entries, saw Sand's suicide attack as the signal for a general uprising, a revolution that would cleanse Germany of all things 'foreign' and pave the way for political unity.[70] They included authors who hoped not just for the expulsion of tyrants but also for the eradication of the Jews, an aim they frequently propagated in their writings. It is hard to see such rabble-rousers as being anything but demagogues.[71]

The Hep-Hep riots in Würzburg

The outbreak of antisemitic riots, in which xenophobia, envy of economic success and aversion to the new governments of the states formed in 1815 came together, occurred in this context. Politicians were held responsible for improving the legal status of Jews, which allowed for Jewish social mobility. The starting point for the so-called 'Hep-Hep' riots was Würzburg, where a secret society had already set fires and issued death threats against representatives of the state and Jewish usurers and profiteers (*Wucherer*) in late 1817 and early 1818. These conflicts re-emerged publicly in 1819 during the continuing economic crisis.

They were unleashed by a formal petition of 2 April 1819 to the first Bavarian Diet by the Würzburg banker Salomon Hirsch, requesting full civil rights for Jews.[72] As had occurred three years before in Frankfurt am Main, this petition sparked a public debate. In the Würzburg *Intelligenzblatt*, a Rechtspraktikant (articled clerk) by the name of Thomas August Scheuring sharply attacked the law professor Sebald Brendel (1782–1844), whom he took for the true author of the petition, and denied that Jews had any right to address demands to the state. Brendel responded in the same newspaper on 15 and 21 July and accused Scheuring of intolerance, inhumanity and anti-Christian views as well as of drawing conclusions while clearly knowing nothing about Jews. Scheuring's insulting reply followed on 29 August, in which he claimed to represent the viewpoint of

184

the majority of Würzburgers.[73] Scheuring, about whom no further biographical details could be found, adopted plainly racist positions, since he did not associate Jewishness with religion, but, following the antisemitic professors Rühs and Fries, spoke disparagingly of 'Asiatic aliens' (asiatische Fremdlinge) who could never become part of the 'native nation' (einheimische Nation).[74] Scheuring used the standard argument of all xenophobes, namely that the 'foreigners . . . rob local, native, national man of his livelihood, his bread and his upkeep, and settle in at the expense of citizens and reproduce at a strikingly rapid rate'.[75]

We can assume that the banker Hirsch's petition had supporters in the highest circles of Bavarian society, since, along with his brother Jakob von Hirsch (1765–1740), who had gained a patent of nobility in 1818, he was among the most important creditors of the Bavarian royal household and state.[76] The king's governors in the Lower Main district, President von Asbeck and Councillor Ernst von Halbritter (1775–1836), and City Commissioner Franz Anton Gessert, supported immediate legal equality for Jews, making them an avant-garde even within the administration.[77] Several university professors, including the jurist Wilhelm Josef Behr, who had also published on the causes of the famine of 1817, also actively promoted Jewish emancipation.[78]

In a letter to his parents of 5 August 1819, the student August von Platen reported on the 'uprising by the rabble against the Jews, the centre of which was Domgasse' (where he lived):

> It began on the night of the 2nd, when it consisted however solely of shouting (Hep Hep, which is the slogan), but on the night of the 3rd the tumult was fierce, most Jews had their windows broken and they were maltreated in the streets. In the crush, a local citizen was shot dead by a police officer. Yesterday at midday the wrath of the rabble was at its height. The rich Jews left the city accompanied by curses. One of them, called Vorchheimer, had his front door blown open, his house looted and his furniture thrown out the windows. This evening the garrison moved out and prevented acts of violence. The cries and crowds in Domgasse lasted until 9.30. Then the cavalry broke them up by force and the infantry pursued individual rioters with their rifle butts. Professor Brendel, who had written in favour of the Jews, fled to Bamberg. This morning, as I write these words, things are almost completely peaceful again.[79]

Varnhagen provided an explanation of the cries of 'Hep Hep': 'Our scholars were, to be sure, on the spot right away and traced the word Hep to the time of the Crusaders, who purportedly marked their crosses with the letters H.e.p., or "Hierosolyma est perdita" (Jerusalem is lost). However, in what secret pantries this mediaeval acronym was kept fresh, only to be revived all of a sudden among the lowest class of the populace, is something they have left unexplained.'[80]

In fact the destruction was not only to property. As in the previous year, threats of murder were issued. A report of 4 August notes that the cries of Hep Hep were combined with explicit calls to 'Beat the Jews to death!'[81] The merchant Abraham Löb Brückner barely escaped with his life when the mob burst into his shop, where he had spent the night to protect his wares. Elieser Kraft wrote in his diary of the danger to Jewish life and limb. The main target was the splendid house of the banker Jakob von Hirsch, a symbol of the economic success and social rise of Jews in Würzburg.[82] The Würzburg city police failed (or were unwilling) to contain the unrest on their own, and only the arrival of the Bavarian military put an end to the terrible episode. The royal guard regiment made short work of the rebels and shortly thereafter arrested their ringleader, the Würzburg civil servant (*Kreiskassensekretär*) Hermann Fleckenstein. At a meeting of the district government, Director Sebastian Andreas Stumpf levied serious accusations against the Würzburg city commandant, who had not intervened in time but gone out for a stroll instead.[83] While the district government was still in session, the unrest broke out in the morning hours on 4 August and numerous Jewish businesses and homes were attacked again.[84]

The government of the Lower Main district responded quickly and sent troops to put the rebellion down. Stumpf and Gessert agreed that the antisemites needed to be suppressed energetically. Fighting broke out during the arrests, in the course of which the Würzburg merchant Josef Konrad was killed by a stray police bullet.[85] Later that morning the troops succeeded in ending the pogrom, while the Würzburg master cobbler Lambrecht mortally wounded a soldier. He was arrested and later sentenced to sixteen years in prison. In the days that followed Gessert ordered more arrests, mostly of inhabitants of Würzburg.[86] On 6 August King Maximilian I Joseph approved all measures by the district government and authorised it to deploy 'all the powers of military force' in case of similar events in future. The king warned the municipal government that 'attacks of this nature' could never be tolerated in Bavaria, and threatened serious consequences in case of repetition. The garrison should remain in the city until all members of the city government, municipal representatives, district and guild chairmen had pledged to cooperate actively in future to prevent such incidents.[87] The king ordered that the Jews be compensated for all losses. These measures proved successful. All those who had fled returned after a few days. In the end, twenty-three people were arrested. Two people were killed during the events, one soldier and one civilian. No Jews were among the dead.[88]

There is general agreement that the riots were fomented by Würzburg merchants and backed by the town council, which recruited its members from the same circles. The city government stood in sharp opposition to the representatives of the Bavarian state. The background to this contrast was Würzburg's recent annexation to Bavaria by the Congress of Vienna after centuries as the capital of an independent state, most recently of the grand duchy of Würzburg.[89] The pain of losing this autonomy was intensified by the obligation to adopt Bavarian legislation: the Jewish Mandate of 1813, which allowed for economic equality and the opening of public shops, went into force in Würzburg in 1816, and additional legal improvements and institutions followed in 1817, 1818 (constitution) and 1819 (parliament). The Würzburg upper classes directly associated the settlement of Jewish merchants – and thus of unwelcome competitors – with Bavarian state policy. The riots, which drew their dynamism from the existential hardships of the Tambora Crisis, were anti-Bavarian and anti-Jewish in equal measure.[90]

Continuing bloodlust

The antisemitic attitudes of these groups in Würzburg persisted even after the suppression of the uprising. This is evident from the printed threatening letters that were distributed in the city in large numbers on 27 August and 2 September 1819. These letters warned Jews of their impending 'annihilation'. Two individuals were even mentioned by name as targets: the merchant Samuel Aron Fränkel and the pawn-broker ('usurer') Abraham Seligmann. The second letter hints at the existence of a secret society 'of more than 3,000', which did not fear even death if it served 'the universal good cause': 'Dagger and fire will soon consume what gold and other bribes have heretofore supported.'[91] It is impossible to know whether there were other suicide assassins – like Sand and Löning – or whether people merely pretended that they existed. There was certainly racism and bloodlust, however, as well as arson attacks. Professor Brendel continued to receive specific threats. A printed threat of murder, the 'Appeal to the Young Men of Würzburg', is signed with the words, 'Emulators and executors of Sand and Löning', thus alluding to that year's suicide attacks.[92]

On 3 September, a letter to the government of the Lower Main district asserted that the opinion people at home and abroad had of the state of public safety in Würzburg could not be a matter of indifference to the city, since this affected attendance at the university as well as the livelihood of the citizenry. The degree to which state suspicions had grown in the meantime is clear from a decree threatening the city and its publicans with high fines if they did not take severe measures against the dissemination of printed threats and support criminal investigations of them. Publicans were threatened with the loss of their licences and the city with the expansion of the garrison. A further letter of 6 September warned of the imposition of martial law and the withdrawal of self-administration. The government's patience was at an end. That it had chosen the proper targets is evident from the sudden disappearance of antisemitic letters in Würzburg in mid-September 1819, probably because of the threatened government sanctions.[93]

In the period that followed, threatening letters appeared elsewhere instead, for example in Lengfurt and Heidingsfeld, and were backed up by actual arson attacks. Heidingsfeld, now part of Würzburg, had been the rabbinical centre of Lower Franconia since the late eighteenth century and at the time of the Hep-Hep riots was home to the second-largest Jewish community in the kingdom of Bavaria, after Fürth.[94] There had already been tumults in Heidingsfeld, the destination of many Jews fleeing Würzburg, on 4 August. The local mayor had bravely stood up to the rioters though. In the surrounding region, however, there were four attempts to set 'Jew villages' on fire. In two smaller towns near Würzburg – Rimpar and Leinach – the synagogues were destroyed by agitated locals. On 12 August the unrest spilled over into the Franconian cities of Bamberg, Ansbach and Bayreuth, themselves former capitals of small territories, now the district capitals of the Upper Main (Upper Franconia) and the Rezat (Middle Franconia). This meant that the pogrom movement had spread to all of the main towns in Franconia. With the addition of Regensburg, this also included the capital of the Regen district (Upper Palatinate), while the Old Bavarian districts (Isar and Lower Danube) and Bavarian Swabia (Iller and Danube districts) were spared.

The pogroms spread

The riots with their battle cry of 'Hep Hep' spread westward from Franconia. The unrest in the free city of Frankfurt am Main, the centre of one of Europe's largest Jewish communities, began on 5 August.

188

After three days, the provocations culminated in an open insurrection, during which houses and businesses in the Jewish quarter were stormed and ravaged. The Nördlingen artist Johann Michael Voltz (1784–1858) produced an engraving of the scene for the Nuremberg publisher of pictorial broadsheets Friedrich Campe; this was not, however, based on his own experience.[95] The Frankfurt riots reached a high point on 10 August. As in Würzburg, the preferred targets were the homes of rich Jews, such as the palace of the banker Amschel Mayer Rothschild (1773–1840),[96] whom Emperor Francis I of Austria had only recently (in 1817) elevated to the hereditary baronage. The fact that bankers were repeatedly attacked during the pogroms may remind us that banks have often been preferred targets during social crises of more recent vintage as well, even where, as in the case of the European Central Bank, this made little sense. While nowadays banks are usually anonymous institutions, at the time of the Tambora Crisis in central Europe banking was dominated by Jewish financiers.

According to an account in the London *Times*, more than 100 coaches carrying the families of wealthy Jews left the city for Hanau and Offenbach on the morning of 11 August. After the Frankfurt police failed, perhaps by choice, to end the unrest, the president of the Diet of the German Confederation, the Austrian ambassador Count Johann Rudolf von Buol-Schauenstein (1763–1834), ordered the deployment of troops from Mainz. It took days to bring the insurrection under control, but even then calls for violence against Jews continued to be issued until the Prussian and Austrian envoys to the Diet increased the pressure. On 14 August the ministers of the various German lands conferred in Carlsbad under the chairmanship of Austrian Chancellor of State Metternich about the most effective means of proceeding against the antisemitic mob. As Frankfurt was preparing for Goethe's seventieth birthday on 28 August, the Jews returned and order was restored. The perpetrators were never prosecuted, however.[97]

The riots found emulators in Fulda (Electoral Hesse), Kassel and above all in Darmstadt (grand duchy of Hesse), where serious violence erupted on 12 and 13 August. Here the tensions lasted weeks. In early September the government still had to take measures to protect Jews. In Marburg, too, antisemitic flyers containing death threats were still being circulated in October.[98] On 12 August the Jews were driven out of Meiningen, the capital of the duchy of Saxe-Meiningen in Thuringia. In the kingdom of Saxony, Leipzig and Dresden were affected. The liberal grand duchy of Baden, which had large Jewish minorities, was especially hard-hit; apart from the

189

Johann Michael Voltz, The Hep-Hep riots in Frankfurt am Main,
August 1819

capital Karlsruhe, the towns of Mannheim, Pforzheim, Bruchsal,
Buehl and Niedergrombach became the scenes of unrest beginning
on 18 August. Grand Duke Karl of Baden demonstratively moved
from his palace to that of the embattled Jewish banker Salomon
von Haber (1768–1839) in Karlsruhe. Especially severe rioting broke
out in Heidelberg, perhaps because the local representative of state
power, Governor Pfister, supported the insurgents. Here the Jews
were defended by 200 sabre-wielding students under the leadership of
two professors, the theologian Carl Daub (1765–1836) and the jurist
Anton Friedrich Justus Thibaut (1772–1840),[99] who bravely faced
down the looters.[100] Following the example of the Bavarian king, the
grand duke demanded compensation and a criminal investigation of
the incidents. But those prosecuted were mainly youthful hooligans,
as a newspaper sarcastically noted: 'The only perpetrators were riffraff and street urchins, they will say here as elsewhere. But it remains
a mystery what it was that so alarmed the ragamuffins in particular
in so many cities.'[101]

In the largest German states – Prussia and Austria – individual
Hep-Hep rioters were rigorously punished and any emulation was
nipped in the bud. In Vienna, Munich and Berlin there were occa-

sional calls of Hep Hep but no riots, which was also the case in Cologne and other large German cities. Some large towns in east Prussia such as Königsberg and Danzig were affected, however, along with Grünberg and Breslau in Silesia. And there were incidents in the Prussian Rhineland in Koblenz, Kreuznach, Hamm, Kleve and Düsseldorf, the seat of the Prussian district government, where on 28 August the Jews were threatened with a bloodbath in the manner of the St Bartholomew's Day massacre.[102] To make matters worse, rumours of ritual murder were spread in Dormagen on 12 October.[103]

Hep-Hep riots also took place in Krakow, Helsinki, Güstrow and above all in Hamburg, where the uprising went on for four days. There, however, the Jews defended themselves. The Jews who had fled Hamburg were protected by Danish troops in Altona. After a rumour that the Hamburg Jews intended to move to Copenhagen, such serious rioting broke out in the latter city that King Frederick VI of Denmark (1768–1839) was forced to flee. After a sailors' mutiny the unrest expanded into an insurrection that extended to cities such as Odense, Helsingör, Hillerod, etc. In the end, hussars and uhlans loyal to the king prevailed over the mutinous troops. Unlike in Germany, Protestant pastors in Denmark supported the Jews from the pulpit. There are some mentions of the rioting spreading to Alsace, Bohemia and the Netherlands, but there is no evidence of this.[104]

The unrest and murderous actions were perpetrated by those on the losing side of the famine: the unemployed, commercial clerks, artisans and indebted peasants who blamed Jews for their suffering and took the opportunity to vent their pent-up rage. The political scientist Eleonore Sterling (1925–1968) spoke of a 'displacement of social protest'.[105] But here the explanation is perhaps not quite so simple, because the arsonists were presumably ideologised by the agitation of the preceding famine years and were familiar with the racist antisem-itism propagated at the time. Rahel Varnhagen wrote in 1819:

> For three years now I have been saying that the Jews will come under attack; I have witnesses . . . The insinuations that have spread through all the newspapers for years; Professors Fries and Rühs, and all the others; Arnim, Brentano, 'Our Crowd' and even loftier personages with prejudices. It is not religious hatred: they do not love their own, how can they hate others; – to what end all the words I could amass end-lessly; it is simply evil, in deed and motive; and not the deed of the common people, whom they taught to shout Hep.[106]

In small German states like Hesse-Darmstadt and Electoral Hesse, Baden, Bavaria and Württemberg the violence often deliberately

191

targeted Jews involved in the grain and cattle trade as well as the business of providing small loans, to whom many people were in debt. While the police often stood idly by as the rabble-rousers attacked, the unrest was ultimately quelled everywhere by the military.[107]

The Carlsbad Decrees

Against the backdrop of the Hep-Hep riots, which endangered lives in many German and Danish cities, the ministers of the German federal states met in the Bohemian spa town of Carlsbad (now Karlovy Vary) from 6 to 31 August 1819 to discuss the political unrest in the German Confederation. The impetus for these meetings was the suicide attack on Kotzebue by the student Sand, as historians have stressed rather one-sidedly. It is important, however, to recall the series of murder threats and assassination attempts which helped lend meaning to Sand's act in the first place. In the course of the violent Hep-Hep riots in August, threats to murder additional 'friends of the Jews' and Jewish representatives were made in many German cities. There were hundreds if not thousands of death threats. That the fear of assassination was not exaggerated had been clear since the failed attempt on the life of the English prince regent, the future George IV, on 28 January 1817,[108] and was underlined by the murder of the Bourbon Prince Charles Ferdinand d'Artois, duc de Berry (1778–1820) on 13 February 1820.[109]

It was not far from Carlsbad in Bohemia to Franconia. Just past the border is the town of Wunsiedel, the home town of the assassin Sand, followed by the towns in which anti-Jewish pogroms took place while the ministers were meeting: Bayreuth, Hollfeld, Ebermannstadt, Pottenstein, etc. In their consultations, the ministers of the ten largest German states assembled in Carlsbad – most of them, like the ministers of state of Prussia and Austria, Prince von Hardenberg and Prince von Metternich, active proponents of Jewish emancipation – concluded that action had to be taken against the demagogues fomenting terrorism as well as their organisations. They formulated measures to this end in the so-called Carlsbad Decrees of 31 August 1819, which were intended to target the milieu of the murderers. The Austrian minister of state Metternich took advantage of the prevailing mood to push through the Decrees at the Diet of the German Confederation in Frankfurt am Main on 20 September 1819. The ministers took matters even further, however, and placed the liberal and nationalist movements under general suspicion. They introduced four laws – a university law, a press law, an investigative law and a federal ordinance to enforce the decrees – to institute surveillance of the press and the universities and to prohibit the student associations (*Burschenschaften*) and the gymnastic practice areas. Meanwhile, a Zentralkommission zur Untersuchung verrätischer Umtriebe (central commission to investigate traitorous activities) with headquarters in Mainz was founded to coordinate prosecutions on a federal level.[110]

Standard histories such as Hans Ulrich Wehler's (1931–2014) *Deutsche Gesellschaftsgeschichte* have interpreted the Carlsbad Decrees as an overreaction to the suicide attack in Mannheim or even as the dark machinations of a great reactionary conspiracy.[111] We may ask what Wehler meant when he referred to the suicide attacks and antisemitic excesses as 'events of third-rate significance'. The notion of a 'secret conference in Carlsbad' or a 'Carlsbad conspiracy' makes about as much sense as calling a G7 or G20 meeting of the leading heads of state a secret conference. In those days all eyes were on Carlsbad, and the newspapers reported freely on the meetings. Everyone knew that the ministers – for instance Goethe – went there to take the waters nearly every summer. The complaint that 'free-thinking, liberal men with blameless pasts' were forced to undergo 'one disgraceful humiliation after another' can scarcely be applied to the sponsors of terrorism in 1819. It was precisely the most liberal states such as the duchy of Nassau, whose chancellor was the victim of an assassination attempt, or Baden, that 'distinguished themselves by overzealousness in applying the Carlsbad Decrees'. It is surely no coincidence that Georg Wilhelm Friedrich Hegel (1770–1831) justi-fied the persecution of the demagogues in the preface to his *Philosophy of Right* as self-defence by the state. It was also no accident that he attacked Fries, the prophet of murder, head-on – a man who wished to see the state founded on a subjective faith and who permitted or even promoted the killing of those who professed another religion.[112]

The misjudgements of historians, which we can recognise more clearly in our own age of terrorism, largely followed the liberalism of the time. The latter, however – much like the conservatism of the time – pursued political strategies in which the victims of terrorism were of secondary importance. It is of course tempting to succumb to the sources. Even liberal Jews and supporters of emancipation preferred not to recall the antisemitic riots. Börne and Heinrich Heine attacked the restriction of freedom. The Carlsbad Decrees indeed signalled a limitation of liberal achievements introduced just a few years before, often by the same politicians. That this change did occur, however, should not be attributed to 'the incoherent delusions' of conservative politicians, but rather to the new states' massive problems in maintaining order, which were of a magnitude that no constitutional state could ignore even today. Thomas Nipperdey (1927–1992) quite correctly referred to the 'Jacobin-totalitarian penchant' of some opponents of the regime. According to him, this also applied to groups within the gymnastic movement and the student associations: 'This radicalism did have revolutionary traits and had the potential within it for the sort of terrorist direct action which has been witnessed in more recent history.'[113]

Against the background of the Tambora Crisis, the Hep-Hep riots in Germany and the widespread unrest and willingness to resort to violence in many regions of Europe, we need to view the Carlsbad Decrees with different eyes. The measures restricting freedom of association, assembly and the press in the German Confederation did not stand in isolation. Similar laws were enacted around the same time in Italy, France and England, since all of these countries were confronted not merely with ideologues calling for action but also with violent organisations that reminded the ruling elites as well as segments of the public of the terror of the French Revolution. The restrictions of civil rights had little to do with the aims of the Holy Alliance. Instead, they represented a reaction to current events that appeared significant to many contemporaries. To be sure, in the struggle for civil liberties these measures later appeared in a less favourable light. The limits on civil liberties were therefore postponed in some countries or implemented only superficially, and often lifted again after only a few years.[114]

The depression of 1819

The famine of 1816/17 had another effect that has gone largely unnoticed: the great depression of 1819. Since the historians of finance and banking who have studied this economic crisis had no interest in famines, the two phenomena have barely been considered together. Conversely, scholars of famine and social protest have had little sympathy with the concerns of investors who had money to burn or large landowners worried about the decline in land and property values after the fall in grain prices. Banking historians have viewed the depression of 1819 purely as a financial crisis in which bursting speculative bubbles and tumbling profit expectations led to the collapse of many enterprises.[115] Others have seen that it began with an overproduction crisis in which the markets were flooded with agricultural products that could no longer be sold. This led to declining incomes for agricultural producers, falling liquidity and diminished buying power among small producers – the farmers. The prices for land and buildings plummeted. Many people could no longer pay the interest on their debts and ended up in debtors' prison. Others had to sell their land and – in the USA – try their luck out west. But the great 'land rush' came to an initial end with the panic of 1819.[116] A decline in financial resources and the prospect of profits led to more dismissals and rising unemployment. In this way, the crisis of overproduction turned into a more general economic crisis or – by another name – a depression. And once again this had nothing to do with the Napoleonic Wars,[117] but was one of the aftershocks of the Tambora Crisis.

The most interesting thing about this depression was its international character. It affected the Russian growing areas in the Baltic as well as Novorossiya with its port at Odessa, whose export services were now less in demand. It affected trade and commerce in central Europe, where merchants directed petitions to the new monarchs or parliaments,[118] and where people sought explanations for economic fluctuations and their significance for future commercial, manufacturing, tax and tariff policy.[119] Naturally the grain blockades and tariff policy now appeared in a new light, and the conflict between free traders and mercantilists entered a new round.[120] Since the famine, people in central and western Europe had tried desperately to boost agricultural production, and the same was true in North America, where within a few months entire new states came under cultivation. Against the background of a more favourable climate – the effects of the Tambora eruption were no longer directly apparent in 1819 – all of these efforts combined led to serious overproduction. And the rapid expansion of trade networks and the improvement of communication channels and methods produced an international economic crisis in which scarcity in one region could not offset overproduction in another.

While societies were still grappling with the health effects of the Tambora Crisis – with malaria, pellagra, typhus and cholera – they already confronted a new crisis. To be sure, crisis managers did not always mention this connection, but they did hint at it. Matthew Carey, for example, estimated that as many people were affected by the crisis as had been during the 'year without a summer', namely one-third of the population of the USA, or about 3 million people.[121] Once again, small farmers who lived from the sale of their produce faced a severe threat to their livelihood. The imagery used by lobbyists recalls the time of the 'Yankee Chill', for instance when Samuel Hopkins, president of the Genesee Agricultural Society, noted 'My first wish would be ... to speak in a tone that should rouse the tenants of every log-house in these counties, and make them stand aghast at the prospect of families naked – children standing in the winter's storm – and the fathers without coats and shoes to enable them to perform the necessary labours of the inclement season.'[122] Once again, soup kitchens had to be set up in American cities like Philadelphia and New York, and the New York Society for the Prevention of Pauperism (SPP) was working at full capacity. Newspapers appealed for clothing donations for the poor and shoe donations for children who could no longer go to school for lack of them.[123]

In 1817, when promoting emigration to the USA, Birkbeck had written, 'Land will long be at a low price, but as produce hardly keeps pace with the population the latter is proportionately dear. Therefore agriculture is and will be a safe and profitable occupation.'[124] Two years later, this prognosis no longer applied. Prices for agricultural products had fallen precipitously and small farmers – and most immigrants – found themselves in dire straits. The effects of the crisis were similar to those of two years before: many people had to mortgage or sell their property. The beneficiaries included the Bank of the United States, whose growing might people watched with unease, since entire communities were deeply in debt, as Senator Benton of Missouri noted: 'I know towns, yea cities . . . where this bank already appears as an engrossing proprietor. All the flourishing cities of the West are mortgaged to this money power . . . They are in the jaws of the monster! A lump of butter in the mouth of a dog! One gulp, one swallow, and all is gone!'[125] Many blamed the banks for the crisis. The richest private banker in America, Stephen Girard (1750–1831), in contrast, blamed the borrowers who had not used their capital wisely enough. Manufacturers and land buyers had incurred high debts in the hope of high yields. Others in turn located the cause in national indebtedness as a result of the long wars.[126]

The Monroe administration declared itself not responsible and – despite the concerns expressed behind closed doors – took refuge in the hope that the crisis would pass and 'time and patience' would heal all wounds, as John Quincy Adams put it in his memoirs.[127] The reaction in the major newspapers was not much different. 'Keep cool' was the motto, even though some people feared the impending exacerbation of class conflict. The country was essentially healthy and could take this opportunity to return to the simplicity of its forefathers. In this way, sickness could be exchanged for health, excess for moderation and vice for virtue. Traders would have to be satisfied with smaller profits, and workers with lower wages in keeping with the new price levels, which had fallen by about one-third. Self-help was the order of the day, but also government assistance.[128] As in every crisis, the hour of the protectionists had come. Along with spending cuts in the bureaucracy and military there were discussions of changes to taxes and tariffs. But there were also genuine improvements. Creditor protection was increased and public savings banks were established in the states to protect small depositors.[129]

Most important for immigrants was the improvement of protection for debtors. It was no longer as easy to send them to debtors' prison, and in many states imprisonment for trifling sums was abolished altogether. Debtors' assets were protected against banks or creditors who sought to exploit their plight. A waiting period of two years was instituted for the compulsory sale of land, during which time the debtor could recover and save his property. If a distress sale still proved necessary, a state agency was to guarantee a fair price. Another result was the lowering of land prices in the areas of settlement in the west, which was combined with the shift to cash payments. This measure reduced the chances of falling into debt, and the westward expansion of the USA was further fuelled – in competition with Spain, England and Russia – during a decisive phase.[130]

The Peterloo Massacre and the Six Acts

In the United Kingdom, the conflict between political radicalism and conservative politics focused on the Corn Laws escalated in 1819. It was joined by the struggle for parliamentary reform, since the existing Parliament elected by restricted suffrage clearly favoured the interests of large landowners. Cruikshank mocked the increasing radicalism of the demagogues by depicting them as a huge, grotesque monster, a walking guillotine, whose massive mouth spewed flames and whose teeth dripped with blood. It also holds a dagger in its hand and cries out 'I'm a coming! I'm a coming! I shall have you . . . come all to me that are troubled with money & I warrant I'll make you easy!' Behind the giant guillotine march many smaller ones calling 'and a hunting we will go', an allusion to Henry 'Orator' Hunt. The 'heads of the nation' flee helter-skelter, led by the prince regent, whose wig flies off his head, followed by the Chancellor of the Exchequer, who cries out 'Never mind, so long as your head's on!' Lord Liverpool has already

George Cruikshank, A Radical Reformer, (ie) a Neck or Nothing Man!
Dedicated to the Heads of the Nation, London 1819

fallen on his face, and gold coins pour from his bag. Castlereagh
brings up the rear, looking over his shoulder and proclaiming 'Och by
the powers! And I don't like the looks of him atall atall.' The cartoon
bears the ironic title 'A radical reformer . . . Dedicated to the heads
of the nation.'

The conflict culminated at Peterloo, named in allusion to Napoleon's
defeat at Waterloo. The massacre committed by a cavalry unit against
people protesting the Corn Laws at St Peter's Fields in Manchester
on 16 August 1819 also became known as the Battle of Peterloo.[131]
Manchester was the centre of textile manufacturing in a region
(Lancashire) that industrialised early and where unemployment had
been particularly high since the Tambora Crisis, a circumstance that
factory owners exploited to cut wages. As elsewhere in England, the
high price of grain could not be reduced by imports because of the
Corn Laws. Widespread hunger fuelled the reform movement.

On Monday, 16 August, a hot, cloudless summer's day, an estimated 60,000–80,000 people gathered for a protest meeting, more
than had ever done so before. Orator Hunt was brought on to convince the crowd to support the political aims, as he had already

done at Spa Fields. Since the secret police had intercepted a letter warning that the heated atmosphere could easily lead to insurrection, a hussar regiment of 600 men was transferred to Manchester. Also present were several hundred infantry, 400 members of the Cheshire Yeomanry, 400 special constables and 120 cavalry. Apart from the usual weaponry, the artillery brought two six-pounder guns.[132]

The crowd gave Hunt a rousing welcome. Around noon the chairman of the magistrates gave the order to arrest Hunt. When the cavalry became stuck in the dense crowd, they lashed out with their sabres and blood flowed. After the arrest of the speaker and organisers, some protesters began to defend themselves by throwing stones, and the military commander in Manchester ordered the meeting to be dissolved. After the assembly had been dispersed with further bloodshed, street fighting and looting began, lasting into the next morning. There was also unrest in Stockport, Macclesfield and Oldham, from where many of the demonstrators had come. We do not know the exact number of dead and wounded, but scholars estimate fifteen dead, including three women. We also know of 654 injured, among them 168 women. One of the demonstrators mortally wounded at Peterloo, John Lees of Oldham, had survived Waterloo as a soldier. Before his death on 9 September he said that at Waterloo he had fought man to man, but the proceedings at Peterloo had been pure murder.[133]

News of these events spread like wildfire throughout Britain, with all of the newspapers reporting on them. Public opinion was against those responsible for the bloodbath. One week afterward, the editor of the *Manchester Observer*, who was close to the meeting's organisers, coined the term Peterloo, which has stuck ever since. His account sold so well that it was impossible to suppress.[134] On 25 August, the government gave orders to arrest the author.[135] Percy Bysshe Shelley, then sojourning in Italy, learnt of Peterloo after some delay, whereupon he penned a manifesto on the non-violent resistance that would vanquish tyranny.[136] He sent it to the publisher of the *Examiner*, but the latter was afraid to publish it since it accused several members of the Liverpool cabinet by name, among them Foreign Secretary Castlereagh, whose masque Murder wears, Home Secretary Sidmouth, clothed as Hypocrisy, or Lord Chancellor Eldon, garbed like Fraud. They are led by Anarchy, a skeleton with a crown. The poem, first published thirteen years later, contains verses of Shakespearean power ('Stand ye calm and resolute, Like a forest close and mute') and propagates the reconquest of liberty with the following words:

Rise like Lions after Slumber
In unvanquishable number,
Shake your chains to earth like dew
Which in sleep had fallen on you –
Ye are many – they are few.

The massacre has gone down in history as a crime perpetrated by the government. Cruikshank depicted it numerous times. One of his cartoons, in which soldiers ride across an open field brandishing sabres and indiscriminately mowing down men, women and children, bears the laconic title 'Manchester Heroes', which could refer either to the victims or to the army that won such a 'valiant' victory over unarmed civilians.[137] Although the number of dead was ultimately not very high, Peterloo became a turning point in English political culture, one which was remembered in a variety of ways, for example by the Anti-Corn Law League, and is still commemorated today.

The initial government response was to proceed against the press and suppress critical voices in the country. Orator Hunt was sentenced to thirty months in prison, and other participants were also incarcerated. The soldiers who perpetrated the massacre, in contrast,

George Cruikshank, A Free Born Englishman! The Admiration of the World!!! And the Envy of Surrounding Nations!!!!!, London 1819

were not merely acquitted but commended by the government and the prince regent. In November 1819, amid renewed fears of insurrection, the Six Acts were passed, laws that, against resistance from the liberal opposition, restricted freedom of speech, assembly and the press. These measures were at least as drastic as the Carlsbad Decrees in Germany. Cruikshank refers to them in his cartoon 'A Free Born Englishman! The Administration of the World!!! And the Envy of Surrounding Nations!!!!!' The etching shows that little remains of English liberties. John Bull stands in tattered clothes and shackles, a padlock through his mouth. At the right in the background we see a crowded debtors' prison; at the left, before the house from which he has been driven by tax collectors, sits a despairing mother with her dead children and a lifeless dog. John Bull's left foot rests on the Magna Charta, his right stands on the Bill of Rights, both of which have been taken from him. In the right foreground lies a Liberty cap, at the left the headsman's axe inscribed 'Law of Libel'.

The Cato Street conspiracy

Probably the greatest murder conspiracy of the era, which originated with one of the main protagonists of the 1816 Spa Fields Riots, illustrates how tense the atmosphere in England remained in 1820. Immediately following his release from prison in July 1817, Arthur Thistlewood reactivated the conspiratorial meetings. He had been further radicalised and was planning a new insurrection for 6 September, after the Bartholomew Fair in Smithfield. He wanted to blow up the Bank of England, occupy the post office – as centres of communication, post offices occupied a position similar to that of television stations in the twentieth century – and take over the artillery. After this plan was betrayed – and the authorities in fact knew from informers about every step the radicals took – the next attempted insurrection was set for 12 October 1817. These coup and assassination plans however destroyed the cohesion of the Spenceans. Reform politicians such as Henry Hunt wanted nothing to do with them, since the attack on the prince regent on 28 January 1817 had turned English public opinion against the conspirators.[138]

In October 1817 a plan was conceived to murder the prince regent and the members of the Privy Council, that is, the entire government, during a dinner. The plan was initially shelved after Thistlewood was imprisoned for one year for threatening Lord Sidmouth. When he was released at the end of May 1819 the thirteen leading members of the protest movement plotted to continue with the assassinations, organising public meetings and demonstrations in order to recruit more supporters. The events of Peterloo and the passing of the Six Acts contributed to the radicalisation process. The conspirators, who were aware that they were under surveillance, made contacts in the North, in Manchester and Lancashire. On 13 December 1819 they appointed an executive committee, which was to work out the details and seek an appropriate opportunity to murder the members of the government. After the assassinations they planned to occupy the Bank of England, set fire to public buildings, capture the Tower of London and form a provisional government. They also prepared a proclamation informing the population that the tyrants had been vanquished. Thistlewood expected a spontaneous uprising of the masses, which would make the revolution a success. They had even chosen a new seat of government, Mansion House, London's town hall.[139]

The death of George III on 29 January 1820 offered an opportunity to strike. A cabinet dinner in Grosvenor Square planned for 23 February was chosen as the occasion. Guns, bombs and hand grenades were to be stored the night before in an attic in nearby Cato Street. The government was informed about every stage of the

George Cruikshank, The Cato Street Conspirators, on the Memorable Night of the 23d of Feb.y 1820 [. . .], London 1820

202

planning, since it had an agent on the executive committee.[140] Most of the conspirators were arrested the evening before while preparing the weapons for the attack. Thistlewood killed a police officer and managed to flee during the tumult, but anonymous tips led to his arrest the next day. The charge was high treason. After a trial lasting three days he was condemned to death by hanging, and executed at Newgate on 1 May 1820. Thistlewood showed no remorse, but said at the end of his trial: 'Albion is still in the chains of slavery; I quit it without regret . . . My only sorrow is that the soil should be a theatre for slaves, for cowards, for despots.'[141] Four additional conspirators were executed with him, and other co-conspirators were sentenced to transportation to Australia.[142]

Protest movements in Scotland followed a similar development, parallel to but independent of those in England and with different emphases. The Scottish social protests against the Corn Laws had also begun with mass meetings in the famine year 1816. The largest of them, with some 40,000 participants, was held in Glasgow. Despite government employment programmes and poor relief the unrest spread throughout the country. As in England, the government succeeded in placing spies within the protest movement. A few conspirators were charged with high treason and transported to Australia as early as 1816 and 1817. In response to Peterloo, the protest movement was revived in Scotland as well and uprisings erupted in many towns in September 1819, which were put down by the cavalry. Alarmed by the Cato Street conspiracy, the authorities unleashed a wave of repression in the spring of 1820. The Scottish protest movement had a leader with military experience in John Baird (1790–1820), who headed a Committee for Organising a Provisional Government, which planned a revolt to liberate Scotland from English rule. On 1 April posters appeared in Glasgow bearing the slogan 'Liberty or Death' and announcing an uprising and the formation of a government. On Monday, 3 April 1820 the Scottish insurrection reached its highpoint with a general strike, mass rallies and demonstrative military manoeuvres by the rebels. Fighting began on 5 April 1820 and regular troops arrived in Glasgow. Two days later all of the leaders had been arrested. As they were being led away, soldiers in the streets were attacked from the houses, there were several deaths and a few prisoners were freed. In August and September several conspirators were executed, and more were transported to Australia.[143]

The final act of the Congress of Vienna

Political murders and assassination attempts in Germany, France and England had shaken the ruling classes, and perhaps not them alone. The murder of Kotzebue in Germany and of the duc de Berry in France, as well as the Cato Street conspiracy in England, drew international notice.[144] As Countess Thürheim wrote in her memoirs, 'The murder of the Duke of Berry reminded all of Vienna once again of the horrors of the French Revolution. One expects the flames to be reignited. Even the Duchess of Angoulême wrote to Vienna that she fears every moment that she will be felled by the blows of the revolutionaries . . . Everyone is suspect and all minds are struck by terror.'[145] The murdered duc de Berry was a son of Charles V (1757–1836), and a brother of Louis XVI, who had been beheaded in 1793, and of the reigning King Louis XVIII. The murderer's objective had been no less than to extinguish the Bourbon dynasty, even though its power had been limited by the constitution of 1814.

The Carlsbad Decrees and the English Six Acts at the end of 1819 were initial responses to actual or imagined conspiracies. In all countries, limits were placed on freedom of assembly and of the press. In the spring of 1820, the justice system dealt with the murderers. On 1 May 1820, the five ringleaders of the Cato Street conspiracy against the government were hanged. On 20 May, the murderer Carl Ludwig Sand was beheaded in Mannheim. And on 7 June the duke's assassin Pierre Louis Louvel (1783–1820) was guillotined in Paris.[146]

This was the climate in which the Final Act of the Congress of Vienna was signed.[147] It integrated the Carlsbad Decrees into the constitution of the German Confederation, thereby 'completing' the German Federal Act. On 8 June 1820 the parliament – the Federal Diet in Frankfurt am Main – unanimously adopted the ministers' submittal. It thereby took effect as the basic law of the German Confederation and remained in force until the Confederation was dissolved. It defined the domestic and foreign policy of the Confederation in sixty-five articles. The German Confederation – 'a union under international law of German sovereign princes and free cities' – was designed for the purposes of self-defence. Its chief task was the preservation of German independence (Article 1). Except for the city republics, the 'monarchical principle' applied, according to which all power resided in the head of state (Article 57). What was new was the Confederation's right to intervene directly in the federal states in case of insurrection – a right of intervention in state crises

(Article 26). The Final Act completed the constitution of the German Confederation by creating the instruments that the experience of the Tambora Crisis had made necessary. The repressive measures that were used in an attempt to stabilise the political order later became a target for reform politicians who aspired to create a free society. The Carlsbad Decrees were not applied in some federal states, and were mitigated in others. Similarly, in Britain, individual measures in the Six Acts were withdrawn after a few years. Other instruments of repression were removed only during the Revolution of 1848. But that is another story.

Yet another story is the impossibility of preventing the evolution towards greater freedom. In the same year, 1820, in which the uprisings caused by the Tambora Crisis came to an end, new sources of unrest emerged which could hardly be associated with it. In Spain and Portugal, mutinies among the troops turned into political movements, which forced their respective kings to accept liberal constitutions.[148] The Carbonari insurrections in Naples, Sardinia and Piedmont took the form of uprisings against foreign domination.[149] Attempts by the Spanish monarchy to restore sovereignty over Latin America engendered liberation movements there, which one by one proclaimed the independence of Chile, Argentina and Gran Colombia.[150] In Europe, the Greek uprising against the Ottoman yoke began; this, too, was a war of liberation against a regular political authority that pushed at the boundaries of the political system of the Congress of Vienna and its notions of legitimacy.[151] Fears of unrest and revolution, which had been widespread during the Tambora Crisis, continued to echo among the governments of the European powers. Since the acute famine was over, however, the sense of crisis increasingly faded.

— 6 —

THE LONG-RANGE EFFECTS OF THE TAMBORA CRISIS

Cultural coping: memories of the 'years of dearth'

The Tambora Crisis generated a plethora of commemorative works that all have one thing in common: they were produced not by order of the authorities but on private initiative, and only later found their way into local history museums and national historical exhibitions. The motivation is neatly summarised in a sermon of thanksgiving: 'Let us never forget the days of hardship that taught us so much, but rather render them salutary and beneficial to us by taking the lessons they provided as worldly wisdom for the future.'[1] Many of these commemorative products record the local peak prices for cereals and potatoes, the basic foodstuffs that had become unaffordable. It is precisely this private form of memoria, which has survived in such large numbers from no other famine, that has proven so interesting for folklorists, whom we can thank for the preservation of and commentary upon these objects after they had lost their significance for private individuals over the course of the twentieth century.

Walter Hartinger has studied the so-called *Teuerungstafel* or inflation panels, large-format picture panels or coloured prints that he refers to as folk art. In the manner of a comic strip, they portray the sellers of various wares and, as a quasi aside, also show the peak prices for the various foods. From today's perspective these overviews also provide information about what, apart from bread (or wheat or rye flour) and potatoes, were considered the basic foodstuffs, namely protein-rich legumes (peas, lentils), white cabbage and turnips, which were eaten in large quantities, or, like oats or six-rowed barley, at least served as substitutes. The price range for meat is quite surpris-

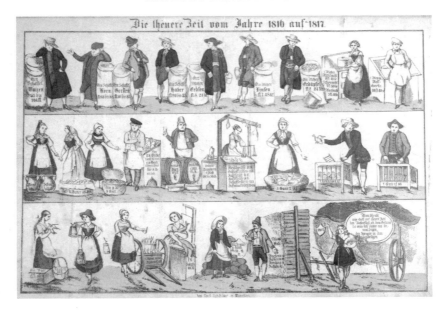

Carl Hohfelder, The inflation time from 1816 to 1817, Neuburg an der Donau, Stadtmuseum

ing, showing that in those days pork was ranked above veal, beef and mutton as well as poultry. Such picture panels were printed and sold by professional *Illuministen* such as the South Tyrolean engraver Vinzenz Zanna (1772–1827), who had settled as an art dealer in Nuremberg.[2] Artists in neighbouring cities, like the Munich lithographer Carl Hohfelder, altered them to create new products, which were reprinted into the 1840s. At the end of Hohfelder's pictorial broadsheet of the inflation era we see the harvest wagon of 1817, alongside which stands a boy holding a cornucopia. The wagon is adorned with a sign reading 'Now grant us God for times of pain, a superfluity of grain. Then with his blessing we shall see, the famine from our land will flee.' Framed or unframed, the printed and coloured pictorial broadsheets hung as wall decorations in private homes, shops or taverns.

To all appearances, the famine broadsheets also served as models for other forms of art. The Historical Museum of St Gall owns a painting by Johann Bartholomäus Thäler (1806–1850) of Hundwil, who made slight alterations to Hohfelder's famine broadsheets in 1825. Instead of market vendors, his version features grain dealers and profiteers

207

Johann Thomas Stettner, Medals commemorating the famine year 1816/17, medals 1 and 2, Mannheim, Reiss-Engelhorn-Museen

Furchtbar rollte der
Donner über den Häuptern
der Menschen; fast jede Wolke
erzeugte vernichtende Blitze;
auch hier nimmt er seinen Lauf
auf eine friedliche Hütte; und
angstvoll fliehen Menschen u:
Vieh ob des gewaltigen Donners

who benefited from the crisis. In the bottom row of his picture, the boy with the cornucopia sits on the harvest wagon, whose inscription he has adopted wholesale. The title of the 'Hundwil Famine Broadsheet' is 'The Great Inflation and Famine in the Year 1817'.[3] A number of such famine broadsheets have survived, such as the 'Herisauer Hungertäfeli', a contemporary calligraphic poster framed by yellow roses, which alongside the peak prices of June 1817 also documented the fact that in Herisau, 'there were more than 950 beggars before a house' on a single day in April 1817.[4] The 'Urnäscher Hungertäfeli' entitled 'Brief Description of the Year of Cheap Prices in 1760 and the Year of Dearness and Unemployment in 1817' manages without illustrations and limits itself to recording the local peak prices, in this case in comparison to a year with a good harvest.[5]

Another typical product of the time was the commemorative coin recalling the famine year. These were based on coins marking political events as well as the coin-like bread tokens issued for example by the Elberfeld corn association.[6] While the bread tokens had practical significance, the commemorative coins served a purely memorial purpose. The Nuremberg medallist Johann Thomas Stettner (1785–1872), whose usual repertoire included commemorative coins featuring Napoleon or the Bavarian King Maximilian I, created a famine coin showing a despairing family under an oak tree on one side, surrounded by the legend 'Oh Lord, have mercy, great is the suffering. 1816 and 1817.' The response on the reverse 'Despair not, God lives yet' conveys the depth of desperation. Another commemorative coin shows the complementary message of thanksgiving for the harvest: a clearly well-heeled citizen, perhaps a local official, stands in a lush field amidst the grain harvest while a child hands him a wreath woven of wheat ears. An angel in the pose of Fama, the Roman goddess of rumour, flies across the sky, pointing to the message 'Realise there is a God'.

Stettner also produced the *Schraubtaler*, coin-like objects that could be unscrewed to reveal a series of illustrated medals on a theme, for example the German Wars of Liberation of the years 1813–1815. Based on these, he created medals commemorating the famine years 1816/17, which because of their peculiar structure are also known as *Dosenmedaillen* (box medals). The nine surviving medals depict the course of the famine in coloured images on the front and corresponding texts on the back:

Medal 1: '1816. Terrible was the devastation spread by the hailstorm in 1816. Thousands stood lamenting, as here the farmer with his wife and

210

children, before the broken seedlings and trees blasted by the savage storm.'

Medal 2: 'The thunder rolls awfully over the people's heads; nearly every cloud produced destructive lightning; here, too, it takes its course towards a peaceful cottage, and the people and animals flee in terror before the mighty thunder.'

Medal 3: 'The rain that poured down almost daily in the summer of this year swelled the waters to an extraordinary height, and thousands watched, wringing their hands, as their homes and belongings were swept away by the mighty stream.'

Medal 4: 'The cold rain in summer produced the most horrible things that can befall human beings, universal crop failure, and the dearth of bread it engenders. Everywhere the people impetuously thronged the bakers' dwellings, and each new morning dawned with miserable laments.'

Medal 5: '1817. The blessed breath of a merciful God awakened the new seeds in the spring of 1817. With jubilant praise all ran out into divine Nature. The old men walked gratefully, the youths and maidens smiling through the rich seedlings and the innocent children danced in the round upon the earth's gleaming carpet.'

Medal 6: 'Great was the suffering that spread among the beasts as well, and it was only with difficulty that one could have meat from the butchers anywhere. It was therefore the most joyous event when the summer of this year yielded an extraordinary harvest of fodder, putting an end to this hardship.'

Medal 7: 'One saw with ineffable delight the full seeds cradled in the earth's maternal bosom, and instead of two rows of grain there were 4 and sometimes even 6, and often even several ears alongside one another on a single stalk. The fathers led their children to the rich plantings and taught them about God's great mercy.'

Medal 8: 'In this year, the inhabitants of towns and villages celebrated the entry of the first harvest wagon with a nameless joy. The admonishments of worthy clerics reminded the people to trust in God's divine providence. Now thank we all our God! rang out everywhere from stirred souls.'

The ninth medal depicts the peak prices of 1817 and 'the moral of the story'.

Alongside these professional objects there were amateurish products such as collages made of newspaper clippings, and sometimes examples of the *Sonderbrote* – the particularly small *Kreuzerwecken* (penny rolls), *Herrenbrote* (white loaves), *Hungerbrote* (famine breads) and *Semmeln* (white rolls) baked during the crisis – were also saved and displayed in their own glass cases. Engravers produced commemorative prints, sometimes with accounts of 'wonder ears' or 'wonder fruits', which were apparently bought by private individuals and hung in their private memorial corners – for instance in the household shrines of Bavarian parlours. Medallists designed decorative coins that could be placed in private collections or hung from watch chains or rosaries.[7]

The inscription on a beam in the belfry of the church at Altdorf in the Palatinate is especially interesting: 'In the year 1817 many mice caused such harm that one can scarce describe it.'[8] In a number of towns one finds commemorative stones recalling the famine year, some of which were later built into the walls of houses. In Heiligenstein in Alsace one can read the inscription, 'This cottage was built in the year 1817, in which one paid 120 fr. for a *Fackel* of wheat, 24 fr. for a sack of potatoes, 100 fr. for an *Ohmen* [c. 150 litres] of wine. Jacob Stiedel.' In Neulautern a commemorative stone comparing the prices of wine, bread and potatoes in the inflation years 1772, 1774 and 1817 was built into the wall of a smallholder's house.[9] Freestanding memorial stones are also referred to as *Hungersteine* (famine stones). The 'Willsbach famine stone', a freestanding sculpture in the shape of a gravestone, bears the dedication 'In memory of the great famine of 1817'. Aside from the peak prices for spelt, oats, barley, potatoes and bread, the stone also bears the entreaty, 'Lord give us our daily bread, of thy mercy forever, and preserve us in future from the scarcity of famine times.' The donor was a J.F. Rudolph.

There were no limits to the imagination in these privately financed memorials, which were, however, generally intended for a local public. This is evident in the shooting target from an Erlangen marksmen's society 'To commemorate the famine of 1817, dedicated by Carl August Adolph Löffler Master Rifleman' (see above p. 47). In the foreground of a landscape, the target depicts a profiteer in frock coat and top hat, pulling a rotten potato plant out of the ground. Looming behind him is a veritable devil with a tail and the legs of a goat, who touches his shoulder in encouragement. The surrounding text comments on the oil painting with the words 'Potato profiteer: "Black through and through, what a pleasure for our kind."' / 'The devil echoes: "Black through and through, what a pleasure for our kind."'

The *Hungerkasten* (famine cabinet) shown in a temporary exhibition at the local history museum of Urnäsch am Säntis (Switzerland) is also noteworthy. The anonymous painter of this late Baroque rustic cupboard, which was built for a newlywed couple, wrote on it not just the peak prices of this 'Notable Year 1817' but also included the information that grain had been imported to Switzerland from

Egypt, Russia and Italy.[10] A *Hungerlied* (famine song) has even come down to us. The author of the text is unknown: 'Oh, the awful, awful time, Oh the great famine. First the long hardship of war, and now the dearness of bread! We scarcely saw such misery in years of war as oppresses us poor, poor folk in times of peace.' The song was to be sung to the melody of Buxtehude's hymn 'Christ the Life of all the Living'.[11]

The lasting effect of the Tambora Crisis may be attributed not least to this intensive commemoration. Its memory was still alive thirty years later, during the famine of 1845/46. Older people could relate their own experiences and the mementoes were honoured again and comforted the afflicted. Many eyewitnesses published their memoirs at that time. One hundred years later, during the First World War famine winter of 1915/16, memories were mobilised once again.[12] A broad wave of scholarly accounts ensued, including editions of original sources and even forgeries of sources.[13] Publications commemorating the sesquicentennial of the famine appeared mainly in France.[14] Two hundred years on, commemorations of the Tambora Crisis no longer revolve around the famine, but rather around our confrontation with climate change.

Frankenstein and the vampires: the invention of the horror story

In the summer of 1816, a curious group of individuals gathered in a villa on Lake Geneva. The tenant that summer was George Gordon Byron (Lord Byron, 1788–1824), who had become mired in scandal and rumours surrounding his sexual predilections – incest, adultery, paedophilia, sodomy and homosexuality – in his homeland and was forced to emigrate before he faced legal repercussions. His entourage included his handsome personal physician John William Polidori (1795–1824), whom a London publisher had commissioned to keep a travel diary.[15] They were joined by the young nobleman Percy Bysshe Shelley (1792–1822), who had been sent down from Oxford for espousing atheist views,[16] his young lover (and future wife) Mary Wollstonecraft Godwin (1797–1851),[17] and her stepsister Claire Clairmont (1798–1879),[18] who was determined to have a romance with Byron. Mary's father and Claire's stepfather was the anarchist William Godwin (1756–1836), much admired by Shelley, and Mary's mother was the feminist Mary Wollstonecraft (1759–1797).[19] Two aristocratic outcasts, a doctor and two unmarried women under the age of twenty were hoping to spend an interesting summer together in agreeable surroundings, away from all conventions.

The company expected the lovely surroundings to afford them relaxation and inspiration, but in the 'year without a summer' they frequently found themselves staying indoors, since it was dark, cold and rainy outside. Warming themselves by the fireside (in high summer!), they read aloud from *Tales of the Dead*, the *Fantasmagoriana* recently translated from the French, and German ghost stories by Johann August Apel (1771–1816) and Friedrich August Schulze (1770–1849).[20] Inspired by these tales, Lord Byron suggested that each of the company should write his or her own story. This competition would have a lasting impact on literature, since it was the birth of the modern horror story. Lord Byron composed his dark poems, Shelley wrote 'Fragment of a Ghost Story', and his future wife Mary constructed a work that would define the horror genre, the story of Frankenstein.[21] Based on a fragment by Byron, Polidori produced the prototype of all romantic vampire tales, which was published as *The Vampyre*.[22]

The invention of the modern horror story has its roots in the horror summer of 1816, as Mary Shelley explained in the preface to the third edition of *Frankenstein*:

> In the summer of 1816 we visited Switzerland, and became the neighbours of Lord Byron. At first we spent our pleasant hours on the lake, or wandering on its shores; and Lord Byron, who was writing the third canto of Childe Harold, was the only one among us who put his thoughts upon paper. These, as he brought them successively to us, clothed in all the light and harmony of poetry, seemed to stamp as divine the glories of heaven and earth, whose influences we partook with him. But it proved a wet, ungenial summer, and incessant rain often confined us for days to the house. Some volumes of ghost stories, translated from the German into French, fell into our hands. There was the History of the Inconstant Lover, who, when he thought to clasp the bride to whom he had pledged his vows, found himself in the arms of the pale ghost of her whom he had deserted. There was the tale of the sinful founder of his race, whose miserable doom it was to bestow the kiss of death on all the younger sons of his fated house, just when they reached the age of promise . . . I have not seen these stories since then; but their incidents are as fresh in my mind as if I had read them yesterday. 'We will each write a ghost story', said Lord Byron; and his proposition was acceded to. There were four of us . . .[23]

The 3rd of June was the only sunny day of that month; on the rest it rained almost incessantly or remained overcast. Overall, the temperatures in Geneva were 2.4°C lower than usual. In July, the figure was even 4° lower, and it rained on nineteen days, with cool north and west winds. The mountains were capped in snow and the sky dark grey. In August, it was 3.2° colder than normal, snowing even at lower altitudes, and the autumnal weather was accompanied by fog.[24] In July 1816 Lord Byron wrote the poem 'Darkness', which begins:

> I had a dream, which was not all a dream.
> The bright sun was extinguish'd, and the stars
> Did wander darkling in the eternal space,
> Rayless, and pathless, and the icy earth
> Swung blind and blackening the moonless air;
> Morn came, and went – and came and brought no day,
> And men forgot their passions in the dread
> Of this their desolation; and all hearts
> Were chill'd into a selfish prayer for light . . .[25]

The sun extinguished, the stars dark, the earth icy, and the people desolate – a perception of the summer of 1816 translated into poetry. Four diaries from this group alone give an account of it. Lord Byron also kept a journal, which tells us how he experienced the summerless summer.[26] He was inspired to write this poem on a day when it was so dark at noon that the chickens retired to sleep, and he had to light candles as one might at midnight.[27] It is unclear whether Byron knew from reading the newspapers of the fears evoked by the dark summer days in England, Holland and Italy, including the worry expressed in Italy that the sunlight might disappear altogether.[28]

The diaries and letters reveal that Byron and the others were deeply impressed by the climatic events. The social hardships and the widespread famine in Switzerland appear either to have escaped the notice of the aristocratic band altogether, or to have been deemed unworthy of mention. After an excursion to Mont Blanc, which began on 29 July, Shelley described only the devastation wreaked by the rain-swelled floods. Vineyards and fields had been swept away and bridges destroyed, the wheat was rotting in the fields, and rain and fog hindered their outing.[29] Mary Godwin, whose diary mentions her work on *Frankenstein* for the first time on 24 July, set the frightening scene where the pitiable monster confronts his maker on the Mer de Glace, of all places.[30]

The growth of the glaciers

The glacial advances triggered an early boom in tourism. Most English travellers, including Byron and Shelley, treated themselves to an excursion to Chamonix in order to visit the Mer de Glace on Mont Blanc. After excursions to the glaciers of Le Bossons, La Source d'Averon, Montanvert and La Mer de Glace, Mary Shelley wrote of the dynamism of the glacier de Montanvert: 'These glaciers flow perpetually into the valley, ravaging in their slow but irresistible progress the pastures and the forests which surround them, performing a work of desolation in ages, which a river of lava might accomplish in an hour ... The vale itself is filled with a mass of undulating ice ... It exhibits an appearance as if frost had suddenly bound up the waves and whirlpools of a mighty torrent.'[31]

In 1818, the Benedictine monk Giulio Battesta Spescha (monastic name Placidus a Spescha, 1752–1833), a pioneer of mountaineering from the Romansh-speaking part of Switzerland, published a book on the Alpine climate (*Das Clima der Alpen*) in which he documented the growth of glaciers in the preceding years: 'According to my thirty-five years of observation (1783 to 1818), for a number of years now, most notably since 1811, the Swiss Alps have become more and more inhospitable. My view is supported by the following observations. 1. Many Alps, which previously offered grazing land, have since become covered with snow and ice. 2. Timber growth has greatly diminished in the Alps. 3. The ice and snow masses have increased markedly and have thrust far into the valleys.' Furthermore, 'Some thirty years ago I ascended Piz Muraun (2899 m) between the Medel and Sumvix valleys. In those days grass and flowers grew on its peak, but for the last several years it has been covered with snow.'[32]

The Valais cantonal and mining engineer Ignatz Venetz (1788–1859) wrote that for some time the glaciers had been shrinking significantly, and the snowline had been especially high in 1811. Only during the cold years 1815–1817, when the glaciers had been loaded with large quantities of snow, had they begun to move.[33] The Breslau counsellor of mines Toussaint von Charpentier (1779–1847) stressed that the glaciers could grow or melt within relatively short spans of time. 'The fact that, namely in recent years, the glaciers have advanced so exceedingly strongly is a result of the four cold and extremely wet years from 1813 to 1816. If a few hot dry summers ensue, the glaciers will surely retreat again, that is, their ends will then melt away more sharply than the increasing ice masses push them forward.'[34] His

216

The Rhône Glacier, 1817, from Jean de Charpentier, *Essai sur les glaciers*,
Lausanne 1841

brother Johann von Charpentier (1786–1855), director of the salt
mines in the canton of Vaud, wrote, similarly, that the universal and
extraordinary advance of the glaciers had begun after the cold and
snowy winters of 1812–1817.[35] The two Charpentiers were the sons
of the Saxon geologist Johann Friedrich Wilhelm von Charpentier
(1738–1805), professor at the Mining Academy in Freiberg, who had
advised the Weimar minister of mines Goethe on the running of his
mines in Ilmenau.[36]

The Swiss naturalist Johann Rudolf Wyss (1782–1839) already
noted the growth of the Upper Grindelwald glacier during an 1814
mountain tour.[37] The same applied to the Lower Grindelwald glacier,
the Gurgler glacier and the Lys glacier. If one follows the overview
by the geologist Eduard Richter (1847–1905), chairman of the international glacier commission, the significant growth of the Sulden
glacier had already been apparent in 1815, as had that of the Giétroz
glacier in the Valais, the Langentauferer glacier in the Tyrol and the
Langenferner glacier. In 1816 the Palue, the Hintereis and Unteraar
glaciers advanced. The du Tour, de Zigiorenova, de Ferpècle and de
Montminé glaciers followed in 1817. In 1818 several glaciers reached
their peaks, for example the Hintereis, Rhône and des Bossons
glaciers. The same was true of the Valais and Mont Blanc glaciers.[38]

Typically, the glacial advances restricted the accessibility of high Alpine passes. This was the case, for instance, at the Col de Fenêtre, which led from the Valais to Piedmont. Venetz wrote that, in 1820, all that was visible there were the ruins of coach houses for a trade road that had become impassable. Mules had to cross the Mont-Durand glacier, which had not been the case in earlier times.[39] The Giétroz glacier had completely closed off the Bagnes valley, so that one could no longer traverse the valley from Chermontane. Four glaciers in all (Zesetta, Mont Durand, Breney and S'Otemma) grew into this valley and had joined in the middle, cutting off the passage from Switzerland to Italy. Many mountain pass roads from tributary valleys of the Upper Rhône valley to Italy were closed, mountain pastures became unusable and mountain forests disappeared under glaciers. In many high valleys, orcharding and other traditional modes of land use vanished. The glacial advance altered the entire ecosystem.[40]

In 1819 some glaciers were still advancing, but there were signs at the same time that the climate was changing. The previous year, some had reached their maximum level, and now they were joined by the Sulden, Lower Grindelwald and Bies glaciers. Some, like the Rhône glacier, began to retreat again, while the Vernagt was still advancing powerfully in 1820. The du Tour and Brenva glaciers reached their maximum. The Sulden and a large number of others began to retreat.[41] The Upper Grindelwald and Vernagt glaciers reached their peaks in 1822, the Mer de Glace on Mont Blanc in 1825, and individual glaciers – like the Oberaar and Aletsch – even continued to advance after that. But the majority of them began to retreat. Richter summarised the findings as follows: 'all known glaciers' were advancing from 1815 to 1820, after which a general retreat began. Like his contemporaries Venetz and Charpentier, he saw a connection between glacier growth and the cold and rainy years 1816 and 1817, which were also years of terrible crop failures and famine. Because of the slow pace of glacial movement, growth continued for a few years in some cases, but on average the maximum extent had been reached in 1818.[42]

The flood disaster in the Val du Bagnes on 16 June 1818

The account of the melting of a glacier lake in the Val du Bagnes in the Lower Valais on 16 June 1818, which devastated the valley below, is remarkable. The cause was the advance of the Giétroz glacier, which, along with the meltwater, ultimately cut off the valley. There had been several major glacier avalanches during the Little Ice Age, and they were known as 'cannonades de Giétroz'. The blocking of the Dranse River by the advancing glacier at the level of the present-day Lac de Mauvoisin reservoir during the Tambora cooling, however, had dramatic consequences.[43]

By 16 June 1818, the glacier lake had attained a length of 2 kilometres, a breadth of 600 metres and a depth of 60 metres. All attempts by Ignatz Venetz, the top hydraulic engineer in the Valais, to create a channel for the water by drilling an artificial tunnel through the ice dam to prevent the reservoir from bursting its banks had failed. The Zurich geologist Hans Conrad Escher (1767–1823),[44] who had recently been engaged in channelling the Linth River and was therefore allowed by his native town to add the attribute 'von der Linth' to his name, described this process in minute detail.[45]

At 4:30 in the afternoon some 20 million cubic metres of water burst the banks and inundated the valley. Several villages with several hundred houses, and forty-four people, thirty-four of them in the town of Martigny, fell victim to the flood disaster. This catastrophe was the direct result of the cooling in the wake of the Tambora Crisis. There had already been a smaller flood on 27 May 1817, but it caused no damage. Not long thereafter, two French publications on the subject by Pastor P.-S. Bridel of Vevey were presented to the German public in Gilbert's *Annalen der Physik*.[46]

The topic of glacial movements continued to appear in the *Annalen der Physik* not least because of further mountain disasters. One year after the glacial lake outburst flood in the Val de Bagnes, the village of Randa in the Matter valley in the Upper Valais was destroyed when part of the Weißhorn glacier collapsed. In all, 119 buildings were flattened. This occurred on 29 December 1819, and once again it was studied and brought to the attention of a broader public by Ignatz Venetz.[47] More recent research shows that earlier disasters had been reported for the same areas, such as the glacial lake outburst flood in the Val de Bagnes in 1595, which destroyed 500 structures and killed 140 people. None of the earlier outburst floods were as well documented as that of 1818, however, when engineers were active around the clock trying to avert the catastrophe.[48]

The Tambora Crisis and the natural sciences

Goethe read about the eruption of Mount Tambora at the height of the crisis, albeit with some delay, in his morning newspaper, Cotta's

219

Morgenblatt für die gebildeten Stände. People in every village in Europe, America and the British Empire knew about the colossal volcanic eruption via the print media. The British East India Company's *Asiatic Journal* reported regularly on volcanic eruptions in the Far East, and its accounts suggest that the explosion on the island of Sumbawa must have been quite an extraordinary event.[49] The Geneva professor of natural philosophy Marc-Auguste Pictet (1752–1825) wrote about it in his respected scientific journal, the *Bibliothèque Universelle*.[50] Sir Thomas Stamford Raffles, now the British governor of Bencoolen, had already published his *History of Java* in 1817, which accords a prominent place to the volcanic eruption, surveys of which he had commissioned during the previous two years.[51] There was thus no lack of information. But although the American ambassador to France Benjamin Franklin, writing in the annual proceedings of a learned society, had already proposed the thesis that the 1783 eruption of the Laki volcano was responsible for the colder temperatures and crop failures that followed on both sides of the Atlantic,[52] his insight did not take root. At first, the worldwide effects of the Tambora eruption remained hidden to contemporaries.

They did, however, notice changes in the climate. The canon of disciplines in those days did not yet include climate science or meteorology. Chemistry was quite a new field, and research in the natural sciences was conducted more at state academies and private learned societies than at the universities.[53] One such scientific society, founded in 1815, was the Schweizerische Naturforschende Gesellschaft, which in 1816 resolved to inspire research by offering a prize. Among the thirteen suggested topics, the following question was selected in October 1817: 'Is it a well-founded fact that our higher Alps have become increasingly wild in the last several years? What are the causes, and how can they be prevented?'[54] The central problem was only ostensibly dairy farming in the higher Alpine pastures, which had fallen off because of the cooler temperatures of recent years. Indirectly, the question addressed recent climate change.

The only author to submit an answer was the Berne forestry official Karl Kasthofer, and he held market forces responsible for the altered use of land. This was not the answer the society had hoped to hear, however; he only received second place, and the prize question was set again. In the second round there were two submissions, and the chief engineer of the canton of Valais, Ignatz Venetz, won the prize. He concluded that the desolation of high mountain pastures was the result of climate change. He took the advance of glaciers in the high mountains as an indicator. It had been the consequence of a cooling period, which also affected mountain dairy farming. As a by-product of his study of the glaciers and their deposits, he discovered that there must have been far greater glacial advances in the past. The prizewinner, whose text was soon published in revised form, was thus one of the pioneers of a theory of ice ages.[55]

From today's perspective, the discussion of the causes of cooling – aside from Franklin's volcanic theory – appears rather chaotic. The debate involved the sunspots discovered in the seventeenth century, but also the influence of the newly invented lightning rod as well as earthquakes and the impact of comets and meteors. In 1817, based on accounts by mariners seeking the Northwest Passage, the president of the Royal Society Joseph Banks (1742–1820) wrote that a substantial and as yet inexplicable climate change must have taken place in the circumpolar waters, a cooling that had led to the formation of towering, insurmountable barriers of ice.[56] The British admiralty thereupon sent four ships to explore the Arctic Sea. They reported on the enormous sheets of ice that had broken off from Greenland since 1815 and whose southward drift could have triggered the cooling in North America and Europe.[57] This theory was shared by the German physicist Chladni, who suggested that the icebergs might be drawing 'caloric substances' (*Wärmestoffe*) from the air as they melted, thus causing the cooling. The perpetual west wind then brought this cold air to Europe. As evidence, Chladni cited the fact that countries outside this air stream, such as Sweden, northern Poland and Russia, did not suffer from the cold wave.[58] The French naturalist and professor of chemistry Joseph Louis Gay-Lussac (1778–1850), however, rejected the theory with the argument that no such iceberg advances had been observed in other particularly cold years.[59]

The invention of the weather map

Another German physicist – Heinrich Wilhelm Brandes (1777–1834) – pointed out on 1 December 1816 that while a number of countries had suffered unusually cold temperatures that year, others had been plagued by drought or even extreme heat. These contradictions made the lack of adequate meteorological data especially unfortunate. Brandes called for more weather stations and the preparation of weather maps: 'If one could illuminate maps of Europe for all 365 days of the year according to the weather conditions, it would probably emerge where exactly the border of the great raincloud lay that covered all of Germany and France in July.'[60] In fact, Brandes

221

published the first weather maps three years later, and he is considered the founder of synoptic meteorology.[61]

From the *Annalen der Physik*, it appears that the unusual weather events inspired a preoccupation with weather and climate phenomena. Apart from articles on meteors, sunspots and clouds, the volume for 1817 contains an increasing number of commentaries on weather phenomena, for example opposite winds at different altitudes,[62] a waterspout on dry land,[63] or the atmospheric physics of thunderstorms and the accompanying cold winds, the latter studied by Count Alessandro Volta (1745–1827), the founder of the modern science of electricity.[64] More attention was now also paid to meteorological instruments, since both the construction and the calibration – for example of mercury thermometers – still presented many challenges.[65]

As minister of state, on 14 December 1817 Goethe issued thirty paragraphs of 'Instructions for the Observers in Ducal Meteorological Institutes', which were intended to put weather observation and analysis on the latest scientific footing with the help of the newest instruments and exact tabular registration. Among other things, these instructions were to serve as guidelines for documenting dry haze (*Höhenrauch*) – the obscuring of the atmosphere that Benjamin Franklin had already identified as a consequence of major volcanic eruptions.[66] A supplement contained a short text 'On the Colours of the Sky', which once again addressed the effects of dry haze: 'In dry haze, the sun appears blood-red as through a much tarnished glass.'[67] In February 1818 Goethe began a many-year process of keeping his own records, especially of his observations on weather conditions, cloud formations and atmospheric chromic phenomena following Howard's cloud classification.[68] An especially intense phase of observation during a stay at the spa in Carlsbad in 1820 gave rise to the essay 'Howard's Cloud Forms', which was published, together with the poem cycle 'In Honour of Howard', in 1821 in issue 3 of his journal *Zur Naturwissenschaft*. At the same time, Goethe displayed a growing interest in geology and volcanic rock formations and prepared several geological essays and drawings.[69]

It was likely no coincidence that Goethe wrote a letter to the society's president Paul Usteri in early March 1817, just when the Schweizer Naturforschende Gesellschaft was offering a prize for the best essay on the connection between cold and glacial movement.[70] As the chairman of a small society of natural scientists in Weimar, Goethe was among the regular readers of Ludwig Wilhelm Gilbert's (1769–1824) *Annalen der Physik*. He also maintained a longstanding interest in a theory of the ice ages. In 1820 he asked a friend who had just returned from a journey to Switzerland whether the glaciers had actually grown as a result of the cooling trend of recent years. In his Berne doctoral thesis, Tobias Krüger concludes that 'Goethe was one of the earliest and most independent proponents of the ice age theory'.[71]

From cloud classification to meteorology

During the first year of the crisis, Marc-August Pictet already noted the unusual distribution of cold and warmth in 1816 to refute the above-mentioned sunspot theory. Pictet argued first of all that sunspots covered only a small portion of the sun; second, that one would have to observe a uniform effect upon the earth; and third, that previous cold years had not always correlated with the appearance of sunspots.[72] The British astronomer W.M. Moseley of Worcestershire essentially agreed with these arguments.[73] The editor of the *Annalen der Physik* considered Pictet's statements on the sunspots so significant that he later summarised them in a separate article.[74]

Throughout the Tambora Crisis, Pictet found himself confronted with extraordinary weather phenomena: constant rain and the growth of glaciers in 1816 and the renewed cold and storms of the summer of 1817.[75] Pictet, who was suffering from rheumatism and migraine in the summer of 1817, discussed the weather phenomena with meteorologists such as Luke Howard, who paid him a visit. But although he reported on the eruption of Mount Tambora on the other side of the world in his *Bibliothèque Universelle*, he saw no connection with the weather in Europe.[76] The editor of the most widely read US magazine, the *Weekly Register*, which reported continuously on the rigours of the climate in North America, also rejected the sunspot theory because it lacked synchronicity. But Hezekiah Niles' (1777–1839) earthquake theory did not provide a usable alternative either.[77] To accept this theory, one had to believe that an earthquake in 1815 had interrupted subterranean electrical currents. Electricity, which was not yet well understood, also played a role in another theory, which held lightning conductors – only recently invented by Benjamin Franklin – responsible for rapid and extreme changes of climate. After all, North America and Europe, where the use of lightning conductors spread most rapidly, had also suffered most from the climate. An Italian scientist at the Milan observatory had claimed that electricity led to cloud condensation. The more electricity was concentrated, the sooner and more heavily it would rain. By conducting electricity, lightning rods would prevent lightning, but trigger protracted rainfall. This theory was repudiated by the Nuremberg experimental physicist Johann Konrad Gütle (1747–1827), one of the most enthusiastic proponents of lightning conductors in Germany.[78]

Historians of science have cited the state of research at the time to explain why contemporaries did not take up the suggestion of a connection between volcanic eruptions and cold phases. Meteorology had started out as a science of meteors, and only began to shed this legacy around 1800.[79] The influence of volcanoes on climate was noted, but only as a local phenomenon. This was a function of the fact that people were not accustomed to regarding weather phenomena in a super-regional context or climate as a dynamic, worldwide phenomenon. The idea that volcanic eruptions could have global impact emerged only after the eruption of Krakatoa,[80] about which the British government had a voluminous dossier prepared.[81] The American atmospheric physicist William Jackson Humphreys (1862–1949) was the first to demonstrate the global climatic effect of the Tambora eruption.[82]

The example of Luke Howard (1772–1864) helps us to trace the path from the observation of nature to meteorology. As an eleven-year-old boy, Howard experienced the peculiar celestial phenomena following the eruptions of Laki in Iceland and Asama in Japan (which people in Europe did not know about), especially the so-called dry haze or *Höhenrauch* that darkened the sky and produced brilliant red sunsets. These impressions would preoccupy Howard for the rest of his life. After leaving school, he began to study chemistry and botany on his own alongside his apprenticeship as an apothecary. In 1793 he opened a shop in Fleet Street that produced and sold chemicals. As a chemist, he became an active member of the Askesian Society, a sort of private academy, in 1796, and as a botanist he was inducted into the Linnean Society in 1802. Increasingly, however, he regarded meteorology as his specialist field of study. Howard had already made a name for himself in 1802 with his *On the Modification of Clouds*, in which he introduced his classification system: stratus, cirrus, nimbus and cumulus clouds and their variants and hybrids. A side-effect of his classification of cloud forms was their use to forecast the weather.[83]

In 1806 Howard began systematic weather observations in London, which he combined with measurements of air pressure and temperature. He began to publish the results in the *Athenaeum Magazine* in 1807 under the title 'Meteorological register', and they were reprinted in scientific journals throughout Europe and discussed by other researchers.[84] Out of these studies he developed the new discipline of urban climatology, which he presented in a two-volume work on the climate of London in 1818/19.[85] At the height of the Tambora Crisis, Howard gave his *Seven Lectures in Meteorology*, which were published with some delay as the first textbook of the new discipline.[86] Given his enthusiasm for studying the weather, the 'father of meteorology' must have deemed it the greatest honour to be inducted in 1821 into the Royal Society, which included the most renowned natural scientists in the world.

To his contemporaries, Howard's taxonomy of clouds seemed every bit as spectacular as Carl Linnaeus' taxonomy of living organisms. Both developed a coherent terminology derived from the Latin, which could be taken up by the vernaculars throughout Europe. Scientific journals published an ongoing commentary on Howard's observations and analyses,[87] which influenced literature and painting as well. From 1815 Goethe classified clouds according to Howard's system, and in 1821, as mentioned earlier, dedicated a poem to him. The two also corresponded. Among painters, it was above all J.M.W. Turner, John Constable[88] and Caspar David Friedrich who drew inspiration from Howard, the last at the suggestion of Goethe.[89]

The emergence of volcanology

The science of volcanology developed as a branch of geology, parallel to the eruption of Mount Tambora and its after-effects. The focus of attention in the new field was Mount Vesuvius – an important stop on the Grand Tour – which experienced a period of protracted activity from the 1770s until the 1830s. At this time, Vesuvius became a kind of pilgrimage site for painters, the sensation-hungry and geologists both amateur and professional. Goethe visited it three times and ascended it twice in March 1787. Along with several visits to the partially excavated cities of Pompeii and Herculaneum, it was one of the highlights of the author's *Italian Journey*, which he happened to be preparing for publication during the year of the Tambora eruption.[90] In 1805, Alexander von Humboldt observed the eruption of Vesuvius and climbed to the top together with the volcano researcher Leopold von Buch (1774–1853)[91] and the aforementioned French chemist Louis Gay-Lussac. In 1822 he ascended the volcano another three times.[92]

The main protagonists of the development of volcanology were two geologists who served as secretaries of the Geological Society in London, George Julius Poulett Scrope (1797–1876) and Charles Lyell (1797–1875).[93] Scrope studied in Cambridge from 1816–1821, and his interest in volcanoes was strongly influenced by a holiday in Naples in the winter of 1817. He returned the next year, and in subsequent years studied the volcanoes in Sicily and the Lipari islands as well. In 1822 he witnessed a large eruption of Vesuvius. In the early 1820s he also visited volcanic regions of France (in the Auvergne) and Germany (in the Eifel). Scrope published the first standard work of vulcanology, *Considerations on Volcanos*, in 1825, which not only analysed the behaviour of volcanoes but ultimately led to a 'new theory of the earth'.[94]

Scrope's book put an end to the old debate between 'Neptunists' and 'Plutonists', which had reached its height between c. 1790 and 1830. The Neptunists believed that basalt rock formations like the Giant's Causeway in Northern Ireland could be explained as the results of maritime sedimentation. The primordial ocean theory, whose main proponent was the geologist Abraham Gottlieb Werner (1749–1817), had the great advantage of being reconcilable with the biblical story of Creation. According to Werner, volcanism was merely an insignificant event in the earth's crust, produced by the combustion of coal seams.[95] Although Werner published little, he had a large group of international disciples, including Goethe,[96] Leopold von Buch, Alexander von Humboldt and the Scottish geologist Robert Jameson (1774–1854), who was so enthusiastic that he founded a Wernerian Natural History Society. In the face of actual volcanic eruptions, however, many followers distanced themselves from Werner's Neptunism, among them Karl Wilhelm Voigt (1752–1821), the counsellor of mines who worked alongside Goethe, Alexander von Humboldt and Leopold von Buch, the latter the founder of scientific stratigraphy and the originator of the term *Leitfossil* (index fossil).[97] Scrope expressed his particular respect for them in the preface to his book.

The Plutonists rejected the primordial ocean theory and proposed instead the theory that fire from the depths of the earth was responsible for rock formation and volcanism. The originator of this theory was the Italian scientist Anton Lazzaro Moro (1687–1764), and it was further refined by James Hutton (1726–1797), who has been called the father of modern geology.[98] His notion, known as uniformitarianism, that the earth was formed according to universal natural laws that also apply in the present,[99] made the study of contemporary conditions the key to understanding the past. Hutton posited that all volcanic eruptions were fuelled by a 'central fire' located deep beneath the earth's surface. This explained the formation of rocks, mountains and continents as well as volcanic eruptions.[100]

Like Scrope, Charles Lyell had also studied from 1816–1821, but in Oxford. Although he subsequently had to work as a lawyer, he retained a keen interest in geology. In 1817 he met Joseph Arnold (1782–1818), who had explored Java two years earlier with Stanford Raffles.[101] Lyell became the secretary of the Geological Society in 1823 and in 1830 began publishing his *Principles of Geology*, the first modern textbook of geology, which he revised personally up to the twelfth edition.[102] It was soon translated into all the major languages, including German as early as 1833.[103] Lyell based his treatment of volcanism on Scrope's ideas, which he integrated into a larger system, primarily using the example of Vesuvius and the neighbouring Phlegraean Fields. He left no doubt, however, that the eruption of Mount Tambora – which he described according to Raffles' *History of Java* – must be counted among the greatest known explosions in human history.[104]

Volcanic eruptions and sunsets in Romantic painting

The influence of the Tambora event on the visual arts is just as ambivalent as its impact on literature. The example most often cited by climate historians is extremely unlikely to convince an art historian. J.M.W. Turner often painted evening atmospheres that corresponded precisely to the celestial phenomena to be expected after a major volcanic eruption: the sun only vaguely contoured, the colours of the sky alternating from yellowish to reddish. Turner painted many such mood paintings; the 'mystic shell of colour' was, after all, a typical characteristic of Romantic painting.[105] This very mood can be found in the 1817 history painting *The Decline of the Carthaginian Empire* (London, Tate Gallery). Everything seems to fit – the time, the subject (the downfall of a culture), the depth of the historical fall and the gloomy evening atmosphere – were it not for the 1815 counterpart to this picture, *Dido Building Carthage, or the Rise of the Carthaginian Empire* (London, National Gallery), which has a similar mood. Here Turner depicts a morning atmosphere, and the subject is the diametrical opposite of the later painting.

Artistic styles and forms follow a logic of their own and do not necessarily depend on external events. Turner was nonetheless demonstrably interested in natural disasters. Thus in 1815 he painted an impressive picture of the eruption of the Soufrière volcano on the

Caribbean island of St Vincent (now the French overseas département of Guadeloupe) on 20 April 1812. The otherwise black sea reflects the explosion, whose projectiles are impressively captured against the black sky. This volcanic eruption must indeed have been an imposing spectacle, and at VEI 4, together with an equally large eruption of Mount Awu in Indonesia the same year, it may well have even exerted a short-term influence on the world's climate.[106] Scrope emphasised the importance of this eruption similarly to that of Tambora.[107] In 1817 Turner painted a sensational watercolour of a volcanic eruption – alas not Tambora, but Vesuvius, which had erupted in 1815 and 1816 (*Vesuvius in Eruption*, New Haven, Yale Center for British Art).[108]

In those years many painters depicted volcanic eruptions, which were a popular theme. We know of at least a dozen versions of the *Eruption of Vesuvius* from close up and afar by Johan Christian Clausen Dahl (1788–1857), based on sketches that the painter made there.[109] One could also mention August Kopisch's (1799–1853) *Crater of Vesuvius with the Eruption of 1828* (Galerie Joseph Fach, Frankfurt am Main). Other, thematically related works, can likewise be viewed in this context of volcanic eruptions, such as the 1830 *Last Day of Pompeii* by Karl Pavlovich Briullov (1799–1825), which evokes a doomsday atmosphere (St Petersburg, Russian Museum of State).

The many sombre cloud atmospheres in the works of John Constable (1776–1837) could be mentioned here, too; for instance the 1816 *Wivenhoe Park* (Washington, DC, National Gallery of Art) or the 1821 *Hay Wain* (London, National Gallery). Similarly the dark cloudburst and rain atmospheres of Turner's 1816 *Solvay Moss* (London, Tate Gallery), and perhaps also Caspar David Friedrich's 1816/17 *Greifswald in Moonlight* (Oslo, National Museum of Art), in which the moon is recognisable only schematically through a layer of black haze. Turner created remarkably sombre mood paintings during his 1817 journey along the Rhine: *Burg Sooneck bei Bacharach am Rhein*, where the river also reflects the black sky, or *At the Confluence of the Rhine and Lahn*, where the viewer cannot tell whether the diffuse light in the sky is supposed to be the sun or the moon. The same is true of the 1819 *St Peter's from the South*, which casts a gloomy light over the Eternal City (London, British Museum). The 1818 *Raft of the Medusa* by Théodore Géricault (1791–1824), which illustrates the gruesome story of a ship carrying French emigrants that foundered off the coast of West Africa in 1816, is also repeatedly cited. The survivors of the *Medusa* managed to cling to a raft, most of them dying of thirst, as the two who came out alive vividly reported after their rescue.[110]

Caspar David Friedrich's 1818 *Woman Before the Setting Sun* (Essen, Folkwang Museum) may have depicted a Tambora evening atmosphere. But whether or not we should consider the endless series of sombre, reddish sunsets by Friedrich, Turner and others to be Tambora pictures is a matter of opinion, which can be neither proven nor disproven. The same is true of the vast number of volcanic eruptions, tempests, snowstorms, floods and dramatic scenes of devastation produced by such painters as John Martin.[111] One image not previously mentioned in the literature seems to me to allude directly to the hardships of 1816–1817: Johann Friedrich Overbeck's (1789–1869) *The Sale of Joseph*, painted in 1816/17. It was part of the fresco cycle *The Seven Lean Years* (today in the Alte Nationalgalerie, Berlin), and the Italian title ('I setti anni di carestia') already suggests an allusion to the 'carestia del 1816–1817', the famine of the Tambora Crisis.[112]

The 'rectification of the Rhine'

Nowadays, when it comes to flooding, the rectification of rivers – forcing them to conform to one riverbed – is repeatedly cited as the root of all evil. It was flooding, however, that led to rectification in the first place. In the case of the Rhine, the high water of 1816 led to the signing of a pact between the kingdom of Bavaria and the grand duchy of Baden on 26 April 1817. The two states resolved to cut through the river's many curves according to plans drawn up by the hydraulic engineer Johann Gottfried Tulla (1770–1828). That same year, Tulla began to straighten the Dreisam River near Freiburg im Breisgau, a tributary of the Rhine. At the time, Tulla, who had already presented plans for the future straightening of the Rhine in 1812, was the leading specialist on river rectification in Europe.[113] But it was only the disasters of 1816 that created opportunities for the implementation of his plans, which went so far as to recommend straightening the Rhine from Switzerland to Hesse, requiring further agreements not just with Hesse but also with France.[114]

The Rhine emerged after the last ice age; its oldest bed that can be dated is 8,000 years old. Over the centuries its meandering loops filled the Rhine valley, which in some places is up to 40 km wide. This is familiar to us from old maps and paintings: the Rhine valley – in David Blackbourn's description – resembled a huge, lagoon-like waterscape. More than 1,600 islands were once counted on the stretch between Basle and Strasbourg alone.[115] In the context of the famine of 1816/17 it appeared sensible to create new, fertile farmland by river regulation. Straightening the river was supposed to render it more predictable, which would also improve its navigability and make it easier to construct quay walls and docks. According to Tulla, the rectification of the Rhine would offer nothing but advantages. 'It was all the more important to gradually populate the shores of this significant river, since the Rhine lowlands . . . consist largely of very fertile soil, and to facilitate shipping, trade and transport.'[116]

Tulla ensured the political implementation of the straightening of the Rhine with remarkable professionalism. He calculated the damage caused by the river's floodwaters since 1816 along its entire length between Switzerland and Hesse, and added the costs that would arise if one sought to protect all the flood-prone towns and villages along the banks from future harm by building embankments. He then calculated the benefits that would probably accrue from the 'rectification of the Rhine' – in commerce and manufacturing, farming and shipping, and finally simply through the rising value of land all along the river. The results were astounding. The more money was invested in the rectification of the Rhine, the higher the profits would be.[117]

The straightening of the Rhine was the largest building project ever undertaken in Germany. The river from Basle to Worms was 345 km long before the rectification, and 273 km after. Dozens of channels were necessary, and they had to be dug by hand, since heavy dredging equipment had yet to be invented. Islands had to be carried away, and embankments erected along the shores. Even in those days such a major project had opponents, both among the population and in the state administration and the public sphere. The inhabitants of Knielingen (now a district of Karlsruhe) feared for their fisheries and resisted, but their protests were put down by military force. Traditional occupations such as gold washing – washing the Rhine gold from the water – or fowling disappeared. For bird fanciers the loss of nesting places at the time was already a disaster. The number of fish species declined, along with the importance of the Rhine fisheries. The advantages outweighed the disadvantages, however. Although it had been expected that draining the marshes in the Rheinaue would mainly diminish the number of foggy days and increase arable land, it transpired that diseases also declined or even disappeared along with the breeding places for insects. The best example was malaria, which in earlier times had regularly cost thousands of lives.[118]

Other states also recognised the advantages of river rectification and canal construction. In Franconia in particular, the river straightening lobby saw it as an opportunity to tackle widespread unemployment.[119] Work on the Regnitz River in Franconia between Forchheim and Bamberg began in 1817, serving not just to improve its navigability for commerce and grain imports but also as an employment programme at a time of 'prevailing hardship'.[120] Attention also turned once again to the construction of a canal between the two great river systems in Germany – the Rhine and the Danube – using the navigable Main: the Rhine-Main-Danube Canal, whose completion remains a political issue today.[121] In northern Germany, plans were made for a canal connecting the North Sea with the Baltic Sea.[122]

The primary consideration in relation to straightening the course of the Salzach River was the fact that it formed the border between Bavaria and Austria from 1816. Planning began that same year.[123] In Austria, the director of the office of waterways engineering, Osterlamm, began a 'General Inspection of the River Danube in Lower Austria', which was intended to facilitate a systematic regulation of the river. This was followed in 1817 by a hydrotechnical study of the Danube near Vienna. The recommended regulation was not undertaken immediately, however. One issue in the discussions was how to get the stagnant waters to flow more rapidly in order to reduce the stench.[124] In Württemberg, the building of the Wilhelmskanal in Heilbronn began in 1818, giving the city a port, making the upper Neckar navigable by installing a system of locks, and removing the necessity of transferring freight onto ships travelling upstream on the river.[125]

The building of the Erie Canal

The US counterpart to the rectification of the Rhine was the building of the Erie Canal, the shipping link between the city of New York and the Great Lakes. Constructing such a link solved several problems at one fell swoop. First, it gave work to tens of thousands of unemployed men, who would no longer be a burden on the relief system. Second, it improved the possibilities for supplying New York and other large cities on the East Coast, since food could be transported cheaply from inland farms. Third, goods could now be moved cheaply from the ports to the Great Lakes regions. Above all, however, it simplified westward migration, which had grown into a mass movement since 1816, further spurred by the many immigrants. The poor roads over the Appalachian mountains were ill-suited to settlers migrating with their families and household goods. Travel by boat was quick, inexpensive and safe.

The building of the Erie Canal had been under discussion for many years. President Thomas Jefferson had rejected the idea as pointless, since the canal only led into the wilderness. Thanks to the shock of the Tambora Crisis, however, the project was able to go ahead. On 15 April 1817, Governor DeWitt Clinton (1769–1828) received approval from the New York state legislature for $7 million to finance his vision of a canal. He believed that the city would, 'in the course of time, become the granary of the world, the emporium of commerce, the seat of manufactures, the focus of great moneyed operations'.[126] The canal opened up the hinterland of New York City, accelerated the settlement of New York state and connected the metropolis with the fertile Ohio Valley, whose main export was grain. The cost of transport from the city to the Great Lakes fell by up to 95 per cent. Each of the lakes in turn allowed access to other waterways, which in turn opened up new areas for settlement.[127] With the help of the Erie Canal, New York managed within just a few years to surpass Philadelphia as the largest city and the most important port in the United States. Before the canal's completion, Buffalo, located at the opposite end, had only 200 inhabitants. By 1840 the town's population had risen to 18,000. The growth of Cleveland, Chicago and Milwaukee was similarly stimulated. The building of the canal fundamentally changed the landscape and the lives of its inhabitants. But only a few people like the author Nathaniel Hawthorne lamented the devastation of nature. Most saw new economic opportunities and celebrated the 'artificial river'. The

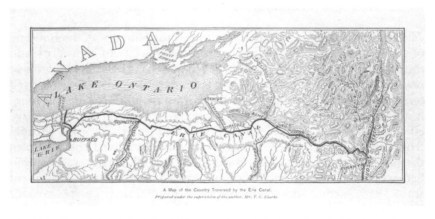

A Map of the Country Traversed by the Erie Canal.
Prepared under the supervision of the author, Mr. T. C. Clarke.

The Erie Canal, built 1817–1825, map from Thomas Curtis Clarke, 'Waterways from the ocean to the lakes', *Scribner's Magazine* 19, no. 15 (1896)

culture of technological progress in the USA has its roots in the era of the canal project.[128]

In comparison to the channelling of the Rhine and other European projects, the building of the Erie Canal was completed in record time. The head engineer was Benjamin Wright (1770–1842), and construction began on 4 July 1817 in his native town of Rome, New York. The first 24 km up to Utica were finished in 1819, but the necessity to clear woodland slowed the pace of construction. Clearing went more quickly after the invention of a 'stump puller' for uprooting trees. The engineer Canvass White was sent to England expressly to study canal building and lock technology. The huge construction site became a training camp, the so-called Erie School of Engineering. The greatest challenge was traversing the Appalachian mountain range. Another difficulty was crossing the Cayuga marshes, where hundreds of workers died of malaria. For that reason, the work was shifted to the winter months, but then the labourers suffered from frostbite. A total of some 50,000 workers found employment on the construction project. Many of them were unemployed Americans or farmers who left the canal at harvest time. As a result, managers increasingly hired immigrants, particularly from Ireland, Wales and Germany.[129]

The 12-metre-wide waterway opened to traffic on 26 October 1825. During the building process, the canal's great competitive advantages for New York had already become apparent to the other coastal cities. As a consequence, canal, road and soon also railway projects arose everywhere.[130] After the successful opening up of the northeast, inland projects were undertaken next. The 496-kilometre Ohio-Erie Canal, which connected Lake Erie near Cleveland with the Ohio River, opened in 1828. As the largest river in the Mississippi River system, the Ohio connects no fewer than fourteen states. This was joined by the 155-kilometre long Illinois Canal further north, which linked the Great Lakes with the Mississippi River system. Many of the labourers involved had already worked on the Erie Canal. This Illinois waterway pushed Chicago closer to the intersection of east-west and north-south traffic, becoming the precondition for its rise as an industrial centre.

The triumph of the steamer

The opening up of the USA by waterways accelerated the development of the recently invented steamboat. Robert Fulton (1765–1815) had patented the first functional 'steam ship' in 1809. That same year, the steamer *Clermont*, powered by a steam engine manufactured by the English company Boulton and Watts, but equipped with a sail just in case, had been the first ship to regularly serve the route on the Hudson River between New York City and Albany. Two years later Fulton and Livingstone, who had secured a steamship monopoly for the interstate waterways from the state of New York, built the first Mississippi steamer, the *New Orleans*. Fulton, however, did not live to see the steamship era unfold. His early death in February 1815 opened the way for the Quaker Henry Miller Shreve (1785–1851), an inventor and transport entrepreneur, who had travelled back and forth between New York and New Orleans with his 'steam boat' since 1814. That same year Daniel French (1770–1853) constructed a far more efficient paddle steamer, the *Enterprise*, in Brownsville, Pennsylvania. On its maiden voyage from Louisville, Kentucky to Pittsburgh, Pennsylvania, it proved that it could travel upstream against strong currents and that it was suitable for use on the Ohio River. Fulton's heirs had the ship impounded because of their steamship monopoly, but a law of January 1817 guaranteed free shipping along the Mississippi – two years after the Congress of Vienna had done the same for waterways in Europe[131] – and ushered in the era of the paddle steamer. It is thus no coincidence that the first steamship for transport on the Great Lakes was built by a New York consortium in 1817 and began service that same year.[132]

Efficient steam-powered vessels became available at just the time they were needed to open up the western USA.[133] In 1816 Shreve and his business partners commissioned the paddle steamer *Washington*, with a motor provided by the steam-engine inventor French. The *Washington* was the first steamer to separate the engineering and passenger decks, and became the prototype for the later showboats, which offered the passengers all manner of entertainments. They travelled on the Mississippi and Missouri Rivers, the Ohio and the Erie Canal. For commercial transports and emigrants before the railway age, the paddle steamer was the safest and most comfortable way to travel west. The figures demonstrate this great leap in mobility: in the 1810s there were just twenty paddle steamers on the American rivers, but by the 1830s there were 1,200. In 1814, only twenty-one steamships docked in New Orleans, while five years later the number was 191, and in 1833, 1,200. Within a few years, the steamship had become a means of regularly scheduled transport.

In the years of the Tambora Crisis steamship travel conquered the world. The first steamer crossed the English Channel on 17 March 1816, and on 12 June the first (English-built) ship steamed up the

Rhine to Cologne. In December of that year the first steamer built in Germany rolled off the line, and in 1818 Professor Stelzhammer of Vienna described the first steamship on the Danube.[134] In 1824, during her visit to southern Russia, Baroness von Krüdener had the opportunity to observe the first Russian steamer on the Volga.[135]

Railway plans

The transformation of steam into motion was of interest not just on water but also on land. The first operational steam locomotive was constructed by Richard Trevithick (1771–1833) in 1804 for use in the mines. It was based on a steam wagon model known as the Puffing Devil that had been built three years before. In 1814 George Stephenson (1781–1848) took this as the basis for his first steam locomotive for use in the Killingworth colliery, where he worked as an engine-wright. The first commercial railway for the transport of goods and passengers famously went into service between Stockton and Darlington in 1825, pulled by a locomotive built by Stephenson.[136] The next railway line, between Manchester and Liverpool, opened in 1830.[137] Thereafter railway construction became a motor of the Industrial Revolution, in England as well as on the continent.

It is a little-known fact that the Tambora Crisis also played a role here. Efforts to introduce steam locomotives in Bavaria began in May 1817, in those days under the fine name 'System der fortschaffenden Mechanik' (System of Transport Mechanics). That is presumably the reason why it was later forgotten. The author of the memorandum introducing the system was the director of mining and engineering Joseph von Baader (1763–1835), who had studied in England around 1790 and maintained good connections there. He began preparing his own railway designs as early as 1807. Ten years later, after a sojourn in Britain in 1815/16 – where he studied a tramroad along a canal in Cardiff – he presented his plans to the public, convinced that this was the technology of the future.[138] He found a supporter in his younger brother Franz Xaver von Baader (1765–1841), who in the 1790s had run mines and steel works in England and Scotland and later entered the Bavarian state service as a counsellor of mines. He was a leading proponent of canal building and particularly supported the construction of the Rhine-Main-Danube Canal.[139] Joseph von Baader presented elaborate plans for building 'the newly invented railways', in which he began with a comparison of the profitability of canal, road and railway construction and emphasised the economic and

235

ecological advantages of railway routes.[140] The railway plans brought the advantages of canal building to regions that could not be served by waterways. Construction offered work for the unemployed, and the railways lowered the cost of transporting bulk goods, including foodstuffs during famines. Those cities, like Munich, that were not located on navigable rivers would benefit particularly.

The continuing propagation of railway construction piqued the interest of King Ludwig I.[141] After a discussion in the Bavarian Diet, and the successful construction of an experimental railway on the grounds of Nymphenburg Palace the year he ascended the throne, Ludwig called upon the merchants of Nuremberg to build a railway line as an alternative to the Rhine-Main-Danube Canal. The merchants declined. But after the success of the first railway lines in England, a joint-stock company was formed in 1833 'to erect a steam railway' between Nuremberg and Fürth on the model of the Liverpool-Manchester line. The locomotive was ordered from Stephenson, complete with an engine driver. When the first German railway line, the 'Bayerische Ludwigsbahn', went into operation in December 1835 it was the result of long preparatory work.[142]

The macadamisation of road construction

While steamships brought improvements only to those regions close to navigable rivers, and railways still lay in the future, in the USA roadbuilding was the first option in infrastructure policy for accessing the new states. The key project, begun in 1818, was the construction of a 'national road' from the Potomac River over the Appalachians to the Ohio River and on into Indiana. This became the first road financed by the federal government.[143] In Europe, a lack of investment meant that the roads were in a lamentable state, despite some improvements. As a result of the Tambora Crisis, they were in an even worse condition than they had been at the end of the eighteenth century. Flooding and landslides or simply abundant rain had damaged the roads throughout the continent, and in many places the surfaces and subsurface were so sodden that vehicles became bogged down. Travel was slow, expensive and unsafe – one need only think of Goethe's summer journey to take the waters in Baden-Baden, which ended after just a few kilometres with a broken axle.[144]

Like the banking crisis of 2008, the Tambora Crisis offered a unique opportunity to rectify the desolate state of infrastructure through a major investment programme. Some towns and villages had to be connected to proper roads for the first time. The large-scale employment programmes were also intended to offer wages for the unemployed so they could support themselves again. This required governments to take on new loans at a time of high national indebtedness, but most of them found the money well spent considering the danger of widespread popular dissatisfaction turning into political revolt. The rising demand encouraged John Loudon McAdam (1756–1836) to present his improved technology for road construction to the public.[145] The McAdam roads were characterised by their three layers of compacted stones of varying sizes. This technique was used to 'macadamise' existing roads.[146]

Germany, Austria, Italy and Switzerland entered the fray in grand style. In the kingdom of Hanover a new era of infrastructure policy began. On 3 October 1816 the government informed the *Landstände* (Estates) of the economic importance of highway construction for the country's development and planned to introduce a road network consisting of nineteen highways for travel and transport between Hamburg and the Rhineland. In addition, twenty-eight roads would serve the needs of regional transport. In the first year alone some 400 kilometres of new 'stone ways' were laid according to the 'Macadam' system.[147] Prussia also began systematic road construction in 1816, with a novel idea: the building of toll roads, where private or public lenders would take over the construction and afterwards be permitted to collect fees from users. In the administrative district of Trier, five new state roads were supposed to provide access to the rest of the Saar region. The social aspect of employment policy also played a role here.[148] The extent to which road construction in Prussia was regarded as part of crisis management is evident from the fact that in the years 1816 and 1817 a state subsidy of 500,000 taler was pumped into the roads, an amount that dropped to 200,000 after the acute emergency ended.[149]

On 5 May 1817 the Bavarian king decreed the improvement of infrastructure through road construction. All roads connecting Class I towns – for example Nuremberg and Bamberg – were to be constructed as 'chaussees'. The regulations stipulated not just the width of roads but also the solidity of their substructure, the type of surface, the curvature needed for water to flow off the roadway and the inclusion of drainage ditches and channels on both sides. This comprehensive road construction programme was a huge employment and infrastructure project, which was to place communications within the kingdom on a new footing. The local upper classes were enlisted for financing. A royal order of 20 December 1817 admonished them not to evade this responsibility, which suggests that 'assistance for the poor and suffering' was the primary aim of these measures.[150] Finding aids for the Württemberg state archives provide information on the plethora of road construction projects initiated there in the wake of the Tambora Crisis.[151]

In northern and eastern Switzerland all manner of road building projects were begun, often by the same groups of people responsible for poor relief.[152] In western and southern Switzerland, the crisis provided the impetus for a road over the more than 2,000-metre-high San Bernardino Pass, designed by the Ticinese engineer Giulio Poccobelli (1766–1843). In just a few days in 1817, he walked the 100-kilometre route to decide where the future road would go.[153] The road pass from Chur to Savognin and then to St Moritz was constructed under the direction of the cantonal engineer Richard La Nicca (1794–1883). The explicit reason for building this particular road was to supply the starving inhabitants of the high valleys with grain – and naturally to provide work for the unemployed.[154]

Similarly in response to the famine, new roads were built in the Habsburg province of Lombardy-Venetia. In 1818, Emperor Francis I issued a decree ordering the establishment of outlines for 'Road Construction over the Rhaetian Alps'. The department of construction in Milan inspected the site that same year and in 1819 prepared detailed plans. The highest in Europe at the time, the breathtaking road over the 2,757-metre Stelvio Pass was built from 1820 to 1824 and connected the Vinschgau in South Tyrol with Valtellina in Lombardy and with Switzerland.[155] The head engineer, Carlo Donegani (1775–1845) of Brescia, received a patent of nobility in recognition of this masterly feat of engineering and was henceforth permitted to style himself 'Carl Donegani von Stilfersberf'.[156] The road over the Splügen Pass (2,115 m) was completed in 1822, connecting Chiavenna in Lombardy with the canton of Grisons. Some road building projects took longer. The Vallarsa road from Vicenza to Rovereto was finished in 1825 and, together with other construction measures, cut the transport time for heavy loads between Innsbruck and Venice in half, from twenty to ten days.[157] The Ampezzo road over the Puster Valley to Belluno was not inaugurated until 1830.[158]

Automobility: from horse to draisine

Among the stranger inventions of the period was the draisine, which some regard as the precursor to the bicycle, the motorcycle or even modern individual transport altogether. The city of Karlsruhe considers Baron Karl Drais von Sauerbronn (1785–1851) to be something akin to a forerunner of Carl Benz. The Prussian ambassador to the court of the grand duke of Baden took a less positive view: 'A hunting squire von Drais contributed in a different manner to the entertainment of society . . . At the Congress of Vienna he already drove a coach without horses set in motion by the feet of those sitting within, later he invented the draisine, which was named after him, a frame with wheels upon which one simultaneously stood and walked, a useless, ridiculous thing that occasioned much mockery.'[159]

If Karl August Varnhagen von Ense was unconvinced of the value of this innovation, other contemporaries were more enthusiastic. In southwest Germany and the centres of the Tambora Crisis the invention of a horseless vehicle made sense, if only because horses were scarce. Not only had the preceding wars decimated their numbers; the constant rain and flooding had led to an acute shortage of fodder. Many farmers had been forced to slaughter their herds of cattle and horses, causing a glut on the market – one of the reasons why the price of meat had not risen as sharply as that of other foods. In addition, epidemics had broken out among the remaining horses.[160]

Cartoonists were quick to take up the draisine, as Cruikshank did in 1819 to make fun of the prince regent and his 'royal hobbies'. He used the association with the hobby-horse to address George's relationship with Lady Hertford, who sits on his back, fat and practically bare-bosomed, while he rides the draisine on his belly. The mistress wears the crown on her head and wields a knotted whip to drive him on. Meanwhile she cries out suggestively, 'Oh dear, this is a delightful Way of Riding' and the regent replies 'Aye, aye, it may be very delightful for you, but it is devilish hard work for me.' In the background, the Duke of York rides in the opposite direction on a draisine and calls out 'Although my Hobby is one of 10,000 yet I had a tumble, so that I advise you both to mind what you are about.' He wears a massive feather on his hat, which, together with his tense posture on the velocipede, lends him the appearance of a rooster. The occasion for the cartoon was an accident the duke had on a draisine, as well as his removal from office because of a scandal surrounding the £10,000 he had received for services at court that were already part of his normal duties. The caricature published on 20 April 1819 was suppressed by the censors and spread all the more as a result.[161] A second cartoon shows the accident in which both the prince regent and his mistress and the Duke of York – once again in the background – are thrown from their vehicles. This caricature alludes to George's relations with the Duchess of Richmond, for he calls out 'this Hertford Road is so d—d rough, I'll not drive on it any more, I'll go the Richmond road next time'.[162]

The draisine was even honoured by Cruikshank a third time to unmask the depravity of court society during the famine. This time, the prince regent sits astride a cook while in the background the crowned Lady Hertford looks on in annoyance. The regent brandishes a bottle of gin and shouts, 'Ha, ha! D— me! This is glorious! This is princely! Better fun than the Hertford Hobby . . . If the rascals caricature me, I'll buy em All up d— me.' In the adjacent panel the Duke of York rides a velocipede towards Windsor with one of his mistresses, her hands on his shoulders, and doffs his hat to the public. In the background, without greeting the Duke, John Bull stands outside a miserable thatched hut, before which his wife and children cower. His arms folded, he expresses his anger at courtly corruption, '£10,000 a year for a son to do his duty to his Father!!!!!! whilst my Children are starving!!!'[163]

Although the draisine did not initially serve any great practical purpose, those who could afford it clearly enjoyed it, since it remained in memory as a model of automobile transport. In order to be transformed into a functional automobile, it required a motor as well as good roads. With its wooden frame and wheels, the *Petroleum Reitwagen* (riding car) motorised by Gottlieb Daimler seventy years later resembled a draisine. And the fact that the other inventor of the automobile, Carl Benz, also came from Karlsruhe, and was initially mocked quite mercilessly for his horseless carriage, at any rate represents a further parallel.[164]

On the way to a common economic area

The reordering of Europe had simplified the map of the continent, since hundreds of tiny territories had been swallowed up by their larger neighbours. The free trade theorists' utopia of duty-free traffic in goods was thus closer to becoming a reality. Moreover, the Austrian chancellor of state envisioned a further easing of regulations for the entire German Confederation. In mid-June 1817 he presented the German Federal Diet with a draft law introducing the free movement of grains, legumes and potatoes as well as cattle for slaughter. His employer, the Emperor Francis I of Austria, however, entered an objection.[165] At the time, tariff barriers existed not only between states, but in the case of larger empires even within them. In 1817, the Prussian government decided to remove all internal customs barriers in response to the large price differences between its eastern and western territories, which made it more difficult and expensive to supply the Rhineland with grain from Prussian Poland and the Baltic.

As Eberhard Weis has emphasised, the Tambora Crisis became the starting point for a unification of the central European economic area: 'An important motivation for efforts to establish a customs union from 1818 was the severe food and sales crisis of 1816/17 ... For both economic and political reasons, the economist Friedrich List recommended the complete removal of economic barriers within Germany.'[166] In 1820, in the name of the Deutscher Handels- und Gewerbeverein (German Trade and Manufacturing Association), founded in 1819, Johann Joseph Eichhoff presented his 'Observations on Article 19 of the German Federal Act', the aim of which was 'to facilitate trade and transport'. In the preface he explained with reference to the negotiations at the Federal Diet: 'Everything revolves around the issue of introducing a state of affairs in Germany that will allow all federal states together to create a whole, with regard to commerce as well. To this end it is necessary for all tariff barriers between the individual states to disappear, and for a general toll border to be drawn between the entire Confederation and foreign countries.'[167]

Since the Federal Act did not provide any basis for coercive action in the economic field, Eichhoff concluded that economic unity could only be pursued on a voluntary basis, that is, through the union of those states prepared to join. He thus formulated principles familiar to us from the European unification process in the early twenty-first century. In today's terminology, what Eichhoff suggested to the German Diet was simply a 'two-speed Germany',[168] a vision that would become a reality with the establishment of the German Customs Union in 1834. The dynamism created by this voluntary foundation stills serves as a model for the process of European unification.

The degree to which the Tambora Crisis was connected with the politics of the customs union can be illustrated by way of the individual protagonists. Goethe's publisher Johann Friedrich Cotta,[169] who was also involved in poor relief and food supply policy in Württemberg, had belonged to the Württemberg Estates since 1815, and from 1819 to 1831 to the second chamber of the Diet in Stuttgart. He was among the supporters and planners of the 1828 customs union between Bavaria and Württemberg, and helped to negotiate the Prussian-Hessian customs union of 1828 as a precondition for the German Customs Union. In 1829, with Cotta as mediator, the two major customs unions decided to grant one another duty-free status on domestic products. This had the advantage for Prussia that its eastern territories were now linked to the Rhineland without customs barriers. The south German states, in turn, now had access to the grain-growing areas in the Prussian regions of Poland and the Baltic.[170]

The globalisation of cholera

Five factors were decisive for the worldwide spread of the cholera epidemic after 1817. First, it was caused by an especially aggressive pathogen; second, the conditions were very favourable (weakened immune systems, high humidity); third, the British East India Company had its headquarters in Bengal; fourth, British troops spread the disease; and fifth, globalised trade networks also facilitated the spread. Sometimes the two last conditions also came together. Thus in 1821 an expeditionary force from India landed in Oman, bringing the epidemic to the Arabian Peninsula and East Africa. Recent studies have shown that Sub-Saharan Africa was also affected by the first pandemic – specifically the island of Zanzibar, which was politically allied with Oman and at that time still a centre of the international slave trade, which had been abolished in Europe but not yet in Arabia. A lack of sources makes it impossible to tell whether, as in all subsequent nineteenth-century pandemics, cholera also spread to the mainland.[171]

The epidemic spread first in Muscat and from there to Bahrain on the Persian Gulf. In 1821, it reached the port city of Basra at the confluence of the Tigris and Euphrates. In this city alone more than 15,000 people died within three weeks. From here the disease spread upriver to Baghdad, at that time part of the Ottoman Empire, and then to Syria along the caravan route, reaching Aleppo in November 1822. A Persian army vanquished an Ottoman army at Yerivan in 1822, but was infected with the cholera and disbanded. The demobilised soldiers spread the disease further, in the summer to Tabriz and Baku in Azerbaijan, among other places. This then Persian province lost some 20,000 people. Cholera arrived in Tiflis in Georgia, which belonged to Russia, and in 1823 in Astrakhan on the Volga. People were also infected in Tehran and all the cities of the Persian high plateau, so that Persia lost 10–20 per cent of its population during this epidemic. Since there was no treatment available, each arrival of the disease led to mass flight.[172] The epidemic ended during the cold winter of 1823/24 only because the pathogen died off.[173]

Cholera had already reached Ceylon by sea in 1819, and from there spread to the island of Mauritius, which had been captured by the British a few years before. There it claimed the lives of some

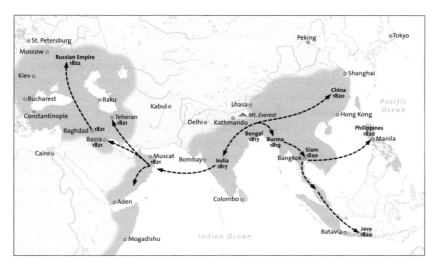

Map showing the spread of cholera during the first pandemic, 1817–1822

6,000 people, mainly African slaves. Via Rangoon, the capital of the kingdom of Burma, it spread to British Singapore, only recently founded by Raffles, and then to Bangkok, capital of Siam (now Thailand), where 30,000 people died.

The epidemic also reached Sumatra and Java in Indonesia. The Sunda Islands, already devastated by the Tambora eruption and the tsunami that followed, were now plagued by the cholera pandemic. Seventeen thousand people died in Batavia, and an estimated 100,000 lives were lost on Java. Cholera spread by sea from Indonesia to the Philippines, to Chinese Hong Kong, and from there to the Japanese islands. The Chinese interior was affected for a second time, with more lasting consequences than the outbreak three years before which had spread by land. In 1820 the epidemic was still being transmitted up the Yangtse and Yellow Rivers. At the start of the reign of Emperor Daoguang (1782–1850, reigned 1820–1850), in 1821 it reached the capital Peking, which, like London, had a population in those days of approximately one million, and soon became the greatest source of transmission for northern Asia. From Peking cholera wandered along the caravan routes, jumping over the Great Wall, crossing Mongolia, which was divided at the time between China and Russia, and arriving in Tomsk, Siberia. The epidemic reached Moscow via Omsk, and then St Petersburg, and thus Europe. Via the Baltic Sea, it finally reached the Baltic and Polish port cities and Prussia.

243

Cholera riots in Russia

The literature generally distinguishes between this first pandemic and a second one in the years 1827–1838, which once again spread through Asia and reached Russia by the land route. In Astrakhan, 400 people succumbed to the epidemic within ten days.[174] Within a month, 2,500 were dead and all of the cities on the Caspian Sea infected. The disease made its way from Astrakhan to Saratov on the Volga, where several Protestant pastors reported on it. Of the 550 German colonists – many of whom had emigrated because of the Tambora Crisis – 400 fled to the countryside. Hardly any of those who remained survived. In Saratov alone, cholera claimed 2,170 lives (8 per cent of the population).[175]

The epidemic visited Russia only briefly in 1823, but in 1830 it unleashed its full horrific potential. The reason for this was not any lack of preparation or backwardness of medical science. The opposite was the case. The Russian doctors had studied at the best European universities, the government immediately set up crisis teams, and the local authorities took every measure available at the time. In 1822 they had already studied Jameson's account of cholera in Bengal.[176] But nothing seemed to help. Old and young, rich and poor died at an alarming rate. And this had consequences. 'Medical horror turned into social anarchy', as a historian of medicine recently noted.[177] Thousands fled the towns, nobody wanted to take responsibility anymore and no one wanted to obey orders. The north German district physician of Saratov, Harry Valentin Haurowitz (1799–1884), reported that the bodies of the dead remained in their houses, since nobody wanted to bury them.[178]

The government brutally implemented cordons sanitaires to prevent the further spread of the epidemic. But force only exacerbated the crisis, since it did nothing to stop the epidemic but intervened massively in the life of the population. The entire Volga region from Astrakhan to Nizhny Novgorod was gripped by social unrest and protest movements. In Sebastopol in the Crimea the rebels even formed their own government and began spreading propaganda among the serfs. The cholera brought with it riots, triggered by rumours that government officials and doctors were deliberately contaminating the population. Angry groups stormed police stations and hospitals and murdered state officials, officers, landowners and nobles. In the provincial capital of Tambov, 450 kilometres southeast of Moscow, the governor was attacked and the army had to be deployed against the insurgents. Similarly, in 1831, a mass demonstration in St Petersburg had to be dispersed by artillery.[179] The cholera riots were a sign not of backwardness, but of helplessness. As Charlotte Henze has shown, order broke down in other places as well when the epidemic proved too devastating. Riots and assaults on doctors occurred in 1831 and 1832 in Germany, Austria, France and England.[180]

The disease reached Moscow in September 1830 despite all precautionary measures. The university and schools were closed, and in all twenty districts of the city cholera committees set up emergency hospitals. After two weeks, 467 people had already died, and anyone who could fled the city. As riots loomed here too, in late September Nicholas I (1796–1855, reigned 1825–1855) drove through the city several times in an open carriage to pacify the people. In all, 4,543 people fell victim to the outbreak before it ended the following February.[181] According to the most recent estimates, the pandemic of 1830–1831 killed some 466,000 people across Russia as a whole. Nevertheless, the tsarist authorities failed to take any measures against future outbreaks. Autocratically ruled Russia could face any enemy, whether Napoleon or a cholera outbreak, but could not prepare adequately for the future. The country paid dearly during the pandemic of 1848, which allegedly claimed precisely 690,150 lives.[182]

Cholera on every continent

Europe was hit very hard indeed in 1831. One centre of infection spread from Russia via the Baltic ports, the other through Egypt and the Mediterranean ports. The disease was also introduced into central Europe in the course of the Polish-Russian War, the first Polish uprising against Russian rule.[183] Some 2,600 people died in Warsaw, and the outbreak reached Vienna in August 1831 via Galicia, claiming some 2,000 lives by December. In the kingdom of Prussia the Baltic ports of Königsberg and Danzig were affected first, before the epidemic reached Berlin in 1831, despite all precautionary and compulsory measures. The victims of the cholera outbreak in Berlin (0.6 per cent of the population) included the philosopher Georg Wilhelm Friedrich Hegel, who died on 14 November 1831. In Breslau, the disease struck down the military theorist Carl von Clausewitz (1780–1831), and in Posen the Prussian military reformer August Neidhardt von Gneisenau (1760–1831).[184]

In December 1831 the cholera epidemic spread to England,

breaking out first in smaller towns such as Sunderland, Gateshead and Newcastle in the northeast. In February 1832 the disease reached London, where 6,536 people (0.34 per cent of the population) succumbed. At the height of the epidemic, riots against medical doctors or the government (or both) erupted in several cities. Between 29 May and 10 June 1832 street battles broke out in the centre of Liverpool, fuelled by the paranoid notion that doctors were deliberately killing people in order to sell their cadavers. Gravediggers were attacked in Exeter for the same reason.[185] France was even more severely affected, losing around 100,000 people to the outbreak, 18,402 (2 per cent of the population) in Paris alone. In 1832 serious rioting again flared up in post-revolutionary Paris.

In early June 1832 English immigrants brought cholera to Quebec in Canada, where despite quarantine measures 1,000 people died in just two weeks. From there the disease spread along the St Lawrence River system to the North American interior. The outbreak began in New York on 23 June, in Philadelphia on 5 July, and thereafter in many other towns in the USA. Cholera remained endemic until 1834, and crossed the Rocky Mountains to the Pacific coast. It also arrived in South America in 1832, reaching coastal cities in Peru and Chile by sea. In 1833 the disease moved from the USA to Mexico, where it reached as far as the highlands. The epidemic reached Cuba, in contrast, via a ship from Spain, and from there attacked the USA a second time, in 1835, now affecting the southern states.[186]

Building the London sewer system

London was the largest city in the world in the early nineteenth century, with a population of more than one million, and given the damage that a deadly epidemic could wreak there people began to take a closer look at solutions. The physician T.J. Pettigrew noted in 1831 that cholera apparently had a peculiar preference for the poorly nourished and clothed, whose living conditions exposed them to 'low and foul situations'.[187] James Adair Lawrie (1801–1859), professor of surgery at the University of Edinburgh and previously stationed in Bengal, also drew a connection between the cholera outbreak and overpopulation, filth and damp.[188] In the new edition of his book on cholera, Reginald Orton conceded that, contrary to his previous views, it probably was an infectious disease – as the Medical Board of Bombay had already asserted in 1818.[189]

Up to that time people had believed that the disease spread via poisonous vapours or miasmas from the canals. After the first cases appeared, the doctor Edwin Chadwick (1800–1890) therefore ordered the flushing of waste water from the smaller canals into the Thames.[190] As a result, cholera spread even more rapidly, since the city's drinking water also came from the Thames. The doctor John Snow (1813–1858) then developed the hypothesis that cholera was spread by living organisms in the drinking water. He proved this in 1855 – following two subsequent cholera outbreaks that had claimed 14,137 lives in 1848 and 10,738 in 1853/54 – using a map showing that cases of cholera occurred mainly in the area around a water pump in Broad Street. After he took the pump out of commission, the outbreak ended.[191] At Snow's request, the microbiologist Arthur Hill Hassall (1817–1894) examined water from the pump, stool samples from cholera patients and water from the Thames and found in them all the *vibrio cholerae* bacterium, which the Italian anatomist Filippo Pacini had recently identified as the infectious agent that caused the disease.[192]

Although the dispute between supporters of the miasma and infection theories remained undecided, the authorities began planning to separate the drinking and waste water systems. The impetus was the 'Great Stink' of 1858, when the purportedly disease-transmitting odours from waste water became so unbearable that Parliament fled London. Planning then began for a 135-metre-long brick-lined sewage system underneath central London. The natural gradient was supposed to guide the effluent out of the city and into the Thames east of London. Today at the same location we find extensive sewage treatment works, but at first the water was not clarified. The sewage system was inaugurated in 1865.[193] Cholera returned to London for the last time in 1866, leading to 5,596 deaths, all of them outside the range of the sewer system.[194] The construction of such sewers ultimately caught on, at first in other major European and North American cities, and later worldwide.[195] The reaction to the cholera outbreak, particularly in London, may be considered one example of how a climate event ushered in lasting changes in modern science, notions of hygiene and town planning.[196]

Saving energy in the wake of famine

One energy-saving invention very much in keeping with our modern concerns made a breakthrough during the crisis. In this case, the energy saving was pursued not for its own sake, but because people were too poor to afford firewood, or depended on public relief. The device was the pressure cooker, invented in the late seventeenth century by Denis Papin, who demonstrated his Papin pot to the Royal Society in London in 1679. The design of his cooking pot was based on the experience that pressure influences the boiling point of water. The pressure could be infinitely adjusted via a valve with the help of a lever. A safety valve prevented the pot from exploding.[197]

On the occasion of a later demonstration to the Royal Society, John Evelyn (1620–1706) noted that 'Papin's digester' could be used to remove meat from the hardest of bones and produce large quantities of meat broth and gelatine. This was precisely what made the pressure cooker so attractive during the Tambora Crisis: one could take bones that would otherwise be discarded to make stock for the soup kitchens. In St Gall the medical doctor Alexander Aepli (1767–1832), town councillor and chairman of the local scientific society, the Bible society and the poor relief commission,[198] acquired a 'Papin pot' to improve the soups served to paupers; for, as Scheitlin noted, 'the small cells of the bones contain very many nourishing fats, marrow juices that are drawn out by the heated and softening water and the steam. This bone broth serves splendidly to enrich the Rumford soup, and the process also yields a large quantity of bone butter.'[199] Private households were supposed to collect leftover bones and bring them every three days to the barracks where the food for the poor was prepared.[200] When that did not work, the bones were collected directly from the wealthy households every day. The aim was to ensure 'that not a single pound of the bones already used by citizens in our native city goes to waste'.[201]

Following Rumford and Papin, other inventors felt inspired to develop better 'cooking, heating and economical stoves', or to improve household heating and cooking technology through new methods of smoke extraction.[202] The objectives of such inventions were not just medical but also ecological and economic, such as 'saving wood'.[203] Professor Johann Christoph Stelzhammer (1750–1840), a naturalist from the circles around the Viennese imperial court, advised public institutions and private individuals to change their cooking habits and introduce the use of pressure cookers to save energy.[204] Stelzhammer also worked on the construction of economical stoves and experimented with using less wood to build curved plank roofs.[205] A Papin pot from this period is on display at the museum of the observatory in Kremsmünster, Austria.[206]

Agricultural reform

One traditional means of responding flexibly to a famine was to expand cropland, which occurred in 1816/17 from Russia to the USA. In the countries with open borders it was easy to create incentives. The governments made land cheaper, or exempted land being cultivated for the first time from taxation. But incentives were possible even in long-settled territories. In Bavaria on 21 February 1817, tax exemptions were granted for wheat, rye (*Korn*), barley and potatoes – 'this root vegetable that truly prevents famine'. The government supported the conversion to potato growing – which was new in many regions – with concrete advice, not only on cultivation itself, but also on how to protect the seeds from theft. Tips on propagation by dividing seed potatoes were disseminated. In the case of cereal cultivation, state specialists were assigned to supervise the quality of the seeds, and starting in March they were expected to provide the government with monthly reports on the progress of the seedlings, in order to prevent them being caught unawares again by crop failures. To this end, the state assisted farmers in purchasing seeds and promoted crop rotation by releasing seeds from the state storehouses for 'beans, vetches, peas, lentils'. Finally, the lower authorities were instructed to allocate money for guards to prevent thefts from the fields. Because of the shorter growing period, the search for faster-growing varieties was also promoted.[207]

In the centre of the crisis – Switzerland – several magazines devoted a series of articles to agricultural reform. These continued beyond 1817 and sought to include all aspects of contemporary knowledge, from technical innovations to the reorganisation of tillage and animal husbandry and the cultivation of alternative crops. *Der Bürger und Bauernfreund* called its series 'Writing about Agriculture'. The misuse of common lands by large farmers for grazing played a surprisingly major role in these articles, 'because it is more convenient for them to keep their livestock on the commons at almost no cost to themselves than to ease the suffering of their brethren'.[208] The anonymous author used this social critique to embroider upon an issue that had already concerned the agricultural reformers of the eighteenth century: the barn feeding of livestock. Barn feeding meant that the fields could be used for other purposes, and provided easily accessible dung for vegetable gardens. The author combined this with the notion that once animals were confined indoors, the poor could use the common lands to grow their own food. 'The better use of our lands, the

249

planting of all manner of foodstuffs, must now be our chief business, and thereby we will establish and maintain a more solid and general prosperity, and one day see healthier and stronger and likely also better people.'[209]

The production and use of fertilisers was a further focus, especially since, according to the latest information, practically anything could be used to make fertiliser: 'The dung from the lanes and roads; the rubble from old buildings: chalk, lime, plaster and the like; the refuse from slaughterhouses and tanneries: hooves, horns, mouldered leather, old shoes and straps; all manner of woollen rags.' It was like alchemy – muck could be turned into gold, and used to promote plant growth.[210] In Switzerland, too, the publications focused particularly on expanding potato cultivation. While Scheitlin wrote in 1817 that people had become accustomed in recent years to potatoes, which could now be seen on the tables of rich and poor alike,[211] that same year the *St. Gallische Kantonsblatt* published an article promising 'Good advice on the planting of potatoes' with the aim 'of cultivating this extremely beneficial fruit in even larger amounts than heretofore'.[212] These publications were connected with the activities of the St Gall Aid Association, which in September 1816 installed an 'agricultural commission' in which leading intellectuals could discuss innovations in the field. In March 1817, the commission informed the Aid Association of their findings. With regard to the impending seedtime, they propagated the 'appropriate planting of potatoes' as well as 'swedes and flax', the last for the workhouses. Able-bodied paupers should also cultivate public land at the Aid Association's expense.[213]

The Tambora Crisis also had a long-term effect through the impression it made upon the young Justus Liebig (1803–1873), who lived through the famine as a thirteen year old. Presumably – and contrary to his self-fashioning – he had to leave the *Gymnasium* in Darmstadt because his father could no longer afford the school fees, as well as the apprenticeship to an apothecary he had begun in 1817 in Heppenheim (Bergstrasse), one of the distressed areas at the time in the grand duchy of Hesse.[214] Liebig began his studies of chemistry in 1819, writing a doctoral thesis 'On the Relationship Between Mineral Chemistry and Plant Chemistry'.[215] After a period studying in Paris, at the age of twenty-one Liebig was appointed professor of chemistry in Giessen, where his research focused on agricultural chemistry.[216] He propagated mineral fertilisers and elucidated their significance for plant yields. Using the image of the 'minimum barrel', later known as Liebig's barrel, he explained how crop yields could be only as great as the nutrient in shortest supply allowed (Liebig's law of the minimum). Using fertilisers judiciously could raise yields and prevent soil depletion. Liebig's textbook on agricultural chemistry went through numerous editions and was translated into thirty-four languages.[217] The fact that Liebig popularised his findings in articles ('Chemical Letters') published in the Augsburg *Allgemeine Zeitung* promoted the reception of his work. In the later 1840s he propagated phosphate fertiliser, which is still in use today. When the daughter of a Munich friend contracted cholera, he developed a form of concentrated nourishment that would also enjoy great commercial success as 'Liebig's extract of meat'. It formed the basis of baby food and stock cubes. Liebig's most significant contribution, however, was as the founder of agricultural chemistry.[218]

Savings banks as keys to self-help

In western Europe and North America, the fall into poverty helped to set the course for changes in banking and insurance, which were intended to protect against extreme hardship and make life easier to plan in future. In 1818, the Wiesbaden 'Manual of Poor Relief' still listed the new institutions under the rubric 'Aid Associations for Special Purposes'.[219] In future crises, savings banks and insurance companies would avert money shortages in private households and especially render them less vulnerable, as Henry Duncan (1774–1846), the founder of the first Scottish savings bank, explained.[220] In 1816 the Provident Institution for Savings in the Town of Boston was founded as the first officially recognised savings bank in the USA, out of the conviction that 'savings bank would enable the less fortunate classes of society to better themselves in a manner which would avoid the dangers of moral corruption traditionally associated with outright charitable institutions'.[221] The second savings bank to be founded in 1816, the Savings Fund Society in Philadelphia, also avoided using the word 'bank' in its name since it awakened such negative associations during the economic crisis.[222]

One problem in early banking history was that banks frequently went bankrupt and could offer no security for small depositors. In England this changed with the passage of the 1817 Savings Bank Act, which encouraged the establishment of savings banks and stipulated that their money be invested only in secure government bonds or the Bank of England.[223] Detailed regulations were later introduced to ensure that savings banks safeguarded depositors' money. These included a state guarantee of the nominal value of deposits, which could be withdrawn at any time; that is, the funds were available to the depositor without restrictions and especially in times of crisis.

Like many other ingredients of the Tambora Crisis, the history of the savings banks also had forerunners. The Hamburg Ersparungskasse (Savings Fund) founded in 1778 is considered the first German institution of this kind.[224] In 1796, the Kiel Spar- und Leihkasse (Savings and Loan Bank) was founded by the local Gesellschaft der freiwilligen Armenfreunde (Society of Volunteer Friends of the Poor), and thus arose in a similar context as the savings banks around 1817.[225] The Tambora Crisis did not just lead to a boom in the founding of new institutions, but also increased their importance. The private savings bank was replaced by a public institution, the state savings bank (*Landessparkasse*). In 1816, at the behest of Grand Duke Karl of Baden, the Leihhaus- und Ersparnis-Kasse (Pawnshop and Savings Bank) was founded in Karlsruhe, at the epicentre of the famine. In 1817, state savings banks were established in Lübeck, Württemberg and Saxony,[226] and the following year the first Prussian savings bank was established by the Berlin city government under the motto 'Helping people to help themselves', which is still in use today. Its location in Berlin's Town Hall symbolised the importance of public services for the poor.[227]

The founding of savings banks in capital cities such as Berlin, Stuttgart or Karlsruhe served as a model for the provinces. The first French Caisse d'Épargne et de Prévoyance was founded in Paris in 1818, and became the prototype for all savings banks in France.[228] In the Dual Monarchy, the Verein der Ersten Österreichischen Spar-Casse (Association of the First Austrian Savings Bank) opened its doors in Vienna in 1819. According to its statutes, its aim was to provide 'factory workers, peasants or otherwise hardworking and thrifty youths or adults with the means to put aside a small capital from time to time from their laborious endeavours, in order to use it at a later date to establish a better livelihood, pay a dowry, assist in cases of illness, in old age or to attain some laudable purpose'. Within just a few years the Erste Österreichische, together with the Allgemeine Versorgungsanstalt (General Pension Institution), expanded their services to the entire Austrian Empire.[229]

In those places that had no savings banks in 1820, writers on economics urged their establishment.[230] Often, they had to be founded against local resistance and required significant advance organisation. Poor-relief officials suggested the founding of a savings bank in the kingdom of Bavaria in November 1816,[231] but it would take five years for the plan to come to fruition. The initiator was Johannes Scharrer (1785–1844), a member of the Nuremberg town council responsible for poor relief. He also played a leading role in the planning of the Customs Union and the construction of the first German railway line between Nuremberg and Fürth.[232] The second savings bank in Bavaria was founded on the initiative of the banker, town council-lor and member of the Bavarian Diet Johann Lorenz von Schaezler, whom we already encountered in relation to his involvement in poor relief in Augsburg.[233] The founder of the Frankfurter Sparkasse von 1822 was the Polytechnic Society established in 1816, whose directors included the banker Simon Moritz von Bethmann (1768–1826).[234] The observation that the founders of savings banks often came from the world of middle-class associations and pursued the secondary aim of 'educating workers in the middle-class virtues of hard work, thrift and strict morals'[235] also applies here. The first savings bank in Hesse was founded in Hanau in 1819 by the Niederländische Diakonie, a Calvinist charity.[236]

In Norway the first *Sparebank* opened in 1822. That same year, the first savings bank in what is now Italy was established under the name Cassa di Risparmio di Venezia in Venice, which then belonged to the Austrian kingdom of Lombardy-Venetia. The above-mentioned Erste Österreichische of 1819 served as a model for the Tyrolean savings bank in Innsbruck (1822), the Bohemian savings bank (Ceska Sporitelna) in Prague (1823) and the Cassa di Risparmio di Milano (1823).[237] The first savings bank in the Prussian Rhine province, modelled on the one in Berlin, opened on 1 January 1822 in Koblenz, the seat of the governor (*Oberpräsident*). The example of Koblenz in turn inspired the district capitals of Düsseldorf, Cologne, Aachen and Trier to follow suit. The city of Elberfeld, which was very active in the area of poor relief, also acquired its own savings bank in 1822.[238]

After January 1824, when the Sparkasse der königlichen Haupt- und Residenzstadt München (Munich Savings Bank) gave small depositors the possibility of making provision for the future, the municipal poor relief institutions in Fulda and Hersfeld also founded savings banks,[239] and by the mid-1820s such institutions existed in several key European countries. Although on the continent they were public and often national institutions, in Britain, Switzerland and the USA a different path was taken with private and local savings banks. As had originally been the case in Karlsruhe, Koblenz, Elberfeld and Cologne, the institutions in the English-speaking countries were often loan and savings banks, which were preceded or accompanied by pawnshops.[240] What all of these new institutions had in common was their association with poor relief. And the outcome of the founding boom was impressive. By 1836, there were already 300 savings banks on the territory of the German Confederation.[241] Developments in other regions were similar. Born of the Tambora Crisis, the idea of the savings bank spread throughout the world as a model for providing greater financial security to all strata of the population through banking services.

Boom in the insurance business

Apart from the establishment of savings banks, Emmermann's 'Handbook of Poor Relief' also recommended the introduction of sickness and death insurance. The latter was an early form of life insurance, which not only helped survivors to pay funeral expenses but also offered assistance in cases of unexpected death and all manner of misfortune. The corn associations – intended to help the needy survive hardship situations, since 'daily bread' was their main foodstuff – were essentially also a form of insurance. Unlike these private mutual aid associations, endowments for the poor, which were based on the capital stock of a private donor and intended to be long-term, were subject to central government oversight, with administrators appointed to supervise the proper 'preservation and safeguarding of the capital fund'.[242]

Pioneering projects also influenced the insurance business. In January 1817 the *Neue St. Gallische Wochenblatt* announced the founding of an old-age insurance policy known as a *Bürger Majorität*, which would give 'young citizens both female and male' the opportunity to acquire 'a legal claim to a continually growing capital for their old age'.[243] In 1818, the first sickness, disability and death insurance fund was founded in Aargau, Switzerland, followed by similar institutions in Zurich, Berne and St Gall. An unusually well-informed article in Krünitz's Encyclopaedia drew attention to the identical aims of death, old-age and life insurance funds and emphasised their kinship with the savings banks. These funds also had precursors reaching back to the last great famine of the 1770s; however, in contrast to those earlier private funds, the insurance companies founded after 1815 had a public character, and thus represented a new stage of development in the insurance business.[244]

Ernst Wilhelm Arnoldi (1778–1841), son of a factory owner and known as the 'father of German insurance', published his first plans for fire insurance in 1817.[245] This project was made possible by the respect Arnoldi had gained through his social engagement during the famine of 1816/17, when he had bought up Russian grain on a grand scale to alleviate suffering. Arnoldi founded the first German commercial school in 1818, and was later involved in building the first *Realgymnasium*, a secondary school with an emphasis on science rather than the traditional Latin and Greek. From 1819, he actively supported the founding of a German Customs Union with a petition to the Federal Diet in Frankfurt, and in the 1830s he promoted the project of the Thuringian railway.[246] The Feuerversicherungsbank für den Deutschen Handelsstand (Fire Insurance Bank for German Commerce) in Gotha, which was founded after extensive consultations in 1819–1820 and whose first director was Arnoldi, would break the previous monopoly of an English insurance society. The advantage of the 'mutual insurance society' was that premiums could be kept lower and depositors could even hope for a share of the profits. The fire insurance fund was followed by further institutions such as the Lebensversicherungsbank (Life Insurance Bank), also in Gotha.

China's decline: the great divergence

The growing gulf in development between the west and other civilisations, referred to as the Great Divergence, appears to have been influenced by the Tambora Crisis. Samuel Huntington (1927–2008) raised the question of why non-western civilisations – the Chinese Empire, the Moghul Empire in India, the Tokugawa Empire in Japan and the Ottoman Empire – did not have an equally successful development in the modern era.[247] The underlying notion that only the western path led to modernity has been disputed in relation to China since the 1990s.[248] The question remains, however: if China followed its own developmental path and was still as strong as Europe in 1800, why did it decline so rapidly thereafter to the status of a semi-colonial developing country while 'the West' gained unprecedented strength and managed to dominate the world for two centuries?[249]

The inclusion of climate and environmental history offers a new twist on this question. For some time now, historians have been exploring the surprising parallels between developmental cycles in China and Europe. One need only think of the period of classical antiquity (Roman Empire/Han China), the crisis of the fourteenth century (Great Plague/collapse of the Yuan dynasty) or the crisis of the seventeenth century (political revolutions in Europe/collapse of the Ming dynasty). When Marxist historiography held sway, there was a widespread impression that 'feudalist' China had existed in a state of underdevelopment ever since the 'early bourgeois revolution' in Europe. Younger Chinese historians, in contrast, argue that China was technologically, economically and commercially equal and in some areas even superior to the west into the eighteenth century.

In that century, the Kangxi-Qianlong period, named after the extremely long reigns of Emperors Kangxi (reigned 1661–1722) and Qianlong (reigned 1736–1795),[250] is considered the golden age of Chinese civilisation. China expanded to the west, subjugating both the province of Sinkiang with its Muslim population and Lamaist Tibet, as well as the island of Taiwan.[251] The population grew from 150 million in 1722 to more than 300 million in 1800, or one-third of the world population in those days. China not only consistently had a larger population than Europe and North America combined, but also clearly underwent a more dynamic development in the eighteenth century. This was possible because of long periods of peace and the introduction of new food crops, new varieties of rice from Southeast Asia and above all potatoes, maize and peanuts from America. Despite the restrictions on foreign trade, the Chinese Empire was the largest economy in the world at the time. China had a positive balance of trade with Europe and America until around 1820, thanks to porcelain, tea and silk exports.[252]

There is some debate about when the decline began.[253] Scholars appear to agree that a quick succession of natural disasters, especially major flooding in the Yangtse and Yellow River valleys, may have played a decisive role. This period during the reign of Emperor Daoguang (reigned 1821–1850) is referred to as the Daoguang depression. According to this view, the catastrophic floods of 1823, 1833 and 1850 followed each other so rapidly that there was insufficient time to recover. They were associated with failed harvests and famines as well as massive material destruction, including a decline in soil fertility.[254] This decline was exacerbated by the British opium trade, which destabilised society, and was sealed by defeats in the Opium Wars as well as by the Taiping Rebellion of 1851–1864, which nearly ended the Qing dynasty.[255] More recently, the search for the causes of the decline has shifted back to the reign of Emperor Jiaqing (1796–1820), which preceded the aforementioned flooding and was marked by ethnically driven rioting, famine, epidemics and corruption. Some scholars now believe that the Tambora Crisis was responsible for these calamities.[256]

We must keep in mind, however, that in China – as in Europe at the time – the growing unrest went back to the eighteenth century, erupting in 1795–1804 and 1811–1813 in two uprisings of the secret White Lotus and Heavenly Principle sects, which were brutally put down. It is hard to avoid the impression that how people coped with the era's climatic stresses played a role in setting the course for the nineteenth century. The process of ending famine and premature death from epidemic diseases had begun in seventeenth-century Europe.[257] The Tambora Crisis represented a setback here, but not a change of direction.

Mfecane: hunger, witch persecutions and migration in southern Africa

At the beginning of the nineteenth century, southern Africa was at a peculiar stage in its development. The former Cape Colony of the Dutch East India Company (VOC) became British in 1806, and the Congress of Vienna affirmed British sovereignty over the Colony in 1815. British immigration and the shift to English as the official language began thereafter. The Boers, farmers of Dutch origin, were unwilling to accept this and undertook long treks to the interior, the Transvaal, to become independent Afrikaners. Around the same time as the British invasion and the exodus of the Boers, Bantu peoples migrated from the north. All of this together led to the displacement of the original population, the Khoi-San (Bushmen). The years following 1815 thoroughly recast not just what is now the Republic of South Africa, but all of southern Africa.[258]

In the literature, this period is known as *Mfecane*, a process of violent change under conditions of extreme drought and famine. The *Mfecane* (literally: crushing), a period of chaos, high mortality, forced migration and military conflicts, began in 1817 and lasted until 1840. There had already been dry periods in southern Africa in 1800–1803 and 1812, but in the years 1816–1818 the drought assumed catastrophic proportions. The famine was so great that there were well-documented cases of cannibalism.[259] During these years the Zulus established a kingdom (on the territory of what is now the South African state of KwaZulu-Natal) to the detriment of the Xhosa people settled there. The dominant figure was the Zulu King Shaka kaSenzangakhona (c. 1787–1828),[260] who set up a professional army after taking power in 1816, thus beginning a policy of conquest that led to the incorporation of ever more clans and chiefdoms until the Zulu kingdom became the most powerful in eastern Africa.[261]

Shaka's policy of conquest led to a widespread exodus. In response to his state-building, the kingdoms of the Swazi (now Swaziland) under King Sobhuza I (c. 1780–1839) and the Basotho (now Lesotho) under its long-lived King Moshoeshoe I (c. 1790–1870) were founded further to the north.[262] The Ndwandwe migrated to Mozambique and established the Gaza kingdom under King Zwide kaLanga (c. 1758–1820).[263] Other Bantu groups migrated north into the regions around Lake Tanganyika and Lake Malawi, founding their own kingdoms there.[264] The Matabele kingdom on the territory of present-day Zimbabwe was formed when the Zulu general Mzilikazi (c. 1790–1868) – one of the main protagonists of the *Mfecane* – split from King Shaka over the latter's attempt to introduce compulsory celibacy for high-ranking military officers.[265]

The catastrophic drought proved devastating to Bantu culture when the mass death of cattle threatened their prosperity. As is not uncommon in Sub-Saharan Africa, people came to associate the unusual circumstances with witchcraft. Although Shaka himself may not have believed in witchcraft, he realised in 1817 that he must take his subjects' complaints concerning the death of their livestock seriously. For that reason, he had some three or four hundred suspects rounded up and executed for sorcery.[266] And he was not alone. Witch hunts also took place in the Kerebe kingdom in East Africa under King Mihigo II (c. 1780–1820).[267] But this response was apparently not the only possible one. Even during the drought King Moshoeshoe I explicitly rejected sorcery as an explanation of the damage to livestock and crops and instead opened his land to Christian missionaries.[268] Shaka in contrast used the widespread fear arising from the terrible drought to install a reign of terror through continued executions.[269]

In South African historiography, debates about the *Mfecane* have been raging since the 1980s. In opposition to John Omer-Cooper's notion from the 1960s, which saw the expansive Zulu kingdom as the cause of the violent upheavals, Julian Cobbing proposed the thesis that this merely serves as a smokescreen to divert attention from the pernicious influence of Europeans on African societies: the Dutch invasion, the Portuguese slave trade and the British conquest.[270] While dogged debates yielded the insight that *Mfecane* was not the invention of a 'white conspiracy', but a contemporary term used by Black African peoples,[271] one aspect was overlooked – that all people living in South Africa were at the mercy of another actor that nobody had yet considered: Tambora. The Tambora Crisis also contributed to the mass migration and scapegoating reactions in South Africa, including the arrival of British settlers.[272]

The invention of Australia

Emigration from the crisis-ridden British Isles was not always voluntary. Britain intervened massively in the culture and ecology of Australia by transporting convicts there. The Australian continent had been discovered by Dutch explorers, and was known from 1644 as New Holland. In 1770, however, the Englishman Captain James Cook claimed the eastern half of the continent for the British Crown, naming it New South Wales. This crown colony gained in significance when the British government began looking for a new territory to send its convicts to after the North American colonies declared their independence. In the age of Enlightenment it had become common to commute death sentences to deportation, known at the time as transportation. As well as those transported for life, the government also preferred to send a whole series of other undesirables, from habitual thieves and petty criminals to prostitutes, to some distant place. The first eleven ships carrying 778 convicts arrived in 1788, and the first penal colony (and later capital) was named after the Home Secretary at the time, Thomas Townshend, 1st Viscount Sydney.

Upon his arrival in 1810, the new governor Lachlan Macquarie (1762–1824) found a penal colony fighting for survival. However, because of the many people transported to New Holland during the Tambora Crisis, new possibilities for development suddenly emerged. Macquarie predicted a boom in New South Wales and began to construct roads, bridges, churches and public buildings. His policy aimed to attract more civilian colonists to Australia and to keep the convicts there after they had finished their period of banishment, since only some 37 per cent of them had been sentenced to life-long banishment, and the average period was less than ten years. The majority of convicts who had come into conflict with the law in Britain between 1816 and 1820 due to economic hardship, as well as those who had been transported because they participated in demonstrations, will have felt little nostalgia for the chilly island in northern Europe. The climate in New South Wales was pleasant and the promise of a livelihood secure. Those who had been exiled by their homeland could begin a new life here. Governor Macquarie made things easy for them, since once they had served their sentences, he did not distinguish between former convicts and voluntary colonists.

The number of ships transporting convicts rose rapidly during the Tambora Crisis. In the first decade of the nineteenth century, only two or three tall ships a year docked in New South Wales. The numbers rose exponentially after 1816, however, peaking at twenty-two ships in the year of the Cato Street Conspiracy. One can observe a similar development in the number of transported convicts and (as a sub-group) of those sentenced to life-long banishment. The passenger lists of some ships mention not a single convict, while other ships were mainly dedicated to their transportation. On 8 October 1816 two ships, each carrying some 200 convicts, set sail from England. The *Fame* reached New South Wales on 8 March 1817 after five months at sea, the *Sir William Bensley* two days later. The largest transports took place on the *Lady Castlereagh* (303 convicts) and the *Baring* (302 convicts) in 1817 and the *Dromedary* (370 convicts) in 1819. The names of the transported convicts, frequently with their crimes and other data, can be found in the British Convicts Transportation Register.

As with voluntary emigration from Britain to North America, a look at penal transportation to Australia reveals that the numbers began to rise sharply in 1816, but did not return thereafter to previous levels, instead continuing at a high rate. During Macquarie's tenure, the number of Britons rose from 5,000 to 36,000 in 1821. That was nearly as many people as the indigenous population, the so-called Aborigines, who lived in the continent's barren interior, and whose numbers had been decimated by epidemics, especially smallpox, brought in by Europeans.[273]

Governor Macquarie was the first person to assert that Australia

Development of Transportations from Britain to Australia[274]

Year	No. of ships	Exiled	Transported for life
1810	3	387	170
1811	3	502	275
1812	4	572	343
1813	7	625	322
1814	8	1,041	470
1815	6	816	309
1816	9	1,118	493
1817	13	1,619	553
1818	18	2,610	772
1819	16	1,964	671
1820	22	2,746	830
1821	17	2,234	671
1822	13	1,734	741
Total		17,968	6,620

was not simply a new continent, but also a British one. In making the claim he referred to a three-year-old map drawn up by Captain Matthew Flinders, the first to circumnavigate the Australian continent and also to suggest the name 'Terra australis'.[275] A British colony could hardly be named after a European rival. When the number of transportations reached an initial high point during the Tambora Crisis, Macquarie suggested in an official report of 1817 that the territory be renamed Australia. Australians now consider the Scotsman from the Inner Hebrides to be the founder of their nation.[276]

Genocide in Tasmania

During the Tambora Crisis Britain exported its troubles to Australia. At first this was not problematic because the continent was so vast, and many Aboriginals died of imported diseases anyway. The situation was quite different on the island at the continent's southern tip, Van Diemen's Land, which until 1854 bore the name of a Dutchman and is now known as Tasmania. When the British arrived there were some 4,000 indigenous people living there.[277] The island soon served the British as a transportation destination and evolved into the empire's most important penal colony.[278] According to the passenger lists, after the first attempts in 1812 transportations to Van Diemen's Land only resumed in 1817 with the ships *Pilot* and *Canada*, which mainly carried people from Ireland. The penal transportations reached a high point that same year with the 303 convicts aboard the *Lady Castlereagh*.[279] Under Governor Thomas Davey (1758–1823) – an alcoholic who invented a delightful punch consisting of rum, brandy and port that he christened 'Blow my Skull' – the colony descended into chaos. Many convicts escaped, living as 'bushrangers' and hunting to survive while killing Aboriginals and abducting indigenous women.[280]

A typical case was that of the sailor Michael Howe (1787–1818) of Pontefract, Yorkshire,[281] who had been sentenced to seven years' transportation for desertion and highway robbery. In Van Diemen's Land he was assigned to a merchant, but refused to serve him and escaped into the bush. He rose to become leader of his own gang, which attacked not just indigenous people but also British settlements until Governor Macquarie imposed martial law over the colony. Howe was killed by his pursuers in 1818, and his head put on display in the principal town of Hobart.[282] The first book ever printed in Australia was an account of his misdeeds.[283] But it was not only

261

the bushrangers who made life difficult for the native Tasmanians. In March 1817, when the Anglican missionary Rowland Hassall (1768–1820) asked why he saw none in Hobart, he was told 'We shoot them whenever we find them.'[284]

Under Governor William Sorell (1775–1848), the civilian settlement of Tasmania developed alongside the penal colony. With some 6,000 settlers in 1824, there were approximately equal numbers of colonists and convicts. Expeditions into the interior and the settlement of sheep farmers proved as disastrous for the native people as the attacks by bushrangers, since they lost their traditional hunting grounds to enclosure. The Tasmanians were killed or expelled to make room for the settlements. Farmers referred to them as 'black crows' and hunted them because they wanted more land on which to plant grain.[285] Many also died as a result of diseases imported from Europe and Asia. In 1836 there were only 123 native Tasmanians left alive, and the intention was to settle them in a reservation and convert them to Christianity. Most of them soon died of influenza, however. The number of British settlers rose to 25,000 in 1830, alongside more than one million sheep. The British export of the problems caused by the Tambora Crisis ultimately led to the genocide of the Tasmanian people.[286]

— 7 —

EPILOGUE: FROM MEANINGLESS TO MEANINGFUL CRISIS

Some readers may be rubbing their eyes in wonder after reading of a worldwide crisis that they never heard about at school or university. Until recently, not a single historical monograph on the Tambora Crisis had been published anywhere in the world. One can count on one hand the collections of essays on the volcanism of the eruption of Mount Tambora, and they are written mainly for geologists. One standard work of history – Wilhelm Abel's *Massenarmut und Hungerkrisen im vorindustriellen Europa* – at least contains a respectable chapter on the 'Famine Years 1816/17',[1] without however any awareness of the causes and momentous implications of this event. None of the standard works on economic and social history or even the history of poverty mention the Tambora Crisis.[2] In his voluminous social history of Germany, Hans-Ulrich Wehler describes famine as a typical trait of pre-industrial society.[3] Thomas Nipperdey at least views it as 'part of the social preamble to the 1848 revolution'.[4]

In order to grasp this phenomenon, we probably need to proceed from Theodor Lessing's notion of 'history as giving meaning to the meaningless'.[5] Those who regard history as a story of progress and for whom the past is merely a kind of prelude to their own present have a particularly hard time with the Tambora Crisis. Historians tend to prefer the troubles of the 1770s or 1780s in France, which as crises of the moribund ancien régime fit neatly into the master narrative and are frequently cited. This is also the case for the famine of 1845/46 as a precondition for the Revolution of 1848. From this perspective, revolutions are interpreted to some extent as a punishment for existing injustices, as symptoms in which the famines stand out.[6] The famine of 1816/17 appeared 'meaningless' in comparison, if not nonsensical. After all, hadn't the 'bourgeois revolution' of 1789, and the transfer of the reforms it instituted to the rest of Europe, ushered in a new era? A new age would dawn after the end of the wars, or so contemporaries thought. What they got instead was the Tambora Crisis.

A major crisis instead of the anticipated reward for sensible and long-awaited reforms and peace treaties made no narrative sense. In fact, it virtually challenged the master narrative. Many historians thus simply retouched it out of existence. Things simply had to improve after revolutions, reforms and peace agreements, before renewed reform bottlenecks produced renewed penalties. German historiography pounced on the 'German question' of an allegedly necessary 'national unification', and blended it with the question of 'political liberty'. The German Confederation had denied freedom-loving Germans a nation-state, and the evil Austrian Chancellor Metternich had suppressed German liberty with the Carlsbad Decrees. The quasi-necessary consequences – according to the nineteenth-century Prussian master narrative – were the Revolution of 1848 and the anti-Austrian founding of a Prusso-German nation-state in 1871.

If we were to remove our nationalist glasses and focus on cultural reactions in Europe, we could write quite different histories. Among the supposed friends of liberty attending the Wartburg festival, those who preferred to abandon enlightened tolerance and take the immediate measure of killing the Jews set the tone. The murder of the author August von Kotzebue and the ensuing Hep-Hep pogroms – as well as similar murderous actions in France and England – revealed a terrorist penchant for violence that the governments of the day had to combat at all costs, and which even today any government dedicated to the public peace needs to nip in the bud. It is hard to avoid drawing a connection between the terrorism of the time and the increasingly ideological quality of politics since the French Revolution on the one hand, and the brutalisation and propensity towards violence of a generation that had lived through twenty years of war on the other. If one wanted to jump to conclusions in the style of the antiquated master narratives, one could assert with some justification that the path embarked upon at the Wartburg festival inevitably led to the Holocaust.[7] The devotees of realpolitik in 1819 were anxious to prevent such developments and sought to keep the 'demagogues' from gaining further influence. Their response was to enact repressive laws, but these were rooted in the need to combat a genuine risk of terrorism, not just in Germany but also in France and England.[8] In his doctoral thesis Henry Kissinger emphasised that Metternich's political system, decried by liberal contemporaries and later historians, kept the peace in Europe for more than a generation.[9]

With his strict focus on foreign policy, however, Kissinger failed to notice the social conflict that Metternich's system had also helped to contain, and that laid the foundations for the murderous fury in Europe.

One could take this reckoning with traditional historiography in the spirit of a new global or world history still further, and list the costs and the drawbacks of a history of human progress that emerged in the course of the Tambora Crisis. One could begin with the starving paupers who were sacrificed to raison d'état in the centre of Europe. The mass emigration sparked by the Tambora Crisis contained all manner of explosive material. One could delve more deeply into the settlement of Novorossiya, in which sect members from Württemberg were used to drive Turks and Tatars out of the Black Sea region and the Caucasus. In parts of Africa, Ceylon and India the wealthy local elites were forced under the yoke of the British Empire. The disenfranchisement of indigenous peoples was repeatedly associated with displacement or genocide, as in the British colony of Tasmania or the westward expansion of the United States. Migration from the eastern states and Europe exacted a high price.

Many of these processes would doubtless have occurred even without the Tambora Crisis, which merely served as a catalyst. Others might have taken a different course. But the inclusion of these atrocities shows that crop failures were not a negligible disruptive factor in the development of a liberal society, but an integral component of an era plagued by problems. The effects of the Tambora Crisis were astonishing in some respects, leading as they did to a return to neglected knowledge from the world of the ancien régime. And some of this recovered knowledge remains valid today – for instance that famines cannot be solved with free trade, adversity is not a private matter and social relief is best organised by local authorities. That people need to put something away for hard times, and a proper legal framework is required for them to do so. That adequate provision of the necessities of life requires a corresponding infrastructure, and creating it is a public task. That there can be no social peace without attending to the social question. Other insights were more recent and suddenly became very topical because of the Tambora Crisis: that there can be no orderly state finances without elections and political participation, and no political stability without combating terrorism. And, naturally, that there can be no progress without freedom.

The apparently 'meaningless' Tambora Crisis makes sense within a new master narrative. Human acts seem small and insignificant in the face of natural disasters, and human beings play no role in deciding when they happen. Politics can only respond to them more or less intelligently. The consequences of a great volcanic eruption present an international challenge, since they affect the climate. Climate events do not follow the logic of historical development, but act upon societies as external factors. The after-effects of the Tambora eruption were not permanent, but for a limited period they altered the entire ecological framework. In some places the weather became colder and vegetation phases shorter; in others it was wetter and certain agrarian products rotted, while elsewhere the climate was drier and livestock died of thirst. Apparently minor changes in temperature and humidity sufficed (and still suffice today) to shake up entrenched ecosystems, but above all entrenched agricultural systems. And without their 'daily bread', people can very quickly become angry. In such a situation it is clear – even in 'absolutist' monarchies or dictatorships – who the sovereign is.

How people respond to such challenges is a function of cultural flexibility. And culture must be understood here in the broadest possible sense, taking in everything including religion and politics, approaches to knowledge resources and social problems, the state of technology and agricultural production, the crops planted and the existing (or non-existent) buffering strategies in the case of crop failures. The Tambora Crisis was a test case of the vulnerability of the civilisations of the day, which still functioned separately despite globalisation. Natural disasters resist moral categorisation. Their effects are unequally distributed; in the case of a volcanic eruption, for example, they depend on the distribution of geological hot spots under the earth, on the continental drift, but also on the direction the wind blows in the days and weeks after the eruption as well as the position of the jet streams in the decisive months. It was pure chance that India and South Africa became dry in 1816, North America cold and dry and western Europe cold and wet, while Russia enjoyed ideal living conditions. Where the Tambora Crisis took hold, reactions to it differed greatly: increased religiosity but also a practical spirit of invention in the USA; witch hunts in southern Africa; hectic social legislation and initial liberal reforms but then repressive measures against protest movements in Europe; an economic boom in Russia; the emergence of class society in Britain; political destabilisation in China; genocide in Tasmania.

A new master narrative might entail an awareness of the vulnerability of human culture to climatic changes in particular, despite progress and advanced technology. The very fact that the Tambora Crisis occurred so inopportunely at a time of optimism about progress may open our eyes to this. Many phenomena of those years – the toppling of governments, mass protests, mass migration, employment programmes, agrarian reforms, the rise of new scientific disciplines, religious renewal, river regulation, pauperism, the introduction of new technologies, the founding of savings banks and life insurance, the power shift in international politics, etc. – only make sense against the background of the Tambora Crisis. The climate, whether influenced by human factors or not, is part of human history. It is no accident that people developed an intense interest in weather observation, volcanism, geology, agricultural chemistry and the microbiology of bodies of water in the years of the Tambora Crisis. If we are to understand human history, we must include 'nature' as a category.

ABBREVIATIONS

ADB	Allgemeine Deutsche Biographie
BLKÖ	Bibliographisches Lexikon des Kaiserthums Österreich
DNB	Dictionary of National Biography
ESSA	Environmental Science Services Administration, USA
fl.	florins, guilders (the main currency in central Europe)
NDB	Neue Deutsche Biographie
SPP	Society for the Prevention of Pauperism
VEI	Volcanic Explosivity Index
VOC	Verenigde Oost-Indische Compagnie (Dutch East India Company)
WA	Weimarer Ausgabe (edition of the works of Goethe)
ZBLG	Zeitschrift für Bayerische Landesgeschichte
ZGO	Zeitschrift für die Geschichte des Oberrheins
ZWLG	Zeitschrift für Württembergische Landesgeschichte

NOTES

1 Introduction: The Tambora Crisis

1 Henry and Elizabeth Stommel, *Volcano Weather: The Story of the Year Without a Summer 1816* (Newport, RI, 1983).
2 John Dexter Post, *The Last Great Subsistence Crisis in the Western World* (Baltimore, 1977).
3 D. Chakrabarty, 'The climate of history: Four theses', *Critical Inquiry* 35, no. 2 (2009): 197–222.
4 Carl Edward Skeen, *1816 America Rising* (Lexington, 2003).
5 Kenneth Pomeranz, *The Great Divergence: China, Europe, and the Making of the Modern World Economy* (Princeton, NJ, 2000).
6 Dominik Collet and Thore Lassen (eds), *Handeln in Hungerkrisen. Neue Perspektiven auf soziale und klimatische Vulnerabilität* (Göttingen, 2012).
7 Henry Kissinger, *A World Restored: Metternich, Castlereagh and the Problem of Peace 1812–1822* (Boston, 1957). The author affirms the thesis of this work, which began as a PhD thesis at Harvard University in 1954, in his *World Order* (New York, 2014).
8 Robert Marjolin, *Essai sur la crise de subsistence de 1816–1817* (Paris, 1931) and 'Troubles provoqués en France par la disette de 1816–1817', *Revue d'Histoire Moderne* 8 (1933): 423–60.
9 Dieter Langewiesche, *Europa zwischen Restauration und Revolution 1815–1849*, 4th edn (Munich, 2004), 31.
10 Gordon A. Craig, *Europe, 1815–1914* (New York, 1961), 57–9 (Austria), 77–8 (France), 101–5 (England).
11 Emile Durkheim, *The Rules of Sociological Method and Selected Texts on Sociology and its Method*, ed. Steven Lukes (New York, 2013), 7.
12 David. G. Myers, *Psychology*, 8th edn (New York and Basingstoke, 2007), chapter 1.
13 Peter Scheitlin, *Meine Armenreisen in den Kanton Glarus und in die Umgebungen der Stadt St. Gallen in den Jahren 1816 und 1817, nebst einer Darstellung, wie es den Armen des gesamten Vaterlandes im Jahr 1817 erging. Ein Beytrag zur Charakteristik unserer Zeit* (St. Gallen, 1820), 14–15 (online edition).

14 Amartya Sen, 'Starvation and exchange entitlements. A general approach and its application to the Great Bengal Famine', *Cambridge Journal of Economics* 1 (1977): 33–59.

15 Spencer R. Weart, *The Discovery of Global Warming* (Cambridge, MA, 2003).

16 Wolfgang Behringer, *Kulturgeschichte des Klimas* (Munich, 2007), 254–64.

17 Michael S. Rampino and Stephen Self, 'Historic eruptions of Tambora (1815), Krakatoa (1883) and Agung (1963), their stratospheric aerosols and climatic impact', *Quaternary Research* 18 (1982): 127–43.

18 Royal Society, Krakatoa Committee (eds), *The Eruption of Krakatoa, and Subsequent Phenomena* (London, 1888).

19 Vilhjalmar Bjarnar, 'The Laki eruption (1783/84) and the famine of the mist', in Carl F. Bayerschmidt and Erik J. Friis (eds), *Scandinavian Studies* (Seattle, 1965), 410–21.

20 William Jackson Humphreys, 'Volcanic dust and other factors in the production of climatic changes, and their possible relation to ice ages', *Bulletin of the Mount Weather Observatory* 6 (1913): 1–34.

21 Hubert H. Lamb, 'Volcanic dust in the atmosphere. With a chronology and assessments of its meteorological significance', *Philosophical Transactions of the Royal Meteorological Society* 266 (1970): 425–533.

22 Claus U. Hammer, H.B. Clausen and Willi Dansgaard, 'Greenland ice sheet evidence of post-glacial volcanism and its climatic impact', *Nature* 288 (1980): 230–5.

23 V.C. LaMarche and K. Hirschboeck, 'Frost rings in trees as records of major volcanic eruptions', *Nature* 307 (1984): 121–6.

24 Tom Simkin and Lee Siebert, *Volcanoes of the World. A Regional Directory, Gazetteer, and Chronology of Volcanism During the Last 10,000 Years*, 3rd edn (Berkeley, 2010), 215–327 (Holocene eruptions) and 361–70 (Pleistocene eruptions).

25 Christopher G. Newhall and Stephen Self, 'The Volcanic Explosivity Index (VEI): An estimate of explosive magnitude for historical volcanism', *Journal of Geophysical Research* 87 (1982): 1231–8.

26 Haraldur Sigurdsson, *Melting the Earth: The History of Ideas on Volcanic Eruptions* (Oxford and New York, 1999), 51–70. The Pliny text is cited on pp. 61–4.

27 Floyd W. McCoy and Grant Heiken, 'The late-bronze age explosive eruptions of Thera (Santorini), Greece: Regional and local effects', in Floyd W. McCoy and Grant Heiken (eds), *Volcanic Hazards and Disasters in Human Antiquity*, Special Papers of the Geological Society of America 345 (Boulder, CO, 2000), 43–70.

28 Michael R. Rampino and Stanley H. Ambrose, 'Volcanic winter in the garden of Eden: The Toba supereruption and the late Pleistocene human population crash', in McCoy and Heiken (eds), *Volcanic Hazards*, 71–82.

29 Stanley H. Ambrose, 'Late Pleistocene human population bottlenecks, volcanic winter and differentiation of modern humans', *Journal of Human Evolution* 34 (1982): 623–51.

30 Michael R. Rampino, Stephen Self and Richard B. Stothers, 'Volcanic winters', *Annual Review of Earth and Planetary Science* 16 (1988): 73–99.

31 Patrick Hughes, 'Eighteen hundred and froze-to-death', *ESSA* 15 (July 1970): 33–5.

32 Lee-Lee Schlegel, 'The year without a summer. 1816, in Maine', www.milbridgehistoricalsociety.org/previous/no_summer.html.
33 Charles M. Wilson, 'The year without a summer', *American History Illustrated 5* (June 1970): 24–9; Stommel and Stommel, *Volcano Weather*, and '1816. Das Jahr ohne Sommer', *Spektrum der Wissenschaft* (1983): 96–103; Willie Soon and Steven H. Yaskell, 'Year without a summer', *Mercury* (May/June 2003): 13–22; Jelle Zeilinga de Boer and Donald Theodore Sanders, *Volcanoes in Human History: The Far-reaching Effects of Major Eruptions* (Princeton, NJ, 2002).
34 Ricardo Garcia Herrera et al., 'Description and general background to ship's logbooks as a source of climate data', *Climatic Change* 73 (2005): 13–36.
35 Clive Oppenheimer, 'Climatic, environmental and human consequences of the largest known historic eruption, Tambora volcano (Indonesia) 1815', *Progress in Physical Geography* 27 (2003): 230–59.
36 Stommel and Stommel, *Volcano Weather*.
37 Charles Richard Harrington (ed.), *The Year Without a Summer? World Climate in 1816* (Ottawa, 1992).
38 Oppenheimer, 'Climatic, environmental and human consequences', 230–59.
39 William K. Klingaman and Nicholas P. Klingaman, *The Year Without Summer: 1816 and the Volcano that Darkened the World and Changed History* (New York, 2013).
40 Gillen d'Arcy Wood, *Tambora: The Eruption that Changed the World* (Princeton, NJ, 2014).
41 Gerald Müller, *Hunger in Bayern, 1816–1818. Politik und Gesellschaft in einer Staatskrise des frühen 19. Jahrhunderts* (Frankfurt am Main, 1998).
42 Myron Echenberg, *Africa in the Time of Cholera: A History of Pandemics from 1817 to the Present* (Cambridge, 2011).

2 The Year of the Explosion: 1815

1 Michael Brouers, *Europe under Napoleon, 1799–1815* (London, 1996); Günther Rothenberg, *Die Napoleonischen Kriege* (Berlin, 2000).
2 Adam Zamoyski, *1812. Napoleons Feldzug in Russland* (Munich, 2012).
3 Jeremy Black, *The War of 1812 in the Age of Napoleon* (London, 2009).
4 Robert A. Rutland, *James Madison: The Founding Father* (New York, 1987), 217–24.
5 Donald Hickey, *The War of 1812: A Forgotten Conflict* (Urbana, IL, 1989).
6 Dieter Langewiesche, *Europa zwischen Restauration und Revolution, 1815–1849* (Munich, 2004), 9.
7 Heinz Duchhardt, *Der Wiener Kongress. Die Neugestaltung Europas 1814/15* (Munich, 2013), 9–11.
8 Thierry Lentz, *Le Congrès de Vienne. Une refondation de l'Europe 1814–1815* (Paris, 2013).
9 Wolf D. Gruner, *Der Deutsche Bund, 1815–1866* (Munich, 2010).
10 Frank Bauer, *Zar Alexander I. von Russland* (Potsdam, 2008).
11 [Sophia Hull Raffles, ed.] *Memoir of the Life and Public Services of Sir Thomas Stamford Raffles, Particularly in the Government of Java 1811–1816, Bencoolen and its Dependencies 1817–1824: with Details of the*

Commerce and Resources of the Eastern Archipelago, and Selections from his Correspondence. By his Widow. A New Edition, in two volumes, vol. 1 (London, 1835).

12 Thomas Stafford Raffles, *The History of Java* (London, 1817).

13 Shanaka L. de Silva, J. Alzueta and G. Salas, 'The socioeconomic consequences of the A.D. 1600 eruption of Huaynaputina, southern Peru', in McCoy and Heiken (eds), *Volcanic Hazards*, 15–24.

14 Vilhjalmar Bjarnar, 'The Laki eruption [1783/84] and the famine of the mist', in Carl F. Bayerschmidt and Erk J. Friis (eds), *Scandinavian Studies* (Seattle, 1965), 410–21.

15 Bernice De Jong Boers, 'Mount Tambora in 1815: A volcanic eruption in Indonesia and its aftermath', *Indonesia* 60 (1995): 41.

16 *Java Government Gazette*, 29 April 1815. Cited in De Jong Boers, 'Mount Tambora', 42.

17 John Crawfurd, *A Descriptive Dictionary of the Indian Islands and Adjacent Countries* (London, 1856), 437.

18 J.T. Ross, 'Narrative of the effects of the eruption from the Tomboro mountain in the island of Sumbawa on the 11th and 12th of April 1815. Communicated by the president of the Batavian Society, 28 September 1815', *Verhandelingen van het Bataviaasch Genootschap von Konsten en Wetenschappen* 8 (1816): 3–4, 12–13.

19 Heinrich Zollinger, *Besteigung des Vulkanes Tambora auf der Insel Sumbawa und Schilderung der Erupzion* [sic] *desselben im Jahr 1815* (Winterthur, 1855), 11.

20 W.A. Petroeschevsky, 'A contribution to the knowledge of Gunung Tambora (Sumbawa)', *Tijdskrift von het Koninklijk Nederlands Aardrijkskundig Genootschap* 66 (1949): 688–703, 695.

21 Rampino and Self, 'Historic eruptions', 127–43.

22 Jürgen G. Nagel, *Der Schlüssel zu den Molukken – Makassar und die Handelsstrukturen des Malaiischen Archipels im 17. und 18. Jahrhundert – eine exemplarische Studie* (Hamburg, 2003).

23 De Jong Boers, 'Mount Tambora', 40.

24 J.C.M. Radermacher, *Korte beschrijving van het eiland Celebes ende eilanden Floris, Sumbawa, Lombok en Bali* (1786), 186; translated and cited in De Jong Boers, 'Mount Tambora', 39.

25 Rik Stoetman and Dan MacLerran, 'Lost kingdom of Tambora', *Past Horizons. Adventures in Archaeology* 11 (2009) (online).

26 Zollinger, *Besteigung des Vulkanes*, 20.

27 De Jong Boers, 'Mount Tambora', 44.

28 Zollinger, *Besteigung des Vulkanes*, 20.

29 De Jong Boers, 'Mount Tambora', 44.

30 Zollinger, *Besteigung des Vulkanes*, 20.

31 Peter R. Goethals, *Aspects of Local Government in a Sumbawan Village (Eastern Indonesia)*, Cornell Modern Indonesia Project (Ithaca, NY, 1961); De Jong Boers, 'Mount Tambora', 46.

32 Zollinger, *Besteigung des Vulkanes*, 102–5.

33 Zollinger, *Besteigung des Vulkanes*, 12.

34 Zollinger, *Besteigung des Vulkanes*, 4–11.

35 M. Eerb, *When Rocks were Young and Earth was Soft: Ritual and Mythology in Northwestern Manggarai* (New York, 1982), 37.

36 De Jong Boers, 'Mount Tambora', 48–9.
37 *Bataviasche Courant*, 26 October 1816.
38 De Jong Boers, 'Mount Tambora', 49.
39 De Jong Boers, 'Mount Tambora', 50.
40 Adrian Vickers, *Bali: A Paradise Created* (Berkeley, CA, 1989), 67.
41 *Java Government Gazette*, 20 and 27 May 1815; De Jong Boers, 'Mount Tambora', 48.
42 Simkin and Siebert, *Volcanoes of the World*, 83–101, 256–8.
43 Simkin and Siebert, *Volcanoes of the World*, 256–8.
44 Wilhelm Christian Müller, *Fünfhundertjährige Witterungsgeschichte, besonders der außerordentlichen Kälte; nebst Beobachtungen ihrer Perioden und Einwirkungen auf die Menschheit* (Bremen, 1823), 74–5.
45 Klaus Fischer, 'Das Hungerjahr 1816/17 in Tirol und der Ausbruch des Vulkans Tambora. Ein Beispiel der Wirksamkeit großer Vulkanausbrüche auf das Klimasystem der Erde', *Der Schlern* 73 (1999): 5–22.
46 George Davis, *Frostiana, or a History of the River Thames in a Frozen State* (London, 1814).
47 Müller, *Fünfhundertjährige Witterungsgeschichte*, 72–3.
48 Hartmut Steger, 'Das Hungerjahr 1817 im Ries', *Rieser Kulturtage* 7 (1988): 299.
49 Fischer, 'Das Hungerjahr 1816/17', 5.
50 Müller, *Fünfhundertjährige Witterungsgeschichte*, 74–5.
51 Paul Henchoz, 'L'année de la misère (1816–1817) dans la région de Montreux', *Revue historique vaudoise* 42 (1934): 69–70.
52 Christa and Wolfgang Jäger, *Die Hungerjahre 1816/17 im heutigen Landkreis Haßberge* (Haßfurt, 2008), 8.
53 F.A. Rollo Russell, 'General list of dates of first appearances of all the optical phenomena', in Royal Society, Krakatoa Committee, *The Eruption of Krakatoa*: 263–312.
54 Joseph Weber, 'Nebensonnen', *Annalen der Physik* 50 (1815): 217–18.
55 Skeen, *1816 America Rising*, 9–10.
56 Jonathan Bate, *The Song of the Earth* (Cambridge, 2000), 97.
57 Reginald Orton, *An Essay on the Epidemic of Cholera in India*, 2nd edn with a supplement (London, 1831), 174.
58 Johann Christoph Daniel Wildt, 'Über den auffallenden Höhenrauch dieses Sommers', *Hannöverisches Magazin*, nos. 72–74 (Hannover, 1819).
59 Leonhard L. Finke, *Naturhistorische Bemerkungen, betreffend eine auf vieljährigen meteorologischen Beobachtungen sich stützende Beschreibung des Moordampfes in Westfalen und seine nachteiligen Einflüsse auf die dortige Witterung; nebst Beurteilung des großen Unterschiedes, der zwischen Moordampf und Höhenrauch stattfindet, und der oft irrigen Verwechslung des letzern mit dem ersten* (Hannover, 1820).
60 Klingaman and Klingaman, *The Year Without Summer*, 21.
61 De Jong Boers, 'Mount Tambora', 53.
62 Klingaman and Klingaman, *The Year Without Summer*, 17–19.
63 Elie Halévy, *The Liberal Awakening, 1815–1830* (London, 1961), 4–5.
64 Norman Gash, *Lord Liverpool: The Life and Political Career of Robert Banks Jenkinson, Second Earl of Liverpool, 1770–1828* (London, 1984), 116–18.

65 See M. Dorothy George, British Museum website (from Catalogue of Political and Personal Satires in the British Museum, IX, 1949).

3 The Year without a Summer: 1816

1 Anonymous, *Schwabacher Intelligenzblatt* (1816): 3. Cited in Müller, *Hunger in Bayern, 1816–1818*, 222.
2 Friedrich Rückert, 'Zum Neujahr 1816', verse 8, in *Die Deutsche Gedichtebibliothek* (online).
3 Jeffrey Vail, '"The bright sun was extinguish'd": The Bologna prophecy and Byron's "Darkness"', *The Wordsworth Circle* 28 (1997): 184.
4 Klingaman and Klingaman, *The Year Without Summer*, 29–30.
5 Johannes Fabricius, *De maculis in sole observatis [...]* (Wittenberg, 1611).
6 John A. Eddy, 'The "Maunder minimum". Sunspots and climate in the reign of Louis XIV', in Geoffrey Parker and Lesley M. Smith (eds), *The General Crisis of the Seventeenth Century* (London, 1978), 226–68.
7 Judit Brody, *The Enigma of Sunspots: A Story of Discovery and Scientific Revolution* (Edinburgh, 2002), 104.
8 Sebastian Wagner and Eduardo Zorita, 'The influence of volcanic, solar and CO_2 forcing on the temperatures in the Dalton minimum (1790–1830). A model study', *Climate Dynamics* 25 (2005): 205–18 (online).
9 Steger, 'Hungerjahr 1817', 294–315.
10 David Müslin, *Ist diese Theuerung von Gott oder ist sie eine blosse Abirrung der Natur? Drei Predigten* (Berne, 1816).
11 Hans Petri, 'Zur Geschichte der Auswanderung aus Württemberg nach Russland', *Blätter für Württembergische Kirchengeschichte* 57/58 (1957/58): 373–9, 376.
12 Joseph von Hazzi, *Betrachtungen über Theuerung und Noth der Vergangenheit und Gegenwart, geschrieben im Herbst 1817* (Munich, 1818) (online), 78–9.
13 Brody, *Enigma of Sunspots*, 174–5.
14 Müller, *Fünfhundertjährige Witterungsgeschichte*, 74.
15 J. David Wood, 'The complicity of climate in the 1816 depression in Dumfriesshire', *Scottish Geographical Magazine* 81 (1965): 5–17, 8.
16 Hans Bach, 'Die Teuerung 1816 und 1817 in Gunzenhausen', *Alt-Gunzenhausen* 21 (1944): 29–33, 29.
17 Fischer, 'Das Hungerjahr 1816/17', 6.
18 Emiel Vanderlinden, *Chronique des événéments météorologiques en Belgique jusqu'en 1834* (Brussels, 1924), 305.
19 P. Placidus Heinrich, 'Auszüge des meteorologischen Tagebuches von Professor Heinrich in Regensburg', *Journal für Chemie und Physik* 17 (1816/17): 368.
20 *Friedens und Kriegs Kurier*, 18 June 1816, cited in Manfred Vasold, 'Das Jahr des großen Hungers. Die Agrarkrise von 1816/17 im Nürnberger Raum', *ZBLG* 64 (2001): 756.
21 Halévy, *The Liberal Awakening*, 9.
22 Halévy, *The Liberal Awakening*, 10.
23 Mary Shelley, *History of a Six Weeks' Tour. Letters Written During a*

Residence of Three Months in the Environs of Geneva, in the Summer of the Year 1816 (London, 1817), Letter 1.

24 Shelley, *History*, Letter 2.
25 Henchoz, 'L'année de la misère', 74.
26 Henchoz, 'L'année de la misère', 76–7.
27 Marc Henrioud, 'L'année de la misère en Suisse et plus particulièrement dans le canton de Vaud 1816–1817', *Revue historique vaudoise* 25 (1917): 116.
28 Fischer, 'Das Hungerjahr 1816/17', 6.
29 Karl Obser, 'Frau von Krüdener in der Schweiz und im badischen Seekreis', *Schriften des Vereins für Geschichte des Bodensees und seiner Umgebung* 39 (1810): 79–93, 90.
30 Jäger and Jäger, *Die Hungerjahre 1816/17*, 8.
31 Heinrich Joachim Jäck, *Beschreibung der Verwüstungen, welche der am 15. Juni 1816 in Tiefenhöchstadt gefallene Wolkenbruch bewirkte [...]* (Bamberg, 1816) (online).
32 Karl Ernst Adolf von Hoff, *Annalen meines Lebens. Die Tagebücher des Gothaer Geologen und Staatsbeamten Karl Ernst Adolf von Hoff. 1771–1837*, ed. Karin Dreißig and Thomas Martens (Weimar, 2012), 287.
33 Bach, 'Die Teuerung 1816 und 1817', 30.
34 Steger, 'Das Hungerjahr', 300.
35 Müller, *Fünfhundertjährige Witterungsgeschichte*, 74–7.
36 Wood, 'The complicity of climate', 8.
37 *The Times*, 20 July 1816.
38 *Norfolk Chronicle*, 20 July 1816.
39 Geoffrey Parker, *Global Crisis: War, Climate Change and Catastrophe in the Seventeenth Century* (New Haven, CT and London, 2013), 688.
40 Stommel and Stommel, *Volcano Weather*, 25–30.
41 Thomas Robbins, *Diary* (online).
42 Stommel and Stommel, *Volcano Weather*, 41.
43 Gisela Mettele, *Weltbürgertum oder Gottesreich. Die Herrnhuter Brüdergemeine als globale Gemeinschaft 1727–1857* (Göttingen, 2009).
44 Adelaide L. Fries (ed.), *Records of the Moravians in North Carolina, 1752–1879*, 11 vols, vol. 7 (1809–1822) (Raleigh, NC, 1947), 3318.
45 *Goethes Werke* (WA), IV. Abteilung: *Goethes Briefe*, vol. 27 (May 1816–February 1817), (Weimar, 1903), 47 (Letter to Eichstädt, 4 June 1816).
46 *Goethes Werke* (WA), vol. 27, 51 (Letter to Zelter, 8 June 1816).
47 *Goethes Werke* (WA), III. Abteilung: *Goethes Tagebücher*, vol. 5 (1813–1816) (Weimar, 1893), 239.
48 Goethe, *Hamburger Ausgabe in 14 Bänden*, vol. 1, 345, commentary, p. 706.
49 *Goethes Werke* (WA), vol. 27, 51, 65, 68, 76.
50 *Goethes Werke* (WA), vol. 5, 245.
51 *Goethes Werke* (WA), vol. 27, 72, 100, 101, 110.
52 *Goethes Werke* (WA), vol. 27, 117–18 (report to Grand Duchess Louise, 22 July 1816), 116–22 (he used virtually the same words to inform his friends and publishers). There is also an almost identical account in the diary: *Goethes Werke* (WA), vol. 5, 255–6.
53 Ernst Florens Friedrich Chladni, *Über Feuermeteore* (Vienna, 1820).
54 *Goethes Werke* (WA), vol. 5, 256.

55 Ernst Florens Friedrich Chladni, 'Über die Ursachen des naßkalten Sommers von 1816, und zum Theil auch 1817', *Annalen der Physik* 62 (1819): 132–6.
56 *Goethes Werke* (WA), vol. 27, 122–36.
57 *Goethes Werke* (WA), vol. 27, 224–6.
58 *Goethes Werke* (WA), vol. 27, 273, 287.
59 *Goethes Werke* (WA), III. Abteilung: *Goethes Tagebücher*, vol. 6 (1817–1818) (Weimar, 1894), 15.
60 Georg Friedrich von Jäger, *Ueber die Missbildungen der Gewächse. Ein Beytrag zur Geschichte und Theorie der Missentwicklungen organischer Körper* (Stuttgart, 1814) (online).
61 *Goethes Werke* (WA), vol. 5, 380. Goethe paid homage to Howard in his poem 'Howards Ehrengedächtnis' (1821). See Richard Hamblyn, *The Invention of Clouds: How an Amateur Meteorologist Forged the Language of the Skies* (New York, 2001).
62 Albrecht Schöne, 'Über Goethes Wolkenlehre', *Jahrbuch der Akademie der Wissenschaften in Göttingen für das Jahr 1968* (Göttingen, 1969): 26–48.
63 *The Times*, 29 July 1816.
64 Vail, 'The bright sun', 188.
65 Report of 29 July in the London *Morning Post*.
66 *Détails sur la fin du monde* (Paris, 1816). On this, see Henrioud, 'L'année de la misère', 173; and John Clubbe, 'The tempest-toss'd summer of 1816. Mary Shelley's *Frankenstein*', *The Byron Journal* 19 (1991): 26–40, 28.
67 *New British Lady's Magazine*, 1 August, 78–89, cited in Vail, 'The bright sun', 186.
68 Thomas Epple, *Der Aufstieg der Untergangsseherin Kassandra. Zum Wandel ihrer Interpretation vom 18. Jahrhundert bis zur Gegenwart* (Würzburg, 1993).
69 'The day the world was to be at an end', in John Cam Hobhouse, *Recollections of a Long Life*, ed. Lady Dorchester, 2 vols (London, 1909), vol. 1, 348.
70 Joseph Farington, *The Diary*, ed. Kenneth Garlick and Angus MacIntyre, 17 vols (New Haven, CT, 1978–1998), vol. 15, 4875.
71 Henrioud, 'L'année de la misère', 173.
72 Tom Bodenmann et al., 'Perceiving, understanding, and observing climatic change: An historical case study of the "year without a summer" 1816', *Meteorologische Zeitschrift* 20 (2011): 577–87, 579.
73 *The Times*, 20 July 1816.
74 Scheitlin, *Meine Armenreisen*, 36–7.
75 Jäger and Jäger, *Die Hungerjahre 1816/17*, 9.
76 Hazzi, *Betrachtungen über Theuerung*, 77–8.
77 Walter Demel, *Der bayerische Staatsabsolutismus 1806/08–1817. Staats- und gesellschaftspolitische Motivationen und Hintergründe der Reformära in der ersten Phase des Königreichs Bayern* (Munich, 1983), 81.
78 Demel, *Der bayerische Staatsabsolutismus*, 81.
79 Fedor de Karacsay, *Freymüthige Gedanken über die Theuerung in Wien* (Vienna, 1816) (online).
80 Maria Palomba, 'La crisi agraria del 1815–1817', in Angelo Massafra (ed.), *Il Mezzogiorno preunitario: economia, società e istituzioni* (Bari, 1988), 149–68, 150.

81 Werner Weidmann, *Die pfälzische Landwirtschaft zu Beginn des 19. Jahrhunderts* (Saarbrücken, 1968), 101.

82 Felix Joseph Müller, *Ueber die gegenwärtige Theuerung der Lebensmittel und ihre Urquellen* (Donauwörth, 1817), 5–6.

83 Daily reports, in Demel, *Der bayerische Staatsabsolutismus*, 81–2.

84 Henrioud, 'L'année de la misère', 118.

85 Eberhard Weis, *Montgelas*, vol. 2: *Der Architekt des modernen bayerischen Staates 1799–1838* (Munich, 2005), 773.

86 Albert Ludwig von Seutter, *Versuch einer Darstellung der höhern Landwirthschaftswissenschaft. Für Cameralisten, Oekonomen und Oekonomieverwalter* (Leipzig, 1813).

87 Albert Ludwig von Seutter, *Über die allgemeine Getreide-Theuerung im Jahre 1816* (Regensburg, n.d.), 6–27.

88 Hazzi, *Betrachtungen über Theuerung*.

89 Ignaz von Rudhart, *Über den Zustand des Königreichs Bayern nach amtlichen Quellen*, 3 vols (Stuttgart, 1825–1827), vol. 1, 118–19.

90 Georg Karl Leopold Seuffert, *Statistik des Getreide- und Viktualienhandels im Königreiche Bayern mit Berücksichtigung des Auslandes* (Munich, 1857), 16, 124, 160, 223 (online).

91 Anonymous (M.R.), *Ansichten über die gegenwärtige Getreid-Theuerung* (Munich, 1817) (online).

92 Although never prohibited altogether, grain imports were subject from October 1816 to increasingly strict controls and restrictions in the form of a series of laws pushed by domestic policymakers. Demel, *Der bayerische Staatsabsolutismus*, 411–13.

93 Ludwig Graf von Montgelas (ed.), *Denkwürdigkeiten des bayerischen Staatsministers Maximilian Grafen von Montgelas (1799–1817). Im Auszug aus dem französischen Original übersetzt von Max Freiherrn von Freyberg-Eisenberg* (Stuttgart, 1887), 542.

94 Hazzi, *Betrachtungen über Theuerung*, 145–6.

95 *Deutsches Rechtswörterbuch* (Weimar 1914–), vol. 7 (1974–1983) (online). The first documented use was by a learned Lutheran pastor in the imperial city of Kempten, Georg Zeämann (1580–1638), who had studied in Wittenberg: Georg Zeämann, *Geitz und Wucher Armee, so zu gentzlicher Verwürr- und Verwüstung Teutschlands vom Sathan auff die Bein gebracht; das ist Zwantzig Thewrungs- und Wucher Predigten* (Kempten, 1622), 269–72, 399 (online), where it appears in the marginalia with a reference to the Biblical passage Luke 12: 19 et seq.

96 Thomas Kaufmann, *Luthers Juden* (Leipzig, 2014).

97 Manfred Gailus, 'Kornjuden', in *Handbuch des Antisemitismus*, 7 vols, ed. Wolfgang Benz, vol. 3 (Berlin, 2010), 178–80 (online).

98 Stefi Jersch-Wenzel, 'Rechtslage und Emanzipation', in Michael Brenner et al. (eds), *Deutsch-Jüdische Geschichte in der Neuzeit*, vol. 2: *Emanzipation und Akkulturation, 1780–1871* (Munich, 1996), 15–56, 26–43.

99 Ludwig Geiger, 'Die Erteilung des Bürgerrechts an die Juden von Frankfurt', *Zeitschrift für die Geschichte der Juden in Deutschland* 5 (1890): 54–74; Inge Schlotzhauer, 'Die bürgerliche Gleichstellung der Frankfurter Juden im Urteil der zeitgenössischen Schriften 1816/17', *Hessisches Jahrbuch für Landesgeschichte* 34 (1984): 129–61.

100 Friedrich Christian Rühs, *Über die Ansprüche der Juden an das deutsche Bürgerrecht* (Berlin, 1815).

101 Jakob Friedrich Fries, *Über die Gefährdung des Wohlstandes und des Charakters der Deutschen durch die Juden* (Heidelberg, 1816), 10 (online).

102 Hazzi, *Betrachtungen über Theuerung*, 77.

103 Hazzi, *Betrachtungen über Theuerung*, 79–80.

104 Paul Leuilliot, 'L'usure judaïque en Alsace sous l'empire et la restauration', *Annales Historiques de la révolution* 7 (1930): 231–50.

105 Weidmann, *Die pfälzische Landwirtschaft*, 104–5.

106 Gabriele Clemens and Daniel Reupke, 'Kreditvergabe im 19. Jahrhundert zwischen privaten Netzwerken und institutioneller Geldleihe', in Gabriele Clemens (ed.), *Schuldenlast und Schuldenwert. Kreditnetzwerke in der europäischen Geschichte 1300–1900* (Trier, 2008), 211–38, 229–32.

107 Clemens and Reupke, 'Kreditvergabe', 232.

108 Gerd Fischer, *Wirtschaftliche Strukturen am Vorabend der Industrialisierung. Der Regierungsbezirk Trier 1820–1850* (Cologne and Vienna, 1990), 273.

109 Cilli Kasper-Holtkotte, 'Kultuspolitik und -verwaltung der Juden', in Christoph Dipper et al. (eds), *Napoleonische Herrschaft in Deutschland und Italien – Justiz und Verwaltung* (Berlin, 1995), 225–43.

110 Kajetan Nadherny, *Vollständige Sammlung aller in den Jahren 1816, 1817, 1818 in dem Königreiche Böhmen kundgemachten und erlassenen Gesetze und Verordnungen*, 3 vols (Prague, 1834), vol. 1, 562 and vol. 3, 589.

111 Demel, *Der bayerische Staatsabsolutismus*, 81.

112 Müller, *Hunger in Bayern*, 201.

113 Adolf Spamer, 'Bairische Denkmale aus der "theueren Zeit" vor 100 Jahren', *Bayerische Hefte für Volkskunde* 3 (1916): 153.

114 Wilhelm Abel, *Massenarmut und Hungerkrisen im vorindustriellen Europa. Versuch einer Synopsis* (Hamburg and Berlin, 1974), 416.

115 Müller, *Hunger in Bayern*, 202.

116 Scheitlin, *Meine Armenreisen*, 152–3.

117 Jäger and Jäger, *Die Hungerjahre 1816/17*, 15.

118 Ernest Labrousse, *La crise de l'économie française à la fin de l'ancien régime et au début de la révolution* (Paris, 1943).

119 Wilhelm Roscher, *Über Kornhandel und Theuerungspolitik*, 3rd edn (Stuttgart, 1852), 160–2.

120 Louis Specker, 'Die grosse Heimsuchung. Das Hungerjahr 1816/17 in der Ostschweiz', *Neujahrsblatt des Historischen Vereins des Kantons St. Gallen* 133 (1993): 16–18.

121 Friedrich List, 'Wider die unbegrenzte Teilung der Bauerngüter' (1816), in List, *Schriften, Reden, Briefe*, vol. 1, part 2 (Berlin, 1933), 580–4.

122 Hans Medick, *Weben und Überleben in Laichingen, 1650–1900. Lokalgeschichte als allgemeine Geschichte* (Göttingen, 1996), 247.

123 Martin Kukowski, *Pauperismus in Kurhessen. Ein Beitrag zur Entstehung und Entwicklung der Massenarmut in Deutschland 1815–1855* (Darmstadt, 1995), 112–14.

124 Hazzi, *Betrachtungen über Theuerung*, 76–7.

125 Marjolin, 'Troubles provoqués', 432.

126 Marjolin, 'Troubles provoqués', 438.

127 Ruprecht Zollikofer, *Das Hungerjahr 1817. Der Osten meines Vaterlandes*

oder die Kantone St. Gallen und Appenzell im Hungerjahre 1817. Ein Denkmal jener Schreckens-Epoche, 2 vols, vol. 1: *Schilderung unseres Elends*, St. Gallen (online), 9–10.

128 Zollikofer, *Das Hungerjahr 1817*, vol. 1, 10–11.
129 Hazzi, *Betrachtungen über Theuerung*, 81–2.
130 Gotthold Emmanuel Friedrich Seidel, *Kanzelrede gehalten am letzten Abend des Jahres 1816 in der Stadtpfarrkirche zu St. Aegidien in Nürnberg*, 2nd edn (Nuremberg, 1817), 8–9 (online).
131 Steger, 'Das Hungerjahr 1817', 306.
132 Hazzi, *Betrachtungen über Theuerung*, 148–9.
133 Scheitlin, *Meine Armenreisen*, 135.
134 Christopher Hitchens, *The Elgin Marbles: Should they Return to Greece?* (London, 1987).
135 George Cruikshank, 'The Elgin Marbles!, or John Bull Buying Stones at the Time his Numerous Family Want Bread!!', London, June 1816. British Museum website.
136 An example is preserved in the Heimatmuseum in Oettingen. See Steger, 'Das Hungerjahr 1817', 311–12.
137 Steger, 'Das Hungerjahr 1817', 314.
138 Müller, *Ueber die gegenwärtige Theuerung*, 6–7.
139 Müller, *Ueber die gegenwärtige Theuerung*, 10.
140 Medick, *Weben und Überleben*, 571–2.
141 Steger, 'Das Hungerjahr 1817', 306.
142 Zollikofer, *Das Hungerjahr 1817*, vol. 1, 297.
143 J.K.F. Falkenberg, *Versuch einer Darstellung der verschiedenen Klassen von Räubern, Dieben und Diebeshehlern mit besonderer Hinsicht auf die vorzüglichsten Mittel sich ihrer zu bemächtigen, ihre Verbrechen zu entdecken und zu verhüten. Ein Handbuch für Polizeibeamte, Criminalisten und Gensdarmen*, 2 vols (Berlin, 1816 and 1818).
144 Post, *The Last Great Subsistence Crisis*, 93–5.
145 Post, *The Last Great Subsistence Crisis*, 95.
146 Post, *The Last Great Subsistence Crisis*, 73–4.
147 Renato Monteleone, 'Il Trentino e la carestia degli anni 1816–17', *Cristallo* 3 (1961): 71–92, 90–1.
148 Müller, *Hunger in Bayern*, 40.
149 Specker, 'Die grosse Heimsuchung', 13.
150 Halévy, *The Liberal Awakening*, 14–15.
151 Thomas Spence, *Property in Land Every One's Right* (London, 1775).
152 P. Mary Ashraf, *The Life and Times of Thomas Spence* (Newcastle upon Tyne, 1983).
153 J.B. Priestley, *The Prince of Pleasure and his Regency 1811–1820* (New York, 1969), 162.
154 Gash, *Lord Liverpool*, 129.
155 Priestley, *Prince of Pleasure*, 162–5.
156 John Belchem, *'Orator' Hunt: Henry Hunt and English Working-Class Radicalism* (Oxford, 1985).
157 William Carr, 'Arthur Thistlewood', in *DNB* 56 (1885), 142–5 (online).
158 Gash, *Lord Liverpool*, 130–1.
159 Priestley, *Prince of Pleasure*, 165.
160 Hazzi, *Betrachtungen über Theuerung*, 88–9.

161 Specker, 'Die grosse Heimsuchung', 16.
162 Henrioud, 'L'année de la misère', 118.
163 Hazzi, *Betrachtungen über Theuerung*, 80–1.
164 Hazzi, *Betrachtungen über Theuerung*, 82–3.
165 Hazzi, *Betrachtungen über Theuerung*, 92–3.
166 Kukowski, *Pauperismus in Kurhessen*, 108–9.
167 Charles Maclean, 'Suggestions for the prevention and mitigation of epidemic and pestilential diseases [. . .]: with some opportune remarks on the danger of pestilence from scarcity', *The Pamphleteer* 10 (1817): 443–82, 449 (online).
168 Scheitlin, *Meine Armenreisen*, 140–1.
169 Wilhelm Joseph Behr, *Das Recht und die Pflicht der Regierungen in Beziehung auf die gegenwärtige Theuerungsangelegenheit* (Würzburg, 1817), 25.
170 John D. Post, 'A study in meteorological and trade cycle history: The economic crisis following the Napoleonic Wars', *Journal of Economic History* 34 (1974): 315–49, 334–9 (statistics).
171 Marjolin, 'Troubles provoqués', 436.
172 Post, *The Last Great Subsistence Crisis*, 72–3.
173 Paul Mantoux, *The Industrial Revolution in the Eighteenth Century: An Outline of the Beginnings of the Modern Factory System in England* (London, 1928; reprint 1961).
174 Charles Officer and Jake Page, *When the Planet Rages: Natural Disasters, Global Warming, and the Future of the Earth* (Oxford, 2009), 5.
175 Henchoz, 'L'année de la misère', 78.
176 Scheitlin, *Meine Armenreisen*, 102.
177 Scheitlin, *Meine Armenreisen*, 360.
178 *Friedens und Kriegs Kurier*, 3 December 1816, 2, cited in Vasold, 'Das Jahr des großen Hungers', 771.
179 Zollikofer, *Das Hungerjahr 1817*, vol. 1, 38.
180 Johann Ernst Müller, *Worte tröstender Aufrichtung und tiefgefühlter dankbarer reger Empfindung: vor einer hohen und sehr zahlreichen Versammlung gesprochen den 23. Juli des Jahres am Eingang der Kirche zu Kreutz-Wertheim, während des feierlichen Hereinbringens des ersten [. . .] Fruchtwagens* (Wertheim, 1817), 5 (online).
181 Hazzi, *Betrachtungen über Theuerung*, 85.
182 Paul Sauer, *Der schwäbische Zar. Friedrich – Württembergs erster König* (Stuttgart, 1984).
183 Paul Sauer, *Reformer auf dem Königsthron. Wilhelm I. vom Württemberg* (Stuttgart, 1997), 127–31.
184 Detlef Jena, *Katharina Pawlowna. Großfürstin von Russland – Königin von Württemberg* (Regensburg, 2003).
185 Fischer, 'Das Hungerjahr 1816/17', 6. On northern Italy, see 8–9.
186 Bach, 'Die Teuerung 1816 und 1817', 31.
187 Wilhelm Gärtner, 'Krieg und Hunger (1816–1817)', *Innviertler Heimatkalender* (1917): 65–8 (online).
188 Stille-Nacht-Museum Mariapfarr, Pfarrstr.19, A – 5571 Mariapfarr (website).
189 Joseph Benedikt Huber, *Topographische Beschreibung der Landschaft Lungau im Fürstenthume Salzburg* (Salzburg, 1786), 2 (online).

190 Ignaz von Kürsinger, *Lungau. Historisch, ethnographisch und statistisch aus bisher unbenützten urkundlichen Quellen dargestellt* (Salzburg, 1853), 512 (online).
191 Max Gehmacher, *Stille Nacht, heilige Nacht! Das Weihnachtslied – wie es entstand und wie es wirklich ist*, 3rd edn (Salzburg, 1968).
192 Scheitlin, *Meine Armenreisen*, 162.
193 Henchoz, 'L'année de la misère', 88–9.

4 The Year of Famine: 1817

1 *Neujahrsblatt der Zürcherischen Hülfsgesellschaft* (Zurich, 1817), 3 (online).
2 Zollikofer, *Das Hungerjahr 1817*, vol. 1, 11–12.
3 Andrej Chrobak, 'New Year greeting cards', in *Joseph Bergler and Graphic Art in Prague, 1800–1830* (Prague and Olomouc, 2007), 47–53, 219–38 (catalogue), 231.
4 Gotthold Emmanuel Friedrich Seidel, *Kanzelrede gehalten am letzten Abend des Jahres 1816 in der Stadtpfarrkirche zu St. Aegidien in Nürnberg*, 2nd edn (Nuremberg, 1817), 15, cited in Vasold, 'Das Jahr des großen Hungers', 764.
5 Sauer, *Reformer auf dem Königsthron*, 154.
6 Josef Carl Bayrhammer, *Erinnerungen an nahrhafte Pflanzen, welche, in das Brod aufgenommen, einen Theil des Brodkorns ergänzen, und, in ganz Europa theils wild wachsen, theils als Gemüse und Futterkräuter in großer Zahl gebaut werden*, 2nd edn (Würzburg, 1817) (online).
7 Josef Carl Bayrhammer, *Practische Anweisung zum Gebrauche der isländischen Flechten . . . als Ergänzungsmittel des Brotkorns* (Freiberg, 1818) (online).
8 Müller, *Hunger in Bayern*, 38–40.
9 Alexander Stollenwerk, 'Der Regierungsbezirk Koblenz während der großen Hungersnot 1816/17', *Jahrbuch für Geschichte und Kunst des Mittelrheins* 22/23 (1970/1971): 109–49, 134.
10 *Nördlinger Intelligenzblatt*, no. 12, March 1817, cited in Steger, 'Das Hungerjahr 1817', 307.
11 'Bemerkungen, veranlaßt durch den gegenwärtigen Mangel an Getreide', *Wöchentlicher Anzeiger für Kunst- und Gewerb-Fleiß im Königreich Bayern* 3, no. 10 (8 March 1817): 145–56.
12 'Bekanntmachung. Mittel zu Vermehrung des Brodes', *Wöchentlicher Anzeiger für Kunst- und Gewerb-Fleiß im Königreich Bayern* 3, no. 17 (26 April 1817): 265–7.
13 Josef Schmid, *Die Kunst, bey gegenwärtiger Theuerung aus allerley wildwachsenden Pflanzen und Baumfrüchten, wie auch aus einigen Feld- und Gartengewächsen mit geringen Kosten sich ein gesundes und nahrhaftes Nothbrod zu verschaffen* (Munich, 1817). On this, see 'Anzeige', *Wöchentlicher Anzeiger für Kunst- und Gewerb-Fleiß im Königreich Bayern* 3, no. 26 (28 June 1817), 404–5.
14 Fischer, 'Das Hungerjahr 1816/17', 6–7.
15 Rahel Varnhagen von Ense, *Ein Buch des Andenkens an ihre Freunde*, part 2 (Berlin, 1834), in *Gesammelte Werke*, 10 vols, ed. Konrad Feilchenfeldt et al., vol. 2, (Munich 1983), 455.

16 Zollikofer, *Das Hungerjahr 1817*, 2 vols.
17 Gerhard Hirschmann, 'Die "Ära Wurm" (1806–1818)', in Gerhard Pfeifer (ed.), *Nürnberg. Geschichte einer europäischen Stadt* (Munich, 1971), 359–66.
18 Vasold, 'Das Jahr des großen Hungers', 763.
19 Müller, *Hunger in Bayern*, 91.
20 Jäger and Jäger, *Die Hungerjahre 1816/17*, 24.
21 Xaver Desch, *Armenversorgung im Landgerichtsbezirke Tirschenreut mit Hinblick auf die Jahre 1816 und 1817* (n.p., 1820).
22 Müller, *Worte tröstender Aufrichtung*, 8–10 (online).
23 Friedrich Wilhelm Emmermann, *Die Armenpflege im Herzogtum Nassau, nach dem Edikt vom 19. Oktober 1816 und den hierauf sich beziehenden allgemeinen Vorschriften. Ein Handbuch für die mit der Armenpflege beauftragten Behörden* (Wiesbaden, 1818) (online). The forms are in the appendix; see especially forms 6: 'Questions to be posed to the poor', and 7: 'Questions that the officials of the poor relief office must answer about the applicant'.
24 Emmermann, *Die Armenpflege im Herzogtum Nassau*, 29–32.
25 Emmermann, *Die Armenpflege im Herzogtum Nassau*, 32.
26 Henrioud, 'L'année de la misère', 135.
27 Tullio Panizza, 'Per la storia della carestia dell'anno 1816 in Trento', *Studi Trentini di Scienze Storiche* 13 (1932): 197–206, 205–6.
28 George I. Brown, *Count Rumford: The Extraordinary Life of a Scientific Genius – Scientist, Soldier, Statesman, Spy* (Gloucester, 2001).
29 Benjamin Rumford, 'Über Speise und vorzüglich über Beköstigung der Armen', in *Kleine Schriften politischen, ökonomischen und philosophischen Inhalts*, vol. 1 (Weimar, 1797), 245–370, 254.
30 Rumford, 'Über Speise', 370.
31 Sophie Wilhelmine Scheibler, *Allgemeines Kochbuch für alle Stände* (Leipzig, 1884).
32 Fischer, 'Das Hungerjahr 1816/17', 7.
33 'Speiseanstalt, Speisehaus, Garküche', in Johann Georg Krünitz, *Oekonomische Enzyclopädie*, vol. 157 (1833), 101–48; soup kitchens for the poor (121–48); a nod to Rumford and his soup (125); the example of the Berlin version of the Rumford soup (143).
34 'Ueber des Hrn. Finanzrath Schätzler in Augsburg Industrie- und Wohltätigkeits-Anstalten', *Wöchentlicher Anzeiger für Kunst- und Gewerb-Fleiß im Königreiche Bayern* 3, no. 17 (26 April 1817): 259–65.
35 Steger, 'Das Hungerjahr 1817', 308.
36 Hazzi, *Betrachtungen über Theuerung*, 150–1.
37 'Beschäftigungs-Institut für weibliche Jugend aus der Armen-Klasse zu Kempten', *Wöchentlicher Anzeiger für Kunst- und Gewerb-Fleiß im Königreiche Bayern* 3, no. 8 (22 February 1817): 118–22.
38 'Beschäftigungs-Institut für weibliche Jugend aus der Armen-Klasse zu Kempten', 121.
39 Michael W. Flinn, 'The Poor Employment Act of 1817', *Economic History Review* 14 (1961): 82–92.
40 P. Straffa, 'Malthus on Public Works', *Economic Journal* 65 (1952): 542–3.
41 Thomas Robert Malthus, *Principles of Economy* (London, 1820), 512. On this, see B.A. Corry, 'The theory of the economic effects of government

expenditure in English classical political economy', *Economica* 25 (1958): 34–48.

42 Flinn, 'The Poor Employment Act of 1817', 82–92.

43 Gash, *Lord Liverpool*, 131.

44 Raymond A. Mohl, 'Humanitarianism in the preindustrial city: The New York Society for the Prevention of Pauperism, 1817–1823', *Journal of American History* 57 (1970): 576–99.

45 George Daitsman, 'Labor and the welfare state in early New York', *Labor History* 4 (1963): 248–56.

46 Gilbert Osofsky, 'The enduring ghetto', *Journal of American History* 55 (1968): 243–55.

47 Ralph J. Caliendo, 'Fiftieth mayor 1810–1811, fifty-third mayor 1815–1818: Jacob Radcliff', in *New York City Mayors*, part 1: *The Mayors of New York before 1898* (New York, 2010), 190–8.

48 Samuel L. Knapp, *The Life of Thomas Eddy* (New York, 1834).

49 David L. Sterling, 'New York patriarch: A biography of John Pintard, 1759–1844'. PhD thesis, New York University, 1958.

50 Mohl, 'Humanitarianism', 587–8.

51 John Griscom, *Memoir of John Griscom, Late Professor of Chemistry. With an Account of the New York High School; Society for the Prevention of Pauperism; the House of Refuge; and Other Institutions*. Compiled from an autobiography and other sources by John H. Griscom (New York, 1859), 157–202, 159 (online).

52 Anonymous [John Griscom], New York Society for the Prevention of Pauperism, *Report of a Committee on the Subject of Pauperism* (New York, 1818) (online).

53 Griscom, *Memoir of John Griscom*, 162.

54 John Griscom, *Discourse on the Importance of Character and Education in the United States* (New York, 1823) (online).

55 Mohl, 'Humanitarianism', 594–5.

56 Harald Beutel, *Die Sozialtheologie Thomas Chalmers' (1780–1847) und ihre Bedeutung für die Freikirchen. Eine Studie zur Diakonie der Erweckungsbewegung* (Göttingen, 2007).

57 Griscom, *Memoir of John Griscom*, 157–202.

58 John Griscom, *Year in Europe. A Journal of Observations. England, Scotland, Ireland, France, Switzerland, the North of Italy, and Holland, in 1818 and 1819*, 2 vols (New York, 1824) (online).

59 Thomas Chalmers, *The Christian and Civic Economy of Large Towns*, 3 vols (Glasgow, 1821–1824).

60 Griscom, *Memoir of John Griscom*, 161–2.

61 Mohl, 'Humanitarianism', 596–7.

62 Zollikofer, *Das Hungerjahr 1817*, vol. 2, 3.

63 Zollikofer, *Das Hungerjahr 1817*, vol. 2, 264–5.

64 Henrioud, 'L'année de la misère', 137.

65 Scheitlin, *Meine Armenreisen*, 239.

66 Zollikofer, *Das Hungerjahr 1817*, vol. 1, 42–3.

67 Scheitlin, *Meine Armenreisen*, 246.

68 Huang Jiayou, 'Was there a colder summer in China in 1816?', in Charles Richard Harrington (ed.), *The Year without a Summer? World Climate in 1816* (Ottawa, 1992), 448–52.

69 Shuji Cao, Yushang Li and Bin Yang, 'Mt. Tambora, climatic changes, and China's decline in the nineteenth century', *Journal of World History* 23 (2012): 587–607, 597.

70 Pei-Yuan Zhang, Wei Chung Wang and Sultan Hameed, 'Evidence from anomalous cold weather in China 1815–1817', in Harrington, *The Year without a Summer*, 448–61.

71 Huang Jiayou, 'Was there a colder summer', in Harrington (ed.), *The Year without a Summer*, 448–52.

72 Zhang, Chung Wang and Hameed, 'Evidence from anomalous cold weather', 448–61.

73 Shuji Cao, 'Tanbola Huoshan Baofa yu Zhongguo Shehui Lishi' [The eruption of Tambora and Chinese society and history], *Xueshuije* [Academies in China] 5 (2009): 37–42 [cited in Shuji Cao et al., 'Mt. Tambora'].

74 Yang Yuda, Man Zhimin and Zheng Jingyun, 'Jiaqing Yunnan Daji, Jiaqing Yunnan Dajihuang (1815–1817) u Tanbola Huoshan Penfa' [A severe famine in Yunan (1815–1817) and the eruption of the Tambora volcano], *Fudan Daxue Xuebao* 1 (2005): 79–85 (cited in Shuji Cao et al., 'Mt. Tambora').

75 Wang Baoning, 'Jiaodong Bandao Nongzuowu Jiegou Brandong yu 1816 Nian de Qihou Tubian' [The change in the structure of food crop cultivation on the Jiaodong peninsula and climate change since 1816], *Xueshuije* 5 (2009): 56–70.

76 Takehiko Mikami and Yasufumi Tsukumura, 'The climate of Japan in 1816 as compared with an extremely cool summer climate in 1783', in Harrington (ed.), *The Year without a Summer*, 462–76.

77 Maclean, 'Suggestions for the prevention', 449–50.

78 Anonymous, 'Handschriftliche Aufzeichnungen eines Älblers über die Teuerung und Hungersnot 1816/17', in Christian August Schnerring, 'Die Theuerungs- und Hungerjahre 1816 und 1817 in Württemberg', *Württembergisches Jahrbuch für Statistik und Landeskunde 1916* (Stuttgart, 1917), 45–78; Christian August Schnerring, *Du suchest das Land heim. Geschichtlicher Dorfroman aus einer Teuerungs- und Hungerzeit* (Stuttgart, 1918).

79 Günter Randecker, 'Die "Laichinger Hungerchronik" – ein Lügengewebe', in Karl Corino (ed.), *Gefälscht! Betrug in Politik, Literatur, Wissenschaft, Kunst und Musik* (Nördlingen, 1988), 74–90.

80 Medick, *Weben und Überleben*, 568–9.

81 Johann Elsässer, *Beschreibung der Menschen-Pocken-Seuche, welche in den Jahren 1815, 1816 und 1817 im Königreich Württemberg geherrscht hat. Aus den Akten gezogen* (Stuttgart, 1818).

82 Hazzi, *Betrachtungen über Theuerung*, 85.

83 This is also noted by Steger, 'Das Hungerjahr', 315.

84 Colette Girard, 'La catastrophe agricole de 1816 dans le département de la Meurthe', *Annales de l'Est* 5 (1954): 133–56.

85 Girard, 'La catastrophe', 18–38.

86 Girard, 'La catastrophe', 31.

87 Girard, 'La catastrophe', 32–5.

88 Christian Pfister, *Im Strom der Modernisierung. Bevölkerung, Wirtschaft und Umwelt im Kanton Bern, 1700–1914* (Berne, 1995), 100–1.

89 Because of their similar causes and symptoms, the two diseases could not be distinguished from one another until 1850, when William Jenner (1815–1898) described the differences in detail.

90 John Bell, 'A history of a contagious fever which has prevailed throughout Italy during the greater part of the year 1817', *The Philadelphia Journal of Medical and Physical Sciences* 1 (1820): 22–34 (online).

91 Zollikofer, *Das Hungerjahr 1817*, vol. 1, 47–8.

92 Zollikofer, *Das Hungerjahr 1817*, vol. 1, 51.

93 William Harty, *An Historic Search of the Causes, Progress, Extent, and Mortality of the Contagious Fever Epidemic in Ireland during the Years 1817, 1818, and 1819* (Dublin, 1820).

94 Anonymous, 'Tracts on the causes, cure and prevention of contagious fever', *The Edinburgh Review* 21, no. 62 (1819): 413–40.

95 Thomas Bateman, *A Succinct Account of the Typhus or Contagious Fever of this Country, Exemplified in the Epidemic which Prevailed in the Metropolis in 1817 and 1818*, 2nd edn (London, 1820).

96 Officer and Page, *When the Planet Rages*, 6.

97 Bell, 'A history of a contagious fever', 22–3.

98 Antonio Raikem, *Sulle malattie che hanno regnato in Volterra negli anni 1816 e 1817 e particolarmente sul tifo contagioso* (Florence, 1818).

99 Franz Weber, *Dissertatio inauguralis medica de Pellagra* (Vienna, 1816); Henry Holland, 'On the pellagra, a disease prevailing in Lombardy', *Medico-chirurgical Transactions* 8 (1817): 317–48; Giuseppe Bellotti, *Congetture sulla cagione efficiente della Pellagra* (Piacenza, 1817); Giovanni Maria Zecchinelli, *Alcune riflessione sanitario-politiche sullo stato attuale della Pellagra nelle due provincie di Belluno e di Padova* (Padua, 1818).

100 Francesco Frapolli, *Mediolanensis nosocomii majoris medici animadversiones in morbum vulgo Pellagram* (Milan, 1771).

101 Holland, 'On the pellagra', 315; G.A. Klein, *Über das Pellagra oder den Scorbutus leprodes* (Würzburg, 1824), 11 (online).

102 Klein, *Über das Pellagra*, 21.

103 Holland, 'On the pellagra', 330.

104 Klein, *Über das Pellagra*, 22–5.

105 A. Quadri, *Prospetto statistico delle provincie venete* (Venice 1826), 16.

106 Holland, 'On the pellagra', 323.

107 Klein, *Über das Pellagra*, 33.

108 Holland, 'On the pellagra', 334 and 336.

109 Holland, 'On the pellagra', 343.

110 A synonym for death by starvation; see Johann Christian August Heyse, *Allgemeines Fremdwörterbuch, oder Handbuch zum Verstehen und Vermeiden der in unserer Sprache mehr oder minder gebräuchlichen fremden Ausdrücke*, part 2 (K bis Z), 7th edn (Hannover, 1835), 40 (online).

111 Zollikofer, *Das Hungerjahr 1817*, vol. 2, 248–50.

112 Scheitlin, *Meine Armenreisen*, 100–101.

113 Zollikofer, *Das Hungerjahr 1817*, vol. 2, 251.

114 Monteleone, 'La carestia', 23–86.

115 Echenberg, *Africa in the Time of Cholera*, 4–5. Echenberg (15–28) provides the following dates for the first six worldwide cholera pandemics: 1817–1826; 1828–1836; 1839–1861; 1863–1879; 1881–1896; 1899–1947.

116 Orton, *An Essay on the Epidemic*, 1–6.
117 Robert Pollitzer, *Cholera, with a Chapter on World Incidence*, ed. World Health Organisation (Geneva, 1959), 11–13.
118 Orton, *An Essay on the Epidemic*, v.
119 Pollitzer, *Cholera*, 17.
120 Orton, *An Essay on the Epidemic*, v–vi.
121 Shoma A. Chatterji, *The Goddess Kali of Kolkata* (Neu Delhi, 2006).
122 Paul D. Nelson, *Francis Rawdon-Hastings, Marquess of Hastings. Soldier, Peer of the Realm, Governor-General of India* (Madison, NJ, 2005).
123 Pollitzer, *Cholera*, 18.
124 David Arnold, *Colonizing the Body: State Medicine and Epidemic Disease in Nineteenth-Century India* (Berkeley, CA, 1993), 162.
125 Mark Harrison, *Climates and Constitutions: Health, Race, Environment and British Imperialism in India, 1600–1850* (Oxford, 1999).
126 James Jameson, *Report on the Epidemic Cholera Morbus, as it Visited the Territories Subject to the Presidency of Bengal, in the Years 1817, 1818, and 1819* (Calcutta, 1820).
127 Orton, *An Essay on the Epidemic*, 164–8. The *Dictionary of National Biography* gives Orton's dates as 1810–1862, but it is highly unlikely that he was already publishing learned treatises at the age of ten (the original edition of the essay on cholera was published in 1820 in Madras). The treatise was written by an uncle of the same name who died in 1835.
128 Harrison, *Climates and Constitutions*, 179.
129 Orton, *An Essay on the Epidemic*, 174.
130 Anonymous [James Sloan], *Rambles in Italy in the Years 1816–17. By an American* (Baltimore, 1818), 63–4.
131 Sloan, *Rambles*, 65.
132 Monteleone, 'La carestia', 23–86.
133 Ferdinand III of Habsburg-Tuscany (1769–1824) was reinstated as grand duke in 1814.
134 Presumably Prince Tommaso Corsini (1762–1856), who received an imperial Austrian patent of nobility in 1809.
135 Francis IV of Austria-Este (1779–1846), who was installed as duke of Modena by the Congress of Vienna in 1815.
136 Sloan, *Rambles*, 364.
137 Sloan, *Rambles*, 68.
138 Mario R. Storchi, 'Grani, prezzi e mercati nel Regno di Napoli (1806–1852)', in Angelo Massafra (ed.), *Il Mezzogiorno preunitario: economia, società e istituzioni* (Bari, 1988), 133–48.
139 Palomba, 'La crisi agraria', 149.
140 Franca Assante, 'Rapporti di produzione e trasformazioni colturali in Basilicata e Calabria nel secolo XIX', in Massafra (ed.), *Il Mezzogiorno preunitario*, 55–70, 63.
141 Renato Monteleone, 'Il Trentino e la carestia degli anni 1816–17', *Cristallo* 3 (1961): 71–92.
142 Sloan, *Rambles*, 73.
143 Wolfgang Behringer, 'Die Krise von 1570. Ein Beitrag zur Krisengeschichte der Neuzeit', in Manfred Jakubowski-Tiessen and Hartmut Lehrmann (eds), *Um Himmels Willen. Religion in Katastrophenzeiten* (Göttingen, 2003), 51–156, 109.

144 Frantisek Graus, *Pest – Geißler – Judenmorde. Das 14. Jahrhundert als Krisenzeit* (Göttingen, 1987).
145 Wolfgang Behringer, 'Climatic change and witch-hunting: The impact of the little ice age on mentalities', *Climatic Change* 43 (1999): 335–51.
146 W. Gregory Monahan, *Year of Sorrows: The Great Famine of 1709 in Lyon* (Columbus, OH, 1993).
147 Post, *The Last Great Subsistence Crisis*, 96.
148 Joshua Bradley, *Accounts of Religious Revivals in Many Parts of the United States from 1815 to 1818* (Albany, NY, 1819).
149 Post, *The Last Great Subsistence Crisis*, 96.
150 Ricardo M. Trigo et al., 'Iberia in 1816, the year without a summer', *International Journal of Climatology* 29 (2009): 99–115.
151 Mariano Barriendos, 'Climate and culture in Spain: Religious responses to extreme climatic events in the Hispanic Kingdoms (16th–19th centuries)', in Wolfgang Behringer, Hartmut Lehmann and Christian Pfister (eds), *Kulturelle Konsequenzen der "Kleinen Eiszeit"* (Göttingen, 2005), 379–414.
152 Fritz Meingast, *Die alpenländischen Nothelfer* (Munich, 1982).
153 Wilhelm Hanseder, 'Tumultuarische Auftritte. Lokale Unruhen in Bayern an der Wende vom 18. zum 19. Jahrhundert', *Oberbayerisches Archiv* 113 (1989): 231–97, 289–90.
154 Müller, *Hunger in Bayern*, 56–8.
155 Andreas Gestrich, 'Religion in der Hungerkrise von 1816/17', in Jakubowski-Tiessen and Lehmann (eds), *Um Himmels Willen*, 292.
156 Sabine Holtz, *Theologie und Alltag. Lehre und Leben in den Predigten der Tübinger Theologen, 1550–1750* (Tübingen, 1993), 93.
157 Rainer Fuhrmann, *Das Reformationsjubiläum 1817. Martin Luther und die Reformation im Urteil der protestantischen Festpredigt des Jahres 1817* (Göttingen, 1973).
158 Carl C. Flatt, *Predigt vor der Wieder-Eröffnung der Versammlung der Stände im Königreich Württemberg, den 3. März 1817 gehalten in der Stiftskirche zu Stuttgart* (Stuttgart, 1817).
159 Gestrich, 'Religion in der Hungerkrise', 281.
160 Johann Heinrich Faber, *Predigt aus Veranlassung der Stiftung des Wohltätigkeits-Vereins. Gehalten am 3. Sonntag nach Epiphaniä 1817* (Heilbronn, 1817).
161 Horst Weigelt, 'Die Allgäuer katholische Erweckungsbewegung', in Martin Brecht (ed.), *Geschichte des Pietismus*, vol. 3 (Göttingen, 2000), 85–111.
162 Joachim Botzenhardt, 'Wann geht die Welt unter? Johann Albrecht Bengel und die Folgen', in Eberhard Gutekunst (ed.), *Apokalypse. Endzeiterwartungen im evangelischen Württemberg* (Stuttgart, 1999), 101–11.
163 Botzenhardt, 'Wann geht die Welt unter', 105.
164 Joachim Trautwein, *Die Theosophie Johann Michael Hahns und ihre Quellen* (Stuttgart, 1969), 203–5.
165 Johann Michael Hahn, *Sammlung auserlesener geistlicher Gesänge*. Cited in Gestrich, 'Religion in der Hungerkrise', 286.
166 Johann Michael Hahn, 'Sendbriefe über einzelne Capitel aus dem Alten und Neuen Testament und Antworten auf Fragen der Herzenserfahrung', in Hahn, *Schriften*, vol. XII (Tübingen, 1830), 138–9.
167 *Landwirtschaftliche Zeitung auf das Jahr 1816, oder der Land- und*

Hauswirth. Cited in Müller, *Hunger in Bayern*, 15.

168 Anonymous, *Täglich Brod in der Theuerung. Warnung und Trost* (Stuttgart and Cannstadt, n.d.); Gestrich, 'Religion in der Hungerkrise', 290.

169 *Die Secte der Pöschlianer in Oberöstreich in dem Jahre 1817. Eine auf Thatsachen gegründete Erzählung von Augenzeugen als ein Beytrag zur neuesten Geschichte der Religions-Schwärmereien in Teutschland* (n.p., 1819) (online).

170 Post, *The Last Great Subsistence Crisis*, 96.

171 Franz Heinrich Reusch, 'Thomas Pöschl', in *ADB* 26 (1888), 454–5 (online).

172 Müller, *Hunger in Bayern*, 202–9.

173 Johannes Goßner, *Das Herz des Menschen ein Tempel Gottes, oder eine Werkstätte des Satans, in zehn Figuren sinnbildlich dargestellt* (Augsburg, 1814).

174 August Friedrich Ludwig, *Die chiliastische Bewegung in Franken und Hessen im ersten Drittel des 19. Jahrhunderts* (Regensburg, 1913), 18–23.

175 Müller, *Hunger in Bayern*, 204–9.

176 Immanuel Wagner, *Geschichte der Gründung der Kolonie Sarata 1822–1832* (Stuttgart, 1967).

177 Debora Sommer, *Eine baltisch-adlige Missionarin bewegt Europa. Barbara Juliane von Krüdener, geb. v. Vietinghoff gen. Scheel (1764–1824)* (Göttingen, 2013), 446–60.

178 Rev. 12: 1–17.

179 Sofia Privalikhina, *Das russische Schicksal einer badischen Prinzessin. Die Kaiserin Elisabeth Alexejewna 1779–1826* (Tomsk, 2006).

180 Talleyrand's memoirs, cited in Sommer, *Eine baltisch-adlige Missionarin*, 287–97.

181 Ernest J. Knapton, *The Lady of the Holy Alliance: The Life of Julie de Krüdener* (New York, 1939).

182 Karl Obser, *Frau von Krüdener in der Schweiz und im badischen Seekreis*, Schriften des Vereins für Geschichte des Bodensees, 59 (Lindau, 1960).

183 Timothy Stunt, *From Awakening to Secession: Radical Evangelicals in Switzerland and Britain, 1815–1835* (Edinburgh, 2000), 29–31.

184 *Zeitung für die Armen*, 5 March 1817, supplement to Karl Obser, 'Frau von Krüdener in der Schweiz und im badischen Seekreis. Nach Mitteilungen des badischen Staatsrats J.A. von Ittner', *Schriften des Vereins für Geschichte des Bodensees und seiner Umgebung* 39 (1910): 79–93, 89–93.

185 Johann Jakob Faesch, *Predigt über 1.Petri 5 v. 6.7, gehalten in der Kirche St. Theodor, den 4. May 1817. Auf Begehren und zum Besten der Armen der St. Theodor Gemeinde dem Druck überlassen* (Basel, 1817).

186 Juliane von Krüdener, *Schreiben der Frau von Krüdener an Herrn von Berckheim, Minister des Innern in Carlsruhe* (n.p., 1817). Cited in Sommer, *Eine baltisch-adlige Missionarin*, 322.

187 Anonymous, *Wer ist die Madame von Krudener? Und was will dieselbige in der östlichen Schweiz? Nur für gemeine und Bauersleuthe* (St. Gallen, 1817).

188 Friedrich Hurter, *Frau von Krüdener in der Schweiz*, (Schaffhausen, 1817), 15–17.

189 Anonymous [Johann Georg Kellner], *An die Armen* (n.p., 1817).

190 Scheitlin, *Meine Armenreisen*, 266–7.

191 Sommer, *Eine baltisch-adlige Missionarin*, 564–5.

192 *Treu niedergeschriebene Rede, welche Frau von Krüdener in einer Versammlung zu Beeskow am 22. Januar 1818 gehalten hat* (Berlin, 1818) (online).

193 Sommer, *Eine baltisch-adlige Missionarin*, 584–604.

194 Hans Körner, 'Berckheim, Karl Christian Freiherr von', in *NDB* 2 (1955), 66 (online).

195 Sommer, *Eine baltisch-adlige Missionarin*, 607–8.

196 Georg von Rauch, 'Juliane von Krüdener', in *NDB* 13 (1982), 95–6 (online).

197 Henri Louis Empeytaz, *Notice sur Alexandre, Empereur de Russie*, 2nd edn (Paris, 1840); Charles Eynard, *Vie de Madame de Krudener*, 2 vols (Paris, Lausanne and Geneva, 1847; P.L. Jacob, *Madame de Krudener, ses lettres et ses ouvrages inédits. Etude historique et littéraire* (Paris, 1880).

198 E.P. Thompson, 'The moral economy of the English crowd in the eighteenth century', *Past and Present* 50 (1971): 76–136, 133.

199 Thompson, 'The moral economy', 129.

200 Monteleone, 'Il Trentino e la carestia', 84–6.

201 Report of 22 May 1817, in Abel, *Massenarmut und Hungerkrisen*, 323.

202 Abel, *Massenarmut und Hungerkrisen*, 416.

203 Thompson, 'The moral economy', 116.

204 Marjolin, 'Troubles provoqués', 428.

205 Abel, *Massenarmut und Hungerkrisen*, 324, based on the account in Louis de Romeuf, *La crise agricole sous la Restauration* (Paris, 1902).

206 Marjolin, 'Troubles provoqués', 429.

207 Marjolin, 'Troubles provoqués', 430–4.

208 Georges Lefebvre, *La Grande Peur de 1789* (Paris, 1932).

209 Marjolin, 'Troubles provoqués', 423–60.

210 Abel, *Massenarmut und Hungerkrisen*, 324.

211 Marjolin 'Troubles provoqués', 435–7.

212 Abel, *Massenarmut und Hungerkrisen*, 324.

213 Marjolin, 'Troubles provoqués', 437–8.

214 Ulrich-Christian Pallach (ed.), *Hunger. Quellen zu einem Alltagsproblem seit dem Dreißigjährigen Krieg* (Munich, 1986), 293–4.

215 Marjolin, 'Troubles provoqués', 456–7.

216 Marjolin, 'Troubles provoqués', 458.

217 Marjolin, 'Troubles provoqués', 448–60.

218 Müller, *Hunger in Bayern*, 181.

219 Müller, *Hunger in Bayern*, 50–1.

220 Müller, *Hunger in Bayern*, 51–4.

221 Baptist Schrettinger, *Der Königlich Bayerische Militär-Max-Joseph-Orden und seine Mitglieder*, vol. 1 (Munich, 1882), 343–5.

222 Theodor Bitterauf, 'Die Zensur der politischen Zeitungen in Bayern, 1799–1825', in Karl Alexander von Müller (ed.), *Festschrift für Sigmund von Riezler* (Gotha, 1913), 305–51, 324.

223 *Korrespondent* (1816), 1479; *The Times* (1817), 1. Cited in Müller, *Hunger in Bayern*, 55–6.

224 Weidmann, *Die pfälzische Landwirtschaft*, 102–4.

225 Müller, *Ueber die gegenwärtige Theuerung*, 5.

226 Müller, *Ueber die gegenwärtige Theuerung*, 14.

227 *Korrespondent* (1817), 829–30.

228 Müller, *Hunger in Bayern*, 122–4.

229 Müller, *Hunger in Bayern*, 114–17.
230 Müller, *Hunger in Bayern*, 127–30.
231 Weis, *Montgelas*, 775–6, quotation 776–7.
232 Karl Otmar von Aretin, *Bayerns Weg zum souveränen Staat* (Munich 1976), 175–7.
233 Hanns Hubert Hofmann, *Adelige Herrschaft und souveräner Staat* (Munich, 1962), 325–8.
234 Weis, *Montgelas*, 791.
235 von Aretin, *Bayerns Weg*, 175–6.
236 *Denkwürdigkeiten des bayerischen Staatsministers Maximilian Grafen von Montgelas (1799–1817)* (Stuttgart, 1887), 547.
237 *Denkwürdigkeiten des bayerischen Staatsministers*, 552–66.
238 In February 1817, however, officials wanted to prevent a pilgrimage to Andechs for fear of rioting. Wilhelm Hanseder, 'Tumultuarische Auftritte. Lokale Unruhen in Bayern an der Wende vom 18. zum 19. Jahrhundert', *Oberbayerisches Archiv* 113 (1989): 231–97, 290.
239 Eberhard Weis, 'Die Begründung des modernen bayerischen Staates unter König Max I. (1799–1825)', in Max Spindler (ed.), *Handbuch der bayerischen Geschichte*, vol. IV/1 (Munich, 1974), 1–86, 69–86.
240 *Allgemeine Zeitung* (1817), 453.
241 August von Platen, *Tagebücher*, ed. G. von Laubmann and L. von Scheffler, vol. 1 (Stuttgart, 1896), 758.
242 Johann Andreas Schmeller, *Tagebücher 1801–1852*, ed. Paul Ruf, vol. 1 (Munich, 1954), 397.
243 Anton Chroust (ed.), *Gesandtschaftsberichte aus München, 1814–1848*, Abt. 3: *Die Berichte des preußischen Gesandten* (Munich 1949), 141.
244 Anton Chroust (ed.), *Gesandtschaftsberichte*, Abt. 1: *Die Berichte des französischen Gesandten* (Munich, 1935), 26.
245 Anton Chroust (ed.), *Gesandtschaftsberichte*, Abt. 2: *Die Berichte des österreichischen Gesandten* (Munich, 1939), 150.
246 Chroust (ed.), *Gesandtschaftsberichte*, Abt. 2, 150.
247 Müller, *Hunger in Bayern*, 119–20.
248 Müller, *Hunger in Bayern*, 143–9.
249 Lefebvre, *La Grande Peur*.
250 C. Johnson, *An Account of the Ely and Littleport Riots in 1816* (Littleport, 1893).
251 A.J. Peacock, *Bread or Blood: A Study of the Agrarian Riots in East Anglia, 1816* (London, 1965).
252 Post, *The Last Great Subsistence Crisis*, 69–89.
253 Gash, *Lord Liverpool*, 132.
254 D.J.V. Jones, 'The Amlwch riots of 1817', *Anglesey Antiquarian Society and Field Club Transactions* (1966): 93–102.
255 Post, *The Last Great Subsistence Crisis*, 72–3.
256 Henrioud, 'L'année de la misère', 139.
257 This entire section is based on Post, *The Last Great Subsistence Crisis*, 73–9.
258 Anonymous, *Patriotische Wünsche bei der bevorstehenden Getreide-Ärndte*, ('Deutschland', 1817), 2.
259 R. Bin Wong, *China Transformed: Historical Change and the Limits of*

European Experience (Ithaca, NY, 1997), 209–29.

260 James C. Scott, *The Moral Economy of the Peasant: Rebellion and Subsistence in Southeast Asia* (New Haven, CT, 1977).

261 H.K. Mishra, *Famines and Poverty in India* (New Delhi, 1991), 66–8.

262 Prafulla Kumar Pattanaik, *The First Indian War of Independence: Freedom Movement in Orissa, 1804–1825* (New Delhi, 2005).

263 N.R. Moharty, 'The Orijya Paika rebellion of 1817', *Orissa Review* (August 2008): 1–3 (online).

264 K.M. de Silva, *History of Ceylon*, vol. 3 (Colombo, 1973), 28.

265 Henry Marshall, *Ceylon. General Description of the Island and its Inhabitants* (London, 1846), 153.

266 Lennox A. Mills, *Ceylon under British Rule 1795–1932* (New York, 1965).

267 Hazzi, *Betrachtungen über Theuerung*, 87–90.

268 Hazzi, *Betrachtungen über Theuerung*, 90.

269 Hazzi, *Betrachtungen über Theuerung*, 94–5.

270 Franz Haecker, *Über die Getraid Theuerung in den Jahren 1816 und 1817* (Nuremberg, 1818), vi.

271 Hazzi, *Betrachtungen über Theuerung*, 96.

272 Palomba, 'La crisi agraria', 166. The price for wheat here is that for *grano duro*.

273 Thomas Stamford Raffles, *Letters during a Tour through Some Parts of France, Savoy, Switzerland, Germany, and the Netherlands in the Summer of 1817* (Liverpool, 1818), 158–9.

274 Anonymous, *Wie schützte sich Elberfeld in den Jahren der Not 1816/17 durch seinen Bürgersinn vor Brotmangel?* (Elberfeld, 1817).

275 Johann Wilhelm Fischer, 'Geschichte des Kornvereins (1816/17) zu Barmen', *Zeitschrift des Bergischen Geschichtsvereins* 48 (1915): 252–312.

276 Hermann Bollnow, 'Johann Caspar Engels', in *NDB* 4 (1959), 527–8 (online).

277 Hortense Martin, 'Soziale Bestrebungen im Koblenzer Katholizismus in der ersten Hälfte des 19. Jahrhunderts', *Jahrbücher für Geschichte und Kunst des Mittelrheins und seiner Nachbargebiete* 4/5 (1952/1953): 74–88.

278 Hans-Heinrich Bass, 'Hungerkrisen in Posen und im Rheinland 1816/17 und 1847', in Manfred Gailus and Heinrich Volksmann (eds), *Der Kampf um das tägliche Brot. Nahrungsmangel, Versorgungspolitik und Protest 1770–1990* (Opladen, 1994), 151–75.

279 Bass, 'Hungerkrisen', 162.

280 J. Neumann, 'The 1810s in the Baltic region, 1816 in particular: air temperatures, grain supply and mortality', in Harrington (ed.), *The Year without a Summer*, 392–415.

281 Christoph K. Neumann, 'Das osmanische Reich in seiner Existenzkrise (1768–1826)', in Klaus Kreiser and Christoph K. Neumann, *Kleine Geschichte der Türkei* (Stuttgart, 2003), 285–95.

282 George Cioranescu, *Bessarabia – Disputed Land between East and West* (Munich, 1985).

283 Scheitlin, *Meine Armenreisen*, 147–8.

284 Johann J. Eichhoff, *Betrachtungen über den 19. Artikel der deutschen Bundesakte* (Wiesbaden, 1820), 34.

285 Chroust (ed.), *Gesandtschaftsberichte*, Abt. 3, 119.

286 Hazzi, *Betrachtungen über Theuerung*, 83–4.
287 Fischer, 'Das Hungerjahr 1816/17', 7–8.
288 Zollikofer, *Das Hungerjahr 1817*, vol. 1, 19.
289 Vernon J. Puryear, 'Odessa. Its rise and international importance, 1815–1850', *Pacific International Review* 3 (1934): 192–215, 192–7.
290 Eichhoff, *Betrachtungen*, 35.
291 Cynthia Cox, *Talleyrand's Successor* (London, 1959).
292 Hans Petri, 'Schwäbische Chiliasten in Russland', *Kirche im Osten* 5 (1962): 75–97, 80.
293 D.A. Schultes, *Chronik von Ulm* (Ulm, 1915), 412.
294 Wolfgang von Hippel, *Auswanderung aus Südwestdeutschland. Studien zur württembergischen Auswanderung und Auswanderungspolitik im 18. und 19. Jahrhundert* (Stuttgart, 1984), 134.
295 Heinz H. Becker, *Die Auswanderung aus Württemberg nach Südrußland, 1816–1830* (Tübingen, 1962), 78–80.
296 Becker, *Die Auswanderung*, 82–4.
297 Abel, *Massenarmut und Hungerkrisen*, 325.
298 Petri, 'Schwäbische Chiliasten', 80–3, based on M.F. Schrenk, *Geschichte der deutschen Colonien in Transkaukasien, zum Gedächtnis des fünfzigjährigen Bestehens derselben* (Tiflis, 1869).
299 Karl Stumpp, *Ostwanderung. Akten über die Auswanderung der Württemberger nach Russland 1816–1822* (Leipzig, 1941), 205–22.
300 Karl August Varnhagen von Ense, *Denkwürdigkeiten des eigenen Lebens*, vol. 3: *1815–1834*, ed. Konrad Feilchenfeldt (Frankfurt am Main, 1987), 133–4.
301 Post, *The Last Great Subsistence Crisis*, 100.
302 Reprints from the *Schwäbischer Merkur* in Karl Stumpp, *Ostwanderung*, 132–204.
303 *Friedens und Kriegs Kurier*, 30 April 1817, 1.
304 Scheitlin, *Meine Armenreisen*, 62.
305 Scheitlin, *Meine Armenreisen*, 62.
306 Scheitlin, *Meine Armenreisen*, 62.
307 Post, *The Last Great Subsistence Crisis*, 100–2.
308 Newspaper clipping, probably from 1820, Stadtarchiv Heilbronn.
309 Moritz Fürstenwärther, *Der Deutsche in Nordamerika* (Stuttgart and Tübingen, 1818), 26 (online).
310 Abel, *Massenarmut und Hungerkrisen*, 325.
311 *Friedens und Kriegs Kurier*, 30 April 1817, 1.
312 Fürstenwärther, *Der Deutsche in Nordamerika*, 47.
313 Kurt E. Leichtle and Bruce G. Carveth, *Crusader Against Slavery: Edward Coles, Pioneer of Freedom* (Carbondale, IL, 2011).
314 Morris Birkbeck, *Letters from Illinois* (Philadelphia, 1819).
315 Morris Birkbeck, *Notes on a Journey in America from the Coast of Virginia to the Territory of Illinois*, 2nd edn (London, 1818), 34 (online).
316 Birkbeck, *Notes on a Journey*, 50.
317 Birkbeck, *Notes on a Journey*, 51.
318 Birkbeck, *Notes on a Journey*, 107.
319 Birkbeck, *Notes on a Journey*, 115.
320 Birkbeck, *Notes on a Journey*, 82.
321 Christopher D. Schröder, 'Dreams of a prairie republic: Morris Birkbeck

and settlement on the Indiana-Illinois frontier, 1764–1860'. PhD thesis, University of Delaware, 2000.

322 Walter Havighurst, *Wilderness for Sale: The Story of the First Western Land Rush* (New York, 1956), 210–17.

323 Birkbeck, *Notes on a Journey*, 66.

324 Eberhard August Wilhelm von Zimmermann, *Johann Maves Reisen in das Innere Brasiliens . . .*, 2 vols (Bamberg and Leipzig, 1816–1817).

325 Maximilian, Prinz zu Wied-Neuwied, *Reise nach Brasilien, in den Jahren 1815 bis 1817* (Frankfurt am Main, 1820).

326 Georg H. von Langsdorf, *Bemerkungen über Brasilien, mit gewissenhafter Belehrung für auswandernde Deutsche* (Heidelberg, 1821).

327 Von Hippel, *Auswanderung*, 175.

328 See library.uwb.edu/guides/USimmigration/1819_steering_act.html.

329 See immigrationinamerica.org/549-history-of-immigration-1783–1891.html.

330 Günter Moltmann, *Aufbruch nach Amerika. Die Auswanderungswelle von 1816/17* (Stuttgart, 1989), 112.

331 Von Hippel, *Auswanderung*, 148 (diagram).

332 Abel, *Massenarmut und Hungerkrisen*, 325.

333 Anonymous, *Einige Worte über Besteuerung im allgemeinen und insbesondere über jene im Großherzogtum Baden* ('Teutschland', 1817), 83 (online).

334 Abel, *Massenarmut und Hungerkrisen*, 325.

335 Weidmann, *Die pfälzische Landwirtschaft*, 30.

336 Gash, *Lord Liverpool*, 131.

337 Post, *The Last Great Subsistence Crisis*, 100.

338 Moltmann, *Aufbruch nach Amerika*, 194.

339 Fürstenwärther, *Der Deutsche in Nordamerika*, 12–13.

340 Moltmann, *Aufbruch nach Amerika*, 212.

341 Fürstenwärther, *Der Deutsche in Nordamerika*, 11–12.

342 Weidmann, *Die pfälzische Landwirtschaft*, 105–6.

343 Monteleone, 'Il Trentino e la carestia', 71–92, 87.

344 Monteleone, 'Il Trentino e la carestia', 90.

345 Frederick Jackson Turner, *The Frontier in American History* (New York, 1920).

346 Noble E. Cunningham, *The Presidency of James Monroe* (Lawrence, KS, 1996).

347 Joseph B. Hoyt, 'The cold summer of 1816', *Annals of the Association of American Geographers* 48 (1958): 118–31.

348 Post, *The Last Great Subsistence Crisis*, 105–7.

349 Frederick Jackson Turner, *The Rise of the New West* (New York, 1906), 78.

350 Birkbeck, *Notes on a Journey*, 31.

351 Thomas Perkins Abernethy, *The Formative Period in Alabama, 1815–1828* (University, AL, 1965).

352 Friedrich Battenberg, *Das Europäische Zeitalter der Juden*, vol. 2 (Darmstadt, 1990), 85–109.

353 Heinz Duchhardt, *Der Wiener Kongress. Die Neugestaltung Europas 1814/15* (Munich, 2013), 107–8.

354 Sylvia Krauss-Meyl, *Das 'Enfant terrible' des Königshauses. Maria*

Leopoldine, Bayerns letzte Kurfürstin (1776–1848) (Regensburg, 1997), 264–5.

355 The Bayerische Hypotheken- und Wechselbank AG was a predecessor to the present-day HypoVereinsbank, which now belongs to the Italian Unicredit Bank.

356 Hendrikje Kilian, *Die jüdische Gemeinde in München, 1813–1871. Eine Großstadtgemeinde im Zeitalter der Emanzipation* (Munich, 1989), 58–61.

357 Müller, *Hunger in Bayern*, 199–200.

358 Müller, *Ueber die gegenwärtige Theuerung*, 15.

359 Anton Baumgartner, *Feyerlicher Auszug zum freyen Pferderennen und zum Vogelschießen bey dem Oktoberfeste 1820 in München. Nebst einer Beschreibung der silbernen Schützen-Ketten und des Dezenniums dieser National-Feste* (Munich, n.d. [1820]).

360 [Anonymous] J.S., *Das Volks-Fest der Baiern im October* (Munich, 1815).

361 Gerda Möhler, *Das Münchner Oktoberfest. Brauchformen des Volksfestes zwischen Aufklärung und Gegenwart* (Munich, 1989), 6–9.

362 Ulrich von Destouches, *Gedenkbuch der Oktober-Feste* (Munich, 1835); Wilhelm Erdmann, *Das Oktoberfest zu München* (n.p., 1838).

363 Statutes of the Association, quoted in Möhler, *Das Münchner Oktoberfest*, 313.

364 Möhler, *Das Münchner Oktoberfest*, 356–7 (Tables 1 and 2).

365 Joseph von Hazzi, *Über die Pferderennen als wesentliches Beförderungsmittel der bessern, vielmehr edlen Pferdezucht in Deutschland und besonders in Bayern* (Munich, 1826).

366 [Andreas Michael von Dall'Armi], *Vorbericht der Gesellschaft der Oktoberfeste in Bayern. Ihre Zwecke, und ihren Fortbestand betreffend, im Oktober 1816* (Munich 1816), cited in Möhler, *Das Münchner Oktoberfest*, 19–20.

367 Möhler, *Das Münchner Oktoberfest*, 17–23.

368 Joseph von Hazzi, *Über das 25 jährige Wirken des Landwirtschaftlichen Vereins in Bayern und des Central-Landwirtschafts- oder Oktoberfestes* (Munich, 1835).

369 Anonymous, *Das Landwirtschaftliche Fest zu Kannstatt. Zum erstenmal gefeyert den 28. September 1818. Mit einem Umrisse der Rennbahn und ihrer Einrichtungen* (Stuttgart, 1818).

370 Andrea Hartl, *Oktoberfest und Cannstatter Volksfest. Vom Nationalfest zum Massenvergnügen* (Munich, 2010), 14–15.

371 Sauer, *Der schwäbische Zar*.

372 Hartl, *Oktoberfest*, 84–7.

373 Sauer, *Reformer auf dem Königsthron*, 156–9.

374 Bernhard Fischer, *Johann Friedrich Cotta., Verleger – Entrepreneur – Politiker* (Göttingen, 2014), 476–84.

375 Sauer, *Reformer auf dem Königsthron*, 158–9.

376 Sauer, *Reformer auf dem Königsthron*, 156.

377 Anonymous, *Patriotische Wünsche bei der bevorstehenden Getreide-Ärndte* ('Deutschland', May 1817).

378 Fischer, 'Das Hungerjahr 1816/17', 6.

379 Anonymous, *Lob- und Danklied zu Gott dem Allmächtigen bey dem Erntefeste zu Bamberg im gegenwärtigen denkwürdigen Jahre 1817* (n.p., n.d. [Bamberg, 1817]); Georg Martin Geiger, *Predigt über Psalm*

CXXXI V.1.2. vom Danke gegen Gott für den glücklichen Anfang der heiß ersehnten Getreideernte nach der großen Theuerung (Bayreuth, 1817); Johann Georg Zimmer, *Predigt über Psalm 119,17, auf das Erntedankfest am letzten Sonntag des Kirchenjahres 1816* (Heidelberg, 1817); Balthasar Rieger, *Hymne bei der höchst gesegneten Getraid-Ernte des Jahres 1817 zur Erweckung frommer Gefühle* (n.p., n.d. [1817]).

380 Johann Michael Sixt, *Wie Schweinfurt den frohen Anfang der dießjährigen Aernte nach der Zeit der Theuerung feyerte* (Schweinfurt, 1817); Johann Christoph Reuß, *Das Theurungs- und Nothjahr von der Ernte 1816 bis zur Ernte 1817* (Wunsiedel, 1819).

381 Elard Hugo Meyer, *Badisches Volksleben im neunzehnten Jahrhundert* (Strasbourg, 1900), 432.

382 Müller, *Hunger in Bayern*, 134.

383 Karl Friedrich Michahelles, *Rede bey der Einfuhr des ersten mit Korn-Getreide von den Fluren zu St. Johannis beladenen Wagens, gehalten Montag am 21sten July 1817* (n.p. [Nuremberg], 1817).

384 Johann Friedrich Häcker, *Rede bey der feierlichen Einführung des ersten Erndtewagens zu Wöhrd den 25. Juli 1817* (Nuremberg, 1817).

385 C.E.N. Kaiser, *Die Feyer des 30. Julius im denkwürdigen Jahr 1817 in der Kreishauptstadt Ansbach beym festlichen Einzuge des ersten Erndtewagens, zum Gedächtnis für die Nachkommen und zur Unterstützung der Hausarmen* (Ansbach, 1817).

386 Thomasius, *Rede bei dem feierlichen Einführen des ersten diesjährigen Erndtewagens zu Uffenheim am 1. August 1817* (n.p., n.d. [1817]).

387 Johann Georg Albert, *Freie Rede über den den 7. August in dem Dorfe Kolmberg feierlich gottesdienstlich eingebrachten ersten Aerndte-Wagen* (Ansbach, 1817).

388 Gottfried B. Clericus, *Feier des Schnitterfestes im Ort Lendershausen, am 11. Sonntag nach dem Dreieinigkeitsfeste 1817* [17 August 1817] *nach dem unglücklichen Hungerjahr 1816 bis 17, nebst einer Predigt über Text Psalm 56, 1.2. gehalten, und auf Verlangen dem Druck übergeben* (n.p., 1817).

389 Johann Michael Sailer, *Zur Feyer des ersten Aerntetages im Jahre 1817. Eine Rede* (Landshut, 1817).

390 *Goethes Werke*, WA, vol. 6, 87.

391 Sauer, *Reformer auf dem Königsthron*, 155–6.

392 Michahelles, *Rede*, 3.

393 Michahelles, *Rede*, 6.

394 Peter Assion, 'Hungerjahr und Erntedank 1817', *Der Odenwald* 23 (1976): 100.

395 Assion, 'Hungerjahr', 100.

396 Post, *The Last Great Subsistence Crisis*, 80.

397 Post, *The Last Great Subsistence Crisis*, 73.

398 Kukowski, *Pauperismus in Kurhessen*, 114–15.

399 Kukowski, *Pauperismus in Kurhessen*, 117–18.

400 Kukowski, *Pauperismus in Kurhessen*, 446–51.

401 Wilhelm Abel, *Der Pauperismus in Deutschland am Vorabend der industriellen Revolution* (Dortmund, 1966).

402 Thomas Sokoll, 'Pauperismus', in *Enzyklopädie der Neuzeit* 9 (2009), 946–9.

403 Müller, *Hunger in Bayern*, 146.

404 Müller, *Hunger in Bayern*, 147 (text). Reproduction of a handwritten copy, 236.
405 Müller, *Hunger in Bayern*, 147–8.
406 Ursula Gehring-Münzel, *Vom Schutzjuden zum Staatsbürger. Die gesellschaftliche Integration der Würzburger Juden 1803–1871* (Würzburg, 1992), 133–64.
407 After the fall of Montgelas, the liberal Maximilian Freiherr von Lerchenfeld (1778–1843) became finance minister in February 1817. *ADB* 18 (1883), 423–4 (online).
408 Gehring-Münzel, *Vom Schutzjuden zum Staatsbürger*, 161.
409 Gehring-Münzel, *Vom Schutzjuden zum Staatsbürger*, 149.
410 Anonymous threatening letter of 5 Sept. 1819, cited in Gehring-Münzel, *Vom Schutzjuden zum Staatsbürger*, 162.
411 Gehring-Münzel, *Vom Schutzjuden zum Staatsbürger*, 163.
412 Hermann Eiselen (ed.), *Brotkultur* (Cologne, 1995), 174.
413 Johann Baptist von Pfeilschifter, 'Standrede am Grabe des Jahres 1817', *Zeitschwingen, oder Weimarisches Unterhaltungsblatt*, no. 1, 2–4 (1818) (online).
414 *Regensburger Wochenblatt*, 8, no. 1 (7 January 1818).
415 Maximilian Joseph Schleis von Löwenfeld, *Das Erntefest zu Rannungen, gefeyert den 3. August* (Schweinfurt, 1817).

5 The Turbulent Years that Followed: 1818–1820

1 Ambrosius Junpertz, *Elegie des Trägers der Düsseldorfer Zeitung* (n.p. [Düsseldorf], 1818) (online).
2 *Neujahrsblatt der Zürcherischen Hülfsgesellschaft* (Zurich, 1818), 3 (online).
3 Weidmann, *Die pfälzische Landwirtschaft*, 107.
4 *Regensburger Wochenblatt*, 8, no. 1 (7 January 1818).
5 Johann Andreas Schmeller, *Bayerisches Wörterbuch*, vol. 1 (Munich, 1827; 1983 reprint of Georg Karl Frommann's revision of the 4th edn [Munich 1872]), 1294–5.
6 Lance Gibson and Garren Benson, 'Origin, history, and uses of corn', Iowa State University, 2002 (online).
7 Latin 'granum', English 'grain', French 'grain', Italian 'grano', Catalan 'gra', Spanish 'grano', Polish 'ziarno'. Friedrich Kluge, *Etymologisches Wörterbuch der deutschen Sprache*, 24th edn (Berlin and New York, 2001), 529.
8 J. Dehnicke, *Geschichte der deutschen Kornbrennerei* (Erfurt, 1936).
9 The Dutch term was *korenjode*, the Danish *kornjoede*.
10 Jacob and Wilhelm Grimm, *Deutsches Wörterbuch* (1838–), vol. 11, 1813–1833, *Korn* and its compounds (online).
11 Sauer, *Reformer auf dem Königsthron*, 161.
12 See www.bruedergemeinde-korntal.de.
13 Julius August Wagenmann, 'Gottlieb Wilhelm Hoffmann', in *ADB* 12 (1880), 495–595 (online).
14 I owe this information to Dr Dieter R. Bauer of Stuttgart, who originally comes from Münchingen.
15 Decree of 28 August 1816, in August Ludwig von Reyscher (ed.),

Vollständige, historisch und kritisch bearbeitete Sammlung der württembergischen Gesetze, vol. 15 (Tübingen, 1846).

16 Georg Smolka, *Die Auswanderung als politisches Problem in der Zeit des Deutschen Bundes, 1815–1866* (Speyer, 1993), 82–3.

17 Gerhard P. Bassler, 'Auswanderungsfreiheit und Auswanderungsfürsorge in Württemberg 1815–1855. Zur Geschichte der südwestdeutschen Massenwanderung nach Nordamerika', *ZWLG* 33 (1974): 117–60, 131.

18 Marionella Wolf, 'Württembergische Rückwanderer aus Ost- und Südosteuropa in der ersten Hälfte des 19. Jahrhunderts', in Mathias Beer and Dittmar Dahlmann (eds), *Migration nach Ost- und Südosteuropa vom 18. bis zum 19. Jahrhunderts. Ursachen – Formen – Verlauf – Ergebnis* (Stuttgart, 1999), 263–90, 288–9.

19 Wolf, 'Württembergische Rückwanderer', 288–90.

20 Willy Andreas, 'Ludwig Winter über eine Reform der Verwaltungsordnung (1817)', *ZGO* 64 (1910): 477–501, 488.

21 Andreas, 'Ludwig Winter', 504.

22 Eberhard Weis, 'Die Begründung des modernen bayerischen Staates unter König Max I. (1799–1825)', in Max Spindler (ed.), *Handbuch der bayerischen Geschichte*, vol. IV/1 (Munich, 1974), 1–86, 48–9.

23 Friedrich Dobmann, *Georg Friedrich Freiherr von Zentner als bayerischer Staatsmann in den Jahren 1799–1821* (Kallmünz, 1962), 103.

24 Weis, 'Die Begründung', 70–1.

25 G. Wahrmut [pseudonym], *Wodurch wird Englands Größe begründet? Eine historische Untersuchung mit Beziehung auf Bayern* (n.p., 1816).

26 Hofmann, *Adelige Herrschaft*, 365–6.

27 Markus J. Prutsch, 'Die Revision der französischen Verfassung im Jahre 1830. Zur Frage der Bewährung des Verfassungssystems der "Charte constitutionnelle" von 1814', *Der Staat. Zeitschrift für Staatslehre und Verfassungsgeschichte, deutsches und europäisches öffentliches Recht* 47 (2008): 85–107.

28 Elisabeth Fehrenbach, *Vom Ancien Regime zum Wiener Kongress* (Munich, 2001), 87–90.

29 Weis, 'Die Begründung', 77–82.

30 Post, *The Last Great Subsistence Crisis*.

31 Cecil-Blanche Woodram-Smith, *Great Hunger: Ireland 1845–1849* (London, 1962); Christine Kinealy, *A Death-Dealing Famine: The Great Hunger in Ireland* (London, 1997).

32 Eleonore O. Sterling, 'Anti-Jewish riots in Germany in 1819: A displacement of social protest', *Historica Judaica* 12 (1950): 118–20.

33 Friedrich Ludwig Jahn, *Deutsche Turnkunst* (Berlin, 1816).

34 Hans Ferdinand Maßmann, *Kurze und wahrhaftige Beschreibung des großen Burschenfestes auf der Wartburg bei Eisenach am 18ten und 19ten des Siegesmonds 1817* (n.p. [Jena], 1817) (online).

35 *Rechtfertigung des Professors Fries gegen die Anklagen, welche wegen seiner Teilnahme am Wartburgs-Fest wider ihn erhoben worden sind. Aktenmäßig dargestellt von ihm selbst* (Jena, 1818).

36 Joachim Burkhard Richter, *Hans Ferdinand Maßmann* (Berlin, 1992), 71–84, 80.

37 F. Gunther Eyck, 'The political theories and activities of the German

academic youth between 1815 and 1819', *Journal of Modern History* 27 (1955): 27–38, 30.

38 Herfried Münkler, *Die Deutschen und ihre Mythen* (Berlin, 2009), 301–27, esp. 318–20.

39 Varnhagen, *Denkwürdigkeiten*, 436.

40 Anonymous, *Authentischer Bericht über die Ermordung des Kaiserlich-Russischen Staatsraths Herrn August von Kotzebue; nebst vielen interessanten Notizen über ihn und über Carl Sand, den Meuchelmörder* (Mannheim, 1819; reprint Berlin 1999, ed. Antonia Meiners).

41 Karl Alexander von Müller, *Karl Ludwig Sand*, 2nd edn (Munich, 1925).

42 *Über die neuen Assassinen. Zwey Schreiben von Otto Schulz und Karl Giesebrecht an August Zeune, nebst dessen Antwort* (Berlin, 1819).

43 Friedrich Ludwig Jahn, *Deutsches Volkstum* (Lübeck, 1810), 398–9.

44 Werner Bergmann, 'Jahn, Friedrich Ludwig', in *Handbuch des Antisemitismus*, ed. Wolfgang Benz, vol. 2/1, Personen A–K (Berlin, 2009), 403–6.

45 Klaus Ries, *Wort und Tat. Das politische Professorentum der Universität Jena im frühen 19. Jahrhundert* (Jena, 2007), 351–2.

46 Hermann Haupt, *Karl Follen und die Gießener Schwarzen* (Gießen, 1907).

47 Walter Grab, 'Demokratie und Deutschtümelei in der Studentenrevolte von 1817–1820', in *Ein Volk muss seine Freiheit selbst erobern* (Frankfurt am Main, 1984), 498–503.

48 August von Kotzebue, *Neue Schauspiele*, 23 vols (1798–1820), and *Sämtliche dramatische Werke*, 44 vols, 1827–9.

49 Johannes Birgfeld et al. (eds), *Kotzebues Dramen. Ein Lexikon* (Hannover, 2011).

50 Otto von Kotzebue, *Entdeckungs-Reise in die Süd-See und nach der Berings-Straße zur Erforschung einer nordöstlichen Durchfahrt in den Jahren 1815 bis 1818*, 3 vols (Weimar, 1821).

51 George S. Williamson, 'What killed August von Kotzebue? The temptations of virtue and the political theology of German nationalism, 1789–1819', *Journal of Modern History* 72 (2000): 890–943.

52 Sterling, 'Anti-Jewish riots', 119.

53 Peter Fasel, *Revolte und Judenmord. Hartwig von Hundt-Radowsky (1780–1835). Biografie eines Demagogen* (Berlin, 2010), 109.

54 August von Kotzebue, *Geschichte des Deutschen Reiches von dessen Ursprunge bis zu dessen Untergange*, 2 vols (Leipzig, 1814/15).

55 Dieter Düding, *Organisierter gesellschaftlicher Nationalismus in Deutschland (1808–1847). Bedeutung und Funktion der Turner- und Sängervereine in der deutschen Nationalbewegung* (Munich, 1984), 79–83, 126–35.

56 Friedrich Gentz, *Tagebücher 1800–1815*, ed. Günter Kronenbitter (Hildesheim, 2004), 269.

57 Joachim von der Thüsen, '"Die Lava der Revolution fließt majestätisch". Vulkanische Metaphorik zur Zeit der Französischen Revolution', *Francia* 23 (1996): 113–43.

58 Stella Gervas, *Réinventer la tradition. Alexandre Stourdza et l'Europe de la Sainte-Alliance* (Paris, 2008).

59 Alexander von Stourdza, *Coup d'œil sur les universités d'Allemagne*

(Aachen, 1818), and *Denkschrift über die gegenwärtige Situation in Deutschland* (Berlin, 1819).

60 Christoph Wilhelm Hufeland, *Makrobiotik oder die Kunst das menschliche Leben zu verlängern*, 6th edn (Berlin, 1842).

61 Varnhagen, *Denkwürdigkeiten*, 391–2.

62 Friedrich von Gentz, *Tagebücher 1800–1815*, ed. Günter Kronenbitter (Hildesheim, 2004).

63 Friedrich von Gentz, *Tagebücher*, vol. 2 (Leipzig, 1843), 315–16.

64 Chroust (ed.), *Gesandtschaftsberichte*, Abt. 3, 206.

65 Varnhagen, *Denkwürdigkeiten*, 440–1.

66 Haupt, *Karl Follen*.

67 Wilfried Schüler, *Das Herzogtum Nassau 1806–1866* (Wiesbaden, 2006), 96–101.

68 Karl Schwartz, 'Lebensnachrichten über den Regierungspräsidenten Karl von Ibell', *Nassauische Annalen* 14 (1875): 1–107.

69 Kissinger, *A World Restored*, 232–5.

70 Eyck, 'The political theories and activities of the German academic youth', 35.

71 Fasel, *Revolte und Judenmord*, 154.

72 *Unterthänigste Bitte des Salomon Hirsch, um allergnädigste Revision derjenigen organischen Edikte und gesetzlichen Anordnungen, welche die staatsbürgerlichen Rechte der Bekenner der mosaischen Religion betreffen* (Würzburg, 1819).

73 Jacob Katz, *From Prejudice to Destruction: Anti-Semitism, 1700–1933* (Cambridge, MA, 1982), 99.

74 Thomas August Scheuring, *Das Staatsbürgerrecht für Juden, eine unpartheiische Würdigung in Beziehung auf die von Salomon Hirsch zu Würzburg an die Ständeversammlung in Baiern eingereichte Vorstellung* (Würzburg, 1819), 43.

75 Scheuring, *Das Staatsbürgerrecht*, 49.

76 Josef Prys, *Die Familie Hirsch auf Gereuth* (Munich, 1931).

77 Gehring-Münzel, *Vom Schutzjuden zum Staatsbürger*, 387–90.

78 Wilhelm Joseph Behr, *Rede zur Feier des ersten Jahrtags der Einführung der Verfassung des Baierischen Staats* (Würzburg, 1819).

79 August von Platen, *Der Briefwechsel*, ed. Paul Bornstein, 2 vols (Munich, 1914), vol. 2, 76–7.

80 Varnhagen, *Denkwürdigkeiten*, 142–3.

81 Rainer Erb and Werner Bergmann, *Die Nachtseite der Judenemanzipation. Der Widerstand gegen die Integration der Juden in Deutschland 1780–1860* (Berlin, 1989), 226.

82 Heinrich Schnee, 'Jakob von Hirsch', in *NDB* 9 (1972), 206–7 (online).

83 Sebastian Andreas Stumpf, *Die Juden in Franken. Denkwürdigkeiten der teutschen, insbesondere fränkischen Geschichte*, vol. 1 (Erfurt, 1802).

84 Gehring-Münzel, *Vom Schutzjuden zum Staatsbürger*, 140–5.

85 Gehring-Münzel, *Vom Schutzjuden zum Staatsbürger*, 136–8.

86 Gehring-Münzel, *Vom Schutzjuden zum Staatsbürger*, 140–3.

87 Gehring-Münzel, *Vom Schutzjuden zum Staatsbürger*, 144.

88 Sterling, 'Anti-Jewish riots', 121–2.

89 Ivo Striedinger, 'Das Großherzogtum Würzburg', *ZBLG* 6 (1933): 250–6 (online).

90 Gehring-Münzel, *Vom Schutzjuden zum Staatsbürger*, 121–31.
91 Gehring-Münzel, *Vom Schutzjuden zum Staatsbürger*, 150.
92 Georg Polster, *Politische Studentenbewegung und bürgerliche Gesellschaft. Die Würzburger Burschenschaft im Kräftefeld von Staat, Universität und Stadt 1814–1850* (Heidelberg, 1989), 73.
93 This is the view of Gehring-Münzel, *Vom Schutzjuden zum Staatsbürger*, 151–2.
94 Lothar Mayer, *Jüdische Friedhöfe in Unterfranken* (Petersberg, 2010), 64–9.
95 Karl Hagen, *Der Maler Johann Michael Voltz von Nördlingen (1784–1858) und seine Beziehung zur Zeit- und Kunstgeschichte in der ersten Hälfte des 19. Jahrhunderts. Nebst einem Verzeichnisse seiner Werke* (Stuttgart, 1863).
96 Manfred Pohl, 'Amschel Mayer Rothschild', in *NDB* 22 (2005), 132–3.
97 Sterling, 'Anti-Jewish riots', 105–42.
98 Dorothee Schimpf, 'Emanzipation und Bildungswesen der Juden im Kurfürstentum Hessen 1807–1866', *Kommission für die Geschichte der Juden in Hessen* 13 (1994): 57.
99 Dörte Kaufmann, *Anton Friedrich Justus Thibaut (1772–1840). Ein Heidelberger Professor zwischen Wissenschaft und Politik* (Stuttgart, 2014).
100 Heinrich Graetz, *Geschichte der Juden von der ältesten Zeit bis auf die Gegenwart*, 11 vols (Leipzig, 1878–1897; 2nd edn 1900), vol. 11, 334–5.
101 *Schwäbische Kronik*, 1 September 1819. Cited in Utz Jeggle, *Judendörfer in Württemberg* (Tübingen, 1999), 90.
102 Heinrich Linn, *Juden an Rhein und Sieg* (Siegburg, 1984), 89.
103 Stefan Rohrbacher, 'Die "Hep-Hep-Krawalle" und der "Ritualmord" des Jahres 1819 zu Dormagen', in Rainer Erb and Michael Schmid (eds), *Antisemitismus und jüdische Geschichte* (Berlin, 1987), 135–47.
104 Gehring-Münzel, *Vom Schutzjuden zum Staatsbürger*, 145.
105 Sterling, 'Anti-Jewish riots', 105–42.
106 Varnhagen, *Denkwürdigkeiten*, 543–4.
107 Battenberg, *Das Europäische Zeitalter*, 123–6.
108 Halévy, *The Liberal Awakening*, 22–3.
109 Paul B. Billecoq (ed.), *Procès de Louis-Pierre Louvel, assassin de Monseigneur le duc de Berry devant la cour des pairs* (Paris, 1844; reprint Paris 2003).
110 Eberhard Weber, *Die Mainzer Zentraluntersuchungskommission* (Karlsruhe, 1970).
111 Hans-Ulrich Wehler, *Deutsche Gesellschaftsgeschichte*, vol. 2: *Von der Reformära bis zur industriellen und politischen 'Deutschen Doppelrevolution', 1815–1845/49* (Munich, 1987), 332–45, quotation 339.
112 Georg Friedrich Wilhelm Hegel, *Grundlinien der Philosophie des Rechts* (Berlin, 1820), online; English: *Elements of the Philosophy of Right*, trans. H.B. Nisbet, ed. Allen W. Wood, rev. edn (Cambridge, 1991).
113 Thomas Nipperdey, *Germany from Napoleon to Bismarck: 1800–1866*, trans. Daniel Nolan (Princeton, NJ, 1996), 246.
114 Nipperdey, *Germany*, 247–48.
115 Samuel Rezneck, 'The depression of 1819–1822, a social history', *American Historical Review* 39 (1933): 28–47.

116 Havighurst, *Wilderness for Sale*, 128.
117 M.C. Buer, 'The trade depression following the Napoleonic wars', *Economica* 1 (1921): 159–79.
118 Anonymous, *Gehorsamste Petition des bürgerlichen Handelsstandes der Haupt- und Residenzstadt München an die erste Ständeversammlung des Königreichs Bayern, den Verfall des Handels und die Abstellung der denselben untergrabenden Mißbräuche und Beeinträchtigungen betreffend* (Munich, 1819).
119 Johann Friedrich Benzenberg, *Ueber Handel und Gewerbe, Steuern und Zölle* (Elberfeld, 1819).
120 Claude Étienne Chaillou-des-Barres, *Essai historique et critique sur la legislation des grains jusqu'à ce jour* (Paris, 1820); William Jacob, *A View of the Agriculture, Manufacture, Statistics and State of Society of Germany, and Parts of Holland and France* (London, 1820); Wilhelm Joseph Behr, *Die Lehre von der Wirthschaft des Staats oder pragmatische Theorie der Finanzgesetzgebung und Finanzverwaltung* (Würzburg, 1822).
121 Matthew Carey, 'Address to the farmers of the United States', in M. Carey, *Essays in Political Economy* (Philadelphia, 1822), 417.
122 Rezneck, 'The depression of 1819–1822', 30.
123 James Flint, *Letters from America* (Edinburgh, 1822), 202.
124 Birkbeck, *Notes on a Journey*, 33.
125 Rezneck, 'The depression of 1819–1822', 33.
126 Oliver Wilson, *Remarks on the Present State of the Currency, Credit, and National Industry* (New York, 1820), 4–6; Rezneck, 'The depression of 1819–1822', 35.
127 Rezneck, 'The depression of 1819–1822', 39.
128 Rezneck, 'The depression of 1819–1822', 40.
129 Rezneck, 'The depression of 1819–1822', 41–7.
130 Turner, *The Rise of the New West*, 141–42.
131 Reginald James White, *Waterloo to Peterloo* (London, 1957).
132 Mark Krantz, *Rise Like Lions* (Manchester, 2011), 12.
133 Joyce Marlow, *The Peterloo Massacre* (London, 1969).
134 James Wroe, *The Peterloo Massacre: A Faithful Narrative of the Events* (Manchester 1819).
135 Marlow, *The Peterloo Massacre*, 6.
136 Percy Bysshe Shelley, 'The Masque of Anarchy. Written on the Occasion of the Massacre at Manchester, 1819'. The poem was only published posthumously in 1832.
137 George Cruikshank, 'Manchester Heroes', London 1819.
138 Halévy, *The Liberal Awakening*, 22–3.
139 George Theodore Wilkinson, *An Authentic History of the Cato-Street Conspiracy* (London, 1820).
140 Gash, *Lord Liverpool*, 154–5.
141 William Carr, 'Arthur Thistlewood', in *DNB* 56 (1885), 142–5 (online).
142 'Execution of Thistlewood and others for high treason', *Morning Chronicle*, 2 May 1820.
143 Seumas Mac a'Ghobhainn and Peter Berresford Ellis, *The Scottish Insurrection of 1820* (Edinburgh, 2001).
144 Goethe, for example, mentioned the assassination of the duc de Berry in his diary entry for 20 February 1820.

145 Lulu Gräfin Thürheim, *Mein Leben. Erinnerungen aus Österreichs großer Welt, 1788–1852*, 4 vols (Munich, 1913), vol. 3, 40.
146 Billecoq (ed.), *Procès de Louis-Pierre Louvel*.
147 *Schluss-Acte der über Ausbildung und Befestigung des deutschen Bundes zu Wien gehaltenen Minister-Conferenzen vom 15. Mai 1820.*
148 Hans Otto Kleinmann, 'Zwischen Ancien Régime und Liberalismus', in Peer Schmidt (ed.), *Kleine Geschichte Spaniens* (Stuttgart, 2000), 253–328, 265–71.
149 [Giuseppe Bertoldi], *Memoirs of the Secret Societies of the South of Italy, particularly the Carbonari*, translated from the original manuscript (London, 1821) (online).
150 Salvador de Madariaga, *Simon Bolivar. Der Befreier Lateinamerikas* (Zurich, 1986).
151 David J. Brewer, *The Flame of Freedom: The Greek War of Independence, 1821–1833* (London, 2001).

6 The Long-Range Effects of the Tambora Crisis

1 Michahelles, *Rede*, 12.
2 Vinzenz Zanna, *Victualien-Preise in dem Theuerungs Jahre 1817* (Augsburg, 1817). Hartinger incorrectly cites his name as Vincenz Zama.
3 Zollikofer, *Das Hungerjahr 1817*, vols 1 and 2.
4 'Herisauer Hungertäfeli' (1817), Kantonsbibliothek Appenzell-Außerrhoden (digital copy online).
5 'Urnäscher Hungertäfeli' (1817), digital copy online at www.zeitzeugnisse. ch/zeitreise/galerie.
6 Fischer, 'Geschichte des Kornvereins', 252–312.
7 Walter Hartinger, 'Teuerungstafeln zu den Hungerjahren 1816/17', *Volkskunst 9*, no. 4 (1986): 5–10.
8 Heinz Bormuth and Hugo Friedel, 'Hungersteine und steinerne Teuerungstafeln', *Der Odenwald 39* (1992): 19–28.
9 After 1930, Neulautern became part of Wüstenrot, in the district of Heilbronn.
10 Specker, 'Die grosse Heimsuchung', 5–56.
11 Anonymous, 'Klage über die Hungerjahre 1816/17', in *Politik & Unterricht*, ed. Landesanstalt für politische Bildung, Baden-Württemberg (Stuttgart, 2001).
12 Fischer, 'Geschichte des Kornvereins', 252–312; Spamer, 'Bairische "Denkmale"', 145–266; Heinrich Bechtolsheimer, 'Die Provinz Rheinhessen in den beiden ersten Jahrzehnten ihres Bestehens', *Quellen und Forschungen zur hessischen Geschichte 4* (1916): 1–143; Maurice Gabbud, 'L'an de misère au Val de Bagnes, 1816–1916', *Annales Valaisannes 1* (1916): 12–25; Theodor Bridler, *Aus schlimmen Tagen unserer Vorväter. Bilder aus der Ostschweiz während der Hungersnot im Jahre 1816/17* (Bischofszell, 1917); Henrioud, 'L'année de la misère', 114–24, 133–42, 171–92; Max Heuwieser, 'Eine Volksspeiseanstalt in Passau vor hundert Jahren', *Niederbayerische Monatsschrift 6* (1917): 81–4; Johann Jakob Hottinger, *Notlage der Hungerzeit, Siebzehntes Neujahrsblatt der Zürcherischen Hilfsgesellschaft* (Zurich, 1917); Georg Kappes, 'Die Hungersnot vor

100 Jahren', *Jahrbuch des Historischen Vereins von Alt-Wertheim* 1917: 48–63; Jakob Kuoni, *Hundert Jahre Hilfsgesellschaft der Stadt St. Gallen, 1816–1916* (St. Gallen, 1918); Theodor von Greyerz, *Das Hungerjahr 1817 im Thurgau*, Thurgauische Beiträge zur Vaterländischen Geschichte 57/58 (Frauenfeld, 1918).

13 Anonymous, 'Handschriftliche Aufzeichnungen eines Älblers über die Teuerung und Hungersnot 1816/17', in Christian August Schnerring, 'Die Theuerungs- und Hungerjahre 1816 und 1817 in Württemberg', *Württembergisches Jahrbuch für Statistik und Landeskunde 1916* (Stuttgart, 1917): 45–78, 72–7. This was a forgery by Schnerring.

14 Maurice Vergnaud, 'Agitation politique et crise de subsistance à Lyon de septembre 1816 à juin 1817', *Cahiers d'Histoire* 2 (1957): 163–77; Paul Leuilliot, 'Les crises économique du XIXe siècle en France: de la disette de 1816–1817 à la famine du Coton', *Annales* 12 (1957): 317–25.

15 John William Polidori, *The Diary*, ed. William Michael Rossetti (Ithaca, NY, 2009).

16 James Bieri, *Percy Bysshe Shelley, a Biography. Exile of Unfulfilled Renown, 1816–1822* (Newark, DE, 2005).

17 Mary Shelley, *The Journals, 1814–44*, ed. Paula R. Feldman and Diana Scott-Kilvert (Baltimore, 1995).

18 Claire Clairmont, *The Journals, 1814–1827*, ed. Marion Kingston Stocking (Cambridge, MA, 1968).

19 Janet Todd, *Mary Wollstonecraft: A Revolutionary Life* (London, 2000).

20 *Tales of the Dead*, trans. Sarah Elizabeth Utterson (London, 1813); *Fantasmagoriana* (Paris, 1812); *Das Gespensterbuch* (Leipzig, 1811). On the authors, see Gero von Wilpert, *Die deutsche Gespenstergeschichte. Motiv – Form – Entwicklung* (Stuttgart, 1994), 230–4.

21 [Mary Shelley], *Frankenstein, or the Modern Prometheus* (London, 1818). The author's name only appeared on the title page of the second edition in 1822. In the preface to the third edition of 1831, Mary Shelley explained how the horror tales came to be written. This edition is freely accessible online at Project Gutenberg.

22 John Polidori, *The Vampyre* (London, 1819).

23 Mary Shelley, *Frankenstein, or the Modern Prometheus* (London, 1831), Introduction (online).

24 Christian Pfister, *Wetternachhersage. 500 Jahre Klimavariationen und Naturkatastrophen* (Berne, 1999), 153–4.

25 George Gordon Byron, 'Darkness' (1816), online at Wikisource.

26 George Gordon Byron, *Byron's Letters and Journals*, vol. V: 'So late into the night', 1816–1817, ed. Leslie A. Marchand (Cambridge, MA, 1976).

27 Morton D. Paley, 'Envisioning lastness: Byron's "Darkness," Campbell's "The Last Man," and the critical aftermath', *Romanticism: The Journal of Romantic Culture and Criticism* 1 (1995): 1–14, 2.

28 Vail, 'The bright sun', 183–92.

29 Hans-Ulrich Mielsch, *Sommer 1816. Lord Byron und die Shelleys am Genfer See* (Zurich, 1998), 169–80.

30 Mielsch, *Sommer 1816*, 177–8.

31 Shelley, *History of a Six Weeks' Tour*, Letter 4, 25 July.

32 Placidus a Spescha, 'Das Clima der Alpen am Ende des vorigen und im

Anfang des jetzigen Jahrhunderts, 1818', *Jahrbuch Schweizer Alpenclub* 5 (1868/69): 494–511.

33 Ignatz Venetz, 'Über die Veränderungen der Temperatur in den Schweizer Alpen, Preisschrift 1821'; *Mémoire sur les variations de la temperature dans les Alpes de Suisse*, Denkschriften der allgemeinen Schweizerischen Gesellschaft der Naturwissenschaften, Abt. 2, vol. 1 (Zurich, 1833), 25.

34 Toussaint von Charpentier, 'Über die Gletscher', *Annalen der Physik* 63 (1819): 388–411, 410–11, and *Über Gletscher* (n.p., 1819).

35 Jean [Johann von] de Charpentier, *Essai sur les glaciers et sur le terrain erratique du bassin du Rhône* (Lausanne, 1841), 26.

36 Wilhelm von Gümbel, 'Johann Friedrich Wilhelm von Charpentier', in *ADB* 4 (1876), 105–7.

37 Johann Rudolf Wyss, *Reise in das Berner Oberland*, 2 vols (Berne, 1816/17), vol. 2, 648–9 (online).

38 de Charpentier, *Essai sur les glaciers*, 26.

39 Eduard Richter, 'Geschichte der Schwankungen der Alpengletscher', *Zeitschrift des Deutschen und Österreichischen Alpenvereins* 22 (1891): 1–74, 65 (online).

40 Richter, 'Geschichte der Schwankungen', 27–8, 66.

41 Venetz, *Mémoire*, 14.

42 Richter, 'Geschichte der Schwankungen', 27–8, quotations 31 and 49.

43 I. Mariétan, 'La catastrophe du Giétroz en 1818', *Bulletin Murithienne* 87 (1971): 12–15.

44 Hans Conrad Escher, 'Notice sur le Val de Bagnes en Bas Valais et sur la catastrophe qui en a dévasté le fond en juin 1818', *Bibliothèque Universelle* (August 1818); 'Bemerkungen über das zerstörende Ereignis im Banien-Tahle; geschrieben im Juli 1818 von dem Staatsrath Escher in Zürich, frei ausgezogen von Gilbert', *Annalen der Physik* 60 (1818): 355–65.

45 Severin Perrig, *Der Traum von einer kanalisierten Welt – Hans Conrad Escher von der Linth und das Linth-Kanalwerk* (Zurich, 2007).

46 'Der im Banien-Thale durch einen Gletscher entstandene See, und verwüstender Abfluss desselben beim Bruch des Eisdammes am 16. Juni 1818. Frei bearbeitet nach zwei kleinen Schriften des Herrn Bridel, Pfarrer bei Vevey, von Gilbert', *Annalen der Physik* 60 (1818): 331–54.

47 'Von dem Schnee, den Lawinen und den Gletschern in den Alpen; und andere Beiträge zur Naturgeschichte des großen St. Bernhards-Berges, von dem Pater Biselx, Prior des Hospizes auf dem großen Bernhard. Mit einigen Zusätzen von Gilbert', *Annalen der Physik* 63 (1820): 183–209; 'Bericht von der Zerstörung des Dorfes Randa in Ober-Wallis, durch Herabstürzen eines Theils des Weißhorn-Gletschers am 29. Dezember 1819, abgestattet dem Staatsrathe des Kantons Wallis von J. Venetz, Wasser- und Wege-Baumeister. Mit einigen erklärenden Zusätzen von Gilbert', *Annalen der Physik* 63 (1820): 210–18.

48 Hans Röthlisberger, 'Eislawinen und Ausbrüche von Gletscherseen', in P. Kasser (ed.), *Gletscher und Klima – glaciers et climat* (Basel, 1978), 170–212.

49 *The Asiatic Journal and Monthly Register for British India and Dependencies* I (1816): 92–3, 116–17, 125, 177–8, 296–7, 322–4, 372; II (1816) 164–6, 421–2.

50 Marc-Auguste Pictet, 'Détails sur une eruption volcanique qui a eu lieu dans l'isle de Sumbava', *Bibliothèque Universelle* 5 (1817): 221-7.
51 Raffles, *The History of Java*.
52 Benjamin Franklin, 'Meteorological imaginations and conjectures', *Memoirs of the Literary and Philosophical Society of Manchester* 2 (1785): 373-7.
53 Bodenmann et al., 'Perceiving', 577-87.
54 Paul Usteri, 'Eröffnungsrede der Jahresversammlung der Allgemeinen Schweizerischen Gesellschaft für die gesamten Naturwissenschaften', *Verhandlungen der Schweizerischen Naturforschenden Gesellschaft* 3 (1817): 3-59, 16.
55 Ignatz Venetz, *Les variations de la température dans les Alpes de la Suisse* (Zurich, 1833).
56 Joseph Banks, President of the Royal Society, London, to the Admiralty, Minutes of the Council (20th November 1817), 8, 149-53.
57 John Barrow, 'Physikalisch-geographische Nachrichten aus dem nördlichen Polarmeer', *Annalen der Physik* 62 (1819): 157-66.
58 Ernst Florens Friedrich Chladni, 'Über die Ursachen des nasskalten Sommers von 1816, und zum Theil auch 1817', *Annalen der Physik* 62 (1819): 132-6.
59 Joseph Louis Gay-Lussac and François Arago, 'Résumé des observations météorologiques de 1817', *Annales de Chimie et de Physique* 6 (1817): 436-44.
60 Heinrich Wilhelm Brandes, 'Aus einem Schreiben des Professor Brandes, meteorologischen Inhalts', *Annalen der Physik* 55 (1817): 112-14.
61 Heinrich Wilhelm Brandes, *Untersuchungen über den mittleren Gang der Wärmeänderungen durchs ganze Jahr; über gleichzeitige Witterungs-Ereignisse in weit voneinander entfernten Weltgegenden; über die Formen der Wolken, die Entstehung des Regens und der Stürme; und über andere Gegenstände der Witterungskunde* (Leipzig, 1820).
62 Thomas Lauder Dick, 'Entgegengesetzte Winde in unterschiedlichen Höhen', *Annalen der Physik* 57 (1817): 217-18.
63 Lukas [Luke] Howard, 'Eine über dem festen Lande heransteigende Wasserhose', *Annalen der Physik* 57 (1817): 219-21.
64 Alexander [Alessandro] Volta, 'Über die periodische Wiederkehr von Gewittern, und über den sehr kalten und außerordentlich trockenen Wind, den man nach Hagelschauern mehrere Stunden lang bemerkt', *Annalen der Physik* 57 (1817): 341-56; Giuliano Pancaldi, *Volta: Science and Culture in the Age of Enlightenment* (Princeton, NJ, 2005).
65 [Kummer], 'Einige Bemerkungen über meteorologische Instrumente; in einem Brief an den königlichen Münzmeister Herrn Studer, in Dresden: 1. Das Thermometer, 2. Das Hygrometer, 3. Das Barometer', *Annalen der Physik* 59 (1818): 301-17.
66 Johann Wolfgang von Goethe, 'Instruction für die Beobachter bei den Großherzoglich meteorologischen Anstalten' (14 December 1817), in *Goethes Werke*, WA, vol. 76 (Weimar, 1896), 203-18; on dry haze, 213 (§ 21).
67 'Über die Farben des Himmels', in *Goethes Werke*, WA, vol. 76, 226.
68 Heinz Nicolai, 'Zeittafel zu Goethes Leben und Werk', in Johann Wolfgang von Goethe, *Hamburger Ausgabe in 14 Bänden*, ed. Erich Trunz, vol. 14 (Munich, 1983), 382-548, 504-5.

69 Nicolai, 'Zeittafel zu Goethes Leben', 509.
70 *Goethes Werke*, WA, vol. 28 (Weimar, 1903), 3 (letter to Paulus Usteri, 8 March 1817); Paul Usteri, 'Eröffnungsrede der Jahresversammlung der Allgemeinen Schweizerischen Gesellschaft für die gesamten Naturwissenschaften', *Verhandlungen der Schweizerischen Naturforschenden Gesellschaft* 3 (1817): 3–59. The latter was also published separately (Zurich, 1817).
71 Johann Wolfgang von Goethe, 'Über das Wachstum der Schweizer Gletscher', in Goethe, *Die Schriften zur Naturwissenschaft*, I. Abteilung, vol. 11, ed. Dorothea Kühn and Wolf von Engelhardt (Weimar, 1970); Tobias Krüger, *Die Entdeckung der Eiszeiten* (Basel, 2008), 143–66, 165.
72 Marc-Auguste Pictet, 'Considerations sur les taches du soleil, et observations de celles qui ont paru l'année dernière et celle-ci', *Bibliothèque Universelle* 2 (1816): 185–93.
73 W.M. Moseley, 'Bemerkungen über die Sonnenflecken des Jahres 1816', *Annalen der Physik* 58 (1818): 406–16.
74 Ludwig Wilhelm Gilbert, 'Etwas von Sonnenflecken. Frei ausgezogen aus Bemerkungen des Herrn Pictet in Genf', *Annalen der Physik* 58 (1818): 417–25.
75 Jean Rilliet and Jean Cassaigneau, *Marc-Auguste Pictet ou le rendez-vous de l'Europe universelle, 1752–1825* (Geneva, 1995), 501.
76 Marc-Auguste Pictet, 'Résumé des observations météorologiques', *Bibliothèque Universelle* 2 (1818): 83–95.
77 Hezekiah Niles, 'Climate of the United States', *Niles' Weekly Register* 10 (1816): 385–6.
78 Johann Konrad Gütle, 'Beleuchtung eines Aufsatzes über Blitzableiter', *Annalen der Physik* 64 (1820): 262–8; Siegfried Kett, 'Johann Conrad Gütle – Mechanicus, Schausteller, Elektrisierer und Wunderheiler, Physiker, Chemiker, Lehrer, Buchautor und Versandhändler', *Mitteilungen des Vereins für Geschichte der Stadt Nürnberg* 96 (2009): 177–228.
79 Vladimir Jankovic, 'The end of classical meteorology, c. 1800', in G.J.H. McCall, A.J. Bowden and R.J. Howarth (eds), *The History of Meteorites and Key Meteoritic Collections: Fireballs, Falls and Finds* (London, 2006), 91–9.
80 Bodenmann et al., 'Perceiving', 583–4.
81 Royal Society, Krakatoa Committee (eds), *The Eruption of Krakatoa*.
82 Humphreys, 'Volcanic dust', 1–34, and *Physics of the Air* (Philadelphia, 1930).
83 Luke Howard, *On the Modification of Clouds* (London, 1802).
84 'Einige von Lukas Howards meteorologische Monatsberichten', *Annalen der Physik* 51 (1815): 66–72; 'Einige meteorologische Beobachtungen in Beziehung auf Lukas Howards und De Luc's Ideen, von Thomas Forster', *Annalen der Physik* 51 (1815): 73–9.
85 Luke Howard, *The Climate of London Deduced from Meteorological Observations Made at Different Places in the Neighbourhood of the Metropolis*, 2 vols (London, 1818/1820).
86 Luke Howard, *Seven Lectures in Meteorology* (Pontefract, 1837).
87 'Versuch einer Naturgeschichte und Physik der Wolken von Lukas Howard [. . .], frei bearbeitet von Gilbert', *Annalen der Physik* 51 (1815): 3–48. Gilbert had already translated Pictet's accounts of Howard's observations

from French into German in 1805 and 1812 for the *Bibliotheca Britannica* published in Geneva, and they were reprinted in the *Annalen der Physik*. His version of 1815 follows an article of 1811 in *Nicholson's Journal*; Adam Müller, 'Über den Howardschen Versuch einer Naturgeschichte der Wolken, in einem Sendschreiben an den Professor Gilbert', *Annalen der Physik* 55 (1817): 102–11.

88 Kurt Badt, *John Constable's Clouds* (London, 1950).

89 John E. Thomes, *John Constable's Skies* (Birmingham, 1999).

90 Johann Wolfgang von Goethe, *Italian Journey, 1786–1788*, trans. Elizabeth Mayer and W.H. Auden (Harmondsworth, 1970), 187–219.

91 Leopold von Buch, *Geognostische Beobachtungen auf Reisen durch Deutschland und Italien* (Berlin, 1809).

92 Alexander von Humboldt, *Über das Universum. Die Kosmosvorträge 1827/28 in der Berliner Singakademie*, at http://www.gutenberg.aol.de/index.htm, cited in Thomas Gransow and Wolf-Ulrich Malm, *Neapel und die Halbinsel von Sorrent. Der Vesuv in Reiseberichten und literarischen Texten*, at www.thomasgransow.de/Neapel/Vesuv/Vesuv_ Briefe.htm.

93 G.L. Herries Davies, *Whatever is Under the Earth: The Geological Society of London 1807 to 2007* (London, 2007).

94 George Poulett Scrope, *Considerations on Volcanos, the Probable Causes of their Phenomena, the Laws which Determine their March, the Disposition of their Products, and their Connexion with the Present State and Past History of the Globe: Leading to the Establishment of a New Theory of the Earth* (London, 1825) (online).

95 Abraham Gottlieb Werner, *Kurze Klassifikation und Beschreibung der verschiedenen Gebirgsarten* (Dresden, 1787), 21–5 (online).

96 Gerd-Rainer Riedel, Jochen Klauß and Horst Feiler, *Der Neptunistenstreit. Goethes Suche nach Erkenntnis in Böhmen* (Berlin, 2009).

97 Sigurdsson, *Melting the Earth*, 117–24.

98 Roy Porter, *The Making of Geology: Earth Science in Britain, 1660–1815* (Cambridge, 1977), 184–93.

99 Sigurdsson, *Melting the Earth*, 147–51.

100 James Hutton, *Theory of the Earth. Or an Investigation of the Laws Observable in the Composition, Dissolution, and Restoration of Land upon the Globe* (Edinburgh, 1788).

101 Leonard G. Wilson, *Charles Lyell. The Years to 1841: The Revolution in Geology* (New Haven, CT and London, 1972), 46.

102 Charles Lyell, *Principles of Geology; Being an Attempt to Explain the Former Change of the Earth's Surface by References to Causes Now in Operation*, 3 vols (London, 1830, 1832, 1833).

103 Charles Lyell, *Lehrbuch der Geologie. Ein Versuch die früheren Veränderungen der Erdoberfläche durch noch jetzt wirksame Ursachen zu erklären. Nach der zweiten Auflage des Originals aus dem Englischen übersetzt von Carl Hartmann* (Quedlinburg and Leipzig, 1833) (online).

104 Charles Lyell, *Principles of Geology*, vol. 1 (London, 1830), chapter 23, 403–4 (online).

105 Werner Hofmann, *Das entzweite Jahrhundert. Kunst zwischen 1750 und 1850* (Munich, 1995), 358.

106 Simkin and Siebert, *Volcanoes of the World*, 257.

107 Scrope, *Considerations on Volcanos*, 255.

108 Simkin and Siebert, *Volcanoes of the World*, 257.
109 Christoph Vitali (ed.), *Ernste Spiele. Der Geist der Romantik in der Deutschen Kunst 1770–1990* (Stuttgart, 1995).
110 Hubertus Kohle, 'Albtraum – Angst – Apokalypse. Das Unheimliche und Katastrophale in der Kunst der Moderne', in Felix Krämer (ed.), *Schwarze Romantik von Goya bis Max Ernst*, exhibition catalogue, Städelmuseum Frankfurt (Ostfildern, 2012), 42–50, 45.
111 William Feaver, *The Art of John Martin* (Oxford, 1975), 16.
112 Monteleone, 'La carestia del 1816–1817', 23–86.
113 Johann Gottfried Tulla, *Die Grundsätze, nach welchen die Rheinbauarbeiten künftig zu führen seyn möchten* (Karlsruhe, 1812).
114 Johann Gottfried Tulla, *Über die Rektifikation des Rheins, von seinem Austritt aus der Schweiz bis zu seinem Eintritt in das Großherzogthum Hessen* (Karlsruhe, 1825) (online).
115 David Blackbourn, *The Conquest of Nature: Water and the Making of the Modern German Landscape* (London, 2006), 75.
116 Tulla, *Über die Rektifikation*, 3.
117 Tulla, *Über die Rektifikation*, 28–48.
118 Blackbourn, *Conquest of Nature*, 97–8, 130–1.
119 Friedrich Fick, *Mein letzter Versuch für die Flöß- und Schiffbarmachung der schönen Regnitz in Franken* (Erlangen, 1816); Heinrich Joachim Jäck, *Einige Worte eines Weltbürgers über die Schiff- und Flossbarkeit der Pegnitz und Rednitz [. . .]* (Bamberg, 1816) (online).
120 Vasold, 'Das Jahr des großen Hungers', 772.
121 Franz Xaver von Baader, *Über die Verbindung der Donau mit dem Main und dem Rhein und die zweckmäßige Ausführung derselben* (Sulzbach, 1822); Friedrich Julius Heinrich Graf von Soden, *Der Maximilian-Kanal. Über die Vereinigung der Donau mit dem Main und Rhein. Ein Versuch* (Nuremberg, 1822).
122 Andreas C. Gudme, *Bemerkungen über die projektierte Verbindung der Ostsee und der Niederelbe mittelst eines Barkenkanals* (Schleswig, 1822).
123 Universitätsbibliothek Salzburg, Flusskarte 7024 (1817).
124 Leopold Mathias Weschel, *Die Leopoldstadt bey Wien* (Vienna, 1826), 482 (online).
125 Sauer, *Reformer auf dem Königsthron*, 332.
126 Roy Finch, *The Story of the New York State Canals: Governor DeWitt Clinton's Dream* (New York, 1925), 7.
127 Peter L. Bernstein, *Wedding of the Waters: The Erie Canal and the Making of a Great Nation* (New York, 2005).
128 Carol Sheriff, *The Artificial River: The Erie Canal and the Paradox of Progress* (New York, 1996).
129 James M. Bergquist, *Daily Life in Immigrant America, 1820–1870* (Westport, CT, 2008), 185.
130 Turner, *Rise of the New West*, 224–35.
131 Reinhard Stauber, *Der Wiener Kongress* (Vienna, 2014), 75–7.
132 Louis C. Hunter, *Steamboats on the Western Rivers: An Economic and Technological History* (Cambridge, MA, 1949).
133 Ross Thomson, *Structures of Change in the Mechanical Age: Technological Innovation in the United States, 1790–1865* (Baltimore, 2009).

134 Johann Christoph Stelzhammer, *Genaue Beschreibung des Dampfschiffes auf der Donau* (Vienna, 1818).

135 Sommer, *Eine baltisch-adlige Missionarin*, 606.

136 Maurice W. Kirby, *The Origins of Railway Enterprise: The Stockton and Darlington Railway 1821-1863* (Cambridge, 2002).

137 Lionel T.C. Rolt, George and Robert Stephenson, *The Railway Revolution* (London, 1960).

138 Josef von Baader, *Über ein neueres System der fortschaffenden Mechanik, als Programm eines über diesen Gegenstand nächstens zu erscheinenden großen Werkes* (Munich, 1817), 18 (online).

139 Baader, *Über die Verbindung*.

140 Josef von Baader, *Neues System der fortschaffenden Mechanik oder vollständige Beschreibung der neu erfundenen Eisenbahnen und Wagen mit verschiedenen andern neuen Verrichtungen, mittelst welcher der innere Transport aller Waren und Produkte fast überall so gut und mit weit geringeren Schwierigkeiten als durch schiffbare Kanäle befördert und erleichtert werden kann* (Munich, 1822) (online), 1-22. This edition was dedicated to Tsar Alexander I of Russia, who had subscribed to one hundred copies, more than any other person.

141 Josef von Baader, *Über die neuesten Verbesserungen und die allgemeinere Einführung der Eisenbahnen* (Munich, 1825).

142 Carl Asmus, *Die Ludwigs-Eisenbahn. Die erste Eisenbahnlinie in Deutschland* (Zurich, 1984).

143 Turner, *The Rise of the New West*, 230.

144 *Goethes Werke*, WA, vol. 27, 117-18 (report to Grand Duchess Louise, 22 July 1816).

145 John Loudon McAdam, *Remarks on the Present System of Road-Making* (London, 1816) (online), and *Practical Essay on the Scientific Repair and Preservation of Roads* (London, 1819).

146 Roy Devereux, *John Loudon McAdam: Chapters in the History of Highways* (Oxford, 1936).

147 Lars Ulrich Scholl, *Ingenieure in der Frühindustrialisierung. Staatliche und private Techniker im Königreich Hannover und an der Ruhr (1815-1873)* (Göttingen 1978), 48-50.

148 Nicole K. Longen, 'Fronarbeiten zur Finanzierung von Infrastruktur: Der Ausbau des Straßennetzes im Kurtrierer Raum, 1716-1841', in Hans-Liudger Dienel and Hans-Ulrich Schiedt (eds), *Die moderne Straße. Planung, Bau und Verkehr vom 18. bis zum 20. Jahrhundert* (Frankfurt am Main, 2010), 23-48, 42-3.

149 Uwe Müller, 'Der Beitrag des Chausseebaus zum Modernisierungsprozess in Preußen', in Dienel and Schiedt (eds), *Die moderne Straße*, 49-76, 53.

150 Jäger and Jäger, *Die Hungerjahre 1816/17*, 32-3.

151 Landesarchiv Baden-Württemberg, Stuttgart, Bestand E 169 c Oberbaurat (online finding aid).

152 Zollikofer, *Das Hungerjahr 1817*, vol. 1, 166-7.

153 Armon Planta, *Verkehrswege im alten Rätien*, vol. 4 (Chur, 1990), 11-33.

154 Gerold Meyer von Knonau, 'Richard La Nicca', in *ADB* 51 (1906), 590-3.

155 Friedrich Springorum, *Die Stilfser-Joch-Straße und ihre Zubringerstraßen* (Munich, 1956).

156 *Wiener Zeitung*, no. 324, 22 November 1840, 1.

157 Monteleone, 'La carestia', 23–86.
158 Heinrich Benedikt, *Kaiseradler über dem Apennin. Die Österreicher in Italien* (Vienna, 1964), 119–20.
159 Varnhagen, *Denkwürdigkeiten*, 487–8.
160 Georg Friedrich Tscheulin, *Beschreibung und Heilung des Nervenfiebers, welches im Frühjahr und Sommer 1817 unter den Pferden hier und in der Gegend geherrscht hat* (Karlsruhe, 1818).
161 George Cruikshank, 'Royal Hobby's, or the Hertfordshire Cock-Horse!' (London, 1819). British Museum website, with additional information.
162 George Cruikshank, 'Accidents in High Life, or Royal Hobby's Brokedown' (London, 1819).
163 Cruikshank, 'Royal Hobby's' (London 1819).
164 Volker Bruse, *Deutsche Motorräder der Kaiserzeit 1885–1918* (Lemgo, 2009).
165 Vasold, 'Das Jahr des großen Hungers', 772.
166 Eberhard Weis, *Der Durchbruch des Bürgertums, 1776–1847* (Berlin, 1975), 400–1.
167 Eichhoff, *Betrachtungen*, ix.
168 Eichhoff, *Betrachtungen*, 46–7.
169 Peter Kaeding, *Die Hand über der ganzen Welt. Johann Friedrich Cotta, der Verleger der deutschen Klassik* (Stuttgart, 2009).
170 Fischer, *Johann Friedrich Cotta*, 729–37.
171 Echenberg, *Africa in the Time of Cholera*, 50–64.
172 Xavier de Planhol and Daniel Balland, 'Cholera', in *Encyclopaedia Iranica*, vol. 5 (1991), 504–11 (online).
173 Pollitzer, *Cholera*, 19–20.
174 Pollitzer, *Cholera*, 21–2; Barbara Dettke, *Die asiatische Hydra. Die Cholera von 1830/31 in Berlin und den preußischen Provinzen Posen, Preußen und Schlesien* (Berlin, 1995), 43, citing an account of 26 October 1830 in the *Vossische Zeitung*.
175 Huber, *Rettung von der Cholera. Tagebuch aus Saratow vom 10. bis 31 August 1830* (Dessau, 1831); *Nachrichten über die Cholera Morbus und ihre schreckliche Verbreitung im Jahre 1830. Mitgetheilt von zwei evangelischen Pfarrern im Gouvernement Saratow* (Basel, 1831); Dettke, *Die asiatische Hydra*, 43–4.
176 Jameson, *Report on the Epidemic Cholera Morbus*.
177 Charlotte E. Henze, *Disease, Health Care and Government in Late Imperial Russia: Life and Death on the Volga, 1823–1914* (New York, 2011), 14. On Jameson's study, see p. 23.
178 Harald Haurowitz, *Topographisch-medizinische Beobachtungen über den südlichen Theil des Saratowschen Gouvernements* (St Petersburg, 1836), 208.
179 Kirsten Mörters, '"Hurra, Cholera!" – Die Cholera-Unruhen in St. Petersburg im Sommer 1831', in Heinz-Dietrich Löwe (ed.), *Volksaufstände in Russland. Von der Zeit der Wirren bis zur 'Grünen Revolution' gegen die Sowjetherrschaft* (Wiesbaden, 2006), 397–426.
180 Henze, *Disease*, 16.
181 Dettke, *Die asiatische Hydra*, 48–56.
182 Henze, *Disease*, 18–20.
183 Henryk Kocój, *Preußen und Deutschland gegenüber dem Novemberaufstand 1830–1831* (Katowice, 1990).

184 Wolfgang U. Eckart, 'Cholera', in *Enzyklopädie der Neuzeit*, vol. 2 (2005), 717–20.

185 Sean Burrell and Geoffrey Gill, 'The Liverpool cholera epidemic of 1832 and anatomical dissection – medical mistrust and civil unrest', *Journal of the History of Medicine and Allied Sciences* 60 (2005): 478–98.

186 Pollitzer, *Cholera*, 23–5.

187 T.J. Pettigrew, *Observations on Cholera, Comprising a Description of the Epidemic Cholera of India, the Mode of Treatment and the Means of Prevention* (London, 1831), 22.

188 James Adair Lawrie, *Essay on Cholera. Founded on Observations of the Disease Made in Various Parts of India, and in Sunderland, Newcastle, and Gateshead* (Glasgow, 1832), 22.

189 Orton, *An Essay on the Epidemic*, 314.

190 Edwin Chadwick, *Report on the Sanitary Condition of the Labouring Population of Great Britain* (London, 1842).

191 John Snow, *On the Mode of Communication of Cholera* (London, 1849), 2nd edn (London, 1855) (online).

192 Filippo Pacini, *Osservazioni microscopiche e deduzioni patologiche sul cholera asiatico* (Florence, 1854) (online).

193 Stephen Halliday, *The Great Stink of London: Sir Joseph Bazalgette and the Cleansing of the Victorian Metropolis* (Stroud, 1999).

194 Halliday, *The Great Stink*, 124, with the figures for all of the cholera outbreaks in London.

195 David S. Barnes, *The Great Stink of Paris and the Nineteenth-Century Struggle Against Filth and Germs* (Baltimore, 2006).

196 Steven Johnson, *The Ghost Map: The Story of London's Most Terrifying Epidemic – and How it Changed Science, Cities and the Modern World* (New York, 2006).

197 Denis Papin, *Recueil de diverses pieces touchant quelques nouvelles machines* (Kassel, 1695) (online).

198 Alexander Aepli, *Wer hat die Pflicht, die Armen zu erhalten?* (St. Gallen, 1817); 'Alexander Aepli', in *Neuer Nekolog der Deutschen* 10, part 1 (1834), 361–3 (online).

199 Scheitlin, *Meine Armenreisen*, 168.

200 Anonymous, D.M., 'Benutzung der Knochen, und Gesuch um Einsendung derselben', *Neues St. Gallisches Wochenblatt*, 17 April 1817.

201 Anonymous, 'Über die Benutzung der Knochen-Gallerte bey den Sparsuppen', *Der Bürger- und Bauernfreund*, 30 April 1817. Cited in Specker, 'Die grosse Heimsuchung', 19.

202 C.G. Demmrich, *Neu erfundene Koch-, Heitz- und Sparöfen, deren Bequemlichkeit durch mehrjährige Erfahrung hinlänglich erprobt wurde* (Leipzig, 1817), and *Neue erprobte Entdeckung, den Rauch, welcher in den Gebäuden die Küchen und Stuben belästigt, nach physischen Grundsätzen abzuleiten* (Leipzig, 1817).

203 C.G. Demmrich, *Heizofen der neuesten Construction, zur Erzeugung einer schnellen und anhaltenden Wärme und beträchtlicher Holzersparniß eingerichtet* (Leipzig, 1817).

204 Johann Christoph Stelzhammer, *Anweisung für die Einführung der papinianischen Kochtöpfe* (Vienna, 1816).

205 'Johann Christoph Stelzhammer', in *BLKÖ* 38 (1879), 193–7.

206 Siegmund Fellöcker, *Geschichte der Sternwarte der Benediktiner-Abtei Kremsmünster. Physikalisches Cabinett. Instrumente und Experimente* (Linz, 1864).

207 Jäger and Jäger, *Die Hungerjahre 1816/17*, 34–8.

208 Anonymous, 'Fortsetzung des Schreibens über die Landwirtschaft', *Der Bürger- und Bauernfreund*, 7 May 1817.

209 Specker, 'Die grosse Heimsuchung', 52.

210 Specker, 'Die grosse Heimsuchung', 52.

211 Scheitlin, *Meine Armenreisen*, 150ff.

212 Anonymous, 'Guter Rath über Pflanzung der Erdäpfel', *St. Gallisches Kantonsblatt für das Jahr 1817* (St. Gallen, 1817), 29. Cited in Specker, 'Die grosse Heimsuchung', 18.

213 Zollikofer, *Das Hungerjahr 1817*, vol. 2, 77.

214 William H. Brock, *Justus von Liebig: The Chemical Gatekeeper* (Cambridge, 1997), 7–8.

215 Martin Kirschke, *Liebigs Lehrer Karl W.G. Kastner (1783–1857). Eine Professorenkarriere in Zeiten naturwissenschaftlichen Umbruchs* (Berlin, 2001). The doctoral diploma from Erlangen is dated 1823.

216 W. Krohn and W. Schäfer, 'Agricultural chemistry: The origin and structure of a finalized science', in Wolf Schäfer (ed.), *Finalization in Science: The Social Orientation of Scientific Progress* (Dordrecht, 1983).

217 Justus Liebig, *Die organische Chemie in ihrer Anwendung auf Agricultur und Physiologie* (Braunschweig) 1840 (online), 5th edn (Braunschweig 1843).

218 Brock, *Justus von Liebig*.

219 Emmermann, *Die Armenpflege im Herzogtum Nassau*, 32–4.

220 Henry Duncan, *Essay on the Nature and Advantages of Parish Banks* (Edinburgh, 1815).

221 Lance Edwin Davis and Peter Lester Payne, 'From benevolence to business: The story of two savings banks', *Business History Review* 32 (1958): 4.

222 James M. Willcox, *A History of the Philadelphia Savings Fund Society 1816–1916* (Philadelphia, 1916), 18.

223 Gash, *Lord Liverpool*, 131.

224 Eckhard Wandel, *Banken und Versicherungen im 19. und 20. Jahrhundert* (Munich, 1998), 3–4.

225 Lars Clausen, '200 Jahre Sparkasse zu Kiel', *Tönnies-Forum* 6, no. 2 (1997): 56–65.

226 Anett Kschieschan, 'Königsbrücker Sparkasse ist älteste im Land', *Sächsische Zeitung*, 10 January 2009, 18.

227 Herbert Krafft, *Immer ging es um Geld. Einhundertfünfzig Jahre Sparkasse in Berlin* (Berlin, 1968).

228 Jean-Dominique de La Rochefoucauld, *Le Duc de La Rochefoucauld Liancourt (1747–1827). De Louis XV à Charles X, un grand seigneur patriote et le mouvement populaire* (Paris, 1980).

229 Wikipedia entry for 'Erste Bank'.

230 Friedrich Julius Heinrich Graf von Soden, *Entwurf zu einer Sparcasse* (Nuremberg, 1820).

231 Hermann Kellenbenz, *Deutsche Wirtschaftsgeschichte*, vol. 2 (Munich, 1981), 150.

232 Rainer Mertens, *Johannes Scharrer. Profil eines Reformers in Nürnberg zwischen Aufklärung und Romantik* (Nuremberg, 1996).
233 Richard Merz, *Stadtsparkasse Augsburg 1822–1997. Ein Beitrag zur Wirtschafts- und Sozialgeschichte der Stadt Augsburg* (Stuttgart, 1997).
234 Franz Lerner, *Bürgersinn und Bürgertat. Geschichte der Frankfurter Polytechnischen Gesellschaft 1816–1966* (Frankfurt am Main, 1966).
235 Hans Pohl, *Die rheinischen Sparkassen. Entwicklung und Bedeutung für Wirtschaft und Gesellschaft von den Anfängen bis 1990* (Stuttgart, 2001), 26.
236 Kukowski, *Pauperismus in Kurhessen*, 292.
237 Luigi De Rosa, *Storia delle Casse di Risparmio e della loro associazione* (Bari, 2003).
238 Pohl, *Die rheinischen Sparkassen*, 31–4.
239 Kukowski, *Pauperismus in Kurhessen*, 292.
240 Winfried Dotzauer, 'Die Triebkräfte einer Sparkassengründung im gesellschaftlichen Umbruch der Napoleonischen Ära: Die städtische Sparkasse Koblenz', *Zeitschrift für bayerische Sparkassengeschichte* 1 (1987): 149–73.
241 Carl August Freiherr von Malchus, *Die Sparcassen in Europa* (Heidelberg, 1838) (online).
242 Emmermann, *Die Armenpflege im Herzogtum Nassau*, 32–4.
243 Anonymous, 'Bürger-Majorat', *Neues St. Gallisches Wochenblatt*, 23 January 1817.
244 'Sterbecasse', in Krünitz, *Ökonomische Enzyklopädie*, vol. 173 (1840), 141–211 (online).
245 Ernst Wilhelm Arnoldi, *Die Idee einer eigenen deutschen Feuerversicherung* (Gotha, 1817).
246 August Beck, 'Ernst Wilhelm Arnoldi', in *ADB* 1 (1875), 589–91.
247 Neumann, 'Das osmanische Reich in seiner Existenzkrise', 285–95.
248 Bin Wong, *China Transformed*.
249 Pomeranz, *The Great Divergence*.
250 Mark C. Elliott, *Emperor Qianlong: Son of Heaven, Man of the World* (New York, 2009).
251 Peter C. Perdue, *China Marches West: The Qing Conquest of Central Eurasia* (Cambridge, MA, 2005).
252 Martin Woesler, *Zwischen Exotismus, Sinozentrismus und Chinoiserie, Européerie*, 3rd edn (Bochum, 2006).
253 John K. Fairbank and Kwang-Ching Liu, *Late Ch'ing, 1800–1911* (Cambridge, 1980).
254 Li Bozhong, 'The Daoguang depression and the 1823 flood: Economic decline, climatic cataclysm and the nineteenth-century crisis in Songjiang', *Shehui Kexue* [Journal of Social Sciences] 6 (2007): 173–8.
255 Robert Bickers, *The Scramble for China: Foreign Devils in the Qing Empire, 1832–1914* (London, 2011).
256 Cao, Li and Bin Yang, 'Mt. Tambora, climatic changes, and China's decline in the nineteenth century', 597–8.
257 Robert William Fogel, *The Escape from Hunger and Premature Death, 1700–2100: Europe, America and the Third World* (Cambridge, 2004).
258 Monica Wilson and Leonard Monteath Thompson, *The Oxford History of South Africa* (Oxford, 1969).

259 Max du Preez, *Warriors, Lovers and Prophets: Unusual Stories from South Africa's Past* (Johannesburg, 2009), 59.
260 John Iliffe, *Africans: The History of a Continent* (Cambridge, 1996), 174.
261 Ernest August Ritter, *Shaka Zulu* (New York, 1955).
262 Elizabeth A. Eldredge, *A South African Kingdom: The Pursuit of Security in Nineteenth-Century Lesotho* (Cambridge, 1993).
263 G.J. Liesegang, *Beiträge zur Geschichte des Reiches der Gaza Nguni im südlichen Mocambique* (Cologne, 1967).
264 John D. Omer-Cooper, *The Zulu Aftermath: A Nineteenth-Century Revolution in Bantu Africa* (London, 1966).
265 The town of Bulawayo was later founded on this site by Cecil Rhodes.
266 Andrew Sanders, *A Deed without a Name* (Oxford, 1995), 137.
267 Wolfgang Behringer, *Witches and Witch Hunts: A Global History* (Cambridge, 2004), 51.
268 Iliffe, *Africans*, 175.
269 Manfred F.R. Kets de Vries, *Lessons on Leadership by Terror: Finding Shaka Zulu in the Attic* (Cheltenham, 2004), 41.
270 Julian Cobbing, 'The Mfecane as alibi: Thoughts on Dithakong and Mbolompo', *Journal of African History* 29 (1988): 487–519.
271 Carolyn Hamilton (ed.), *The Mfecane Aftermath: Reconstructive Debates in Southern African History* (Bloomington, IN, 1995).
272 Norman Etherington, *The Great Treks: The Transformation of Southern Africa, 1815–1854* (Abingdon, 2001).
273 The calculations are based on the figures in www.convictrecords.com.au/timeline.
274 Judy Campbell, *Invisible Invaders: Smallpox and Other Diseases in Aboriginal Australia, 1780–1880* (Melbourne, 2002).
275 Matthew Flinders, *A Voyage to Terra Australis, with an Accompanying Atlas*, 2 vols (London, 1814).
276 Peter Butler and Harry Dillon, *Macquarie: From Colony to Country* (Milsons Point, NSW, 2010).
277 Lloyd Robson and Michael Roe, *A Short History of Tasmania*, 2nd edn (Melbourne, 1997).
278 Arthur Phillip, *Australien. Die Gründung der Strafkolonie*, ed. Rudolf Plischke (Göttingen, 2001), 189.
279 The calculations are based on the figures in www.convictrecords.com.au/timeline.
280 P.R. Eldershaw, 'Davey, Thomas', in *Australian Dictionary of Biography* (Melbourne, 1996) (online).
281 The only man of that name on the passenger lists was transported to Van Diemen's Land on the *Indefatigable* on 9 May 1812 and arrived there on 19 October.
282 K.R. von Stieglitz, 'Howe, Michael', in *Australian Dictionary of Biography* (Melbourne, 1966), 2 (online).
283 Thomas Wells, *Michael Howe, the Last and Worst of the Bushrangers* (Hobart Town, 1818).
284 Lyndall Ryan, 'List of multiple killings of Aborigines in Tasmania, 1804–1835', *Online Encyclopedia of Mass Violence* (last modified 5 March 2008).
285 Ryan, 'List of multiple killings of Aborigines in Tasmania'.

286 Lloyd Robson and Michael Roe, *A Short History of Tasmania*, 2nd edn (Melbourne, 1997).

7 Epilogue: From Meaningless to Meaningful Crisis

1 Abel, *Massenarmut und Hungerkrisen*, 514–43.
2 Christoph Sachsse and Florian Tennstedt, *Geschichte der Armenfürsorge in Deutschland. Vom Spätmittelalter bis zum 1. Weltkrieg* (Stuttgart, 1980).
3 Wehler, *Deutsche Gesellschaftsgeschichte*, vol. 2, 27–30, 51.
4 Nipperdey, *Germany from Napoleon to Bismarck*, 126.
5 Theodor Lessing, *Geschichte als Sinngebung des Sinnlosen* (Leipzig, 1919). See Elke-Vera Kotowski (ed.), *'Geschichte als Sinngebung des Sinnlosen'. Zum Leben und Werk des Kulturkritikers Theodor Lessing (1872–1933)* (Hildesheim, 2006).
6 Labrousse, *La crise de l'économie française à la fin de l'ancien régime et au début de la Révolution.*
7 Katz, *From Prejudice to Destruction*, 102.
8 Craig, *Europe, 1815–1914*, 77–8 (France), 101–5 (England).
9 Kissinger, *A World Restored*.

SELECT BIBLIOGRAPHY

Abel, Wilhelm, *Massenarmut und Hungerkrisen im vorindustriellen Europa. Versuch einer Synopsis*. Hamburg and Berlin, 1974.

Assion, Peter, 'Hungerjahr und Erntedank 1817', *Der Odenwald* 23 (1976): 93–105.

Birkbeck, Morris, *Notes on a Journey in America from the Coast of Virginia to the Territory of Illinois*. London 1817, 2nd edn, London 1818 (online).

Cao, Shuji, Li Yushang and Yang, Bin, 'Mt. Tambora, climatic changes, and China's decline in the nineteenth century', *Journal of World History* 23 (2012): 587–607.

Demel, Walter, *Der bayerische Staatsabsolutismus 1806/08–1817. Staats- und gesellschaftspolitische Motivationen und Hintergründe der Reformära in der ersten Phase des Königreichs Bayern*. Munich, 1983.

Echenberg, Myron, *Africa in the Time of Cholera: A History of Pandemics from 1817 to the Present*. Cambridge, 2011.

Emmermann, Friedrich Wilhelm, *Die Armenpflege im Herzogtum Nassau, nach dem Edikt vom 19. Oktober 1816 und den hierauf sich beziehenden allgemeinen Vorschriften. Ein Handbuch für die mit der Armenpflege beauftragten Behörden*. Wiesbaden, 1818 (online).

Fischer, Klaus, 'Das Hungerjahr 1816/17 in Tirol und der Ausbruch des Vulkans Tambora. Ein Beispiel der Wirksamkeit großer Vulkanausbrüche auf das Klimasystem der Erde', *Der Schlern* 73 (1999): 5–22.

Fürstenwärther, Moritz von, *Der Deutsche in Nordamerika*. Stuttgart and Tübingen, 1818 (online).

Gash, Norman, *Lord Liverpool: The Life and Political Career of Robert Banks Jenkinson, Second Earl of Liverpool, 1770–1828*. London, 1984.

Gehring-Münzel, Ursula, *Vom Schutzjuden zum Staatsbürger. Die gesellschaftliche Integration der Würzburger Juden 1803–1871*. Würzburg, 1992.

Girard, Colette, 'Les conséquences démographiques de la famine de 1816–1817 dans le département de la Meurthe', *Annales de l'Est* 7 (1956): 18–38.

Halévy, Élie, *The Liberal Awakening, 1815–1830*. London, 1961.

Harrington, Charles Richard (ed.), *The Year without a Summer? World Climate in 1816*. Ottawa, 1992.

Havighurst, Walter, *Wilderness for Sale: The Story of the First Western Land Rush*. New York, 1956.

Hazzi, Joseph von, *Betrachtungen über Theuerung und Noth der Vergangenheit und Gegenwart. Geschrieben im Herbste 1817*. Munich, 1818 (online).

Henchoz, Paul, 'L'Année de la misère (1816–1817) dans la région de Montreux', *Revue historique vaudoise* 42 (1934): 66–89.

Henrioud, Marc, 'L'Année de la misère en Suisse et plus particulièrement dans le Canton de Vaud 1816–1817', *Revue historique vaudoise* 25 (1917): 114–24, 133–42, 171–92.

Holland, Henry, 'On the pellagra, a disease prevailing in Lombardy', *Medico-chirurgical Transactions* 8 (1817): 315–48 (online).

Hornthal, Franz Ludwig von, *Vorschlag, wie der herrschenden Theuerung abzuhelffen sein dürfte*. Bamberg, 1817 (online).

Howard, Luke, 'Notes of a journey on the continent, 1816', in Douglas F.S. Scott (ed.), *Luke Howard, (1772–1864), his Correspondence with Goethe and his Continental Journey of 1816*. York, 1976.

Humphreys, William Jackson, 'Volcanic dust and other factors in the production of climatic changes, and their possible relation to ice ages', *Bulletin of the Mount Weather Observatory* 6 (1913): 1–34.

Jäger, Christa and Wolfgang, *Die Hungerjahre 1816/17 im heutigen Landkreis Haßberge*. Haßfurt, 2008.

de Jong Boers, Bernice, 'Mount Tambora in 1815: A volcanic eruption in Indonesia and its aftermath', *Indonesia* 60 (1995): 37–60.

Klingaman, William K. and Nicholas P. *The Year Without Summer: 1816 and the Volcano that Darkened the World and Changed History*. New York, 2013.

Kukowski, Martin, *Pauperismus in Kurhessen. Ein Beitrag zur Entstehung und Entwicklung der Massenarmut in Deutschland 1815–1855*. Darmstadt, 1995.

Leibbrandt, Georg, *Die Auswanderung aus Schwaben nach Russland, 1816–1823*. Stuttgart, 1928.

Marjolin, Robert, 'Troubles provoqués en France par la disette de 1816–1817', *Revue d'Histoire Moderne* 8 (1933): 423–60.

Medick, Hans, *Weben und Überleben in Laichingen, 1650–1900. Lokalgeschichte als allgemeine Geschichte*. Göttingen, 1996.

Mohl, Raymond A., 'Humanitarianism in the preindustrial city: The New York Society for the Prevention of Pauperism, 1817–1823', *Journal of American History* 57 (1970): 576–99.

Moltmann Günter (ed.), *Aufbruch nach Amerika. Die Auswanderungswelle von 1816/17*. Stuttgart, 1989.

Monteleone, Giulio, 'La carestia del 1816–1817 nelle Province Venete', *Archivio Veneto* 86/87 (1969): 23–86.

Müller, Felix Joseph, *Ueber die gegenwärtige Theuerung der Lebensmittel und ihre Urquellen*. Donauwörth, 1817 (online).

Müller, Gerald, *Hunger in Bayern, 1816–1818. Politik und Gesellschaft in einer Staatskrise des frühen 19. Jahrhunderts*. Frankfurt am Main, 1998.

Nipperdey, Thomas, *Germany from Napoleon to Bismarck: 1800–1866*, trans. Daniel Nolan. Princeton, NJ, 1996.

Oppenheimer, Clive, 'Climatic, environmental and human consequences of the largest known historic eruption: Tambora volcano (Indonesia) 1815', *Progress in Physical Geography* 27 (2003): 230–59.

Orton, Reginald, *An Essay on the Epidemic Cholera of India*, 2nd edn, with a supplement. London, 1831 (online).

Peacock, A.J., *Bread or Blood: A Study of the Agrarian Riots in East Anglia, 1816*. London, 1965.

Pollitzer, Robert, *Cholera. With a Chapter on World Incidence*, ed. World Health Organization. Geneva, 1959.

Post, John Dexter, *The Last Great Subsistence Crisis in the Western World*. Baltimore, 1977.

Raffles, Thomas Stamford, *The History of Java*. London, 1817 (online).

Rampino, Michael S. and Self, Stephen, 'Historic eruptions of Tambora (1815), Krakatau (1883) and Agung (1963), their stratospheric aerosols and climatic impact', *Quaternary Research* 18 (1982): 127–43.

Rezneck, Samuel, 'The depression of 1819–1822, a social history', *American Historical Review* 39 (1933): 28–47.

Ross, J.T., 'Narrative of the effects of the eruption from the Tomboro mountain in the island of Sumbawa on the 11th and 12th of April 1815. Communicated by the president [of the Batavian Society, 28 September 1815]', *Verhandelingen van het Bataviaasch Ge-nootschap von Konsten en Wetenschappen* 8 (1816): 3–25 (online).

Royal Society, Krakatoa Committee (eds), *The Eruption of Krakatoa, and Subsequent Phenomena*. London, 1888.

Sandkaulen, Wilhelm, *Das Notjahr 1816/17 mit besonderer Berücksichtigung der Verhältnisse am Niederrhein*. Münster, 1927.

Sauer, Paul, *Reformer auf dem Königsthron. Wilhelm I. von Württemberg*. Stuttgart, 1997.

Scheitlin, Peter, *Meine Armenreisen in den Kanton Glarus und in die Umgebungen der Stadt St. Gallen in den Jahren 1816 und 1817, nebst einer Darstellung, wie es den Armen des gesamten Vaterlandes im Jahr 1817 erging. Ein Beytrag zur Charakteristik unserer Zeit*. St. Gallen, 1820 (online).

Simkin, Tom and Siebert, Lee, *Volcanoes of the World. A Regional Directory, Gazetteer, and Chronology of Volcanism During the Last 10,000 Years*. 3rd edn, Berkeley, 2010.

Skeen, Carl Edward, *1816 America Rising*. Lexington, 2003.

Sommer, Debora, *Eine baltisch-adlige Missionarin bewegt Europa. Barbara Juliane von Krüdener, geb. v. Vietinghoff gen. Scheel (1764–1824)*. Göttingen, 2013.

Spamer, Adolf, 'Bairische Denkmale aus der "theueren Zeit" vor 100 Jahren', *Bayerische Hefte für Volkskunde* 3 (1916): 145–266.

Specker, Louis, 'Die grosse Heimsuchung. Das Hungerjahr 1816/17 in der Ostschweiz', *Neujahrsblatt des Historischen Vereins des Kantons St. Gallen* 133 (1993): 9–42; 135 (1995): 5–56.

Steger, Hartmut, 'Das Hungerjahr 1817 im Ries', *Rieser Kulturtage* 7 (1998): 294–315.

Sterling, Eleonore O., 'Anti-Jewish riots in Germany in 1819: A displacement of social protest', *Historia Judaica* 12 (1950): 105–42.

Stommel, Henry and Elizabeth, *Volcano Weather. The Story of the Year Without a Summer: 1816*. Newport, RI, 1983.

Vail, Jeffrey, '"The bright sun was extinguis'd": The Bologna Prophecy and Byron's "Darkness"', *The Wordsworth Circle* 28 (1997): 183–92.

Varnhagen von Ense, Karl August, *Denkwürdigkeiten des eigenen Lebens*, 3 vols, ed. Konrad Feilchenfeldt. Frankfurt am Main, 1815–1834.

Vasold, Manfred, 'Das Jahr des großen Hungers. Die Agrarkrise von 1816/17 im Nürnberger Raum', *ZBLG* 64 (2001): 745–82.

Vergnaud, Maurice, 'Agitation politique et crise de subsistance à Lyon de septembre 1816 à juin 1817', *Cahiers d'Histoire* 2 (1957): 163–77.

Wehler, Hans-Ulrich, *Deutsche Gesellschaftsgeschichte*, vol. 2: *Von der Reformära bis zur industriellen und politischen 'Deutschen Doppelrevolution', 1815–1845/49*. Munich, 1987.

Weidmann Werner, *Die pfälzische Landwirtschaft zu Beginn des 19. Jahrhunderts*. Saarbrücken, 1968.

Weis, Eberhard, *Montgelas*, vol. 2: *Der Architekt des modernen bayerischen Staates 1799–1838*. Munich, 2005.

Wood, Gillen D'Arcy, *Tambora: The Eruption that Changed the World*. Princeton, NJ, 2014.

Zollikofer, Ruprecht, *Das Hungerjahr 1817. Der Osten meines Vaterlandes oder die Kantone St. Gallen und Appenzell im Hungerjahre 1817. Ein Denkmal jener Schreckens-Epoche*, 2 vols, vol. 1: *Schilderung unseres Elends*. St. Gallen, 1818 (online); vol. 2: *Denkmäler des Wohlthuns*. St. Gallen, 1819 (online).

Zollinger, Heinrich, *Besteigung des Vulkanes Tambora auf der Insel Sumbawa und Schilderung der Erupzion [sic] desselben im Jahr 1815*. Winterthur, 1855.

PICTURE CREDITS

INDEX

Americans, Germans, and War Crimes Justice

Law, Memory, and "The Good War"

James J. Weingartner

PRAEGER

AN IMPRINT OF ABC-CLIO, LLC
Santa Barbara, California • Denver, Colorado • Oxford, England

Library of Congress Cataloging-in-Publication Data

Weingartner, James J., 1940–
    Americans, Germans, and war crimes justice : law, memory, and "the good war" / James J. Weingartner.
        p. cm.
    Includes bibliographical references and index.
    ISBN 978-0-313-38192-8 (alk. paper) — ISBN 978-0-313-38193-5 (ebook)
    1. World War, 1939–1945—Atrocities.   2. World War, 1939–1945—Atrocities—Germany—Borkum.   3. World War, 1939–1945—Atrocities—Germany—Voerde (North Rhine-Westphalia)   4. War crimes—Germany—Borkum.   5. War crimes—Germany—Voerde (North Rhine-Westphalia)   6. Prisoners of war—Crimes against—Germany.   7. Prisoners of war—Crimes against—United States.   8. War crime trials—Germany.   9. World War, 1939–1945—Moral and ethical aspects.   I. Title.

    D803.W44   2011
    341.6'90268—dc22   2010052047

ISBN: 978-0-313-38192-8
EISBN: 978-0-313-38193-5

15   14   13   12   11   1   2   3   4   5

This book is also available on the World Wide Web as an eBook.
Visit www.abc-clio.com for details.

Praeger
An Imprint of ABC-CLIO, LLC

ABC-CLIO, LLC
130 Cremona Drive, P.O. Box 1911
Santa Barbara, California 93116-1911

This book is printed on acid-free paper (∞)

Manufactured in the United States of America

Contents

Introduction

In December 2009, an op-ed piece entitled "The Real Rules of War" appeared in the *Wall Street Journal.* It is a commentary on war crimes and the rules that seek to limit the savagery that is a common and perhaps inevitable part of armed conflict. Laws governing behavior in war are well and good, the author argues, but only so long as both sides respect them, a rare occurrence. And he suggests that the law of war is problematic in a more general sense. It applies the behavioral standards of civilian society to soldiers who are exposed to stresses that civilians who have never experienced combat can scarcely imagine. Although the author declares the rules of war to be "important," his primary message seems to be that efforts to govern the behavior of soldiers in battle are often impractical.

The essay appears to have been inspired by recent American experiences in Iraq, including cases of allegedly illegal conduct by U.S. forces. Ahmed Hashim Abed was beaten by Navy SEALs who captured him, but, after all, he was the mastermind of the brutal murders of four civilian contractors in Fallujah. Although they violated the rules, do the Americans who beat him deserve to be punished? The three SEALs accused of the violations have since been acquitted by military courts. But most of the historical evidence that the author uses to flesh out his argument is drawn from the experience of World War II. U.S. troops murdered German soldiers who had surrendered during the Battle of the Bulge, the author concedes, but Germans had murdered American prisoners earlier in the battle. Surrendered SS men were massacred by American forces at the Dachau concentration camp, but "the obscene horror of the Nazis" was in full evidence all around them.[1] Should soldiers abide by the international law of war when their adversaries do not? Unfortunately, American (and all other) soldiers in World War II did not always need the provocation of enemy atrocities to commit their own, a point that the author does not address.

The essay sparked spirited reaction from readers. Some of these were published in a column provocatively entitled "Do the Realities of War Turn Warriors into Criminals?"[2] The essay and the responses to it indicate that the depressing history of war crimes and their punishment in World War II remains relevant to the contemporary world, fraught as it is once again with armed conflict and controversy surrounding the bringing of suspected war criminals to justice. This book is offered as a contribution to a better understanding of that history, which may be more complex than the author of the essay realizes.

What follows is a story of crime and punishment. The perpetrators and victims are soldiers and civilians who were caught up in modern history's most devastating war. Literature on war crimes committed during World War II and the trials that some of them occasioned is plentiful, but this book is different. The Holocaust, that most horrendous of crimes associated with the Second World War II and the focus of most war-crimes literature, is mentioned only in passing and the "rape of Nanking" and the Katyn Forest massacre not at all. The atrocities that form the focus of this book each cost the lives of only a handful of victims, far fewer than the notorious Bataan "Death March" or the "Malmédy massacre." It is safe to say that they are unknown to the great majority of professional historians working in this period and to most if any of that vast throng of World War II enthusiasts. Yet, the legal and moral issues raised by these crimes and, in particular, by their judicial processing far transcend the very limited scope of the atrocities themselves.

This book is different in another way. Unlike almost all literature dealing with World War II war crimes, it concerns in part atrocities perpetrated by American soldiers. Those crimes and the way in which the U.S. Army regarded them will be compared with the character and legal treatment of *similar* crimes committed by Germans. "Similar" is a critical qualifier that must be emphasized. In no way should this book be interpreted to suggest even approximate moral equivalence between the wartime records of the United States and Nazi Germany. The Holocaust, German genocidal war against the Soviet Union, and murderously brutal German occupation policies that afflicted much of Europe during the dark period between September 1939 and May 1945 have no counterparts in the conduct of U.S. forces during World War II.[3]

But all countries that participated in World War II committed war crimes, and to this generalization the United States is no exception. This may be difficult to reconcile with the mythologized and celebratory image of the U.S. war effort to which all Americans have been long exposed. Paul Fussell, once a young platoon leader with the U.S. 103rd Infantry Division in France who had experienced the "Real War," has written that "For the past fifty years [he was writing in the late 1980s] the Allied war has been sanitized and romanticized almost beyond recognition by the sentimental, the loony patriotic, the ignorant, and the bloodthirsty."[4] But, in the immediate aftermath of the war, perhaps before memory had congealed into patriotic myth, it was possible to read in a mass-circulation middlebrow American magazine such as the *Atlantic Monthly* a bitter article written by Edgar L. Jones, an American ambulance driver and war correspondent. Jones mused:

> What kind of a war do civilians suppose we fought, anyway? We shot prisoners in cold blood, wiped out hospitals, strafed lifeboats, killed or mistreated enemy civilians, finished off the enemy wounded, tossed the dying into a hole with the dead, and in the Pacific boiled the flesh off enemy skulls to make table ornaments for sweethearts or carved their bones into letter openers. . . . As victors we are privileged to try our defeated opponents for their crimes against humanity, but we should be realistic enough to appreciate that if we were on trial for breaking international law, we should be found guilty on a dozen counts.[5]

In fact, Americans *were* sometimes tried for war crimes. Some U.S. airmen, including eight captured members of the Doolittle raid of April 1942, were tried by the Japanese for alleged attacks on civilians in trials that, by Anglo-American standards, were travesties on justice, and some defendants were executed.[6] But this book concerns trials of a different sort. As is generally known, the U.S. Army conducted hundreds of war-crimes trials of Germans, both military and civilian, between 1945 and 1947, involving more than 1,600 defendants. What is less widely known is that the Army also occasionally tried its own members for atrocities committed in the course of the war, and some of these atrocities were similar in scope and character to crimes for which the Army tried and punished its enemies.

This book has as its primary focus two such war crimes and the trials that resulted from them. The defendants in one were German and in the other, American. Both were conducted by the U.S. Army in the months immediately following the end of the war in Europe, and one case would unexpectedly impinge upon the other. But did the Army approach the two cases in the same way? Was the evidence required to bring defendants to trial in the two cases of approximately equal weight? Were the two trials conducted according to similar procedural standards, and were verdicts and punishments based on equally rigorous standards of judgment? In other words, did the U.S. Army mete out equal justice in their trials of these men, American and German? These questions can be answered only by a careful examination of the two crimes and of the trials that resulted from them.

The answers to these questions have important implications that go beyond the assessment of two criminal cases. By means of war-crimes trials, the United States intended not only to punish Germans for their offenses, the worst of which beggared (and continue to beggar) the imagination, but also to educate the German people as to the criminal nature of the regime that most of them had supported or at least tolerated. It was also hoped that an example of fair trials conducted for the vanquished by the victors would help convince Germans of the virtues of a democratic society based on respect for law.[7] But, if the victors were unwilling to apply the same standards of judgment for war crimes to themselves, the educational value of the trials would be seriously diminished. Sixty years later, the announced intention of the U.S. government to try accused terrorists before military commissions in the absence of some of the legal protections ensured to American citizens, including American soldiers tried by court-martial, has sparked vigorous debate.[8] The appearance of hypocrisy and the application of a double standard in the matter of judging wartime atrocities were as potentially damaging to a nation's moral standing in 1946 as they are today.

A number of people made contributions to the completion of this book. Robin Smith, historian of the 486th Bombardment Group, provided valuable documents and photographs relevant to B-17 #909 and its crew and to the dedication of the memorial to them on Borkum. For his assistance and for his unfailing interest in this project, he has my gratitude. Linda J. Erickson of the U.S. Army Judiciary supplied vital court-martial documents generated by the Voerde atrocities, and Carol Martin and Randy Sowell of the Harry S. Truman Library located correspondence related to the Schneeweiss case. Michelle Romero of the Snell Library at Northeastern University provided permission to use material from the papers of Edward F. Lyons Jr. To Jens Westemeier go my thanks for a stimulating exchange of views on the subject of war crimes and, in particular, for valuable insights on the contemporary German perspective on that subject. Riccardo Giannola provided me with his father's account of the massacre of Italian prisoners on Sicily, while Danny S. Parker shared with me important documentary material from his own research. I thank *The Atlantic Monthly* for permission to quote from Edgar L. Jones's "One War Is Enough." Quentin F. Ingerson kindly gave permission to use his photograph of the crew of B-17 #909, of which he had been a member. Praeger's Michael Millman proved a supportive editor and thanks are due to Apex for their perceptive copyediting.

Finally, I am deeply grateful to my wife, Jane Vahle Weingartner, for her invaluable assistance as literary critic, grammarian, and word processing expert and for her patience with a sometimes ill-tempered and preoccupied husband. Of course, any errors of fact or interpretation are solely my responsibility.

James J. Weingartner
Edwardsville, Illinois
April 21, 2010

NOTES

1. Warren Kozak, "The Real Rules of War," *The Wall Street Journal,* December 23, 2009.
2. "Do the Realities of War Turn Warriors into Criminals?," ibid., January 5, 2010.
3. Racial hatreds and the dehumanization of the enemy evident in the attitudes and conduct of many Americans toward the Japanese do, however, bear some uncomfortable similarities to German perspectives and conduct regarding the peoples of the Soviet Union. The crucial difference, however, is that, unlike Germany, genocide never became U.S. policy. On this subject, see John Dower, *War without Mercy: Race and Power in the Pacific War* (New York: Pantheon, 1986); Omer Bartov, *The Eastern Front, 1941–45: German Troops and the Barbarization of Warfare* (New York: St. Martin's Press, 1985); James Weingartner, "War against Subhumans: Comparisons between the German War against the Soviet Union and the American War against Japan," *The Historian* 58 (Spring 1996): 557–73.

4. Paul Fussell, *Wartime: Understanding and Behavior in the Second World War* (New York: Oxford University Press, 1989), ix.

5. Edgar L. Jones, "One War Is Enough," *Atlantic Monthly*, February 1946, 49–50.

6. Craig Nelson, *The First Heroes: The Extraordinary Story of the Doolittle Raid—America's First World War II Victory* (New York: Penguin, 2003), 280–83; "Trial of General Tanaka Hisakasu and Five Others," *Law Reports of War Criminals, Selected and Prepared by the United Nations War Crimes Commission* 6 (London: His Majesty's Stationery Office, 1948): 66–70.

7. Frank M. Buscher, *The U.S. War Crimes Trial Program in Germany, 1946–1955* (Westport, CT: Greenwood Press, 1989), 2.

8. See, for example, Kevin J. Barry, "Military Commissions: Trying American Justice," *The Army Lawyer* (November 2003): 1–9; Colonel Frederic L. Borch III, "Why Military Commissions Are the Proper Forum and Why Terrorists Will Have 'Full and Fair' Trials," ibid. (November 2003): 10–16.

1

War Crimes and the Law of War

Borkum and Voerde are two towns in northwestern Germany. They are separated by little more than 100 miles as the crow flies but differ significantly. Since the 19th century, the island of Borkum, part of the North Sea Frisian archipelago, has been a popular (and, prior to World War II, notoriously anti-Semitic) vacation retreat, with the town of Borkum's economy centered on catering to a flourishing tourist trade. But Borkum in the early 20th century had a schizophrenic character. Sharing the island with hotels and shops serving vacationers and residents in the town on Borkum's southwestern corner were heavy coastal defense guns to the north, forming part of the defensive chain protecting Germany's North Sea coast. A German officer stationed there during World War I poetically called upon Borkum to "protect the ships that seek safe haven, defend the mainland with your strong arm."[1] By the start of World War II, Borkum's "strong arm" included the two 240 mm guns of Battery Oldenburg and the four 280mm weapons of Battery Coronel. Complementing Borkum's big-gun defenses against seaborne assault was an array of antiaircraft batteries and air defense radar that offered protection against the newer threat from the air. Foreign forced laborers were put to work strengthening fortifications against an Allied attack that never came. Borkum was able to ride out the war in relative safety and never fully lost its prewar character as a seaside resort. At least two Allied aircraft crashed on Borkum in the course of the war, and stray bombs jettisoned by bombers in distress sometimes fell in the North Sea close by or even on the island itself, although little damage was done. The island was occupied by Canadian forces at the end of the war.[2]

Voerde, on the other hand, was a small town on the lower Rhine not far from the border with the Netherlands to the west and the heavily industrialized (and heavily bombed Ruhr Valley) to the east.[3] The town was home to a 19th-century military installation, the Friedrichsfeld *Truppenübungsplatz* (troop training area), which had served as a prisoner-of-war camp during the Franco-Prussian War, and the Buschmannshof compound, a grim barracks-like structure that housed not soldiers but small children. Its tiny inmates—the oldest were no more than two years old—were the children of Eastern European women who were employed as slave laborers by the huge Krupp industrial complex in Essen, a short distance away. The Buschmannshof facility had been established in 1943, when Krupp's own hospital could no longer accommodate the growing numbers of children born to its female captive workers. The children were cared for by a staff of Russian women under German direction, but the quality of care given to them was minimal. Disease and malnutrition caused the death of close to 100 of these small prisoners, 48 of them in a diphtheria epidemic in the fall and winter of 1944, before a pitiful remnant was evacuated in the face of advancing Allied forces. How many, if any, survived is unknown.[4]

What brings Borkum and Voerde together in this book is the fact that both were the scenes of war crimes. As World War II atrocities go, they were small in terms of the number of victims each claimed—small even in comparison to the loss of life due to criminal negligence incurred at Buschmannshof. The crimes that will be addressed here, however, were not the products of negligence but were willful acts of murder. One was perpetrated by Germans and the other, by troops of the U.S. Army, and both would occasion postwar trials of the alleged perpetrators. In that context, the two crimes would converge in an unexpected but meaningful way.

By August 1944, the tide of war was running strongly in the Allies' favor. The Anglo-American forces that had landed in Normandy two months before were ashore to stay, and Patton's Third Army was fanning out into the interior of France. In the East, the Red Army had driven German forces from most Soviet territory and was threatening the border of East Prussia. In the south, Rome had fallen to Mark Clark's Fifth Army two days before the start of Operation Overlord, and, on August 4, British forces had entered Florence, 140 miles to the north. The threat of German U-boats had been mastered the year before, and, in the air, vast fleets of American and British bombers operated against often little more than token opposition from German fighters. Missions over Germany were much safer than they had been a year earlier when, in twin attacks by the U.S. Eighth Air Force on August 17, 1943, on the ball-bearing works at Schweinfurt and the Messerschmitt factory at Regensburg, 60 heavy bombers had been shot down and more than twice that number damaged, many beyond repair. More than six hundred crewmen had been lost. But flak, occasional German fighters, and accidents ensured that operating a bomber on missions in German skies remained dangerous business until the end of the war.

The Eighth Air Force was to be up in strength on the morning of August 4, 1944. From their bases in East Anglia and the Midlands, more than 1,300 bombers were assigned to strike targets in northern Germany. One of these aircraft was B-17 #909 of the 486th Bombardment Group (Heavy), based at Sudbury. The crew was composed of recent arrivals in the European Theater of Operations, having joined the 486th late in July. Under the command of Second Lieutenant Harvey M. Walthall of Baltimore, they were hastily integrated into a group then making the transition from flying Consolidated B-24 "Liberators" to Boeing B-17 "Flying Fortresses," which, although built to an older design than the B-24, had a higher operational ceiling and were more stable bombing platforms. Walthall's crew had flown its first mission two days earlier. The fledgling #909 returned safely, but Walthall had shown himself to be a less than satisfactory formation flyer, having had difficulty holding position in his element and, in the process, frightening the crews of neighboring planes. The August 4 mission began inauspiciously; takeoff was delayed by fog, and assembly was complicated by a malfunctioning radio beacon. But, by a few minutes past 11 A.M., the bombers were crossing the English coastline at 13,000 feet and climbing on a northeasterly heading to their bombing altitude of 25,000 feet.

The 486th's primary target was the 5,000-ton-per-month capacity Ernst Schliemann oil refinery at Hamburg, an objective that was part of a campaign against the German oil industry then in the process of rapidly "demodernizing" the Nazi war effort to a premotorized state. Each B-17 carried a bomb load of 20 250-pound general-purpose bombs. These were light missiles, but effective against a refinery's fragile network of storage tanks, pipes, and retorts. The Schliemann refinery, however, would be spared #909's bombs. Shortly before 1 P.M., the 486th crossed the German coast north-northwest of Bremen, where flak sent #949 spinning to earth. One parachute was observed. A few minutes later, as the formation was executing a turn east of Bremen, two planes collided, perhaps the result of a flak burst that propelled one into the other and/or pilot error. In any case, #145 fell out of control and disintegrated in midair. The other B-17 was Walthall's #909. In the terrifying moments following the collision, two crewmen, flight engineer Sergeant Kazmer Rachak and navigator Second Lieutenant Quentin Ingerson, took to their parachutes. The rest of the crew might have followed, had it not been for #909's initially uncontrolled dive that trapped them in their positions. But, fatefully, as events would prove, Walthall and his copilot, Second Lieutenant William Myers, succeeded in bringing #909 under control and swinging the damaged plane around in an attempt to nurse it home to England. There were no surviving witnesses to the effort, but Walthall undoubtedly would have ordered #909's bomb load jettisoned in order to lighten the aircraft as it struggled westward. It was not enough. By the time it had passed the German coastline, Walthall's bomber had lost too much altitude to permit it to cross the 250 miles of the North Sea to British soil. Beneath its wings lay the inviting beaches of Borkum. Walthall brought his plane in from the northeast and executed a wheels-up landing on tidal flats north of the town, known to locals as the *Muschelfeld*. It was a harrowing conclusion to a terrifying mission, for #909 had been fired upon by naval antiaircraft gunners on its approach, and some German witnesses claimed that fire had been returned by the B-17's defensive .50-caliber machine guns. Yet, #909 had suffered little additional damage, and the remaining seven crewmen surrendered peacefully and without further incident to German personnel who had been dispatched to the scene.[5]

The emergency landing of #909 on Borkum brought into collision not only aircraft and earth but also asymmetrical elements of the laws of war. To the degree that the vast and mutual dealing of death and destruction characterizing World War II was influenced by international law, it was affected primarily by conventions concluded in the periods immediately preceding and following World War I. One of these was Hague Convention IV of 1907, "Convention Respecting the Laws and Customs of War on Land," a slight revision of a similar treaty completed in 1899. In explaining the intentions of its signatories, its preamble notes that they had been "Animated by the desire to serve . . . the interests of humanity and the ever progressive needs of civilization" and "inspired by the desire to diminish the evils of war, *as far as military requirements permit* [author's italics]." Nevertheless, the convention notes that "The right of belligerents to adopt means of injuring the enemy is not unlimited" (Article 22). The protections due prisoners of war are stated unambiguously: "They must be humanely treated," (Article 4) and "it is especially forbidden . . . to kill or wound an enemy who, after having laid down his arms, or having no longer means of defense, has surrendered at discretion" (Article 23). Article 25, however, contains an element that also seems unambiguous in regard to civilians and their property: "The attack or bombardment, by whatever means, of towns, villages, dwellings or buildings which are undefended is prohibited," although the definition of "defended town" might be subject to a variety of interpretations. The inclusion of the phrase "by whatever means" was clearly intended to address the recently invented airplane, for it was the only change made to a similar article in the Hague Convention of 1899, four years before the Wright brothers' first heavier-than-air flight. Aerial warfare had been addressed at the 1899 conference, however, in the form of a five-year prohibition on the employment "of balloons or similar new machines for throwing projectiles or explosives," due to their indiscriminate nature. This, of course, had expired by 1907.[6]

But, if attack on an undefended town (however that might have been understood) was an illegal operation of land warfare, what was one to make of Hague Convention IX, "Bombardment by Naval Forces in Time of War," which was signed on the same day as "Hague IV"? An apparently similar prohibition of the bombardment of "undefended ports, towns, villages, dwellings, or buildings" was followed by a body of exceptions large enough to allow the passage of a battleship. A naval commander, according to Article 2, was free to destroy with his big guns "military works, military or naval establishments, depots of arms or war materiel, workshops or plants which could be utilized for the needs of the hostile fleet or army." Moreover, "He incurs no responsibility for any unavoidable damage which may be caused by a bombardment under such circumstances." And even undefended places devoid of military significance were open to bombardment if, "after a formal summons has been made to them, [local authorities] decline to comply with requisitions for provisions or supplies" (Article 3).[7]

In sharp contrast to existing primitive aircraft, warships, particularly battleships, were the most sophisticated and destructive weapons systems of the day. The revolutionary HMS *Dreadnought,* placed in service with the Royal Navy less than a year prior to the signing of

Hague IX, was capable of firing 10 850-pound projectiles per minute to a range of 12 miles. The greater effectiveness of naval gunfire and long experience with its employment against shore targets going back to the 16th century may account for the unwillingness of the conferees to impose significant restrictions upon its use. Comparatively primitive bombardment by heavier-than-air aircraft, on the other hand, would not be introduced to international conflict for another four years, when Italy employed a handful of planes against Turkish forces in Libya; these dropped their first bombs on enemy positions on November 1, 1911. The tiny missiles, weighing no more than five pounds, had little physical effect, but the first lines of a new and terrifying chapter in the history of warfare had been written. When aircraft were again used against their army in the Balkan War of the following year, the Turks threatened to execute any of the attacking airmen whom they might capture.[8]

World War I threw into high relief the destructive potential of aerial bombardment and saw the application to it, in practice, of the relatively permissive standards that already regulated naval bombardment. The shelling by German battle cruisers of British coastal towns in December 1914 resulted in substantial loss of civilian life and property and earned for the Germans condemnation as "baby killers" in the British press, although some of these towns were fortified and, therefore, seemingly legitimate targets under existing international law.[9] In 1915, raids on British cities by Zeppelins were followed two years later by the operational advent of the Gotha, history's first strategic bomber, capable of carrying a 660-pound bomb load at 80 miles per hour at altitudes up to 15,000 feet. An attack on London on June 13, 1917, by 14 Gothas resulted in the deaths of 160 people, about half of them women and children, when a bomb struck the Liverpool Street Station.[10] Such raids were condemned in Allied propaganda as examples of a uniquely German barbarity, although the British carried out similar attacks of their own and their naval blockade of German ports resulted in the deaths by malnutrition of hundreds of thousands of civilians.[11] By the end of the war, the British had succeeded in dropping a 1,650-pound bomb (far larger in terms of explosive payload, if not gross weight, than the biggest naval projectiles of the time) from a bomber and were planning an aerial assault on Germany with hundreds of Handley Page V/1500 four-engine bombers capable of reaching Berlin from bases in England and able to carry maximum bomb loads of 7,500 pounds.[12] All of these acts exemplified an accelerating destructive dynamic in which the economic base of modern industrialized war provided both the means and the justification for mass assaults on civilian populations.

Something more than 8.5 million men had died in combat during World War I, primarily the victims of the machine guns and artillery pieces produced in the industrial centers of Europe. Some theoreticians concluded that the airplane, whose enormous destructive potential was suggested by aircraft such as the V/1500, could provide the means of avoiding such battlefield carnage in future wars. Fleets of heavy bombers could strike devastating blows at enemy cities, crippling industrial infrastructures and demoralizing populations, bringing conflicts to quick and relatively inexpensive conclusions, victorious conclusions at least for those best prepared materially and psychologically to wage war in this manner. Yet, the fact that what came to be known euphemistically as "strategic bombing" inevitably involved the killing of civilians—perhaps in very large numbers—was troubling to many. Delegates to the Washington Conference on the Limitation of Armament, whose most notable achievement was the establishment of fixed ratios of strength among the world's leading naval powers, decided, in 1922, to establish a commission composed of representatives of Britain, France, Italy, Japan, and the United States to determine whether the existing rules were adequate in light of recent innovations in the waging of war, particularly in the air. The result was a 62-article document entitled "The Hague Rules of Air Warfare," which proposed to regulate the future employment of aircraft in international conflict. Most important was a series of provisions that sought to restrict the latitude of combatants to bomb population centers. Aerial bombardment was to be limited to military objectives, defined as "military forces; military works; military establishments or depots; factories constituting important and well-known centres engaged in the manufacture of arms, ammunition, or distinctively military supplies; lines of communication or transportation used for military purposes." Attacks on population centers not in the immediate vicinity of the operation of ground forces were prohibited unless they contained military objectives so defined, but those objectives might be attacked only if the "indiscriminate bombardment of the civilian population" could be avoided. Population centers that *were* in the immediate vicinity of such forces might be bombed "provided that there exists a reasonable presumption that the military concentration is sufficiently important to justify such bombardment, having regard to the danger thus caused to the civilian population." Although the restrictive provisions, in practice, would have been open to broad interpretation and would have allowed considerable freedom to the new breed of air warriors, the proposed rules nevertheless threatened to complicate and to some degree constrain the employment of a new technology of possibly war-winning potency, and this the major powers were unwilling to risk. The Hague Rules of Air Warfare remained a dead letter.[13]

International law regulating the treatment of prisoners of war was a different story. Hague IV of 1907 had stated simply that prisoners "must be humanely treated" and then specified in 16 articles the particulars of their required treatment. World War I had seen prisoners of war taken in unprecedented numbers and held, in some cases, for more than four years. Some had suffered terribly. The Convention of July 27, 1929, Relative to the Treatment of Prisoners of War of 1929 (the "Geneva Convention," in the discourse of World War II) was inspired, according to its preamble, by the recognition that, "in the extreme case of a war, it will be the duty of every Power to diminish, so far as possible the unavoidable rigors thereof and to mitigate the fate of prisoners of war." The 1929 convention spelled out in much greater detail than had Hague IV the conditions under which prisoners were to be held, down to a long list of the specific injuries and illnesses that were to qualify them for repatriation prior to the end of hostilities. But the fundamental requirement of the convention was that prisoners of war not be harmed. "They must at all times be humanely treated and protected, particularly against acts of violence, insults and public curiosity. Measures of reprisal against them are prohibited" (Article 2). And "Prisoners of War shall be evacuated within the shortest possible period after their capture, to spots located in a region far enough from a zone of combat for them to be out of danger" (Article 7). Unlike the proposed rules for aerial bombardment, with their numerous qualifiers in regard to the safety of civilians, the 1929 Geneva Convention was unambiguous. Moreover, unlike the abortive air rules, it was adhered to by most of the world's independent states. Of the major powers, only the Soviet Union and Japan (the latter signed but did not ratify) refused to become parties to it.[14]

On the eve of World War II, then, it seems appropriate to speak of a significant asymmetry in the laws of war. The protected status of prisoners under all circumstances was clear. Those countries that had not become parties to the Geneva Convention of 1929 might be written off as existing on the fringes of the "civilized" world. Civilians, on the other hand, had little, if any, formal legal protection against aerial attack; pre–World War I treaty law and custom were in general agreement that injuring civilians was not a good thing but was acceptable if it could not be avoided in the pursuit of "legitimate" military objectives. And advocates for "strategic" bombing suggested that civilian casualties might actually serve humanity by bringing wars to quick conclusions, thus avoiding the prolonged mass slaughter that had characterized World War I. The will to impose meaningful limitations on a new technology whose potential had only begun to be explored was lacking. The killing of prisoners of war was not likely to produce victory, but airpower might!

Among the most enduring icons of the Second World War are scenes of vast urban devastation wrought by aerial bombardment. Never before or since have so many great places of human habitation and endeavor been subjected to destruction of similar magnitude. Approximately one million human beings, as a rough estimate, died as a consequence, many of them in overwhelmingly horrible ways. Germany initiated the air war on European cities, and its willingness to use urban bombing as a conscious instrument of terror is beyond serious dispute.[15] What is also beyond dispute, however, is that British and American air forces inflicted vastly greater damage on German cities and their civilian populations than the Luftwaffe visited upon Germany's enemies. More Germans died in two series of raids (those on Hamburg in July 1943 and Dresden in February 1945) than did British civilians in all German air attacks, including V-1 and V-2 missile bombardments, during the whole of World War II. Although German aircraft manufacturers produced prototypes of bombers capable of crossing the Atlantic, the cities of the United States emerged from the war unscathed by aerial assault.

If there was no clear prohibition of urban bombing in international law, were the Allies *morally* justified in demolishing German cities and killing hundreds of thousands of civilians in the process? Opinion is by no means unanimous on this contentious issue. Applying the standard of proportionality in the context of genocidal German policies that resulted in the murders of millions of human beings, policies most expeditiously terminated by the fastest possible termination of the criminal regime that gave rise to them, might suggest an unambiguous "yes." Yet, it may be difficult to resist some degree of empathy with Hamburg policeman Otto Müller who, following the firestorm produced by the British attack of the night of July 27–28, 1943, encountered a young girl who had been wandering for days dragging the body of her little brother. "I got so angry at this incident," he later recalled, "that I would have shot any enemy airman who had parachuted down. I also think that any English or American person would have felt the same way."[16] At least one American agreed. U.S. Army Major Burton F. Ellis, an attorney sent to Germany after the war to assist in the trial of German war criminals, wrote to his wife in August 1945: "On Sunday I went through Darmstadt, a place about the size of Fresno. It was leveled. Block after block with nothing but burned out skeletons of apartment houses. If your family, your home, your possessions were buried there—what would your reaction be? These people that lived there beat some airmen to death. I can see why they did what they did. I would have done likewise."[17]

But it was not only bombing that assailed civilian populations. Less widely known and discussed than urban bombing is the fact that fighter pilots commonly attacked "targets of opportunity" as they flew over enemy territory. Such targets were sometimes human beings, and not always military personnel. This issue was frankly addressed in one of the documentary films produced by the U.S. War Department for showing to service and civilian audiences. Director William Wyler's *Thunderbolt* portrays the routine operations of a U.S. Army Air Forces fighter-bomber group flying the Republic P-47 "Thunderbolt" from bases on the island of Corsica against targets in German-held territory in Italy during the bloody Allied struggle to break through German defenses south of Rome in the first half of 1944. Viewers of the film are placed "in the head" of one pilot, whose voice is supplied by an actor as he flies to the day's target (a bridge), drops his bombs, and heads for home. On his way back to base, he sees a group of people on the ground, although he is unable to identify them. He muses in the clipped, unemotional tones affected by this film, "Somebody in that field. Don't know who they are. No friends of mine." With that, he opens fire with his plane's eight .50-caliber Browning machine guns, collectively spewing bullets a half-inch in diameter at the rate of one hundred per second. Continuing on, he sees rural Italian houses and comments on the supposed German practice of storing munitions in such structures. He proceeds to strafe them, initially without explosive effect, commenting, after each attack, "Nothing there" (except, perhaps, one is tempted to observe, an Italian family). Finally, one of the houses detonates, revealing the presence of enemy munitions and presumably justifying the attacks on the others.[18]

Wartime fighter pilot and famed postwar test pilot Chuck Yeager recalls orders received by his fighter group in the fall of 1944:

> Our seventy-five Mustangs [P-51 fighter planes] were assigned an area fifty miles by fifty miles inside Germany and ordered to strafe anything that moved. The object was to demoralize the German population. Nobody asked our opinion about whether we were actually demoralizing the survivors or maybe enraging them to stage their own maximum effort. . . . We weren't asked how we felt zapping people. It was a miserable, dirty mission, but we all took off on time and did it. If it occurred to anyone to refuse to participate (nobody refused, as I recall), that person would have probably been court-martialed. . . . We were ordered to commit an atrocity, pure and simple.[19]

Such attacks, delivered at low altitude and against small groups and, in some cases, individuals, seemed more personal than bombs dropped from altitudes of four or five miles and were possibly more frightening and infuriating to the intended victims. Pastor Florenz Siekermann of Voerde declared, "One can only call it a crime against humanity that low-flying fighters [*Tiefflieger*] began more and more to fire on peaceful people in the streets and even in their fields." His judgment was probably influenced by an incident toward the end of 1944 in which a 10-year-old boy of the village was machine-gunned on his way home from school.[20]

Some Germans were able to view the ruination being rained upon them as just retribution for the criminal actions of their own government and people. One remarked long after the fact, "I shouldn't really say this but I felt a wild joy during those heavy British raids. That was our punishment for our crimes against the Jews."[21] Such reactions were almost certainly exceptional. It would be unrealistic to expect most German civilians who were on the receiving end of Allied bombs and bullets to regard them as their just desserts. On the contrary, it would be remarkable if occasional violence against downed Allied airmen had not occurred, as attacks on German airmen had sometimes taken place when they had fallen into the hands of the enemy.[22] Desire for revenge and frustration over the inability of the Nazi regime to retaliate in kind grew as German cities were progressively reduced to rubble.[23] But, in the later stages of the war, the regime openly encouraged and sought to legitimize the ill treatment and murder of captured Allied aircrew, which served as a means of releasing anger and deflecting it from the dictatorship that was unable to protect the German people from increasingly devastating attack from the air. It also had the effect of making ordinary Germans participants in Nazi criminality, thus giving them seemingly no alternative but to support the regime as it fought desperately to fend off defeat and Allied retribution. By the end of the war, perhaps 350 downed U.S. and British airmen had been murdered by German civilians, military personnel, or police and party officials.[24] Although the number killed represents only a small fraction of the total number of Allied airmen captured on German soil during that period and although some of the murders would probably have occurred in the absence of official encouragement, such encouragement was clearly provided. On August 10, 1943, SS commander and German police chief Heinrich Himmler ordered police officials not to intervene if civilians attacked captured Allied aircrew. On May 21, 1944, Hitler directed that downed Allied airmen be summarily executed if they had fired on German airmen parachuting from stricken aircraft or German aircrew who had crash-landed or if they had attacked trains or individual civilians.[25] And, in an editorial published in the Nazi Party newspaper *Völkischer Beobachter* during the following week, Propaganda Minister Josef Goebbels, in "a word on the enemy air terror," accused British and American airmen of the willful murder of German civilians. German morale was the primary objective of Allied bombing, he asserted, and 99 percent of the physical damage was to the civilian sector. The consequence of this "murder of women and children" was likely to be that the German people would be moved to take matters into their own hands and pay back in their own coin Allied flyers who had bailed out over German territory. But Goebbels reserved most of his venom for Allied flyers who strafed civilians with their machine guns and cannon, not wholly a figment of the propaganda minister's malignant imagination, as we have seen. "That has nothing more to do with war," he declared. "That is sheer murder." Goebbels went on to describe one incident "out of thousands" that had allegedly occurred the previous Sunday (thus, presumably, particularly dastardly) somewhere in Saxony in which groups of children were attacked, causing numerous casualties. If such criminals were to be shot down and captured, Goebbels continued, it would be inappropriate for German soldiers to protect them from civilians and their just desire for vengeance.[26] In fact, according to an order by Hitler (of which Goebbels may have been unaware), troops who captured airmen guilty of such acts were to kill them. At the end of the month, Hitler's private secretary and Nazi Party chancellery chief Martin Bormann circulated a secret memo to party leaders down to the district level. Provocatively entitled "Re: Justice Exercised by the People against Anglo-American Murderers," it, too, referred to the strafing of civilians, including children, while the latter were engaged in innocent pursuits and directed that no prosecution or punishment of citizens who participated in the killing of such airmen was to take place. Local party bosses or *Ortsgruppenleiter* were to be notified orally of the contents of the memo. By early July 1944, the German high command had issued a top-secret order discouraging military personnel from intervening to protect captured Allied air crew from civilian attack and made specific reference to Goebbels's editorial.[27]

Goebbels was guilty of hypocrisy of staggering proportions when he contrasted the "unlimited barbarity" of the Allied air campaign with the alleged German wish "that the war should be conducted in a chivalrous manner." The air war *was* barbarous. Genocide was far worse. And he was simply wrong when he claimed that "There is no rule of international law which the enemy can call on in this matter. The Anglo-American pilots place themselves through such a criminal code of warfare outside the pale of every internationally recognized rule of warfare."[28] Goebbels had conflated instances of fighter planes machine-gunning civilians with urban bombing, but the fact was that international law constraining aerial warfare was thin at best, while that regulating the treatment of prisoners of war and mandating their protection was well established. There was little in international law to counter the dominant Allied perspective that extreme and often indiscriminate force from the air was justified in defeating an enemy extreme in its evil.

By the summer of 1944, Germans had been subjected to years of increasingly devastating aerial assault. In spite of the ambiguities in Goebbels's editorial, they had every reason to believe that they were free to do with any of their tormentors who fell into their hands as they pleased. Yet, it would appear that relatively few Germans actually participated in or facilitated attacks on captured U.S. flyers. Given the provocation of Allied bombing and strafing and the encouragement of lawlessness from Nazi leaders, it is remarkable that so many captured American airmen (in excess of 32,000) survived the war.[29] But seven members of the crew of #909 would not be among them.

Since all seven crewmen aboard #909 when it crash-landed on Borkum on August 4, 1944, were murdered that day, the only witnesses to their murders and the events immediately preceding them were Germans or, in a few cases, non-Germans held as captive laborers. Dozens of residents of Borkum, members of the Wehrmacht stationed there and civilians, produced descriptions of what they claimed to have seen and done. These descriptions were recorded in the context of an investigation by the U.S. Army of the murders and the trials of those believed to have been perpetrators. Added, therefore, to the normal distortions to which human memory is subject was the powerful motivation of self-preservation.

Sworn statements and trial testimony describe a wartime American-German encounter that began with deceptive calm but culminated in brutality, terror, and death. Early on the afternoon of August 4, 1944, pilot Second Lieutenant Harvey Walthall, his copilot, Second Lieutenant William J. Myers, bombardier Second Lieutenant Howard S. Graham, radioman Sergeant Kenneth Faber, ball turret gunner Sergeant James W. Danno, waist gunner Sergeant William F. Dold, and tail gunner Sergeant William W. Lambertus exited #909 where it had come to rest on the *Muschelfeld*. With the exception of one crewman who had apparently suffered a slight head wound, all had survived the crash landing uninjured. They were taken prisoner by personnel of the nearby Ostland antiaircraft battery, one of whom, a Corporal Roesing, bandaged the head of the injured American. The prisoners were then marched to the battery position about a kilometer away, where they were searched by the battery commander, Lieutenant Jakob Seiler. An English-speaking officer, Lieutenant Erich Wentzel, briefly interrogated them, after which they were marched under armed guard from the beach along a route that led through the town of Borkum. The captives were required to walk with raised hands, and, although the day was a hot one, they were forced to maintain a fast pace with the encouragement of shoves and blows from rifle butts. Encountering a detachment of the Nazi Labor Service (*Reichsarbeitsdienst* or "RAD"), the prisoners were beaten with spades, although not seriously injured, by its members. Then, incited by the mayor and local Nazi Party leader Jan Akkermann, a mob of townspeople kicked and beat them with fists and sticks. Throughout their ordeal, their guards offered them no protection. After a march of slightly more than three and one-half miles, the guards were equally passive when an off-duty German soldier approached the column near the town hall with drawn pistol and shot Lieutenant Graham, who had tripped and fallen, in the head. The column moved on another mile and a half, pursued by the soldier, who methodically and fatally shot the remaining six prisoners near the town's *Sportsplatz* (athletic field). The seven murdered flyers were buried the following day.[30]

The incident had clearly been encouraged by Nazi statements that had categorized downed Allied airmen as war criminals who, by their own actions, had removed themselves from the protected status of prisoners of war under international law. Prior to the fatal march, Goebbels's editorial of the previous spring, transformed in the minds of some Borkumers into a "decree," had been adopted as a guide for the treatment of the captives. And yet, the incident had not fully conformed to Goebbels's model. Walthall's B-17 had not been a strafing fighter plane. The naval personnel responsible for the prisoners had not provided them protection against civilian assault, but the actual murders had been committed by a member of the Wehrmacht, a scenario not addressed in the propaganda minister's editorial. This may account for the falsification of the incident contained in a report drafted immediately after the killings, according to which the guards had allegedly been overwhelmed by an enraged civilian mob, which had beaten the airmen to death. The fallacious report was signed by the guards and possibly transmitted to Gestapo agents on the mainland, although a report of the examining physician at the naval hospital on Borkum to which the bodies had been transported correctly noted the cause of death as gunshots to the head. Not surprisingly, however, German authorities made no effort to punish anyone for the murders, although an uneasy atmosphere descended on Borkum. Guards were ordered to neither speak nor write of the incident and to avoid entering the town. As the war neared its conclusion, fear of likely Allied retribution intensified uneasiness. Naval Captain Kurt Goebell, the senior officer on the island, claimed at his trial to have instituted a court-martial in March 1945 to try those responsible for the murders and to have taken up a collection for the maintenance of the graves of the U.S. flyers, probably a desperate effort to mitigate Allied punishment. No German trial had begun when Canadian forces occupied the island early in May 1945. The graves of the seven airmen neatly marked with white crosses bearing the name of each man and the date of burial, August 5, 1944, were found in Plot D of Borkum's Lutheran cemetery.[31]

As ghastly as the murder of seven American airmen in Borkum was, it is a minor entry in the vast catalog of German crimes committed during World War II. The Holocaust that consumed much of Europe's Jewish population and genocidal German policies directed against the Slavic peoples of Europe, with their millions of victims, created a new paradigm of modern state-directed criminality approached only by the example of Stalin's Soviet Union. The magnitude of German crimes has rendered difficult the discussion of World War II war crimes as an international phenomenon. It constitutes a kind of historical black hole from which the attentions of historians cannot escape. Moreover, to mention the crimes of others in the same breath with those of Germany may appear to relativize and therefore diminish the gravity of Nazi offenses. Nazi genocide also distorts perspectives on German war crimes. Not all German criminality was motivated by a uniquely Nazi ideology of race, lawlessness, and the glorification of brutality. Some of it was the product of psychological forces generated by the stresses of war that affected all participants in approximately similar ways, no matter what their national or ideological affinities. Unfortunately, these distinctions tended to be obscured in the postwar U.S. program of wholesale war-crimes trials that tried many hundreds of Germans for offenses ranging from the leadership of *Einsatzgruppen,* the murder squads that ranged behind the German army in the Soviet Union, killing more than a million Jews, and the operation of concentration camps where vast numbers perished to the shooting of American POWs and the wearing by German soldiers of Allied uniforms while in combat. In the minds of many Americans, all tended to be indiscriminately subsumed in a uniquely horrific Nazi conspiracy of evil. But many war crimes committed by Germans were hardly unique to them. If nothing on the Allied side matched the Holocaust or the genocidal policies adopted toward Slavic peoples, all parties to World War II commonly murdered prisoners of war. But here, too, there are important distinctions to be made. Russians and Germans routinely shot each other's captured personnel, and vast numbers of Soviet POWs died in German captivity, while, in the Pacific, little mercy or respect for international law was shown by either side. On the more "civilized" battlefields of Western and Central Europe, on the other hand, where ethnically similar combatants found it easier to recognize in one another a common humanity, the murder of surrendered enemy soldiers was less frequent and on a much smaller scale, although not uncommon. The widely publicized Malmédy massacre of surrendered GIs by troops of the 1st SS Panzer Division in December 1944 during the Battle of the Bulge had a rough parallel in the lesser-known murders of

Axis POWs by members of the U.S. 45th Infantry Division on Sicily in July 1943. Both war crimes had been encouraged by inflammatory statements made by commanders prior to combat. In the case of the Malmédy incident, SS men had received pre-attack "pep talks" urging the creation of a "wave of fright and terror" and highly ambiguous directives not to "worry" about taking prisoners. The Germans were also encouraged to regard the offensive as an opportunity to wreak vengeance on Americans for the bombing raids that had taken the lives of many thousands of German women and children, although the killing of approximately 80 American prisoners was probably more an act of convenience on the part of mechanized troops on a very tight schedule than revenge. The U.S. 45th Infantry Division had been a part of the U.S. Seventh Army, commanded by Lieutenant General George Patton. Prior to the Anglo-American invasion of Sicily, Patton had openly discouraged the taking of prisoners under some circumstances. "Kill the bastard," the division's commander remembered Patton saying, when the enemy continued to resist within two hundred yards of an American advance, even if he subsequently offered to surrender.[32]

There were survivors of both massacres. Their narratives reflect a common experience of helplessness and terror that transcends national divisions. Lieutenant Virgil P. Lary described having been taken prisoner along with other members of the 285th Artillery Observation Battalion's Battery B on December 17, 1944. The lightly armed motorized American unit came under heavy fire from a powerful armored element of the 1st SS Panzer Division and quickly surrendered. All of the American POWs were assembled by their German captors in a field adjacent to a road intersection south of the Belgian town of Malmédy. Three vehicles parked on the road in front of the assembled prisoners. At the apparent signal of two pistol shots fired by one of the Germans, machine gun fire was opened on the captured GIs. Lary was slightly wounded and fell face down in mud, feigning death. He listened to the agonized screams of the wounded, while German soldiers moved among the recumbent forms, finishing off those who showed signs of life. After the Germans departed, Lary succeeded in slipping away and joining American forces in Malmédy.[33]

When Anglo-American forces invaded Sicily on July 10, 1943, Italian airman Giuseppe Giannola was stationed at the air base of San Pietro di Caltagirone (known to the Allies as the Biscari airfield), a short distance inland from the Gulf of Gela, where troops of Patton's Seventh Army had come ashore. On July 14, he and a number of other Italian soldiers found themselves surrounded by U.S. forces and surrendered to them. They were strip searched, allowed to retain only their trousers, then marched to join another group of prisoners. The approximately 50 men were lined up, then mowed down by submachine gun fire delivered by a noncommissioned officer while 7 other GIs armed with rifles prevented their escape. Giannola was wounded in the right arm and lay motionless under corpses for about two hours, while the Americans lingered to deliver the coup de grace to the wounded and the dying. After the killers had left, he managed to crawl away but was shot in the neck by another GI. More merciful U.S. soldiers picked him up shortly thereafter and took him to a U.S. field hospital at Scoglitti.[34] Giannola had survived one of at least two mass murders of Axis POWs.

The Malmédy and Biscari atrocities are unusual in that detailed written records have survived, a result of the fact that both gave rise to formal trials of the alleged perpetrators. But most incidents involving the murders of prisoners of war did not become the subjects of methodical investigations and judicial proceedings. Individual prisoners or small groups of surrendered enemy soldiers were casually murdered in the rage and "heat" of combat, in revenge for fallen comrades, or as the consequence of the rational if also brutal calculation that the efficiency of the capturing force would be diminished by burdening itself with prisoners. Sometimes captured soldiers were murdered in reprisal for real or imagined enemy atrocities or because they were perceived as unnecessarily prolonging a ghastly war. For some combatants, the perverse joy young men may derive from killing an overpowered adversary was motivation enough, as might be the reluctance to grant a surrendered enemy the relative safety of captivity while their captors continued to be exposed to the hazards of combat. Men were killed, their bodies commingled with those of men fallen in battle, while the killers moved on. Since the perpetrators were rarely brought to trial, most accounts are anecdotal, preserved in the memories of participants and witnesses. Stephen G. Fritz describes an incident in which an American captain invited seven German soldiers to surrender, then methodically shot each of them in the head. Fritz adds that "the memoirs of most GIs reveal such episodes." Infantry platoon leader Paul Fussell recalls an event that occurred in his company in which 15 or 20 Germans trapped in a crater and attempting to surrender were killed. "Laughing and howling, hoo-ha-ing and good-old-boy yelling, our men exultantly shot into the crater until every single man down there was dead." Ninety-ninth Infantry Division veteran Grady Arrington describes the murder of a German POW by a platoon commander "still hysterical with hate and fright" and his own participation in the killings of wounded German soldiers while filled with fury over the deaths of his buddies. In his *Citizen Soldiers,* the late Stephen Ambrose notes that he had interviewed more than a thousand U.S. combat veterans. Of these, one-third reported having witnessed German prisoners with their hands in the air being shot by American soldiers, although only one admitted his own participation.[35] German conduct in Western Europe was no better and in the East, where war merged with genocide, far worse.[36] In the Pacific, many GIs regarded the Japanese as little more than animals, due to widespread racism and the crimes committed by Japanese combatants. Japanese prisoners of war were few. This was due in part to expectations of the Japanese high command that Japanese soldiers fight to the death, rather than surrender and in part to overwhelming U.S. firepower. But, even when the opportunity to capture Japanese soldiers presented itself, it was frequently rejected. Charles Lindbergh, while serving as a technical adviser in the Pacific, was told by a U.S. Army officer on New Guinea in regard to the taking of Japanese prisoners, "Oh, we could take more if we wanted to, but our boys don't like to take prisoners." "It doesn't encourage the rest to surrender," Lindbergh continued, "when they hear of their buddies marched out on the flying field and machine guns turned loose on them." A Marine Corps veteran of the fighting on Okinawa remembers, "Nine Marines in ten would shoot them. If you saw a Jap trying to surrender, you'd let him have it fast." The importation of Japanese body parts as souvenirs—skulls, ears, noses, and the ever-popular gold teeth—became so common that it came to the attention of the U.S. Customs Service and was widely reported in the American press.[37]

That Allied troops as well as their enemies had committed battlefield atrocities created crises of conscience in the minds of some commanders after the war, as their governments moved to the trial and punishment of Axis war criminals. Canadian general Chris Vokes, while considering a plea for clemency by Kurt Meyer, former commander of the 12th SS Panzer Division, who had been sentenced to death for the murder of Canadian POWs on the Normandy front, observed, "There isn't a general or colonel on the Allied side that I know of who hasn't said, 'Well, this time we don't want any prisoners.'" Following the conclusion of the Malmédy massacre trial, in which all 73 German defendants were found guilty and 43 sentenced to death, the chief defense counsel wrote to his family that the president of the court, Brigadier General Josiah Dalbey, had told him that presiding over the trial was the most difficult thing he had ever done, because he knew that American soldiers had been guilty of similar crimes.[38] To its credit, the U.S. Army had brought to trial some of its own members who had violated the laws of war, but it treated them with comparative leniency. The Biscari massacre resulted in court-martial proceedings for two soldiers of the 45th Infantry Division in September and October 1943. The first of these had as its sole defendant Sergeant Horace T. West of Company A, 180th Infantry Regiment. West was charged under the 92nd Article of War with having "with malice aforethought, willfully, deliberately, feloniously, unlawfully and with premeditation" killed 37 prisoners of war with a Thompson submachine gun. West's battalion commander testified that he had turned over to West more than 40 prisoners who had been flushed from a hillside cave near the Biscari airfield, which Giannola identified as the base near San Pietro di Caltagirone. Assembling a guard detail of nine men, West had marched the prisoners a short distance, then shot most of them with a submachine gun borrowed from one of the guards. None of the accompanying GIs had apparently attempted to restrain West. The sergeant offered a defense that combined his own fatigue and frayed nerves and Patton's alleged "orders" with the claim that he had witnessed the murder of two captured GIs by the enemy, an experience that had filled him with uncontrollable rage. Nevertheless, he was found guilty of murder and was sentenced to life imprisonment. In fact, he remained incarcerated for little more than a year and was then returned to active duty.[39]

The second trial for the Biscari murders had as its sole defendant Captain John C. Compton, commander of the 180th's Company C. In an incident separate from that involving West, approximately 40 Italians had surrendered to men of Compton's company. Compton ordered the prisoners shot, an order that was executed by a firing party of about two dozen men, some of whom had volunteered for the assignment. But the 45th Infantry Division's inspector general recommended court-martial proceedings against Compton alone on the grounds that it was "certain" that the members of the firing squad had believed that they were following a lawful order. Compton was acquitted on essentially the same grounds. Patton had ordered the killing of enemy soldiers who continued to resist to within two hundred yards of an American advance, even if they subsequently offered to surrender. Compton's closing statement made the point succinctly: "I ordered them shot because I thought it came directly under the General's instructions. Right or wrong a three star general's advice, who has had combat experience, is good enough for me and I took him at his word."[40]

Respondeat superior or "let the master answer"—the principle that culpability for an illegal act rests with the commander who orders it— was a viable defense for an American soldier in 1943. Article 347 of the 1940 edition of the U.S. Army's *Basic Field Manual: Rules of Land Warfare*, in discussing the liability of soldiers for violations of the laws of war, states that "Individuals of the armed forces will not be punished for these offenses in case they are committed under the orders or sanctions of their governments or commanders." By the time the United States was ready to begin trying Axis war criminals, however, the standard had been significantly changed. As of November 1944, superior orders were no longer to be deemed a complete defense, although they might be considered in determining the degree of a defendant's culpability and in mitigation of punishment.[41] This provision was incorporated in the Charter of the International Military Tribunal of August 1945 and was applied not only to defendants in the Nuremberg Trial of November 1945–October 1946 but in lesser war-crimes trials, as well. American soldiers accused of atrocities, however, were acquitted on the grounds of superior orders as late as July 1945 in a case involving the murders of German civilians committed several months earlier in Voerde.

There, troops of the U.S. 8th Armored Division randomly shot and killed at least six and probably eight persons, two of them women, who had been arbitrarily chosen for death. The murders were motivated by the desire of a junior officer, possibly encouraged by the intemperate or careless language of a superior, to "hunt Germans" or "shoot Krauts." As was true of the Biscari atrocities, the Voerde case required the U.S. Army to confront the fact that not all war crimes were committed by a uniquely brutal enemy. The murders in Voerde were as blatant a violation of international law as was the slaughter of the crew of Walthall's B-17 in Borkum. Article 46 of the 1907 Hague Convention (IV) requires an occupying army to respect the lives of persons in occupied territory. Article 19 of the U.S. Army's own *Rules of Land Warfare* of 1940 stated that "Inhabitants who refrain from acts of hostility . . . must not be injured in their lives or property."[42] The Voerde atrocities and the courts-martial that they occasioned will be addressed in subsequent chapters.

By the time of the Voerde trials, U.S. prosecution of German war criminals had already begun. The U.S. program to try German war criminals was rooted in the "Moscow Declaration" of August 1943, in which Great Britain, the Soviet Union, and the United States declared their intention to apprehend and punish those responsible for Nazi atrocities. That resolve eventually involved the United States in a three-tiered system of war-crimes justice in Germany. The best-known component of this system—synonymous in the minds of many with the entire process of bringing Nazis to justice—was the International Military Tribunal that sat in Nuremberg for almost a year, from the fall of 1945 until the fall of 1946. There, a panel of American, British, French, and Soviet judges heard evidence against 22 German leaders and a number of organizations. Twelve defendants were sentenced to death by hanging. Seven received prison sentences ranging from 10 years to life. Three were acquitted. But the fewer than two dozen defendants tried by the IMT represented but a tiny fraction of the total number of accused German war criminals in whose trial the United States participated. A series of 12 subsequent trials conducted at Nuremberg before American judges passed judgment on 185 lesser German leaders between 1946 and 1949. By far the largest number of defendants, 1,672, were tried in 489 proceedings conducted from 1945 to 1948 before courts established and run by the U.S. Army for accused war criminals of lesser importance than those tried at Nuremberg.[43] In their totality, these trials were wide ranging and included defendants held responsible for the operations of the concentration camps at Buchenwald, Dachau, Flossenbürg, Mauthausen, Mühldorf, and Nordhausen and the Hadamar "euthanasia" facility; the Malmédy massacre case; the Skorzeny case, involving the use by Germans of American uniforms in combat; and more than two hundred "flyers cases," in which Germans were tried for the abuse and murder of downed American airmen.[44]

A very early trial conducted by the U.S. Army involved an incident similar to the Borkum atrocity. On August 24, 1944, 20 days after Walthall's B-17 had come down on the *Muschelfeld,* an 8th Air Force B-24 commanded by Second Lieutenant Norman J. Rogers was shot down while taking part in an attack on Hannover. The nine-man crew took to their parachutes and were promptly captured. A seriously wounded member was given first aid by a German farm family, then hospitalized for further treatment, while the remaining eight men were placed on a train for transportation to a POW facility. They were forced to detrain at Rüsselsheim due to damage to the rail line and were marched through part of the town, which had been heavily bombed by the RAF the previous night.[45] In spite of shouts from crew members that "We didn't bomb Rüsselsheim" and "I am not Jewish," they were brutally clubbed and beaten by enraged townspeople, while their guards gave them no protection. Four were shot by a local Nazi Party official. Two survived.[46]

Eleven alleged perpetrators, including two women, were put on trial in July 1945 in Darmstadt, a town devastated by a British night attack the previous September that had killed 8,500 residents and left 70,000 homeless.[47] The defense argued that they had been incited to commit the crime by Goebbels's propaganda and that he, not they, bore the preponderance of guilt. But the prosecution led by Lieutenant Colonel Leon Jaworski, who would achieve national fame three decades later as the special prosecutor in the Watergate case, insisted on the individual responsibility of the defendants for the murders, observing that "They were all grown men and women. If they are called on to commit murder and they do, they are just as responsible as any other murderers." The officers hearing the case agreed. Ten of the defendants were found guilty, and seven, including the two women, were sentenced to death. One defendant was acquitted.[48]

Like the Rüsselsheim case, the Borkum incident and trial involved important legal and moral issues growing out of atrocities spawned by an atmosphere of total war. Both tested the capacity of the U.S. Army to do justice to a defeated enemy that, in violation of international law, had murdered surrendered American soldiers. The Voerde case presented a no less significant challenge, probing the willingness of the U.S. Army to apply to its own soldiers the standards by which it was judging and punishing its enemies. Both of these cases must be carefully examined in order to draw valid comparative conclusions. In the immediate postwar years, the German people, whom the United States was intent upon "reeducating" in the ways of democracy, were watching and making comparisons of their own.

NOTES

1. Carl Lange, ed., *Kriegszeitung der Festung Borkum: Auswahl aus zwei Jahrgängen* (Berlin: R. v. Decker's Verlag, 1917), vii.

2. J. E. Kaufmann and R. M. Jurga, *Fortress Europe: European Fortifications of World War II* (Conshohocken, PA: Combined Publishing, 1999), 77; Jacob Borut, "Antisemitism in Tourist Facilities in Weimar Germany," *Shoah Resource Center,*

http://www.yadvashem.org/odot_pdf/microsoft%20word%20-%203123.pdf, 13; Holger Bloem and Wilke Specht, *Borkum: Nordseeinsel unter Weitem Himmel* (Norden: Verlag Soltau-Kurier-Norden, 2009), 7.

3. Voerde on the lower Rhine shared a name with a village to the southeast that, after the war, became a camp for Eastern European refugees, many of whom had been employed as slave laborers in German industry. On this Voerde, see Dieter Wiethege, *Und als der Krieg zur Ende Schien . . . Krieg, Überrollung und Ausländerlager in Voerde* (Meinerzhagen: Meinerzhagener Druck und Verlagshaus, 1985), 65–67, 81.

4. "Fahrtbericht 22.08.2009," 1, http://www.vdk.de/kv-am-niederrhein/mime/00057407D1252005573.pdf; Ulrich Herbert, "Labor as Spoils of Conquest, 1933–1945," in *Nazism and German Society, 1933–1945,* ed. David F. Crew (New York: Routledge, 1995), 250; Karl Göllmann, "Die Entstehung Friedrichsfelds," http://www.friedrichsfeld.net/Entstehung.pdf.

5. "Report of Operations Office—Mission of 4 August 1944—Hamburg, Germany, Headquarters 486th Bombardment Group (H)," August 4, 1944, Entry 7, Mission Reports, Records of the U.S. Army Air Forces, RG 18 (National Archives, College Park, MD). I use this report courtesy of Robin Smith; "Report: Murder of Seven American Airmen on Borkum Island, 4 August 1944," *United States of America v. Kurt Goebell et al.* (microfilm, frames 66–67, 240, Reel 1), Record Groups 338 and 153 (National Archives, Washington, DC); "Walthall's Crew," http://www.486th.org/B5832/Walthall.htm; Kazmer Rachak to Helmut Scheder, n.d. (in James J. Weingartner's possession; courtesy of Robin Smith).

6. "Laws of War: Laws and Customs of War on Land (Hague IV)," October 18, 1907, *The Avalon Project at Yale Law School,* http://www.yale.edu/lawweb/avalon/lawofwar/hague04.htm; Adam Roberts, "Land Warfare: From Hague to Nuremberg," in *The Laws of War: Constraints on Warfare in the Western World,* ed. Michael Howard, George J. Andreopoulos, and Mark R. Shulman (New Haven, CT: Yale University Press, 1994), 119–23; Peter Karsten, *Law, Soldiers, and Combat* (Westport, CT: Greenwood Press, 1978), 23.

7. "Laws of War: Bombardment by Naval Forces in Time of War (Hague IX), October 18, 1907, *The Avalon Project,* http://avalon.law.yale.edu/20th_century/hague09.asp; Tami Davis Biddle, "Air Power," in *The Laws of War: Constraints on Warfare in the Western World,* ed. Michael Howard, George J. Andreopoulos, and Mark Shulman (New Haven, CT: Yale University Press), 143.

8. Lee Kennett, *The First Air War, 1914–1918* (New York: Free Press, 1991), 18–19.

9. Paul G. Halpern, *A Naval History of World War I* (London: Routledge, 1995), 40; Martin Gilbert, *The First World War: A Complete History* (New York: Holt, 1994), 110; "Scarborough Raid, 16 December 1914," http://www.Historyofwar.org/articles/raid_scarborough1914.html.

10. Noble Frankland, "The Emergence of Air Power," in *The Encyclopedia of Twentieth Century Warfare,* ed. Noble Frankland (New York: Orion Books, 1989), 194, 196; Kennett, *First Air War,* 57–62. The British regarded German Zeppelin crews as war criminals. See Karsten, *Law, Soldiers and Combat,* 23.

11. Holger H. Herwig, *Hammer or Anvil? Modern Germany 1648–Present* (Lexington, MA: Heath, 1994), 204.

12. "Handley Page V/1500," in *Encyclopedia of Twentieth Century Warfare,* ed. Noble Frankland (New York: Orion Books, 1989), 185; "The War in the Air—Bombers Britain," http://www.firstworldwar.com/airwar/bombers_britain.htm.

13. "The Hague Rules of Air Warfare," http://wwi.lib.byu.edu/index.php/The_Hague_Rules_of_Air_Warfare; W. Hays Parks, "Air War and the Laws of War," in *The Conduct of the Air War in the Second World War: An International Comparison,* ed. Horst Boog (New York: Berg, 1992), 337–39; Biddle, "Air Power," 148.

14. "Convention between the United States of America and Other Powers, Relating to Prisoners of War; July 27, 1929," http://avalon.law.yale.edu/20th_century/geneva02.asp; Adam Roberts, "Land Warfare," in *The Laws of War: Constraints on Warfare in the Western World,* ed. Michael Howard, George J. Andreopoulos, and Mark Shulman (New Haven, CT: Yale University Press), 127–28.

15. Olaf Groehler, "Strategic Air War's Impact on German Civilians," in *The Conduct of the Air War in the Second World War: An International Comparison,* ed. Horst Boog (New York: Berg, 1992), 281–83; Olaf Groehler, *Bombenkrieg gegen Deutschland* (Berlin: Akademie Verlag, 1990), 8–14; cf. Horst Boog, "The Luftwaffe and Indiscriminate Bombing to 1942," *The Conduct of the Air War in the Second World War: An International Comparison,* ed. Horst Boog (New York: Berg, 1992), 373–96.

16. For a powerful moral indictment of Allied bombing policy, see A. C. Grayling, *Among the Dead Cities: The History and Moral Legacy of the World War II Bombing of Civilians in Germany and Japan* (New York: Walker, 2006). A more nuanced recent appraisal is Randall Hansen, *Fire and Fury: The Allied Bombing of Germany, 1942–1945* (New York: North American Library, 2008); Martin Middlebrook, *The Battle of Hamburg: Allied Bomber Forces against a German City in 1943* (New York: Scribner's, 1981), 323.

17. Burton F. Ellis to Dee Ellis, August 29, 1945, Burton F. Ellis Papers, Manuscript Group 409 (University of Idaho Library, Moscow). I use this letter courtesy of Danny S. Parker.

18. *Thunderbolt,* dir. William Wyler (War Department, 1944), DVD, Galam Americas, 2001.

19. Chuck Yeager and Leo Janos, *Yeager: An Autobiography* (New York: Bantam, 1985), 62–63.

20. Wiethege, *Und als der Krieg zu Ende Schien . . .,* 38.

21. Middlebrook, *The Battle of Hamburg,* 303.

22. Alfred de Zayas, *Die Wehrmacht-Untersuchungsstelle: Deutsche Ermittlungen über alliierte Völkerrechtsverletzungen im Zweiten Weltkrieg* (München: Universitas/Langen Müller, 1979), 256–58.

23. David Welch, *The Third Reich: Politics and Propaganda* (New York: Routledge, 1993), 115–18.

24. Barbara Grimm, "Lynchmorde an alliierten Fliegern im Zweiten Weltkrieg," in *Deutschland im Luftkrieg: Geschichte und Erinnerung,* ed. Dietmar Süss (Oldenbourg: Institut für Zeitgeschichte, 2007), 75. Bryan T. van Sweringen, who arranged the Borkum trial records for microfilming while employed by the U.S. National Archives, has written that the U.S. Army tried

"about 600 persons, mostly German civilians, . . . for the killing of some 1200 U.S. nationals, mostly airmen." "Introduction," 4, *U.S. v. Goebell* (microfilm, frame 4, reel 1).

25. Patrick Brode, *Casual Slaughters and Accidental Judgments: Canadian War Crimes Prosecutions, 1944–1948* (Toronto: University of Toronto Press, 1997), 105; Jörg Friedrich, *The Fire: The Bombing of Germany, 1940–1945*, trans. Allison Brown (New York: Columbia University Press, 2006), 433–34; Vasilis Vourkoutiotis, *Prisoners of War and the German High Command: The British and American Experience* (New York: Palgrave Macmillan, 2003), 188; Whitney Harris, *Tyranny on Trial: The Evidence at Nuremberg* (Dallas, TX: Southern Methodist University Press, 1954), 232–39; *Flieger-Lynchmorde in Zweiten Weltkrieg*, http://www.flieger-lynchmorde.de/Text/auflistung.htm.

26. "Document No. 1676-PS," in *Trial of the Major War Criminals before the International Military Tribunal*, 42 vols. (Nuremberg: International Military Tribunal, 1948), 27: 436–39.

27. "Rundschreiben 125/44g, May 30, 1944, ibid., XXV, 112–13; Szymon Datner, *Crimes against POWs: Responsibility of the Wehrmacht* (Warsaw: Western Press Agency, 1964), 198.

28. "Document No. 1676-PS," 438–39.

29. David A. Foy, *For You the War Is Over: American Prisoners of War in Nazi Germany* (New York: Stein and Day, 1984), 12. Some downed airmen were shown great kindness. See, for example, the experience of Matthew Radnosky in Lewis H. Carlson, *We Were Each Other's Prisoners: An Oral History of World War II. American and German Prisoners of War* (New York: Basic Books, 1997), 51–52.

30. See James J. Weingartner, "Americans, Germans, and War Crimes: Converging Narratives from the 'Good War,'" *Journal of American History* 94 (March 2008): 1167.

31. "Report: Murder of Seven American Airmen on Borkum Island, 4 August 1944," June 27, 1945; "Short Statement of Facts," January 24, 1946, *U.S. v. Goebell* (microfilm, frames 66–67, 240, 540, reel 1); Rachak to Scheder, n.d.; Maximilian Koessler, "Borkum Island Tragedy and Trial," *Journal of Criminal Law, Criminology, and Political Science* 47 (July–August 1956): 184–89.

32. On the Malmédy and Biscari massacres, see John M. Bauserman, *The Malmedy Massacre* (Shippensburg, PA: White Mane, 1995); James J. Weingartner, *Crossroads of Death: The Story of the Malmédy Massacre and Trial* (Berkeley: University of California Press, 1979); James J. Weingartner, "Massacre at Biscari: Patton and an American War Crime, *The Historian* 52 (November 1989), 24–39; Stanley P. Hirshson, *General Patton: A Soldier's Life* (New York: HarperCollins, 2002), 372–76, 453–56; Rick Atkinson, *The Day of Battle: The War in Sicily and Italy, 1943–1944* (New York: Holt, 2007), 116–21.

33. *U.S. v. Valentin Bersin, et al.* (microfilm, frames 419–36, reel 1), Records of the United States Army Commands, 1942–, RG 338 (National Archives, Washington, DC).

34. Statement of Giuseppe Giannola, March 4, 1947 (in author's possession). I use this document courtesy of Riccardo Giannola.

35. Stephen G. Fritz, *Endkampf: Soldiers, Civilians, and the Death of the Third Reich* (Lexington: University of Kentucky Press, 2004), 73–74; Paul Fussell,

Doing Battle: The Making of a Skeptic (Boston: Little, Brown, 1996), 124; Grady P. Arrington, *Infantryman at the Front* (New York: Vantage Press, 1959), 165–66, 226–27; Stephen E. Ambrose, *Citizen Soldiers: The U.S. Army from the Normandy Beaches to the Bulge to the Surrender of Germany, June 7, 1944–May 7, 1945* (New York: Simon and Schuster, 1997), 352–53; Justin Michael Harris, "American Soldiers and POW Killing in the European Theater of World War II," M.A. thesis, Texas State University, 2009, 13–22.

36. See, for example: Omer Bartov, *The Eastern Front, 1941–1945: German Troops and the Barbarization of Warfare* (New York: St. Martin's Press, 1985); Christian Streit, *Keine Kameraden: Die Wehrmacht und die sowjetischen Kriegs-gefangenen 1941–1945* (Stuttgart: Deutsche Verlags-Anstalt, 1978); Richard J. Evans, *The Third Reich at War* (New York: Penguin Press, 2009), 182.

37. John Dower, *War without Mercy: Race and Power in the Pacific War* (New York: Pantheon, 1986), 52–73; Charles A. Lindbergh, *The Wartime Journals of Charles A. Lindbergh* (New York: Harcourt Brace Jovanovich, 1970), 856; George Feifer, *Tennozan: The Battle of Okinawa and the Atomic Bomb* (New York: Ticknor and Fields, 1992), 485; James J. Weingartner, "Trophies of War: U.S. Troops and the Mutilation of Japanese War Dead, 1941–1945," *Pacific Historical Review* 61 (February 1992): 53–67. For an effort to apply game theory to the issue of sur-render and capture, see Niall Ferguson, "Prisoner Taking and Prisoner Killing in the Age of Total War: Towards a Political Economy of Military Defeat," *War in History* 11 (2004), 148–92.

38. Brode, *Casual Slaughters and Accidental Judgment*, 105; Willis M. Ever-ett to family, n.d., Papers of Willis M. Everett Jr. (in James J. Weingartner's possession).

39. "Record of Trial of West, Horace T., Sergeant," September 2, 1943, 4, 9, 11, 25, 35–38, 40–43, 84–100, 112–13; *United States v. West, Sgt. Horace T.* (Clerk of Court, U.S. Army Judiciary, Arlington, VA).

40. "Report of Investigation of Shooting of Prisoners of War under Direc-tion of Captain John T. Compton, 0-406922, Co. A, 180th Inf. On July 14, 1943 in the Vicinity of the Biscari Airport, Sicily," August 5, 1943, 1–2; "Record of Trial of Compton, John T., Captain, Infantry," October 23, 1943, 63, *United States v. Compton, Capt. John T.* (Clerk of Court, U.S. Army Judiciary, Arlington, VA).

41. U.S. War Department, *Basic Field Manual: Rules of Land Warfare* (Wash-ington, DC: U.S. Government Printing Office, 1940), 86–87; James B. Insco, "Defense of Superior Orders before Military Commissions," *Duke Journal of Comparative and International Law* 13 (Spring 2003): 404, http://www.law. duke.edu/journals/cite.php?13+Duke+J.+Comp.+&+Int'l+L.+389.

42. "Laws of War: Laws and Customs of War on Land (Hague IV)," Article 46; *Basic Field Manual: Rules of Land Warfare*, 6.

43. Frank M. Buscher, *The U.S. War Crimes Trial Program in Germany* (West-port, CT: Greenwood Press, 1989), 9, 21, 31.

44. Ute Stiepani, "Die Dachauer Prozesse und ihre Bedeutung im Rahmen der alliierten Strafverfolgung von NS-Verbrechen," in *Der Nationalsozialismus vor Gericht: Die alliierte Prozesse gegen Kriegsverbrecher und Soldaten 1943–1952*, ed. Gerd R. Ueberschär (Frankfurt am Main: Fischer Taschenbuch Verlag, 1999), 229.

45. August Nigro, *Wolfsangel: A German City on Trial* (Washington, DC: Brassey's, 2001), 17–24; Winston G. Ramsey, "The Rüsselsheim Death March," *After the Battle* 57 (1987): 1–4.

46. Nigro, *Wolfsangel,* 24–25, 46–51; Gladwin Hill, "11 Germans Tried for Killing Fliers," *New York Times,* July 26, 1945.

47. Groehler, *Bombenkrieg gegen Deutschland,* 374, 410.

48. "7 Germans Doomed for Killing Fliers," *New York Times,* August 1, 1945.

2

Building a Case

Borkum was in the British zone of occupation and came under the control of Canadian forces in the waning days of the war. The Canadians were given a handwritten statement by Dirk Johan Hendrik Dreux, a Dutch prisoner who had been held on the island by the Germans for labor on the fortifications. On "August 3, 1944," Dreux had watched Walthall's B-17, which he described as already visibly damaged, make a crash landing after having been "shot down" by Borkum's antiaircraft guns. He and several other Dutch prisoners then watched as "three" crewmen exited the plane and were marched off in the direction of the town by German soldiers. Dreux learned later that day from another Dutchman, named Lubbers, that the American prisoners had been paraded around the town with hands behind their heads while townspeople, including some members of the Hitler Youth, yelled and spat at them. In front of the railway station, a spectator had kicked one of the prisoners who had retaliated by punching his assailant in the face. The prisoners had then been attacked by a mob that struck them with "shovels, stones and other things." Lubbers claimed to have heard pistol shots, but he could not see who had fired them. In any event, all of the Americans had been killed. Subsequently, Dreux had heard people talk nervously about the murders, and one had pointed out to him a "butcher" and local Nazi leader who had allegedly played a leading role in fomenting the incident, clearly the mayor and local party boss, Jan Akkermann.[1]

Dreux's statement was based partly on hearsay and was wrong on the date of the incident, the number of victims, and some of the particulars, but it was soon supplemented by a CIC (U.S. Counter Intelligence Corps) report containing testimony by Thomas J. Lyons, a recently liberated U.S prisoner of war. Lyons was a slightly built 22-year-old native of Buffalo who had served as the dorsal turret gunner of an Eighth Air Force B-17 shot down by flak, on November 6, 1944, while on a raid against Hamburg. He had parachuted from his stricken aircraft, coming to Earth about nine miles from Emden, breaking his left leg and cracking seven ribs in the process. His treatment had differed radically from that accorded #909's crew on nearby Borkum. His German captors took him to the Marine Hospital at Emden, where he remained until liberated by Canadian troops the following spring. While recuperating, he was told a story by a number of other POWs, including a Serb who claimed to be an eyewitness, about seven American airmen who had made an emergency landing on Borkum. According to Lyons's informants, they had been paraded around the island under the direction of the mayor, abused, and finally shot without justification and buried in a mass grave.[2]

Additional information was provided in a report by Lieutenant (jg) J. W. Gould of the U.S. Navy that was based on statements made to him by several Germans. These noted the names of German naval personnel who had allegedly been present at the killings and specified a Lieutenant Weber as the officer allegedly responsible for ordering the American airmen shot.[3] But by far the most complete description of the atrocity to date was supplied on May 22 by Roger Guillon, a French prisoner who had been employed on Borkum at the time of the incident. It is not clear how many of the events of August 4 Guillon had actually witnessed and to what degree his statement was based on what he had heard from others, but Guillon had been held on the island for two years, spoke fluent German, and had established associations—perhaps even friendships—with some residents. Not only were major components of the incident described with considerable precision, but key names were provided, as well. Naval Captain Kurt Goebell, the top-ranking officer on Borkum, had arrived at the crash site and had ordered the prisoners marched to an air base on the other side of the island approximately seven miles away, ostensibly for evacuation to POW facilities on the mainland. Guillon observed that the prisoners might have been transported by means of a narrow-gauge railroad that passed close to the crash site, a point that would later prove an important component in the prosecution case. As the column of seven Americans and their dozen guards approached the town, officers of the Labor Service seized spades from their men and attacked the prisoners. Abuse continued at the hands of townspeople, who beat and stoned the prisoners, egged on by Mayor Jan Akkermann with shouts of "Kill them, kill them like dogs!" Guillon, whose testimony clearly indicated that he had been an observer of this part of the march, claimed to have then been threatened by a "Corporal Langer," one of the Germans who guarded the foreign laborers on the island, who had ordered him at pistolpoint to stand aside. Guillon testified that he had subsequently heard from multiple witnesses that Langer shortly thereafter had shot and killed one of the prisoners. Accompanied by their guards, who provided no protection against continuing assaults, the prisoners stumbled on, collapsing one by one, then were "finished off" with further pistol shots. The bodies were allowed to remain where they had fallen until evening, when they were transported by wagon to nearby sand dunes and stripped of their clothing. They were then taken to the town cemetery and buried in a common grave.[4]

Guillon's statement would be proved wrong on some details, but it was compelling testimony. He was able, moreover, to provide the names of several Germans whom he characterized as "anti-Nazi" who might provide additional information. Motivated by substantial evidence that a war crime had occurred on Borkum, an investigation was begun by naval Lieutenant Guin Fisher, a legal officer attached to the U.S. Navy Flag Officer for Western Germany stationed at Buxtehuda, a short distance southwest of Hamburg. Assisted by Sub-Lieutenant D. McDonald of the Royal Navy as interpreter, Fisher interviewed more than 40 Germans, both military and civilian, from June 11 to June 18.[5]

If any doubts lingered that a war crime had been committed on Borkum the previous August, they were erased by Fisher's interrogations, on the basis of which a coherent narrative emerged that broadly corroborated Guillon's recollections. A "Short Summary of the Facts" based on those interrogations noted that:

> On 4 August 1944, about 1300 hours, an American flying fortress was hit by flak and was forced to land on Borkum island. The crew consisted of three Second Lieutenants and four Sergeants, all of whom were immediately taken prisoners [*sic*]; six of the men were uninjured and the seventh suffered only a minor forehead injury. Upon his arrival at the scene of the landing shortly thereafter, the Military Commander of the Island ordered that the prisoners be marched through the town of Borkum to the airfield situated on the other side of the island about seven miles distant, although it would have been easy for rail transportation to have

been provided. Seven German soldiers were ordered to march with the prisoners and guard them. At the entrance to the town, the Americans were forced to march with their hands over their heads and to pass between members of the German Labor Corps, who beat them with spades at the order of their Commanding Officer. Many civilians of the town also beat the men with sticks and fists and threw stones at them. The Burgomaster of Borkum incited the mob to fever pitch, shouting "Kill them, kill them like dogs." At the center of the town, after the prisoners had been badly beaten, a German soldier ran up and shot one of them in the back of the head. The remaining six prisoners were forced to continue their march and to receive additional beatings from both the civilians and their guards. Finally, these men collapsed on the street and were also killed where they lay by shots through the head.

Contained in the report was a list of 29 Germans suspected of participating in the atrocity. U.S. Navy Reserve Lieutenant Morton E. Rome, who authored the report, declared the existing evidence probably sufficient to support convictions for murder of 14 of these and verdicts of mistreatment of the prisoners for the remainder. Nine of the suspects were already in custody.[6]

Further investigation of the Borkum case now became the responsibility of the U.S. Army, which, under Joint Chiefs of Staff Directive 1023/10 of July 8, 1945, was authorized to establish courts in the U.S. occupation zone to try Germans suspected of having committed war crimes.[7] These tended to be lesser offenders than those who would be tried at Nuremberg and included Germans accused of crimes committed against U.S. combatants. Both the U.S. Third and Seventh Armies were to conduct trials, the former primarily at the former Nazi concentration camp at Dachau outside Munich and the latter at Ludwigsburg, near Stuttgart, although, in October 1946, the process would be centralized and all subsequent trials held at Dachau. U.S. Army Air Forces Major Abraham Levine, investigator-examiner for War Crimes Investigation Team #6837, arrived on Borkum on October 5. Although he claimed to have "found the people as a whole very uncooperative," by October 22, with the assistance of German-born interpreter Private Rudolph Kaufman, he had nevertheless assembled 47 sworn statements that presented, he believed, "a clear picture of what happened on the 4th day of August, 1944."[8] In the ensuing weeks, Levine would secure dozens more.

Many of the interrogations occurred at the British 102 Civil Internment Camp at the site of the German Navy's former POW enclosure at Westertimke or 103 Civil Internment Camp at Esterwegen, previously a Nazi concentration camp. These were of persons already strongly suspected of participation in the atrocity. Other interrogations were conducted in the town of Borkum itself. Ex-mayor Jan Akkermann, one of those in custody, was vague on many details of the events of August 4 but admitted having yelled, as the prisoners were led past him and a crowd of civilians, "Murderers, murderers, murderers, beat them on their necks." He also had observed Raender Haksema and Joseph Hanken each strike at least one of the Americans.[9] Haksema testified in excellent English that he had heard Akkermann shout "hit them, hit them" but denied having struck a prisoner or having seen anyone else do so.[10] Hanken, however, admitted that he had been in a state of high agitation over the fact that he had lost his home, possessions, and job in an air raid on Hamburg and, consequently, had been moved to hit one of the flyers. He also claimed that Akkermann had informed him that the American bomber had fired on Nazi Labor Service men as it descended, killing one and wounding another.[11] Fifty-one year-old air-raid policeman Gustav Mammenga also admitted to having struck the smallest of the prisoners, who struggled throughout the march to keep an oversize pair of pants from falling to his ankles, but only "two or three times" with his open hand.[12]

On August 4, 1944, 34-year-old Heinz Witzke had been an enlisted man serving searchlight # 3 of Battery 7, Antiaircraft Battalion 216. He was ordered to serve as one of the guards as the POWs were marched through Borkum. Lieutenant Jakob Seiler, commander of the battalion's Ostland Battery, near which the B-17 had come down, directed the guards to withhold protection from the prisoners should they come under civilian attack and to beat them if they lowered their hands, although Witzke denied having personally struck anyone. Following the murders of the seven Americans, Witzke testified, all of the guards were required to sign a statement to the effect that the prisoners had been beaten to death by enraged civilians and were ordered neither to speak nor to write of the incident.[13] In his own sworn statement, Seiler admitted only to having ordered the guards not to "shoot" civilians if they should attack the prisoners, but he denied having required the beating of prisoners who lowered their hands during the march.[14] Former lieutenant Karl Weber witnessed the march through the town, Akkermann's efforts to incite the crowd, and attacks by "four or five" citizens on the prisoners. Although Major Levine confronted him with testimony alleging that he had been seen riding a bicycle at the head of the column of prisoners while yelling, "Beat them to death, beat them to death," Weber denied all wrongdoing and claimed, in fact, to have helped a fallen prisoner to his feet.[15]

Frigate Captain Walter Krolikovski had commanded the 216th Naval Antiaircraft Battalion on Borkum when Lieutenant Harvey Walthall had put #909 down on the *Muschelfeld*. Although the second-highest ranking officer on Borkum, when questioned by Levine in Esterwegen on October 29 he claimed to have played only a tangential role in the events of August 4, 1944, largely limited to having been informed by others of assaults on the prisoners, ordering subordinates to investigate, and notifying his superior, Captain Kurt Goebell, that trouble was afoot. That the prisoners had been shot to death he had not discovered until later, having been told initially by the guards that they had been fatally beaten by civilians. But Levine confronted Krolikovski with Johann Schmitz, the senior noncommissioned officer among the guards, who stated that he had informed Krolikovski almost immediately that the Americans had been shot by an unnamed soldier and Petty Officer Jakob Wittmaack, a member of the guard detail.[16] Krolikovski's assertion of ignorance in regard to the fate of the prisoners was implicitly called further into question by the sworn statement of the former deputy commander of the battalion, ex-lieutenant Emil Sobiech. Sobiech had been at battalion headquarters in the Dorf Hotel after the prisoners had passed and had learned almost immediately of the shooting of the first American at the town hall. He had witnessed Krolikovski's "very excited" reaction after having spoken to civilians returning from the scene of the subsequent murders. Sobiech testified that Krolikovski had then dispatched him to investigate but had declared that he already "knew all about it" when Sobiech attempted to report the deaths of the remaining Americans. He also identified Goebell as the source of the orders to march the prisoners on the seven-mile route to and through the town.[17]

Forty-four-year-old former Lieutenant Erich Wentzel, adjutant and personnel officer of the 216th Naval Antiaircraft Battalion, was one of those already under detention at Esterwegen. At the time of #909's emergency landing on Borkum, he had been in his office in the Dorf Hotel but had hurried on his own volition to the crash site, he testified, meeting Captain Goebell and several other officers on the way. Wentzel spoke English and was ordered by Goebell to briefly question the prisoners at the Ostland Battery, to which they had been brought. Goebell was primarily interested in learning who had been responsible for shooting down #909. In fact, probably no one had been, the primary damage to #909 having been caused by its collision with another B-17, although that information apparently was not elicited from the prisoners. Following the interrogation that Wentzel recalled as having lasted about 15 minutes, the prisoners were assembled for the march to the airfield. Lieutenant Seiler, the battery commander, ordered the guards to see to it that the prisoners kept their hands raised and refrained from talking to one another, but Wentzel denied having heard him direct that the Americans were not to be protected if attacked by civilians. Petty Officer Johann Schmitz, who was appointed leader of the guard detail, doubted his ability to find the prescribed route through the town, and Wentzel volunteered to accompany the procession as guide. As the prisoners and their guards marched from the Ostland Battery around the *Muschelfeld* and on to the Promenade that ran along the beach, all was peaceful. Then, Schmitz made a wrong turn onto Victoria Strasse, whereupon Wentzel ordered him to turn the column back along the Promenade toward Strand Strasse. That maneuver brought the prisoners and their guards into contact with a company of the Nazi Labor Service equipped with spades then engaged in exercises. Someone—Wentzel professed not to know who—ordered the Labor Service men to form two lines on either side of the street. As the column of prisoners marched between them Wentzel, pedaling ahead on his bicycle, heard shouts but claimed not to have seen any acts of violence. He paused briefly while the column passed him, did not see any evidence of injury to the Americans, then followed in the company of Lieutenant Weber down Strand Strasse, turning right on Bahnhof Strasse. At the corner of Bahnhof Strasse and Franz Habich Strasse stood a mob of civilians, shouting, Wentzel recalled, "Knock them down, kill them dead, they killed our sisters, brothers, and children." He observed prisoners being struck by civilians and claimed to have attempted to protect the Americans by riding his bicycle between them and the mob. Once again at the head of the column, Wentzel heard a shot in the vicinity of the town hall. Turning back to investigate, he found a prostrate prisoner and several men preparing to carry him inside the office of the air-raid police. Wentzel proceeded to the Dorf Hotel, where he reported to Captain Krolikovski what he had seen, then continued along the route of march to Reede Strasse, where he observed the bodies of the remaining prisoners and spoke to Schmitz, who explained that they had been beaten to death by the mob. But Wentzel's effort to portray himself as the innocent observer of criminal acts that he had been helpless to prevent was undermined by his reluctant admission in the face of sarcastic questioning by Levine that he had composed a report on the incident incorporating the tale of beatings by civilians as the sole cause of the prisoners' deaths in the knowledge that at least one of the prisoners had been shot and had read the report aloud to the guards prior to their having been required by Krolikovski to sign it.[18]

Forty-nine-year-old Kurt Goebell was Borkum's senior military officer on August 4, 1944. He had watched #909 descending and being fired upon by the batteries under his command. He went to the crash site, then proceeded to the Ostland Battery, where the American prisoners had been assembled. Goebell was evasive in his responses to Levine's questions. He claimed not to remember whether or not he had ordered Wentzel to interrogate the prisoners or if he had posed any questions himself, nor could he remember ordering Seiler to direct the guards not to intervene if the Americans were attacked by civilians, although he admitted that he had been aware of Propaganda Minister Goebbels's "decree" on the subject. He did concede, however, that he had relieved one of the guards for his failure to be "strict" enough with his prisoner and, more critically, that he had ordered Seiler to march the prisoners through the town. In response to Levine's question as to why he had ordered the prisoners marched to the airfield rather than transported by the island's narrow-gauge railroad, he replied that the train was being used by foreign workers and civilians and that he did not want the Americans to come in contact with them. When asked why a separate car could not have been used for the prisoners, Goebell could only manage, "I did not think about it." After the column had marched off, Goebell went to his office and phoned Borkum's police chief, Heinrich Rommel, to notify him of the imminent arrival in the town of the American prisoners. Rommel testified that Goebell had said, "Unfortunately, I have taken seven prisoners," which, when queried by Levine, he denied, but he admitted the possibility of having said to Rommel, "I point out to you the decree of Dr. Goebbels." Goebell attempted to defend himself against the sinister interpretation that Levine assigned to the statement by claiming the sole motivation of wanting to alert the man responsible for the maintenance of law and order in the town, to which his interrogator responded with heavy sarcasm, "You were responsible for the care and safety of these prisoners of war who had surrendered according to the Geneva Convention." Goebell conceded that, "in the final analysis," that was true and assured Levine that, if he had had reason to anticipate trouble, he would have avoided marching the prisoners through the town in daylight.[19]

Hermann Wulff was a 41-year-old plumber who had been employed by Borkum's gas works at the time of #909's emergency landing. He had been returning from a job to the gas works at about 4:30 P.M. and nearing the town hall when he had encountered a crowd of about 20 civilians and soldiers. Alighting from his bicycle, he asked two of the soldiers what was going on and was told that captured airmen were about to be led through the town and that they were to be beaten. Wulff rode down Seldte Strasse to the drug store at its intersection with Neue Strasse, where he stopped to observe the approaching column of prisoners. They were clearly exhausted, he recalled, staggering from side to side as they "jogged" down the street, with hostile civilians both beside and in front of them. One prisoner, the tallest, had a bloody face. Although Wulff did not see civilians attack the prisoners, he did observe that one prisoner who had fallen was struck with the rifle butt of a guard, whom Wulff professed himself unable to identify. The smallest prisoner, the last in line, struggled to keep a pair of oversized trousers around his waist. Lowering his hands to reposition them, he was struck and knocked to the ground by his guard, also unknown to Wulff, who jerked him to his feet and shoved him forward with a shout of "Go on, gangster, criminal!" As the column moved down Seldte Strasse, the witness heard a shot and, as the crowd dispersed, saw a prisoner lying on the pavement in front of the air-raid police office. This would later be identified as #909's bombardier, Lieutenant Howard Graham, the "little flyer" with the falling pants and the first victim of the Borkum atrocity. Wulff claimed to have repulsed one guard's invitation to participate in beating the prisoners and to have finally witnessed the murder of the remaining Americans by a pistol-wielding soldier who, with a "wild look in his eye" and yelling "I can't go on anymore," shot each in the back of the head, the last as he attempted to flee the carnage.[20]

Karl Fick was a 45-year-old policeman who had lived on Borkum island since 1939. Under questioning by Levine, he provided a succinct account of what he had witnessed on the afternoon of August 4, 1944. Between 3 and 4 P.M., he had been on the Promenade investigating an incident unrelated to the captured airmen. He encountered an air-raid policeman, Klaas Wegmann, who informed him that the

American prisoners were to be led through the town on their way to the airfield and that he had been directed by Mayor Akkermann to alert Fick about the prisoners' approach. Fick also observed a large group of young Labor Service men, perhaps as many as 100, exercising with their spades on the promenade between Victoria and Strand Strassen. As he was conversing with Wegmann, the prisoners and their guards hove into view—hands raised, walking fast but obviously exhausted—led by an officer mounted on a bicycle. The Labor Service contingent assembled on either side of the promenade, although Fick could not hear an order for them to do so. The prisoners were made to march between the ranks of spade-wielding men, although the witness remembered seeing only one American—the last or next to last—actually struck. Fick then proceeded to the police station, where, about 15 minutes later, a phone call from his wife informed him of the shooting of six of the prisoners near the athletic field (Graham, of course, had been mortally wounded earlier on the march). Fick bicycled to the scene along with Heinrich Rommel, the police chief, blocked off the street, and watched as an ambulance removed the bodies.[21]

Rommel was 54 years old and had been a resident of Borkum for 22 years. When #909 landed on the *Muschelfeld,* he had been at home. He had not seen the plane descend, but he had heard the air-raid siren and proceeded to his office. At about 3 P.M., he informed Levine, he had received a phone call from Captain Goebell. Goebell's message, as Rommel recalled it, was to be central to the case that U.S. Army prosecutors were to formulate: "An airplane has come down and unfortunately I took seven prisoners. They will be taken to the airport and I draw your attention to the decree of Dr. Goebbels." Being unfamiliar with the "decree," Rommel was made uneasy by Goebell's statement, and he phoned the Gestapo office in Emden for instructions. Commissioner Struwe asked whether the prisoners had been taken by the police or the military and, when told the latter, instructed Rommel to remain uninvolved. Although allegedly ignorant of the nature of the Goebbels "decree," he oddly neglected to query Mayor Akkermann when the latter phoned to essentially repeat the message given to Rommel earlier by the island's commandant. It was a passive police chief who briefly observed the marching prisoners, claimed to have witnessed no abuse of them as they passed the police station, but was shortly thereafter notified by Fick of the prisoners' murder, whereupon he proceeded to the scene and observed the removal of the bodies.

Rommel's testimony included an insight into the tensions among Borkumers created by the murders and their fear of American retribution. Following war's end, Captain Goebell, obviously apprehensive, had questioned Rommel on the tenor of opinion among Borkumers on the murders of the American flyers the previous summer. Rommel replied that the people were "worried and sorrowful" and believed that Goebell could have prevented them. "Me?" Rommel remembered Goebell responding. "I had nothing to do with it." In what was clearly an increasingly heated exchange, Rommel replied that if Goebell was not responsible, he couldn't imagine who might be. Goebell could; he blamed Rommel for not having protected the prisoners from attack and categorically denied having brought the "decree" of Dr. Goebbels to the police chief's attention.[22]

On the afternoon of August 4, 1944, 29-year-old Heinrich Heinemann was making sausages in his father's butcher shop on the corner of Neue and Franz Habich Strassen. He had served in the German Navy but had been released due to his father's having been awarded a contract to supply meat products to the military. Learning from passers-by that prisoners were to be led through the town, he and six foreign prisoner-workers employed in the shop went outside to watch. Heinemann remembered that the Americans seemed weary, that a tall prisoner had a bandage over his eye, and that the smallest flyer, the last in the column, had trouble keeping his pants in place. Although he estimated that about 20 civilians "were running all around," he saw none of them strike the prisoners but stated that some of the guards repeatedly hit the prisoners with their rifle butts. Heinemann returned to work. After about 15 minutes, a woman entered the shop with the news that one of the prisoners had been shot near the city hall. He took to his bicycle to investigate but found no one there. Pedaling on to the old lighthouse just beyond the Dorf Hotel, he observed the six surviving prisoners, their guards, and a crowd of civilians. Also present were Lieutenants Wentzel and Weber and Captain Krolikovski, who looked on as guards continued to force the exhausted prisoners on with blows from their rifle butts. Heinemann continued to follow the procession to the fence along the sports field when he heard shots. An infantryman whom Heinemann described as tall with a thin face and "a brutal look in his eyes" and armed with a pistol was running up the line of prisoners shooting each man in the back of the head. His final victim, the prisoner at the head of the line, attempted to flee but was pursued by his assailant and shot from a distance "of about two or three meters." Heinemann then observed one of the noncommissioned officers among the guard detail, described as a short, older man with a thick moustache, shoot two of the fallen Americans a second time with his 9mm *Pistole 08*. In distress and agitation, Heinemann testified, he immediately rode home. But Heinemann might have been less the innocent observer than his testimony implied. Another witness interrogated by Levine claimed to have seen Heinemann—easily identified by his white butcher's apron—rush into the crowd as the prisoners passed. Questioned a second time, Heinemann told an unconvincing story of having "stumbled" and put his hand on the shoulder of one of the Americans, pushing him "twice so I would not fall."[23]

Klaas Meyer-Gerhards was a 50-year-old merchant and a lifelong resident of Borkum who, on August 4, 1944, was leader of the island's air-raid police. He had seen the approach of #909 and proceeded with seven subordinates to the landing site, where they blocked off an area of about 150 meters from the aircraft to secure it from curious residents. Finding no more to do, Meyer-Gerhards accompanied his men back to town and went home for lunch and a nap. His slumber was interrupted by a phone call from one of his men. He was informed that Mayor Akkermann was attempting to reach him and that he needed to come to his office in the Central Hotel, across the street from the city hall. His arrival coincided with that of the American prisoners and their escort, along with a crowd of onlookers whose number he estimated at "about a hundred or more and a lot of children, too." As Meyer-Gerhards was about to enter his office, he saw a soldier whom the witness identified as Langer run toward an American who had fallen and shoot him in the back of the head. Meyer-Gerhards had the victim, clearly Lieutenant Graham, carried into his office, followed by a wild-eyed Langer, who asked to be allowed "to finish him off." Meyer-Gerhards claimed to have responded, "Are you crazy? He isn't an animal! Get out of my office!" Detaining Langer, however, does not seem to have occurred to the witness, and Langer was free to pursue the remaining prisoners. Meyer-Gerhards called for an ambulance, which transported the still breathing but unconscious Graham to the naval hospital on the island, and summoned yet another ambulance when informed that the remaining prisoners had also been shot. Before leaving his office, at around 6 P.M., Meyer-Gerhards testified, he phoned the hospital and learned that Graham was, at that point, still alive.[24]

That an atmosphere of tension and fear had developed among Borkumers concerning the possible consequences of the murders of the

American flyers was hardly surprising. Many of the sworn statements gathered by Levine were obvious efforts to portray the deponents' conduct on August 4, 1944, in the best possible light, and some of them certainly contained serious distortions, if not outright falsifications. That some witnesses, motivated by conscience, personal animosity, or a desire to conceal their own guilt or that of family members, were willing to make (or, possibly, invent) damaging revelations about their neighbors was evident. Erna Garrels testified that her husband, Gerhard, already arrested for participating in the beating of the prisoners, had in fact been in Emden on August 4, 1944, but that she had seen Klaas Wegman, a neighbor, kick one of the Americans. In a second statement, she revealed a series of mutual recriminations that had been stimulated by earlier American investigations of the murders. Shortly after Lieutenant Guin Fisher's preliminary inquiry, in June 1945, Frau Garrels had learned of a heated exchange between Klaas Meyer-Gerhards and Heinrich Heinemann, whose father had been imprisoned on suspicion of having assaulted the Americans. In the course of the confrontation, the younger Heinemann apparently imputed guilt to Meyer-Gerhards, to which the latter allegedly replied: "You keep still! If I open my mouth, you will be in it, too. You were one of the first at City Hall who did the beating." After Levine's arrival on Borkum, Frau Garrels had threatened Meyer-Gerhards with disclosure to the Americans of what she had heard about the latter's actions on August 4, 1944. According to Garrels, Meyer-Gerhards had replied: "I'll deny everything. Your husband wouldn't want that if he was [*sic*] here. I'd sooner go to jail for five years before I would report somebody," to which Frau Garrels had responded tartly, "So far neighborly love doesn't go, that you would go to prison for a guilty one." Frau Garrels's husband, Gerhard, interned at Westertimke, although identified by Agnes Fischer as having beaten Lieutenant Graham and by Hendireka Gemsa as having been present on Borkum rather than in Emden, claimed that the witnesses had confused him with Gustav Mammenga, whom he closely resembled.[25]

Other residents supplied Levine with additional detail regarding the attacks on the American prisoners. On August 4, 1944, Rudolf Erdwiens, a 16-year-old carpenter, had been working when Borkum's air-raid sirens sent him to a shelter. He heard the firing of the island's antiaircraft batteries and, shortly thereafter, the sounding of the all-clear, after which he returned to work. Knocking off at around 5 P.M., he gathered up some wood from the shop for his personal use and began to walk to his home, at 54 Deich Strasse. Reaching Reede Strasse, he saw the American prisoners with their guards. As the column drew opposite him, a tall male civilian dressed in white shirt and gray trousers whom he did not know grabbed a piece of wood about two feet long and two inches square from Erdwiens and used it to beat one of the prisoners on his shoulders and back.[26] Johann Grupengiesser, a 48-year-old machinist who had witnessed the attack described by Erdwiens, identified the assailant as a certain "Rimbach." He also claimed to have witnessed *two* of the guards who were armed with pistols shooting two of the prisoners a second time after they had been felled by Langer. These men he was able to describe but not identify. Grupengiesser also observed two officers on bicycles, one of whom he identified as Lieutenant Weber (the other was certainly Wentzel), who rode up to the scene, made a cursory inspection, then rode away.[27]

Johanna Wybrands, age 51, told a dramatic story that, if true, indicated that, on August 4, 1944, not all Borkumers had approved of the assaults on the American prisoners and that at least one of the prisoners had attempted a measure of self-defense. Looking out the kitchen window in the building at 26 Reede Strasse shared by the grocery store she operated with her husband, Frau Wybrands saw "a crowd of people" and went outside to investigate. She witnessed an onlooker (presumably the Rimbach identified by Grupengiesser) seize a stick from a youngster (who must have been Erdwiens) and strike a prisoner on the head with it. Another prisoner, she testified, grabbed the stick, at which point someone from the crowd yelled, "Now shoot him!" She then claimed to have seen a private shoot "the flyer" (which one is unclear) in the back of the head. At this point, Frau Wybrands fled back into her store, although she re-emerged some time later to see "four" more dead Americans. As an interesting coda to her sworn statement, Frau Wybrands added that, at the time of the assault on the prisoner with the stick taken from Erdwiens, she had attempted to pull the assailant away from his victim, for which she was reviled by several bystanders with the accusation that she was "not fit to be a German woman," a now useful distinction also claimed by another female witness critical of the beatings, Elizabeth Biermann. Wybrands had been confronted by Langer, who, she asserted, had appeared at her door as she was about to enter the store and put his hand menacingly on his pistol, at which point Frau Wybrands was pulled inside by her husband, Eldbert, who in his own statement confirmed her testimony in its essentials.[28]

Fritz Fidelak claimed to have been in Emden on August 4, 1944, but was well acquainted with Langer, the principal (and possibly sole) murderer of the American prisoners. Fidelak had been Langer's immediate superior in an army company responsible for guarding the prisoners of war who worked on Borkum's fortifications. Fidelak testified that he had received a phone call from Langer in which the latter had described the circumstances of his shooting of the American prisoners. He had been off duty and in town shopping when he had encountered the marching column of Americans and their guards. He had joined the procession and had shot the Americans "while they were attempting to escape." Fidelak claimed to have reported the conversation to the captain in command of the company but then to have lost track of Langer after he had been transferred to the mainland, although he had received a postcard at some point in which Langer explained that he was being sent to the front.[29]

Other witnesses contributed additional incriminating detail. Fifty-one-year-old Klaas Adel was bicycling home from work at the town hall at around 6 P.M. when he encountered an officer whom he identified as Lieutenant Weber riding his bicycle in the opposite direction and yelling, he recalled, "Beat them to death! Here come the pigs!" Following at some distance were six prisoners and their guards. Adel saw one uniformed German beating the next-to-last American with his fists, but he saw no assaults by civilians. About 30 minutes later, he saw the bodies of the six Americans lying on Reede Strasse along the athletic field between Wybrand's store and Grupengiesser's house.[30] Fifteen year-old Hilde Glashoff had been out walking when she had seen the seven exhausted American prisoners under armed guard coming down Seldte Strasse. She estimated that "about 25 or 30" civilians were looking on, one of whom, a tall, slim man in a white shirt, had hit one of the Americans in the face with his fist. Although Captain Krolikovski was present, he had done nothing to prevent the assault or restrain the civilian.[31] Jenni Glashoff, probably Hilde's mother, had witnessed assaults by two civilians on the prisoners. One of them was likely the same one described by Hilde, and both had been carried out in the presence of a passive Krolikovski.[32] *Paterfamilias* Alfred Glashoff described the same attacks and identified not only Krolikovski but also Lieutenant Erich Wentzel as having made no effort to intervene.[33] Gerhardt Stindt, a 61-year-old hotel owner, had served as assistant to the commander of Borkum's air-raid police, Klaas Meyer-Gerhardts. On the afternoon of August 4, 1944, Stindt had received two phone calls from Mayor Akkermann, who was trying to contact Meyer-Gerhardts to tell him of the impending march of the prisoners through town. Akkermann, according to Stindt, was anxious to see "how tough the air-raid policemen were."[34] Dorothea Viehring, age 41, ran a tobacco shop and had watched the column of prisoners and guards, accompanied by Wentzel on his bicycle, moving down Strand Strasse. She denied having seen any violence inflicted on the Americans but related that, sometime later, Rimbach had come into her shop. He had held out his hand with the comment, "I also got a bloody hand out of this." In response to Frau Viehring's request for an explanation, Rimbach allegedly answered, "I have had my revenge."[35] Some testimony suggested behavior closer to harassment than criminal assault. In addition to the shouted insults and threats attested to by many witnesses, Jan Klieviet claimed to have seen one of the prisoners kicked in the shins.[36] Some testimony was potentially exculpatory. Gerhardt Akkermann (not to be confused with mayor Jan Akkermann) was employed at the naval air base on the island. He recalled having been informed by a non-commissioned officer at around 4:00 or 4:30 P.M. that the night crew would have to guard seven prisoners who were to be brought to the base and evacuated to the mainland the next morning, suggesting that there had been no overt intent to murder the Americans.[37] Some testimony was hearsay of dubious value. Anne Akkermann reported that her sister had been told by Jean LaPierre, a French POW working on Borkum, the names of civilians who had beaten Americans and identified a Richard Kutscher as the murderer of Lieutenant Graham.[38] In his own sworn statement, Kutscher claimed to have been working at the air base all day. In the end, he would not be charged, nor would any of the other persons implicated by LaPierre.[39]

Major Levine had also gathered evidence more tangible and less ambiguous in its import than the testimony of frightened suspects and often self-serving witnesses. Major Murray M. Braff was a medical doctor and pathologist by training who had been assigned to Levine's War Crimes Investigation Team. On October 8, 1945, he visited Plot D in Borkum's Lutheran cemetery, where, close to the cemetery wall and surrounded by a low enclosure of brick, were nine white crosses, each mounted on a small concrete pedestal. On seven was inscribed "U.S. Army," the name of the deceased, and "beerd" (*beerdigt* or buried) and the date of burial, with, according to German custom, the day preceding the month, "5.8.44." Striking a discordant note was a misreading of James Danno's given name, rendered by those who had consigned him to his grave as "Jannes." The seven members of #909's crew were not alone in this corner of the cemetery. Present to the immediate right of Graham's grave (he was in death, as on the march, again at the end of the line) were two more, one that of a member of the Royal Canadian Air Force and the other that of a British Royal Air Force crewman. The bodies of the Americans were exhumed by German civilians and examined by Major Braff in situ. All had been buried uncoffined and, after more than a year in Borkum's damp, sandy soil, were badly decomposed. The apparent circumstances of their deaths had already been described to Braff by Levine and were readily confirmed by Braff's cursory examination. In five cases, bullet wounds that had entered the back of the skull were present. Danno's skull had completely disintegrated, making the identification of a cause of death impossible, while no wound could be found in Faber's remains, leading Braff to speculate that he had been shot in the neck. There was no evidence of a second bullet wound to any of the bodies, although, given their condition, that was clearly a possibility. The remains of the seven Americans were placed in zinc-lined coffins and temporarily reburied in the graves the Germans had provided for them.[40]

The evidence assembled by Levine, if not devoid of the ambiguity present in many criminal cases, strongly indicated that some civilians had expressed murderous hostility toward the captured airmen that in a few cases had extended to assaults, while the naval personnel assigned to escort the prisoners had been ordered to withhold protection from them if they came under civilian attack. Some of the guards had struck the Americans with their rifle butts. But the actual murderer had belonged to neither group and had not been apprehended. On December 28, 1945, a case analysis was completed by Captain Charles D. Mathews of the Prosecution Subsection, Deputy Theater Judge Advocate's Office, War Crimes Branch. Two charges were preferred on January 8, 1946, against 23 Germans, alleging that they "did willfully, deliberately and wrongfully encourage, aid, abet and participate in the killing of" and "did willfully, deliberately encourage, aid, abet and participate in assaults upon" the seven crewmen of #909. The case was assigned the reference number 12-489 and referred by the Deputy Theater Judge Advocate's War Crimes Branch, United States Forces, European Theater (USFET), to the U.S. Seventh Army which, along with the Third Army, was then in control of the U.S. occupation zone, for trial.[41]

NOTES

1. "War Crimes, Island of Borkum," May 16, 1945, I Echelon, 21 Army Group, *U.S. v. Goebell et al.* (microfilm, frames 47, 52–54, reel 1).

2. "Memorandum for the Officer in Charge," ibid. (frames 59–60).

3. "Murder of Seven American Airmen on Borkum Island, 4 August 1944," June 27, 1945, ibid. (frame 68).

4. "Exhibit 1," ibid. (frames 90–91).

5. "Report," June 27, 1945, ibid. (frames 66–163).

6. "A Short Summary of the Facts: Murder of Seven American Airmen— Mistreatment of American Prisoners of War on Borkum Island," ibid. (frames 165–67).

7. "Introduction," 3, ibid. (frame 3).

8. "Memorandum to Lt. Col. B. F. Ellis," October 22, 1945, ibid. (frame 270).

9. "Testimony of Jan J. Akkermann," October 24, 1945, 4, ibid. (frame 287).

10. "Testimony of Raender Haksema," October 26, 1945, 2–3, ibid. (frames 291–92).

11. "Testimony of Josef Peter Hanken," November 2, 1945, 3, ibid. (frame 301).

12. "Testimony of Gustav Mammenga," November 5, 1945, 3, ibid. (frame 296).

13. "Testimony of Heinz Witzke," October 27, 1945, 2–4, 6, 11, ibid. (frames 305–7, 309, 314).

14. "Testimony of Jakob Valentin Seiler," November 1, 1945, 4, ibid. (frame 328).

15. "Testimony of Karl Weber," October 28, 1945, 3–7, ibid. (frames 318–22).

16. "Testimony of Walter Krolikovski," October 29, 1945, 2–7, ibid. (frames 333–38).

17. "Testimony of Emil Sobiech," October 27, 1945, 3–6, ibid. (frames 343–46).

18. "Testimony of Erich Wentzel," October 29, 1945, 2–14, ibid. (frames 350–62).

19. "Testimony of Kurt Goebell," October 29, 1945, 2–8, ibid. (frames 366–72).

20. "Testimony of Hermann Wulff," October 16, 1945, 2–6, ibid. (frames 379–83).

21. "Testimony of Karl Fick," October 16, 1945, 2–5, ibid. (frames 385–88).

22. "Testimony of Heinrich Rommel," October 16, 1945, 2–6, ibid. (frames 391–95).

23. "Testimony of Heinrich Heinemann," October 17, 1945, 2–5; "Testimony of Heinrich Heinemann," November 5, 1945, 2, ibid. (frames 402–5, 408).

24. "Testimony of Klaas Meyer-Gerhards," October 13, 1945, 2–4, ibid. (frames 416–18).

25. "Testimony of Erna Garrels," October 18, 1945, 2–3; "Testimony of Erna Garrels," October 19, 1945, 2, ibid. (frames 424–25, 428).

26. "Testimony of Rudolf Erdwiens," October 11, 1945, 2–3, ibid. (frames 446–47).

27. "Testimony of Johann Grupengiesser," October 12, 1945, 2–4, ibid. (frames 450–52).

28. "Testimony of Johanna Wybrands," October 11, 1945, 2–3; "Testimony of Elizabeth Biermann," October 12, 1945, 3; "Testimony of Elbert Wybrands," October 11, 1945, 3, ibid. (frames 455–56, 460, 472).

29. "Testimony of Fritz Fidelak," October 13, 1945, 2–3, ibid. (frames 467–68).

30. "Testimony of Klaas Adel," October 18, 1945, 2–3, ibid. (frames 475–76).

31. "Testimony of Hilde Glashoff," October 11, 1945, 2–3, ibid. (frames 479–80).

32. "Testimony of Jenni Glashoff," October 11, 1945, 3, ibid. (frame 484).

33. "Testimony of Alfred Glashoff," October 14, 1945, 3, ibid. (frame 487).

34. "Testimony of Gerhardt Stindt," November 5, 1945, 2–3, ibid. (frames 490–91).

35. "Testimony of Dorothea Viehring," October 9, 1945, 2–4, ibid. (frames 530–32).

36. "Testimony of Jan Klieviet," October 15, 1945, 3, ibid. (frame 508).

37. "Testimony of Gerhardt Akkermann," October 10, 1945, 2, ibid. (frame 521).

38. "Testimony of Anne Akkermann," October 10, 1945, 2, ibid. (frame 524).

39. "Testimony of Richard Kutscher," October 20, 1945, 2, ibid. (frame 496).

40. "Testimony of Murray M. Braff, Major, Medical Corps," October 8, 1945, *Record of Testimony,* 264–68, ibid. (frames 816–20); exhibits 56–63, ibid. (frames 783–90, reel 2).

41. "Case Analysis, Deputy Theater Judge Advocate's Office, War Crimes Branch, United States Forces, European Theater," ibid. (frames 231–44, reel 1); "Military Government Charge Sheet," January 8, 1946, ibid. (frames 537–39); "Memorandum to Theater Judge Advocate," n.d., ibid. (frame 254).

3

A Town Brought to Trial

U.S. v. Kurt Goebell et al. opened on the morning of February 6, 1946, in the ceremonial hall of the palace of the kings of Württemberg in Ludwigsburg. Lighted by high, graceful windows flanked by marble columns and hung with crystal chandeliers and lavish baroque wall decorations, it was an incongruous venue for the trial of a brutal case of mass murder. The evidence would be heard by a general military government court composed of seven officers of the U.S. Seventh Army holding the ranks of colonel and lieutenant colonel. Prosecution of the case was in the hands of a trial judge advocate, Major Joseph D. Bryan, and three assistant trial judge advocates, while the defense of the accused was to be directed by defense counsel in the person of Lieutenant Colonel Samuel M. Hogan and three officers in support. All of these were appointed from a pool of officers with legal training who had been assigned to the theater judge advocate for employment in war-crimes trials.[1] Supplementing Hogan's defense team were nine civilian German attorneys. At least in terms of manpower, the defense of the Borkum accused would not be found wanting.

Although 23 Germans had originally been charged in the case, only 15 defendants were actually present in the dock. American investigators had failed to locate and apprehend the remaining eight, although one would be found later and tried individually in a subsequent proceeding. The 15 defendants were equally distributed among three distinct groups: those who had held military rank as officers (Kurt Goebell, Walter Krolikovski, Erich Wentzel, Karl Weber, and Jakob Seiler); the guards, all of whom had been noncommissioned officers or enlisted men (Johann Schmitz, Johann Pointner, Günther Albrecht, Karl Geyer, and Heinz Witzke); and civilians (Jan Akkermann, Klaas

Meyer-Gerhards, Heinrich Rommel, Gustav Mammenga, and Heinrich Heinemann).[2] The most glaring absence from the courtroom was
that of Langer, by universal agreement the prime and, perhaps, sole
murderer of the seven American prisoners. The defendants would be
tainted with the guilt that belonged primarily to him. Some of them
would pay a heavy price.

At least one member of the prosecution team was aware of the moral
ambiguities inherent in his assignment. Captain Edward F. Lyons was
a sensitive 46-year-old New York attorney who continued to lament
the alleged injustice of the Sacco-Vanzetti trial of a quarter-century earlier and enjoyed reading poetry with his wife. In postwar Germany, he
agonized over the devastation around him and the dropping of atomic
bombs on Japan against the background of his reading of Thoreau's
idyllic *Walden* and was troubled by conversations with American officers who expressed opposition to the trial of German soldiers for
violations of the laws of war, because "we, too, lined up prisoners,
decided how many we wanted to send in tonight . . . and unconcern-
edly turned machine guns on the rest." He was distressed by the exploitation of German women by U.S. Army officers and lamented that
"your typical officer over here seems to regard a woman as a utility
and not as a human being."[3] But, involvement in other cases, including
those concerning the operation of concentration camps, made him and
his colleagues acutely conscious of the profound evil that had infected
German society under the Nazis. As an atrocity, the seven Borkum
murders bore little comparison to the sufferings and deaths of many
thousands in Buchenwald, but those accused of having perpetrated
them would be prosecuted with equal vigor, and some would suffer
comparable punishment.

But it would not be not for want of an energetic defense. The proceedings had been under way for less than 10 minutes when Captain
Jim Phelps abruptly demanded the opportunity to individually interrogate the panel of officers sitting in judgment for possible bias, a
self-evident possibility in a case in which officers of the U.S. Army
were called upon to judge the accused murderers of brother officers.
The request was peremptorily refused by the court's president, Colonel Edward F. Jackson, who, although not a lawyer, would act as law
member throughout the trial. Defense counsel had to content itself
with Jackson's simple "no" to the question of the presence of prejudice
on the bench.[4] Further largely pro forma procedural challenges by the
defense that persisted into the afternoon gave further notice that the

defendants would be vigorously represented. The trial proper began with the reading of the charges, to which all defendants pleaded innocent.[5] Major Bryan then delivered the prosecution's opening statement. It was a sober account of the events of August 4, 1944, that emphasized those collusive actions by the defendants that had allegedly turned the ostensible effort to deliver the seven prisoners to Borkum's airport into torment for the Americans and, ultimately, into a "death march."[6] That it had been the actions of one man not in collusion with the defendants who had made the procession a "death march" was a fact awkwardly skirted. Langer's name was not mentioned and would be heard only rarely during the balance of the trial.

The prosecution's case continued with the key testimony of Major Abraham Levine, the war-crimes investigator who had secured the sworn statements on which the case against the defendants was based. Each defendant was identified by Levine as having been interrogated by him and was required to rise from his place in the dock as his name was called. Collectively, they accounted for 15 of the vital statements. But Levine testified that he had collected a total of 75–80 sworn statements, only a small fraction of which were included in the body of trial evidence. That discrepancy attracted the attention of defense counsel in the person of Captain Albert Hall. Under cross-examination, Levine explained that he had submitted the statements to the war-crimes branch of the judge advocate general's office and that the prosecution section of that agency had made the selection in building its case, although he also revealed that there had been some statements that he had not submitted on the grounds of irrelevance. But Levine assured the court that "My job . . . is to find the facts relating to a certain incident, and it makes no difference to me whether a witness tells me something for or against a certain individual."[7]

Those sworn statements were now to be supplemented by the testimony of prosecution witnesses. Unlike the pretrial sworn statements, this testimony was subject to defense scrutiny during cross-examination, although much of it was neither skillful nor effective. Robert Viehring had been serving with a naval artillery unit on the island and had watched #909 as it descended for its crash landing on the *Muschelfeld.* He had gone to the crash site and, as others had testified to Levine, had heard Captain Goebell exclaim to the noncommissioned officer who reported to him the capture of the Americans, "And you bring them to me alive?" Inflection was obviously crucial in interpreting the ambiguous rhetorical query. Viehring testified that he had understood Goebell to mean, "Why do you bring them to me at all?" Ambiguity was not eliminated, although, in light of the later abuse and murder of the American prisoners, it was not difficult to assume a sinister connotation. Viehring had clearly been called by the prosecution to lay the first stone in the foundation of its theory that a murderous conspiracy had been hatched on August 4, 1944, that had resulted in the murders of seven American airmen. The witness was cross-examined by Dr. Ottmar Weber, one of the German attorneys hired to assist in the defense of the accused. It is unfortunate that the original testimony and Weber's challenges of it in German are not included in the trial record but only the extemporaneous and often awkward translations into English of court interpreters. What seems ambiguous in translation may have been less (or more) so *auf Deutsch*. Yet, it was the translations upon which the Army judges would reach their verdicts. German attorneys, moreover, were unfamiliar with Anglo-American adversarial trial procedure and often seemed confused, particularly at this early stage in the war-crimes trial program. In his cross-examination of Viehring, Weber appeared to egregiously misunderstand the witness's testimony when he accused him of contradicting himself and asked, "Do you mean to say that he did not care to receive any prisoners altogether? In that case why did he tell them to bring the prisoners to him alive?" Viehring was understandably perplexed by the question. Weber persisted: "Put yourself in such a predicament where you don't care to receive any prisoners, would you tell the men to bring the prisoners to you alive?"[8] Listeners to the exchange must have been scratching their heads, and not for the last time.

But other efforts by the defense to cast doubt on prosecution testimony were more effective. Sixteen-year-old Walter Hawich had been attached to the air-raid police and had gone to the scene of #909's crash landing on August 4, 1944, identified the plane as American by, as he testified, "the star" and assisted in the posting of *Eintritt Verboten!* (Entry Forbidden!) signs around the wreck. He had then returned home, eaten and, reflecting the relatively idyllic conditions still prevailing on Borkum, gone to the beach for a swim. He had just come out of the water when he heard someone yell, "The American flyers are coming!"

He, along with other bathers, had hurried up to the Promenade, which ran along the beach, to watch the procession. The young Hawich described how the "one or two platoons" of Labor Service men, who had been drilling on the Promenade, broke formation, apparently in response to an order, lined up on both sides of the street, and beat the passing prisoners with spades and shovels while their guards made no effort at intervention. The witness testified that he followed the procession, observed the tragic-comic travail of "the little flyer" and his falling trousers ("the pants kept falling down on his heels," Hawich noted), and Mayor Akkermann's efforts to incite the crowd with cries of "Beat the dogs" or "Beat the murderers," in response to which some of the onlookers had struck the prisoners with, again, the apparent acquiescence of the guards. At the point in the march at which the prisoners reached the city hall, where the little flyer collapsed, Hawich ceased his pursuit, although he heard a single shot, presumably Langer's mortal wounding of Graham. But, under cross-examination by Lieutenant John Davis, Hawich admitted that he had not actually heard any orders given to the Labor Service contingent exercising on the Promenade to form up on either side of the prisoners, nor did he believe that many blows had been struck by them. On the route to the city hall, moreover, he had seen only two civilians hit any of the prisoners; he maintained that the guards had occasionally "shoved" or "pushed" the men they were guarding with their rifle butts rather than hitting them, an admittedly subtle and subjective but nevertheless potentially significant distinction. Mayor Akkermann had not personally assaulted anyone, Hawich testified, nor had his inflammatory shouts apparently had much influence on the conduct of bystanders.[9] The defense had enjoyed an early, if minor, victory in somewhat diluting the image of the march as a well-coordinated exercise in brutalizing defenseless American POWs.

But this success was trivial when measured alongside the dense body of evidence represented by Levine's sworn statements, and it was to these that the prosecution team now turned. Levine was recalled to the stand and asked to identify the pieces of evidence generated by his team that were now to be formally introduced into evidence. In addition to the crucial sworn statements, Levine had personally taken photographs relevant to the case, and his editorializing on some of them called into question his earlier assurances of objectivity. When asked by Major Bryan to identify one photograph, Levine replied that it showed a part of the sea wall facing the *Muschelfeld* and the Ostland Battery, as well as part of the road along which the American prisoners had been marched on their way to the town. "On this road," Levine added, describing events he had not witnessed, "the prisoners were led with their hands over their heads at a fast rate of march and were mishandled on the way." Captain Hall's immediate objection was sustained by the court's president, Colonel Jackson, although Levine continued to offer commentary on evidentiary photographs, including grisly scenes of the disinterment of the Americans' decomposed corpses that, the defense argued, also went far beyond his personal knowledge.[10]

But the sworn statements were potentially far more damaging than photographs, no matter how gruesome, and the defense made a desperate effort to exclude them from evidence. There would be no allegations at this point that torture or other forms of duress had been employed in securing them, as would be claimed by the defense in the controversial Malmédy massacre case that would come to trial a few months later, but the defendants and others who had been interrogated by Levine during the investigation had been without legal counsel and undoubtedly were badly frightened, certainly, in some cases, deservedly so. The statements, moreover, had almost all been made in German, while the documents introduced by the prosecution were translations into English, leaving open the possibility that important nuances had been lost or distorted in the process. But on what legal grounds could the defense move that the statements be excluded as evidence?

Levine's earlier assurances of impartiality would be qualified by his later testimony that he and other leaders of war-crimes investigation teams had been given to understand that they were to conduct their interrogations in such a manner that cases could be tried on affidavits alone, making investigators in practice instruments of the prosecution. A prosecution objection to the rather quixotic defense query as to whether the rights of the accused had been protected during the investigation was sustained by the president of the court.[11] In fact, the question of whether the defendants had "rights" in any meaningful sense was moot. Germany had ceased to exist as a sovereign entity, authority having passed wholly to the occupying powers, which were free to operate as they chose.[12] In principle, prisoners of war were protected by international law, most notably by the Geneva Convention Relative to Prisoners of War of 1929. But the sworn statements, whether made by military or by civilian suspects, all were prefaced by a formula that identified each deponent as "a German civilian." The U.S. Army, in other words, did not recognize the defendants who had held military rank as prisoners of war. But this awkward reality was not openly addressed in the Ludwigsburg courtroom. Instead, the defense argued, in opposition to the introduction of the first statement, that of Kurt Goebell, both that it was not the "best evidence" available, since the deponent could be readily questioned and cross-examined in court, and that, in any case, the sworn statement was not admissible under . international law against those defendants who had been members of the German armed forces. The latter argument was rooted in Article 63 of the 1929 Geneva Convention, which stated that prisoners of war must be tried according to the same standards and procedures used by the detaining power in trying its own soldiers and that, under the U.S. Army's rules of court-martial, the sworn statements would be inadmissible as evidence. Moreover, inasmuch as the military government court sitting in Ludwigsburg differed in some significant respects from a U.S. Army court-martial (much looser rules of evidence governed in the former, for example), it lacked jurisdiction over the military defendants.[13] A similar argument had been recently offered in an application to the U.S. Supreme Court for leave to file for a writ of habeas corpus in the case of Japanese general Tomoyuki Yamashita and had been rejected on the grounds that Article 63 applied only to the trial of captured enemy combatants for offenses committed while in captivity. Yamashita would be hanged on February 23, 1946, while the Borkum trial was still in progress. As the defense surely had anticipated, its objections were overruled by Colonel Jackson, although they would be restated as additional sworn statements were introduced by the prosecution and, in most cases, with equal futility.[14]

Having failed to exclude the sworn statements from evidence, defense counsel could at least cross-examine witnesses and compare their courtroom testimony with their earlier responses to Levine's interrogations. This produced some discrepancies and possibly weakened the prosecution's case for the existence of a conspiracy or common design whose intentional or at least foreseeable result was the death of the American prisoners. Policeman Karl Fick had told Levine that, on the approach of the prisoners and their guards, the Labor Service contingent had separated into two groups on either side of the Promenade, requiring the Americans to run a gauntlet of spade-wielding Germans, although he had seen only one prisoner actually struck. His courtroom testimony was slightly different. Now, it seemed, the Labor Service men had broken formation and surrounded the prisoners "helter-skelter." He reiterated that he had seen only one German actually strike a prisoner with his spade, while a few others had raised their implements, although "it was impossible to determine whether they intended to beat the flyers or really [*sic*] intended to threaten them." He had seen no blood on the faces of the Americans.[15] This version hardly suggested an organized assault. The English translation of Hermann Staats's affidavit stated that the witness had seen guards "hit" the prisoners with their rifle butts and that he was "sure" that Lieutenant Wentzel, riding at the head of his column on a bicycle, had seen it but had done nothing to prevent it. In court, however, Staats testified that he had seen "the small flyer" and one other prisoner "pushed" by their guards with rifle butts but did not believe "excessive force" had been employed. Moreover, Staats now "could not say" whether Wentzel had been aware of the guards' treatment of the prisoners.[16] Gerhardt Stindt's affidavit stated that he had seen "the small flyer's" guard "always" hitting him with the butt of his rifle (although he amended that observation to "at least two times") and that, in front of the Dorf Hotel, "two or three" soldiers had come out of the building, "jumped" on one prisoner, and beat him. From the witness stand in Ludwigsburg, however, Stindt initially testified that the small flyer had been "either pushed or hit" twice by his guard and another prisoner kicked by a single soldier in front of the hotel. Under defense cross-examination, he then modified his testimony in regard to the treatment of the small flyer to an unambiguous "hit" rather than "push," but with the qualifier that "It was not brutal."[17]

To be sure, most courtroom testimony was generally consistent with statements made earlier to Major Levine, and discrepancies were generally minor, although suggestive of evidence that deserved to be taken with a degree of skepticism. Klaas Adel steadfastly maintained on both occasions that one of the defendants, Lieutenant Weber, had encountered him on the afternoon of August 4, 1944, and had declared, "There the pigs are coming, beat them to death." In both venues, too, Adel testified that he had seen a man in uniform, but possibly not one of the guards, punch a prisoner.[18] On the other hand, while Johann Grupengiesser confirmed his earlier testimony to Levine that he had seen the shadowy Rimbach hit a prisoner with a piece of wood and a soldier who was clearly Langer shoot the last of the prisoners with a pistol, the *two* guards who in his sworn statement of the previous October had allegedly shot *two* of the Americans a second time had been reduced in his trial testimony to a single guard and a single prisoner.[19]

Grupengiesser was not challenged on the discrepancy, but Elizabeth Biermann was grilled by assistant defense counsel Lieutenant Davis because she had testified to Levine that she had seen three bodies on coming out of Wybrand's store, whereas, in court, she claimed to have seen only two. In explanation, Frau Biermann suggested vaguely that "It is possible that I saw the three but the whole thing was too foggy in the distance to determine exactly what I saw." But she recounted without inconsistency or hesitation her comment critical of the mistreatment of a prisoner who had fallen to the pavement, undoubtedly Graham, and her having been reviled and threatened by a guard wearing a steel helmet (whom she was unable to identify) in response. She had then retreated with her daughter into Wybrands' grocery store.[20] Eldert Wybrands, the owner of the store, in contrast, testified that he had not seen Frau Biermann near or in his shop and that it had been *his* wife who had condemned the rough handling of the prisoners and been castigated in language virtually identical to that claimed by Frau Biermann to have been directed at her and threatened by a soldier in a soft cap, who had then proceeded to shoot down "three or four prisoners."[21]

A minor discrepancy between Wybrands's courtroom testimony and his statement made to Major Levine five months earlier led to a suggestion by Lieutenant Davis that the witness be shown his earlier affidavit to refresh his memory. That produced an interesting colloquy between two members of the defense team and Major Bryan for the prosecution, who objected to allowing the court interpreter to translate into German the relevant passage in Wybrands's sworn statement on the grounds that the interpreter might produce a version that differed from the German in which the witness had originally spoken to Levine. That possibly unwise although certainly apposite remark permitted the defense to renew its attack on this critical block of prosecution evidence.

> HALL: If the court please, how else would the witness find out what the language meant unless the court interpreter translates the statement in question to the witness? The prosecution has objected on the ground [*sic*] that he might translate it differently than the investigator's interpreter did. If that is true it might be well that we should have all the statements of the prosecution reinterpreted.
>
> PHELPS: Sir, can the defense have an objection to all of the statements introduced, because it is possible that the witness did not know what he was signing?

BRYAN: That is distinctly not the basis of the prosecution's objection.

DAVIS: For the purpose of avoiding any further argument on an extremely minor question, I will withdraw the question.[22]

One suspects sarcasm on Davis's part. It was not, in fact, a minor question, but the president of the court had already made abundantly clear that any effort by the defense to exclude the sworn statements as they had been submitted would be futile, as Davis certainly knew.

The problematic character of some of the sworn statements when placed alongside courtroom testimony was thrown into high relief by the appearance of Erna Garrels, called as a witness by the prosecution. Frau Garrels, it may be recalled, had made two sworn statements to Levine in October of the previous year. In the first, she had asserted that her husband, Gerhard, had been in Emden on the day of the murders. She had also accused a neighbor of having kicked one of the Americans and testified to having seen one of the guards strike a prisoner with the butt of his rifle.[23] In the second statement, she had described a visit in the company of her husband and another, unnamed, person to the home of Klaas Meyer-Gerhards in June 1945. Meyer-Gerhards had allegedly told the Garrels couple of a confrontation between himself and Heinrich Heinemann, in which mutual recriminations of involvement in the attacks were exchanged. Frau Garrels also claimed that Meyer-Gerhards later tried to persuade her to reveal nothing of what he had shared with the couple to American investigators, an effort that had seemingly failed and that contributed to the fact that both he and Heinemann became defendants.[24] In spite of his wife's assurances that he had been in Emden on the day of the murders, Gerhard Garrels had been among the accused, but he was not in the defendants' dock in Ludwigsburg, apparently because, although arrested, he could not be produced for trial.

Under direct examination for the prosecution by Captain John A. May, Frau Garrels presented a coherent repetition of both of her statements to Major Levine.[25] Cross-examination by the defense, however, made the picture somewhat murkier. In response to questioning by Dr. Metzler, one of the German defense attorneys, Frau Garrels first stated that she had told Levine that she had not been present when her husband had visited the home of Meyer-Gerhards but, in the next breath, testified that in fact she had been.[26] That contradiction might have been the result of momentary confusion on the part of the witness, but subsequent questioning by Captain Phelps suggested the possibility of perjury. Meyer-Gerhards had been Gerhard Garrels's superior in the wartime air-raid police, and Phelps had secured information indicating that bad blood had developed between the two men, which Frau Garrels admitted under cross-examination. Meyer-Gerhards had, in fact, been instrumental in Gerhard Garrels's having spent three days in jail for an undefined minor offense. Phelps probed the fact that Frau Garrels had made two statements to Levine on succeeding days. At the conclusion of the first, he pointed out, she had been asked by Levine if she had anything further to say, to which she had answered an unambiguous "no." Why, then, the second statement on the following day? When the witness answered evasively, Phelps proposed an explanation. Following the first sworn statement to Levine, Frau Garrels had approached Meyer-Gerhards and had asked him to sign an attestation to the effect that Gerhard Garrels had not been on Borkum on August 4, 1944. This, Meyer-Gerhards had refused to do, which Frau Garrels admitted. Moreover, Phelps indicated that he was in possession of an affidavit from the third man present at the alleged conversation involving the Garrels couple and Meyer-Gerhards, now identified as Franz Fleitner, asserting that the exchange described in Erna Garrels's second sworn statement had never taken place. But on this crucial point Frau Garrels refused to yield.[27]

Erna Garrels's cross-examination had indicated the possibility not only that she had committed perjury but also that interpersonal conflicts and tensions within the closely knit and isolated population of Borkum might be influencing testimony. That hypothesis was supported by information presented shortly after court convened on the morning of February 19. Karl Fick, who had already testified for the prosecution, had approached members of the prosecution staff with the allegation that relatives of the accused present in Ludwigsburg and witnesses were in contact with one another in a dining room apparently provided by the U.S. Army for German witnesses and family members of defendants and that the testimony of witnesses was in danger of being tainted thereby. No evidence was presented that witnesses had been influenced by such contact, however, and Fick's motives in bringing the supposed problem to the attention of the prosecution are unclear. As a witness for the prosecution, he may have been expressing his own discomfort at being in contact with relatives of the accused, many of whom he undoubtedly knew well. In any event, Colonel Jackson directed that measures be taken to ensure the future segregation of witnesses from members of defendants' families, a possibly impractical undertaking, as Major Bryan pointed out, due to severe limitations on available space. A warning to members of defendants' families to abstain from attempting to influence the testimony of witnesses may have been all that was attempted.[28]

The testimony of prosecution witnesses continued with mixed effect. Housewife Henni Eilers had told Levine a simple story of having been with her two children on the corner of Franz Habich and Bahnhof Strassen on the afternoon when #909 had descended on Borkum. She had seen the American prisoners and their guards approaching "in good order" with their hands raised, when Mayor Akkermann arrived and began to shout, "There you come, you murderers. How many women and children have you killed today? Civilians, beat them, kick them, and knock them down." But the only violence she had personally seen was a guard striking a prisoner in the side with the butt of his rifle for having lowered an arm and a civilian delivering a body punch to another American. Distressed, she had then retreated with her children into a shoemaker's shop until the tumult had subsided. Frau Eilers's testimony for the prosecution conformed in all essentials to the sworn statement she had made for Levine, but, under questioning by Captain Lyons, she added some significant detail. She and her children had been alone on the street corner when Mayor Akkermann had arrived, but, in response to his inflammatory shouting, people had begun to stream from their houses to a total, Eilers estimated, of "twenty to thirty." On the other hand, what had been a blow from a rifle butt in the statement to Levine now had become a "push" and the punch delivered by the civilian, a strike with the flat of the hand. Beyond Akkermann and a now deceased "Herr Wegman," whom she belatedly remembered having seen kick a prisoner, Frau Eilers was able to identify no one as an assailant.[29]

Perhaps the most articulate and in some ways the most compelling witness called by the prosecution was Fritz Vomel, a 44-year-old physician and a resident of Borkum since 1937. Vomel testified to having visited Mayor Akkermann after he had heard from some of his patients that seven American prisoners of war had been shot to death that afternoon and that the mayor had encouraged the population to attack them. Vomel claimed to have reproached Akkermann for his behavior, to which Akkermann had supposedly replied, "Do you perhaps have pity for these people who kill our women and children and have destroyed our cities? I don't understand your point of view."

Vomel's objections may not have been based on the moral nature of the atrocity but, rather, on its aesthetics. He testified that he had responded by pointing out that people under 15 years of age were not allowed to enter the town's slaughterhouse, yet defenseless prisoners had been murdered in the presence of women and children. If Akkermann had made a rejoinder, Vomel did not describe it.[30] Vomel also testified to having confronted August Haesiker, the commander of the Labor Service detachment on Borkum, as he was returning from his conversation with Akkermann. According to Vomel, he had declared to Haesiker that the people of Borkum would not have resorted to violence if the Labor Service men had not set an example by attacking the prisoners with their spades. Haesiker allegedly replied with a candor that suggested pride that he had given the order for the assault, to which Vomel claimed to have responded that, in that case, he should be ashamed.[31]

In its cross-examination, defense counsel made no effort to challenge Vomel's testimony but, rather, required him to expand upon it to the benefit of some of the defendants. Captain Hall elicited from Vomel a statement that Haesiker had not implicated anyone else in the decision to turn his Labor Service men loose on the prisoners, while, in response to questioning from Dr. Magenau, one of the German defense attorneys, the witness testified to Akkermann's basically decent, although "easily excited," personality. There had been people residing on Borkum who had been bombed out of their homes on the mainland (including Vomel's own mother), while Allied bombers passing overhead on their way to attack targets on the continent had driven Borkumers to air-raid shelters almost every day and night. All of this, plus the fact that occasional bombs jettisoned by aircraft in distress had produced scattered damage on the island may have made residents excitable and susceptible to incitements to violence.[32]

On the afternoon of February 19, the prosecution wrapped up its case with two witnesses who were questioned about neither the murderers nor the alleged perpetrators. Otto Mennenga (not to be confused with defendant Gustav Mammenga) had been a naval chief petty officer and medic at Borkum's naval hospital at the time of the murders. The bodies of the murdered crew members of #909 had been brought there (Graham had been alive when he arrived at the hospital but died shortly after his arrival), and Mennenga was ordered to examine the corpses and prepare a report. When questioned on the witness stand more than a year and a half later, he remembered that each victim had been wounded in the head and had a bloody and swollen face but no other wounds or bruises.[33] Mennenga's testimony was followed by that of Johann Eilgs, a 62-year-old gravedigger at Borkum's Lutheran cemetery. On August 5, 1944, he had driven to the naval hospital to collect the corpses of the murdered Americans, by now sewn into shrouds, and to transport them to the cemetery for burial. There, the bodies had been interred, each in its own grave, and the victims' names entered in the church registry by Pastor Doebbles, who conducted a burial service for the men of #909. Each grave had been marked with a simple white cross bearing the name of the deceased and the date of his death.[34]

Among the perceived advantages to the prosecution of Mennenga's and Eilgs's testimony may have been the idea that, inasmuch as the two men were the last witnesses called by the prosecution, they were appropriate figures with whom to close the case by underlining the mortal consequences of the defendants' conduct. At the same time, however, their testimony, particularly that of Eilgs, served to humanize, if not the defendants, then at least the community in which the murders had taken place. The bodies of #909's crew had clearly been accorded dignified treatment, although one of the judges, Colonel Robert N. Hicks, may have been disturbed that the corpses had been interred in canvas shrouds, rather than coffins, and questioned Eilgs on that point. Eilgs responded simply that Germans on Borkum were being buried in that manner also, because the supplies of wood on the island for coffins had been exhausted. Hicks seemed satisfied.[35]

Defense counsel now chose to revert to the stratagem that it had employed at the start of the trial—a challenge to the authority of a military government court to try defendants who were members of Germany's armed forces. The court had already spoken clearly on this issue, and the defense could not have been optimistic as to the likely outcome of Captain Hall's motion that all charges against Kurt Goebell, the senior military defendant, be dismissed on the grounds that the court lacked jurisdiction to try him. Perhaps it reflected a desire to demonstrate lawyerly ingenuity or a conscientious determination to pursue every conceivable avenue of defense in a case likely to have grim consequences for the defendants. In any event, Captain Hall's arguments were intriguing, if also, in practical terms, a waste of time.

Once again, the foundation of the challenge to the court's jurisdiction was Article 63 of the 1929 Geneva Convention on the treatment of prisoners of war, of which both the United States and Germany had been signatories. That article, it may be recalled, specified that prisoners of war were to be tried by the same courts and according to the same procedures as members of the armed forces of the detaining power.

As Hall must have known, trial by U.S. Army court-martial, with its stricter standards of evidence, would not have guaranteed a more favorable outcome for the military defendants. In 1944, for example, seven captured German U-boat crewmen held in the United States were tried by court-martial for the murder of another German POW suspected of collaborating with his captors amid allegations that confessions had been extracted under torture. All were convicted and hanged at Fort Leavenworth.[36] Unlike the Borkum defendants, there had been no question of the status of those seven Germans sailors as prisoners of war to whom Article 63 of the Geneva Convention applied. According to Captain Hall, there should have been none either in the case of Captain Goebell and, by implication, the other defendants who had held military rank at the end of the war. Discharging those men as prisoners of war and reducing their status to that of civilians on suspicion of their having committed war crimes, and thus denying them the protections of the Geneva Convention, was comparable, Hall argued, to annulling the citizenship of an American upon charging him with a crime for which the penalty is loss of that citizenship.[37] Major Bryan's response skirted the issue of status, preferring the citation of U.S. regulations in *Rules of Land Warfare* and *Technical Manual for Legal and Prison Officers* that permitted the trial by military government courts of persons suspected of having committed war crimes and the observation that the German government had ceased to exist, its authority, including that to try German citizens, having passed into the hands of the occupying powers.[38] In any event, whether or not the defendants were prisoners of war was, from a juridical standpoint, irrelevant. A majority of the U.S. Supreme Court had already held that Article 63 applied only to offenses committed by prisoners of war subsequent to capture (the situation of the captured U-boat crewmen), although Associate Justice Wiley Rutledge had found that conclusion invalid and the arguments in support of it strained and unconvincing.[39] But no one in the Ludwigsburg courtroom could have been surprised when the president of the court, Colonel Jackson, denied the defense motion.[40] Similar motions on behalf of the remaining military defendants were similarly rejected.

In making largely pro forma motions to dismiss charges against defendants who had not held military rank and to whom the Geneva

Convention offered no protection, the defense adopted a more mundane stratagem. Following the opening of court on the morning of February 20, Captain Phelps moved that murder charges against Heinrich Heinemann and Gustav Mammenga and all charges against Heinrich Rommel and Klaas Meyer-Gerhards be dropped on the grounds of insufficient evidence. Phelps pointed out that the only evidence against Heinemann and Mammenga was that they had struck a prisoner, Mammenga admitting having done so. Neither could have foreseen the appearance of the hate-filled Langer with his pistol. Phelps caustically noted that he had witnessed the beating and stoning of German POWs as they had been marched through French towns with no expectation that someone in the crowd would shoot them. As far as Rommel and Meyer-Gerhards were concerned, there was no evidence that either had committed any acts of violence whatsoever against the Americans. Meyer-Gerhards, in fact, had ordered the mortally wounded Graham carried into the air-raid police office and had called for an ambulance.[41]

Phelps's motion gave the prosecution the opportunity to further develop a critical element in its case, one that had not been clearly articulated in the original charges brought against the defendants. Quite apart from acts of violence that each personally might or might not have committed, all had allegedly participated in an illegal common design or conspiracy, the outcome of which had been the ill treatment and deaths of the seven captured crewmen of the B-17, and all were, consequently, guilty of those crimes.[42]

Conspiracy is a slippery legal concept, easy to state—an agreement between or among two or more persons to perpetrate a crime—but often problematic to prove, inasmuch as there is seldom unambiguous evidence to demonstrate its existence.[43] To a greater degree than many other offenses, its presence may lie in the eye of the beholder. The temptation to stretch the concept beyond the point warranted by the evidence may be particularly strong in cases involving collective threats or injuries to the nation.[44] It is an efficient means of dealing judicially with multiple enemies.

In arguing the charge of criminal conspiracy, both prosecution and defense relied heavily on the venerable *Wharton's Criminal Law*, first published in the mid-19th century (and still in print). What May's opening citation sounded like in the rough and not always ready translation of the courtroom to Germans who were unfamiliar with

Anglo-American legal concepts is difficult to imagine: "All those who assemble themselves together with an intent to commit a wrongful act, the execution whereof makes probable in the nature of things a crime not specifically designed but incidental to that which was the object of the confederacy, are responsible for such incidental crime."[45] But how was the existence of the "confederacy" to be proved? According to *Wharton's*:

> The actual fact of conspiracy may be inferred . . . from circumstances and the concurring conduct of the defendants need not be directly proved. Any joint action on a material point or collocation of independent but cooperative action by persons closely associated with each other is held to be sufficient to enable the jury to infer concurrence of sentiment, and one competent witness will suffice to prove the cooperation of any individual conspirator.[46]

In regard to membership in "riotous and tumultuous assemblies," as the crowds that lined Borkum's streets on the afternoon of August 4, 1944, arguably had been, May quoted *Wharton* to the effect that "All persons who are present and not actually assisting in their suppression may, where their presence is intentional and where it tends to the encouragement of the rioters, be *prima facie* inferred to be participants."[47]

According to this principle, it appeared that only those Borkumers in attendance who had attempted to intervene on behalf of the prisoners, as Elizabeth Biermann had claimed to have done, were clearly excluded from the conspiracy so defined. But did their guilt extend to actual murder? There was no doubt of that, argued May:

> Of course, the Defense will contend that Langer is the guilty man, that he fired the shots. Let us look into that for a moment. Why did Langer do this? You know a mob sometimes gives courage to a coward. A coward will do things when incited by a mob that he would not do otherwise. . . . Was not the coward Langer encouraged to do what he did by the action and, as the law says, the accessory? The man who aids and abets it is just as guilty if he stood by and aided and abetted in the commission of the crime. Yes, there was a common design in this case, all equally guilty. A damnable plan . . . that they designed there to torture, to abuse, and to murder these American flyers.[48]

Whether Langer's actions are best characterized as those of a coward rather than a man crazed with grief and hatred is debatable, but the defense could also quote *Wharton*. Phelps noted that May had been selective in his citation of the section dealing with the liability of members of a conspiracy or common design. *Wharton*, he pointed out, also argues that

> Where, however, a homicide is committed collaterally by one or more of a body unlawfully associated, from causes having no connection with the common object, the responsibility for such homicide attaches exclusively to its actual perpetrators. . . .[49]

Had the prosecution offered any evidence, asked Phelps, that the defendants had conspired to murder the prisoners? *Wharton*, he pointed out, also holds that "a rioter is not responsible . . . for a death accidentally caused by officers engaged in suppressing the riot , nor in an affray are the original parties responsible for a death caused by strangers wantonly and adversely breaking in."[50]

The latter characterization seemed to fit Langer's role reasonably well. Phelps accepted *Wharton*'s dictum that, in a riot, "all present and not suppressing are participants," but that, he argued, meant merely that his clients had been rioters, not murderers, and that there were many other Borkumers in that category who were not on trial.[51] Similar motions to dismiss charges were made on behalf of the remaining civilian defendants. Dr. Magenau, civilian German defense counsel for ex-mayor Jan Akkermann, in a gesture to which the adjective "quixotic" might be appropriately applied, argued that his client was subject only to German law, inasmuch as "it is a basis of law throughout the world that a criminal can only be punished by the law of the scene where the crime was committed." Under German law, he continued, a person can be punished only for a crime in which he has taken an active part or that he has encouraged, aided, or abetted. Akkermann might have encouraged, aided, or abetted the beating of the prisoners, but no evidence supported the notion that Akkermann intended that the prisoners were to be shot to death. His later apparent approval of the murders was legally irrelevant.[52] But the brutal reality was that sovereignty in Germany had passed to the major Allied powers, who were free to do as they pleased. The prosecution did not deign to comment, and the court summarily denied all motions to dismiss.[53]

Defense counsel, as its members had certainly anticipated, had no recourse but to call witnesses to rebut the evidence that the prosecution had presented in the course of the previous two weeks. But it was unprepared to do so. This was due, not to the attorneys' lack of industry but to the enormous burden of bringing to some kind of trial the huge numbers of Germans under suspicion of having committed war crimes. All American members of the defense team had been engaged in other trials until almost literally the eve of the Borkum proceedings, and they had had barely time to identify the witnesses they would require, much less locate and secure them, while the prosecution case had, in effect, been in preparation since the previous June. They had raised this as an objection to going to trial at the scheduled time but had been told that they might request a continuance if that should prove necessary by the time the prosecution had completed presenting its case. It was necessary. Not only would defense witnesses not begin to arrive before Saturday (it was now Wednesday), but also others would be even later. Moreover, the U.S. defense team had been ordered to prosecute another case before the conclusion of the Borkum trial. Little wonder that trials of multiple defendants alleged to have been parties to conspiracies or common designs were commonplace. In no other way could the Army hope to process the masses of Germans awaiting trial, but justice sometimes suffered as a consequence. A continuance already having been assured, the court adjourned until February 27.[54]

NOTES

1. "Special Orders Number 33," February 2, 1946, Headquarters Seventh United States Army, *U.S. v. Goebell et al.* (microfilm, frame 259, reel 1); "Record of Testimony," 1, ibid. (frame 551); Maximilian Koessler, "American War Crimes Trials in Europe," *Georgetown Law Journal* 39 (1950–51): 30.

2. "War Crimes Branch, Summary Work Sheet," November 16, 1945, *U.S. v. Goebell et al.* (microfilm, frames 266-67, reel 1).

3. "Incidents Noted by E. F. Lyons," *Edward F. Lyons, Jr. Papers*, M14, 7, 13, 46, 80, and various unpaginated fragments, Snell Library, Northeastern University, Boston, MA.

4. "Record of Testimony," 2–3, *U.S. v. Goebell et al.* (microfilm, frames 552–53, reel 1). The fact that there was no lawyer among the officers hearing the case was in violation of military government regulations. See Military Government Germany, *Technical Manual for Legal and Prison Officers* (n.p., n.d.), Document XII-A, 1.

5. "Record of Testimony," 11–12 (frames 561–62).

6. Ibid., 14–19 (frames 564–69).

7. Ibid., 19–30 (frames 569–80).

8. Ibid., 50–51, 59 (frames 600–601, 609).

9. Ibid., 68–80 (frames 618–30).

10. Ibid., 87–88, 97–99 (frames 637–38, 647–49).

11. Ibid., 312–13 (frames 864–65).

12. Richard Wiggers, "From Supreme Authority to Reserved Rights and Responsibilities: The International Legal Basis of German-American Relations," in *The United States and Germany in the Era of the Cold War,* ed. Detlef Junker, vol. 1 (New York: Cambridge University Press, 2004), 103–5.

13. On rules of evidence, see *Technical Manual for Legal and Prison Officers,* Document XII-A, 5; War Department Technical Manual 27–255, *Military Justice Procedure* (Washington, DC: U.S. Government Printing Office, 1945), 88–89; United Nations War Crimes Commission, *Law Reports of Trials of War Criminals* 1, Annex 2 (London: His Majesty's Stationery Office, 1947), 117–18; Koessler, "American War Crimes Trials in Europe," 69–76.

14. "Record of Testimony," 100–113 (frames 650–63); A. Frank Reel, *The Case of General Yamashita* (Chicago: University of Chicago Press, 1949), 218; Koessler, "American War Crimes Trials in Europe," 48–49.

15. "Testimony of Karl Fick," October 16, 1945, 2–3, *U.S. v. Goebell et al.* (microfilm, frames 385–86, reel 1); "Record of Testimony," 345, 364–65, 367, ibid. (frames 900, 919–20, 922).

16. "Testimony of Hermann Staats," October 11, 1945, 3, ibid. (frame 281); "Record of Testimony," 371–72, ibid. (frames 926–27).

17. "Testimony of Gerhardt Stindt," November 5, 1945, 3–5, ibid. (frames 491–93); "Record of Testimony," 377A, 380, ibid. (frames 933, 937).

18. "Testimony of Klaas Adel," October 18, 1945, 2–3, ibid. (frames 475–76); "Record of Testimony," 387–88, ibid. (frames 944–45).

19. "Testimony of Johann Grupengiesser," October 12, 1945, 2–3, ibid. (frames 450–51); "Record of Testimony," 397–98, 402, ibid. (frames 955–56, 960).

20. "Testimony of Elizabeth Biermann," October 12, 1945, 3, ibid. (frame 472); "Record of Testimony," 405, 407, ibid. (frames 963, 965).

21. Ibid., 419, 421 (frames 977, 979).

22. Ibid., 424–27 (frames 982–85).

23. "Testimony of Erna Garrels," October 18, 1945, 2–3, ibid. (frames 424–25).

24. "Testimony of Erna Garrels," October 19, 1945, 2, ibid. (frame 428).

25. "Record of Testimony," 431–32, ibid. (frames 989–90).

26. Ibid., 433 (frame 991).

27. "Record of Testimony," 435–46, ibid. (frames 993–1004).

28. Ibid., 451–54 (frames 1009–12).

29. "Testimony of Henni Eilers," October 17, 1945, 2–4, ibid. (frames 412–14); "Record of Testimony," 455–56, 459, ibid. (frames 1013–14, 1017).

30. Ibid., 462 (frame 1020).

31. Ibid., 463–64 (frames 1021–22).

32. Ibid., 464–66, 468–70 (frames 1022–24, 1026–28).

33. Ibid., 476–77 (frames 1034–35).

34. Ibid., 478–80 (frames 1036–38).

35. Ibid., 482 (frame 1040).

36. Richard Whittingham, *Martial Justice: The Last Mass Execution in the United States* (Annapolis, MD: Naval Institute Press, 1971), 153–219, 287.

37. "Record of Testimony," 482–85, ibid. (frames 1040–43).

38. Ibid., 486–88 (frames 1044–46).

39. *Yamashita v. Styer*, December 4, 1946, 6, "International Humanitarian Law, National Implementation," http://www.icrc.org; A. Frank Reel, *The Case of General Yamashita* (Chicago: University of Chicago Press, 1949), 267–69.

40. "Record of Testimony," 490, ibid. (frame 1048).

41. Ibid., 491–95 (frames 1049–53).

42. On the concepts of conspiracy and common design and their roles in the Army's war crimes trials, see Koessler, "American War Crimes Trials in Europe," 82–83. In the Borkum trial, the two terms appear to have been used interchangeably.

43. "Conspiracy," *Oxford Companion to American Law*, ed. Kermit L. Hall (New York: Oxford University Press, 2002), 144–45.

44. On this point, see Marie E. Siesseger, "Conspiracy Theory: The Use of the Conspiracy Doctrine in Times of National Crisis," *William and Mary Law Review* 46 (December 2004): 1177–78.

45. "Record of Testimony," 497 (frame 1055).

46. Ibid., 497–98 (frames 1055–56).

47. Ibid., 498 (frame 1056).

48. Ibid., 499 (frame 1057).

49. Ibid., 500–501 (frames 1058–59).

50. Ibid., 501 (frame 1059).

51. Ibid., 502 (frame 1060).

52. Ibid., 506–7 (frames 1064–65).

53. Ibid., 508–9, 52 (frames 1066–67, 1079).

54. Ibid., 521 (frame 1079).

4

"Worms on the Ground"

When court reconvened, the defense opened with testimony from the defendants, which, like that of prosecution witnesses, sometimes differed from the sworn statements they had made to Major Levine the previous fall. Gustav Mammenga had testified to Major Levine the previous November that he had been on duty in the office of the air-raid police on the afternoon of August 4, 1944. Mayor Akkermann had telephoned the office and, according to Mammenga, had said to someone whom he had claimed not to know, "Now we will see what you air-raid policemen are made of." The meaning of the statement was unclear, even nonsensical, but it was apparently uttered in the context of notifying the air-raid police that the American prisoners were about to be marched through town. In light of the fate that was about to befall the crew of #909, Akkermann's words assumed a sinister import, an interpretation supported by other elements of Mammenga's testimony. He admitted that, as the prisoners and their guards approached, he had left his office and had struck the small flyer who was having trouble with his pants "two or three times" with his open hand. This, he had told Levine, had been in response to the "order" that had been received by his office from Akkermann. Shortly thereafter, he had heard a shot and seen a soldier with pistol in hand standing over the prostrate form of "the little flyer." Mammenga's, superior, Klaas Meyer-Gerhards, had then ordered the mortally wounded Graham carried inside the air-raid police office. But, when under direct examination by defense counsel, Mammenga had testified that *he* had taken the phone call from Akkermann, had not attached any significance to it, and had "slapped" one of the prisoners twice on the back when he had heard someone yell, "Beat them, beat them, they killed my wife and my child," which brought to his mind his son, who had been killed in action. He had not hit the prisoner very hard, however, as he had been recovering from injuries suffered in a motorcycle accident. As he was about to return to his office, Mammenga testified that he heard a shot, turned, and saw a soldier holding a pistol, the same soldier, he thought, whom he had heard yelling. In this version of the events, Mammenga denied that the American who had been shot was the same one he had hit. The prisoner was carried into the air-raid police office, where Mammenga claimed to have provided him with a pillow and wiped blood from his face. When questioned by the defense concerning the inconsistencies between his courtroom testimony and that given earlier to Levine, Mammenga's explanations were vague.[1] But, by giving the witness the opportunity to testify that he and his comrades had attached no particular importance to Akkermann's phone call and that some solicitude had been shown for the mortally wounded Howard Graham, the testimony may have made somewhat less plausible the prosecution's contention that the murders of the American airmen had been the products of a criminal conspiracy.

Heinrich Heinemann testified that, on the afternoon of August 4, 1944, he had been working in his father's butcher shop when he learned from customers that downed American flyers were being marched through Borkum and would be passing the shop in a few minutes. Heinrich summoned two French prisoners of war who were employed in Heinemann's shop to accompany him to watch the procession.[2] When questioned by Levine on October 17, 1945, Heinemann had described a chaotic scene in which, as the prisoners and their guards marched by, civilians were running around the street but not attacking the prisoners. Heinemann had returned to the butcher shop but then set out on his bicycle to catch up to the procession after having been told by a customer that one of the prisoners had been shot at the town hall. On arriving there, he found no one and continued on, finding six prisoners, their guards, and a crowd near the Dorf Hotel. There, he saw "mostly all" of the guards hitting the Americans with their rifle butts while Lieutenants Weber and Wentzel and Captain Krolikovski looked on impassively. Heinemann claimed to have paused for a chat with some of the onlookers, taking the opportunity to denounce the brutal treatment of the prisoners. Pedaling on, he heard shots and saw a tall soldier with a long face and "a brutal look in his eyes" methodically shoot each of the remaining prisoners in the back of the head with a 7.65 mm pistol. One of the guards, whom he described as a petty officer with a heavy mustache, shot two of the Americans a second time with his *Pistole 08*. "Upset and excited," he hurried home.[3]

In the weeks that followed, Heinrich Heinemann had found reasons to reconsider elements of his self-exculpating statement. One of these was probably the fact that, subsequent to his sworn statement to Levine of October 17, Karl Weber had sworn to having seen Heinemann beat a prisoner. On November 5, he reappeared in Levine's office to make a supplementary statement. Civilian spectators, including himself, had not been entirely passive, it appeared. In a revision of his account of having pursued the procession on his bicycle, Heinemann alleged that he had tried to pass the prisoners and their guards but had lost his balance and, trying to avoid falling, had "pushed" the shoulder of one of the Americans twice, propelling him to one side. He had also seen a now deceased civilian named Wegman hit some of the prisoners.[4] On the stand in Ludwigsburg, Heinemann was clearly nervous and apprehensive. When questioned about the alleged "accident" and whether he had actually hit one of the Americans, Heinemann responded with frantic defensiveness: "No, I did not hit any one of them. I am not guilty and I just got into this thing!" When asked why he had made a second statement to Levine about the allegedly inoffensive shoving of the American, Heinemann replied piously, "Because my conscience told me that it was only the right thing to do, to tell the whole truth." He denied that his "conscience" might have been stimulated by Levine's suggestion that he had witnesses to Heinemann's beating of a prisoner, but he was no longer willing to assert that almost all of the guards had struck the prisoners, and some of the blows had possibly become mere "pushes." Melodrama thickened with Heinemann's irrelevant assertion that he had resigned from the SA (Storm Troopers) as a consequence of a boycott against his father's shop by the Nazi Party and SA because his family were "half-Jews."[5] Ironically, an ethnic status that, a year earlier, had brought peril to the holder was now sought for protection.

Major Bryan's cross-examination was heavy with sarcasm, as he led Heinemann through a recounting of his pursuit of the column on his bicycle, "because of sheer curiosity, I never had seen foreign soldiers before." Bryan's mocking reaction to that explanation was followed by a savaging of the witness's description of his "accidental" contact with a prisoner as he allegedly attempted to prevent himself from falling:

BRYAN: You merely placed your hand on one, is that all you did?

HEINEMANN: That is true. I was going past the column of flyers in front of the Rathaus, [and] all of a sudden one man from the crowd of people jumped in front of my bicycle and I commenced to fall, so I supported myself with my left hand on the flyer's right shoulder. . . .

BRYAN: So all you did was place your hand on the flyer's shoulder, is that all?

HEINEMANN: Yes.

BRYAN: And you saw the guards just push the flyers with the butts of their rifles, is that all you saw?

HEINEMANN: Either push them or tap them.

BRYAN: And is that just as true as everything else you have testified about?

HEINEMANN: Yes.[6]

If Heinrich Heinemann's testimony was a gift to the prosecution, Heinrich Rommel's was more likely to elicit a measure of sympathy from the court. Heinemann had been free to avoid personal involvement in the events of August 4, 1944, but not Rommel. He, along with Karl Fick, had constituted Borkum's tiny police force on that fatal afternoon. Rommel, but not Fick, was a defendant because he had been in the police station at around three o'clock when the telephone had rung. The caller had been the senior naval officer on the island, Captain Goebell. Rommel's testimony did not diverge significantly in its essentials from his sworn statement made to Levine the previous October, but questions from multiple defense attorneys, both U.S. Army and German civilian, elicited additional detail. Rommel was questioned closely on the exact language used by Goebell in his phone call and expressed certainty that Goebell had used the word "unfortunately" in regard to the capture of the seven Americans and had drawn his attention to the "edict" of Reich Minister Goebbels. Rommel professed ignorance of the intent of Goebell's phone call and testified that he had been "worried" by the information that the prisoners were going to be marched through town, rather than transported by vehicle, as had been earlier practice. He claimed in Ludwigsburg, as he had done in his earlier statement to Major Levine, that he had never heard of Goebbels's "edict," which in any event had not been a formal directive but merely an editorial opinion. That such distinctions had been seriously blurred in the administrative and moral chaos of the Third Reich was an important issue that, however, was not broached. But, if he had been in the dark about the purpose of Captain Goebell's phone call and concerned about the mode of transportation, why had he not asked for clarification? When pressed on those points, Rommel answered incongruously that "I never gave it a second thought" and lamely added, "What could I have answered or told the commander of the island, the highest officer present?"[7] Rommel also provided a more dramatic account of his post-surrender confrontation with Goebell. He had sought out Goebell in his office as he investigated an incident in which a resident of Borkum had been killed after wandering into a minefield that had presumably been laid by the island's naval forces during the war. Goebell took the opportunity to ask Rommel about the mood of the townspeople, observing, "I never get a chance to get out of here and see anything." Rommel responded that the populace was apprehensive about the possibility of Allied retaliation for the killing of the Americans and was blaming the naval commander for having failed to prevent it. That, Rommel testified, had precipitated an explosive exchange:

GOEBELL: I? It was not my fault. I had nothing to do with it. It was the fault of those who incited the population and those who hit the flyers.

ROMMEL: Captain, in that case, why did you speak to me over the telephone about it?

GOEBELL: It was your job to protect the flyers.

ROMMEL: Then, Captain, why did you refer me to the edict of Reichminister Goebbels?

GOEBELL: I never did such a thing.

ROMMEL: Captain, I have nothing else to speak to you about in this matter.

In fact, Rommel testified, he had an additional request for Goebell. "Then," he testified to have said, "you better [sic] give me a pistol and I will kill myself because I don't want to have anything to do with this whole mess." Rommel had not killed himself at that time and became very much a part of the "whole mess." While being transported by British occupation forces to the mainland for the trip to Ludwigsburg, however, he had jumped from the boat into Emden harbor in an apparent attempt at suicide.[8] It was unsuccessful, and Rommel found himself on trial, possibly for his life.

Subsequent to his brief phone conversation with Goebell on August 4, 1944, as he had informed Levine four months earlier, Rommel had telephoned Gestapo commissioner Struwe on the mainland for guidance and was informed that the transport of the American prisoners was a military matter, for which the police had no responsibility. He had then taken a call from Mayor Akkermann, who directed Rommel to inform the commander of Borkum's emergency service, identified only as "Boelts," of the prisoners' impending arrival in the town and to mention that Goebell had made reference to Reich Minister Goebbels's "edict." Rommel had then set out on his bicycle for Boelts's house, intending to continue on to the police station. He found Boelts wary, declaring that he knew nothing about a Goebbels edict, although admitting that he had read "once or twice" in the newspaper and perhaps heard on the radio that protection should not be given to downed Allied aircrew because of the prevailing state of "total war." Nevertheless, Rommel testified, Boelts had declared that he and his men would have nothing to do with any demonstration against the captured Americans and believed that the police should hold themselves aloof, as well, a position with which the witness had expressed agreement. Proceeding from Boelts's house to the police station, Rommel claimed to have encountered a few soldiers who told him that Labor Service men had been fired on by #909 as it approached the *Muschelfeld* for its emergency landing.[9] It seems unlikely that aircrewmen about to carry out an emergency landing in enemy territory would have been so foolish as to fire at persons at whose mercy they were likely to soon find themselves, although the possibility cannot be entirely excluded. One or more of the B-17's gunners might have fired reflexively at Germans on the ground in response to heavy fire from Borkum's guns. Another defendant claimed that he had found expended American .50-caliber ammunition on the beach near the crash-landed bomber. Even if the Americans had fired, of course, their captors would not have been justified in abusing and ultimately killing them after capture, although, if civilians had been the apparent targets, Goebbels's oft-cited "edict" would appear to have applied. But Rommel had not included this allegation in his statement to Levine the previous October, and why he should have presented it now is unclear, as it was of little value to his own defense. In any event, no effort was made by either prosecution or defense attorneys to probe the matter more deeply. Nor, at this point in the trial, did either the defense or the prosecution appear to have been aware of Himmler's earlier and more relevant order to police officials not to intervene in situations in which civilians attacked captured Allied airmen, and Rommel did not raise it, suggesting the possibility that he, if not Gestapo commissioner Struwe, was unaware of it. Rommel went on to testify that he had been at the police station when he learned of the murder of the prisoners and had proceeded to the scene, where he blocked off the area where the bodies lay at the behest of one of the naval officers who was present.

Rommel's degree of responsibility, if any, for the protection of the American prisoners was the issue central to his presence in Ludwigsburg as a defendant. His defense was based on the directive he had received from Struwe to the effect that the transport of the prisoners was a purely military affair and on the argument that he, as a policeman, lacked jurisdiction over military personnel. But, if the matter of the American prisoners was a purely military affair, asked Captain May for the prosecution, why had he accepted orders from a naval officer to secure the murder scene? And what was the nature of the authority over him wielded by Akkermann? Had it been as mayor or as local leader of the Nazi Party? When Rommel was pressed to respond to the question of whom he would have obeyed—the naval commander of the island or the mayor/party leader—if the two had given him contradictory orders, this simple official was reduced to responding with a plaintive "Everything happens to me now at this time. I never thought about it before." In any case, it was irrelevant to the fact that Rommel had made no effort to protect the Americans because he had been told by his police superior on the mainland that the conveying of the prisoners through the town was a purely military responsibility.[10]

Klaas Meyer-Gerhards's testimony in Ludwigsburg went well beyond his sworn statement made to Major Levine the previous October. Questioned by German civilian defense counsel Metzler about his activities as chief of Borkum's air-raid police, Meyer-Gerhards explained that he had been asked to join the organization in 1940 because he was the only person on the island who was able to drive an automobile and had assumed the position of leadership of a force of 32 men and 8 female nurses in August 1943. His men had been unarmed until near the end of the war, when they had been conscripted into the Nazi last-ditch militia, the *Volkssturm*. Number 909 had not been the first Allied bomber that Meyer-Gerhards had seen on Borkum. In 1942, an RAF bomber had crashed about 30 meters from the main motor route outside town. When Meyer-Gerhards arrived on the scene with medical personnel in an ambulance, he found the aircraft in flames but managed to extract four of the crew alive. Two of them subsequently died, possibly the occupants of the graves in Borkum's Lutheran cemetery alongside of which the murdered crewmen of #909 had been buried. At least prior to their absorption into the *Volkssturm*, the defendant emphasized, the job of the air-raid police was "saving lives and extinguishing fires"—"Saving Lives Is the Main Job" was their motto, he claimed. As he had informed Levine, Meyer-Gerhards testified in Ludwigsburg that he had seen #909 descending towards the *Muschelfeld* on August 4, 1944, and had driven to the crash site with several of his subordinates. By the time they arrived, the prisoners had been removed. Meyer-Gerhards ordered "keep-out" signs to be posted, then departed. In his statement to Levine the previous October, he testified that he had gone home for lunch and a nap. His siesta had been interrupted by a phone call from one of his men with the information that Akkermann had telephoned the air-raid police office wanting to speak with him. He tried to return the call but found the mayor's line busy and left for his headquarters in the Central Hotel on Seldte Strasse. It was at this point that that his courtroom testimony diverged significantly from his sworn statement. In the latter, his narrative went directly to a description of his encounter with the column of prisoners and their guards near his office, the shooting of Graham, and the carrying of the mortally wounded "little flyer" into the air-raid police office, where Meyer-Gerhards claimed to have prevented Langer from delivering the coup de grace. Testifying in Ludwigsburg, Meyer-Gerhards embellished his story with a suspiciously self-exculpating account of a phone conversation with Akkermann that had supposedly occurred after the defendant had reached his office but before the prisoners had arrived. Akkermann had allegedly informed him of Goebell's decision to march the prisoners through the town, of Dr. Goebbels's "decree" in regard to downed Allied airman, and his desire that "an example be set." Meyer-Gerhards claimed to have indignantly rejected any suggestion that the air-raid police should participate in a demonstration against the prisoners with a peremptory "You can't give me such an order."[11]

Meyer-Gerhards's account of subsequent events was also more dramatic and favorable to himself (and other Borkumers) than his statement to Levine. He testified that, on hearing the approach of the American prisoners and their guards, he terminated his conversation with Akkermann and stepped outside. Almost immediately, he saw

Howard Graham fall to the pavement about three meters from the door to his headquarters and a German soldier push his way through the crowd of onlookers and fire a pistol at the fallen American. General pandemonium ensued, with spectators shouting "That's low," "That's dirty," and "That's unfair," while Meyer-Gerhards ordered Graham carried into the air-raid police office. Two of his subordinates took Graham by the head and feet, while Meyer-Gerhards supported his midsection. Ordering personnel in his headquarters to administer immediate first aid, he went to his phone to summon an ambulance but was interrupted by Langer, who had entered the office with pistol in hand and the offer to "finish him off." As Meyer-Gerhards had told Levine, he responded with outrage and told Langer to "get the hell out of here" and "that man is not an animal." Langer ran outside and Meyer-Gerhards, locking the door, called for an ambulance. Anticipating an obvious query from the prosecution, Metzler asked why Meyer-Gerhards had made no effort to arrest or restrain Langer. The air-raid police were unarmed, he explained, and lacked the authority to arrest anyone. He claimed, moreover, to have been in shock. "I am fifty years old. I participated in the First World War. In other words, I have participated in eleven years of war. That was the most terrible experience I have ever had in my life."[12]

It was in the interest of all of the defendants that the court be reminded that it had been the absent Langer, and not they, who had actually murdered the American prisoners. Meyer-Gerhards testified that, while he had not known Langer personally, a friend of his had and had described him as a man with an "evil personality," some of which was attributable to head injuries suffered in World War I, although the loss of his wife and children had made him "crazier yet." Langer's problematic behavior was illustrated by a bizarre anecdote involving a cat he had been given and on which he seemed to dote. After having showered affection on the animal and catching small fish for it to eat, he suddenly seized it and placed it in a barrel of tar, where it died. "This man was the harm [sic] of our island," Meyer-Gerhards observed.

Yet, the "harm of the island" might have been prevented from killing the remaining prisoners if he had been restrained after his assault on Graham, and Meyer-Gerhards had, arguably, been in the best position to have done that. Why, Major Bryan asked for the prosecution (as Metzler had anticipated), had he made no effort to do so? The defendant repeated that he had had no authority over military personnel and that, in any event, he had been unarmed and concerned primarily with protecting Graham from further harm. When asked why, if he had ordered Langer to leave the air-raid police office, he had not also demanded that Langer surrender his pistol, Meyer-Gerhards replied not without plausibility, "That a man in such a rage would have never given me his pistol. That was an impossibility." Although admitting that if Langer had been "exterminated," "the rest of it could have been prevented," the damaging fact was that he had made no effort whatever to restrain the murderer.[13]

The morning of Monday, March 4, saw the appearance in the witness chair of one of the key defendants and a central figure in the Borkum atrocity, former mayor and local Nazi Party leader Jan Akkermann. Under questioning by Dr. Magenau, one of the German civilian defense lawyers, Akkermann described his roots in the petit bourgeoisie, one of the mainstays of support for the Nazi Party as it was struggling to come to power. He had been born on Borkum in 1892 and had lived almost all of his life there, running a grocery store and rooming house and, along with his wife, raising two daughters and two sons. He had been a public-spirited resident, too, having become a member of Borkum's School and Resort Councils in 1924. But "public spirit" had had a sinister political dimension. Akkermann had joined the Nazi Party in December 1930, a few months after it achieved its first great electoral success in national politics. In 1932, he had become *Ortsgruppenleiter* or local party boss of Borkum, antecedent to his assumption of the office of mayor, in 1935. Akkermann did his best to portray himself as an honorable citizen and family man, which, in his own restricted terms, he may well have been. He had not used his positions as mayor and party leader to enhance his business, he assured the court, nor did he lie, steal, cheat, or "whore." His multiple responsibilities resulted in chronic overwork, and this, combined with an impulsive personality, he implied, helped explain his behavior on the afternoon of August 4, 1944. His own experience a few days before had also been relevant. He had visited Emden, where his meal in a restaurant had been interrupted by an air-raid alarm. Returning to the scene the following day, he found the area flattened by bombs.[14]

While Akkermann had attempted to offer extenuating circumstances for his conduct on August 4, 1944, he made no effort to seriously challenge what other witnesses had testified about it as, indeed, he had abstained from doing in his sworn statement to Major Levine. He had been at home when a phone call from Goebell's headquarters informed him of the capture of the Americans and the intention to march them through the town "in accordance of the decree of Dr. Goebbels." He had phoned the air-raid police office and encouraged them to "show now the kind of guys you are" but passed it off as the kind of "drastical" [sic] joke that he was known to frequently make. He admitted having encouraged his employees to take to the street on the approach of the Americans; he also acknowledge having observed to one of them that "You lost everything in Hamburg, in your block of houses over 40 children have been killed" and querying Rommel about the so-called Goebbels decree. Most damaging to Akkermann's legal prospects was his candid admission that, as the column of prisoners and their guards passed his house, he had shouted, "There are the murderers, the ones that killed your women and children, the ones that bombed your homes, beat them on the neck [sic], beat them!" He denied having personally assaulted the prisoners and suggested that he had not intended that any serious harm should come to the Americans. Rather, Akkermann, testified, "It was more or less an outlet. Everybody was yelling there, everybody in his own way, to let those flyers who had come over there every day at 8000 meter altitude, to show them how we feel, as worms on the ground." Moreover, Akkermann added in response to a question from Magenau, he had assumed that the prisoners would be protected, a blatant falsehood in light of his earlier admission that he had raised the matter of the Goebbels "decree" or "edict" with Rommel. He claimed to have been both "scared" and "shocked" when he learned that all seven American prisoners had been murdered.[15]

Scared and shocked, perhaps, but had Akkermann been remorseful? The earlier testimony of Dr. Fritz Vomel for the prosecution had suggested that he had not been. Vomel, it may be recalled, had described a meeting with Akkermann in which he had condemned the mayor's conduct during the prisoners' march through town. Akkermann had replied, in effect, that "these people who kill our women and children" had gotten what they had deserved. While not denying in Ludwigsburg that he had expressed that sentiment, Akkermann and his attorney attempted to place those words in a context that would diminish their damaging impact. To the annoyance of the prosecution but with the indulgence of the court, Akkermann described the events of August 5, 1944, the day following the murders. The defendant had been in his office around noon when Borkum's air-raid alarms sounded. Initial reports were contradictory. Some indicated that bombs had fallen into the sea; others suggested that they had fallen in the vicinity of the rail-road station. The latter proved to be the case, although it is clear that this was not a serious attack and may, indeed, have been the chance result of an Allied bomber in distress jettisoning its bombs, an event that the people of Borkum had experienced in the past. Akkermann accompanied Meyer-Gerhards to the scene. Ten bombs had fallen, one of which, a dud, had struck a locomotive and killed one of the crew. The post office had been badly damaged, as had a number of nearby houses. One of these, Akkermann testified, was his own. His wife and daughter, he claimed, had been "under a rubble of glass." He did not indicate that they had been seriously injured, if at all, but it was while this experience was fresh in his mind that he had been reproached by Dr. Vomel for his role in encouraging attacks on the prisoners, and Akkermann freely admitted that he might have said something like, "If things like this happen, why is it not right?"[16] The prosecution saw no need to cross-examine, and Akkermann's self-destructive candor continued in the face of questioning by the judges. When asked by Colonel Jackson whether he had anticipated that the prisoners would be beaten by the mob, Akkermann conceded that he had but added that "I never figured that there would be any killing." Akkermann suggested that, if his intentions had been genuinely murderous, he could have done much more than merely stand on a street corner and yell a few imprecations. As Nazi *Ortsgruppenleiter,* he could have mobilized Borkum's party members to form a gauntlet through which the Americans would have had to march.[17] That thin evidence of restraint was unlikely to have impressed the panel of officers who would determine Akkermann's fate.

When questioned by Major Levine more than four months earlier, Walter Krolikovski, on August 4, 1944, commander of the 216th Anti-aircraft Battalion, had delivered a self-exculpating statement according to which he had been uninvolved in the murderous events of that day and had been the innocent victim of a fallacious report of the murders made to him by a noncommissioned officer, although the non-com, Sergeant Schmitz, had denied it.[18] In Ludwigsburg, this theme was much embellished. He testified that he had first become aware of trouble on August 4, 1944, while dining at around 5 P.M. in the officers' mess, situated in an annex to the Dorf Hotel, where his own office was located. An orderly interrupted his meal to inform him that the American prisoners were being led down the street and that "something was happening." Although, as he emphasized, he had no role to play in the movement of the prisoners to the air base and had been entitled to finish his meal, a sense of "responsibility to look after them" impelled him to leave his table and run outside.

He saw a crowd of "30 to 40 people" and one prisoner on the pavement trying to get up and, simultaneously, to pull up his pants. He also observed a civilian who appeared to have just kicked the helpless prisoner. Finding such conduct against his "nature as an old soldier," Krolikovski professed to have been outraged and to have pushed the civilian away, "coming close to hitting him and knocking him down"; he also reproved the mob, shouting, "Damned business, what's going on here?" and admonishing people to "hurry up and beat it and that they should be ashamed." The crowd dispersed, and Krolikovski claimed to have been satisfied that the prisoners would be able to proceed unmolested. He was allegedly "shocked" to learn from Lieutenant Erich Wentzel a short time later that all of the prisoners had been shot. Krolikovski phoned the information to Captain Goebell, who replied with a dismissive "I can't change anything "and ordered him to question the guards and draft a report. The entire guard detail was called into Krolikovski's office, he testified, and its commander, Sergeant Schmitz, directed to relate the incident. Schmitz allegedly stated that the prisoners had been attacked by Labor Service personnel and that one of them had been "shot at"; then, they had been beaten to death by a mob near the athletic field. Schmitz's statement was then typed up by Wentzel, Krolikovski's adjutant, who delivered the report to Goebell, although the defendant admitted that he had made no effort to verify its contents.[19]

Krolikovski's claim of shock and moral outrage at the abuse and ultimate murder of the American prisoners was seemingly contradicted by testimony to the effect that, on the day following the murders, he reproved members of Searchlight #3 of Battery 7, near whose position #909 had landed and who had made the initial capture, for not having killed its crew immediately, thus sparing everyone the complications that had followed from their apprehension. When questioned on this matter by German civilian defense counsel Wacker, Krolikovski explained unconvincingly that he had been speaking under the influence of rumors that had then been current to the effect that #909 had been firing its guns as it had descended and that he had simply scolded members of the searchlight battery for not having made use of a machine gun located at the battery to return fire.[20]

Whether or not the bomber had been firing as it approached the *Muschelfeld* was legally irrelevant, but, then, so were the remarks that Krolikovski was alleged to have made the day following the murders. The defendant's cross-examination on more substantive issues would reveal an important and troubling facet of the Borkum trial.

NOTES

1. "Testimony of Gustav Mammenga," November 5, 1944, 3, *U.S. v. Goebell et al.* (microfilm, frame 296, reel 1); "Record of Testimony," 523–27, ibid. (frames 1081–85).

2. "Record of Testimony," 539 (frame 1097).

3. "Testimony of Heinrich Heinemann," October 17, 1945, 2–5, "Testimony of Gustav Mammenga," (frames 402–5).

4. "Testimony of Heinrich Heinemann," November 5, 1945, 2, ibid. (frame 408).

5. "Record of Testimony," 542–45, ibid. (frames 1100–1103).

6. Ibid., 552–53 (frames 1110–11).

7. Ibid., 562, 572–73 (frames 1120, 1130–31).

8. Ibid., 573–74 (frames 1131–32).

9. Ibid., 562, 569 (frames 1120, 1127).

10. Ibid., 580–82, 586 (frames 1138–40, 1144).

11. Ibid., 599–604 (reel 2, frames 13–18); "Testimony of Klaas Meyer-Gerhards," October 13, 1945, 3–4, ibid. (reel 1, frames 417–18).

12. "Record of Testimony," 613–14, ibid. (reel 2, frames 18–21).

13. Ibid., 613–14 (frames 27–28).

14. Ibid., 630–34 (frames 44–48).

15. Ibid., 632, 635–38 (frames 49–52).

16. Ibid., 639–40 (frames 53–54).

17. Ibid., 647–48 (frames 61–62).

18. "Testimony of Walter Krolikovski," October 29, 1945, 2–7, ibid. (reel 1, frames 333–38).

19. "Record of Testimony," 657–66, ibid. (reel 2, frames 71–80).

20. Ibid., 667 (frame 81).

5

Divided Counsel

Krolikovski was subjected to a tough cross-examination for the prosecution by Major Bryan, who pressed him vigorously on the matter of having submitted a false report on the circumstances surrounding the prisoners' deaths.[1] This, of course, had no direct bearing on the killing of the Americans, happening of necessity after the murders had taken place, but it served to damage the images of those involved and supported the notion of a criminal conspiracy that had been sustained after the crime to which it had given rise had taken place. But it was in the nature of a trial in which multiple defendants of varying status and levels of authority were being prosecuted simultaneously that Krolikovski had to try to defend himself against attacks on his testimony not only by the prosecution but by members of the defense counsel, as well. These men, both U.S. Army and German civilian attorneys, were defending not the 15 defendants collectively but categories of defendants or even specific individuals. This sometimes meant that they attempted to lessen or refute the apparent guilt of their clients by imputing responsibility to other defendants, a situation that necessarily worked to the advantage of the prosecution. Defense counsel Lieutenant John Davis attempted to destroy Krolikovski's credibility with questions as bitingly sarcastic as Bryan's about the report that had falsely placed blame for the killings exclusively upon civilians who had allegedly beaten the prisoners to death. Krolikovski's confused and contradictory responses to Davis's probing as to when he had learned the actual circumstances of the murders could have done him little good in the eyes of the panel of Army officers who would judge him:

DAVIS: Later you found out that they were shot, did you not?

KROLIKOVSKI: No. I didn't find that out later. A copy of the
police reports were [*sic*] handed to me. . . .
DAVIS: At that point, you knew that the flyers were shot, didn't
you?
KROLIKOVSKI: No. I didn't know that they had been shot.
I doubted the whole affair.
DAVIS: You still thought that they were beaten to death by the
civilians, didn't you?
KROLIKOVSKI: No. Not that alone. I testified that I doubted
the whole affair.

Davis asked sarcastically if Krolikovski believed that the American
prisoners could have been both beaten to death and shot to death.

DAVIS: Does that seem perfectly compatible to you?
KROLIKOVSKI: Both could be true, yes.

Krolikovski had not learned the truth, he claimed, until after the war
had ended, nine months later.[2]

The first witness to testify on the morning of March 6 was defendant
Erich Wentzel, a particularly problematic and even tragic figure in the
prosecution's narrative of criminal conspiracy. Like those of millions
of men on both sides, his peacetime life had been profoundly altered
by the outbreak of war. At the time of his trial, he was 45 years old and
married and had two children, a 10-year-old daughter and a 4-year-old
son. As a teenager near the end of an earlier world war, Wentzel had
received training as a naval artilleryman and had been called up for
service in that capacity as an enlisted man on the eve of Germany's
invasion of Poland in 1939. The war had interrupted Wentzel's career
in a sporting-goods business established by his parents in Neuwied,
control of which he had assumed. He had made regular business trips
to Great Britain and spoke English, a fact that went far toward explaining his presence in Ludwigsburg as a defendant. Wentzel had been
assigned to Borkum's 216th Flak Battalion and remained with that
unit throughout the war, rising to the status of commissioned officer
in January 1944, at which time he was also appointed adjutant to the
battalion commander, Walter Krolikovski.[3]

Wenztel had made a sworn statement to Major Levine on October 29,
1945, while being held at Esterwegen. Levine's questioning had been
aggressively hostile and Wentzel's replies, evasive. Many of the events

of August 4, 1944, he claimed not to remember. Levine had closed his interrogation with a blunt "You know that you have lied through this entire interrogation, didn't [*sic*] you?"[4] Under more sympathetic questioning by German defense counsel Dr. Schoeck more than four months later, Wentzel demonstrated an improved memory. He explained that he was in his office in the Dorf Hotel on August 4, 1944, when he heard Borkum's antiaircraft guns open fire and someone yelling from a neighboring office that an aircraft was visible and clearly the target. He ran to his window and saw the plane losing altitude and turning left toward the island. Borkum's old lighthouse blocked his view of #909's final moments in the air, but he was certain that the B-17 had come down on the island. Curiosity, rather than duty, prompted him to bicycle to the crash site, which he correctly guessed to be the *Muschelfeld*. On the way, he testified, he encountered Captain Goebell, who ordered him to proceed to the nearby Ostland Battery, where the American crewmen had been taken, to conduct an interrogation. Wentzel observed that questioning captured air personnel was a function of the Luftwaffe, to which Goebell replied that he merely wanted to ascertain whether the bomber had been shot down by Borkum's guns. When he arrived at the battery, Wentzel found the prisoners being searched and their personal belongings deposited in large envelopes, one for each man. The interrogation took place in front of the battery's mess bunker and, Wentzel recalled, lasted no more than 15 minutes, as the Americans refused to provide much information beyond identifying themselves. One revealed his position on the bomber, and another asserted that #909 had crashed because of "the blocking of the connection from the wheel," possibly an attempt by the American airman to mislead his interrogator. Wentzel testified that he quickly abandoned the effort as clearly futile.[5]

A fateful moment for Wentzel occurred when he overheard the commander of the Ostland Battery, Lieutenant Jakob Seiler, giving directions to the guard detail that was to escort the prisoners through town to the airfield for transportation to the mainland. "Are you clear on all points? Is it clear to you which way to take?" Wentzel recalled having heard Seiler ask. The noncommissioned officer appointed to lead the group, Sergeant Josef Schmitz, confessed that he was unfamiliar with part of the route, whereupon Wentzel, whose bicycle had been left leaning against the sea wall and who had been ordered by Krolikovski to return to his office, volunteered to show the way at least as far as Borkum's hotel district. But he was in no hurry. As the column marched from the battery, around the *Muschelfeld,* and toward the sea wall in the direction of town, Wentzel veered off to examine the skid marks left by #909 as it slid along the sand toward its resting place. He had been motivated to do this, he testified, because of assertions he had heard by members of the battery that they had been fired on by the B-17 as it came in to land. He claimed, in fact, to have earlier found "quite a few" empty .50-caliber machine-gun cartridge casings in the sand. He caught up with the column, he testified, shortly before it reached the sea wall.

At this point in his narrative, Wentzel made an admission that would weigh heavily against him. He observed, he said, that one guard, Witzke, was not maintaining the five-meter intervals between the prisoners that he had been ordered to do, with the result that the last American in the column was coming close to stumbling over the heels of the man in front of him. Wentzel repeatedly reprimanded the guard and ultimately recommended to Sergeant Schmitz that he be replaced. He had thus voluntarily assumed a degree of command authority over the column and, it could plausibly be argued, responsibility for the prisoners and their well-being.[6]

Initially, according to Wentzel, there was no difficulty with the people of the town. As the column approached the seawall, bathers ran up from the beach to gawk but did not behave in a threatening manner. Wentzel recovered his bicycle and pedaled ahead along the Promenade, which ran atop the seawall. He passed a group of Labor Service men drilling with spades in front of the Kaiserhof Hotel, where they normally exercised at around 4 P.M. each afternoon. This, too, was a perilous element in Wentzel's testimony. He was about to turn onto Strand Strasse as the route of march specified when his attention was attracted by someone waving. Looking over his shoulder, he noticed that the column of prisoners and guards led by Sergeant Schmitz was turning prematurely at Victoria Strasse. According to Wentzel's trial testimony, he then rode back to the column to redirect it on to the Promenade. That, however, would take it past the Labor Service men before reaching Strand Strasse. By that time, Wentzel testified, the Labor Service detachment had been dismissed from its drilling, and its members were in "wild disorder" as they streamed—so Wentzel thought—toward the nearby Victoria Hotel, where they were quartered. Secure in the belief that Schmitz would now follow the correct route, he rode on well ahead of the column and observed no difficulty with the Labor Service members; he did not stop to talk with the leader of the detachment as some witnesses claimed to have observed.[7]

Wentzel now sought out Lieutenant Karl Weber, the commander of another of Borkum's flak batteries, whose headquarters were on the Strand Strasse. His purpose in seeking Weber was not explained but the two, according to Wentzel, discussed the crash landing of #909 and whether any of Weber's guns had been involved in what they believed had been the "shoot-down." During the conversation, the prisoners and guards overtook and passed the two men. According to Wentzel, the column was out of sight as he, accompanied now by Weber, climbed on his bicycle and followed. The two men caught up with the procession as it was crossing the railroad tracks at the corner of Bahnhof and Franz Habich Strassen, where Wentzel recalled having seen a crowd of Borkumers, among whom was Mayor Akkermann, in a state of considerable agitation. From the mob had come yells to the effect that the prisoners should be beaten as "the murderers of our women and children."[8] There followed Wentzel's primary effort to refute the prosecution's contention that he had been a party to a conspiracy to mistreat the American captives. He had attempted to move once again to the head of the column but found his way impeded by the crowd, which, he testified, was pressing toward the prisoners in a threatening manner. Some townspeople were evidently punching the Americans. His objective now was to protect the prisoners and to move the column through the mob as quickly as possible, which he was able to do after about a half-minute, escaping the press of spectators at the corner of Franz Habich and Neue Strassen. He now claimed to have been intent on proceeding with Weber to their superior, Captain Krolikovski, to report that the crowd had become hostile and had attacked the flyers. As he approached the Dorf Hotel, he heard someone shout that one of the prisoners had "fallen" in front of the town hall. Hurrying to the scene, Wentzel testified, he saw one of the prisoners lying on the pavement and overheard members of the air-raid police announcing that an ambulance had been summoned and that their intention was to carry the American into their headquarters opposite the town hall. Believing the situation to be well in hand, Wentzel resumed his ride to Krolikovski's headquarters. The prisoners and their guards had again passed him, he testified, and he was able to see ahead of him the raised hands of the Americans. Reaching his destination, he encountered Krolikovski running from the building, evidently in pursuit of the column. While Wentzel was parking his bicycle, Krolikovski returned. As the two men conversed, passersby coming from the direction in which the column had marched shouted that the remaining prisoners were lying in front of the athletic field. Wentzel and Weber were sent to investigate, and they encountered Sergeant Schmitz, who had led the column, on his way back to the Dorf Hotel. Wentzel claimed to remember Schmitz's verbatim reply when asked what had happened: "I don't know that myself. There was a big crowd there. All of a sudden we were pushed away by the crowd and then it happened. The flyers were all lying on the ground having been beaten to death by the populace."[9]

Wentzel testified that he rode forward to where the murdered Americans lay, then returned to the Dorf Hotel and related to Krolikovski what he had learned. Krolikovski replied that he had already ordered the men who had escorted the American prisoners to report to him. Sergeant Schmitz made an oral statement, a summary of which Krolikovski had Wentzel reduce to writing. This was then read to the remaining guards, who, according to Wentzel, were invited to make additions or corrections. None did. Krolikovski wrote a report of his own, and both were sent to Captain Goebell, the island's commandant.[10]

Wentzel knew that he was on trial for his life and naturally attempted to place his conduct on August 4, 1944, in the most favorable light. Not surprisingly, he was subjected to a brutal cross-examination. Major Bryan confronted him with a number of differences between his sworn statement made to Major Levine and his trial testimony. Some of these discrepancies resulted from the fact that Levine had put often very different questions to Wenzel than had his civilian defense attorney, Dr. Schoeck. Bryan noted that Wentzel, in response to a query by Levine, had conceded that he had been aware of Dr. Goebbels's screed discouraging protection by German military personnel of captured Allied airmen who came under attack by civilians, an issue that Wentzel had not addressed in his trial testimony. Bryan probed the implications of that awareness for Wentzel's conduct on August 4, 1944. Why, he asked, did Wentzel think Goebbels's commentary had been published? Wentzel answered evasively. "The truth of it was," Bryan countered, "that it was issued because Allied airplanes bombed German cities, isn't that true?" Wentzel allowed that it might have been a factor.[11] Dr. Schoeck had asked Wentzel whether he had been aware of cases of violence against prisoners of war prior to the events of August 1944, an obvious effort to suggest that there had been no reason to take unusual precautions with the crew of #909. Wentzel replied ingenuously,

"Not in Borkum. But it was known to me that in France or Belgium prisoners had been mistreated."[12] Schoeck had moved quickly on, but Bryan had taken note. What was the policy in regard to Allied airmen captured on Borkum, Bryan wanted to know. "As far as I can remember," Wentzel answered, "there was a provision whereby all prisoners belonging to the Allied Air Force [*sic*] had to be taken over the shortest and quickest route to the nearest air force authorities. I am speaking from the island to the mainland." That, Wentzel continued, required transporting prisoners to the air base on Borkum and flying them to the nearest airfield on the mainland. "What would be the shortest and quickest route to the airport on Borkum Island from Ostland Battery?" asked Bryan. "Doubtlessly the railroad," Wentzel freely conceded. The purpose of Bryan's line of questioning quickly became clear:

> Now, having heard about prisoners having been mistreated in Belgium and France, and knowing about these regulations concerning the transport of Allied flyers, didn't it occur to you that there was something strange about the route chosen in this case? . . . And yet, having knowledge of Dr. Goebbels' decree, you volunteered to accompany that column without being ordered to do so, isn't that right?[13]

Wentzel replied that, at the time, he had seen no connection among the Goebbels decree, the abuse of flyers in France and Belgium, and the march of the seven American prisoners through the town of Borkum, the purpose of which, he believed, was simply to show the prisoners to the populace. "Here prisoners are taken. You can see by that [*sic*] that we have protected you." But even that, Bryan was quick to point out, was a violation of the Geneva Convention, which forbade the exposing of POWs to public curiosity.[14]

Bryan next turned to the matter of the prisoners' violent encounter with the detachment of Labor Service men. How had it happened that they had been given the opportunity to assault the Americans with spades? Wentzel had testified that Schmitz had led the column down the wrong street before he reached the detachment. In redirecting it, Wentzel inadvertently exposed the prisoners to attack. Bryan would have none of it. In Ludwigsburg, Wentzel had testified that his attention had been drawn by two waving uniformed figures to the fact that Schmitz had misdirected the column. But his account of that stage of the march earlier given to Levine had been a bit different. In that statement, "two men in uniform" had "beckoned" to him, in response to which he had ordered Schmitz to redirect the column, and it was this new direction that led the prisoners past the exercising unit. It was on Wentzel's earlier (and potentially more incriminating) description of the rerouting of the prisoners at the apparent behest of the Labor Service members that Bryan focused. Had Wentzel determined who these two men were? He had not, nor could he now remember what color uniform they were wearing. "Well, was there any similarity between those uniforms and the uniforms the Labor Service wore?" Bryan wanted to know. Wentzel could not remember that, either. What had he thought their gesticulations meant? "I thought that they meant to indicate that this one particular road was to be taken and for that reason I looked around where the column was going, and at that time I saw that they had turned into Victoria Strasse." Bryan apparently thought the implausibility of outsiders knowing the prescribed route would be evidence enough to obviate the need for further exploration of that point, and he moved on to the march of the American prisoners between two rows of spade-wielding Labor Service men, the violent consequences of which Wentzel claimed not to have seen, as he had been riding well ahead of the column.[15]

On the matter of the actual murder of the crew of #909, Bryan's cross-examination reached an intensity that the chief of the defense team, Lieutenant Colonel Hogan, characterized as "approaching something like the third degree," and Wentzel's plausibility, always tenuous, was clearly wilting. His claim that he had not known how the flyers had died, in spite of having admitted to Levine knowledge of Graham's shooting death, and assertion that he had made no effort to view the victims, although he was within a few feet of them, stretched credibility beyond the breaking point, as Bryan was at pains to emphasize. "Having given instructions to the guards about keeping civilians away and seeing the corpses of these pilots [*sic*] on the ground, you did not bother to find out what happened to them, did you?" Wentzel admitted that was true, although explicable on the grounds that "I had to return [to Krolikovski's office] immediately."[16]

On the following morning, March 7, Dr. Schoeck, on redirect, attempted to repair some of the damage that Bryan had done. But the little he accomplished was more than neutralized by the questioning of Lieutenant Davis, who, although a member of the defense team, was defending the guards and was clearly not interested in exculpating Wentzel. If anything, his examination was more hurtful to the defendant's cause than Bryan's cross-examination for the prosecution had been. Davis caustically challenged Wentzel's central contention that his function on the march had been solely that of showing the uncertain Schmitz the prescribed route. He pounced on Wentzel's crucial revelation that he had reprimanded the guard Witzke for failing to keep the prescribed distance between the prisoner he was guarding and the American ahead of him: "that was the method which you had intended to use to show Schmitz which was the route to be used?" Refusing to accept the contention that Wentzel had lacked authority to alter the route at his discretion, Davis pressed him on his failure to circumvent the hostile crowds through which the American POWs had been forced to march. Not only had he directed the column past the Labor Service contingent but, some guards had testified, he had redirected it a second time to lead it in front of the town hall, where additional assaults had taken place: "Don't you think it is rather a coincidence that every time you interfered and made the guards change the route they wanted to take, that the flyers got beaten as a result?" The objection of Captain Hall for the defense to the combative and purely rhetorical question posed by a fellow member of the defense team was overruled by Colonel Jackson, and the best that Wentzel could manage in response was the unhelpful observation that, after all, the prisoners had "allegedly" been beaten all along the route through Borkum. A scornful questioning of the defendant on his acceptance of Schmitz's report that the Americans had been beaten to death by the mob capped Davis's devastating "defense" examination.[17]

In the bizarre circumstances prevailing in the Borkum trial, it was now up to Hall, defense counsel for the officers, to attempt to undo the damage done by his colleague and codefense counsel. In questioning Wentzel about Sergeant Schmitz's report on the manner in which the prisoners had been murdered, Davis had asked sarcastically, "Can you think of any reason why a man would tell a stupid lie like that?" Wentzel could offer no explanation, but Hall tried. Among the sworn statements assembled by Major Levine was one taken from Karl Geyer on October 25, 1945, in the British 101 Civil Internment Camp, the former Nazi concentration camp at Esterwegen. On August 4, 1944, the Austrian Geyer had been an enlisted man assigned to Searchlight #3 of Battery 7 on Borkum and had served as one of the guards on the fatal march. He had, of course, witnessed the shooting of the American prisoners by Langer. When asked by Levine to elaborate on what he had seen, he replied, "As I heard the next shot, I turned around and saw Sgt. Schmitz with a pistol in his hand shoot one of the flyers in the back of the head." Civilian defense counsel Dr. Kerchbaum objected to the introduction of Geyer's assertion on the grounds that it was irrelevant to Wentzel's testimony. Hall argued that the prosecution and defense counsel for the guards

> are attempting to show that these officers are lying when they say the report was made to them that the flyers were beaten to death. I would like to [*sic*], at a time when the point is fresh in all our minds, show the court that there is positive basis for Schmitz and all the guards to do a little lying on their own.

The objection was overruled, and Kerchbaum's skepticism that Schmitz would have independently fabricated the story while knowing, as he must have, that the true cause of the prisoners' death would quickly become evident, is not compelling.[18]

Wentzel's claim that he had had no official responsibility for the column as it marched from the Ostland Battery through the town was further undermined by the testimony of Karl Weber. Weber had been interrogated by Levine at Esterwegen on October 28, 1945, and testified that he had first seen the column of prisoners and guards on Strand Strasse, in the vicinity of the headquarters of the medium antiaircraft battery he commanded. He had spoken to Wentzel and, on the basis of the latter's statement that he was directing the column in its march through Borkum, concluded that he was in charge, a conclusion he repeated in the Ludwigsburg courtroom. He had then ridden on his bicycle after the column on his way to deliver a report to battalion headquarters.[19] But, under questioning by civilian defense counsel Dr. Dreher, Weber provided additional information. Contrary to the testimony of many other witnesses, he claimed that he had seen the guards making a genuine effort to protect the prisoners when they came under attack from civilians. "Yes, they tried to prevent it time and time again. They tried to push the civilians away from the flyers with the butt [*sic*] of their rifles," he asserted. Geyer had distinguished himself by seizing "a 15- or 16-year-old fellow by his collar and [throwing] him literally off the street." When queried by Dreher as to why he had not included this in his earlier sworn statement, Weber replied simply that Levine had not asked. In his own sworn statement, Geyer had claimed simply to have "tried to push the civilians away." Weber was less commendatory of his own conduct. "All I could do was attempt to push my bicycle through the crowd."[20] Municipal employee Klaas Adel had been considerably less complimentary. In his sworn statement to Major Levine, he had asserted that Weber had declaimed from his bicycle, "Beat them to death. Here come the pigs!"[21]

In his cross-examination, Major Bryan reacted skeptically to Weber's description of Geyer's efforts to protect the prisoners. Levine might not have questioned Weber on the subject, he noted, but, at the end of the interrogation, he had asked Weber, as he had asked all witnesses he had questioned, if there was anything he wanted to add. Why had he not taken advantage of that opportunity? Weber replied that he had not thought of it at the time and added, "I must also say that the interrogation took place in Esterwegen, where morally and physically we were pretty beaten down." With presumably unintentional irony, Bryan followed this question with one concerning Weber's knowledge of the Geneva Convention.[22]

Defendant Jakob Seiler was examined by Dr. Engelhorn and provided detailed information on the capture and processing of the American prisoners. Seiler had recently been promoted to the command of the 216th Flak Battalion's Ostland Battery. The battery had joined in the firing at #909 as it approached Borkum, and Seiler had watched as the big plane touched down on the beach and became entangled in a barbed-wire fence. He testified that he had received orders by telephone to bring the American crew to his battery's position, a task that was accomplished in less than an hour of the landing by a few enlisted men led by a senior noncommissioned officer named Hoppe. Seiler also dispatched the battery's medic, a Corporal Roesing, in case any of the crew had been injured in #909's rough meeting with the sands of the *Muschelfeld*. Roesing reported that only one crewman had been even slightly injured, having sustained a minor head wound, which the medic had bandaged. With hand gestures, Seiler directed the Americans to empty their pockets. One prisoner retained a map, Seiler noticed, leading to individual searches of each of the Americans. It was a fairly relaxed procedure, with the prisoners not required to keep their hands raised except when being "frisked." As the searches progressed, Captain Goebell and several other officers, including Wentzel, arrived. At that point, Seiler testified, the atmosphere became tenser. Goebell ordered that a guard be provided for each of the prisoners, all of whom were to keep their hands raised at all times. That Goebell could be a difficult commander was suggested by the consequences of a concomitant decision that the prisoners' shoes would have to be removed as part of the search. One of the guards proceeded to untie the shoes of the Americans, only to be reprimanded by Goebell for performing so undignified a task. Goebell then ordered Seiler to have each prisoner's belongings placed in a large brown envelope inscribed with the owner's name. Seiler observed that his ignorance of English might produce problems, to which Goebell replied that the English-speaking Wentzel would now take over.

Goebell then turned his attention to the movement of #909's crew for evacuation to the mainland once Wentzel's brief interrogations were completed. Seiler testified that Goebell ordered the guards to take the prisoners through the town according to a specified route and that the Americans were to keep their hands raised throughout the march, were forbidden to talk, and were to maintain an appropriate interval between each captive and the man ahead of him. Any attempt to escape was to be dealt with by the use of weapons. More relevant to the case at hand, Seiler asserted that he had been ordered to "make clear to the guards" that, should civilians attack the prisoners, they were to take no action against them, although he was uncertain as to whether Goebell had made specific reference to the editorial on the treatment of downed Allied flyers issued by Dr. Goebbels. In any event, he thought that unimportant, inasmuch as the propaganda minister lacked authority to issue orders to the military. The fact that the Wehrmacht high command had itself issued orders that harmonized with Goebbels's screed went unmentioned. In fact, it may have been unknown to the naval defendants, who presumably would have included it as part of their defense had they been aware of it.

Seiler testified that he had designated Sergeant Schmitz as the leader of the column, a good choice, he thought, in that Schmitz had proven himself to be a reliable subordinate and had had experience transporting Russian POWs who had been employed as laborers on Borkum to another assignment on the mainland. Schmitz had professed his unfamiliarity with the prescribed route, whereupon Wentzel had offered his assistance. But, in spite of Captain Goebell's order that the guards were to take no action against hostile civilians, Seiler anticipated no difficulty. Borkumers had not been subjected to heavy Allied bombing and were usually placid. He believed that Goebell's motive in ordering the prisoners marched through town had been to demonstrate to the populace "that Borkum's entire [sic] aircraft defenses that been successful for once, because they had always been negatively judged."[23]

Seiler's testimony had been coherent and plausible, but members of the defense team representing other defendants sought to discredit it. For example, Dr. Weber, representing Goebell, undertook to impeach Seiler by exposing his Nazi associations. He freely admitted to having joined the Nazi Party in December 1932, before Hitler had come to power, and to having served as a leader in the Hitler Youth from 1935 until 1939. He had also been employed in a store operated by *Kraft durch Freude* (Strength through Joy), the organization within the German Labor Front that provided German workers with cut-rate theater tickets and vacations and promised to provide them with an affordable "people's car," the Volkswagen. Seiler's explanation that he had accepted party employment as a consequence of having been unable to find a job as an electrician, a job for which he had been trained, seemed implausible, given Germany's booming war production economy in the years immediately preceding the outbreak of war. In an effort to accelerate what amounted to defense cross-examination of Seiler and Dr. Engelhorn's efforts to repair the damage caused by it, the prosecution's Major Bryan objected that testimony of this nature was irrelevant, inasmuch as the defendant was not on trial for his party associations.[24]

Bryan's own cross-examination turned to more substantive issues. What had Seiler understood to be the significance of Captain Goebell's order that the prisoners were not to be protected against hostile civilian action? Had he not anticipated that something bad might occur? Seiler answered blandly that he had regarded it "as an order just like any other and I passed it on as such." Moreover, it was unusual to find many civilians on the streets of Borkum unless a train had arrived or a movie was letting out, an observation that seemed to clash with Seiler's earlier suggestion that the purpose of conducting the prisoners through the town was to demonstrate the success of the island's antiaircraft defenses to the populace. But, Bryan wanted to know, had Seiler been unaware of the terms of the Geneva Convention, according to which POWs were to be treated "humanely and protected against violence, insults, and public curiosity"? Seiler responded that, although he had heard of the Geneva Convention, he had never received any formal instruction on the proper treatment of prisoners. He added that, while the Americans had been in his custody, he had treated them humanely. Bryan clearly overreached when he belabored Seiler for not knowing that, under Article 6 of the Geneva Convention, prisoners were to be allowed to keep their personal effects, a provision that was commonly violated on both sides. Captain Hall for the defense puck-ishly requested that the trial record show that Bryan had been reading from a copy of the Army's *Rules of Land Warfare*.[25]

Kurt Goebell, on August 4, 1944, the commander of Borkum's military forces, was the defendant central to the drama being played out in Ludwigsburg. If a conspiracy to mistreat the American POWs had existed, he, as the source of the order to march the prisoners through town and as the person who had notified Mayor Akkermann of his intentions, with an alleged reference to Dr. Goebbels's inflammatory remarks, had been the initiator. When interrogated in Esterwegen on October 29, 1945, he had responded to many of Levine's provocative questions with "I don't remember."[26] In Ludwigsburg, more than four months later, his memory was much improved. His testimony began on the morning of March 11 with questioning by civilian defense counsel Dr. Weber. Goebell, an engineer and chemist in civilian life, had been a recent arrival on the island, having been transferred to Borkum from command of a flak battalion in Wilhelmshaven. He had been at home, an apartment in the barracks, with his wife as #909 approached and had run outside with his binoculars in response to the roar of Borkum's antiaircraft batteries. The plane had seemed to be taking evasive action when a shell exploded just above it, close enough, he thought, to be considered a hit. It then swung around, seemingly in preparation for landing, although hills prevented Goebell from seeing the final phase of #909's descent. He immediately proceeded to the crash site on the *Muschelfeld* but found that the crew had already been removed. Goebell was informed by one of Seiler's men, possibly Hoppe, that seven American prisoners had been taken. This puzzled him, as he knew that a B-17 normally carried a crew of 9 or 10. Not knowing that Kazmer Rachak and Quentin Ingerson had bailed out from #909 over the mainland, Goebell suspected that dead or wounded crewmen might still be on board and searched the plane. Instead, he found material presumably intended to facilitate escape of the crew if brought down over enemy territory, including road maps and water-purifying tablets. Goebell claimed to have immediately recognized the import of these and other items as a result of having earlier examined other American aircraft and their crews shot down around Wilhelmshaven. These investigations, he testified, had uncovered European currencies, German ration cards, compasses concealed in buttons, and, implausibly, swords contained in rubber packages. As a consequence, Goebell claimed to have been wary of the possibility of an escape attempt by

#909's crew, although escape from an island in the North Sea would appear to have been highly unlikely. Goebell categorically denied having asked any of the men who had effected the capture why they had brought the prisoners to him alive and conjectured that the witness who had made that assertion had misinterpreted a query by Goebell as to whether there might be crewmen still alive inside the B-17.[27]

The issue of Goebell's subsequent communication with Mayor Akkermann was of critical importance to the prosecution's theory that a conspiracy or common design to humiliate and physically harm the American prisoners had been initiated by the two men. What information had Goebell transmitted to Akkermann and why? Goebell explained that, when he had assumed military command of the island, he and Akkermann had agreed to share information on occurrences on the island if one became aware of it before the other. As best he could remember, he testified, he had instructed his adjutant, Lieutenant Dr. Baier, to "Inform the burgomeister that a plane had been shot down and that the prisoners would be taken to the pier." Notable by its absence was any reference to Propaganda Minister Goebbels's rant on the treatment of captured Anglo-American airmen.[28]

What, then, of the route through town that Goebell had prescribed? There had been nothing at all sinister in that, Goebell was at pains to emphasize. There was, to be sure, a shorter route, but that would have taken the column past construction sites where hundreds of forced laborers—Dutch, Belgian, French, Italians, Poles, and Russians—were employed in the building of fortifications. Goebell claimed that he had feared trouble, possibly an escape attempt by the Americans facilitated by the forced laborers if the two groups of captives had been brought into contact or proximity. If escape from the island was unlikely, the possibility of a sympathetic demonstration by the forced laborers did not seem implausible. Why, then, had Goebell not ordered the American prisoners transported by rail? The witness conceded that railroad tracks passed very close to the Ostland Battery and that two apparent ways to employ that mode of conveyance had existed. One involved the use of a small gasoline-powered railcar— described by Goebell as a "track automobile," probably a Wismar *Triebwagen* and possibly the same buslike vehicle now gaily painted red and yellow that one can ride on Borkum today.[29] But, at that stage of the war, Goebell explained, gasoline was so scarce that such an option had been out of the question. Only wounded military personnel were allowed to be transported by gasoline-powered vehicles. Borkum's officers themselves traveled by foot, bicycle, or horse. There was also a scheduled train, powered by a coal-fired steam locomotive, but that would not have been available before the evening and, in any event, was used to transport the foreign workers, contact with whom Goebell was determined to avoid. Goebell further asserted that he had prescribed a route different from the one actually taken. If his original instructions had been followed, the Labor Service contingent, as well as the crowds on Franz Habich Strasse and the town hall would have been avoided.[30]

Goebell estimated that he had remained at the Ostland Battery for about 20 minutes, then departed to return home. On the way, he paused to inspect the marks #909 had left on the shore as it skidded to a halt. As other witnesses had done, Goebell claimed to have found numerous empty cartridge casings indicating, he thought, "that the crew had been shooting to the very last moment." Once in his apartment, Goebell phoned the commander of the Luftwaffe air base on the island, a Lieutenant Colonel Plachte, to alert him to the fact that seven American prisoners were on the way and were likely to arrive in approximately an hour and a half and to tell him to make preparations to transport the captured airmen to Emden, on the mainland. From there, they would be taken to the Luftwaffe's interrogation center at Oberursel, near Frankfurt am Main. He followed up the call to Plachte with one to Police Chief Rommel, notifying him that the column of prisoners and their guards would shortly march through town. This, he testified, had been purely routine and similar to an alert that might have been issued to the fire brigade in case of approaching thunderstorms or a warning to the air-raid police should enemy aircraft be picked up on radar. These parallels with potentially destructive phenomena, natural and manmade, were probably ill chosen and clashed with Goebell's subsequent testimony that he had had no reason to anticipate trouble on the march. Borkum was a peaceful place, and the number of bombs that had fallen on the island had been minimal. Testimony to the contrary, he thought, had been greatly exaggerated. But Goebell seemed to equivocate when asked by Weber whether he had mentioned Dr. Goebbels's inflammatory statement in his conversation with Rommel. While he had denied having made such a reference when Rommel had made his bizarre visit to Goebell in June 1945, as a consequence of which the police chief had requested a pistol for the purpose of suicide, he now wanted not "to preclude the possibility that I mentioned this speech [*sic*] at that time." When asked why he might have mentioned Goebbels's comments to Rommel, Goebell responded vaguely that "he wanted to place the police on alert for security reasons," seemingly contradicting his earlier statement that he had had no reason to anticipate trouble in the course of the march. Yet, he had been "shocked" when informed by Krolikovski that the Americans had been "beaten to death."[31]

Goebell claimed to have initiated an investigation, although what that entailed was not explained, nor had any other witnesses mentioned such an effort. He reported the fatal "beatings" to his superior on the mainland, Admiral Scheuerlin, who initially told him to do nothing pending the receipt of further orders, then informed him that the investigation would be assumed by the Emden office of the Gestapo, presumably because the report had stated, falsely, that the murders had been committed by civilians. He attempted nothing further until near the end of the war, by which time he had assumed complete control of the island, including the civilian population. Goebell claimed to have then referred the case to a court-martial shortly before Borkum was occupied by Canadian forces, implying that he, in effect, had initiated the process that was now being played out in Ludwigsburg. But, from the start, rumors and the alleged hostility of the civilian population to the garrison had obstructed (and, by implication, continued to obstruct) efforts to get at the truth.[32] Goebell concluded his questioning by Weber with a rambling and largely irrelevant effort at self-justification:

> The incident or the incidents were surrounded by a tremendous mass of rumors and these rumors were exaggerated to such an extent that one was no longer able to differentiate between truth and rumor. In conclusion, I want to cite the following example. There existed a drive in Borkum from unknown sides to work against the armed forces, and for that reason the rumor was spread that all the flyers that had been shot were buried under a manure pile . . . and that they had been undug [*sic*] at a later time when they were buried in the cemetery; that an investigation to get behind the truth of this rumor was started by Brigadier Patrie and myself, but when the grave digger and the navy chaplain were interrogated the lie was uncovered immediately. . . . And a further thing which I would like to add is that before the war was concluded I had asked the population to contribute for the purpose of keeping up this cemetery.[33]

Indeed, Major Levine had found the graves of the murdered Americans well manicured. Unfortunately for Kurt Goebell, respect for the corpses of the crew of #909 was not at issue but, rather, how the crew had *become* corpses.

Once again, a defendant was exposed to vigorous cross-examination by defense lawyers representing other accused. In an effort to challenge the credibility of Goebell's testimony that he had had no reason to anticipate trouble during the march, German civilian defense counsel Baur asked why he had specified that seven guards were to accompany the prisoners. Wouldn't two have been adequate? Goebell exploded in exasperation

> if I had sent along twenty guards you would have asked me now why so many; if I would have sent two guards you would have asked me why so few. Where should I find the right number? The right number is one guard per man. It's very easily done afterwards to make uncountable [*sic*] propositions. Believe you me that if I had known what was coming off I would have done everything possible and everything within my power to prevent it.[34]

Baur zeroed in on Goebell's assertion that the route along which the prisoners had been marched had been chosen to minimize opportunities for escape. Borkum, after all, was an island. To where could the Americans have escaped? As before, Goebell defended himself energetically:

> The size of Borkum is being underestimated [*sic*] by this question. Borkum has 36 square kilometers; the whole northern part of it was a chain of dunes with old pill boxes from the last war; and I want to guarantee you that conditions existed at that time to leave the island unseen at any time and go either to the continent or to Holland. This problem concerned me very much. I therefore gave an order to a tech sergeant to go to Emden and back and not get caught, without traveling papers or money or any other material you would take, and he carried out that task.[35]

Baur did not bother to raise the obvious point that escape for a single native speaker of German familiar with local conditions and clothed inconspicuously bore little resemblance to the challenge that would have confronted seven Americans clad in U.S. Army Air Forces flight suits.

The grilling to which Goebell had been subjected by members of the defense team left the prosecution with little to do, and it contented itself with a brief and perfunctory cross-examination.[36] It was left to the U.S. Army officers sitting in judgment to pose a fundamental question as to the location of the primary weight of responsibility for the fate of #909's crew. "The court would like to know," began Lieutenant Colonel Versace, "who was the person that showed the greatest negligence in the conduct of this march?" Versace's use of the word "negligence" is interesting, in that negligence is a matter very different from conspiracy. Was Versace, in effect, offering Goebell the opportunity to accept guilt for a lesser offense? Goebell was initially evasive. "I can practically not [*sic*] answer that question because it was one continuous chain of events, one following the other, and a differentiation or distinction of events can hardly be made in this connection." But Versace was persistent. "You have admitted that the responsibility of protecting these flyers lay in the military. Who disallowed that responsibility [*sic*], in your opinion?" Goebell responded more imaginatively, but with no greater specificity:

The happenings . . . could not be foreseen by anybody, and I should like to put . . . it to be the forces of a higher power. If a marching order is given to troops and these troops march along and on the way there is a dud, a bomb that has not been exploded, when by the shaking of the ground by the marching troops this bomb comes to an explosion [*sic*] and men are . . . killed, the responsibility does not lay [*sic*] with the man who ordered the march because nobody knew about this dud.

Colonel Versace seemed incredulous. "From your remarks, you would like us to believe that this was an act of God?" "No," replied Goebell, "I only mean to say that those were circumstances that you could not have foreseen."[37]

Colonel Barden adopted a different approach, asking Goebell whether it was not true that, had the column adopted the march route he had originally prescribed, the Labor Service detachment, as well as the crowds on Franz Habich Strasse and in front of the town hall, would have been avoided, to which Goebell, who had already testified to that effect, agreed. And was it not Lieutenant Seiler who had specified the route actually taken? Goebell hesitated to accept the apparent invitation to pin the blame on a subordinate. While agreeing that Seiler was the only person to whom he had given instructions with regard to the route, he refused to condemn Seiler on the grounds of ignorance of "what further circumstances" might have been involved. But the purpose of Barden's line of questioning quickly became evident. Was not Goebell attempting to suggest that the events of August 4, 1944, were the consequences of a conspiracy hatched by several of his subordinates, including Seiler, and aided and abetted by Wentzel and Weber? And wasn't he simply trying thereby to cover up the fact that he himself "was the key man who actually engineered this whole route of march and course of events?" Goebell, of course, indignantly denied it: "Never have I had the idea to send those men on a death march. Never!"[38]

Defendant Johann Pointner had been questioned by Major Levine at Esterwegen on October 26, 1945. The 24-year-old Austrian had commanded one of the big antiaircraft searchlights on the island and had seen #909 make its crash landing approximately one kilometer from his position at around 2 P.M. on the afternoon of August 4, 1944. He and two other men had proceeded to the site and had found the seven Americans standing "in formation" outside the plane. One requested permission to bandage the head of a crewmate (at variance with other testimony, which credited a German medic with the bandaging), which Pointner granted, while "the small flyer," clearly Graham, voluntarily surrendered a pistol. Responsibility for the prisoners was quickly assumed by a squad from the Ostland Battery, which escorted them to their position, while Pointner and his comrades were left to guard the big bomber until about 4 P.M., when he was notified that he, Witzke, and Geyer were to serve as part of the escort for the POWs. On arrival at the Ostland Battery, Pointner stated that he had reported to Lieutenant Seiler, who informed him that the prisoners were to be marched through the town, "and if the civilians wanted to do anything to these flyers, then we must not protect the flyers in any way." Moreover, the prisoners were to keep their hands raised throughout the march, and any American who lowered his hands, much less attempted to escape, was to be shot. The first guard to shoot a POW would be rewarded with a bottle of *schnaaps*. At sharp variance with Wentzel's testimony was Pointner's claim that he had been appointed to lead the column because he was familiar with the prescribed route. Wentzel's defense suffered further damage from Pointner's assertion that it had been he who had redirected the column past the RAD detachment and again when Pointner sought to lead it on a shorter and less congested route to the airport. Following the murder of the flyers, all guards had been ordered to report to Krolikovski's headquarters in the Dorf Hotel. There, Wentzel had read aloud a statement to the effect that the Americans had been beaten to death by civilians, in spite of efforts by the guards to protect them. Pointner and his comrades were directed to sign it and did so.[39]

In Ludwigsburg, under questioning by defense counsel Dr. Baur, Pointner confirmed the essentials of his earlier sworn statement, but with at least one significant addition. The order that #909's crew was not to be protected from civilian attack had apparently not been the first time the issue of allowing prisoners to be assaulted had been addressed. Pointner testified that some time prior to the crash landing, a Lieutenant Ahrens, who was not identified further, had informed a meeting of position leaders in his battery that, in the event that prisoners were taken in future, they were not to be protected. As soon as Pointner had returned to his duty station following the murders, he found a message to the effect that no one was to talk about the incident, and censorship of personal mail would be tightened to ensure that news of it would not spread outside Borkum. Absent was Pointner's earlier claim that Seiler had offered a bottle of *schnaaps* to the first guard to shoot a prisoner. And, under questioning by other civilian defense attorneys, Pointner admitted that he had arrived late at the Ostland Battery and might not have heard the instructions that Seiler had given as to the precise route to be taken.[40] Wentzel's deviations, therefore, might not have been deviations at all but simply efforts to adhere to orders issued by a superior officer. Major Bryan's cross-examination was limited to a perfunctory extraction from Pointner of a confirmation that the sworn statement he had made in Major Levine's presence had, to the best of his knowledge, been truthful.[41]

Günther Albrecht had been questioned by Major Levine in Esterwegen on October 25, 1945. He was the equivalent of a private and was serving with the Ostland Battery when #909 landed on Borkum. Ordered by Seiler to serve as one of six guards during the search and interrogation of the prisoners, he had witnessed the abuse of one of them when Petty Officer Jakob Wittmaack, apparently annoyed by the American's gum chewing, knocked the wad out of his mouth with a blow to the face. He had not heard Seiler give orders that the prisoners were not to be protected if attacked by civilians, but he had heard later from Geyer and Witzke that such orders had been given. As the column was leaving the Ostland Battery, however, Seiler had allegedly ordered Albrecht to hit one prisoner with his rifle butt for not holding his hands high enough. He had refused to do so, Albrecht informed Levine, and had been threatened with disciplinary action by Seiler. Sometime later, he received a similar order from Sergeant Schmitz, which he claimed to have again defied, limiting himself to the benign admonition in English, "Boys, hands up." When Howard Graham ("the small, fat flyer" to Albrecht), struggling with his pants, fell in front of the Rathaus, Albrecht testified that he was attempting to help him to his feet when he was pushed aside by an army private who shot the American behind the right ear. He had then helped to carry the mortally wounded Graham into the office of the air-raid police.

Albrecht's effort at self-exoneration was matched by his willingness to incriminate others. Wentzel, whom Albrecht assumed was in charge of the column, had done nothing to protect the prisoners. Wittmaack had beaten the Americans, while Schmitz had expressed satisfaction when told that the six remaining POWs had been murdered. Moreover, he and Wittmaack had requested ammunition for their pistols following the march, suggesting that they might have expended some in helping Langer to accomplish his murderous purpose.[42]

In the witness chair in Ludwigsburg more than four months later, Albrecht had the opportunity to expand his description of the events of August 4, 1944, particularly his own allegedly blameless role. Under the benevolent questioning of civilian defense counsel Dr. Dieterich, the 23-year-old Albrecht revealed that he had been a recent arrival on Borkum, having been drafted from his civilian job as a shipyard worker in November 1943. On Borkum, he had been assigned to the flak battery commanded by Lieutenant Seiler and, on August 4, 1944, as he had informed Levine, had been ordered to serve as a guard for the prisoners, although he professed to have had no knowledge of where they were to be taken. As the column proceeded along the Promenade to Victoria Strasse, he recalled having seen a group of Labor Service men a short distance ahead. Just as the column was turning onto Victoria Strasse, he heard some of them shout, "Bring them here, bring them here." It was at that point, Albrecht testified, that Wentzel redirected the column towards the Labor Service members.

> All of a sudden we were surrounded by men of the RAD. I heard
> a voice telling the RAD men to beat the flyers. . . . Later on I found

out that he was the man in charge of the RAD platoon. He used the following words and I quote, "Beat them boys, beat them." I did see several spades up in the air and I assumed that some of the flyers were actually hit.

Albrecht was unable to protect the prisoner he was guarding because he had been "pushed away" by several of the Labor Service men. He denied ever having struck an American, limiting himself to a gentle admonition in English when the prisoner he had been guarding lowered his hands, but he accused Wittmaack of having hit a POW on three occasions. "It is not my nature to hit defenseless persons," Albrecht intoned. When Graham fell over his loose trousers in front of the town hall, Albrecht turned to help him to his feet, although "the little flyer" was not the man whom he had been assigned to guard. While he had been rendering assistance, Albrecht claimed, he had been shoved aside by a figure in the uniform of an army private, who had shouted "Go away, go away!" That had been followed immediately by the sound of a shot, and Albrecht observed, in variance with his earlier sworn statement to Levine, that Graham had "received a shot into the *left* rear part of his head." Dieterich asked him why he had not at least tried to identify the assailant, to which Albrecht responded with well-prepared pathos:

> At that moment I was so much shocked by what happened that I couldn't think straight. You can put yourself into this kind of predicament [*sic*], you are trying to assist somebody and all of a sudden that somebody is shot by somebody else. It was all strange to me. The flyer was still moving when at that time the people from the SHD [air raid police] office came and one of them said we should help grab [*sic*] the flyer. . . . The first thing that injured flyer needed was aid.

Albrecht testified that he tried to catch up with the column but found the remaining prisoners already dead on the Reede Strasse near the athletic field. He was then instructed by Wittmaack to report to battalion headquarters in the Dorf Hotel, where Wentzel read to the assembled guards the statement fallaciously describing the beating deaths of the POWs on the Reede Strasse by civilians. Wentzel directed the guards to sign the document. But why had Albrecht been willing to sign it? Albrecht answered that he had assumed that the statement had been based on an oral report made to Krolikovski by Schmitz and that the latter had been acquainted with the circumstances of the prisoners' deaths. Dieterich was quick to guide Albrecht into a modified restatement of his assertion that the document had referred only to the killings of the six prisoners on the Reede Strasse and not to the shooting of Graham near the town hall, the circumstances of which Albrecht had just dramatically described, a version of the statement not in agreement with the testimony of other witnesses. When he and his comrades returned to the Ostland Battery, Albrecht remembered "positively" that he had been ordered by Seiler not to speak or write about the incident and also, somewhat contradictorily, commanded to state that the flyers had been beaten to death if he was ever asked about the means by which they had been killed. Follow-up questioning by other defense counsel and members of the prosecution team failed to move Albrecht significantly from his testimony.[43]

Thirty-four year-old Heinz Witzke was arrested on June 16, 1945, and interrogated under oath by Major Levine at Esterwegen on October 27. He testified that on August 4, 1944, he had been serving with Searchlight #3, Battery 7, of the 216th Naval Antiaircraft Battalion and had seen #909 come down on the *Muschelfeld* some 700 to 800 meters from his position. He and Private Johann Pointner were the first Germans to arrive at the scene and found Walthall's crew standing alongside the aircraft with their hands raised. Witzke and Pointner were shortly joined by a contingent from the Ostland Battery. The two thereupon returned to their searchlight position. At around 3:30 that afternoon, Witzke and Pointner, along with Karl Geyer, were ordered to report to the Ostland Battery for service as guards for the march that was to take the American POWs to the airfield for transportation to the mainland. Witzke recalled that, before the march began, Seiler had issued an order to the effect that

> The flyers must go with their hands over their heads at a fast pace. If any one of them stepped out of line, then they were attempting to escape and we must shoot them at once. In the event that the civilians attacked these flyers, we must do nothing to prevent them from doing so. And further he said that in the event that the flyers did not hold their hands over their heads correctly, we were to beat them with our rifles.

The procession set out at around 4:30 P.M. and was commanded, he believed, by Lieutenant Wentzel.

Witzke testified to having begun the march guarding "the little flyer," Howard Graham, but claimed that Wentzel had ordered him to change places with Geyer as the column was proceeding down Strand Strasse after he refused to beat Graham for having lowered his hands. Graham, the recipient of the most abuse due to his wayward trousers and the first POW to be killed, was obviously someone from whom Witzke was at pains to separate himself. Levine had challenged him on this assertion, noting that other witnesses had testified to the contrary. Witzke admitted the lie but stoutly denied having beaten Graham and claimed that, at the time that Graham had been shot, the prisoner had no longer been under his supervision. In front of the athletic field, he recalled, an army private had jumped out of the crowd, yelled, "You have killed my wife and children," then shot the prisoner he was guarding at that time, as well as the prisoner next in line, who was guarded by Geyer. He had heard additional shots but had not seen additional POWs fall. Witzke concluded his sworn statement with the familiar description of having been required to sign a fallacious account of the murders.[44]

Questioned by civilian defense attorney Dr. Baur in Ludwigsburg, Witzke offered testimony that differed only in minor respects from the sworn statement he had given Levine. Now he and *two* other men from his searchlight position had been the first to arrive at #909's crash site, and Witzke presented a fuller, if not more plausible, explanation of the shifting responsibility for guarding Graham as the march had proceeded. Wentzel had switched Witzke to the prisoner ahead of him, but, as the column marched through the hostile Labor Service contingent, Graham had moved ahead, making him once again Witzke'e responsibility, which he remained until they reached the town hall, where a disorderly press of civilians forced the two apart just before Graham was shot by Langer. At the athletic field, Witzke now claimed to have been "jumped from behind" by a figure shouting "You took my women [*sic*] and children" as he put a pistol to the neck of the prisoner Witzke was then guarding and fired. And, although he had earlier testified that he believed that Wentzel had been in charge of the march, he undermined that statement by testifying that he had not seen Wentzel between the time that he was relieved of responsibility for Graham and the arrival of the column at the athletic field. Under later questioning by defense lawyer Captain Hall, he now testified that he thought Sergeant Schmitz had been in charge of the guards.[45]

Once again, another member of the defense team energetically probed the defendant's testimony. Hall was the only attorney on either side to raise a pertinent point: Witzke and others had testified that Seiler had ordered the guards to provide no protection to the prisoners should they come under attack by *civilians*. But Langer was a member of the Wehrmacht and was clearly identifiable as such by his uniform. Why had no effort been made to protect the prisoners against him? Witzke answered that Langer had taken him and his comrades by surprise. "Then you assume that from one end of the column to the other, in all this crowd and shooting, that everybody was completely surprised, is that correct?" asked Hall sarcastically. "I cannot judge the situation as it was," responded Witzke, who, of course, had just done precisely that.[46]

Johann Schmitz had been the senior noncommissioned officer in the procession that had conducted the crew of #909 through Borkum. Whether he had been the actual commander of the group and what he had told his superiors about the deaths of the POWs were central issues in the trial. The 52-year-old Schmitz, a veteran of World War I, had been questioned by Major Levine in Esterwegen on October 27, 1945. He recalled having seen #909 come down on the *Muschelfeld* and had seen the crew brought into the Ostland Battery about an hour later. After some two hours had elapsed, Seiler had ordered him to serve as one of the guards for the prisoners and had personally lined up the column in preparation for departure. Schmitz did not recall an order requiring the prisoners to keep their hands above their heads but confirmed that Seiler had ordered that any prisoner attempting to escape be shot and that civilian attacks on the Americans not be resisted. Schmitz claimed ignorance of who had been in command of the column, obviously attempting to minimize his own responsibility but also seeming to confirm Wentzel's story of his own fortuitous inclusion in the march. When Seiler began to explain to him the route that was to be taken, Schmitz (who was implicitly admitting to at least having been designated the leader of the column) had professed unfamiliarity with the town, whereupon Wentzel had volunteered to show the way. In the course of the march, Schmitz denied having done any more than "push" some of the prisoners and claimed that, when the Americans had been attacked by the Labor Service men, he had yelled, "Don't do that." And, although implicating Wittmaack in having fired at a prisoner near the athletic field, the scene of the murders of six Americans, he asserted that his own pistol "went off accidentally" when he tried to keep civilians "from taking things from the flyers." Nor had he misled Krolikovski as to the circumstances of the POWs' deaths. He had informed him that they had been shot by an army private and Wittmaack but had then signed a false statement typed out by Wentzel without having read it. Of all of the affidavits extracted by Levine, Schmitz's was probably the most blatantly implausible.[47]

Schmitz was no more noteworthy for consistency than he was for persuasiveness. When questioned by German civilian defense counsel Dr. Kerschbaum in Ludwigsburg, he denied that Seiler or anyone else had organized the column prior to its departure, asserting that "there was no formation formed actually." In direct contradiction of his statement to Levine, he now testified that Seiler *had* ordered that the prisoners be required to keep their hands above their heads and that, at the march's fatal conclusion, he had not actually seen Wittmaack fire at a prisoner but had simply observed him with pistol in hand. When challenged on the latter discrepancy, Schmitz claimed that deafness had prevented him from hearing the statement he had made to Levine when it was read back to him, and he denied having made the accusation against Wittmaack. On his own innocence of wrongdoing, he was, of course, adamant.[48]

In a bizarre departure from the testimony of the accused, Lieutenant Davis called to the stand Willi Gutermuth, a doctor of medicine currently interned by the British. He proceeded to question Dr. Gutermuth on the effects of smoking on the human body, on which subject he professed to be an expert. What, Davis asked, would be the impact of smoking a cigarette on a smoker who had been deprived of tobacco for an extended period and who was called upon to testify immediately thereafter? Gutermuth answered that result might be euphoria intense enough to diminish his reasoning abilities and self-control, and he supported his contention with a description of a personal experience. After not having smoked for an extended period, he was given an American cigarette, which he proceeded to smoke. "The effect was that I became more or less dizzy, that is, I felt a kind of joyousness and did things which ordinarily I would not have done. This condition is increased by malnutrition." As a consequence, Gutermuth had recommended that prisoners who were about to be interrogated not be given cigarettes.

It was a desperate ploy that sought to bring into consideration the conditions under which many of the defendants had been held, including being given inadequate food, prior to their interrogations by Major Levine. But the issue of malnutrition, pressed by German defense counsel Dr. Wacker, went too far for Davis, and his objection to that line of questioning as irrelevant was sustained by Colonel Jackson. Major Bryan, cross-examining Gutermuth for the prosecution, endeavored to undermine whatever impact the witness's testimony had by suggesting that he was an antismoking fanatic who had been relieved of his duties as head of a camp hospital for that reason. Gutermuth denied the charge of fanaticism, noting that he was simply opposed to smoking by people in ill health, a condition in which he clearly believed many of the prisoners to have been.[49]

Defendant Karl Geyer had made his statement to Levine on October 25, 1945. On the day of #909's landing on Borkum, Geyer had been serving in Pointner's searchlight battery and had seen the B-17 skid to a halt on the *Muschelfeld* about 200 meters from his position. He had not gone to the plane but saw others run to it and make prisoners of the crew. He watched as they were then marched to the Ostland Battery. At around 4 P.M. he, Pointner, and Witzke were ordered to report to the battery to serve as escorts for the Americans and were directed not to interfere if the POWs came under attack from civilians. But Geyer added additional dramatic detail. Seiler asked the arrivals where they had come from. "The searchlight battery," Geyer replied. That was not quite what Seiler had meant.

> He then asked two of us [again] where we came from and if our houses had been bombed. We told him Austria and that our homes were not bombed. He then asked why we didn't shoot the prisoners right away. I said our planes go out and pick flyers up from the water, so why should we shoot them here. He said that was no excuse.

Then, according to Geyer, Seiler had asked who among the assembled group knew the way from the battery through the town. Apparently assuming that Seiler was interested primarily in a route to the air base, Geyer and Pointner had recommended a road that circumvented populated areas. Seiler was alleged to have brusquely rejected the suggestion, along with Geyer's subsequent query about the possible use of the railroad. Geyer claimed also to have interceded several times for Graham in the course of the march, requesting of Wentzel a pause so that "the little flyer" could fix his pants, all to no avail. He was also "positive" that Schmitz had shot one of the prisoners in the back of the head during the final bloodletting at the *Sportsplatz* because he had seen him do so. He confessed to no wrongdoing of his own, nor had Levine explored that issue.[50]

When questioned by members of the defense team in the Ludwigsburg courtroom, Geyer deviated from his earlier sworn statement in some noteworthy respects. Gone was the account of Seiler's inflammatory remarks upon his arrival at the Ostland Battery, and Geyer now claimed to have tried to protect the American he was guarding by shoving some of the hostile Labor Service men aside with his rifle. When his prisoner was approached by a civilian intent upon beating him, Geyer described having grabbed the man by the collar and shoved him aside. And he no longer testified that he had actually seen Schmitz shoot a prisoner; rather, he asserted that he had simply witnessed Schmitz pulling a pistol away from the head of an American. Geyer, according to his own account, had neither hit nor even pushed anyone. In both his statement to Levine and in the witness chair in Ludwigsburg, Geyer described a visit by Captain Krolikovski to Searchlight #3 a day or two after the murders in which the battalion commander had reproved him and his comrades for not having killed #909's crew as soon as they had stepped out of the plane, a remark that Geyer claimed to have protested.[51]

Captain Hall pressed Geyer on that part of his sworn statement for Levine in which he had claimed to have seen Schmitz shoot a prisoner in the head, an allegation that he had modified in his courtroom testimony. Geyer responded vaguely that he had requested that his sworn statement be revised when he arrived at Ludwigsburg. The exchange went to the critical issue of the reliability of the sworn statements, on which the prosecution case was largely based. In order to repair the potential damage to their credibility, the prosecution's Captain May questioned Geyer sharply on the circumstances under which he had produced the statement. Had he requested that Levine make any changes to the document before he had signed it?

No. But I told Major Levine from the very beginning that I received a very poor education. I have called for witnesses to testify to that. My own company chief gave me orders never to do any phone duty because I couldn't write. I was in no way able to listen and write at the same time. For that reason, I asked Major Levine to read [the statement] back to me very slowly.

This, Geyer testified, Levine had not done, creating for Geyer a problem in comprehension aggravated by alleged poor hearing.[52] Once again, the credibility of the sworn statements had been challenged, although this effort was to be as futile as those earlier in the trial had been.

NOTES

1. "Record of Testimony," 682–84, *U.S. v. Goebell et al.*, 682–84 (microfilm, frames 96–98, reel 2).

2. Ibid., 694–99 (frames 108–9).

3. Ibid., 719–20 (frames 133–34).

4. "Testimony of Eric Wentzel," October 29, 1945, ibid. (frames 355–56, 363, reel 1).

5. "Record of Testimony," 721–24, ibid. (frames 135–38, reel 2).

6. Ibid., 728–29 (frames 142–43).

7. Ibid., 729–33 (frames 143–47).

8. Ibid., 733–34 (frames 147–48).

9. Ibid., 738–41 (frames 152–55).

10. Ibid., 742–43 (frames 156–57).

11. Ibid., 759 (frame 172).

12. Ibid., 726 (frame 140).

13. Ibid., 760–62. (frames 173–75).

14. Ibid., 762, (frame 175).

15. Testimony of Erich Wentzel," October 29, 1945, 6, ibid. (frame 354, reel 1); "Record of Testimony," 763–66, ibid. (frames 176–79, reel 2).

16. Ibid., 768–70 (frames 181–83).

17. Ibid., 771–82 (frames 184–95).

18. Ibid., 193, 202, 784–85 (frames 745, 754, reel 1; frames 197–98, reel 2).

19. Testimony of Karl Weber," October 28, 1945, ibid. (frames 318–19, reel 1).

20. Record of Testimony," 798, ibid. (frame 210, reel 2); "Testimony of Karl Geyer," October 25, 1945, 200, ibid. (frame 752, reel 1).

21. Testimony of Klaas Adel," October 18, 1945, 2, ibid. (frame 475); "Record of Testimony," 805–6, ibid. (frames 217–18, reel 2).

22. Ibid., 811–12 (frames 223–34).

23. Ibid., 819–29 (frames 232–43).

24. Ibid., 833–34, 838 (frames 247–48, 252).

25. Ibid., 841–44 (frames 255–58).

26. "Testimony of Kurt Goebell," October 29, 1945, 3–4, 6–8, ibid. (frames 367–68, 370–72, reel 1).

27. "Record of Testimony," 854–57, ibid. (frames 268–71, reel 2).

28. Ibid., 857–58 (frames 271–72).

29. Holger Bloem and Wilke Specht, *Borkum: Nordseeinsel unter Weitem Himmel* (Norden: Verlag Soltau-Kurier-Norden, 2009), 5.

30. "Record of Testimony," 859–62 (frames 273–76, reel 2).

31. Ibid., 863–64 (frames 277–78).

32. Ibid., 865 (frame 279).

33. Ibid., 866 (frame 280).

34. Ibid., 877 (frame 291).

35. Ibid., 878 (frame 292).

36. Ibid., 886–90 (frames 300–303).

37. Ibid., 896–97 (frames 309–10).

38. Ibid., 897, 899 (frames 310–312).

39. "Testimony of Johann Pointner," October 26, 1945, "Record of Testimony," 220–29, ibid. (frames 772–81, reel 1).

40. Ibid., 906, 918, 921–22 (frames 319–331, 334–35, reel 2).

41. Ibid., 934 (frames 347).

42. "Testimony of Günther Albrecht," October 25, 1945, "Record of Testimony," 206–16, ibid. (frames 758–68, reel 1).

43. Ibid., 935–38, 941–48, 950–58 (frames 348–51, 354–61, 363–71, reel 2).

44. "Testimony of Heinz Witzke," October 27, 1945, 2–11, ibid. (frames 305–14, reel 1).

45. "Record of Testimony," 965–73 (frames 378–86, reel 2).

46. Ibid., 974–75 (frames 387–88).

47. "Testimony of Johann Josef Schmitz," October 27, 1945, "Record of Testimony," 169–77, ibid. (frames 719–27, reel 1).

48. Ibid., 989, 995, 997–98 (frames 402, 408, 410–11, reel 2).

49. Ibid., 1020–25 (frames 433–38). On Nazi attitudes toward smoking, see Robert N. Proctor, *The Nazi War on Cancer* (Princeton, NJ: Princeton University Press, 1999), 173–247.

50. "Testimony of Karl Geyer," October 25, 1945, "Record of Testimony," 193–94, ibid. (frames 745–46, reel 1).

51. Ibid., 1027–36 (frames 440–49, reel 2).

52. Ibid., 1036, 1043 (frames 449, 456).

The crew of #909, standing from left to right (back row) Lieutenants Quentin F. Ingerson, Harvey M. Walthall, William J. Myers, Howard S. Graham, (front row) Sergeants Kazmer Rachak, J. Hesner (not on the August 4, 1944 mission), Kenneth Faber, James W. Danno, William W. Lambertus, William F. Dold. (486th Bombardment Group Association and Quentin F. Ingerson)

A nun makes her way through the streets of Würzburg, devastated by Allied bombing. (U.S. National Archives)

Site of the Ostland battery with the tracks of Borkum's railroad clearly visible. (U.S. National Archives and 486th Bombardment Group Association)

At Borkum's Rathaus (town hall) Lieutenant Howard S. Graham, the "little flyer," was mortally wounded. (U.S. National Archives and 486th Bombardment Group Association)

Major Abraham Levine testifies during the Borkum trial. (U.S. National Archives)

Defendants in the Borkum trial leave the courtroom under guard. (U.S. National Archives)

Few photos were taken of U.S. Army courts-martial. This one shows a World War II trial. (U.S. National Archives)

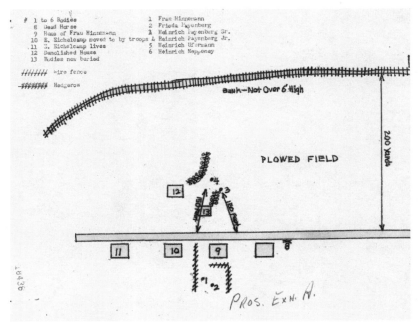

Prosecution Exhibit A shows the locations of the murders of Voerde civilians. (U.S. National Archives)

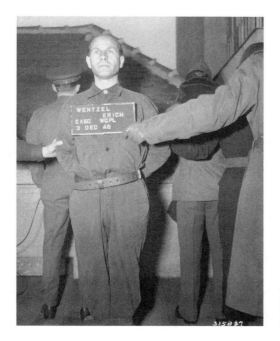

Erich Wentzel is about to be hanged at Landsberg prison. (U.S. National Archives)

The monument to the murdered crewmen of #909 was dedicated on August 4, 2003. (486th Bombardment Group Association)

6

Fed to the Lions

The court adjourned on Thursday, March 14, for a long weekend. When it reconvened on March 18, the prosecution recalled as a rebuttal witness Major Levine, perhaps reflecting the perceived seriousness of Geyer's challenge. Under questioning by Major Bryan, Levine described the process by which the statement had been presented to the witness for verification prior to signature. Although written in English, the statement was read to the witness in German by the interpreter, Rudolph Kaufman, a German-born U.S. Army private who had come to the United States with his parents in 1938. The witness, according to Levine, had been urged to listen carefully and to correct any errors. After the answer to each question had been read, Levine had asked the witness in German if it was true. "When the statement came to that part of the testimony where Geyer described how Schmitz had shot one of the flyers I went over it personally three times and asked him three times whether or not he was positive that what he said was the truth and each time he said 'Yes, that's the truth.'"[1]

In its cross-examination of Levine, the defense pointed out that statements by other witnesses had fingered Langer as the sole shooter, one of many inconsistencies probably inevitable in a trial of 15 defendants and the testimony of a good many more witnesses. In any event, Levine was scheduled to depart for the United States the following day and had no further role to play in the trial whose evidentiary foundation he had laid.[2]

By March 18, the Borkum trial had dragged on for almost six weeks, and Colonel Jackson was becoming impatient. He therefore announced that afternoon that, beginning the following day, court would be in session from 9 A.M. until 10 P.M., with recesses for lunch and dinner.

This would be a grueling schedule for all participants, but particularly so and even dangerous for German civilian counsel, which resided in Stuttgart, nearly 10 miles away via a transportation system still devastated by a war less than a year past. A 10 P.M. adjournment, Dr. Baur pointed out, would not permit a return to Stuttgart before the curfew that had been imposed by U.S. military government. Colonel Jackson's terse "we will arrange for passes" was probably cold comfort.[3]

Emil Sobiech had been deputy commander of the 216th Naval Antiaircraft Battalion and had watched as #909 had made its descent onto the *Muschelfeld*. When interrogated by Major Levine in Esterwegen on October 27, 1945, he explained that he had been ordered by his immediate superior, the battalion commander Walter Krolikovski, to investigate the crash. He bicycled initially to the Ostland Battery, where he encountered several other officers, including Seiler, Wentzel, and the island commander, Goebell. Sobiech noted the presence of the seven American prisoners, who were in the process of emptying their pockets, and observed Goebell replace one of the guards who was not being "strict enough." He remained at the battery long enough to hear Goebell order the prisoners marched over the beach and through the town, specifying the streets that were to be used, directions that, according to Goebell's own testimony, were later changed. Sobiech then visited the crash site to inspect the bomber, pedaled home, then went on to his office in the Dorf Hotel. Searching for Krolikovski in order to make his report, he encountered several soldiers, who informed him that one of the POWs had been shot at the town hall and that the Americans had been beaten by Labor Service men and civilians in the course of the march. Krolikovski went back inside to take a phone call, then returned to the street, where he talked to a group of passing civilians. In great excitement, he directed Sobiech to proceed to the athletic field to ascertain what had transpired. Sobiech again took to his bicycle. On reaching the field, he found a crowd standing around the dead Americans. Sobiech rode back to the Dorf Hotel to report but was brushed off by Krolikovski with a dismissive "I know all about it." Sometime later, he was ordered by the battalion commander to refrain from talking or writing about the incident and to convey the order to the rest of the battalion.[4]

Under questioning by defense counsel in Ludwigsburg, Sobiech provided a more nuanced account of his experiences, one that, not surprisingly, was more favorable to himself. After he had arrived at the Ostland Battery, he testified, he had engaged one of the prisoners in friendly conversation, asking the American where he had been born, a subject of interest to Sobiech as he had once visited the United States. He claimed to have interceded for the prisoners with Goebell, requesting that they be allowed to lower their hands after they had been searched and questioned, and assured the court that, had he been in a position to do so, he would have taken steps to protect the prisoners from attack. Goebell, however, had insisted on strict treatment of the POWs, not only reprimanding and replacing guards considered lax but snarling about "these damned German humanitarian ideas and just now when women and children are being killed in Bremen." In its cross-examination, the prosecution was content to elicit from Sobiech a confirmation of the truthfulness of his sworn statement to Major Levine.[5]

The problem of conflicting defenses among the 15 defendants was never better demonstrated than in the testimony of former general of infantry Hans-Karl von Scheele, brought from U.S. Internment Camp 78 at Zuffenhausen to serve as a witness for the enlisted men. A soldier since 1911, von Scheele not only had much experience as a combat commander but had served at the end of the war as president of Nazi Germany's highest military court. Under questioning by Lieutenant Davis and several of the German defense attorneys, von Scheele explored the command relationship between German enlisted men and their officers. When confronted with the "hypothetical" situation in which seven enlisted men under the command of a sergeant were ordered to conduct prisoners of war to a given destination and were accompanied by an officer who had volunteered to show them the way, von Scheele reached a conclusion dangerous to the officer, Wentzel: under those circumstances, the enlisted men would be justified in assuming that the officer was effectively in command. While the enlisted men would also have been required to refuse to carry out an illegal order, such as withholding protection from the prisoners if they came under attack, and "punishment for not having carried out any such order would have been impossible," liability for an illegal order lay with the officer who had issued it, while the enlisted man would have been acquitted if he could have convinced the court that he had not realized the illegal nature of the order. But what if the order had been justified on the basis of a statement by a high government official, such as Dr. Goebbels? Von Scheele replied that, while Hitler was the "supreme power in the German state" and had the power to issue orders to anyone in that polity, Goebbels had not shared in that power and, more to the point, had possessed no authority over the armed forces. The more pertinent question of what orders concerning the treatment of captured Allied airmen might have come down through the armed forces chain of command was once again not explored.

But clearly the Borkum incident had not played out according to von Scheele's principled analysis. No one, officer or enlisted man, had been punished or even reprimanded for the assaults and murders, and Langer, who had turned an ugly demonstration into a massacre, had been removed from the island, while Borkum's naval authorities had been permitted to sweep the matter under the rug. That, von Scheele opined, had been due to extralegal factors, "the incessant attacks upon German cities and [the] German people. . . . You have to consider that in consideration of the situation at that time. . . I do consider that this was the reason." Von Scheele, it might be assumed, was probably well acquainted with the "extralegal" murder of prisoners of war, given his own wartime service on the Eastern Front, where huge numbers of Soviet POWs had been murdered by the Germans.[6]

Forty-one-year-old Oscar Born was not a defendant, although, as adjutant to Goebell, the island commander, he had been intimately associated with one of the principals in the case. It is difficult to believe that he had not been interrogated by Major Levine but, if he had been, a copy of his sworn statement had not been entered into evidence, nor is one present in the voluminous documentation of the Borkum case. In any event, his account of Goebell's conduct on August 4, 1944, was in sharp variance with the testimony of other witnesses. Under questioning by Dr. Weber, civilian attorney for Goebell, Born testified that he had gone to the Ostland Battery following #909's emergency landing and found Goebell already there. Goebell, it would appear, had been a largely passive spectator. Born had not heard Goebell order the prisoners marched on a specific route through Borkum or telling the guards that protection was to be withheld in case of civilian attack. To Born's knowledge, Goebell had never spoken of Dr. Goebbels's "decree" on the treatment of downed Allied airmen, either, although he had mentioned to Born a speech made by Goebell's immediate superior, Admiral Scheuerlen, in which the latter had complained that "too many prisoners were being taken." Goebell, however, had rejected the implications of Scheuerlen's comments out of hand. In regard to Goebell's decision not to adopt a march route that bypassed the town or to transport the prisoners by rail, Born explained, as Goebell had earlier done, that bypassing the town would have put the

Americans in contact with sympathetic foreign laborers and that fuel shortages had prevented the use of the small, gasoline-powered locomotive. The persuasiveness of the latter argument, however, was weakened by Born's revelation that Goebell had traveled to the crash site by automobile, which he had then sent to bring a war correspondent to the scene.[7] And, on the matter of the mendacious report on the manner in which the American prisoners had been murdered, Born's credibility crumbled under sharp questioning by Lieutenant Davis.

DAVIS: Now, as a matter of fact, when did you find out that these Flyers were shot and not beaten to death?

BORN: I found out about that much later.

DAVIS: How much later?

BORN: At the time when investigations were conducted after the capitulation.

DAVIS: At that time you found out that the seven Flyers had been shot and not beaten to death?

BORN: Yes.

DAVIS: And up until that time you hadn't heard that the Flyers had been shot to death?

BORN: No.

DAVIS: Do you remember one Flyer who died by the Rathaus?

BORN: No.

DAVIS: You never knew that one Flyer had been shot to death at the Rathaus? (the witness hesitates a while before answering)

BRYAN (prosecution):   I'm just wondering what we're waiting for. Does the witness understand that there is a question pending and that he is expected to answer?

BORN: Yes. I believe to remember now that in the report a Flyer that had been shot was mentioned.

DAVIS: You believe now to remember that?

BORN: Yes.

DAVIS: But you never saw Captain Krolikovski's report, did you?

BORN: I had to work on the report in which there was contained the statement of the guards.

DAVIS: As a matter of fact, don't you know that that report that contained the statement of the guards had nothing to say about the Flyer at the Rathaus?

BORN: I can't remember that.

DAVIS: I thought you just said that you remembered that it told about a Flyer being shot at the Rathaus?

BORN: It's possible I am mixing up these things with the stories that were told later that were regarded by us as rumors.

DAVIS: Then there were rumors circulating on Borkum Island, were there, about the way the Flyers died?

BORN: Yes.

DAVIS: But you didn't believe them?

BORN: No.[8]

Once again, a member of the divided and mutually antagonistic defense team had succeeded in discrediting a defense witness. Cross-examining for the prosecution, Major Bryan needed only to continue Davis's line of questioning.

BRYAN: As a matter of fact, it was a matter of common knowledge all over Borkum Island on 4 August and 5 August 1944, among civilians as well as military personnel, that all seven of these Flyers had been shot to death and not beaten to death, isn't that true?

BORN: So many rumors circulated on Borkum Island you didn't know what to believe and you didn't believe anything.

BRYAN: Did you hear or didn't you hear that the Flyers had been shot and not beaten to death on either 4 August or 5 August, 1944.

BORN: As I said before there were so many rumors you could believe them all or believe none.

BRYAN: I move to strike out the answer as not responsive.

PRESIDENT: The witness will answer the question.

BORN: By way of rumors I heard both, either believing both or not believing both.[9]

The degree to which personal animosities and petty disputes might have played a role in the accusations and counteraccusations contained in some of the evidence against the defendants was the theme of testimony provided by a series of tangential witnesses called by defense counsel as the trial struggled toward its conclusion. Jakob Klein, a tax expert in civilian life and an observer in Borkum's radar installation on August 4, 1944, testified that it was well known among the enlisted men of Borkum's naval garrison that Goebell was disliked by his subordinate officers, although Klein was unable to supply specifics to buttress that assessment.[10] Leni Meyer-Gerhards, wife of one of the accused, Klaas Meyer-Gerhards, testified to the long-standing animosity between her family and that of Erna Garrels, one of the witnesses against her husband, due to business competition between the two families, and between Garrels and the Heinemann family, also represented in the prisoners' dock in the person of Heinrich, the latter hostility rooted in Heinemann's refusal or inability to supply parts for a bicycle belonging to the Garrels family. Frau Garrels, she believed, would willingly impute guilt for attacking the Americans to members of either family in order to protect her own husband.[11]

Important testimony concerning the responsibility of police personnel to protect prisoners of war was provided by Heinrich Fisher, a 39-year-old policeman from Emden who held the rank of major. A police official since the days of the Weimar Republic, Fisher was at the time of the trial commander of the Emden gendarmerie under the authority of British occupation forces. Fisher confirmed that civilian policemen such as the defendant Rommel would have had no authority to arrest military personnel guilty of crimes against prisoners of war, but he was evasive on the question of police competence with regard to civilians who had committed offenses against POWs who were in military custody. The air-raid police, as mere auxiliaries, Fisher testified, had no independent arrest authority over military personnel or civilians. When confronted with the situation that had occurred following the shooting of Howard Graham in front of the Rathaus, in which Langer had offered to "finish off" the American but had been chased away by Meyer-Gerhards, Fisher was ambivalent. The air-raid police leader had not been "required" to make an arrest, leaving open the possibility that he might have had the legal authority to do so. In a brief but sharp cross-examination, Major Bryan probed the issue of police authority over civilians who were assaulting prisoners in military custody, to which Fisher continued to respond evasively. Bryan scored a minor victory with the witness's answer to his final question:

BRYAN: So then the truth of it is that both the Wehrmacht, the guards, would owe a duty as well as the policeman [*sic*] to prevent an attack from civilians?
FISHER: Yes.[12]

But it was a member of the defense counsel, Lieutenant Davis, who finally raised a significant issue related to the status of the police in Nazi Germany. Since 1936, *Reichsführer-SS* Heinrich Himmler had been the German national chief of police (*Chef der deutschen Polizei*). The German police, therefore, although they had continued to perform "traditional" police functions, had also been part of the broader SS imperium that was the primary executor of murderous Nazi ideological goals, reflected in the concentration and extermination camp system, in which millions had perished. Himmler had, in fact, anticipated Goebbels by almost a year with regard to captured Allied aircrew, and in an administratively more substantial, less rhetorical form. On August 10, 1943, almost a year prior to the Borkum murders, he had ordered police personnel not to intervene in cases of civilian attacks on downed Allied airmen, a fact clearly more relevant to Rommel's passivity than Goebbels's editorial. This directive was among the thousands of incriminating documents gathered in Nuremberg for the four-power trial of major German war criminals, although how it had come to the attention of Davis is not clear. He queried Fisher about his knowledge of orders from Himmler with regard to police conduct in such situations. Fisher initially claimed ignorance, but Davis was persistent.

> DAVIS: To the best of your memory, no orders were issued as to the treatment of captured flyers, is that correct?
> FISHER: Only the order was issued that in case a plane should crash and members of the crew of this plane should be captured or taken prisoner by the police, they were to be taken to a camp, a prison camp, and the wounded men were to have medical attention right away and that the police were to contact the nearest Luftwaffe agency and hand these prisoners over to the Luftwaffe.
> DAVIS: ... as a matter of fact, isn't it true that orders were passed down by Himmler to the police chiefs of the various towns to the effect that if civilians wanted to make a demonstration against the Flyers, the police were not to protect them?
> FISHER: That order is not known to me since I was doing front-line duty from 1943 to 1944.

The answer indicated Fisher's possible prevarication, as Davis had not specified the date of Himmler's directive. That possibility was

promptly confirmed by Fisher's clearly rattled and implausible response to Davis's final question.

DAVIS: But you have heard of the order, haven't you?
FISHER: Afterwards, when I returned, but not written orders;
it was just talk among the population. It was not known to the
police where this order came from, but it was generally known
among the population also.[13]

The trial wound down with the sweeping together of miscella-
neous bits of testimony and evidence. Emil Sobiech was recalled to
the witness stand by the defense and offered testimony to the effect
that Goebell had expressed regret for having given orders that had
led to tragedy, lamenting that "One has done so many good things
in life and once one has failed, that decides one's fate." Much of
whatever impact Goebell's alleged expression of self-pitying remorse
might have had was lost when, under questioning, Sobiech was unclear about the circumstance under which he had heard or learned of
the remark.[14] The defense attempted to turn one of the sworn statements secured by Levine to its advantage by reading it into the record. Gerhardt Akkermann (not to be confused with defendant Jan
Akkermann) had informed Levine that he had been a machinist employed at Borkum's airfield on August 4, 1944. At around 4 P.M. that
afternoon, he was told by a sergeant that the night crew would have
to guard seven POWs who were to arrive later for transportation to
the mainland the following day, suggesting that the death or serious injury of the Americans had not been intended by Goebell and
his subordinates. Several hours later, the same sergeant had informed
Akkermann that the prisoners had been shot to death, which high-
lighted the implausibility of the claims by Goebell, Wentzel, and others that they had remained ignorant of the true causes of the deaths
of #909's crew.[15] The prosecution read into the record the sworn statement of Emil Fokuhl, an electrician who had also been the driver of
the small, gasoline-powered locomotive that operated on a line that
passed near the Ostland Battery and ran to the airfield. In fact, Fokuhl
had made a run on the afternoon of August 4, 1944, to an electric cable
break apparently caused by #909's crash landing. Although the car
attached to the locomotive was capable of carrying only six people,
Fokuhl testified that a passenger car of larger capacity had been readily available.[16]

Court opened on Thursday, March 21, 25 minutes late due to undefined "trouble with the armored cars" that escorted the truck conveying the defendants to the palace, apparently a not uncommon
occurrence and evidence that the U.S. Army considered the German
defendants (or, perhaps, their supporters) serious threats.[17] The time
had arrived for prosecution and defense to summarize their respective
evidentiary narratives and deliver final arguments. Captain Lyons led
off for the prosecution team with a relatively dispassionate summary
of the evidence against each defendant.[18] It was left to Captain May
to interpret the evidence and to breathe life and passion into a case
that may have demonstrated nothing more than intemperate remarks,
isolated rough treatment of the Americans by a few individuals, and
a callous, although officially encouraged, negligence that had unwittingly set the stage for Langer's murderous assault, rather than the
conscious homicidal conspiracy argued by the prosecution.

May characterized the trial as one addressing "a great tragedy that
has been committed against our country . . . in savage violation of
the rules and usages of war." Images of a Christlike journey to the
place of death were evoked by May's recalling "the cross those seven
American boys had to bear" and "the poor flyers with their hands over
their heads, their faces bloody, with the guards hitting and prodding
them along [sic] with their rifles, civilians . . . rushing into the mob,
hitting and beating, with Krolikovski occupying the grandstand seat,
like a Roman emperor watching the Christians of old being fed to the
lions."[19]

More important than lending pathos to the evidence was assembling it into a context demonstrating conspiracy or common design
that would make all of the defendants guilty of criminal assault and
murder. How the actions (or inactions) of the defendants resulted in
the deaths of #909's crew could best be understood, May argued, in
terms of the dynamics of mob action.

> They did not all participate in exactly the same manner. Members
> of mobs seldom do. One will undertake one special or particular
> action and another will perform another particular action. It is
> the composite of the actions of all that results in the commission
> of a crime. Now, all legal authorities agree that where a common
> design of a mob exists and the mob had carried out its purpose,
> then no distinction can be drawn between the finger man and
> the trigger man. No distinction is drawn between the one who,

by his acts, caused the victims to be subjected to the pleasure of the mob or the one who incited the mob or the one who dealt the fatal blows.[20]

Goebell's call to Akkermann had initiated a series of events that had culminated in Langer's fatal shots in front of the athletic field. Using mechanical imagery that would be employed in other U.S. Army mass trials of Germans accused of war crimes, May continued: "Yes, may it please the court, we have the civilians, we have the officers, and we have the guards, 'C' for civilians, 'O' for officers and 'G' for guards. C-O-G, and cogs they were. Cogs in the wheel of common design, all equally important, each part doing the part assigned to it. And the wheel of wholesale murder could not turn without all the cogs."[21]

Adding an additional helping of melodrama, May concluded with a recitation of the names of the victims—William Lambertus, William J. Myers, James W. Danno, William P. Dold, Harvey M. Walthall, Kenneth Faber, and Howard S. Graham—and a summons to recognize that the Borkum trial served a purpose that transcended the punishment of 15 persons complicit in their murders.

Where they were from we do not know. Some, perhaps from the great North, some, perhaps, from the industrial East, some, perhaps, from the golden West, and perhaps some from the sunny Southland. We know not where, except they were just Americans, their young lives sacrificed on the altar of German Nazism . . . yes, victims of a system we now seek to destroy for all time to come.[22]

The Borkum defendants, it appeared, were to suffer for more than the deaths of seven American airmen.

Major Bryan concluded the prosecution's summation with a discussion of the finer points of law relevant to the charge of conspiracy or participation in a common design. According to Bryan's reading of the venerable *Wharton's Criminal Law,* the threshold for proving conspiracy was modest. It need not be proved that the defendants had formulated a plan to commit criminal acts but, rather, a conspiracy could be inferred from the actions of two or more persons apparently directed towards the commission of a crime. But not only actions were relevant. All persons intentionally present at the scene of criminal acts and not assisting in their suppression might be assumed prima facie to have been participants. Moreover, all participants, active or passive, were liable for "incidental" felonies that might not have been objectives of the original conspiracy but that were consequences of it. Under the prosecution's interpretation of conspiracy, much of the population of Borkum might have been charged with the murders of #909's crew.[23]

Bryan could not avoid an allusion to the ticklish issue of "superior orders." Although the military defendants, by and large, had simply denied having mistreated the prisoners or having intentionally withheld protection from them, frequent references to Dr. Goebbels's "decree" had seemed to imply the influence of higher authority in the atrocity (with the existence of more relevant Wehrmacht orders either ignored or unknown). The issue was an awkward one because, until November 15, 1944, the U.S. Army's own *Basic Field Manual: Rules of Land Warfare,* in discussing the liability of soldiers for violations of the laws of war, had stated that "individuals of the armed forces will not be punished for these offenses in case they are committed under the orders or sanction of their government or commanders."[24] Had the tables been turned and had Americans soldiers been tried for the murders of POWs on August 4, 1944, a defense of superior orders might well have led to an acquittal as, in fact, it had for Captain John Compton when he had been court-martialed for the murder of Axis POWs in Sicily in 1943.[25] But, as Bryan was quick to point out, this provision of the manual had been fundamentally changed. Superior orders were no longer to be deemed a complete defense but might be taken into consideration in determining the degree of a defendant's guilt and in mitigation of his punishment. He might also have noted that the London Charter of the International Military Tribunal, which was trying the major German war criminals at Nuremberg, had incorporated the same standard. Bryan closed his argument by observing that "the old Mosaic law demanding an eye for an eye, a tooth for a tooth and a life for a life has not been repealed by any legislative body of any civilized nation and is fully accepted by the judicial systems of such nations. . . . Thus and only thus can justice be meted out."[26]

The defense rebuttal, not surprisingly, was directed primarily at undermining the credibility of the prosecution's theory that the Borkum killings had been the products of a conspiracy or common design to which the defendants had been party. Success would be determined by the impact of their efforts on the minds of the officers sitting at the front of the courtroom who would judge the defendants and assign punishment—if those minds were open to arguments in defense of former enemies accused of the murders of other American officers and men. The German civilian attorneys, to whom the American concept of conspiracy was largely unfamiliar, engaged in ponderous and often poorly translated analyses and refutations of the evidence against the specific individuals whom they had defended. Captain Phelps, however, delivered a sometimes sardonic critique of the prosecution case as it applied to the civilian defendants.

If all persons consensually present at a mob action were guilty of the criminal consequences, Phelps wondered, why was the number of defendants so small? And, if May had been prosecuting a lynching case in his native South Carolina, would he have presented the "mob theory" so eloquently? The first point was hardly compelling, and the second was a cutting though fundamentally irrelevant aside, as racist southern jurisprudence was not on trial in Ludwigsburg. More to the point was Phelps's construction of a much tighter set of criteria for conspiracy than the prosecution had offered. To be sure, Mayor Akkermann had stood on the corner of Franz Habich and Bahnhof Strassen, attempting to incite the crowd, but had he "set into force a series of acts which could have been reasonably foreseen and did ultimately result in this unlawful homicide?" Had the prosecution demonstrated that Langer had shot the prisoners *because* he had been incited to do so by Akkermann? There was no evidence that Langer had even heard Akkermann's shouts, and, Phelps pointed out, prisoners had been beaten before the procession had reached the place along the march route where Akkermann had placed himself. Nevertheless, Phelps was willing to concede that there might have been a conspiracy between Akkermann and some of the officers to encourage the beating of the prisoners by civilians, but there was no evidence of a conspiracy to kill them. The evidence against the other civilian defendants, he argued, was even thinner. Delicately avoided as it had been in all of the arguments by the defense as well as the prosecution was the obvious point that the apparent loss of Langer's wife and children to Allied bombing would appear to have provided more than adequate stimulus for Langer's deadly assault.[27]

Phelps closed his argument with an effort to put the Borkum trial into broader context. Following World War I, he noted, the Allies had permitted Germany to try its own war criminals, and the results had been farcical. A handful out of hundreds of men accused by the Allies had been tried, half of whom were acquitted, and the remainder given light sentences. Phelps feared that the pendulum, now under Allied control and in an atmosphere of war-bred hatred, had swung too far in the other direction. The policy was not only "reactionary" but hypocritical. Phelps revealed that he had commanded an infantry platoon at Anzio and knew from personal experience that the U.S. Army had not always treated German POWs in accordance with the laws of war. American violations had either gone unpunished or had been visited with lenient penalties. Phelps illustrated the point with the case of a GI who had been court-martialed for mistreating German POWs, sentenced to two years' imprisonment, then pardoned after outraged congressional intervention. "Gentlemen, is it any less a war crime if we commit the act than if our enemy violates the rules of land warfare?" Phelps's rhetorically expressed confidence that the Ludwigsburg court would deal with Germans no more severely than it would with Americans accused of similar offenses was in fact, as he must have known, a slim hope.[28]

Further critiques of the prosecution's conspiracy theory were delivered by Lieutenant Davis and Captain Hall. The notion that a conspiracy existed to kill the American POWs was, on its face, incredible, Davis argued. Preparations had been made to receive the prisoners at the airfield that evening in anticipation of their movement to the mainland the following day. The guards may have obeyed illegal orders to withhold protection from the prisoners, but it would not have been unreasonable for them to have supposed that the Americans, characterized by Goebbels as murderers of German women and children, were themselves war criminals undeserving of the rights due POWs under international law. And, of course, the actual murderer, Langer, had been a wholly independent force totally unconnected to the defendants. Were the guards to be condemned, Davis declared dramatically, the sacrifice of #909's crew, who "flew their last mission to help make our system of law a reality in the world," would be desecrated.[29] The officers may have used poor judgment, Hall conceded, but the tragic outcome of the march was a result of the irresponsible conduct of Akkermann and the unforeseen intervention of a madman. The evidence for conspiracy was so thin, Hall observed mockingly, that the prosecution was obliged to bring in Roman emperors and the throwing of Christians to the lions![30] The fear that the officers sitting in judgment might not weigh the evidence dispassionately or be free to do so was implicit in Davis's admonition to the bench to resist "pressure from above," the "sudden spotlight of publicity," and "veiled threats" and in Hall's urging that the judges overcome "the understandable prejudices of our time."[31]

It was 8:15 P.M. on the evening of March 22 when Colonel Jackson, president of the court, ruled that no further argument would be heard. The court was closed six minutes later, and the panel of officers hearing the case retired to reach their verdicts.[32]

There is no record of the deliberations of the seven officers who decided the Borkum case. The court was reconvened at 11:05 P.M., the panel having spent an average of approximately 10 minutes in determining the guilt or innocence of each defendant. Given the reams of convoluted testimony that had been given over the previous six weeks, not to mention the sworn statements that had been secured by Major Levine, it is difficult to avoid the conclusion that the deliberations were superficial. Colonel Jackson ordered the court interpreter to call the name of each accused, who was to stand as his verdict was pronounced. Goebell, the top-ranking defendant, was first. "Kurt Goebell, the Court in closed session at least two thirds of the members present at the time the vote was taken concurring in each finding of guilty, finds you of the particulars to charge one [murder] guilty; of charge one, guilty; of the particulars to charge two [assault] guilty; of charge two, guilty"[33]

Over the next 25 minutes, the same form was followed for the remaining 14 Germans. The other four officers—Krolikovski, Weber, Wentzel, and Seiler—were also pronounced guilty of both charges and their particulars, as was Schmitz, the senior noncom. Pointner, Geyer, Albrecht, and Witzke, all enlisted men, were acquitted of murder but found guilty of assault. The civilians Rommel, Mammenga, and Heinemann received like verdicts, but Akkermann was convicted on both charges. Meyer-Gerhards was acquitted of both.[34]

Although it was now approaching midnight, Colonel Jackson was determined to bring the proceedings to an end before adjourning. The convicted defendants were invited to present statements of extenuating circumstances—essentially pleas for mercy—before sentencing. Whether out of despair, exhaustion, or recognition of guilt, none did. The court closed for 40 minutes, then reconvened in the early minutes of a new day. Goebell rose as Colonel Jackson called his name. "Kurt Goebell, the Court, in closed session, at least two thirds of the members present at the time the vote was taken concurring, sentences you to death by hanging at such time and place as higher authority may direct."[35]

Wentzel and Seiler heard the same grim formula, while Krolikovski was sentenced to life in prison and Weber to 25 years. Schmitz was condemned to the gallows, while Pointner, Albrecht, Geyer, and Witzke were given prison sentences ranging from 4 to 11 years. Of the civilians, Rommel, the policeman, received a sentence of 2 years, Heinemann 18, and Mammenga 20. Akkermann was sentenced to hang. The Borkum trial officially concluded at 12:30 A.M.[36]

NOTES

1. "Record of Testimony," 1045–47, *U.S. v. Goebell* (frames 459–61, reel 2).
2. Ibid., 1047–55 (frames 461–70).
3. Ibid., 1069 (frame 484).
4. "Testimony of Emil Sobiech," October 27, 1945, 2–7, *U.S. v. Goebell* (frames 342–47, reel 1).
5. "Record of Testimony," 1072–73, 1084, ibid. (frames 488–89, 500, reel 2).
6. Ibid., 1085–93 (frames 501–8).
7. Ibid., 1096–1100, 1103 (frames 511–15, 518).
8. Ibid., 1107–08 (frames 522–23).
9. Ibid., 1111–12 (frames 526–27).
10. Ibid., 1116, 1120–21 (frames 530, 534–35).
11. Ibid., 1135–36 (frames 549–50).
12. Ibid., 1143–1148a (frames 557–59, 562–63).
13. Ibid., 1148b–49 (frames 564–66); Vasilis Vourkoutiotis, *Prisoners of War and the German High Command: The British and American Experience* (New York: Palgrave Macmillan, 2003), 188.
14. "Record of Testimony," 1156, 1161–62, *U.S. v. Goebell* (frames 573, 578–79, reel 2).
15. "Testimony of Gerhardt Akkermann," October 10, 1945, 1169–70, ibid. (frames 586–87).
16. "Testimony of Emil Fokuhl," October 12, 1945, 1173–74, ibid. (frames 590–91).
17. Ibid., 1176 (frame 593).
18. Ibid., 1178–85 (frames 595–602).
19. Ibid., 1187 (frame 604).
20. Ibid., 1186 (frame 603).
21. Ibid., 1188 (frame 605); James J. Weingartner, *Crossroads of Death: The Story of the Malmédy Massacre and Trial* (Berkeley and Los Angeles: University of California Press, 1979), 101.
22. "Record of Testimony," 1189, *U.S. v. Goebell* (frame 606, reel 2).
23. Ibid., 1190–92 (frames 607–9).
24. U.S. War Department, *Basic Field Manual: Rules of Land Warfare* (Washington, DC: U.S. Government Printing Office, 1940), 87.
25. *United States of America v. Compton, Capt. John T.,* Clerk of Court, U.S. Army Judiciary, Arlington, VA, 63.

26. "Record of Trial," 1193–94, *U.S. v. Goebell* (frames 610–11); "Charter of the International Military Tribunal," Article 8, *The Avalon Project at Yale Law School,* http://avalon.law.yale.edu/imtconst.asp.

27. "Record of Testimony," 1203–06, *U.S. v. Goebell* (frames 620–23).

28. Ibid., 1206–07 (frames 623–24).

29. Ibid., 1269, 1273, 1276–77 (frames 686, 690, 693–94).

30. Ibid., 1278–79 (frames 695–96).

31. Ibid., 1268, 1279 (frames 685, 696).

32. Ibid., 1280 (frame 697).

33. Ibid., 1280–81 (frames 697–98).

34. Ibid., 1281–83 (frames 698–700).

35. Ibid., 1283 (frame 700).

36. Ibid., 1284–86, (frames 701–3).

7

Germans as Victims

War-crimes trials were common events in the immediate aftermath of World War II, an almost unimaginably savage conflict. The overwhelming majority of them, such as the Borkum trial, were held to punish the recently defeated enemy, but not all. In July 1945, four American soldiers were tried by U.S. Army courts-martial in Czechoslovakia for offenses committed the previous March in the German town of Voerde. Unbeknownst to the participants, these proceedings would have important implications for Germans' assessment of the Borkum case and for post–World War II U.S. war-crimes justice in general.

The U.S. Eighth Armored Division, the "Thundering Herd," was a latecomer to the European war, entering combat in eastern France in January 1945 against a German army fast coming to the end of its resources, both human and material. Within the month, the division was moved north to the Netherlands to take part in the drive of Lieutenant General William Simpson's Ninth Army to the Rhine, which was crossed on March 26.[1] On the following morning, elements of the division, the 49th Armored Infantry Battalion reinforced by Company B of the 36th Tank Battalion, entered the German town of Voerde. Shortly after breakfast, Second Lieutenant Robert A. Schneeweiss, the 24-year-old commander of one of Company B's tank platoons, ordered 18-year-old Private Francis Nichols and 19-year-old Private Glen Joachims to accompany him to test their weapons or, more ominously, to hunt for Germans. Approaching a nearby house, they were informed of the presence inside of two male civilians. Declaring that he would "take care of them," Schneeweiss entered the dwelling with the young privates. Under orders from Schneeweiss, Joachims and Nichols took the Germans into the basement and shot them to death.

Schneeweiss also directed 19-year-old Private William Peppler to shoot two women who had been discovered a short distance away. Through the window of a house, Peppler observed the women rummaging through a chest of drawers. He fired into or around the window but stated that he could not bring himself to fire directly at the women. Reporting his reluctance to Schneeweiss, he was ordered to return to the house with Nichols and to kill them. As the two GIs approached, the terrified women attempted to flee but were cut down by M-3 "grease gun" submachine-gun fire in the backyard of the house. Schneeweiss joined the two privates and, finding the women still alive and groaning and thrashing about, killed them both with his .45-caliber pistol. Nichols then departed for a "KP" (kitchen patrol) assignment, while Schneeweiss and Peppler continuing hunting "Krauts." Finding two male civilians crossing a plowed field, Schneeweiss opened fire with an M-1 rifle. Both men fell wounded along a hedgerow at the edge of the field. Peppler appears to have fired in the direction of the victims but, perhaps still resisting orders to murder civilians, might not have aimed at them. In any event, it was Schneeweiss who once again finished the job with bursts from Peppler's M-3. One or possibly two more German civilians apparently were also murdered, but the circumstances of these killings, for reasons that are not clear, were not investigated.[2]

Like the Borkum murders, the killings in Voerde were not classic "heat-of-battle" atrocities, in which the victims were done to death during or immediately after the rage, fury, and confusion of combat. The U.S mechanized group to which Schneeweiss's platoon belonged had traveled from Venlo in the Netherlands to Voerde without encountering enemy resistance other than a lightning-fast strafing run on the night of March 26–27 by a German jet aircraft (probably a Messerschmitt 262) in the vicinity of Herongen, a raid that, although alarming, had done little damage to the column and none to Company B. Schneeweiss had seen virtually no combat. His only experience of being under fire from German ground forces had occurred when he had test-fired the guns of his tank from the west bank of the Rhine at targets on the far side and had received some German mortar fire in return. He had attempted to fire the .50-caliber machine gun mounted atop the turret of his tank at the marauding German jet but had failed to get the weapon into operation before the enemy plane was gone. Nor had Schneeweiss viewed evidence of Nazi mass atrocities in liberated concentration camps, an experience that often filled GIs with hatred of all things German. There had, in fact, existed nearby a facility for the infant children of Eastern European women employed as slave laborers at Krupp's gigantic manufacturing complex in Essen where large numbers had died of disease and neglect, but that had been evacuated before the arrival of the Americans. No German forces had been present in Voerde to contest the GIs' advance, and the only shooting that had accompanied the capture of the town had been from GIs dispatching the local population of chickens.[3]

Most atrocities in World War II went unreported and unpunished. But, unlike the German failure to take action against Langer or anyone else involved in the Borkum atrocity, the U.S. Army, to its credit, moved swiftly to investigate most of the Voerde murders. These were glaring violations of Article 46 of the Hague Convention (IV) of 1907, which requires an occupying army to respect the lives of persons in occupied territory, while Article 19 of the U.S. Army's *Rules of Land Warfare* states that "It is now universally recognized that hostilities are restricted to the armed forces of belligerents. Inhabitants who refrain from acts of hostility . . . must not be injured in their lives or liberty, except for cause and after due trial."[4]

Killing large numbers of enemy civilians by remote and impersonal air attack, if not simply ignored or denied, was rationalized as an unavoidable necessity of war, but the face-to-face murder of peaceful residents of a small town, including two women, could apparently still disturb. The incident was reported to the intelligence officer of the Eighth Armored Division's Combat Command B, Major John Elting, at around 10 A.M., by Lieutenant Georgi, his prisoner interrogation officer, and by Captain Coleman, the command's military government officer, both of whom may have been more sensitive to atrocities than combat troops. Elting reported what he had been told to the commander of Combat Command B, Colonel Edward Kimball, who ordered Elting to conduct a preliminary inquiry. Witnesses were interviewed and probable responsibility fixed on a lieutenant from the 36th Tank Battalion's B Company. All of the company's lieutenants were assembled for scrutiny by the witnesses, and Schneeweiss was identified as the culprit. Elting had Schneeweiss disarmed and arrested and reported his findings by telephone to the Eighth Armored's inspector general, Lieutenant Colonel Harold G. MacAdams, along with the information that Schneeweiss was being sent to XIX Corps headquarters in nearby Lintfort.[5] MacAdams found him there in military police custody and questioned him that evening and for much of the following day. Schneeweiss initially denied his guilt:

> Well, all I can say is I can't believe I am here to be tried for some-thing like that. I didn't kill any civilians. . . . Everything seems to be all jumbled up to me, I can't figure it out for myself. These two men that were with me can vouch for the fact that I didn't shoot those civilians.[6]

Schneeweiss claimed that he had been on an innocent excursion with some enlisted men of his platoon who had wanted to test-fire their small arms. He had seen dead civilians, but only after having been told about them by unidentified informants. Schneeweiss con-ceded that, as a German civilian had bicycled past, he had "made a crack to the fellows that I would get him on the second bounce" but observed that, had he been intent on killing civilians, he would have shot the man immediately.[7] Lieutenant William Kellner of Head-quarters Company, 49th Armored Infantry Battalion, had been one of "the fellows," and he told MacAdams a somewhat different story. He had been speaking to Schneeweiss about what to do with civilians in order to free up housing for the occupying forces. Schneeweiss had allegedly observed, "Well, in the 36th [Tank Battalion] we either shoot them or kick them out," to which he had added, "I just got two." The cyclist had then pedaled by, prompting Schneeweiss to ask Kellner if he had seen the man. In response to Kellner's answer that he had, Schneeweiss had replied, "Well, he's not going to come back."[8] Tech. 5 Nathan Schumer remembered Schneeweiss asking how civilians were treated, to which Schumer had replied that they followed orders and moved civilians if that was necessary. He recalled Schneeweiss responding with "we don't want any part of them, we either shoot them or drive them in front of us."[9] Sergeant Donald J. Welch of the 49th Armored Infantry Battalion offered a more expansive narrative:

> It was on the 27th of March, we were looking for billets, and we were down at this one house, and there was [*sic*] two dead civil-ians down in the basement, and then we waited for our platoon sergeant . . . and while we were standing there, this officer and three enlisted men walked by us . . . and this officer said "see that fellow coming down the road on the bicycle? Well, we're going to shoot him." So I said to the other sergeant that was

with me, "he won't shoot him," and the officer said, "the hell I won't. . . ." But he didn't shoot him and let him go on past him. And then somebody from the rear hollered up that he wanted one of the KP's with him, so he said "get the hell back there," and he [Nichols?] said, "no, I want to go with you." So he told him to get the hell back, and this guy turned around and went back. Then he walked on up the road and, in the meantime, me and the two sergeants went back in the house and I said, "let's turn around and see if he is really going to shoot him." So we went out . . . and we saw him stop, and there were two civilians there close to an orchard, and he shot three times. They dropped over dead and he went over to them with a submachine gun and shot them five or six times.

MacAdams questioned Welch about the killing of the two women. The sergeant replied that he hadn't witnessed those murders but that Schneeweiss had mentioned that he had "killed five of them" that morning.[10] The other two sergeants, Francis Stemock and John Dauphinis, testified similarly to Welch.[11]

Schneeweiss had assured MacAdams that the "two" men who had been with him on the morning of the 27th would vouch for his innocence; when questioned by MacAdams the following day, Private Glen Joachims did precisely that. Schneeweiss had not fired a shot while in his presence, he claimed, and the only dead civilians he had seen had been in the basement of the house. When asked directly by MacAdams whether he himself had shot civilians, Joachims flatly denied it. He had fired his submachine gun, but only to test it.[12]

But Private William Peppler testified with greater candor, although reluctantly and with considerable circumlocution. He had seen dead civilians in a field where he had been firing, had been told by Schneeweiss that they were going to "shoot Krauts," and had also seen Schneeweiss firing an M-1 rifle, but, when asked by MacAdams whether he had seen anyone shoot the civilians, he initially declined to answer. But when asked whether *he* had shot civilians, Peppler surprisingly replied that he had, although he quickly withdrew his answer when reminded of article 24. Candor reasserted itself at the close of the interrogation.

MACADAMS: Do you have anything else to say before we close this part of the investigation?

PEPPLER: I think not. I had no reason for killing any civilians
as they didn't have rifles.
MACADAMS: I though you said a minute ago that you did kill
some?
PEPPLER: Well, that was under orders.[13]

Private Nichols was even more forthcoming, although with a greater
effort to claim extenuating circumstances. He had seen civilians killed
and, although reminded of his right not to incriminate himself, admitted that he had participated. But he claimed, without elaboration, that
the two men murdered in the basement had been "Heinie soldiers in
civilian clothes," of whom Schneeweiss had said, "Take the bastards
downstairs and shoot them." The women, in Nichols's mind, had become looters who had been shot while trying to escape. In any event,
he claimed, the commander of the 36th Tank Battalion, Major John van
Houten, had said that the outfit's "first job is to kill civilians."[14]
On March 30, MacAdams confronted Schneeweiss with the overwhelming evidence against him. After having heard a synopsis of the
testimony, Schneeweiss seemed close to incoherence, responding with
a feeble "I can't figure it out" and "I don't know what to do, Colonel,"
then "I don't know what to say. I have no more witnesses. It is a good
way to fight for your country." Finally, in a quasi-confession combined
with an effort to protect Joachims, Nichols, and Peppler, Schneeweiss
declared:

I don't know what has come over me. I've been in a fog ever since
it happened. It wasn't their fault, they would listen to any officer.
They shouldn't suffer for anything I did. They were just obeying
orders, that's all. They are as foolish as I am, I guess.[15]

But what of the German victims who, in the testimony gathered
from the GIs, had been faceless ciphers for whom scant sympathy
had been shown? The bodies had been identified and buried by the
temporary mayor of Voerde, Johann Hellmich, and Ernst Eichelkamp.
MacAdams questioned the two men, along with some unidentified
residents of the town, on April 1. Some of the dead had been personally known to Hellmich, while the names of others were provided by
relatives. The two men who were shot in the basement of the house
visited by Schneeweiss, Nichols, and Joachims were the householder,
Heinrich Ufermann, and his son-in-law, Heinrich Neppeney, while

the two women were Therese Hinnemann and her sister, Frieda Payenberg. Hinnemann had resided in the house behind which she had been killed, and she had been cleaning the dwelling with Payenberg's help. Heinrich Payenberg Sr. and Heinrich Payenberg Jr., presumably related to Frieda, although MacAdams did not probe the matter, were the men shot in the open field. A Dietrich or Fritz Lorberg (Eichelkamp was uncertain) was one of possibly two other civilians murdered on March 27 under circumstances that were not investigated. The Germans were not asked whether they had witnessed any of the killings, although Eichelkamp volunteered that "We didn't see anything so we don't have anything [more] to say."[16]

The case against the Borkum defendants had been based on the theory that they had consciously and willfully engaged in a criminal conspiracy to ill treat American prisoners of war and that that conspiracy had led directly to the prisoners' deaths. The U.S. Army approached the Voerde killings very differently. The four suspects were held in custody in the Ninth Army stockade while the war ground on to its conclusion, on May 7–8, 1945. Later that month, the men were subjected to psychiatric examinations intended to determine whether they had been sane and capable of distinguishing right from wrong at the time of the murders. This was standard procedure in court-martial proceedings stemming from serious offenses under the Articles of War, although it was nowhere in evidence in the Army's preparation of war-crimes cases against German defendants. Some of the witnesses whom MacAdams had questioned had characterized Schneeweiss's demeanor on the day of the murders as odd and had suggested that the lieutenant had been "battle happy," in spite of the fact that he had not been involved in significant combat. There seems to have been an implicit reluctance to accept that "normal" American soldiers were capable of the murders of unarmed persons who posed no threat to them, although no questions had been raised as to the sanity of the Germans accused of complicity in the Borkum killings. A three-member board of Army psychiatrists found Schneeweiss, Peppler, Nichols, and Joachims "free from mental defect, disease or derangement" that would have prevented them from distinguishing right from wrong and adhering to the right and refraining from the wrong at the time of the murders.[17]

The movements of the Eighth Armored Division in the immediate postwar period for occupation duty in the Harz Mountains area of central Germany and then in Czechoslovakia delayed the opening of the courts-martial until July.[18] Schneeweiss was to be tried separately from Joachims, Nichols, and Peppler, another significant difference with the Borkum trial. There would be no conflicting defenses between officer and enlisted men in their trials, nor was there a hint of alleged conspiracy in the cases brought against them, although it would not have taken much imagination to have constructed such a theory including others besides the four men actually tried. The battalion commander had allegedly said *something* that had seemed to encourage the killings, and there had been no apparent effort from other GIs to discourage Schneeweiss's openly proclaimed murderous ambitions, and at least one of them had passively watched as he had shot the two male civilians in the open field. Major Bryan's conception of conspiracy as applied to the Borkum defendants would have embraced a good many more men than Lieutenant Schneeweiss and the three privates.

Schneeweiss appeared before a general court-martial convened on July 21 in Rokycany, Czechoslovakia, charged with violation of the 92nd Article of War, which dealt with the crimes of murder and rape, in the killings of the two Heinrich Payenbergs, Frieda Payenberg, and Therese Hinnemann, but strangely, not with the basement murders of Neppeney and Ufermann. The 92nd Article mandated the death penalty or life imprisonment for those found guilty. Technically, therefore, Schneeweiss was charged not with a war crime under international law but with an offense under the U.S. Army's own internal code. Early in the trial, however, "judicial notice" was taken of Article 19 of the Army's *Rules of Land Warfare*, which echoed the Hague (IV) Convention's protections of civilian populations.[19]

Serving as judges and jury were nine officers, most holding the rank of lieutenant colonel, with Brigadier General and West Pointer Charles F. Colson as law member (and, as the senior officer, presumably president). A single defendant, however, required much smaller prosecution and defense teams than would 15. Responsible for prosecuting Schneeweiss were trial judge advocates Captain Roger Joseph and Captain John Putnam, while defending him were Captain Albert Joven and Captain William Behrens.[20] More striking was the difference in tone between the two trials. At Rokycany, there was none of the pathos and drama or expressions of moral outrage on the part of the prosecution that had been so much in evidence in Ludwigsburg. The Borkum trial had been in part a morality play enacted before an audience, whose purpose was the exposure and punishment by the forces of good of a thin slice of the Nazi evil. A substantial photographic record of the Borkum atrocity and trial was created by the U.S. Army that keeps alive the tragedy and drama of the events. We are able, many decades later, to recoil in horror at photographs of the decomposed corpses of the victims, view the route of the "death march" as it was little more than a year after the atrocity, and look upon the faces of the defendants, including those who were hanged seconds before they dropped into eternity. The courts-martial in Rokycany, by contrast, were closed, prosaic, and tightly controlled exercises by the U.S. Army in the maintenance of internal discipline that brought to trial only those men accused of personally violating the 92nd Article of War. There are no photographs of the victims, of the locations of the murders, or of the courts-martial themselves. The only visual evidence of the Voerde atrocity is a crude hand-drawn map of the tiny area in which the murders had taken place, introduced by the prosecution in Schneeweiss's court-martial as "Exhibit A."

The trial of Robert Schneeweiss began with the testimony of the first prosecution witness, First Lieutenant Richard Redmon of the 49th Armored Infantry Battalion. Redmon described having viewed the bodies of six German civilians on the morning of March 27. He had descended into the cellar of the Ufermann house in the company of Captain Pfister, the battalion dental officer, and Captain Gaulet, its medical officer, and had discovered the bodies of two male civilians lying side by side on the concrete floor, one face up and the other face down. Considerable blood was in evidence, along with several spent .45-caliber shell casings. When asked whether the bodies had still been warm, the witness replied that he had not touched them, but he was prevented from relating what Captain Gaulet had told him, that being hearsay evidence, which was excluded from courts-martial, although freely admissible in the war-crimes trials of enemy personnel. Similarly, Redmon's testimony that the positions of the bodies of the two men in the field and the two women in the yard of the Hinnemann house suggested that they had been running at the time of their having been shot was stricken as "opinion." The defense limited itself to inquiring whether Redmon knew the identities of the bodies he had viewed, which he denied.[21]

The prosecution next called Major Morris Labess who, on March 27, had been the surgeon of the Eighth Armored Division's Combat Command B. He had been approached that morning by Lieutenant Georgi, who had invited him to come along and "see something." Labess may have examined the bodies of all of the murdered civilians, but he was questioned only about the four of whose killings Schneeweiss was accused. Of the two "females," one had been young and the other, middle aged. The two were lying close together. The older woman had been shot through the head, with brain matter protruding from the exit wound at the back of the skull. Her companion had been shot through the breast, and no exit wound had been visible. Labess estimated that they had not been dead for more than an hour to an hour and a half, as the bodies had still been warm. Uncongealed blood had dripped from their wounds. The two men whose bodies were found in the field had been also middle aged. The face of one of them had been partially shot away. They, too, had been killed recently. Labess was confident that all four had died by small-arms fire, rather than by shrapnel from exploding artillery shells.[22]

Having established the deaths and the means thereof of the four German civilians, the prosecution turned to establishing the responsibility of Schneeweiss for their murders. Private Francis Nichols, one of the alleged participants and soon to face his own court-martial, appeared as a prosecution witness, assured of his right not to be forced to incriminate himself. The prosecution's original intent was to allow the witness to offer, in his own words, a narrative of his experiences that morning. The defense, however, objected that to allow Nichols to speak freely and at length might create "a good chance that the witness will bring into evidence certain facts that should not be brought out at this trial." What these "facts" might have been was not explained, although the objection probably referred to the danger of self-incrimination. In any event, the objection was sustained, and Nichols began carefully controlled testimony under prosecution questioning.[23]

Nichols testified that he had been a member of Schneeweiss's platoon and on KP duty with Company B's field kitchen when the company had entered Voerde on the morning of March 27. The kitchen had been placed between two houses, one of which he, Schneeweiss, and several other unnamed GIs had entered with the apparent intention of requisitioning it for use by U.S. troops. Present also were two civilians, one of whom was described by Nichols as wearing "regular civilian clothes" and the other a "civilian shirt" and what "looked like a pair of German army shoes and sort of black pants with a stripe on the side." When asked what had happened to the two civilians, Nichols declined to answer, as he did when asked about the cause of death of the two "females" whose bodies he admitted having seen that morning. Both refusals were accepted by the prosecution without comment.[24]

Precisely how members of Schneeweiss's platoon had been instructed to behave toward German civilians was of obvious importance to the prosecution case and to Schneeweiss's defense. In his statement to MacAdams four months earlier, Nichols had asserted that the 36th Tank Battalion's commander, Major John van Houten, had declared that the battalion's "first job is to kill civilians" as the unit was about to cross the Rhine. The defense evidently saw in this potential mitigation of Schneeweiss's responsibility for his conduct. Nichols was given a copy of the earlier statement and invited to read it. Having done so, he observed that "there was an error." Asked to explain, he replied, "Where it says about our job was to kill civilians [*sic*], that was wrong, he said to kill Germans. He said our first job was to kill the enemy, that was the Germans, and his job was to see that we all got through all right and could get back to the states again." But when asked what he understood van Houten to have meant by "Germans," whether "soldiers, women, men," Nichols answered, "He talked about both," immediately qualifying that statement with "I don't remember exactly what he said." On redirect, the prosecution succeeded in obscuring the issue even further by eliciting from Nichols that he thought van Houten had been encouraging the killing of "mostly" German soldiers and that, in any case, he was uncertain that Schneeweiss had been present to hear the major's ambiguous pep talk. Ironically, it had been van Houten who, as a matter of administrative form, had brought the charges against the defendant.[25]

Nichols' testimony was followed by that of Private Peppler, whose questioning by the prosecution was also prefaced by a reminder of the protections against self-incrimination contained in the 24th Article of War. Peppler immediately attempted to avail himself of it by refusing to reveal what Schneeweiss had said to him on March 27 or even whether he had been in his company. Directed by the court to answer, he replied that he had been approached by Schneeweiss at around 7 A.M. and told "to go down the road and get a few Krauts." When asked what he had understood the lieutenant to have meant, Peppler answered, "I understood him to mean to kill the Krauts," an interpretation that had been based, he added, on his awareness that two civilians had already been shot in the basement of their home. How he had acquired this prior knowledge was a matter not pursued, although the fact that he had "heard" of their killing resulted in the testimony being stricken as hearsay, again, a category of evidence readily admissible in U.S. Army proceedings against Germans, such as the Borkum trial.[26]

> I went down the road, he said they were in the first house. I looked in the first house, but there was no one there. I went to the second house and there were two women in there. It looked like they were looting. I could see through the window. I fired a few rounds around the window panes and they went to the back of the house. I got scared and came back to the company. I told him I can't do it [*sic*]. He told me to go out anyway, male or female, kill them.[27]

Peppler sought to continue his narrative but was again reminded of his right not to incriminate himself and stopped. Under continued questioning by the prosecution, he described the location of the bodies of the two women, still alive although wounded in the legs before Schneeweiss killed them with his .45, but not his own role in wounding them, and Schneeweiss's shooting of the two male civilians in the field.[28]

In its cross-examination of Peppler, the defense attempted to elicit testimony suggesting that Schneeweiss's actions had been the consequence of temporary insanity. Peppler seemed willing to help, but the 18-year-old, when asked to describe Schneeweiss's demeanor, could only answer vaguely that "he seemed a little unusual" or "peculiar," testimony the insubstantial nature of which the prosecution emphasized in its redirect. Peppler's observation that Schneeweiss had not slept for 24 hours prior to the killings did little to resuscitate the case for diminished responsibility. Sleep deprivation is one of the more common afflictions of men at war. The defense touched on Major van Houten's "pep talk" prior to the Rhine crossing but made no effort to exploit Peppler's recollection that "He said that the Germans will be eliminated and it was his job to get us over and it was his duty to get us back."[29]

Before Peppler left the witness stand, one of the judges succeeded in eliciting from him testimony that reflected a bit of the horror of that bloody morning in Voerde.

> COURT: You testified a while ago that you and Lieutenant Schneeweiss saw these two women and you further said you

thought they were wounded at that time. Were they standing, sitting, walking, lying, running, what were they doing?

PEPPLER: They were lying.

COURT: You further testified that they were not dead, but injured. How do you know if they were lying down?

PEPPLER: They were jumping around [*sic*] and making noise.

COURT: After the Lieutenant fired, did you see them jump, did you see the missiles hit them?

PEPPLER: I saw the holes and the blood.[30]

Sergeants Welch and Dauphinis recounted what they had witnessed on the morning of March 27 (and told MacAdams), Dauphinis adding that, as Schneeweiss had fired his M-1 at the two civilians in the field, he had heard a GI shout, "You got him!"[31] Colonel MacAdams described his interrogations of Schneeweiss, noting in response to questions by the defense that the defendant had seemed rational and emotionally stable.[32]

Van Houten did not testify on the critical issue of what he might have told Schneeweiss, for he was not present, nor was his absence explained. Instead, his then-executive officer, Major Frank E. Moore, appeared as a witness for the prosecution. Moore remembered that Schneeweiss had asked van Houten "what his policy was towards the Germans." The battalion commander had replied that "our mission was to destroy the Germans," although Moore assumed that both Schneeweiss and van Houten had understood "Germans" to mean the German army.[33] But would so seemingly self-evident a point have required elucidation or even mentioning? No one asked the question. Major Malcolm J. Dugas of the 49th Armored Infantry Battalion, to which Schneeweiss's company had been attached in Voerde, testified that the battalion's policy toward German civilians had been to treat them "justly, firmly and fairly."[34]

The court adjourned at midafternoon at the request of the prosecution to permit the appearance of the Eighth Armored Division's psychiatrist, a crucial witness in light of the defense's introduction of Schneeweiss's alleged mental derangement. The trial resumed on the morning of July 23 with Major Nathan N. Root, a psychiatrist with pre-war experience in New York's famed Bellevue psychiatric hospital, on the witness stand. Root had been a member of a three-man board that had included two other Ninth Army divisional psychiatrists. It had examined Schneeweiss on May 26, questioning him on his background, his family life, "and his mental processes at the time of the alleged offenses." This was standard procedure, Root pointed out, in cases involving serious infractions of the Articles of War. Schneeweiss had been found to have been able to distinguish right from wrong and of adhering to the right and refraining from the wrong; he was also found capable of cooperating in his own defense.[35] His defense counsel might have legitimately questioned whether an obviously rather superficial examination had much probative value but limited itself to noting that the psychiatrists had interviewed Schneeweiss two months subsequent to the murders.[36]

Major Root's testimony marked the conclusion of the prosecution phase of the trial. The defense introduced several witnesses who testified as to their impressions of the defendant's mental state at the time of the murders. In the absence of a plausible claim of superior orders, demonstrating some degree of mental incapacity was Schneeweiss's only conceivable defense in a case in which the murders in question were incontrovertible and that multiple witnesses had seen the defendant commit. These witnesses, while testifying that Schneeweiss had seemed nervous, unstable, or abnormal, also emphasized that their impressions were based on very brief contact.[37] One explained that his conclusion that Schneeweiss "was a little off" was based on the crimes themselves—that only an unstable personality would have been capable of committing them, although a factor contributing to that instability might have been sleep deprivation.[38] This was pretty thin stuff and unlikely to neutralize the report of the psychiatric board, superficial as its examination might have been.

The defense had nothing to lose by calling upon Schneeweiss to speak for himself. His defense counsel led him through a lengthy biographical disquisition that was patiently tolerated by the court and by the prosecution. He had been one of five children—the next to youngest—of a working-class Milwaukee family. His father had been a heavy drinker, he testified, often spending his paycheck on booze, leading to "pretty stiff arguments" between his parents and the necessity of his mother's taking a job, leaving the children to fend for themselves. Schneeweiss recalled nightmares about "large animals and falling off buildings" and frequently wet his bed. He had been an indifferent student and, at the age of 15, had spent "a week or two" in a detention home for truancy, following which he had completed his formal education in a vocational school. Childhood surgery for osteomyelitis, he testified, had made him reluctant to engage in fights, resulting in mockery from other boys.

If Schneeweiss had found employment following technical school in the Depression-wracked U.S. economy, it did not enter into his testimony. He had enlisted in the Wisconsin National Guard in February 1939 and had become a soldier in the U.S. Army following the federalization of his Guard unit the following year. The 32nd Infantry Division, made up of the federalized Wisconsin and Michigan National Guard, trained at Camp Beauregard, Louisiana, before shipping out for the Pacific in the fall of 1942. Schneeweiss had not accompanied the division, however, because of a hip injury sustained in a motorcycle accident. Following his recovery, he applied for admission to Officer Candidate School, from which he graduated as a second lieutenant in April 1943. But he was shuffled from one training assignment to another, not reaching the European Theater until early 1945, where he was posted for about a week to the Second Armored Division before being transferred to the Eighth shortly before it crossed the Rhine.

Schneeweiss's marriage had been less peaceful than most of his army career. From the start, he testified, it had been tumultuous, with divorce threatened frequently by both parties. Nevertheless, he revealed, his wife was currently pregnant and due to deliver within a week or two. His two brothers had both been discharged from the service, one from the army because of an unspecified "nervous condition" that resulted, his mother had informed him, in spasms and foaming at the mouth, the other from the Marine Corps due to "combat fatigue."

Schneeweiss's testimony, carefully guided by defense counsel, painted a self-portrait of an insecure young man whose problems were the result of a chaotic early life. Against that background, his conduct upon entering a combat zone was understandable and, he and his defense counsel no doubt hoped, excusable, particularly in the light of the battalion commander's alleged directive prior to the crossing of the Rhine from the Netherlands. Schneeweiss testified that van Houten had said that "everything on the other side of the Rhine was considered a Kraut, a German," and that "our mission was to kill Krauts." When cross-examined by the prosecution on his interpretation of van Houten's instructions, Schneeweiss responded, "I don't know, to me a German is a German, that's the way I felt about it all the time. If the Germans were going to fight, there was no sense of [*sic*] us sitting back and being as good-hearted as we had always been . . . and if they were going out for total war, we could do the same." When asked if he had considered unarmed civilians a personal threat, Schneeweiss answered, "Well, I was afraid of them all. I didn't trust any of them."[39]

Schneeweiss's testimony was followed by the reappearance of Major Root, but this time as a defense witness. A lengthy questioning by defense counsel that clearly tried the patience of the divisional psychiatrist probed the likely response of a "hypothetical" subject whose life mirrored that described by Schneeweiss to the circumstances that the defendant encountered when his outfit had crossed the Rhine into Germany. But the effort of the defense to elicit from Root an unambiguous concession that such a man might have lapsed into temporary insanity was unsuccessful, although Root admitted that the "hypothetical" subject "was emotionally unstable to a certain degree."[40] In its cross-examination, the prosecution contented itself with leading Root through a restatement of the psychiatric board's conclusion that Schneeweiss had been able to distinguish right from wrong and to adhere to the former while abstaining from the latter.[41]

The trial ended with closing arguments from defense and prosecution, which, unfortunately, were not recorded in the transcript. The court was closed for an unspecified period, and, upon reconvening, the president announced that Schneeweiss had been found guilty of all four charges, but with an important reservation. The defendant was guilty of killing four German civilians but without malice aforethought and premeditation. It was clearly a compromise verdict, probably indicating a degree of acceptance of the argument that Schneeweiss's mental faculties had been diminished at the time. It was a crucial distinction in that, in effect, it found the defendant not guilty of an offense under the 92nd Article of War, which would have mandated a death penalty or, at least, life imprisonment. Instead, he was declared guilty of violating Article 93, a catch-all provision that covered numerous offenses ranging from manslaughter to sodomy and for which a court-martial could impose any penalty it chose. The court that had tried Lieutenant Schneeweiss chose to dismiss him from the service with forfeiture of all pay and allowances and to sentence him to prison at hard labor for 25 years.[42]

Privates Nichols, Joachims, and Peppler were tried jointly three days later accused, as Schneeweiss had been, of violating the 92nd Article of War in the killings of the six German civilians. Peppler was charged with the killings of the two women and the Payenberg males, while Joachims and Nichols were accused of the murders of Ufermann, Neppeney, and the two women. The inclusion of Joachims in the killing of

Therese Hinnemann and Frieda Payenberg is odd, in that no recorded pretrial testimony had implicated him in their deaths, and the error was later recognized.[43] Many of the same witnesses who had testified in the Schneeweiss court-martial appeared on the witness stand in the trial of the three privates.

One of them was Major Root, who had participated in a psychiatric examination of the defendants, which had found all three capable of telling right from wrong and adhering to the former. All three seemed to have been normal American teenagers of the period, although one had revealed a childhood fear of large dogs, while another complained of shyness. All three reported having girlfriends. One admitted to still being a virgin, while another confessed to having contracted gonorrhea at age 16. Only one of the defendants had graduated from high school, while the remaining two had eight and nine and a half years of formal education. In the course of his psychiatric examination, one of the young men had apparently revealed another incident, which, unaccountably, had not been included among the charges brought against either him or Lieutenant Schneeweiss. Private Peppler reported that "later," possibly after the killings of the two women and the Heinrich Payenbergs, he had been ordered by Schneeweiss to "clean out another house" containing German civilians. Proceeding to the dwelling, he found six women, four children, and one adult male. Protesting to Schneeweiss that he could not "take action" against these civilians, Peppler was ordered to "call the man out of the house." He "feels sick," he informed the board, whenever he thought of the incident, suggesting that the male civilian may also have been murdered. Schneeweiss had seemed generally antagonistic toward civilians, had thrown stones at children to keep them from his tank, and had once fired into the ground to frighten away Dutch children. Nichols informed the examining board that no one had seemed to know what to do with Voerde's civilian population and that Schneeweiss had opined that they should all be killed. Nichols expressed the belief that killing civilians was wrong but also that, if he were to be given orders in future to kill civilians under similar circumstances, he would obey them.[44]

The leading prosecution witness was the recently convicted Schneeweis, who, however, seemed confused and often offered vague answers to the questions put to him. He had difficulty remembering the names of the three defendants and was unable to identify the town where the killings had taken place. He could not recall which of the privates he had ordered to kill Ufermann and Nippeney in the basement of their house, nor could he remember what words he had used in issuing the order. His memory failed him when he was asked who had accompanied him in the killings of the two Heinrich Payenbergs, although he testified that there had been "a large group of men around." When asked what order he had given that resulted in their deaths, he replied, perhaps sarcastically, "Fire!"[45] Schneeweiss may have been more valuable to the defense. In its cross-examination, it elicited from Schneeweiss the information that Peppler had resisted when he had ordered the three men to accompany him for the obvious purpose of killing civilians and that, in response, "I made it clear in the platoon that whenever I gave an order it would be carried out."[46] That testimony provided support for a defense motion to dismiss the case, on the grounds that the defendants had reluctantly participated in the killings in obedience to superior orders. While the defense conceded that "a man must exercise judgment and be reasonable," it argued that there were limits to a subordinate's liability when an order to which he had expressed reservations was repeated. The prosecution responded with the observation that an "illegal order does not have to be obeyed" and maintaining that the fact that some of the defendants had protested the orders demonstrated that they thought them unreasonable and unjustified. The motion to dismiss was denied.[47]

The primary defense witnesses were the defendants themselves, who had expressed a desire, presumably on the advice of defense counsel, to testify on their own behalf. Private Joachims testified that he had arrived in Scotland from the United States on February 15, 1945, having thereafter been shuttled to England, shipped across the English Channel to France, then to Belgium, and finally to Holland, where he joined the Eighth Armored Division at Venlo. He could have been with the Eighth only a few days before his unit had moved into Voerde on February 27. Joachims described having had "chow" at the field kitchen that morning, then joining another man in the cleaning of the guns of their Sherman tank. He was interrupted by Lieutenant Schneeweiss, who ordered him to get his "grease gun" (M-3 submachine gun) and accompany him to a nearby house. Joachims testified that he objected on the grounds that he had not yet finished the maintenance of the guns but that Schneeweiss "told me to get it and come anyway." Once at the house, where he found an undetermined number of GIs, he was ordered by Schneeweiss to take two German civilians into the basement and to shoot them. Asked by defense counsel what he had thought of the order, he replied, "I didn't think it was right. I didn't want to do it." Whether or not he had expressed that opinion to Schneeweiss at the time is not clear, but it was obviously useful for counsel to assume it. "What did he say?" Joachims was asked. "Take them down and shoot them anyway," the defendant replied. The Americans then left the house and were standing outside when, according to Joachims, Schneeweiss commented that he had seen some women in a neighboring residence. "He wanted some guys to go with him." Joachims testified that he told the lieutenant that "I didn't want to" and, while Schneeweiss was engaged in conversation, "took off and went back to the tanks," where he claimed to have remained for the remainder of the day.[48]

Joachims's testimony was a mixed bag, in that it both indicated that he had recognized that the order to shoot Ufermann and Nippeney in the basement had been improper but also that he had carried it out nevertheless, while having refused to accompany Schneeweiss in a hunt for the women. In its cross-examination, the prosecution homed in on the crucial issue of a subordinate's willingness to carry out patently illegal orders.

PROSECUTION: When Lieutenant Schneeweiss gave you the order, did you think it was a proper order?

JOACHIMS: It wasn't a proper order, but he is a superior officer.

PROSECUTION: Did you think he had the authority to order you to kill a civilian?

JOACHIMS: I have always been taught to follow an order.

PROSECUTION: Have you been taught to follow an order no matter how illogical or outrageous that order might be?

JOACHIMS: What do you mean by that, sir?

PROSECUTION: Have you been taught to follow any order an officer might give you, no matter how outrageous it might be? For example, if he you ordered you to commit suicide, would you feel yourself obligated to carry out that order?

JOACHIMS: I had the Articles of War read to me and I believe there is an Article of War on that, sir.

That was an ambiguous answer. It is not clear whether Joachims was conceding fault or offering a defense. He likely had in mind Article 64, defining the offense of "assaulting or willfully disobeying superior officers," which carried with it the possibility of the death penalty. The punishable offense, however, was disobedience to a *lawful* order, which Schneeweiss's clearly was not. The dialogue continued.

> PROSECUTION: If you thought an officer were intoxicated or insane, would you feel obligated to obey his orders?
> JOACHIMS: No, sir.
> PROSECUTION: If you thought an officer were in his right mind and completely sober, would you feel obligated to obey every order he gave you even if that were an order that was manifestly outrageous, if it outraged your sense of righteousness and justice and fairness?
> JOACHIMS: No, sir.
> PROSECUTION: Did you hesitate on this occasion when Lieutenant Schneeweiss gave you the order?
> JOACHIMS: I did.
> PROSECUTION: Do you consider yourself a reasonable man of normal understanding?
> JOACHIMS: Yes, sir.
> PROSECUTION: What is your education please?
> JOACHIMS: I went through grammar school and high school, twelve years.[49]

It had been a sober and decorous exchange, far removed from the open hostility and sarcasm that often characterized prosecution (and sometimes defense) examinations of defendants in the Borkum trial. The testimony of Private Peppler was somewhat earthier, although his treatment was no less gentle. Under questioning by defense counsel, Peppler described his initial involvement in the events that had resulted in his arrest and court-martial. He had gone to the kitchen truck for "chow" and had encountered Schneeweiss, who indicated a desire to speak with him after he had eaten.

> I went over to him and he was talking with Corporal Jones and he said there is [*sic*] a couple of women at the first house down the road and he said go get them. I looked at him and thought he was kidding at first, then he said go and get them so I went down the road by myself. I went to the first house where he said they were supposed to be and they weren't in the first house. . . . I went to the next house and there was [*sic*] two women in the front room going through drawers or something.

Peppler had then "fired around the window panes of the house to scare them," after which he returned to Schneeweiss to report, "I couldn't do it. They were women." Schneeweiss had replied, he testified, "Women or male, Krauts alike [*sic*], shoot them."[50] Defense counsel did not question Peppler on his role in the killing of the women or, later, in the deaths of the two Heinrich Payenbergs in the field. These would be explored by the prosecution in its cross-examination.

Upon returning with Nichols to the house where he had found the women, Peppler testified, he had found them "in the driveway" about 50 feet from the road. He admitted to having fired at them but "hit them in the legs and knocked them down."

Schneeweiss, who had been following Peppler and Nichols, walked to within 10 feet of the women and fired "about a clip and a half" from his pistol into them. Peppler admitted having subsequently accompanied Schneeweiss "up the road," where the two Heinrich Payenbergs had been killed. After Schneeweiss fired at them with an M-1 rifle, Peppler testified, the lieutenant ordered him "to go out and finish them off" but claimed only to have "fired a few shots in the general direction" without, he believed, hitting them. Seemingly assuming the role of the defense, the prosecution asked the defendant if he had hesitated to obey the order to shoot the two women. Peppler replied that he had. When asked why, he responded plaintively "I just didn't think it was right." Then, volunteering the reason why he had complied, "I didn't know no [*sic*] better." The prosecution's final question to Peppler elicited an answer that poignantly expressed the stresses and moral inversions to which men (and boys) at war are exposed.

> PROSECUTION: Do you consider yourself a reasonable man of ordinary understanding?
> PEPPLER: When I was back in civilian life, yes.[51]

Private Nichols's testimony in his own defense further explored the central issue of a private's understanding of the degree of his obligation to obey orders.

> DEFENSE: Were you ever told you had no right to question an order of an officer?
> NICHOLS: Not until we carried out the order, sir.
> DEFENSE: What were your instructions on that point?
> NICHOLS: When it came to an officer we were supposed to carry out the order and ask questions afterwards.

Nichols explained how, on the morning of March 27, he had been ordered to "take those two Germans who were in the house down in the basement and kill them." The defendant's initial reaction, he testified, was to do nothing. "When he told me I stood there, I didn't know what to say or do and then he told me again." The fatal consequences of the repetition were left undescribed by Nichols, but not so Schneeweiss's order to the defendant and Peppler to "get" the two women following Peppler's initial refusal to shoot them, although with an obvious effort at self-justification. When the two young soldiers reached the house, Nichols testified, "it looked like they were looting to me, going through everything in the front room, drawers and everything . . . they seen [sic] us coming and took off on a dead run." Peppler had then opened fire.[52] It was left to the prosecution to elicit from Nichols a description of his own contribution to the killing of the women. He had fired as they had run but had only wounded them. It was Schneeweiss who fired the fatal shots. Nichols, too, claimed to have "hesitated" before carrying out Schneeweiss's orders, but, when asked whether he believed Schneeweiss had had the authority to order him to kill unarmed civilians, he answered with a mildly equivocal "I would say so, yes."[53]

Prosecution and defense made statements in summation, which, as in Schneeweiss's trial, were not recorded. The court closed for an unspecified period of time and, upon reopening, announced that the three defendants had been found innocent of the charge and specifications.[54]

Both the Borkum trial and the courts-martial of Schneeweiss, Joachims, Nichols, and Peppler were precipitated by indisputable violations of the laws of war. In Borkum, seven prisoners of war in the custody of the German armed forces were subjected to public abuse, both verbal and physical, then shot to death. In Voerde, six (and probably two more) German civilians engaged in activity in no way threatening to U.S. Army forces occupying the town were arbitrarily murdered by American soldiers. Was one crime more heinous than the other? Comparisons are difficult to make and not likely to produce useful conclusions, although many might agree that the wanton killing of peaceful noncombatants is particularly repugnant, if no more a violation of international law than the murders of POWs. What is beyond serious dispute, however, is that the U.S. Army addressed the two incidents in radically different ways.

The United States regarded the trials of Germans accused of war crimes as the culmination of its crusade against the Nazi evil, the depths of which we still struggle to comprehend. That moralistic zeal, fully justified when directed against genocide, the mass starvation, sadism, and murder perpetrated in the concentration camps, and the killings of helpless thousands of the mentally ill and handicapped in "euthanasia" facilities, may have been less appropriate in its application to lesser crimes that were in large part the spontaneous by-products of the stresses of war. The Borkum atrocity, to be sure, had been stimulated by official encouragement and facilitated by orders to military and police personnel that clearly contravened international law. Moreover, the failure of German authorities to punish the perpetrators had been tantamount to tacit approval of what they had done, but it is not unreasonable to suppose that the murderous foray of Langer, the actual killer of #909's crew, was the action of a man traumatized by the death of his family in an Allied air raid and probably needed no external instigation.

The psychological conditions of the four defendants in the Voerde courts-martial was investigated by U.S. Army psychiatrists in an effort to determine their state of mind at the time of the murders. A finding that they were not able to distinguish right from wrong when they entered Voerde would have presumably led to acquittal on the grounds of insanity, temporary or otherwise. In the Borkum case, the actual murderer was not on trial because he could not be found. The defendants, all alleged to have been accessories to the ill treatment and murders of the American POWs, were assumed a priori to have been capable of distinguishing right from wrong, with no allowance being made for the psychological impact of years of progressively heavier Allied bombing, in addition to the open encouragement of the atrocity by a criminal regime, under which they had lived for more than 10 years.[55] The Borkum trial included 15 defendants divided into three categories—civilians, officers, and enlisted men. Their defenses were frequently antagonistic, meaning that efforts to defend members of one group often cast blame on members of another. Examinations of defendants belonging to one group by defense attorneys defending another were often as damaging as the questioning by prosecutors. Two separate courts-martial, on the other hand, heard the cases against the American officer, Schneeweiss, and his enlisted subordinates, Joachims, Nichols, and Peppler, and, although the defendants were used as prosecution witnesses in one another's trials, their cases did not directly impinge upon one another. Hearsay evidence, freely admissible in the Borkum trial, was expressly excluded by the rules under which the Americans were tried.

The contrast in overall tone between the Borkum trial and the Voerde courts-martial is dramatic. In the former, of course, the U.S. Army was trying the enemy for the murders of American soldiers and did so with ferocious determination. In the latter, the Army was trying its own for the unlawful killing of Germans, who, although noncombatants, were nevertheless citizens of the nation with which the United States only a few months before had been at war. The Army, to its credit, nonetheless brought those men to trial, but it proceeded against them with a moderation suggesting a degree of reluctance, perhaps even sorrow, that was far removed from the vengeful zeal shown by the prosecution in the Borkum trial. German witnesses to the Voerde murders, whose testimony might have enhanced the emotional impact of the case against the defendants, were not called. There were no allusions in the Voerde courts-martial to a Christ-like martyrdom of the victims. But, again to the U.S. Army's credit, prosecutorial zeal in the Borkum case was matched by a zealous if also internally conflicted defense, which was forced by the structure of the mass trial to do some of the work of the prosecution. Most significant, of course—certainly from the perspective of the defendants— was the difference in outcome of the trials: for the Borkumers, 14 out of 15 convictions with five death sentences; for the GIs, three acquittals and one 25-year prison sentence. Posttrial processing of the two cases would reflect once again a double standard of justice that sometimes clashed with an apparent commitment to due process for a defeated enemy.

NOTES

1. Charles R. Leach, *In Tornado's Wake: A History of the 8th Armored Division* (Nashville, TN: Battery Press, 1992), 60, 83, 138.

2. "Review by Staff Judge Advocate," n.d., 4, *United States v. Second Lieutenant Robert A Schneeweiss* (Clerk of Court, U.S. Army Judiciary); "Statement of Investigating Officer," April 2, 1945, ibid.; "Division Judge Advocate's Review," September 10, 1945, *United States v. Private Glen Joachims, Private William Peppler, and Private Francis F. Nichols,* ibid. Trial records specify the location of the crime as "Vorde," but Voerde was clearly the scene of the murders. The likelihood of two additional killings is indicated by Voerde's archivist. Günther Wabnik to James J. Weingartner, e-mail, July 24, 2006 (in Weingartner's possession).

3. "Review by Staff Judge Advocate," November 9, 1945, 1–2, *U.S. v. Schnee-weiss*; Ulrich Herbert, "Labor as Spoils of Conquest," in *Nazism and German Society*, ed. David F. Crew (New York: Routledge, 1995), 250.

4. "Laws of War: Laws and Customs of War on Land (Hague IV)," October 18, 1907, Article 46, *The Avalon Project at Yale Law School*, http://www.yale.edu/lawweb/avalon/lawofwar/hague04.htm; U.S. War Department, *Basic Field Manual: Rules of Land Warfare* (Washington, DC: U.S. Government Printing Office, 1940), 6.

5. "Testimony of Major John R. Elting," March 28, 1945, *U.S. v. Schnee-weiss*; "Record of Trial," 29, 44, ibid.

6. "Testimony of 2nd Lt. Robert A. Schneeweiss, 01017469, Company B, 36th Tank Battalion, 8th Armored Division, APO-258, U.S. Army, taken by Lt. Col. Harold G. MacAdams, Inspector General, 8th Armored Division, at Lintford [sic], Germany on 27 March, 1945," *Pre-Trial Investigating Officer's Report*, 1, *U.S. v. Schneeweiss*.

7. Ibid., 2.

8. "Testimony of Lieutenant William W. Kellner, 04473345, Headquarters Company, 49th Armored Infantry Battalion, 8th Armored Division, APO 258, U.S. Army, taken by Lt. Col. Harold G. MacAdams, Inspector General, 8th Armored Division, on 28 March, 1945, at Bruckhausen, Germany," ibid., 7.

9. "Testimony of Tec. [sic] Nathan Schumer, 39410382, Headquarters Company, 49th Armored Infantry Battalion, 8th Armored Division, APO 258, U.S. Army, taken by Lt. Col. Harold G. MacAdams, Inspector General, 8th Armored Division, on 28 March, 1945, at Bruckhausen, Germany," ibid., 8.

10. "Testimony of Sergeant Donald J. Welch, 36301956, Headquarters Company, 49th Armored Infantry Battalion, 8th Armored Division, APO 258, U.S. Army, taken by Lt. Col. Harold G. MacAdams, Inspector General, 8th Armored Division, on 28 March, 1945 at Bruckhausen, Germany," ibid., 16.

11. "Testimony of Sergeant Francis Stemack, 33594770, Headquarters Company, 49th Armored Infantry Battalion, 8th Armored Division, APO 258, U.S. Army;" "Testimony of Sergeant John. W. Dauphinis, 32852384, Headquarters Company, 49th Armored Infantry Battalion, 8th Armored Division, APO 258, U.S. Army," both "taken by Lt. Col. Harold G. MacAdams, Inspector General, 8th Armored Division, on March 28th, 1945 at Bruckhausen, Germany," ibid., 19–23.

12. "Testimony of Private Glen D. Joachims, 37698990, Company B, 36th Tank Battalion, 8th Armored Division, APO 258, U.S. Army, taken by Lt. Col. Harold G. MacAdams, Inspector General, 8th Armored Division, on 28 March, 1945 at Bruckhausen, Germany, ibid., 27–29.

13. "Testimony of Private William Peppler, 36913733, Company B, 36th Tank Battalion, 8th Armored Division, APO 258, U.S. Army, taken by Lt. Col. Harold G. MacAdams, Inspector General, 8th Armored Division, on 28 March, 1945, at Bruckhausen, Germany," ibid., 31–34.

14. "Testimony of Private Francis F. Nichols, 36913735, Company B, 36th Tank Battalion, 8th Armored Division, APO 258, U.S. Army, taken by Lt. Col. Harold G. MacAdams, Inspector General, 8th Armored Division, on 28 March, 1945, at Bruckhausen, Germany," ibid., 35–36.

15. "Further Testimony of 2nd Lt. Robert A. Schneeweiss, 01017469, Company B, 36th Tank Battalion, 8th Armored Division, APO 258, U.S. Army, taken by Lt. Col. Harold G. MacAdams, Inspector General, 8th Armored Division, on 30 March, 1945 at Loberich, Germany," ibid., 41–42.

16. "Testimony of Johann Hellmich, temporary Burgomeister of Vorde [sic], Germany " and "Testimony of Ernst Eichelkamp, Holshausen, Vorde [sic], Germany," both "taken by Lt. Col. Harold G. MacAdams, Inspector General, 8th Armored Division, on 1 April, 1945 at Vorde [sic], Germany," ibid., 43–47.

17. "Report of Proceedings of Board of Medical Officers," May 26, 1945, ibid.; "Reports of Proceedings of Board of Medical Officers," May 26, 1945, *U.S. v. Joachims, Peppler and Nichols*.

18. Leach, *In Tornado's Wake*, 188–89.

19. "Proceedings of a General Court Martial," 4, 9, *U.S. v. Schneeweiss*.

20. Ibid., 2.

21. Ibid., 6–9.

22. Ibid., 9–11.

23. Ibid., 12–13.

24. Ibid., 13–14.

25. Ibid., 5, 14–16.

26. Ibid., 16–18.

27. Ibid., 18.

28. Ibid., 18–20.

29. Ibid., 20–22, 24.

30. Ibid.

31. Ibid., 28.

32. Ibid., 31.

33. Ibid., 33.

34. Ibid., 35.

35. Ibid., 37–38.

36. Ibid., 38.

37. Ibid., 39–44.

38. Ibid., 46–47.

39. Ibid., 48–59.

40. Ibid., 60–65.

41. Ibid., 66–67.

42. Ibid., 67–68; U.S. War Department, *The Articles of War* (Washington, DC: U.S. Government Printing Office, 1920), 24.

43. "Arraignment," *U.S. v. Joachims, Peppler and Nichols*; "Division Judge Advocate's Review," September 10, 1945, ibid.

44. "Record of Trial," 17–20; "Report of Neuropsychiatric Examination," May 26, 1945, Subject: Private Glen D. Joachims"; "Report of Neuropsychiatric Examination, May 26, 1945, Subject: Private William Peppler"; "Report of Neuropsychiatric Examination, Subject: Private Francis F. Nichols," ibid.

45. "Record of Trial," 21–23, ibid.

46. Ibid., 24–25.

47. Ibid., 33.

48. Ibid., 35–37.

49. Ibid., 37–38.
50. Ibid., 39–40.
51. Ibid., 40–42.
52. Ibid., 43–45.
53. Ibid., 45–46.
54. Ibid., 46.
55. Ellery C. Stowell, an eminent American legal scholar, argued in 1945 that allowances should be made for "the emotional strain of bombed civilians who have lost their homes and loved ones through what they erroneously believed were acts in violation of the laws of war." Maximilian Koessler, "American War Crimes Trials in Europe," *Georgetown Law Journal* 39 (1950–51): 92.

8

Posttrial Drama

The Borkum and Voerde trials as legal processes did not end with the handing down of verdicts and the subsequent sentencing of those found guilty. Both were subjected to review, a much more protracted process for the former than for the latter. Trials before U.S. Military Government Courts that resulted in penalties more severe than two weeks in prison or fines in excess of 250 Reichsmarks underwent multilayered scrutiny by lawyers, who often reached conclusions from the evidence that were very different from those of the line officers who had served both as judges and juries. Cases in which the death sentence had been imposed required additional review and confirmation by the Theater Commander.[1] It was also possible for dissident attorneys and members of the court to interject themselves into the posttrial process. The most notable example is that of Colonel Willis M. Everett Jr., chief defense counsel in the Malmédy massacre trial, in which 73 former members of the Waffen-SS were tried and found guilty of murdering U.S. POWs and Belgian civilians during the Battle of the Bulge. Forty-three were sentenced to death and the rest to varying terms of imprisonment. Everett fought for 10 years to overturn what he was convinced had been a miscarriage of justice.[2] Four days after the Borkum court adjourned, three members of the nine-member panel of officers that had heard the case filed a petition for clemency on behalf of the lead defendant, Kurt Goebell, the island commander who had been sentenced to death. Colonels Barden, Miller, and Versace had not been persuaded of Goebell's guilt beyond a reasonable doubt by the evidence presented against him and requested that his death sentence be commuted to something "less severe."[3] But posttrial reviews were a process influenced not only by purely juridical perspectives but also by

political considerations. Although Germany had surrendered uncon-
ditionally to the Allies and had, for a time, been deprived of national
sovereignty, the United States could not afford to ignore German opinion, particularly as relations with the Soviet Union deteriorated and
Germany—at least those parts under the control of the Western allies—
made a gradual transition from enemy to be punished to potential ally
to be courted.[4] The Borkum trial and many other U.S. war-crimes trials
would not be fully played out until well into the decade of the 1950s.
Death sentences were commonly commuted and prison sentences substantially reduced. Goebell's death sentence, for example, was reduced
to life imprisonment in 1948, and he was released on parole in 1956.[5]
Jakob Seiler was also spared the gallows and eventually freed.[6] Jan
Akkermann, Johann Schmitz, and Erich Wentzel, however, were
hanged at the U.S. War Crimes Prison No. 1 at Landsberg in the fall of
1948. Akkermann died essentially because he had incited the crowd
against the American airmen and Schmitz because he had led the
guard detail that had failed to protect the prisoners and may have shot
one of them a second time after Langer's attack. Wentzel's death was
due to his having been the only officer accompanying the prisoners on
their fatal march and the allegation he had intentionally led them into
harm's way. Why these men, particularly Akkermann and Wentzel,
should have been hanged while Goebell and Seiler, described by an
American reviewer as "the wire pullers of the atrocious incident," had
their death sentences commuted is far from clear. The disapproval of
Rommel's conviction, on the other hand, seems appropriate. No credible evidence had linked the policeman to the mistreatment and eventual murders of the crew of #909.[7]

While the review process lumbered on, a second "Borkum trial"
was conducted more than a year after the first one had ended. This
was a much briefer affair than the "parent" proceeding and was confined to a single day, June 26, 1947. Its brevity was due in large part to
the fact that it involved a single defendant and was based on the mass
of evidence that had been presented in the earlier trial, an arrangement that was employed in a number of U.S. Army war-crimes trials
of Germans. Standing trial was August Haesiker, one of those persons
who had been identified as a suspect during the investigation that
had preceded the mass trial of the previous year. Trial procedure had
been refined in the intervening year and a half and progressed more
smoothly. It is likely, too, that some of the zeal that had been evident in
earlier prosecutions had, by mid-1947, faded.

Haesiker had held the rank of *Oberstfeldmeister* (Captain) in the *Reichsarbeitsdienst* (National Labor Service) and was serving on Borkum at the time of the murders. He had been identified during the investigation that preceded the first trial as the RAD leader who had arranged the first assault on #909's crew, a gauntlet of men armed with spades through which the hapless POWs had to march. In a sworn statement made to Major Levine, Fritz Vomel described a conversation with Haesiker, in which he claimed to have reproved the latter for having ordered his men to beat the Americans, an act that Haesiker had allegedly admitted.

Haesiker was tried before a General Military Government Court under the presidency of Colonel Charles F. Johnson to which 10 officers (3 more than had tried Haesiker's 15 predecessors) holding the ranks of colonel and lieutenant colonel had been appointed, although only 6 were actually present as the trial commenced. Its site was the former Nazi concentration camp at Dachau, where U.S. Army war-crimes trials had been centralized in October 1946. Unlike the court for the main Borkum trial of the previous year in Ludwigsburg, this one had an officer with formal legal training to serve as "law member," Lieutenant Colonel David H. Thomas. As the earlier 15 had been, Haesiker was charged with "violations of the laws and usages of war" for allegedly having aided and participated in assaults upon #909's crew and in their subsequent murders, to which he pleaded "not guilty." The case against him would be presented by an American civilian attorney, Harry D. Pitchford, while his defense was in the hands of Captain William Gordon. In contrast to the earlier trial, no German attorneys participated.[8]

The prosecution case was simplicity itself. No witnesses were called; instead, Pitchford introduced into evidence 14 of the sworn statements secured by Major Levine prior to the main trial. The first of these had been made by Major Murray M. Braff, the pathologist who had examined the bodies of the American flyers after they had been exhumed from Borkum's Lutheran cemetery in October 1945, followed by two statements by Heinz Klinger, a German surgeon who had been on duty at Borkum's naval hospital on August 4, 1944, and who had examined the bodies of #909's crew, and Otto Mennenga, a medical aide. These statements served to establish the fact that the Americans had been murdered and, through Klinger's second statement and in Mennenga's, that there had been evidence of trauma other than bullet wounds. A statement by Johann Eilts, the sexton of the Lutheran cemetery, described the burial of the victims accompanied by a service read by Pastor Doebbels, a German naval chaplain.[9] Other statements described the attack on the flyers by the Labor Service detachment, while only Fritz Vomel's identified Haesiker as the instigator.[10] No challenges to the admissibility of these statements were offered by defense counsel. Haesiker's defense was simpler still—his own testimony; the testimony of two defense witnesses, Rita Hinterberger and Charlotta Hochmuth, that he had been lounging on the beach with them at the time the American POWs had been marched through Borkum; and his denial that he had admitted to Vomel that he had orchestrated the Labor Service beatings.[11] It took the court 20 minutes to find Haesiker guilty of having participated in the beatings but innocent of the murder charge and another 10 minutes to agree on a sentence of 10 years in prison, to be calculated from July 5, 1946, presumably the date of his apprehension.[12] Had he stood trial in Ludwigsburg a year earlier, his sentence would almost certainly have been far more severe.

Erich Wentzel had allegedly conferred with Haesiker and had contrived to alter the march route in order to lead the prisoners through the gauntlet prepared by the RAD members. Wentzel's case is a particularly problematic example of the administration of justice to Germans accused of war crimes by the U.S. Army. He had been the highest ranking German on the march through Borkum and had arguably led the American prisoners into danger while doing nothing to protect them. No one had accused him of personally injuring any of #909's crew. Yet, according to the theory employed by the prosecution, he had participated in a common design that had resulted in the murders of seven POWs. He was therefore guilty of murder and deserved to die. And die he would, but only after having spent 38 months in prison. During that period his case, like many others, underwent a multilayered review. The justice dispensed to its enemies by the U.S. Army may have been harsh and sometimes seemingly arbitrary, but it was not precipitous.

Wentzel was 45 years old at the time of his trial, married, with two children. His social background was solidly middle class. Wentzel's parents had owned a business dealing in sporting equipment in which he had become a principal and stockholder, often traveling abroad in the prewar years on company business, in the course of which travels he had become proficient in English. It was this facility that got him involved with the American prisoners in the first place. His prewar international business associations were mobilized postwar to save him from the gallows. In response to entreaties from his wife, Wera, British businessman E. W. Thompson wrote of Wentzel's "gentlemanly" demeanor and his certainty that "he would not be implicated in any plot to murder any person. He came from Norwegian stock and was quite different from the usual aggressive German type."[13] London sportswear manufacturer Ernest Hinton, who had known Wentzel since 1929, remembered him as "not pro-Nazi" and "incapable of the action alleged against him."[14] Ragnar Laurel of Stockholm had found Wentzel to have been someone with "an undoubtedly healthy feeling for what is right and wrong. I only know too well that he, with his quiet ways, would never do any harm to anybody."[15] Copenhagen businessman Victor Skjold Heyde concluded that Wentzel had been "anti-Nazi" and, according to his observations, someone who had "treated everybody decently."[16] A Swiss representative of Wentzel's firm, Max Schneider, thought it significant that correspondence from Wentzel had not been signed with "Sieg-Heil" or "Heil Hitler."[17] With the assistance of Toni Kloewer, a Christian Democratic deputy in the reviving postwar German political system, Wera Wentzel succeeded in contacting Erich Loewenstein, a possibly Jewish schoolmate of her husband's who, as Eric Livingston, was living in San Francisco. Livingston-Loewenstein pronounced Wentzel "absolutely respectable and unable to take part in such an atrocious deed."[18]

Although these letters were superficially impressive, coming as they did from persons who, for the most part, had no reason for charitable feelings toward Germans, they were, from a purely legal standpoint, irrelevant, as was a letter from Hans Carls. Father Carls was director of the Roman Catholic charity Caritas and, as political prisoner 29400, an inmate of Dachau concentration camp from 1941 until 1945. He knew Wentzel and thought it "impossible" that he could have been involved in the murder of the American airmen. His execution, Carls was convinced, would be an act of judicial murder, and he begged U.S. authorities for a reconsideration of the case, which he was certain would exonerate Wentzel.[19] But that would require more than the character references, no matter how poignant, that Frau Wentzel forwarded to Army lawyers who would review the case. Within a month of her husband's conviction and sentencing, she had directed an international "Appeal to the Sense of Justice" to persons as diverse as President Truman, Eleanor Roosevelt, General Dwight Eisenhower, the president of the International Red Cross, and Pope Pius XII, urging them to intervene on behalf of her husband, in order that "to the millions of human sacrifices exacted by this dreadful war and its shattering effects, the life of a husband and father . . . who was among the few who always stood up for justice and human dignity and who had nothing to do with the crime of which he was accused, not be added."[20]

More practically if less dramatically, Frau Wentzel attempted to engage Albert Hall, a member of the defense team during the trial and now a civilian, to represent her husband, an effort that seems to have been unsuccessful.[21] Instead, Rolf Galler, a German lawyer based in Heidelberg, was secured for the purpose at the end of 1946 and would represent Wentzel for almost two years in a vain attempt to save him from the gallows.[22]

In an appeal dated February 22, 1947, and directed to U.S. Army reviewers, Galler argued that Wentzel had been convicted on flimsy and primarily circumstantial evidence that failed to demonstrate that he had been a party to a conspiracy to harm the Americans and that should not be accepted as proof of guilt "where the question of life or death is involved." Not only had Wentzel not been proved to have been a conspirator but, according to Galler, no direct evidence (as opposed to inferential evidence) had been offered to prove that a conspiracy had ever existed. "Incriminating" orders (i.e., to abstain from interfering should the prisoners be attacked by civilians) may have been issued, but this had occurred before Wentzel's arrival at the battery where the Americans were being held prior to the march. Evidence of Wentzel's noninvolvement in the alleged conspiracy, he argued, had been available in the form of eyewitnesses who would have testified to that effect had they been called upon to do so, testimony that Galler had secured in a number of sworn affidavits. Wentzel's reason for participating in the march was an innocent willingness to serve as guide along the prescribed route.[23] Haesiker's arrest and incarceration at Dachau in preparation for his upcoming trial permitted Galler to secure a sworn affidavit from the former RAD leader. Although concerned primarily with his own exculpation, Haesiker testified not only that he had not spoken to Wentzel during the march, as Schmitz had claimed, but that he considered it "absolutely improbable" that any attack on the prisoners by the RAD had occurred at all.[24]

But multiple witnesses more impartial than Haesiker, who was obviously more concerned with his own survival than Wentzel's, had testified that it had, although the prosecution's argument that Wentzel had been a party to the attack had been based on rather thin circumstantial evidence. Moreover, it was clear that none of the Americans had been seriously injured in the alleged assault or, for that matter, in any of the other attacks by individual civilians that had taken place prior to the shootings by Langer. But U.S. reviewing authorities remained fundamentally unmoved by the avalanche of paper directed their way by Wentzel's supporters. Wentzel's presence as the highest ranking German on the march, his failure to protect the prisoners from attack, and his complicity in the production of a false report on the cause of the Americans' deaths were irrefutable and decisive. The "Review and Recommendations" of the Deputy Judge Advocate's Office, 7708 War Crimes Group, dated August 1, 1947, found the evidence against him sufficient to sustain both the verdict and sentence, on the grounds that "the accused very actively furthered and contributed to the plan which resulted in several illegal killings."[25] Wentzel seemingly could not escape from the tentacles of the prosecution's conspiracy theory.

Yet, the U.S. Army moved slowly, partly because of the large volume of cases that had to be reviewed on multiple levels. Those involving death sentences were subjected to three reviews. Following their scrutiny at the Deputy Judge Advocate's office, cases moved on to the Theater Judge Advocate before finally reaching the Theater Commander (and head of military government in the U.S. zone of occupation), where they received their final reviews. In light of the 489 trials that had been conducted by the U.S. Army by the end of 1947, this was a daunting task.

But, in a larger context, the Army's dilatory approach to executing the Borkum death sentences was likely the consequence of growing general criticism of the Army's war-crimes trial program coming from the United States. This had been stimulated by controversy surrounding the high-profile Malmédy massacre case, in which 73 former members of the Waffen-SS had been convicted by a U.S. Army military government court in July 1946 of the "killing, shooting, illtreatment, abuse and torture of members of the armed forces of the United States, and of unarmed Allied civilians" during the Battle of the Bulge.[26] Although the alleged offense was on a much larger scale than the Borkum murders—in addition to a substantial number of Belgian civilians, approximately 80 U.S. POWs were slaughtered in the central event that gave the massacre its name—the issues were not dissimilar. The defendants were accused of having "acted together in this shooting and killing of prisoners of war, each man a cog-wheel in a monstrous slaughter machine."[27] Of the accused, 43 were sentenced to death and 22 to life imprisonment. The remaining 8 received prison sentences ranging from 10 to 20 years.[28] But Colonel Willis M. Everett Jr., chief defense counsel in the trial, refused to accept the outcome, alleging that the defendants had been convicted largely on the basis of pretrial statements that had been secured only because the interrogators employed various forms of deception and duress, including mock trials and beatings. In addition Everett, although not a combat soldier, had heard enough from men who were in a position to know that American soldiers, too, were guilty of sometimes killing prisoners of war but in most cases had escaped punishment for it. At the end of the trial, he wrote to his family that the president of the court, a brigadier general, had approached him to say that judging the Malmédy defendants had been "the hardest thing he had ever done," because he had been aware of U.S. guilt for similar crimes.[29]

Everett's public campaign of criticism following his return to the United States eventually resulted in a full-blown investigation of the Malmédy trial by the U.S. Senate, in which Senator Joseph McCarthy played an inflammatory role. Everett's allegation of gross mistreatment of German war-crimes suspects may have encouraged the Borkum convicts to make similar claims of pretrial abuse. On May 18, 1948, for example, Johann Schmitz declared in an affidavit that he had been beaten about the head with a pistol during his preliminary interrogation by Lieutenant Fisher and threatened with being shot while interrogated later by Major Levine.[30] Others convicted in the Borkum trial made similar allegations and worse. Karl Weber complained of being kept in solitary confinement and given starvation rations while in pretrial custody in Esterwegen and asserted that his weight had fallen from 160 to 106 pounds.[31] Erich Wentzel composed a lengthy statement cataloging the various abuses to which he claimed to have been subjected beginning while he was still on Borkum:

> The interrogation lasted about one hour. All of a sudden, Fisher jumped to his feet, got his pistol out of his pocket and put it against my heart. He called me names—fokking [*sic*] bastard, etc.—and said he was going to shoot me at once. He yelled and raged so that I told him that I could not get all his words. Another lieutenant came into the room and told Fisher: "Stop that, put that gun away" [clearly, the "good cop, bad cop" routine]. But Fisher shouted: "No, I"ll do it right away," putting his pistol against my forehead. After a while, he calmed down. . . . Interrogation commenced at 22:00 (10:00) P.M.; at around 2:00 A.M. I was allowed

to go to my quarters. . . . On 16 June 1945 I was arrested and taken to Esterwegen camp. About the end of October 1945, I was interrogated by Major Levine. . . . Right after my first answers Major Levine shouted at me: "You are a liar," and this went on like that through the interrogation. . . . He kept twisting around every answer . . . and several times he said: "Now you have put the rope round your neck." I hardly knew what to say anymore and all my objections and explanations were shouted down, only that part being recorded in the minutes that Levine himself had formulated. Whenever I wanted some amendments to be made, he said: "That is not important."[32]

Even allowing for the possibility, even the likelihood, of exaggeration by a man desperate to escape the gallows, it is probable that the pretrial interrogations of the Borkum defendants were not the calm and decorous events suggested by the sworn statements that were placed in evidence. That brutal tactics were sometimes employed is not unlikely, although the veracity of these allegations more than 60 years after the events is beyond verification.

The fight for survival eventually led Wenztel, as it did many other convicted Axis war criminals, to file a petition for a writ of habeas corpus with the U.S. Supreme Court. Prospects for success were not good. In February 1946, the Court had rejected a similar petition filed on behalf of Japanese general Tomoyuki Yamashita, who had been sentenced to hang by a U.S. Army court sitting in Manila for war crimes committed in the Philippine capital by Japanese troops. Frank Reel, Yamashita's attorney, argued that Yamashita had not received a fair trial as mandated by the Fifth Amendment to the U.S. Constitution. By a six-to-two vote, the Court refused to grant certiorari, holding that the trial was not reviewable by civilian courts, but only by military authorities. Justice Frank Murphy, in a dissenting opinion, argued eloquently to the contrary in language that is relevant to the contemporary "war on terror."

no exception is made as to those who are accused of war crimes or as to those who possess the status of enemy belligerent. Indeed, such an exception would be contrary to the whole philosophy of human rights which make the Constitution the great living document that it is. The immutable rights of the individual, including those secured by the due process clause of the Fifth Amendment, belong not only to the members of those nations that excel on the battlefield or that subscribe to the democratic ideology. They belong to every person in the world, victor or vanquished, whatever may be his race, color or beliefs.[33]

The Court continued to reject similar appeals by convicted enemy war criminals, although by diminishing margins. Willis Everett's petition on behalf of the Malmédy defendants failed in May 1948 on a four-four vote, with Justice Robert Jackson, former U.S. chief prosecutor at Nuremberg, abstaining.[34] But the odds of success seemed to be improving and, in any event, appeals to the Supreme Court delayed the execution of death sentences. Consequently, a petition for a writ of habeas corpus was submitted on behalf of Erich Wentzel by Rolf Galler on July 30.

It was a densely argued document in excellent English of nearly 100 pages. Galler challenged Wentzel's conviction on multiple grounds. The Ludwigsburg court had lacked jurisdiction, he asserted, and its trial procedure had been, in any event, contrary to international law. The prosecution case had been based largely on pretrial statements secured under duress, and "the totality of departures from the principles of fair trial and due process of law vitiated the entire proceedings, trial and sentence." Finally, "even if the verdict of guilty should be upheld, the facts and evidence before the court did not warrant the penalty of death."[35]

The concluding element of Galler's brief was probably the most persuasive. Was Wentzel deserving of the death penalty, particularly in light of the fact that the death sentence of Kurt Goebell, the island's former commander, had by this time been commuted to life imprisonment? Even if the prosecution's theory of conspiracy or common design was to be taken seriously, Goebell, as the instigator of the march through town, had to be seen as at the center of it. But the accusation of conscious participation in a criminal design was far from credible, Galler argued. Wentzel had had nothing to do with the organization of the march or the issuing of orders as to how it was to be conducted, nor had he been placed in command of the column. When he volunteered to accompany the prisoners and their guards as a guide, he had no reason to anticipate the attacks that were to follow, which, in any event, were of little consequence until Langer, an entirely independent actor, intervened. Galler must have recognized that Wentzel's collaboration in the production of a report that falsely placed blame for the killings on the civilian population could be construed as tangible as opposed to circumstantial evidence of participation in a criminal conspiracy and argued less persuasively that his client had been at the time genuinely ignorant of the true cause of the prisoners' deaths. But it is hard to quarrel with Galler's conclusion that, however the evidence against Wentzel might be construed, a sentence of death was excessive.[36] Galler's carefully crafted arguments on the defects in the case against Eric Wentzel proved nugatory. As it had done repeatedly in other war-crimes cases, the Supreme Court during its October 1948 term refused to accept jurisdiction.[37]

But Washington had intervened in Wentzel's case in another way. Controversy over the quality of the U.S. Army's war-crimes justice, particularly in regard to the Malmédy massacre trial, had led Secretary of the Army Kenneth C. Royall to order a stay of all executions and to appoint a three-man commission chaired by Texas Supreme Court justice Gordon Simpson to investigate the more than 100 death sentences that had been handed down in war-crimes cases by U.S. Army courts and sustained on review. The commission was established in July 1948 and submitted its report in September, after having selectively examined trial records and posttrial reviews and appeals that included Galler's Supreme Court brief. If they read it, the commission's members seem not to have been impressed. A relatively small number of death sentences was recommended for commutation, but Wentzel's was not among them.[38]

It appeared that all that now stood between Erich Wentzel and the gallows at Landsberg prison was Theophil Wurm, the 80-year-old Protestant bishop of Württemberg, whose moral authority was enhanced by a record of modest resistance to the Nazi regime. In postwar Germany, Wurm had emerged as one of the spokesmen for Germans who believed that they had become victims of Allied injustice.[39] The Cold War, moreover, was heating up dramatically. In June 1948, in an effort to block the Western Allies from establishing a West German state, the Soviet Union cut off land access to West Berlin, an event that did much to change U.S. perceptions of Germans from enemies to be punished to crucial allies in a struggle to contain communism. Bishop Wurm made several appeals on behalf of Wentzel, the latest in the form of a telegram to Secretary of the Army Royall. Even though Wentzel's petition to the Supreme Court had been denied and his death sentence upheld by the Simpson Commission, Colonel James Harbaugh, European Command judge advocate, was respectful enough of Wurm's influence to caution that "we had better keep Wentzel on the protected list until we know what he [Wurm] does as a result of the Department of the Army cable to him [of] 16 October 1948." That message had noted the Simpson Commission's recommendation but had added that "you may, of course, take the matter up with the Commanding General European Command who is the final reviewing authority and has complete jurisdiction over all war crimes cases."[40] If Wurm attempted further action, it did not impress Harbaugh, who instructed a subordinate a month later to inform "the Evangelical people" that they had until November 26 to submit materials on behalf of Wentzel.[41] The condemned man himself meticulously penciled in both English and German a "Petition for Clemency" to General Clay, European commander and military governor, emphasizing the devastating impact his execution would have on his ailing mother, his wife, and his two children, ages 6 and 12, and expressing the belief that conscience would shortly compel those who had given damaging testimony against him to save their own skins "to testify and clear up the events of August 4, 1944, which I personally regret very much."[42]

But General Clay personally reviewed Wentzel's case on November 23 and gave his death sentence its final confirmation. A desperate telegram to Clay from Wentzel's wife, Wera, was answered coldly by Clay's chief of staff, Lieutenant General Clarence Huebner: "It is regretted that the executive clemency which you requested in your telegram of 30 November, 1948 cannot be granted."[43]

A telegram from Rolf Galler, Wentzel's German attorney, to General Clay crossed Huebner's reply to Wera Wentzel. It read in its entirety:

STARS AND STRIPES EDITION TWENTY NOVEMBER PAGE ELEVEN REPORTS THAT US JUSTICE DEPARTMENT PAROLE BOARD WASHINGTON PAROLED US LIEUTENANT WHO MARCH 1945 SHOT DOWN FOUR GERMAN CIVILIANS IN COLD BLOOD AFTER REDUCING ORIGINAL SENTENCE FROM TWENTYFIVE TO EIGHT YEARS STOP URGENTLY PRAY THAT EQUAL JUSTICE BE APPLIED IN BORKUM ISLAND CASE US VERSUS GOEBELL BY YOUR EXCELLENCY GRANTING CLEMENCY TO ACCUSED ERIC WENTZEL WHO IN AUGUST 1944 DID NOT PERSONALLY KILL OR MALTREAT OR OTHERWISE ACT IN COLD BLOOD STOP SUPREME COURT DENIED DECISION FOR WANT OF

JURISDICTION STOP EXECUTION WENTZEL SIXXED [*sic*]
FOR FRIDAY THIRD DECEMBER LANDSBERG PRISON STOP[44]

It is not clear how Galler had gotten access to the U.S. Army newspaper, but the brief article of about 130 words, entitled "Board Frees
Officer in German Slaying," which shared a page with a much longer article bemoaning higher prices for Thanksgiving turkeys in the
United States, revealed that a U.S. Army lieutenant who had been
sentenced to 25 years' imprisonment for "allegedly" participating
in the murders of four German civilians had been paroled and was
on his way home to rejoin his wife and two children. The lieutenant's defense counsel, the article explained, had argued that the defendant had been "fired by Kraut-killing propaganda" and had not
been "really responsible for his actions."[45] Huebner was unmoved.
He replied to Galler that the case against Wentzel had to be judged
on its own merits and that the evidence against him had been found
"amply sufficient" to support the sentence.[46] A final petition for stay
of execution, this time from the Roman Catholic Bishop of Limburg
with supporting affidavits, reached the European Command's Judge
Advocate General's office at 11:20 A.M. on the morning of December 3,
1948. Major Floyd Lundberg noted matter-of-factly that "inasmuch as
the execution had been performed prior to receiving the petition . . . it
is recommended that they be filed with the record of trial and that no
[review] board action be taken."[47]

The American lieutenant whose release had come to Rolf Galler's
attention was, of course, Robert Schneeweiss. Schneeweiss's case, too,
had undergone multiple posttrial reviews. Lieutenant Colonel Sam
Russ, the Eighth Armored Division's judge advocate, produced an
analysis of Schneeweiss's court-martial dated August 4, 1945, in which
he found the evidence adequate to support the court's findings and
recommended that "in view of the atrocious nature of the accused's offenses" the sentence of 25 years in prison be approved, a recommendation that was accepted by Major General John M. Devine, the division's
commander.[48] Captain Abraham Hyman, an assistant staff judge advocate with USFET (U.S. Forces, European Theater), concurred but added
the tart observation that "there was no recommendation for clemency
in this case and there is nothing in this record that persuades me that
the accused deserves any clemency beyond that which has already
been extended to him by the court." The opinion that Schneeweiss

had not been adequately punished was shared by USFET's staff judge advocate, Brigadier General E. C. Betts, who appended to Hyman's review the recommendation that "the court be criticized for the inadequacy of the sentence."[49]

As required for cases of this nature under Article of War 48, Schneeweiss's trial records were then forwarded to the field army to which the Eighth Armored Division belonged for final confirmation. In the waning months of 1945, that happened to be none other than General George S. Patton Jr., then languishing in relative inactivity and disgrace following his relief from command of the Third Army as a result of his occupation policies in Bavaria, widely regarded as being "soft" on Nazism. The Schneeweiss case reached his desk as he was serving as temporary commander of the rapidly shrinking USFET. On November 13, 1945, a Patton less bloodthirsty than the combat commander who had encouraged war crimes by U.S. troops in Sicily more than two years earlier signed a confirmation of Schneeweiss's 25-year sentence, noting, however, that it was "wholly inadequate punishment for an officer guilty of such grave offenses. In imposing such meager punishment the court has reflected no credit upon its conception of its own responsibilities." Schneeweiss, since December 26, 1945, a civilian, was transported to the United States, where he was to be incarcerated in the federal penitentiary at Lewisburg, Pennsylvania, although, in fact, he seems to have served his sentence in the U.S. penitentiary in Leavenworth, Kansas.[50]

As in the case of Erich Wentzel, efforts were made to ameliorate Schneeweiss's less ominous prospects. Leading the campaign for revision or clemency was Robert Schneeweiss himself. Prior to the final confirmation of the outcome of his court-martial, Schneeweiss had sought but had not gotten an appointment to plead his case personally with Patton. Presumably to aid him in the framing of appeals, the Army had provided Schneeweiss with a copy of his trial record shortly after his conviction, although, in a floridly hand-printed letter, he requested that his wife be provided with one as well, "if a spair [sic] copy is available" (it would cost $15.40, he was informed).[51] Unlike Erich Wentzel and his wife, Wera, Robert Schneeweiss and his wife, Fannie, were able to turn to legislators of their own national government for assistance, although the Wisconsin senators and congressmen seem to have limited their intervention to requesting information about the case from the U.S. Army. Among the interested lawmakers was the state's still relatively obscure junior senator, who, after having been briefed by the War Department on the case, declared that he "wished to have the brutal nature of this affair made clear."[52] In this context, it is interesting to note that, in 1949, Joseph McCarthy would play a prominent role in a Senate investigation of the controversial Malmédy massacre trial and express outrage at what was alleged to have been Army brutality in extracting confessions from the German defendants.[53]

Private American citizens, however, were more sympathetic to Schneeweiss. The Milwaukee chapter of the American Veterans of World War II (later AMVETS), petitioned President Harry Truman to "use your influence" to suspend Schnweeweiss's sentence.[54] On January 25, 1947, 15 employees of the Burbank (California) *Evening Review*, reacting to an unidentified article on the Schneeweiss case, sent an indignant letter to the War Department protesting the subject's imprisonment.

> We think the sentence itself a far greater crime than the supposed offense warranting the sentence. The article mentioned that he killed these people WHILE IN COMBAT [*sic*]. What about all the German civilians killed in the bombings over Nazi territory? What about the common soldier, the other men who have killed German civilians? Are they all in prison too? A 25 year prison term is a serious enough sentence on any basis, regardless of the crime committed. It is not even thanks enough, [*sic*] however, to an honest man who has fought for his country. This matter is offending our sense of justice, right and Americanism. Please give it the consideration it is due.[55]

The letter would have made interesting reading in Voerde and Borkum, although a better understanding of the Voerde killings might have tempered the outrage of writers whose "sense of justice, right and Americanism" seemingly embraced the belief that the deaths of civilians incidental to combat were acceptable, at least if those civilians were *enemy* nationals. Colonel Hubert Hoover, the assistant judge advocate general, responded with a brutally frank description of the circumstances under which the murders of which Schneeweiss had been convicted had occurred. Schneeweiss's unit had not been "actively engaged with the enemy," and the killings of two women and two "elderly" male civilians had been "deliberate and entirely unprovoked."[56] The directors of Milwaukee's Algonquin Club seem to have been under a misapprehension similar to that of the Burbank journalists. In a conceptually confused letter of April 2, 1947, addressed to Wisconsin's congressional delegation, the club's secretary, expressing the wishes of the directors, requested that the circumstances of the "alleged crime of killing four German civilians" be investigated and Schneeweiss retried, believing that a retrial would "more than likely warrant his complete pardon." Congressman John C. Brophy, representing Wisconsin's Fourth Congressional District, forwarded the letter to the War Department's congressional liaison officer, with the observation that he had had "considerable correspondence in connection with this case," which he had passed on to the War Department with the request that "when this boy's [*sic*] case is again reviewed the various expressions of interest may be noted."[57]

Schneeweiss was to be neither retried nor pardoned, but Major General Thomas H. Green, army judge advocate general, signaled early in 1947 that he was not likely to serve out his full sentence. In a letter to Louisiana senator Allen J. Ellender, who, for reasons that are obscure, had been contacted by Schneeweiss, Green explained that the former lieutenant's case would be regularly reexamined and that "by continued good conduct and the demonstration of his rehabilitation he may be able to earn a reduction in his sentence."[58] The occasion to demonstrate "rehabilitation" had already come in the form of a research program exploring treatments for malaria, which required participants to be infected with the disease and for which Schneeweiss volunteered. It was an opportunity for redemption not available to Erich Wentzel, and it led to a reduction of Schneeweiss's sentence to 12 years on July 30, 1948, and to his parole, on November 12, three weeks before Wentzel climbed the steps of Landsberg's gallows. Schneeweiss remained on parole until August 1952, when the secretary of the army ordered the remainder of his 25-year sentence remitted.[59]

NOTES

1. Eli E. Nobleman, "Procedure and Evidence in American Military Government Courts in the United States Zone of Germany," *Federal Bar Journal* 8 (January 1947): 238, 246.

2. James J. Weingartner, *A Peculiar Crusade: Willis M. Everett and the Malmedy Massacre* (New York: New York University Press, 2000), 49–217.

3. "Petition for Clemency for Kurt Goebell," March 26, 1946, *U.S. v. Kurt Goebell et al.* (frame 13, reel 3). In trials before military government courts, only a two-thirds majority of the judging officers was required for verdicts and sentences, including the death penalty. In U.S. Army courts-martial, capital

punishment demanded unanimity. Maximilian Koessler, "American War Crimes Trials in Europe," *Georgetown Law Journal* 39 (1950–51): 28–29.

4. On this subject, see Frank M. Buscher, *The U.S. War Crimes Trial Program in Germany* (Westport, CT: Greenwood Press, 1989), 69–86. See also Kerstin von Lingen, *Kesselring's Last Battle: War Crimes Trials and Cold War Politics, 1945–1960,* trans. Alexandra Klemm (Lawrence: University of Kansas Press, 2009), 174–83.

5. Colonel J. L. Harbaugh Jr. to Elizabeth Goebell, March 5, 1948, *U.S. v. Goebell* (frame 201, reel 3); "Order of Parole," February 14, 1956, ibid. (frames 955–57, reel 4).

6. "Order of Parole," December 30, 1953, ibid. (frames 959–61, reel 6).

7. Maximilian Koessler, "Borkum Island Tragedy and Trial," *Journal of Criminal Law, Criminology, and Political Science* 47 (July–August 1956): 192–93.

8. "Record of Testimony," 2, *United States v. August Haesiker* (frame 527, reel 7), Records of the United States Army Commands, 1942–, RG 338 (National Archives, Washington, DC).

9. "Testimony of Major Murray M. Braff," October 8, 1945; "Testimony of Heinz Klinger," October 14, 1945; "Testimony of Heinz Klinger," October 15, 1945; "Testimony of Otto Mennenga," October 15, 1945, ibid. (frames 587–605).

10. "Testimony of Fritz Vomel," October 10, 1945, ibid. (frames 677–79).

11. "Record of Testimony," 20–23, 32–34, 48, ibid. (frames 539–42, 551–53, 567).

12. Ibid., 57–59 (frames 576–78).

13. E.W.C. Thompson to Wera Wentzel, April 24, 1946, "Erich Wentzel: Clemency Petitions, II; Mar. 20, 1946–April 2, 1948," *U.S. v. Goebell* (frame 345, reel 5).

14. Ernest C. Hinton to Colonel Bard, April 25, 1946, ibid. (frame 348).

15. Ragnar Laurel to Wera Wentzel, April 23, 1946, ibid. (frame 276).

16. Victor Skjold Heyde to Wera Wentzel, April 22, 1946, ibid. (frame 262).

17. "Eidesstattliche Erklärung," April 5, 1946, 3, ibid. (frame 357).

18. Toni Kloewer to Wera Wentzel, August 18, 1946, ibid. (frames 352–53).

19. Hans Carls to Col. Bard, May 2, 1946, ibid. (frame 317).

20. "Denkschrift (Appell an den Gerechtigkeitssinn)," April 14, 1946, ibid. (frames 260–61).

21. Wera Wentzel to Albert W. Hall, September 15, 1946, ibid. (frames 277–79).

22. Heidelberg was a center for German lawyers active in war-crimes cases. See Robert Sigel, "Die Dachauer Prozesse und die deutsche Öffentlichkeit," in *Dachauer Prozesse: NS-Verbrechen vor amerikanischen Militärgerichten in Dachau 1945–48. Verfahren, Ergebnisse, Nachwirkungen,* ed. Ludwig Eiber and Robert Sigel (Göttingen: Wallstein Verlag, 2007), 75.

23. "In re: United States vs. Goebell et al. Petition in Supplement to Petition of Review Filed on Behalf of Erich F. Wentzel," February 22, 1947, *U.S. v. Goebell* (frames 374–92).

24. "Eidesstattliche Erklärung," May 15, 1947, ibid. (frames 410–12).

25. "United States v. Kurt Goebell, et al. Review and Recommendations," August 1, 1947, 21, ibid.

26. "Record of Trial," 5, *U.S. v. Valentin Bersin et al.* (frame 10, reel 1).

27. Ibid., 76 (frame 81).

28. Ibid., 3251–67 (frames 738–54, reel 4).

29. Willis M. Everett to family, n.d., Papers of Willis M. Everett Jr. (in author's possession).

30. "Affidavit by Johann Schmitz," May 18, 1948, *U.S. v. Goebell et al.* (frame 147, reel 5).

31. "Affidavit by Karl Weber," May 20, 1948, ibid. (frames 155–56).

32. "Affidavit by Erich Wentzel," April 28, 1948, ibid. (frames 144–45).

33. *Yamashita v. Styer,* Sec. 56, *Open Jurist,* openjurist.org/327/us/1/yamashita-yamashita-v-styer-us; A. Frank Reel, *The Case of General Yamashita* (Chicago: University of Chicago Press, 1949), 219.

34. *United States Supreme Court, Lawyers' Edition, Advance Opinions, 1947–1948, 92, No. 17* (Rochester: Lawyers' Cooperative, 1948), 1051–52.

35. "In the Matter of United States vs. Kurt Goebell et al.," 3–5, *U.S. v. Goebell,* 3–5 (frames 31–33, reel 5).

36. Ibid., 86, 93–97 (frames 114, 121–25).

37. "Memorandum for Colonel Fleischer," October 18, 1948, ibid. (frame 494).

38. Buscher, *The U.S. War Crimes Trial Program in Germany,* 38; Colonel J. L. Harbaugh to Chief, War Crimes Trial Branch, Civil Affairs Division, Department of the Army, August 11, 1948, *U.S. v. Goebell* (frame 468, reel 5).

39. Norman J. W. Goda, *Tales from Spandau: Nazi Criminals and the Cold War* (New York: Cambridge University Press, 2008), 76.

40. "HQ Department of the Army from Chief Civil Affairs Division to CINCEUR," October 16, 1948; "HQ Department of the Army from Chief Civil Affairs Division to EUCOM," October 16, 1948; "Memorandum for Colonel Fleischer," October 18, 1948, *U.S. v. Goebell* (frames 494–96, reel 5).

41. "Memorandum for Colonel Schiller," October 18, 1948 (with notation dated November 18, 1948), ibid. (frame 487).

42. "Petition for Clemency (Gnadengesuch)," November 14, 1948, ibid. (frames 584–85).

43. General Huebner to Wera Wentzel, December 2, 1948, ibid. (frame 507).

44. Rolf Galler to General Lucius D. Clay, ibid. (frame 513).

45. "Board Frees Officer in German Slayings," *Stars and Stripes* (European ed.), November 20, 1948.

46. Huebner to Galler, December 3, 1948, *U.S. v. Goebell* (frame 490, reel 5).

47. "Memorandum of Major Floyd M. Lundberg," December 6, 1948, ibid. (frame 532).

48. "Division Judge Advocate's Review," August 4, 1945, 5–6; "Headquarters U.S. Forces, European Theater," December 26, 1945, 2, *U.S. v. Schneeweiss.*

49. "Review by Staff Judge Advocate," November 9, 1945, 4, ibid.

50. "Headquarters U.S. Forces, European Theater," December 26, 1945, 3, ibid.

51. Robert A. Schneeweiss to the Adjutant General's Department, May 23, 1946; Major Frank C. Alfred to the Warden, U.S. Penitentiary, Leavenworth, Kansas, September 16, 1946, ibid.

52. "Memorandum for the Judge Advocate," April 9, 1947; Major Alfred to General Hoover, n.d., ibid.

53. *Malmedy Massacre Investigation: Hearings before a Subcommittee of the Committee on Armed Services, United States Senate, Eighty-First Congress, First Session, Pursuant to S. Res. 42* (Washington, DC: U.S. Government Printing Office, 1949), 217, 247, 367, 782.

54. Milwaukee County Council of Veterans of Foreign Wars to the President, February 11, 1947, General File, box 2161, White House Central Files, Harry S. Truman Papers (Harry S. Truman Library, Independence, MO).

55. Employees of the *Burbank Evening Review* to the Provost General [*sic*], War Department, January 25, 1947, *U.S. v. Schneeweiss.*

56. Colonel Hubert D. Hoover to publisher, *Burbank Evening Review,* n.d., ibid.

57. Algonquin Club Inc. to Senators Wiley and McCarthy, Representatives Kersten and Brophy, April 2, 1947; John C. Brophy to Liaison Officer, War Department, April 7, 1947, ibid.

58. General Thomas H. Green to Senator Allen J. Ellender, January 24, 1947, ibid.

59. "AGPK-CR 201, Schneeweiss, Robert A.," July 30, 1948; "AGPK-CR 201, Schneeweiss, Robert A., August 15, 1952, ibid.; "Board Frees Officer in German Slayings," *Stars and Stripes,* November 20, 1948.

9

Two Kinds of Justice?

Eric Wentzel (and two other men) died for their association with the murders of seven American POWs, although only one of them may have actually shot a prisoner (the evidence was ambiguous). Lieutenant Robert Schneeweiss suffered three years of imprisonment for having personally killed four German civilians, and three young accomplices were acquitted of charges that they had murdered six. Given the fact that Joachims, Nichols, and Peppler were still in their teens, it is hard to find fault with their acquittals, although U.S. Army courts convicted Germans who had been as young as 16 at the time they had committed their offenses.[1] We must confront the glaring disparity between the outcomes of the two cases while, at the same time, avoiding any suggestion of moral equivalence between the overall German and American records of criminality during World War II.

That the U.S. Army judged war crimes committed by its own members by a more indulgent standard than that applied to comparable crimes committed by the enemy is suggested not only by a comparison of the Voerde and Borkum cases. Had the Biscari massacre of 1943 been judged by standards similar to those applied in the Malmédy massacre trial, George Patton would have been sentenced at least to life in prison, if not death, Sergeant Horace West and Captain John Compton would certainly have faced death, and many other officers and men would have been subject to a wide range of punishments for having played various roles in a conspiracy or common design to murder Axis POWs. The Malmédy massacre was characterized by Army lawyers as the work of "hardened and dangerous criminals," while the War Department's Bureau of Public Relations urged that no publicity be given to the Biscari murders, partly on the grounds that to do so "would arouse a segment of our own citizens that are so distant from combat that they do not understand the savagery that is war." German atrocities, it appears, were the products of undeniable Nazi depravity, while comparable American crimes were merely the regrettable but unavoidable consequences of war.[2]

To be sure, some GIs expressed their disgust at the Biscari murders. The chaplain of the 45th Infantry Division reported that

> several of the men . . . came to me to make a strong protest against the treatment of prisoners they were observing. They stated that they would not care to go on fighting if such brutal treatment [as] the shooting down of men who had their hands up and the shooting down of prisoners who were being escorted to the rear was to continue. They stated that they had come into the war to fight against that sort of thing, and they felt ashamed of their countrymen who were doing those very things.[3]

But others voluntarily participated in the murders, and there is no evidence that any U.S. soldiers attempted to prevent them. Patton was not tried, West was sentenced to a life term but released after a year, and Compton was acquitted on the grounds that he had simply been following orders. The source of those alleged orders, Lieutenant General George S. Patton, accompanied by legal counsel, was questioned in April 1944 by Lieutenant Colonel Curtis Williams of the Inspector General's Department to answer allegations "prejudicial to his character and standing."[4] Patton was worried. His own recorded recollection of his exhortations to the officers of the 45th Infantry Division prior to the invasion of Sicily was that he had gotten "pretty bloody, trying to get an untried division to the sticking point," but that nothing that he had said could have been construed "by the wildest stretch of the imagination" as directing the murder of prisoners of war. This was clearly disingenuous and was contradicted by his own words. In a letter Patton wrote to his wife, Beatrice, the day before his meeting with Colonel Williams, he observed, "Now some fair-haired boys are trying to say that I killed too many prisoners. Yet, the same people cheer at the far greater killing of Japs. Well, the more I killed, the fewer men I lost, but they don't think of that. Sometimes I think that I will quit and join a monastery."[5]

It would be unrealistic in the extreme to expect a state in the midst of a desperate war to sacrifice one of its most effective commanders on the eve of the decisive campaign of the war in Western Europe as a consequence of his killing the enemy, even if it had been in violation of the laws of war. And bloody-mindedness was not undesirable in a commander, at least if he was on *your* side. In a letter written to the Army's inspector general, Major General Everett S. Hughes, a West Point classmate of Patton's, observed: "I am convinced that Patton is a fighter for he looks at war realistically and does what few men in our army have yet dared to do—talk openly about killing. George believes that the best way of shortening the war is to kill as many Germans as possible and as quickly as possible."[6] It may have been a similarly "realistic" view of war that was expressed by Major van Houten to Lieutenant Schneeweiss.

Patton's career was not seriously jeopardized by his role in the killing of enemy POWs on Sicily. On the other hand, he came close to ending his career with the notorious incidents involving the slapping of two psychologically traumatized GIs whom he had encountered in field hospitals on Sicily (whose "shell shock" he considered an "invention of the Jews"), an act which prompted Eisenhower to send him a letter containing "the strongest words of censure written to a senior American officer during World War II."[7]

The double standard applied by the U.S. Army to comparable war crimes committed by its own members and those done by its adversaries is striking. The truism that the wrongs that one suffers generally seem more reprehensible than the wrongs that one inflicts, while undoubtedly relevant, is an inadequate explanation. It should come as no surprise that a nation involved in a life-and-death struggle against a ruthless and genocidal enemy, a struggle articulated and justified to its people as an apocalyptic moral struggle pitting absolute good against total evil, should strive to minimize its own transgressions while visiting upon its enemies draconian punishment for theirs. Might it be plausibly argued that, on the level of macrojurisprudence, the normative disparity shown in the fates of Erich Wenzel and Robert Schneeweiss were morally justified on the grounds that Schneeweiss had committed his crimes in the context of an effort to destroy one of human history's greatest evils, while Wentzel's seemingly less egregious offenses were committed in defending that evil against seven American airmen who had been engaged in bombing it into morally necessary rubble? That is a proposition with which many, perhaps most, Americans would probably have agreed in the immediate postwar years. Many probably still would.

And it is equally unsurprising, if lamentable, that a nation should value the lives of its own citizens more highly than those of "foreigners." This seems true even if the foreigners were not recent enemies but victims of that enemy's malevolence. Joachim Peiper, the lead defendant in the Malmédy massacre trial and the commander of the SS battlegroup responsible for the murder of American POWs, had also been adjutant to *Reichsführer-SS* Heinrich Himmler and almost certainly was consensually present as genocide was being planned. He confessed to having been a witness to the experimental gassing of prisoners. Yet, the United States saw fit to try him only for his role in the murders of surrendered American soldiers, to which the killing of Belgian civilians by his battlegroup was distinctly secondary.[8] It is relevant, too, that the legal systems under which the Borkum and Voerde cases were tried served different purposes, as did the trials themselves. The Articles of War (since superseded by the Uniform Code of Military Justice) under which Schneeweiss was tried had been adopted to preserve discipline and good order within the U.S. Army, while war-crimes trials were imbued with a spirit of retribution for German atrocities, among the worst ever perpetrated. The punishment imposed on Schneeweiss may have served the ends of discipline adequately, but the most severe of the Borkum penalties were certainly excessive; the Borkum massacre, for all of its horror, was hardly comparable in moral terms to the operation of the Nazi concentration camps at Mauthausen, Dachau, and Buchenwald or the "euthanasia" facility at Hadamar, whose staff members were also tried and some hanged by the U.S. Army.

Some defense attorneys suspected that U.S. Army officers hearing cases against Germans accused of war crimes were under pressure to deliver verdicts of guilty. They may have been, but *United States v. Kurt Goebell et al.* was not a sham trial designed, like Stalin's show trials of 10 years before or the trials conducted before the "Peoples' Court" of Hitler's Germany, to deliver predetermined verdicts in the face of nonexistent or purely pro forma defenses. Although not as well protected as U.S. soldiers tried for similar crimes by court-martial, Germans being tried before U.S. Military Government Courts were assured the fundamentals of due process. Defendants were to be advised of charges prior to trial and to be represented by counsel of their choosing, in addition to an officer of the U.S. Army in cases in which the death penalty might be imposed. They were free, in most cases through their attorneys, to cross-examine witnesses against them and to summon defense witnesses with the assistance of U.S. authorities.

In the event of convictions, defendants might file petitions challenging the court's findings and sentences and setting forth reasons why they should be set aside, but multiple reviews by the Army's legal staff were automatic.[9] That process, in company with a changing political and international environment, kept Erich Wentzel alive and in hope of reprieve for more than two years and reduced the sentences of most of his codefendants, sparing two of them the grim walk to Landsberg's gallows. Yet, in the face of much more compelling evidence in the Voerde case, three American soldiers were acquitted of murder charges on the grounds that superior orders had relieved them of personal liability for their acts, and a fourth, sentenced to 25 years in prison, was released after three. The defense of superior orders was raised in the Borkum trial, too, but was brushed aside by the prosecution and by posttrial Army reviewers in rebuttals stunning in their hypocrisy. It is true, it was argued in "Review and Recommendations" related to the Borkum trial of August 1, 1947, that, at the time of the murders of #909's crew, U.S. combatants were protected by superior orders from prosecution for crimes against persons protected by international law, but that was a pragmatic provision in the Army's field manual that did not nullify the principle of individual responsibility. "Formerly under the Rules of Land Warfare only the commanders ordering the commission of such illegal acts were responsible therefore," Major Bryan declared in his summation for the prosecution, "but the world is progressing and such is not the case today."[10] Perhaps, but only, it appears, if the defendants were enemy combatants. Captain John Compton was acquitted of his role in the murders of Axis POWs on Sicily in 1943 on the grounds that he had been following orders from General George Patton. But, a few months prior to the Borkum trial, a U.S. Army military commission tried German General Anton Dostler for having ordered the deaths of 15 members of the U.S. Army who had been captured while on a sabotage mission behind German lines in Italy. Dostler based his defense on a *Führerbefehl* of October 18, 1942, in which Hitler ordered that, in reprisal for alleged Allied orders issued to commandos that Axis prisoners taken in the course of operations be killed, Allied commandos were to be "exterminated to the last man" in the course of combat or pursuit. Dostler was found guilty of violations of the laws of war and put to death by firing squad.[11] If similar punishments for similar crimes judged according to similar standards are necessary components of justice, the U.S. Army did not do justice in these cases.

But U.S. Army courts did not always judge their enemies harshly and inequitably. In the late summer of 1947, a nine-member U.S. general military government court heard a case against the notorious former *SS-Obersturmbannführer* (Lieutenant Colonel) Otto Skorzeny and nine other defendants. Skorzeny was well known to the Allies as the rescuer of Mussolini following the overthrow of his regime and as commander of an effort during the Battle of the Bulge to capture bridges over the Meuse River and sow confusion behind American lines by employing English-speaking German soldiers wearing captured U.S. uniforms. The operation, code-named *Greif* (Griffin), was a dismal failure but has provided raw material for the imaginations of popular historians and movie makers. It also provided Army prosecutors with the makings of a war-crimes trial.

Skorzeny and his codefendants were charged with violations of "the laws and usages of war" for having illegally used American uniforms and insignia, misappropriated property belonging to the International Red Cross, and, most serious, murdered more than 100 U.S. prisoners of war.[12] The charge of murder was loosely associated with the Malmédy massacre, for which 73 Germans had been tried and convicted the previous year. Skorzeny's U.S. Army defense team was permitted to call Allied witnesses, who testified that they had used German uniforms in combat operations in probable violation of international law and had been ordered not to take prisoners.[13] In his summation for the defense, Lieutenant Colonel Donald McClure argued that the laws of war had changed through universal practice since the Hague Convention (IV) of 1907. "Once there were days of chivalry," he intoned. "In the Second World War, there were no days of chivalry." The Skorzeny case, McClure argued, could not be judged by the standards of 1907, for in the intervening 40 years there had been two world wars that had altered the rules according to which war is waged.[14] Whether or not the nine officers sitting in judgment of the case agreed is unknown, but they produced the verdict desired by the defense. The defendants were acquitted.[15]

Why the dramatic difference in outcomes between the Borkum and the Skorzeny trials? Beyond the attitudes of the officers who judged the cases—unknowable at this point—there are a number of relevant factors. The most important, clearly, is that the Skorzeny prosecution team had dropped the most serious charge—that of the murder of American POWs—as it concluded its presentation. That element of the case had been based primarily on a single affidavit, for which little corroborating evidence could be found. Moreover, more than a year had passed since the Borkum trial, a year during which wartime passions had cooled and criticism of the quality of U.S. Army justice applied to Germans accused of war crimes, most evident in regard to the Malmédy massacre trial, had mounted. The prosecution noted pointedly that it did not care to base that element of its case on affidavits alone, as had been largely done in the now suspect Malmédy case.[16]

There was a link between the two proceedings in the person of Colonel Abraham Rosenfeld. Rosenfeld had served as law member of the Malmédy court and led the prosecution team in the Skorzeny trial, which experience he was to describe as "interesting" but "unpleasant." He noted in a letter of October 8, 1947, to Willis M. Everett Jr., who had led the defense of the Germans accused of the Malmédy massacre, that "things have changed in the year since you were here."[17] What was in Rosenfeld's mind is uncertain, but there are undeniable differences between the Borkum and Malmédy trials of 1946 and the Skorzeny trial of more than a year later. Perhaps most noteworthy is the fact that, in the Skorzeny trial, the defense was permitted to offer evidence that the Allies had been guilty of offenses similar to those with which the defendants in the case at hand had been charged. Testimony regarding U.S. violations of the laws of war had been explicitly excluded from the Malmédy trial and merely hinted at in the Borkum courtroom. In what was perhaps the dramatic high point of the proceedings, RAF Wing Commander Forrest Yeo-Thomas was questioned on his wartime efforts to organize French resistance activities, as well as his involvement in espionage and sabotage behind German lines. German uniforms obtained "by hook or crook" had often been employed, and Yeo-Thomas and his men, while so attired, had been prepared to engage in combat, in the course of which prisoners were not to be taken. It was with considerable relish that defense counsel explored this issue.

> DEFENSE: In the event of discovery of danger [*sic*] or the prevention of discovery, what would the practice be?
> YEO-THOMAS: Bump off the other guy!
> DEFENSE: Did the court get the answer?
> PRESIDENT: Yes, the court got it.[18]

It has been alleged that German criminality in World War II, for largely cynical and opportunistic reasons, was inadequately punished and that the wartime Allied commitment to pursue the German authors of atrocities "to the uttermost ends of the earth . . . in order that justice may be done" was a "pledge betrayed."[19] It may have been, although one may legitimately ask whether "justice" for the worst of German crimes could ever have been achieved or, indeed, what it would have looked like. But the evaluation of postwar war-crimes justice has hitherto been incomplete. Surely a comparative appraisal of the manner in which the victors dealt with lesser crimes committed by their own personnel as well as by the enemy should enter into the analysis without fear that German criminality will thereby be "relativized" and in some sense excused on the grounds of rough moral equivalence. Nazi Germany's crimes, of which the Holocaust and genocidal war in Eastern Europe are paramount, will always stand alone as constituting the nadir of human conduct during World War II.

NOTES

1. James J. Weingartner, *Crossroads of Death: The Story of the Malmédy Massacre and Trial* (Berkeley and Los Angeles: University of California Press, 1979), 35.

2. James J. Weingartner, "Americans, Germans, and War Crimes: Converging Narratives from 'the Good War,'" *Journal of American History* 94 (March 2008): 1166.

3. "Statement of Lieutenant Colonel William E. King, Chaplain, 45th Infantry Division, July 16, 1943," *United States of America v. West, Sgt. Horace T.* (Clerk of Court, U.S. Army Judiciary, Arlington, VA).

4. Orders to Lieutenant Colonel Curtis L. Williams, March 24, 1944; Brigadier General Philip E. Brown to the Deputy Chief of Staff, March 21, 1944, Record Group 159, File 333.9, Records of the Office of the Inspector General (National Archives II, College Park, MD).

5. Martin Blumenson, ed., *The Patton Papers, 1940–1945* (Boston: Houghton Mifflin, 1974), II: 431. Patton had attempted to cover up the massacre by suggesting that it be portrayed as the consequence of an attempt to escape by the prisoners. Ibid., 288.

6. Major General Everett S. Hughes to Major General Virgil L. Peterson, April 7, 1944, Record Group 159, File 333.9, Records of the Office of the Inspector General.

7. Stanley P. Hirshson, *General Patton: A Soldier's Life*, 393, 399; Carlo D'Este, *Patton: A Genius for War* (New York: HarperCollins, 1995), 533–36.

8. Jens Westemeier, *Joachim Peiper: Zwischen Totenkopf und Ritterkreuz* (Bissendorf: Biblio Verlag, 2006), 25–55; Richard Breitman, *The Architect of Genocide: Himmler and the Final Solution* (New York: Knopf, 1991), 95–168.

9. Eli E. Nobleman, "Procedure and Evidence in American Military Government Courts in the United States Zone of Germany," *Federal Bar Journal* 8

(January 1947): 214–15; Maximilian Koessler, "American War Crimes Trials in Europe," *Georgetown Law Journal* 39 (1950–51): 67–69.

10. "Review and Recommendations," 4, *U.S. v. Goebell* (frame 30, reel 3); "Record of Trial," 1193, ibid. (frame 610, reel 2).

11. "The Dostler Case. Trial of General Anton Dostler, Commander of the 75th German Army Corps," United Nations War Crimes Commission, *Law Reports of Trials of War Criminals* (London: His Majesty's Stationery Office, 1947), I: 29, 32–33. The prosecution argued that Dostler's defense of superior orders was invalid on the grounds that the *Führerbefehl* was illegal and that, in any event, Dostler had violated the order by having held the Americans prisoner for 45 hours before having them shot. Ibid., 33.

12. "Record of Trial," *U.S. v. Otto Skorzeny et al.,* 1, 5 (fiche 1), National Archives Record Group 153, Microfilm Publication 1106.

13. Ibid., 526 (fiche 11).

14. Ibid., 778 (fiche 14).

15. Ibid., 799 (fiche 14).

16. Ibid., 452 (fiche 9).

17. Abraham Rosenfeld to Willis Everett, October 8, 1947, Everett Papers (in author's possession).

18. "Record of Trial," 526–31, *U.S. v. Skorzeny* (fiche 11).

19. The theme and title of Tom Bower, *The Pledge Betrayed: America and Britain and the Denazification of Postwar Germany* (New York: Doubleday, 1982). See also Frank M. Buscher, *The U.S. War Crimes Trial Program in Germany* (Westport, CT: Greenwood Press, 1989), 159–64.

10

Memory

Erich Wentzel's ashes were buried on the afternoon of Wednesday, December 15, in Wuppertal's Vohwinkel cemetery. The *Wuppertaler Rundschau* reported that "over a thousand mourners . . . followed the urn with silent emotion." The Borkum prosecutors were not alone in employing religious imagery to sanctify the dead. In his eulogy delivered in the cemetery chapel, Pastor Posth likened Wentzel to Christ, crucified between the two thieves. "Seen in this light," the article continued, "Wentzel's tragic death receives its meaning." Speaking at the graveside, Caritas director Hans Carls embellished the image of Wentzel's Christ-like martyrdom by recalling the last words allegedly spoken by the deceased: "Lord, thy will be done." The mournful strains of *Ich hatt' einen Kameraden*, the traditional lament for a soldier fallen in battle, echoed over a grave that was covered by what was described as "a mountain of flowers."[1]

Other published accounts were less ethereal. A bitter commentary that appeared in an unidentified German newspaper struck hard at the alleged injustice of Wentzel's conviction in Ludwigsburg and hanging in Landsberg and their possible consequences.

The German public has the right to be informed of what took place behind the closed doors of the American war tribunals, and what is taking place inside the walls of the Landsberg prison. The German public has this right, because one cannot assert that one wants to punish war crimes, while one is committing grave injustices oneself. We consider it our conscientious duty to take care that the future relations between Germans and Americans are not poisoned by the names of Dachau, Ludwigsburg and Landsberg,

and we fear that a dangerous hatred and nationalism can be engendered in the murky confusion of guilty and innocent. Therefore, we take up the case of Erich F. Wentzel of Wuppertal in order
to show with what means and in what a spirit the Americans conducted many trials. Wentzel has meanwhile been executed; he
died innocent, and he is not the only one.

There followed a recapitulation of the defense case for Wentzel and
a provocative reference to a lurid accusation that Wentzel's wife had
leveled against Major Abraham Levine, the chief of the Borkum investigation team. Wera Wentzel had claimed that, in the course of a visit
to Borkum to learn something about her husband's condition during
Levine's pretrial investigations, Levine had attempted to "seduce" her.
Frau Wentzel's resistance to Levine's advances, the article asserted,
had resulted in Erich Wentzel's solitary confinement for 14 days. And
the author may have been aware of the Schneeweiss case. "It is significant in this context to learn from the American Army . . . ," he observed
sarcastically, "what the law is like that American soldiers are subject
to." He continued:

> They wanted to teach us Germans, they unrolled the horrors of
> the Hitler regime before our eyes. Now we have a right to know
> what really happened in Dachau, Ludwigsburg and Landsberg.
> We want to know what the standards were for the justice that
> engendered such "errors." The Americans must make it clear that
> justice is indivisible for victors and vanquished.[2]

It was a fair point. The article reflects the damage done to the image
of U.S. Army war-crimes justice by proceedings such as the Borkum
trial and its aftermath when compared to the Army's handling of the
Voerde atrocity. The double standard applied by the United States in
comparable atrocity cases in which Germans and Americans were perpetrators provided an all too facile means by which Germans could seek
to minimize their own enormous burden of guilt for crimes that were
very much worse. "What really happened" at Dachau, where most
war-crimes trials conducted by the U.S. Army took place, included
not only the prosecution and the sometimes draconian sentencing of
Germans for crimes for the like of which Americans were commonly
punished more leniently if at all but also trials involving offenses that
were at the core of the Nazi system of mass murder—the operation

of the concentration camps at Dachau, Mauthausen, and Buchenwald and the Hadamar "euthanasia" facility where hundreds of thousands had been done to death.

The Borkum trial, with particular emphasis on the fate of Eric Wentzel, was the subject of a tendentious book published in 1952 under the title *Landsberg: Henker des Rechts? (Landsberg: Hangman of Justice?)*. The question mark was disingenuous, as the author, K. W. Hammerstein (apparently a pseudonym used by Erich Wentzel's brother, Kurt) left no doubt as to his conviction that justice had gone to the gallows along with Wentzel. But a forward was contributed by Rudolf Aschenauer, defense attorney in numerous war-crimes trials, including the *Einsatzgruppen* case, in which 24 SS officers were tried for participating in the killing squads that murdered hundreds of thousands of Jews in Russia.[3] Aschenauer was also a prolific propagandist who railed against alleged Allied injustices in the investigation and prosecution of Germans for war crimes, and the trial and execution of Erich Wentzel was prime grist for his mill. Wentzel, he declared, was "one of many" victims of Allied hatred and lust for vengeance, which had subjected Germans of all ages and social classes to brutal mistreatment and unjust trials, setting them on a path of suffering that led to the gallows or prison. Hammerstein/Wentzel's book would, he claimed, "prove that men like Erich Wentzel were not criminals, but victims of a justice system manipulated for political ends."[4] In Aschenauer's hands, the death of Erich Wentzel became a weapon that, like the flawed Malmédy massacre trial, could be used to defame the whole of the Allied war-crimes trial program and, by implication, exonerate Germans for the horrendous crimes of the Third Reich.

Hammerstein/Wentzel's book offered a highly dramatized, semifictional account less of the Borkum atrocity itself, which he made no effort to deny, than of the subsequent investigation of the incident and trial of its alleged perpetrators by the U.S. Army. The anti-Semitism that had been at the foundation of the Holocaust was clearly evident in Hammerstein/Wentzel's treatment of Major Abraham Levine, leader of the investigation team. In an affidavit, Wera Wentzel had asserted that Levine had attempted to "seduce" her when she had approached him for information on her husband and a request that he deliver to him a letter.[5] Hammerstein/Wentzel's lurid and heavily dramatized version of the alleged event would not have been out of place in the pages of Julius Streicher's virulently anti-Semitic Nazi newspaper, *Der Stürmer*. Having invited Wera Wentzel, "an elegant blond woman," to his hotel room for a cigarette, the "dark eyed" Levine allegedly informed her of her husband's perilous situation and boasted of his amorous successes with German women. Then, according to the author, he attempted to undress Frau Wentzel and forced her onto his bed. The account has Frau Wentzel succeeding in escaping Levine's clutches with an indignant "I am not one of your loose girls! I am a German woman, Herr Major! Among our officers it was self-evident that along with the uniform went the obligation to behave decently, and I believed that to be true throughout the world." She then resolved to leave the island rather than risk another encounter with Levine, convinced that her resistance to his advances had seriously damaged her husband's prospects.[6]

How closely Hammerstein/Wentzel's account approximates reality is now impossible to ascertain. Wera Wentzel had waited two and a half years after the alleged event to execute an affidavit of which her likely brother-in-law's description is a highly dramatized version. Her motives are clear—to weaken the case against her husband by revealing, exaggerating, or fabricating an incident that cast aspersions on the investigator who had secured the sworn statements that formed a major part of the prosecution case. In Hammerstein/Wentzel's hands, it became a device that degraded justified criticism of genuine abuses in U.S. war-crimes trial policy with the racism that had been the cornerstone of the Third Reich and the motivation for its most heinous crimes. Persons of all faiths except Jews had urged mercy for the Borkum convicts, the author pointedly noted, seemingly unconscious of the grotesqueness of the statement or, perhaps, confident that it would resonate positively with his readers.[7]

Hammerstein/Wentzel admitted that not all of the Germans held in Landsberg prison were innocent.[8] That grudging concession, contained in a sparse three-sentence paragraph, hardly conveyed the enormity of the crimes of which some of them had been convicted. One of the last inmates of Landsberg to keep an appointment with its gallows was Oswald Pohl, wartime chief of the SS Economic and Administrative Main Office, a typically benign-sounding bureaucratic structure whose responsibilities included the brutal exploitation of hundreds of thousands of concentration-camp prisoners and the utilization of the "byproducts" of the murder of millions of Jews in the extermination camps. The injustices allegedly visited on Erich Wentzel and other Borkum defendants, on the other hand, were described in lurid detail. Beatings, starvation rations, and primitive living conditions not dissimilar to those inflicted on prisoners in Nazi concentration camps were allegedly inflicted by Esterwegen's new masters on the suspects in the Borkum case being held there, while U.S. investigators extracted "confessions" in brutal interrogations and contrived to "misplace" inconvenient witnesses whose stories threatened to undermine the prosecution's case.[9] Erich Wentzel had been singled out for a "frame-up" by Levine, the author implied, as revenge for Wera's resistance to his advances. Sergeant Schmitz, who had led the guard detail during the fatal march, bore the major burden of responsibility for the failure to protect the prisoners but, with Levine's connivance, had attempted (unsuccessfully) to save himself by shifting the blame to Wentzel. During the trial, the defense had been inept, while the officers sitting in judgment, the author claimed, had gotten drunk while deciding on the sentences to be imposed.[10]

It was a badly distorted account of the investigation and trial and an example of the inclination of many postwar Germans to regard themselves as victims, rather than the perpetrators or accomplices of Nazi criminality. Four years later, a very different appraisal of the Borkum trial was published in the United States by Maximilian Koessler in the scholarly *Journal of Criminal Law, Criminology, and Political Science.* Koessler was an Austrian-born lawyer who had been employed by the War Crimes Branch of the Army's Judge Advocate General's Department. Koessler was nothing if not a meticulous analyst of judicial proceedings. He had been assigned the Malmédy massacre case for review, a task that his boss hoped he would complete in three to four months. Six months later, he had completed evaluations of the convictions of only 15 of the 73 former SS men who had been tried and found guilty. He was not afraid to find fault with Army investigative and court procedure. Some of the Malmédy defendants, he concluded, had been convicted on inadequate evidence, and some pretrial sworn statements shared suspiciously similar wording, perhaps related to questionable interrogation techniques, including the use of false witnesses and mock trials.[11]

Koessler's analysis of the Borkum trial, which he declared "was one of the most interesting among those American war-crimes cases which were tried outside Nuremberg," was apparently motivated by personal interest, rather than the result of an official assignment. He rightly passed off Hammerstein/Wentzel's book as "mostly based on hearsay and colored by the attempt to eulogize one of the defendants"; it, in fact, closed with an epitaph for Wentzel, the "victim of judicial murder by an American military court." Koessler entitled his article "Borkum Island Tragedy and Trial," but his tragedy was not Hammerstein/Wentzel's but, rather, the "cruel ordeal" and murder of #909's crew. He accepted as factual the description of the events of August 4, 1944, as they had been presented by the prosecution: the prior inflammatory editorial by propaganda minister Goebbels, elevated in the minds of the defendants to the status of a "decree"; the capture of the bomber's crew by members of the Ostland Battery under Lieutenant Seiler's command and its interrogation by Wentzel; the orders to the guard detail to conduct the prisoners by the longest possible route to the point of embarkation to the mainland; the assault on the prisoners by members of a Labor Service detachment with Wentzel's tacit approval, if not actual connivance; Mayor Akkermann's incitement of the crowd to attack the prisoners and the failure of the guards to protect them; Langer's shooting of the "little flyer," Howard Graham, and the failure to arrest the assailant, giving him the opportunity for a second attack in which he murdered the remaining prisoners; and, finally, the drafting of an official report on the incident that falsified the manner in which the crew of #909 had been done to death. But Koessler had serious reservations about the conclusions that the court had drawn from the narrative.[12]

An analysis of the thinking behind the verdicts was, as Koessler pointed out, impossible inasmuch as the officers who arrived at them had offered no explanation as to how they had reached their conclusions. But he was able to reasonably infer that the prosecution's theory of criminal conspiracy had played an important role in determining the Borkum trial's outcome, and with that he disagreed on both legal and evidentiary grounds. It was inappropriate, he argued, for the court to have applied American common-law concepts of conspiracy, concepts unknown to legal systems based on civil law, such as Germany's. Moreover, even under the American concept of criminal conspiracy, Koessler believed, there had been inadequate evidence to convict four of the five defendants, including Wentzel, of the murder charge. He doubted that the "spontaneous action of Langer" could be reasonably construed as a natural or foreseeable consequence of a scheme to expose the Americans to abuse by the civilian population.[13]

Koessler was more cautious in judging the matter of sentencing, although he clearly believed that the prison terms given to the defendants found guilty only on the assault charge were excessive. On the graver issue of the five death sentences, however, Koessler refused to express an opinion, perplexing in view of his skepticism with regard to the evidentiary bases for those verdicts. The commutations of Goebell's and Seiler's sentences, however, seemed to him "highly questionable" in view of the two men's roles as the "wire pullers" behind the march that had resulted in the deaths of the seven American prisoners. Perhaps reflecting reluctance as a German-speaking immigrant to the United States to question the fundamental integrity of the trial, Koessler hastened to add that "nothing herein is meant to deny or question that all those who had to make decisions in the case discharged their duties in a most conscientious way, with the honest intention to find the truth, to be just, and to be fair."[14]

Hammerstein/Wentzel, surprisingly, made no reference to the Voerde murders and Schneeweiss's prison sentence and early release, although he may have been in contact with Rolf Galler, Erich Wentzel's German attorney, who had brought the disparity between the fates of the two men to General Clay's attention. Indeed, beyond noting that Langer's wife and children had been killed in an air raid on Hamburg, Hammerstein/Wentzel said nothing about German sufferings at the hands of the Allies *during* the war. In addition to the brief article in *Stars and Stripes* that announced Schneeweiss's parole and the unidentified article referred to by the employees of the Burbank *Evening Review*, which led them to conclude incorrectly that the German civilians for whose murders Schneeweiss had been convicted had been killed during a combat operation, there is a clipping in the Truman Library containing a photograph of Fannie Schneeweiss and her two children, ages 3 and 17 months, with an inset of a moderately handsome Robert Schneeweiss in his second lieutenant's uniform. The caption notes prosaically that a petition had been filed "in Washington" requesting the commutation of his 25-year sentence.[15] But there is nothing on the Voerde murders comparable to Koessler's analysis of the Borkum case, although the former seems inherently no less interesting or significant than the latter. A routing slip in the Schneeweiss file dated February 20, 1950, at which time the file was classified "restricted," notes that a "technical historian" employed by the "Research Office of the Army" planned to consult the documents for a paper on the "Geneva Convention and its effect on physiological [*sic*] warfare," but a later addendum declares that "the historian found nothing she could use in her paper and so she made no notes."[16] If the author had been interested more broadly in the effect of international law on the conduct of troops in battle, she might have found something worthy of note in the Schneeweiss trial record. When asked by a member of the court if he had ever heard of the War Department's Field Manual 27-10 *Rules of Land Warfare* in the course of his military experience, Schneeweiss answered in the negative and added that not only had he never been required to read it but he had never seen a copy of it prior to his court-martial.[17]

Evidence that public memories of World War II are selective should shock no one. Why the Army's "technical historian," identified only as a "Dr. Bartimo," scrawled in pencil on a slip of paper, should have elected not to include the Schneeweiss case in her paper is not known, but to many Americans with a modicum of historical consciousness, the consumers of the never-ending flow of popular literature and visual treatments of World War II, the preservation of a sanitized image of their country's conduct of the war is a sacred obligation. To do otherwise, as was demonstrated by the controversy surrounding the proposed Smithsonian Air and Space Museum's exhibit to commemorate the 50th anniversary of the atomic bombing of Hiroshima, is to be guilty of "revisionism."[18] That revising beliefs about the past on the basis of new information and altered perspectives, what historians must do in order to elevate their product above the perpetuation of what its consumers find familiar and comfortable, can generate high levels of resistance when it is applied to what is perhaps the most positively regarded collective experience in U.S. history is not surprising. But it imposes unfortunate and harmful limitations on public understanding of this most terrible of all wars and of war in general. The moral balance between the United States and its enemies in World War II is not significantly altered by the recognition that U.S. combatants, too, were sometimes guilty of gross violations of the laws of war but escaped the punishment for them that was often imposed on their enemies. When the author served as a consultant and "talking head" for a documentary television program on the Malmédy massacre, his suggestion to the producers that a broader perspective be provided by including at least a brief reference to similar atrocities committed by U.S. forces was received with something close to horror and peremptorily rejected. Information on the Biscari atrocities that recently appeared in a leading Italian newspaper and on Italian state television seems not to have registered with U.S. news media.[19] Although some Germans have also resisted confronting aspects of their nation's far worse record of war crimes—the fact, for example, that the German Army willingly cooperated with Heinrich Himmler's SS and police in waging a racial war of almost unimaginable barbarity in Eastern Europe—the broad outlines of German genocide are denied only by a lunatic fringe. More characteristic of present-day Germans seems to be a compulsive need to express remorse for the criminal acts of the Third Reich.

NOTES

1. "Die Beisetzung von E.F. Wentzel," *Wuppertaler Rundschau*, December 16, 1948, *U.S. v. Goebell* (frame 521, reel 5).

2. "Unabdingbare Fragen an einem Grabe," ibid. (frame 526). On German consciousness of an American double standard in regard to war crimes, see Richard L. Merritt, *Democracy Imposed: U.S. Occupation Policy and the German Public, 1945–1949* (New Haven, CT: Yale University Press, 1995), 168.

3. Norbert Frei, *Adenauer's Germany and the Nazi Past: The Politics of Amnesty and Integration*, trans. Joel Golb (New York: Columbia University Press, 2002), 110, 119, 121; Kurt Tauber, *Beyond Eagle and Swastika: German Nationalism since 1945* (Middletown, CT: Wesleyan University Press, 1967) I: 519, 714–15; Kerstin von Lingen, *Kesselring's Last Battle: War Crimes Trials and Cold War Politics*, trans. Alexandra Klemm (Lawrence: University of Kansas Press, 2009), 184.

4. K. W. Hammerstein, *Landsberg: Henker des Rechts?* (Wuppertal: Abendland Verlag, 1952), "Vorwort."

5. "Eidesstattliche Erklärung," April 16, 1948, *U.S. v. Goebell* (frames 136–37, reel 5).

6. Hammerstein, *Landsberg*, 113–15.

7. Ibid., 199.

8. Ibid.

9. Ibid., 93–96, 100–106.

10. Ibid., 117–19, 125, 150–51, 169, 170, 191–92.

11. U.S. Senate, *Malmedy Massacre Investigation: Hearings before a Subcommittee of the Committee on Armed Services, United States Senate, Eighty-First Congress, First Session, Pursuant to Senate Resolution 42* (Washington, DC: U.S. Government Printing Office, 1949), 1338–66.

12. Maximilian Koessler, "Borkum Island Tragedy and Trial," *Journal of Criminal Law, Criminology and Political Science* 47 (July–August 1956): 183–89.

13. Ibid., 193–96.

14. Ibid., 196.

15. Schneeweiss photo, Official File, White House Central File, Harry S. Truman Papers, Harry S. Truman Library, Independence, MO.

16. "Routing Slip," Hattie Wright, February 20, 1950; handwritten note on slip, February 26, 1951, *U.S. v. Schneeweiss*.

17. "Record of Trial," 59–60, *U.S. v. Schneeweiss*.

18. Edward T. Linenthal and Tom Engelhardt, eds., *The Enola Gay and Other Battles for the American Past* (New York: Holt, 1996).

19. Gianluca di Feo, "I prigionieri italiani uccisi? Dite che erano cecchini," *Corriere Della Sera,* June 24, 2004, http://archiviostorico.corriere.it/2004/ giugno/24/prigionieri_italiani_uccisi_Dite_che_co_9_ . . . ; "Il 'Prigioniero' Giannola el il Silenzio sui Caduti di Biscari," ibid., September 24, 2009, http:// archiviostorico. corriere.it/2009/settembre/24/Prigionero_Giannola_Silenzio_ sui_Cad. . .; Riccardo Giannola to James J. Weingartner, e-mail, September 1, 2009 (in Weingartner's possession).

11

August 4, 2003

On August 4, 2003, a small memorial was dedicated on Borkum to the seven American airmen who had been murdered there 59 years earlier. It is an incongruous intrusion in a resort community normally preoccupied with serving a thriving tourist trade. Current vacation literature entices the reader with the prospect of "sun on your skin, an endless vastness in view, sand between your toes, wind in your hair. . . . Borkum invites you to an unforgettable summer holiday." Should the North Sea be uncooperatively calm, "the Flow Rider, the only indoor surfing facility in Northern Germany," is available to simulate the waves that had sometimes washed onto Borkum's wartime beaches the bodies of downed airmen.[1] The events of August 4, 2003, evoked memories of that grimmer Borkum.

Wilfried Krahwinkel, one of the island's permanent residents and an employee of the narrow-gauge railroad that might have been used to safely transport the crew of #909 to the point of departure for the mainland, had developed an interest in Borkum's World War II history. Some older residents casually mentioned to him that a number of "Canadian" prisoners had been murdered on the island, an issue unaddressed in local historical literature. Further research revealed that the victims had belonged to the U.S. Army Air Forces and introduced him to the webpage of the 486th Bombardment Group and its historian, Robin Smith, who provided him with the names of #909's crew. Dr. Helmer Zühlke, one of Borkum's physicians and the honorary director of its museum of local history, had been educated on the events of August 4, 1944, by Krahwinkel and by Bryan van Sweringen, an American historian who had become familiar with the records of the Borkum trial while serving as an intern at the U.S. National Archives in the 1970s. He and his German-born wife had visited Borkum in the summer of 2002 and, in a dramatic gesture, had walked the route followed by #909's crew and their guards, placing a yellow rose at the scenes of their murders. Before leaving Borkum, van Sweringen deposited a summary of the atrocity at the museum. The contents of the document, Zühlke later recalled, had seized him and had refused to let go.[2]

Krahwinkel and Zühlke initiated a campaign to erect a memorial on Borkum to the murdered American airmen, whose bodies had long before been moved either to the United States or to the Ardennes American Cemetery in Belgium.[3] Town councilmen and business people reacted hesitantly at first. Many Borkumers held ambivalent views on the events of August 4, 1944, and their aftermath, recognizing the inhumanity of marching #909's crew through the town without protection but also seeing injustice in the death penalties imposed for Langer's murderous acts. But it was also recognized that the American airmen bore no responsibility for flaws in U.S. Army justice. A decision was made to purchase a small stone monument, its cost defrayed by Borkum's Rotary Club. The memorial was erected in Borkum's war memorial square on Hindenburg Strasse and dedicated in a ceremony conducted on August 4, 2003, the 59th anniversary of the murders of #909's crew.[4] Among the several hundred persons in attendance, many of whom were probably curious townspeople and vacationers, was a handful with a more compelling interest. Present were Quentin F. Ingerson, #909's navigator, and Kazmer Rachak, its flight engineer, both of whom had bailed out of their damaged B-17 in the vicinity of Bremen and fallen into the hands of less wrathful captors, thereby avoiding the death march on Borkum. They were accompanied by surviving relatives of the murdered airmen and the 486th's historian, Robin Smith. Also in attendance were representatives of the German government and the U.S. Air Force, the former to offer expressions of contrition for a criminal act for which they bore no responsibility, the latter to extol the sacrifice involuntarily made almost six decades earlier by #909's crew.[5]

The language of memory reflects the tensions inherent in the event that evoked it. A bronze plaque affixed to the rough-hewn stone contains the names and ranks of the seven victims, rendered in large capital letters. They are preceded by a statement in smaller characters in both German and English. The latter reads:

In Memory
of those US-Airmen

who were killed under tragic
circumstances on August 4th 1944
after being captured on our island.

But by whom? And what was the nature of these "tragic circum-stances"? An uninformed visitor to Borkum might suppose that the prisoners had been run over by an out-of-control truck or crushed by a collapsing wall. Beneath the names of the murdered Americans, but in German only, is a statement that reads, "With them, we also remem-ber the millions of soldiers in many countries who, in violation of in-ternational agreements regarding the treatment of prisoners of war, had to give up their lives [*ihr Leben lassen mussten*] in captivity."[6] Un-mentioned was the fact that the most numerous of these were Soviet prisoners taken by Germany, of whom roughly 3.3 million of the ap-proximately 5.7 million captured (58 percent) perished.[7] By that stan-dard, the Borkum atrocity—indeed, all atrocities inflicted by Germans on Americans—were minor. In any case, the monument seemed to suggest that the U.S. airmen had died as part of an impersonal and universal wave of wartime brutality.

German speakers at the dedication ceremony were less ambiguous than the text of the monument. Pastor Joachim Jannsen expressed re-morse for a shameful act that occurred as "part of the darkest chapter in German history."[8] The murder of seven airmen who were engaged in an aspect of World War II that is not without a high degree of moral ambiguity was thereby implicitly linked to what is arguably the great-est crime in modern history, the Holocaust and the German genocidal war in Eastern Europe. Pastor Jannsen's oratory alongside the obfus-cating text of the monument exemplifies the extraordinary difficulty Germans experience in reconciling their own wartime suffering with the unparalleled catastrophe that Germany inflicted on Europe and doing it without alienating people with divergent perspectives in Ger-many itself and affected non-Germans, some of whom were among the spectators and participants.

Brigadier General Stanley Gorenc and Colonel Kerry Taylor, rep-resenting the U.S. Air Force in Europe and the U.S. Eighth Air Force, which had borne the brunt of the U.S. aerial assault on Germany, ex-pressed a less ambivalent perspective. General Gorenc praised the people of Borkum for having confronted their history and lauded the murdered airmen for having made "the highest sacrifice for peace and freedom," while noting darkly the willingness of Borkumers to "allow a bitter inheritance to live on" in the form of the monument.[9] Colonel Taylor recalled "the constellation of fighters and bombers" that had carried 350,000 airmen deep into Europe, of whom 26,000 had paid "the ultimate price."[10] Borkum provided an ideal venue for reaffirming the comfortable proposition that the cost, both in American lives and in the products of U.S. industrial predominance, had been exacted in a war that in a moral sense had been self-evidently necessary.

That many more German civilians than American airmen paid the "ultimate price" was an aspect of the war central to the monument's historical context addressed by neither German nor American speakers. Reinhold Robbe, Social Democratic chairman of the Bundestag's Defense Committee, however, came close. With a brutal frankness unique in an otherwise delicately articulated event, Robbe raged against "blind Nazis," "guards devoid of decency," and civilians who had "humiliated and attacked" the American airmen. But, of course, there was also Langer, "a German soldier obsessed with hate who had executed the Americans one after the other." That Robbe used the German verb *hinrichten* (to execute), rather than *ermorden* (to murder), to describe Langer's act may have reflected a certain ambivalence, perhaps subconscious. In any event, no overt reference was made to the source of Langer's hatred—the death of his wife and children in an Allied bombing raid on Hamburg.[11]

To have alluded to any of the roughly half-million civilians killed in Allied air attacks on Germany during World War II would have been awkward. Although in recent years Germans have felt increased freedom to grieve openly for their sufferings under American and British bombing, any reference to them while dedicating a memorial to the murdered crew would have seemed precariously close to an attempt to lessen the gravity of the Borkum atrocity and perhaps to relativize other German crimes that were infinitely worse. German-born author W. G. Sebald has observed that "a nation that had murdered and worked to death millions of people in its camps could hardly call on the victorious powers to explain the military and political logic that dictated the destruction of German cities."[12] But Sebald has also noted that "our vague feelings of shared guilt prevented anyone . . . from being permitted to remind us of such humiliating images as the incident in the Altmarkt in Dresden, where 6, 865 corpses were burned on pyres in February 1945 by an SS detachment which had gained its experience at Treblinka."[13] To have pointed out that the physical results of mass killings, irrespective of their motivation and methodology, are much the same would have violated the spirit of "shared guilt" that had produced the monument.

And there was the memory complex of the American guests to consider. While strategic bombing failed to live up to the full promise held out for it by its proponents, American airpower and the industrial and technical virtuosity that gave rise to it contributed significantly to a victory that was relatively economical of American lives, if profligate in its toll on enemy civilians, as well as on the citizens of countries under German occupation. The romance of clear-eyed young Americans waging high-tech war in the light of day (in contrast to their surreptitiously night-bombing British counterparts) in the face of sometimes crippling losses has not lost its appeal. The stirrings of conscience that have animated and embittered the American debate over the morality and necessity of bombing Japanese cities, particularly the atomic bombings of Hiroshima and Nagasaki, are not matched in postwar American ruminations over the appropriateness of the means by which Nazi Germany was brought down, surely in part a gauge of the horror that German genocide continues to evoke, and the "conventional" nature of the bombs employed against its authors. The onus for "indiscriminate" urban bombing, moreover, is borne primarily by the British, a not entirely equitable assessment, as even the modest degree of "precision" with which American bombers dropped their loads on German targets early in their war was partially abandoned in that war's latter stages. "Blind" bombing through thick cloud cover, using the primitive on-board radar then available, permitted a degree of accuracy that differed little from that of RAF Bomber Command's "area bombing." This led ball turret gunner Sergeant John Briol of the 457th Bomb Group to note grimly in his diary, "If we fall into most German hands now, they will kill us."[14] The same realization prompted Bernerd Harding of the 492nd Bombardment Group to bury his pilot's wings following the shooting down of his B-24 over Germany on July 7, 1944.[15] Even daylight bombing in conditions of good visibility often devastated areas far beyond the intended target. Briol's group was dispatched to bomb the marshalling yard at Mayen, "a little city of about 2000 people. We blasted the yards all right and the entire city with it. I saw the whole city disappearing and I suddenly realized again what a rotten business this was."[16] But such brutal candor was remote from the atmosphere surrounding the dedication of the monument. The national anthems of the two countries were played, while members of the U.S. and German armed forces stood at attention. The two elderly survivors of #909's crew saluted the memorial to their murdered comrades, while many in the audience wept, although, perhaps, not all for the same thing.[17]

The elaborate binational memorialization of the murdered crewmen of #909 stands in stark contrast to remembrances of the German civilians murdered in Voerde. The history of the 36th Tank Battalion, to which Lieutenant Schneeweiss had belonged, recalls Voerde only as a stop en route to an assembly area near Bruckhausen, a way station on the battalion's triumphant drive to victory over Germany less than two months later. The history of the Eighth Armored Division does not mention the town at all.[18] As far as American memory of World War II is concerned, the Voerde atrocity is a nonevent. Interestingly, and no doubt for different reasons, the people of Voerde, although they have memorialized the martyred children of Buschmannshof, have repressed or, at least, have failed to register public memory of their own murdered citizens. When asked if German records dealing with the murders were available, city archivist Günter Wabnik replied to the author:

> The city archives has previously been unaware of the event you describe. Records in this office give the cause of death of the six persons whose names you provided as having died through the effects of war. As a result of some research—information provided by residents at the time of the event—I now know that seven or eight civilians were shot to death by American soldiers. Besides those whom you named, Heinrich Tittmann and Gertrud Neukäter (?) (not yet fully clarified) also died.[19]

Gefallen durch Kriegseinwirkungen—died through the effects of war. That minimally informative language in Voerde's archives constitutes the memorial for perhaps eight of its citizens, eight among the many millions of civilian victims of World War II.

NOTES

1. "Borkum: Nordseeinsel mit Hochseeklima," http://ew.borkum.de/.

2. Jürgen Petschull, "Der Fliegermord von Borkum," *Biographie* 3 (2004): 90.

3. Robin Smith to James J. Weingartner, e-mail, March 27, 2010 (in Weingartner's possession).

4. Tönjes Akkermann, "Späte Ehrung für amerikanische Flieger," *Borkumer Zeiting*, July 1, 2003.

5. Wilke Specht, "Borkum erinnert an ermordete US-Gefangene," *Borkumer Zeitung*, August 5, 2003.

6. Petschull, "Fliegermord," 91.

7. Richard G. Evans, *The Third Reich at War* (New York: Penguin Press, 2009), 185.

8. Specht, "Borkum erinnert."

9. Ibid.

10. Colonel Kerry Taylor, "Borkum Commemoration Comments," August 4, 2003 (in Weingartner's possession; courtesy of Robin Smith).

11. Petschull, "Fliegermord," 91.

12. W. G. Sebald, *On the Natural History of Destruction*, trans. Anthea Bell (New York: Random House, 2003), 13–14.

13. Ibid., 98.

14. Donald L. Miller, *Masters of the Air: America's Bomber Boys Who Fought the Air War against Nazi Germany* (New York: Simon and Schuster, 2006), 366.

15. "World War II Pilot Will Return to Germany, Seek Lost Wings," *Belleville News-Democrat*, September 5, 2009.

16. Miller, *Masters of the Air*, 365.

17. Petschull, "Fliegermord," 91.

18. Frederick W. Slater, *Invincible: A History of the Men and Armored Might of the Thirty-sixth Tank Battalion*, 4, http://www.8th-armored.org/books/36tk/36h-pg04.htm; Charles R. Leach, *In Tornado's Wake: A History of the 8th Armored Division* (Nashville, TN: Battery Press, 1992), 138.

19. Wabnik to Weingartner, e-mail, July 24, 2006 (in Weingartner's possession).

Epilogue

German memorialization of the American airmen murdered on Bor-kum and American amnesia regarding the murdered civilians of Vo-erde reflect the very different collective memories of World War II held by the two peoples. To generalize about anything as complex as the perspectives of millions of human beings on events now more than 60 years in the past is hazardous in the extreme, but it is probably not too daring to suggest that German and American collective mem-ories regarding the Second World War are approximate opposites of each other. For most Germans, World War II was a profoundly nega-tive event, in which a war caused by German aggression resulted in the deaths of approximately four million of their countrymen and cit-ies reduced to vast landscapes of rubble. The war also earned for Ger-mans the moral condemnation of much of the world for a campaign of genocide that murdered not only six million Jews but millions of others categorized as *Untermenschen*, while Germany subjected much of Europe to a brutal occupation.

To be sure, the precise character of this negative memory has man-ifested itself in changing forms over the decades since May 1945, a fact complicated by Germany's division between communist east and capitalist west until 1990. Germans' initial preoccupation with their own wartime and postwar suffering, understandable but intensely of-fensive to surviving victims of German aggression, exploitation, and genocide, gave way by the late 1960s and 1970s among a younger gen-eration to a sharper consciousness of widespread German wartime criminality.[1] Some young Germans came to identify with Nazism's Jewish victims, learned Hebrew, and visited Israel. The American political scientist Daniel J. Goldhagen's controversial *Hitler's Willing*

Executioners: Ordinary Germans and the Holocaust, which posited that most Germans had been imbued with anti-Semitism and willingly accepted, if they did not actively participate in, the Holocaust, was published in 1996 and in translation became a best seller in newly reunified Germany, winning for its author a prestigious prize.[2] Jörg Friedrich's *Der Brand. Deutschland im Bombenkrieg 1940–1945,* which described in lurid detail the sufferings and deaths of hundreds of thousands of German civilians and the destruction of a rich material heritage under years of merciless bombing, also recognized that it was Hitler who was ultimately responsible for Germany's destruction.[3] Yet, Friedrich's emphasis on the terrible toll exacted by the Allied aerial assault, couched in descriptive terms suggestive of the Holocaust, made some readers uneasy. An exhibition entitled "War of Extermination: Crimes of the Wehrmacht 1941 to 1944," which opened in 1995 and was seen by hundreds of thousands of visitors in 34 German and Austrian cities, revealed widespread resistance to its message that the German Army and not only the SS had been heavily implicated in the murders of millions of Jews and non-Jews in the Soviet Union.[4] But, at the end of the first decade of the 21st century, well into the seventh decade after the start of World War II, Germans are still bringing to trial very old men for crimes committed during that war, although many war criminals have gone unpunished. Ninety-year-old Josef Scheungraber was convicted in August 2009 of having been responsible as a 25-year-old lieutenant for the murders of 10 Italian civilians in 1944 in reprisal for the killing by partisans of two German soldiers. He was sentenced by a Munich court to life imprisonment. On quite another level of criminality, the German trial of 89-year-old John Demjanjuk, charged with having been a party to the murders of 27,900 Jews in the Sobibor extermination camp, where he had served as a guard, began in Munich on November 30 of the same year.[5]

And Borkum is not the only German town to have memorialized murdered U.S airmen. Little more than a year after the dedication of the Borkum monument, the industrial city of Rüsselsheim, home of the Opel automotive plant, unveiled a memorial to the seven B-24 crewmen killed there by a mob on August 24, 1944. It is a more imposing and emotionally compelling structure than the stone erected on Borkum's war memorial square, consisting of a wall more than six feet high on which appear larger-than-life-size photographs of the youthful American crew. Memory of the murders had percolated beneath the surface of life in Rüsselsheim for many years. Far more Rüsselheimers than the 11 defendants who had been brought to trial by the U.S. Army in July 1945 had played supporting roles in the murderous assaults. Widespread fear of awakening a potentially dangerous sleeping dog had enforced silence until the chance encounter of an artist with a talkative older resident in the early 1990s resulted in the incorporation of the incident in a painting commissioned by city leaders and the opening of the murders to public discussion. The memorial was the eventual result.[6] German guilt produces monuments to men who came not only to bomb but also, some Germans now believe, to liberate them.

The collective memory of World War II held by most U.S. citizens, by contrast, is dramatically different. To the majority of white Americans, World War II was "the Good War," and challenges to that image are bitterly resisted. A notable example of this resistance is the uproar sparked by the Smithsonian Air and Space Museum's proposed exhibit to commemorate the 50th anniversary of the dropping of an atomic bomb on Hiroshima, which, along with the nuclear attack on Nagasaki three days later, was the culminating event in the evolution of indiscriminate urban bombing during World War II. The original plan for the Smithsonian's exhibit centered on a portion of the fuselage of the Enola Gay, the plane that carried the bomb to Japan, accompanied by artifacts from the devastated city, including a child's scorched lunchbox and other evidence of the effects of the bomb on the civilian population. Accompanying text questioned the necessity of "nuking" Japanese cities and alluded to the postwar nuclear arms race that development and use of the bomb unleashed. News of the planned exhibit precipitated a storm of protest and invective from veterans' groups, journalists, and politicians, who argued that "truth" had been distorted and the memory of American wartime heroism besmirched.[7] The *New York Times* was moved to observe that the proposed exhibit's critics would accept nothing less than "uncritical glorification of the American war effort."[8] Many academic historians defended the original plan and deplored the Smithsonian's efforts to satisfy its critics. No satisfactory middle ground could be found. The original 10,000-square-foot exhibit was canceled and replaced by a minimalist display of the Enola Gay's fuselage, accompanied by a bland identifying plaque.[9]

Cards left by visitors to the exhibit reflected a variety of responses, ranging from the inane ("It's pretty stupid here. My legs hurt.") to echoes of wartime hatreds ("They deserved what they got—should have been sooner.") and the simplistically patriotic ("Please do not ever remove this. This is why we are here and free today."). But there were also statements of varying degrees of sophistication that were critical of the dropping of the bomb and the sanitized exhibit commemorating it. "A whitewash," declared one. "Murder by any other name is still murder. It is about time we admit the blood on our hands," proclaimed another. A similar conviction was expressed by the visitor who wrote: "The exhibit should never have been scaled back. This is an important if dark part of our history, and to not pay it its full due is a disgrace. I'm ashamed the museum gave in to outside pressure." Another asked more colloquially, "Why are we so chicken to own part of our action, fellas?"[10]

But, for most Americans, World War II is not history in any analytical sense but, rather, uncritical, patriotic myth, the stuff of celebration and self-congratulation. While many personal accounts of war experiences contain references to American atrocities and a few recent screen productions have alluded to them, these have not entered the dominant popular narrative of the war. Americans have constructed a memorial to the victims of the Malmédy massacre, located at the site of the atrocity, in the form of a rustic stone wall on which are mounted 86 plaques, each bearing the name of a murdered GI. It is much visited by American tourists. The dead now lie in cemeteries in Europe and the United States. The Italian victims of the Biscari massacre, on the other hand, have disappeared. Family members are unable to visit their graves, whose locations are unknown.[11]

Unlike Germans, Americans have lacked a powerful motivation to critically assess this phase of their national history. A war experience that *did* occasion considerable critical self-assessment, the Vietnam conflict, with its American atrocities that were punished only nominally, if at all, seems to have more deeply embedded selective memory of World War II as the contrasting "Good War," a kind of retrospective antidote to those poisonous years of the late 1960s and early 1970s. Then, unlike in the Vietnam war, the enemy seemed unambiguously evil and the United States, which was attacked by the evil enemy, unambiguously good, and the war ended in the unambiguous victory of good over evil, for which the United States, in the minds of most Americans, was primarily responsible.[12] Threats to that treasured system of collective memory are greeted with outrage and rejected as "revisionist," an epithet (when used in this context) that overlooks the fact that all advances in human knowledge are and must be revisionist and that assumes that "true" historical understanding must be a fixed reality.

Surely one reason why the image of the Good War is so resistant to change is that, beyond its serviceability to the American collective ego, it is, in its broad outlines, true. The United States, while not the sole author of victory, was an indispensable factor in its achievement, and the enemy, certainly in the manifestation of Nazi Germany, *was* profoundly evil. Casual murders of prisoners of war—even the mass slaughter of noncombatants by aerial attack as part of a brutal effort to subdue an implacable and, in the case of Germany, genocidal foe— are in a different and morally far less reprehensible category from the programmatic extermination for its own sake of entire racial groups. Yet, the victims of the Voerde atrocity were neither combatants nor the civilian casualties of a combat operation. In the absence of any evidence to the contrary or a crude belief in the undifferentiated collective guilt of *all* Germans for Nazi crimes, it appears that they were at least as undeserving of their violent deaths as the crewmen of #909 were of theirs. Should they be memorialized, as well? Or has selective historical memory consigned them to oblivion?

NOTES

1. Robert G. Moeller, "The Politics of the Past in the 1950s: Rhetorics of Victimization in East and West Germany," in *Germans as Victims: Remembering the Past in Contemporary Germany*, ed. Bill Niven (Hound-Mills and New York: Palgrave Macmillan, 2006), 27–28; Bill Niven, "The GDR and Memory of the Bombing of Dresden," ibid., 113–17; Ruth Wittlinger, "Taboo or Tradition? The 'Germans as Victims Theme' in the Federal Republic until the Mid-1990s," ibid., 65–69; Jeffrey Herf, *Divided Memory: The Nazi Past in the Two Germanys* (Cambridge, MA: Harvard University Press , 1997), 27, 307–12; Atina Grossmann, *Jews, Germans and Allies: Close Encounters in Occupied Germany* (Princeton, NJ: Princeton University Press, 2007), 40; Bernhard Schlink, *Guilt about the Past* (Toronto: House of Anansi Press, 2009), 23–42.

2. Daniel Jonah Goldhagen, *Hitler's Willing Executioners: Ordinary Germans and the Holocaust* (New York: Knopf, 1996), trans. Klaus Kochmann as *Hitlers willige Vollstrecker: Ganz gewöhnliche Deutsche und der Holocaust* (Berlin: Siedler, 1996). For a thoughtful locating of the Goldhagen phenomenon within the evolution of postwar German memory, see Michael Zank, "Goldhagen in Germany: Historians' Nightmare and Popular Hero. An Essay on the Reception of *Hitler's Willing Executioners in Germany*," *Religious Studies Review* 24 (July 1998): 231–40.

3. Jörg Friedrich, *Der Brand: Deutschland im Bombenkrieg 1940–1945* (München: Propyläen Verlag, 2002), 76. This book has appeared in English translation as *The Fire: The Bombing of Germany 1940–1945,* trans. Allison Brown (New York: Columbia University Press, 2006).

4. The complicity of the German army in genocidal war in the Soviet Union had been made clear earlier by German scholars in publications such as Helmut Krausnick and Heinz-Heinrich Wilhelm, *Die Truppe des Weltanschauungskrieges: Die Einsatzgruppen des Sicherheitspolizei und des SD* (Stuttgart: Deutsche Verlags-Anstalt, 1981), and Christian Streit, *Keine Kameraden: Die Wehrmacht und die sowetischen Kriegsgefangenen 1941–1945* (Stuttgart: Deutsche Verlags-Anstalt, 1978). On the storm generated by the exhibit, see Omer Bartov, "The Wehrmacht Exhibition Controversy. The Politics of Evidence," in *Crimes of War: Guilt and Denial in the Twentieth Century,* ed. Omer Bartov, Atina Grossmann, and Mary Nolan (New York: New Press, 2002), 41–60; Hannes Heer, *"Hitler War's": Die Befreiung der Deutschen von ihrer Vergangenheit* (Berlin: Aufbau Verlag, 2005), 237–91.

5. Judy Dempsey, "Former Nazi Officer Convicted of Murdering Italian Civilians," *New York Times,* August 11, 2009. Demjanjuk was convicted and sentenced to death by an Israeli court in 1988 but was released in 1993 on the grounds of mistaken identity. Nicholas Kulish, "Man Tied to Death Camp Goes to Trial in Germany," ibid., November 30, 2009.

6. Kevin Dougherty, "Memorial Honors Victim of World War II Mob," *Stars and Stripes* (European ed.), August 25, 2004.

7. Edward T. Linenthal, "Anatomy of a Controversy," in *History Wars: The Enola Gay and Other Battles for the American Past,* ed. Edward T. Linenthal and Tom Engelhardt (New York: Henry Holt and Company, 1996), 28–52.

8. "The Smithsonian and the Bomb," *New York Times,* September 5, 1994.

9. "Official Resigns over Exhibit of Enola Gay," ibid., May 3, 1995; Richard Kohn, "History at Risk: The Case of the Enola Gay," in *History Wars: The Enola Gay and Other Battles for the American Past,* ed. Edward T. Linenthal and Tom Engelhardt (New York: Henry Holt and Company, 1996), 161.

10. "A Collection of Comment Cards Left by Visitors to the Enola Gay Exhibit at the National Air and Space Museum," http://digital.lib.lehigh.edu/trial/enola/files/round4/commentcards.pdf.

11. John N. Bauserman, *The Malmedy Massacre* (Shippensburg, PA: White Mane, 1995), 111–15; Ricardo Giannola to James J. Weingartner, e-mail, September 1, 2009 (in Weingartner's possession).

12. See Marilyn B. Young, "Dangerous History: Vietnam and the 'Good War,'" in *History Wars: The Enola Gay and Other Battles for the American Past,* ed. Edward T. Linenthal and Tom Engelhardt (New York: Henry Holt and Company, 1996), 199–209.

Bibliography

Trial Records

Records of the Office of the Inspector General, Record Group 159, National Archives and Records Administration, National Archives II, College Park, MD.

Trial of the Major War Criminals before the International Military Tribunal, Nuremberg, 14 November 1945–October, 1946. 42 vols. Nuremberg: International Military Tribunal, 1947–49.

United States of America v. August Haesiker, Record Groups 153 and 338, National Archives and Records Administration Microcopy 1103, Washington, DC.

United States of America v. Compton, Capt. John T., Clerk of Court, U.S. Army Judiciary, Arlington, VA.

United States of America v. Kurt Goebell et al., Record Groups 153 and 338, National Archives and Records Administration Microcopy 1103, Washington, DC.

United States of America v. Otto Skorzeny et al., Record Groups 153 and 338, National Archives and Records Administration Microcopy M1106, Washington, DC.

United States of America v. Private Glen Joachims, Private William Peppler, and Private Francis F. Nichols, Clerk of Court, U.S. Army Judiciary, Arlington, VA.

United States of America v. Second Lieutenant Robert A. Schneeweiss, Clerk of Court, U.S. Army Judiciary, Arlington, VA.

United States of America v. Valentin Bersin et al., Record Group 153, National Archives and Records Administration Microcopy A3390, Washington, DC.

United States of America v. West, Sgt. Horace T., Clerk of Court, U.S. Army Judiciary, Arlington, VA.

Manuscript Collections

Burton F. Ellis Papers, Manuscript Group 409, University of Idaho Library, Moscow, ID.
Willis M. Everett, Jr. Papers, in author's possession.
Edward F. Lyons Papers, M14, Snell Library, Northeastern University, Boston, MA.
Harry S. Truman Papers, Harry S. Truman Library, Independence, MO.

U.S. Government Publications

Military Government Germany. *Technical Manual for Legal and Prison Officers.* No place or date of publication; no publisher.
U.S. Senate. *Malmedy Massacre Investigation: Hearings before a Subcommittee of the Committee on Armed Services, United States Senate, Eighty-First Congress, First Session, Pursuant to Senate Resolution 42.* Washington, DC: U.S. Government Printing Office, 1949.
U.S. War Department. *The Articles of War.* Washington, DC: U.S. Government Printing Office, 1920.
U.S. War Department. *Basic Field Manual: Rules of Land Warfare.* Washington, DC: U.S. Government Printing Office, 1940.
U.S. War Department. *Military Justice Procedure.* Washington, DC: U.S. Government Printing Office, 1945.

Books

Ambrose, Stephen E. *Citizen Soldiers: The U.S. Army from the Normandy Beaches to the Bulge to the Surrender of Germany, June 7, 1944–May 7, 1945.* New York: Simon and Schuster, 1997.
Arrington, Grady P. *Infantryman at the Front.* New York: Vantage Press, 1959.
Atkinson, Rick. *The Day of Battle: The War in Sicily and Italy, 1943–1944.* New York: Holt, 2007.
Bartov, Omer. *The Eastern Front, 1941–1945: German Troops and the Barbarization of Warfare.* New York: St. Martin's Press, 1985.
Bartov, Omer, Atina Grossmann, and Mary Nolan, eds. *Crimes of War: Guilt and Denial in the Twentieth Century.* New York: New Press, 2002.
Bauserman, John M. *The Malmedy Massacre.* Shippensburg, PA: White Mane, 1995.
Bloem, Holger, and Wilke Specht. *Borkum: Nordseeinsel unter Weitem Himmel.* Norden: Verlag Soltau-Kurier-Norden, 2009.
Blumenson, Martin, ed. *The Patton Papers, 1940–1945.* Boston: Houghton Mifflin, 1974.
Boog, Horst. *The Conduct of the Air War in the Second World War: An International Comparison.* New York: Berg, 1992.

Bower, Tom. *The Pledge Betrayed: America and Britain and the Denazification of Postwar Germany.* New York: Doubleday, 1982.

Breitman, Richard. *The Architect of Genocide: Himmler and the Final Solution.* New York: Knopf, 1991.

Brode, Patrick. *Casual Slaughters and Accidental Judgments: Canadian War Crimes Prosecutions, 1944–1949.* Toronto: University of Toronto Press, 1997.

Buscher, Frank M. *The U.S. War Crimes Trial Program in Germany.* Westport, CT: Greenwood Press, 1989.

Carlson, Lewis H. *We Were Each Other's Prisoners: An Oral History of World War II. American and German Prisoners of War.* New York: Basic Books, 1997.

Crew, David F., ed. *Nazism and German Society, 1933–1945.* New York: Routledge, 1995.

Datner, Szymon. *Crimes against POWs: Responsibility of the Wehrmacht.* Warsaw: Western Press Agency, 1964.

Dower, John. *War without Mercy: Race and Power in the Pacific War.* New York: Pantheon, 1986.

D'Este, Carlo. *Patton: A Genius for War.* New York: HarperCollins, 1995.

Eiber, Ludwig, and Robert Sigel, eds. *Dachauer Prozesse: NS-Verbrechen vor amerikanischen Militärgerichten in Dachau 1945–1948. Verfahren, Ergebnisse, Nachwirkungen.* Göttingen: Wallstein Verlag, 2007.

Evans, Richard G. *The Third Reich at War.* New York: Penguin Press, 2009.

Feifer, George. *Tennozan: The Battle of Okinawa and the Atomic Bomb.* New York: Ticknor and Fields, 1992.

Foy, David A. *For You the War Is Over: American Prisoners of War in Nazi Germany.* New York: Stein and Day, 1984.

Frankland, Noble, ed. *The Encyclopedia of Twentieth Century Warfare.* New York: Orion Books, 1989.

Frei, Norbert. *Adenauer's Germany and the Nazi Past: The Politics of Amnesty and Integration.* Trans. Joel Golb. New York: Columbia University Press, 2002.

Friedrich, Jörg. *The Fire: The Bombing of Germany, 1940–1945.* Trans. Allison Brown. New York: Columbia University Press, 2006.

Fritz, Stephen G. *Endkampf: Soldiers, Civilians and the Death of the Third Reich.* Lexington: University of Kentucky Press, 2004.

Fussell, Paul. *Doing Battle: The Making of a Skeptic.* Boston: Little, Brown, 1996.

Fussell, Paul. *Wartime: Understanding and Behavior in the Second World War.* New York: Oxford University Press, 1989.

Gilbert, Martin. *The First World War: A Complete History.* New York: Holt, 1994.

Goda, Norman J. W. *Tales from Spandau: Nazi Criminals and the Cold War.* New York: Cambridge University Press, 2008.

Goldhagen, Daniel Jonah. *Hitler's Willing Executioners: Ordinary Germans and the Holocaust.* New York: Knopf, 1996.

Grayling, A. C. *Among the Dead Cities: The History and Moral Legacy of the World War II Bombing of Civilians in Germany and Japan.* New York: Walker, 2006.

Groehler, Olaf. *Bombenkrieg gegen Deutschland.* Berlin: Akademie Verlag, 1990.

Halpern, Paul G. *A Naval History of World War I.* London: Routledge, 1995.

Hammerstein, K. W. *Landsberg: Henker des Rechts?* Wuppertal: Abendland Verlag, 1952.

Hansen, Randall. *Fire and Fury: The Allied Bombing of Germany, 1942–1945.* New York: North American Library, 2008.

Harris, Whitney. *Tyranny on Trial: The Evidence at Nuremberg.* Dallas, TX: Southern Methodist University Press, 1954.

Heer, Hannes. *"Hitler War's": Die Befreiung der Deutschen von ihrer Vergangenheit.* Berlin: Aufbau Verlag, 2005.

Herf, Jeffrey. *Divided Memory: The Nazi Past in the Two Germanys.* Cambridge, MA: Harvard University Press, 1997.

Herwig, Holger. *Hammer or Anvil? Modern Germany 1648–Present.* Lexington, MA: Heath, 1994.

Howard, Michael, George. J. Andreopoulos, and Mark Shulman, eds. *The Laws of War: Constraints on Warfare in the Western World.* New Haven, CT: Yale University Press, 1994.

Junker, Detlef, ed. *The United States and Germany in the Era of the Cold War.* New York: Cambridge University Press, 2004.

Karsten, Peter. *Law, Soldiers and Combat.* Westport, CT: Greenwood Press, 1978.

Kaufmann, J. E., and R. M. Jurga. *Fortress Europe: European Fortifications of World War II.* Conshohocken, PA: Combined Publishing, 1999.

Kennett, Lee. *The First Air War, 1914–1918.* New York: Free Press, 1991.

Krausnick, Helmut, and Heinz-Heinrich Wilhelm. *Die Truppe des Weltanschauungskrieges: Die Einsatzgruppen des Sicherheitspolizei und des SD.* Stuttgart: Deutsche Verlags-Anstalt, 1981.

Lange, Carl, ed. *Kriegszeitung der Festung Borkum: Auswahl aus zwei Jahrgangen.* Berlin: R. von Deckers Verlag, 1917.

Leach, Charles R. *In Tornado's Wake: A History of the 8th Armored Division.* Nashville, TN: Battery Press, 1992.

Lindbergh, Charles A. *The Wartime Journals of Charles A. Lindbergh.* New York: Harcourt Brace Jovanovich, 1970.

Linenthal, Edward T., and Tom Engelhardt, eds. *The Enola Gay and Other Battles for the American Past.* New York: Holt, 1996.

Von Lingen, Kerstin. *Kesselring's Last Battle: War Crimes Trials and Cold War Politics.* Trans. Alexandra Klemm. Lawrence: University of Kansas Press, 2009.

Merritt, Richard L. *Democracy Imposed: U.S. Occupation Policy and the German Public, 1945-1949.* New Haven, CT: Yale University Press, 1995.

Middlebrook, Martin. *The Battle of Hamburg: Allied Bomber Forces against a German City in 1943.* New York: Scribner's, 1981.

Miller, Donald L. *Masters of the Air: America's Bomber Boys Who Fought the Air War against Nazi Germany.* New York: Simon and Schuster, 2006.

Nelson, Craig. *The First Heroes: The Extraordinary Story of the Doolittle Raid—America's First World War II Victory.* New York: Penguin, 2003.

Nigro, August. *Wolfsangel: A German City on Trial.* Washington, DC: Brassey's, 2001.

Niven, Bill, ed. *Germans as Victims: Remembering the Past in Contemporary Germany.* Houndsmills and New York: Palgrave Macmillan, 2006.

Proctor, Robert N. *The Nazi War on Cancer.* Princeton: Princeton University Press, 1999.

Reel, A. Frank. *The Case of General Yamashita.* Chicago: University of Chicago Press, 1949.

Schlink, Bernhard. *Guilt about the Past.* Toronto: Anansi Press, 2010.

Sebald, W. G. *On the Natural History of Destruction.* Trans. Anthea Bell. New York: Random House, 2003.

Streit, Christian. *Keine Kamaraden: Die Wehrmacht und die sowetischen Kriegsgefangenen 1941–1945.* Stuttgart: Deutsche Verlags-Anstalt, 1978.

Süss, Dietmar, ed. *Deutschland im Luftkrieg: Geschichte und Erinnerung.* Oldenbourg: Institut für Zeitgeschichte, 2007.

Tauber, Kurt. *Beyond Eagle and Swastika: German Nationalism since 1945.* Middletown, CT: Wesleyan University Press, 1967.

Ueberschär, Gerd, ed. *Der Nationalsozialismus vor Gericht: Die alliierte Prozesse Gegen Kriegsverbrecher und Soldaten, 1943–1952.* Frankfurt am Main: Fischer Taschenbuch Verlag, 1999.

United Nations War Crimes Commission. *Law Reports of Trials of War Criminals.* Vol. 1. London: His Majesty's Stationery Office, 1947.

Vourkoutiotis, Vasilis. *Prisoners of War and the German High Command: The British and American Experience.* New York: Palgrave Macmillan, 2003.

Weingartner, James J. *Crossroads of Death: The Story of the Malmédy Massacre and Trial.* Berkeley and Los Angeles: University of California Press, 1979.

Weingartner, James J. *A Peculiar Crusade: Willis M. Everett and the Malmedy Massacre.* New York: New York University Press, 2000.

Welch, David. *The Third Reich: Politics and Propaganda.* New York: Routledge, 1993.

Westemeier, Jens. *Joachim Peiper: Zwischen Totenkopf und Ritterkreuz.* Bissendorf: Biblio Verlag, 2006.

Whittingham, Richard. *Martial Justice: The Last Mass Execution in the United States.* Annapolis: Naval Institute Press, 1971.

Wiethege, Dieter. *Und als der Krieg zur Ende Schien. . . . Krieg, Überrollung und Ausländerlager im Voerde.* Meinerzhagen: Meinerzhagener Druck und Verlags-Haus, 1985.

Yeager, Chuck, and Leo Janos. *Yeager: An Autobiography.* New York: Bantam, 1985.

De Zayas, Alfred. *Die Wehrmacht-Untersuchungsstelle: Deutsche Ermittlungen über alliierte Völkerrechtsverletzungen in Zweiten Weltkrieg.* Munich: Universitas/Langen Müller, 1979.

Articles and Chapters

Barry, Kevin J. "Military Commissions: Trying American Justice." *Army Lawyer* (November 2003): 1–9.

Biddle, Tami Davis. "Air Power." In *The Laws of War: Constraints on Warfare in the Western World*. Edited by Michael Howard, George J. Andreopoulos, and Mark Shulman, 140–59. New Haven, CT: Yale University Press.

Borch, Colonel Frederic L. "Why Military Commissions Are the Proper Forum and Why Terrorists Will Have Full and Fair Trials." *Army Lawyer* (November 2003): 10–16.

Ferguson, Niall. "Prisoner Taking and Prisoner Killing in the Age of Total War: Towards a Political Economy of Military Defeat." *War in History* 11 (2004): 148–92.

Grimm, Barbara. "Lynchmorde an allierten Fliegern im Zweiten Weltkrieg." In *Deutschland im Luftkrieg: Geschichte und Erinnerung*. Edited by Dietmar Süss, 71–84. Oldenbourg: Institut für Zeitgeschichte, 2007.

Herbert, Ulrich. "Labor as Spoils of Conquest, 1933–1945." In *Nazism and German Society, 1933–1945*. Edited by David F. Crew, 219–73. New York: Routledge, 1995.

Insco, James B. "Defense of Superior Orders before Military Commissions." *Duke Journal of Comparative* and *International Law* 13 (Spring 2003): 389–418.

Jones, Edgar. "One War Is Enough." *Atlantic Monthly* (February 1946): 48–53.

Koessler, Maximilian. "American War Crimes Trials in Europe." *Georgetown Law Journal* 39 (1950–51): 18–112.

Koessler, Maximilian. "Borkum Island Tragedy and Trial." *Journal of Criminal Law, Criminology and Political Science* 47 (July–August 1956): 183–96.

Nobleman, Eli E. "Procedure and Evidence in American Military Government Courts in the United States Zone of Germany." *Federal Bar Journal* 8 (January 1947): 238–46.

Petschull, Jürgen. "Der Fliegermord von Borkum." *Biographie* 3 (2004): 85–91.

Ramsey, Winston G. "The Rüsselsheim Death March." *After the Battle* 57 (1987): 1–20.

Roberts, Adam. "Land Warfare: From Hague to Nuremberg." In *The Laws of War: Constraints on Warfare in the Western World*. Edited by Michael Howard, George J. Andreopoulos, and Mark Shulman, 116–39. New Haven, CT: Yale University Press.

Stesseger, Marie. "Conspiracy Theory: The Use of the Conspiracy Doctrine in Times of National Crisis." *William and Mary Law Review* 46 (December 2004): 1177–89.

Stiepani, Ute. "Die Dachauer Prozesse und ihre Bedeutung im Rahmen der allierten Strafverfolgung von NS-Verbrechen." In *Der Nationalsozialismus vor Gericht: Die allierten Prozesse gegen Kriegsverbrecher und Soldaten 1943–1952*. Edited by Gerd R. Ueberschär, 227–39. Frankfurt am Main: Fischer Taschenbuch Verlag, 1999.

Weingartner, James J. "Americans, Germans, and War Crimes: Converging Narratives from 'the Good War.'" *Journal of American History* 94 (March 2008): 1164–83.

Weingartner, James J. "Massacre at Biscari: Patton and an American War Crime." *The Historian* 52 (November 1989): 24–39.

Weingartner, James J. "Trophies of War: U.S. Troops and the Mutilation of Japanese War Dead, 1941–1945." *Pacific Historical Review* 61 (February 1992): 53–67.

Weingartner, James J. "War against Sub-humans: Comparisons between the German War against the Soviet Union and the American War against Japan." *The Historian* 58 (Spring 1996): 557–73.

Zank, Michael. "Goldhagen in Germany: Historians' Nightmare and Popular Hero. An Essay on the Reception of *Hitler's Willing Executioners* in Germany." *Religious Studies Review* 24 (July 1998): 231–40.

Unpublished Thesis

Harris, Justin Michael. "American Soldiers and POW Killing in the European Theater of World War II." M.A. thesis, Texas State University, 2009.

Newspapers

Belleville (Illinois) *News-Democrat*
Borkumer Zeitung
Corriere Della Sera
New York Times
Stars and Stripes (European edition)
The Wall Street Journal
Wuppertaler Rundschau

Index

About the Author

JAMES J. WEINGARTNER is a professor of history emeritus, recently retired from full-time teaching at Southern Illinois University, Edwardsville. He began his career as a researcher with a focus on recent German history, particularly the Nazi period, shifting subsequently to a concentration on World War II war crimes. His previous books have been published by Southern Illinois University Press, the University of California Press, and New York University Press. His articles have appeared in *The Journal of American History, Journal of Military History, The Historian, Central European History,* and the *Pacific Historical Review,* among others.